Iran and the Rise of Reza Shah

IRAN AND THE RISE OF REZA SHAH

From Qajar Collapse
to Pahlavi Rule

Cyrus Ghani

I.B.Tauris *Publishers*

LONDON • NEW YORK

Published in 1998 by I.B.Tauris & Co Ltd
Victoria House, Bloomsbury Square, London WC1B 4DZ
175 Fifth Avenue, New York NY 10010

In the United States and Canada distributed by St. Martin's Press
175 Fifth Avenue, New York NY 10010

ISBN 1 86064 258 6

A full CIP record for this book is available from the British Library
A full CIP record for this book is available from the Library of Congress

Library of Congress catalog card: available

Typeset in Bookman by Dexter Haven, London
Printed and bound in Great Britain by WBC Ltd, Bridgend, Mid Glamorgan

For Caroline, Ali, Vida, Touraj and Laila

Contents

List of Illustrations

Style and Usage

The spelling of names of persons and places has been transliterated as they are pronounced in the Persian language.

The name Iran is used for the most part throughout the book except where direct quotes and paraphrases refer to the country as Persia. The word 'Persian' has been used consistently as the language of the country.

Titles and family names have been used in the following manner. Iranians who lived before the passage of the 1925 Law of Identity and Status are simply referred to by titles. Those who were born before passage of the law and who lived thereafter have been referred to by their titles as well as adopted family names. When this work deals with the years after 1925 only family names have been used. All names have been cross-referenced with titles in the index. Mirza, when it comes after the first name, denotes a Qajar prince. Iranian military officers are identified by the highest rank which they attained.

Iranian books and other writings in Persian mentioned in either text or end-notes have been transliterated followed by the translation in parenthesis. Their dates are given in the Iranian solar calendar and corresponding Christian era calendar.

References and source notes appear at the end of each chapter. Biographical sketches of individuals who played a role in the period under study, for reasons of significance and ease, are incorporated at the bottom of the corresponding pages of text.

Abbreviations used in the text are:

APOC	Anglo-Persian Oil Company
Foreign Office	Refers to British Foreign Office
Norperforce	North Persian Expeditionary Force
PRS	Persian Railway Syndicate

Abbreviations used in the end notes are:

CAB	Cabinet documents
DBFP	Documents on British Foreign Office Policy, 1919–1930, edited by Rohan Butler and J.P.T. Bury, London, 1963.
DoS	United States Department of State, Papers on Foreign Relations. Papers Relating to the Foreign Relations of the United States; United States Government Printing Office. Confidential

Preface

The years 1921 to 1926 encompass one of the most important and engrossing chapters in twentieth-century Iranian history. The period begins with a bizarre coup d'etat engineered in great haste by a British general who knew virtually nothing of the country or her people. Seldom has the British military acted so freely to formulate policy, let alone promote a coup, without the express direction of the civilian government. Equally bizarre is the role played in the coup by the British Minister to Iran who from the moment he reached Tehran initiated and carried out polices at complete variance with the dictates of the Foreign Office and ultimately totally lost the confidence of his Foreign Secretary. The coup d'etat of 1921 and the emergence of Reza Khan were the direct result of the British Government's pursuance of an unrealistic and nineteenth-century policy, epitomised by the 1919 Agreement, in a post World War I Iran in which a new nationalism had taken root.

The coup brought to power an obscure military officer, Reza Khan, who had no prior political experience but adapted and learned so quickly that he could have given Machiavelli lessons in statecraft. This novice politician within five years brought about the downfall of a dynasty which had ruled Iran for over 130 years and installed himself as the new Shah. The first ten years after the coup was a period of innovation and bold measures, great hopes and growing confidence, self-esteem and self-reliance. By the late 1920s all signs indicated that Iran was becoming independent and free of foreign domination. Despite the recognition by Reza Shah of the British role in the coup and despite the pre-eminent position Britain enjoyed in Iran, he could deal as an equal with Britain and the governments of the other powers. This study ends in 1926 after the coronation, although the epilogue briefly touches upon the major events up to Reza Shah's abdication in September 1941.

The promise held forth by the coup on the whole went unfulfilled due to a variety of factors. Not the least of these were flaws in Reza Shah's character and the decision by Britain and Russia to invade Iran in 1941, rendering the progress initiated by Reza Shah at best incomplete and at worst all but lost. The 'modernism' introduced during the Reza Shah era was more profound and consequential than the measures implemented or even envisaged during the 1960s and 1970s. The period witnessed the most concentrated effort to limit the power of the clergy and it may have succeeded further had it not been for the invasion of and occupation of the country in 1941.

The wartime policy of the Allies during their occupation not only altered the secularist path the country had adopted but also negated some key measures Reza Shah had sought to implement.

The rule of Reza Shah laid the foundation of the present day government structure. Despite a concerted effort for change by the current rulers of Iran the main frame of that apparatus is still intact. The body of laws and regulations enacted in that period, including the comprehensive Civil Code, still define and govern relationships between government and people and amongst individuals.

The period under review in this book, 1919–1926, has been dealt with sparingly and unevenly by historians and social scientists. Although there are excellent works in English on the separatist and Communist movements of those years there is very little on the coup, the prominent figures who helped Reza Shah to topple the Qajars, and their later roles in formulating and implementing a new agenda for the country. The writings in Persian are more detailed and varied and also include some competent works, but what they suffer from is a lack of reliance on primary sources. This has led writers to perpetuate versions of events which are totally at variance with existing archival documents both in Iran and abroad.

With the fall of the Pahlavi dynasty in 1979 there has been, perhaps not surprisingly, a conscious effort by adherents of the new regime in Iran to paint as dark a picture as possible of the founder of the dynasty. This is not the first time history has been evoked and slanted to justify the government of the day. This in itself may be understandable in the light of Reza Shah's secularist policies. What is unconscionable is the denial of his contributions to the creation of modern Iran. Too many spurious accounts have surfaced since the abdication of Reza Shah and most particularly since the 1979 revolution. The present study is an attempt to present a balanced picture of one of the foremost rulers of twentieth-century Iran. Any writer of history inevitably interprets material according to his or her own perceptions. Total objectivity is an illusion, but by rigorous research one should attempt at least to establish some small truths and differentiate between fact and fiction.

The responsibility of the writer of history is great: 'History is to the nation rather as memory is to the individual. As an individual deprived of memory becomes disoriented and lost, not knowing where he has been or where he is going, so a nation denied of a conception of its past will be disabled in dealing with its present or future.'*

---

*   Arthur Schlesinger Jr, *The Disuniting of America*, USA, 1992, pp 45–46.

Acknowledgements

The idea for this study came to me in 1992. The years 1992–1994 were spent researching and copying dispatches at the London Public Record Office and United States Archives in Washington DC and Maryland. Almost all the books I have relied on were in my own library. Later friends and acquaintances were kind enough to send me their articles. I had a superb editor in my wife, Caroline, who patiently read and reread every chapter and skillfully moved sentences and paragraphs up or down or from page to page. She gave invaluable suggestions and not least of all made the tedious spelling and typing corrections. Her moral support was of inestimable value.

Many friends encouraged me to pursue my work. Dr Alinaghi Alikhani, a keen student of contemporary Iranian history, was especially helpful and encouraging. He read the first three chapters and offered many useful suggestions. Dr Gholam Reza Moghadam, whose own doctoral dissertation at Stanford University in 1956 was 'Iran's Foreign Trade Policy and Economic Development in the Inter War Period', helped me greatly by a careful reading of the major part of the manuscript and offering helpful suggestions. Dr Hassan Kamshad, the author of several books on Persian literature as well as superb translator of several important works of history and philosophy from English to Persian, also read most of the manuscript. Farrokh Ghaffari, a man of letters who had met many of the people mentioned in my work, guided and introduced me to several references to the period under study in the works of lesser-known Iranian and French writers. My thanks are due to Ebrahim Golestan, a widely cultured man who encouraged me along the way and offered differing perspectives of certain events. My thanks also to Dr Ali Touran, who is knowledgeable in Iranian history, for kindly reading part of the manuscript. I owe a great debt to each of the above-mentioned friends. I am grateful to Iradj Bagherzade, my able and learned publisher (my Maxwell Perkins) for having read the entire manuscript and offering valuable suggestions. My thanks to Professor James Bill, who provided transcripts of his interviews with prominent Iranians active in the Reza Shah era. I also am grateful to Cyrus Samrad, a friend of long standing who gave me the idea that a new study of the Reza Shah era was due and furnished me with some of the photographs used in this work. Dr Mehran Tavakoli and Kambiz Atabai also gave me encouragement in the initial stages. I must thank Homayoun Katouzian, a knowledgeable writer on Iran who was kind enough to help in identifying certain sources. My conversations with Amir Khosrow Afshar and Sa'id Hedayat, gentlemen of long experience, provided me with further insight.

A book does not become a book by the efforts of the writer alone. Many others helped. Majid Tafreshi, a PhD candidate on Iranian history at London University, was extremely helpful in finding and placing at my disposal many articles in various periodicals and several unpublished doctoral theses. My thanks to Zahra Shadlou, who typed the first draft of the manuscript on an antiquated computer. I wish to acknowledge the courtesy extended to me by the people at Her Majesty's Public Record Office at Kew Gardens. Finally, I must express my appreciation to the staff of I.B. Tauris.

INTRODUCTION

Iran Under Qajar Rule

The history of Iran spanning 25 centuries is a trying one. She suffered all the adversities to which a nation may be exposed, including numbers of invasions and the imposition of an alien religion. On the positive side, however, Iran endured her despots, assimilated the various invading cultures and altered the imposed religion. Most importantly, the national frame endured and sustained all hardships to remain a viable entity.

The Qajar dynasty ruled Iran from the end of the eighteenth century to the early twentieth century. From a Turkic tribe in north-east Iran, the great body of them had settled at Astarabad (present day Gorgan) near the south-eastern corner of the Caspian Sea. When Nader Shah Afshar died in 1747 with no living heirs, the Qajar tribal leaders were among the contenders for the throne. From the ensuing 50 year struggle one Aqa Mohammad Khan Qajar (c.1742–c.1797) emerged the undisputed ruler in 1794. He was crowned in 1796 and founded the dynasty. Aqa Mohammad Khan had been castrated in childhood by the enemies of his father and was one of the cruelest kings even by eighteenth-century Iranian standards. In his quest for power he razed cities, massacred entire populations, and in an act of singular cruelty blinded some 20,000 men in the city of Kerman solely because the local populace had chosen to defend the city against his siege.[1] He was, however, an extraordinary leader and the last of the great conquerors of Central Asia, basing his strength on tribal manpower in the mould of Genghis Khan, Teimur (Tamurlane)

1

and Nader Shah.[2] He is in many ways the initial architect of Iran as we know it today. The mere fact that the dynasty he founded and the country managed to survive into the twentieth century free of official colonial status says something of his abilities.

Aqa Mohammad Khan was assassinated by one of his military commanders in 1797 and the throne passed to his nephew who was crowned Fath Ali Shah.* Fath Ali contributed little to the country and is remembered for his ruinous wars with Russia in which Iran lost all her territory on the west coast of the Caspian Sea. Beginning in the eighteenth century Russia's foreign policy was aimed at territorial expansion. With Poland and Sweden to the west having lost their former power and no longer posing a threat, Russia drove towards expansion in the south and east: Turkey, Iran, Afghanistan, India, Tibet and China. Russia annexed Georgia at the turn of the nineteenth century. Iran, which had ruled the land for centuries, fought to retain Georgia but was badly defeated. Peace came in 1813 and under the Treaty of Golestan Iran renounced all claims to Georgia and lost most of her Caucasian provinces including Derbent, Baku and Shirvan. The Caspian Sea became virtually a Russian lake. Peace was short-lived and in 1825 the Russians seized the territory between Erivan and Gochka Lake. This time Iran reluctantly went to war and in 1826 was again defeated. Through the Treaty of Turkamanchai in 1828 Iran ceded further provinces in the Caucasus, including Erivan and Nakhjavan, and made other political concessions, among them the disastrous grant of extra-territorial rights to the Russians. In return for these concessions, the north-western boundaries of Iran and Russia were permanently fixed and the Russians, who had earlier guaranteed the survival of the Qajar dynasty, reiterated the commitment. The treaty also stipulated that the line of succession for future kings of Iran would devolve from the male issue of Abbas Mirza.

Abbas Mirza, Fath Ali Shah's son and heir apparent, died a year before his father. Abbas Mirza, 1787–1833, was the second son of Fath Ali Shah but became heir to the throne because his older

---

*   Fath Ali Shah, c.1771–1834, is also remembered for the number of his offspring. At his death he left behind some 5,000 descendants from some 700 wives, concubines and other liaisons. As in the case of Charles II of England he was in more than one way the father of his country.[3]

†   Mirza Abol Qasem, Qaem Maqam II, c.1779–1835, was the son of Mirza Issa Qaem Maqam I who had earlier served as First Minister. These two, father and son, established the machinery of government of the Qajar dynasty.[4]

brother's mother was of Georgian descent and not from the Qajar tribe. In his brief life he had shown great valour in battle and administrative skill in governing the north-western provinces. He appears to have been one of the earliest Qajar princes to have had an inkling of what was being accomplished in the Western World in industry and science. Abbas Mirza aroused the enmity of the clergy for sending a few Iranians abroad to learn modern science, for his plans to bring foreign military advisers to create a standing army and for plans to establish small industries. This opposition hampered his efforts. He surrounded himself with some very able men, principally Abol Qasem Qaem Maqam.[†] Abbas Mirza, sensing his imminent death and wanting to ensure sound government, had prevailed upon Qaem Maqam to continue to serve his son. The future Mohammad Shah in turn had promised his father that he would never harm or 'shed the blood of his Minister'.

At Fath Ali Shah's death the crown passed to Abbas Mirza's eldest son who was proclaimed Mohammad Shah. Mohammad Shah's rule had begun on a hopeful note principally because Qaem Maqam served as his chief First Minister. But Mohammad Shah could tolerate neither a strong character nor a dissenting voice. Before a year had passed he had his First Minister suffocated in a felt carpet, presumably shedding no blood. He replaced him with a mystic fool from Erivan, Haji Mirza Aqasi,[#] and ruled miserably for 13 years. Mohammad Shah's rule witnessed an unnecessary and unsuccessful war with the Afghans for the capture of Herat and the growing influence of the Russians and the British.

Mohammad Shah died in 1848 and was succeeded by his son Naser al Din Shah. Born in 1831, he ascended the throne at the age of seventeen. The death of kings in nineteenth-century Iran always presented problems. There were claimants and pretenders. Had it not been for the acumen of Mirza Taqi Khan Amir Nezam (later Amir Kabir), who soon became Naser al Din Shah's First Minister, the path to the throne would not have been smooth. Amir Kabir was probably the ablest Iranian public servant of the nineteenth century. An intelligent and thoughtful man, he had the advantage of having visited Russia and Ottoman Turkey on diplomatic missions earlier

---

[#] Haji Mirza Aqasi, c.1783–1849, was born Abbas and later became known as Haji Mirza Aqasi. He studied theology and became the teacher of the children of Abbas Mirza, including the future Mohammad Shah. He married the future Shah's aunt and was instrumental in helping smooth the way for Mohammad Shah to ascend the throne, as there were several other claimants. Aqasi was rewarded by being appointed First Minister.[5]

in his career. These trips convinced him of the necessity of measures
to drag Iran out of its isolation and backwardness.* But within four
years he met the fate of his predecessor and mentor, Qaem Maqam,
and was murdered at the order of the Shah. Several Iranian writers
believe the country never fully recovered from this loss. What is certain is that Amir Kabir's murder deprived Iran of a fine administrator
and its first systematic planner, and left foreign powers an even freer
hand to meddle in the country's affairs.

In addition to cultural and historical reasons, the Shahs of Iran
were able to get away with arbitrary power over life and death because
there was no well-defined aristocracy in Iran comparable in composition and function to that of Europe. This lack of hereditary
aristocracy allowed for no other power bases, vesting totally unre-
strained power in the Shah. The land-owning elite often changed when
the king changed. The property of no-one was secure and could be
taken away at the Shah's pleasure. Ministers and government officials were the personal servants of the Shah, the populace his serfs.

Naser al Din Shah had some difficult years after Amir Kabir's
death. He became entangled in foreign wars and faced serious turmoil at home, but sheer longevity gradually made him a proficient
preserver of the status quo. More significantly he kept both Britain
and Russia satisfied and maintained an equilibrium in the award of
concessions. Although the country remained stagnant, the last forty
years of his rule was a period of relative stability and peace, and
whether by chance or his acumen the territorial boundaries of Iran
remained substantially intact.

A quarter of a century after Amir Kabir's death, another First Minister, Mirza Hosein Khan Moshir al Dowleh, attempted to introduce

---

*   Mirza Taqi Khan Farahani (Amir Kabir), c.1800–1852, travelled abroad
on three known occasions. In February 1829 he accompanied Khosrow
Mirza, son of the Crown Prince Abbas Mirza, on a peace mission to St
Petersburg. He stayed about a year and in that period visited a variety of
institutions, educational and industrial. In 1838 he went to Erivan and
Teflis as an emissary, accompanying the Crown Prince Naser al Din. In
1844 he was a middle ranking member of the Boundary Commission in
Erzerum in Ottoman Turkey. Robert Curzon who took part in the conference comments on Amir Kabir in his book *Armenia: A Year at Erzeroom
and on the Frontiers of Russia, Turkey and Persia*, London, 1854, p 55,
'He was beyond all comparison the most interesting of those assembled
at the Congress of Erzeroom'. On this trip, Amir Kabir saw more factories and military schools. Once in office he encouraged development of
the mining industry and established small factories in Esfahan, Tehran
and Sari. He also established the first European-modelled polytechnic
school in Tehran.[6]

some reforms, initially with the Shah's blessings. He persuaded the Shah to visit Europe, hoping he would witness the progress of the West. Naser al Din Shah, as his journals attest, did not really like Europe and was fearful of what he saw, particularly Western forms of government. After his second trip he attempted to dissuade Iranians from going abroad, and frowned upon and distrusted those who ventured to do so. He visited Europe three times in his life, saw most of the major capitals, but little resulted except another round of concessions to British entrepreneurs. In 1892 there had been an uprising over the granting of a tobacco concession to a British national and Naser al Din Shah had been forced to cancel it. In 1896, at the time of Naser al Din Shah's death, Iran was hardly different to how it had been in 1848. Nothing had been done to improve the condition of its people and the administrative structure remained antiquated.

On 1 May 1896 Naser al Din Shah, who had ruled Iran as an absolute monarch for over forty-eight years, was assassinated while on a visit to a religious shrine about four miles from Tehran. The length of his rule had made him a father-figure both feared and respected. On this and earlier visits there had been no need for special protection. A presumed petitioner approached him in the shrine and shot the king at point-blank range.

The First Minister, Ali Asghar Khan Atabak,† carried the half-live body of the Shah to the waiting carriage and told the attendants that the bullet had just grazed his shoulder and that the Shah would be fine once he was back in the capital. In the short ride to Tehran, Atabak propped up the body in a sitting position and would occasionally lift the arm of the Shah as if waving to the crowd. The Shah died that night, but not before the Crown Prince had been notified in Tabriz to proceed at once to Tehran and messages had been sent to the British and Russian legations. Naser al Din Shah was succeeded by his son Mozaffar al Din Shah. The transition was smooth in the circumstances.

The assassin, Mirza Reza Kermani, was initially believed to have been either mentally deranged or a religious fanatic and soon after a cursory interrogation was hanged. He was born in 1847 in Kerman

---

† Ali Asghar Khan Atabak, 1858–1907, was the son of Ebrahim Amin al Soltan, the Shah's butler who had risen to become Naser al Din Shah's Minister of Court. When his father died in 1883, Ali Asghar was given the title Amin al Soltan and became Minister of Court. He was later given the pre-Qajar title of Atabak and became the First Minister under three successive kings. Atabak was the most resourceful politician of his time. He was assassinated by an anarchist in 1907.[7]

to a minor land-owning family. He attended religious seminaries and became a disciple of the pan-Islamic leader Jamal al Din Afghani. As punishment for writing a threatening letter to Naser al Din Shah he had been imprisoned and tortured. In assassinating the Shah he carried out his master's famous edict, 'Reciprocate tyranny with tyranny'. The records of his interrogation reveal something extraordinary.[8] His motive for assasinating the 'Shadow of God' and the 'Pivot of the World', as Qajar kings had come to be called, was neither revenge nor personal grievance. Kermani's answers reveal his deep revulsion to the corruption of Iranian society. He had concluded that the only way things could be changed was for despots to be overthrown and eliminated. He blamed the state of affairs on British speculators, corrupt Iranians and especially the king. The Iranian assassin was beginning to think like a European nationalist and revolutionary. Kermani seemed to be questioning the validity of despotic monarchies. He ridiculed the attribution of God-like qualities to the king and wanted an end to the presence and influence of foreign powers in Iran. Naser al Din Shah's death constituted an end of an era.

Naser al Din Shah's children were vastly inferior to him. His eldest surviving son, Mas'oud Mirza Zell al Soltan, could not inherit the throne because his mother was a commoner and did not come from the Qajar tribe. The throne passed to the next surviving son, Mozaffar al Din, 1853–1907, who was an aging and ailing man when his father died. He had waited many years to become king and had virtually been ignored by his father for a quarter of a century. He had surrounded himself with some of the most inept people of the day and when he ascended the throne these same people accompanied him from Tabriz to Tehran and became his advisers, ministers and confidants. He was pathologically superstitious. Thunder and storms, which he believed were signs of anger from the heavens against those who had transgressed, terrified him, and he would ask his favourite soothsayer to confirm that they were not directed at him. He was timid and lazy, and greatly resented his father for having lingered on for so long.

From the moment he was proclaimed king his sole and fervent wish was to travel to Europe, ostensibly for health reasons, but first he had to raise money. The Russian bank in Iran, a branch of the Russian Ministry of Finance whose operations were not always conducted on a strictly business-like basis, was happy to extend loans to the king. A first loan of the rouble equivalent of £2,400,000 at 5% interest was raised and the customs receipts of the major ports were pledged as security. Other loans followed to finance a second trip.

By 1906 the total financial resources of the government were pledged to the Russians. Before 1900 Iran's only external debt was £500,000 borrowed from the British Imperial Bank in 1892 to pay off the compensation claimed by the British-owned Tobacco Regie after the cancellation of its concession by Naser al Din Shah. By 1914 the foreign debt had shot up to the equivalent of £6.8 million, of which £2.6 million was owed to Britain. It had risen to the equivalent of £10.6 million by 1919.[9]

In 1901 a British national, William Knox D'Arcy, obtained a concession for the exploration, production and sale of oil and other mineral deposits which in a few years proved to be more profitable than anything any foreign power had hitherto been granted. When oil was struck in 1908 it was clear that the British political and military presence would become permanent.

In earlier protests against the award of concessions, there had come about an alliance between religious leaders and lay reformers. At the turn of the century a new alliance comprising substantially the same elements was asking for an end to despotic rule and the establishment of a House of Justice to check the powers of the Shah. By 1903 there was a full-grown movement asking for political reform. What had started in Europe with the French Revolution, setting in motion a series of challenges to despotic regimes, had finally come to the East. In 1905 the Czar had been forced to grant sweeping concessions and a Consultative Assembly had been established. Turkey was in the throes of agitation which led to the overthrow of its king in 1908. There was also less fear of the two powers by the Iranians. The Japanese victory over the Russians at Port Arthur had done away with the belief in the inevitable victory of a European nation in conflict with an Asian nation. The successful revolt of the Boers in South Africa had humiliated Britain and tarnished the myth of the invincible British Lion.

By late 1904 the demand for a House of Justice had grown to a demand for a proper parliament modelled on the British House of Commons. In 1906 there were mass demonstrations. The Shah, who up to then had resorted to repressive measures, had to give in. On his birthday, 5 August 1906, he granted a form of constitution and permitted the convention of a constituent assembly which promptly met to draft an electoral law. In October 1906 the assembly had drafted and passed a constitution which was ratified by the Shah. The supplement, i.e. an Iranian version of a Bill of Rights, was enacted later in October 1907.

Mozaffar al Din Shah died in January 1907 and in February was succeeded by his son Mohammad Ali. Mohammad Ali Shah, born in

1872, was very different from his cautious and ailing father. He was impulsive, vain and a stern autocrat. During his years in Tabriz as Crown Prince he had ruled oppressively and was not in the habit of seeking advice or sharing power. He believed his father had made an error in giving in to the constitutionalists and felt the movement could have been dispersed if greater force had been used. He was unwilling to accept any diminution of his powers and is supposed to have said, 'It is fine to have a parliament provided it does not interfere in matters of state and politics'. From the beginning of his rule he did everything to subvert the constitution and he had strong allies among the notables and certain elements of the clergy. Some prominent clerics opposed all democratic institutions which they considered too secular and European, and as members of an elite group they were apprehensive of egalitarian change. The clergy on the whole never accepted nationalism or even nationhood which they considered a form of idol worship, and monarchy the elevation of mortals to the level of deity. Some amongst them had supported the constitutional movement only for its anti-imperialist and anti-foreign features and because they felt their interests were being threatened under an unyielding autocratic Shah.

Russia was unequivocally opposed to parliamentary rule in Iran. Britain also preferred dealing with a single individual and not being bogged down by governments and parliaments. There were some dissenting voices in the British Government which viewed the change favourably but for entirely different reasons. Britain's influence was at a low ebb in Iran, and Russia had gained ascendancy since the turn of the century. Thus perhaps a weakening of the monarchy would even the scales between Britain and Russia. There were also a few voices in the British parliament which were sympathetic because of their own parliamentary structure, and felt it better in principle to have an accountable government. The treatment of Iranians who had sought asylum in the British Legation during the struggle preceding the granting of parliamentary rule had greatly enhanced Britain's popularity. In fact it was higher than at any point before and probably since. At this very time, however, Britain was contemplating an agreement with the Russians to divide Iran into spheres of influence.

Russia's defeat by the Japanese in 1905 had left her in a state of shock and made her more amenable to co-operate with Britain in devising a structure for the protection of their respective interests in Iran. The emergence of Germany as a world power and a potential threat to Britain and Russia was probably another incentive to conclude an agreement. Without consultation or even a hint to the

Iranians the two powers in August 1907 entered into an agreement which dealt with their differences in Afghanistan, Tibet and Iran. In the case of Iran they in effect carved up the country between themselves. Iran was divided into three zones, Russian in the north, British in the south and a neutral zone in between. With the logic that comes from naked power the preface to the Convention stated:

> ...the sole object of the arrangement is the avoidance of any misunderstanding on the ground of Persian affairs between the contracting parties. The Shah's government will be convinced that the Agreement... can not fail to promote prosperity, security and interior development of Persia in the most efficacious manner.

Lord Grey, Britain's Foreign Minister at the time, stated:

> Persia had always attempted to play one power off against another thus creating tension between the two great imperial powers. Only a cordial understanding would prevent such a state of affairs from becoming worse...

The reference to the integrity and independence of Persia in the preamble was merely a formality. Grey went on to say, 'Persia was honeycombed by concessions... and was not in reality a viable entity'. He concluded, 'Persia tried my patience more than any other subject'.[10]

From the moment the purports of the Convention were made public, Britain lost whatever temporary popularity she had gained and was viewed with increased suspicion. The British concentrated their efforts toward the southern oil fields. They ignored the central Government and entered into various agreements with local tribes to protect the drilling and export of oil. The Russians inspired even greater fear. Another consequence of the agreement was to give the Russians an almost completely free hand in their relations with the Iranian Government, something the Russians were happy to exploit in the face of demands for a constitution.

Mohammad Ali Shah, who had been close to the Russians from his days as Crown Prince in Azarbaijan, actively sought their intervention to dismantle parliament. There were some abortive attempts in 1907 and finally in 1908 he staged a bloody coup. The parliament building was shelled by the Iranian Cossack Brigade under Russian officers. Prominent constitutionalists were arrested, most tortured and some murdered. Others fled the country or went into hiding.

The torture and extreme repression after the shelling of parliament contributed to greater discontent, and soon there was a full-scale uprising in Tabriz, the capital of Azarbaijan. This province being nearer to European Russia was more conversant with Western thought and ideas. The people of Tabriz, although more religious than the inhabitants of central Iran, could read pamphlets written in Turkish issued by members of nationalist and reformist movements in Russia and Turkey. Mohammad Ali Shah, unable to quell the revolt, laid siege to the city. Provinces on the southern shores of the Caspian also rose against the Shah. Esfahan in central Iran came into the picture as well. The Bakhtiari tribe had a blood feud with the Shah's uncle Zell al Soltan, who had murdered one of their chieftains, Hosein Qoli Khan, in 1881. Troops led by Sardar As'ad,* a tribal elder, began to march into Esfahan. Another body of troops led by Mohammad Vali Khan Tonokaboni (Sepahsalar),† a landed grandee from Mazandaran who had espoused the cause of the constitutionalists but who also had personal grievances against the Shah, marched from the shores of the Caspian toward Tehran.[11]

In June 1909 there was a decisive battle some 20 kilometres from Tehran in which the forces of the Shah were defeated. On 16 July the Shah abdicated in favour of his twelve-year-old son Ahmad (Shah). The former Shah accepted a pension and under the protection of Russian troops left Iran to settle in Odessa on the Black Sea.

The arrival of Bakhtiari tribesmen in the capital was not regarded as cause for rejoicing, but at least the tyrant Shah had fallen. The victors were magnanimous in victory and there was little persecution of the royalists and absolutists. Sheikh Fazlollah Nouri, a learned

---

*   Ali Qoli Khan Sardar As'ad II, c.1856–1917, was probably the best and most honourable of Bakhtiari chieftains. Unlike the others he was fair and impartial in administration of tribal affairs. Self-educated, he spent several years in Paris in self-imposed exile. Probably with encouragement from the British, fearful of growing Russian influence he returned to Iran in 1909 and led the southern and western flank attack on Tehran.[12]

†   Mohammad Vali Khan (Nasr al Saltaneh, later Sepahdar A'zam, still later Sepahsalar A'zam), c.1847–1926, was born in Tonokabon, a small town on the road to the Caspian Sea. His father and grandfather had held high positions in the army from the days of Mohammad Shah. He also headed the local army in Mazandaran and led local military campaigns for Naser al Din Shah. During the rule of Mozaffar al Din Shah he became Administrator of Customs and later held several governorships. He was an ally of Mohammad Ali Shah in trying to put down the constitutionalist revolt in Tabriz but soon changed sides and led the northern flank attack on Tehran that toppled the Shah. After the removal of the Shah he became Prime Minister briefly in 1910; received the highest military title of Sepahsalar and was again Prime Minister briefly in 1915. He committed suicide in 1926 over financial problems. He contributed little during his periods in office. He was brave and forceful but also autocratic, avaricious and cruel.[13]

senior clergyman who had become a vocal supporter of Mohammad Ali Shah, was the most prominent of those against whom retribution was sought. He was hanged in 1909 in a public square.

Ali Reza Azd al Molk,[#] a respected Qajar elder, was appointed regent. Sardar As'ad and Sepahsalar were the dominant political figures and together governed the country. Elections were held and a new parliament was convened. Sepahsalar who had vast holdings in the Caspian region soon lost interest in matters of state and the Bakhtiaris effectively ruled over the country from 1910 to 1912.

In 1910 the octogenerian regent died. Through intense pressure from the British Abolqasem Naser al Molk[§] was appointed regent, although the majority of deputies and the constitutionalists wanted Hassan Mostofi al Mamalek. Naser al Molk, who came from a land-owning family and had been a contemporary of Lord Grey at Balliol

---

[#] Ali Reza Khan Azd al Molk, c.1822–1910, was the son of Mousa Khan an uncle of Naser al Din Shah. He became close to the Shah and accompanied him on his trips abroad to the holy shrines in Najaf and Karbela in 1870-71 and twice to Europe in 1873 and 1878. He became governor of several provinces including Mazandaran, (where Reza Shah's father had served in the provincial army) and later served as Minister of Justice. He was not especially well educated or particularly intelligent, but carried himself well and acquired a reputation for probity, honesty and as a devout Moslem. Towards the end of his life he was affectionately refered to as 'Khan Daii' ('Honourable Uncle').[14]

[§] Naser al Molk (Abolqasem Qaragozlou), c.1863–1927, came from a tribal family in western Iran. His grandfather Mahmoud Khan Naser al Molk, a grandee of the Qaragozlou tribe, became a high functionary at the court of Naser al Din Shah, and later as Minister of Foreign Affairs accompanied the Shah on his second trip to Europe in 1878. During this trip the grandfather took his grandson with him and the young Abolqasem stayed in England to attend Balliol College, Oxford between 1879 and 1882. His classmates included Edward Grey, future Foreign Minister, and Cecil Spring Rice, subsequently British Minister in Tehran and later Washington. On his return he became a personal translator for Naser al Din Shah and was given his grandfather's title upon the latter's death. He was Minister of Finance, Governor and Prime Minister very briefly in 1907. Under pressure from constitutionalist elements he tendered his resignation as Prime Minister without the permission of Mohammad Ali Shah, who had him imprisoned. It was Britain's intervention that secured his release and probably saved his life. He fled to England where he stayed until 1910, when he returned to Iran to become regent until 1915. He returned to Europe and remained until the last year of his life. He acted as an adviser to Curzon on the 1919 Agreement. It is doubtful whether Naser al Molk ever thought of himself as an Iranian. Iran happened to be where his considerable property was located. He left behind a very competent Persian translation of Shakespeare's Othello.[15]

College, was a confirmed anglophile and saw his primary role as keeping the two powers satisfied.

In December 1910 the Government, in despair over the political and financial condition of the country, decided to employ an American, Morgan Shuster,* to improve financial management and tax collection. Americans with their history of good works as missionaries were admired and regarded as people of integrity. The move toward utilising the services of nationals of a third country was not entirely new. Earlier unsuccessful attempts had been made to involve a third country in Iran and lessen the influence of the two powers. It was France in the Napoleonic era, Germany and Austria in the 1880s and now the United States. In employing Shuster the Iranians did not want a mere functionary. The primary goal was to engage the United States in Iran in order to loosen the Anglo-Russian hold over the country.

Accompanied by four assistants, Shuster arrived in early 1911 with the title of Treasurer General and Financial Adviser. From the outset he was viewed with deep suspicion by the British and Russians. The powers, having divided Iran into two zones of influence, had difficulty in accepting an independent third party not answerable to them. Shuster went to work immediately and performed near-miracles, though ultimately for a lost cause. In June 1911, in a pre-planned two-pronged attack with Russian support the former Shah landed at Anzali on the Caspian Sea and one of his brothers, Salar al Dowleh,† led a force into Iran from Mesopotamia. In addition to mercenaries the former Shah had counted on the support of rebel tribes in the north-east and west of Iran. It was the combination of Shuster's independence and his innovations in financial matters that allowed the government to pay its soldiers,

---

*   Morgan Shuster, 1877–1960, was a lawyer from Washington DC who had previously served as Collector of Customs in Cuba, adviser on customs and immigration in the Philippines and later as a member of the US governing body in the Philippines. He was highly regarded by William Howard Taft, Governor of the Philippines (later President of the United States, then Chief Justice of the Supreme Court). In 1910 the Iranian Minister in Washington, Ali Qoli Khan Nabil al Dowleh, asked the US Government for assistance. Although the US Government officially stayed clear of the selection process, Shuster was recommended with the understanding that he was assuming his new post in a private capacity. Shuster's brief stay in Iran and his formidable services made him a legendary figure among Iranians and led to the beginning of the Iranian nationalists' attempts to have the United States act as a third force in Iran to counterbalance the Russians and British. During the early Pahlavi era unsuccessful attempts were made to re-employ Shuster as financial adviser.

enabling the army to repel Mohammad Ali Shah. Not only was the Persian Government able to pay its troops, but Shuster also devised plans whereby wherever the rebel forces advanced he ordered government funds withdrawn lest they fall into rebel hands.[16]

The British, who had for several decades considered southern Iran part of their empire and had appointed officials who acted as autonomous rulers of the region, now went a step further. They landed troops in the south, ostensibly to provide safety for their nationals. The Russians, in reponse, landed several thousand troops and occupied cities in the northern provinces.

After several months of fighting the forces of the former Shah were defeated in September 1911 and Mohammad Ali Shah once again escaped to Russia and his brother to Mesopotamia. After Mohammad Ali Shah's defeat, Shuster attempted to seize the property of Sho'a al Saltaneh,[#] another brother of Mohammad Ali Shah, in lieu of back taxes. Sho'a al Saltaneh had been a participant in the recent invasion and also had escaped to Russia. The Russians who

---

† Abolfath Mirza Salar al Dowleh, 1881–1959, was the third son of Mozafar al Din Shah. He became Governor of Kermanshah in 1897 but was removed by the Shah for excessive zeal in expropriating other people's property. He was soon forgiven and became Governer of Zanjan in 1899, Khuzestan and Lurestan in 1901. In 1907 he led a rebellion against his older brother who had a few months earlier ascended the throne. The rebellion was put down by Atabak and he was brought to Tehran and placed under house arrest. For past services to British Petroleum he was given protection by the British Consul in Kermanshah and was allowed to leave Iran. In 1911, ostensibly to aid his brother in taking back the throne, but with personal ambitions of his own, he entered Hamadan and began a march to Tehran. In the interim he declared himself Shah. His army suffered great losses about 100 miles southwest of Tehran, and after his defeat he escaped abroad and lived in Switzerland. He secretly entered Iran in 1926 and attempted to oust Reza Khan but again escaped to Europe. He was given a subsidy of 1500 tomans per month by Britain. The subsidy ended in 1933 and he lived in Haifa until 1935. The last fourteen years of his life he lived in Egypt where he died. People who knew and have written about him uniformly believe he was out of touch with the realities of the world, and at times his instability approached derangement.[17]

Malek Mansour Mirza Sho'a al Saltaneh, c.1874–1920, was the second son of Mozaffar al Din Shah. He became Governor of Fars in 1900 and 1904 and both times the Shah was forced to recall him in the face of uprisings. He was considered briefly to replace his older brother Mohammad Ali Mirza as heir to the throne, but the Russians intervened and Mohammad Ali Mirza remained heir. At the time of his death he was one of the wealthiest Iranians of his day.[18]

had placed him and his property under their protection objected and issued an ultimatum demanding Shuster's immediate dismissal and an undertaking by Iran not to employ any foreign subject without the consent of the Russian and British Legations. To support their threat the Russians amassed more troops at the border. The Iranian parliament defied the ultimatum. The Russians countered by sending troops into all northern provinces. As well as reiterating the demand for the immediate dismissal of Shuster they demanded payment for expenses incurred in the deployment of troops. The British, by virtue of the 1907 Convention, sat by idly. Lord Grey, in a speech in the House of Commons on 14 December 1911, defended Russian actions:

> Russia played fair... (Shuster) should not have appointed treasury officials at Esfahan and Tabriz which are in the Russian Zone... That won't do... Russia is entitled to demand indemnity for [mobilising troops but I hope she decides] not to seek prompt payment.

On 10 July 1912 Grey, again addressing the House of Commons argued that Persia was now 'more independent because of the (1907) Convention'.[19] In March, to enforce demands, Russian troops shelled the most holy site in Iran, the Imam Reza shrine in Mashhad. There were atrocities in Tabriz, where a senior cleric and several prominent people were hanged in a public square for expressing anti-Russian sentiments. The subservient regent forced parliament to delegate its powers to a commission which then accepted the Russian ultimatum and its terms. Shuster left Iran in December 1911 and parliament was closed.

The constitutional period brought forth very few men of ability, and the nationalist fervour and reformist zeal were extinguished early. It appeared, as it had many times before, that Iran was doomed and nothing could save her. Every major attempt at reform had been defeated by forces the Iranians could not control. The constitutional movement had been thwarted by the shelling of parliament and the murder of a number of its leading figures. It had reduced the power of the monarch, but instead had allowed Bakhtiari tribesmen, who owed greater loyalty to British interests than to Iran, to dominate the political scene. The Bakhtiaris were in fact one of the guardians of British oil in the South and had even been given shares in the Anglo-Persian Oil Company (APOC). Britain in 1909 had reached an agreement with the Bakhtiari tribal elders for the payment of £650 per year for ten years, paid in advance, and a loan of £10,000 for the right of passage through their lands and for providing security in the oil region. It had further been agreed that the tribe would receive 3% of APOC's profits. The 3% would be deducted from the Iranian

Government's share of profits. These arrangements had been made without the consent or even knowledge of the Iranian Government.[20]

The period 1911–1921 was probably the bleakest period in Iranian history since the Afghan invasion in the 1720s. The constitutional movement which had as one of its aims the curtailment of foreign intervention had ironically increased the hold of foreign powers by bounds. The 1907 Convention had brought home the reality that Iran was in no way independent. Many leaders of the constitutional movement lost hope and reverted either to their self-seeking ways or general apathy. When the nationalists had attempted to appoint an independent regent, the British had interfered and had appointed the docile Naser al Molk who never seemed comfortable in Iran and probably owed little loyalty to her. Then there was the Shuster chapter which was an attempt to salvage the country's economy and finances and to assert symbolically a vestige of independence. The episode had ended in a humiliating defeat.

Iran had not had a national military force since the days of Naser al Din Shah. In 1878, on his second trip abroad, Naser al Din Shah had seen a parade by Cossack soldiers in Russia. Greatly impressed, he asked the Czar whether a similar force could be established in Iran. In 1879 under a 40-year agreement the Russians established a Cossack Brigade manned by Iranians and commanded by Russian officers. The brigade thereafter was always a tool of Russian imperialist designs and Persian autocracy, serving primarily as a bodyguard for the Shah. In 1916 during World War I the force was expanded into a division composed of 7,866 men, 50 senior and 66 junior Russian officers and 202 Persian officers. Until late 1920 it was always headed by a Russian officer. It was to be disbanded and integrated into the united national army by Reza Khan in 1922.[21]

The Gendarmerie was created in 1911 by the second parliament during the brief constitutional period. In 1910 the Iranian Government approached the Swedish Government to organise a highway police. The idea had been given by the Russians. The British did not favour such a force but made no objection. By 1914, the Gendarmerie comprised 200 officers and 7,000 men. During World War I its size was reduced because of the pro-German sympathies of some of its Swedish officers. At the end of the war only a few Swedish officers remained. All returned by 1924.[22] Although commanded by ostensibly neutral Swedish officers, it was not free from Russian and British influence. The British also had their Indian troops in the south and encouraged tribal leaders to act independently of the central Government.

In June 1914 elections were held and parliament, forced to close over the Shuster affair in 1911, was reconvened. By 1915 Ahmad Shah, having reached the age of 18, was crowned and Naser al Molk, the regent who had been a dominant figure, left Iran.

By the beginning of the Great War the Iranian flag flew over only a few principal cities. Whatever vestiges of independence had remained all but vanished in August 1914 with the outbreak of war in Europe. In October 1914 Turkey entered the war on the side of the Germans and in November occupied parts of north-western Iran. Iran declared its neutrality a few days after Turkish occupation. In that same month the Iranian Legation in Washington DC transmitted to the State Department Iran's declaration of neutrality and requested the United States Government to do what it could to prevent hostilities from spilling over onto Iranian territory. On 11 November the State Department gave 'a general pledge to support Persian neutrality'.[23] It was obvious, however, that none of the belligerents would pay any heed to the declaration of neutrality and that Iran was to be a battlefield. The British and Russians with their total control over Iran's political figures and institutions could have induced the Iranian Government to declare war on Germany and join the Allies, but they had no desire to do so. They were wary of what Iranian expectations were likely to be after the war and did not want to limit their freedom of action in Iran when the war ended.

Britain and Russia had already begun talks concerning their interests in the East in the post-war era and reached accord in what is now called the Constantinople Convention. The agreement is not a single document but a series of diplomatic exchanges between 4 March and 10 April 1915 whereby the parties agreed, *inter alia*, for Britain to have control over Iran's neutral zone specified in the 1907 Convention in return for Russian control of the Dardanelles and the European domains of the Ottoman Empire.

The British, who already had troops in the south, landed more and occupied Abadan and Bushehr. The Russians also landed troops in north-west Iran and shortly thereafter in Gilan province. The Germans, who had no troops in the Middle East, played a subtle game. Their aim was to incite Moslems in India, Afghanistan and Iran to side with their Turkish Moslem brothers and destabilise the Allied presences, forcing the British to divert troops to quell uprisings. During and after the war Britain greatly exaggerated the dimension of German operations in Iran mainly to justify her post-war plans for the area.[24] With clever use of the tribes the Germans did indeed cause some problems for the British in southern Iran and even in the oil region of the south-west. In 1915 elements of the Bakhtiari tribe, with the help of Turkish and German agents, damaged several oil pipelines. The British Government and APOC (now totally controlled by Britain) which had ignored the Iranian Government and had sought security from the Bakhtiari tribe, held the Iranian Government responsible for the damage and asked for about £700,000 in indemnity . The fact that Iran had declared its neutrality and that the damage had been caused by the very people with whom the British had an agreement was ignored.[25]

Soon Russian and British troops were fighting the Turks in all regions except central and eastern Iran. Famine and epidemics were widespread in western Iran. In Hamadan and Kermanshah people were forced to live in caves.[26] Over 100,000 people died of starvation and more than 10,000 villages were deserted.[27] Carpet-making centres in western Iran disappeared. Iran's declaration of neutrality continued to be ignored. Harold Nicolson has stated, 'Persia had been exposed to violations and suffering not endured by any other neutral country'.[28]

The Government of Hassan Mostofi (Mostofi al Mamalek),* a respected politician and member of the dominant faction in parliament, the Democrats, leaned toward the Germans and the Turks.[30] With Russian troops having actually entered Tehran, a movement began to transfer the entire machinary of government from Tehran to Qom and to form a government partially free of British and Russian dominance. Mostofi advised the deputies to move to Qom and Ahmad Shah, who may briefly have been in sympathy with the Democrats, appeared to agree with the suggestion. The plans were soon aborted as the British and Russian Ministers in Tehran warned the Shah against moving. Any possible chance of forming an independent government was dashed. Nonetheless, some prominent members of the Democrat Party did go to Qom and established a National Defence Committee. The founders of the committee, fearful

---

* Hassan Mostofi, c.1871–1932, one of the most popular Iranian politicians of this century, was the son of Mirza Yousef Mostofi al Mamalek, c.1812–c.1885. From 1858 Mirza Yousef served as the Minister of Finance and from about 1863 was regarded as equal with the First Minister. In 1880 he was finally made First Minister and retained the post until his death in 1885. In 1881, at the request of Mirza Yousef, the Shah bestowed the title of Mostofi al Mamalek (Chancellor of the Realm) on the ten-year-old Hassan. Both father and son carried themselves as gentlemen. Both were kind, honest, steadfast friends, humble and generous. As Prime Minister Hassan Mostofi stood up to both Britain and Russia in World War I, giving credence to his reputation as a person of character and integrity. Mostofi lived in Europe, mostly in Paris, from 1900–1907. After his return he served six times as Prime Minister.[29]

of being apprehended by the Allies, soon moved to Kermanshah in western Iran and formed a government in exile. Parliament was dissolved not to meet until 1921. To counter the formation of a government in exile the British installed a pronounced anglophile, Abdol Hosein Mirza Farmanfarma,* as Prime Minister.[30]

There was no longer any pretence as to who ruled Iran. The zones of influence had become zones of occupation.

---

* Abdol Hosein Mirza Farmanfarma, 1857–1939, who adopted the family name Farmanfarmaian, was one of the most influential Iranian politicians from the end of the nineteenth century until the early 1920s. He was the second son of Firouz Mirza, son of Abbas Mirza, the Crown Prince. His mother was the grand-daughter of Fath Ali Shah. He married Ezat al Dowleh, the daughter of Mozaffar al Din Shah around 1888. His own sister, Hazrat-e-Olya, was married to Mozaffar al Din Shah. From the 1880s onward he held high positions in the military, numerous governorships and ministries. He was briefly Prime Minister at a difficult period in 1915. He was well disposed to British interests in Iran and received the GCMG (Grand Companion of the Order of St Michael and St George) from the British Crown. He was highly intelligent and shrewd and was far superior to other princes of his generation. Virtually all of his children received higher education in Iran and abroad and were successful in their fields, many achieving prominence. His eventful and interesting life deserves a full-length biography.

NOTES ON INTRODUCTION
Further details of publications and documents in Bibliography

1   John Malcolm, *History of Persia*, vol. 2. p 271.
2   G.R.G. Hambly, 'Aqa Mohammad Khan and the Establishment of the Qajar Dynasty,' *Journal of Royal Central Asian Society*, p 1.
3   George N. Curzon, *Persia and the Persian Question*, vol. 1, pp 410–411.
4   Ghasem Ghani, *Yaddasht ha-e-Dr Ghasem Ghani (Memoirs of Dr Ghasem Ghani)*, vol. 9, pp 230–239.
5   Mehdi Bamdad, *Tarikh Rejal Iran Quroun 12, 13, 14 (Dictionary of National Biography of Iran: Twelfth, Thirteenth, Fourteenth Centuries)*, vol. 2, pp 203–209.
6   Abbas Amanat, *Pivot of the Universe: Naser al-Din Shah Qajar and the Iranian Monarchy, 1851–1896*, p 34; Abbas Eqbal, *Mirza Taqi Khan Amir Kabir*, pp 24–82.
7   Mehdi Bamdad, *Tarikh Rejal Iran Quroun 12, 13, 14 (Dictionary of National Biography of Iran: Twelfth, Thirteenth, Fourteenth Centuries)*, vol. 2, pp 387–425.
8   *Ibid.*, vol. 2 pp 11–23.
9   L/PS/10/872, Cox to Curzon, 3 December 1919 (L designates India Office Library). Quoted by Houshang Sabahi, *British Policy in Persia 1918–1925*, p 12. This is a well-researched book which has brought to light many previously overlooked documents..
10 Edward Grey, *Twenty Five Years 1892–1916*, vol. 2, pp 166–169.
11 Some Iranian historians regard Sepahsalar as anti-Russian since he was partly responsible for the fall of Mohammad Ali Shah in 1909 and resisted his attempt to retrieve the crown in 1911. However, in the archives of the British Foreign Office there is the translation of a letter from the Czarist Minister to Tehran, together with a copy of the Persian original dated April 1916, stating that the Imperial Russian Legation takes under its protection all the properties and interests of Sepahsalar A'zam to protect him against all internal and foreign molestations. FO 248/1321, 4 October 1920 (FO designates Foreign Office).
12 Mehdi Bamdad, *Tarikh Rejal Iran Quroun 12, 13, 14 (Dictionary of National Biography of Iran: Twelfth, Thirteenth, Fourteenth Centuries)*, vol. 2, pp 448–451.
13 *Ibid.*, vol. 4, pp 17–33.
14 *Ibid.*, vol. 2, pp 435–442.
15 *Ibid.*, vol. 1, pp 66–70.
16 Robert A. McDaniel, *The Shuster Mission and the Persian Constitutional Revolution*, p 159; Morgan W. Shuster, *The Strangling of Persia*, pp 85–133.
17 Mehdi Bamdad, *Tarikh Rejal Iran Quroun 12, 13, 14 (Dictionary of National Biography of Iran: Twelfth, Thirteenth, Fourteenth Centuries)*, vol. 1, pp 48–50; FO 416/98, Bullard to Halifax, 7 February 1940.
18 *Ibid.*, vol. 4, pp 156–158.
19 Sir Edward Grey, *Speeches on Foreign Affairs 1904–1914*, ed. Paul Knaplund, pp 172–184. See also pp 70 and 100.
20 L.P. Elwell-Sutton, *Persian Oil*, pp 19–21; R.W. Ferrier, *The History of the British Petroleum Company*, vol. 1, pp 67, 120–122, 126–128. The subsidies to the Bakhtiaris were far higher than cited as was the British Government payment to them during World War I, although the exact amounts have never been fully documented.

21 Rouhollah Ramazani, *The Foreign Policy of Iran 1500–1941*, p 178.

22 Andreas Adhal (ed.), *Iran Through the Ages – A Swedish Anthology*, pp 129–135.

23 Documents relating to 'Foreign Relations of the United States, 1914', supplement, Washington DC, 1928, quoted by Benson Lee Grayson, *United States-Iranian Relations*, p 27.

24 L.I. Miroshnikov, *Iran in World War I*, p 15. See also Sykes, *Wassmuss, the German Lawrence*, wherein he unconvincingly argues that a single German and a few German Consuls assigned to the provinces by the German Government before the war caused 'unending misery' for the British Empire.

25 L.P. Elwell-Sutton, *Persian Oil*, pp 26.

26 M.H. Donohoe, *With the Persian Expedition*, pp 118–119. See also Donald N. Wilber, *Riza Shah Pahlavi*, p 17. For famine and starvation in Hamadan see Maj. Gen. Dunsterville, *The Adventures of Dunsterforce*, p 108. For a general account see same author in *Stalky's Reminiscences*, pp 270– 286.

27 Donald N. Wilber, *Riza Shah Pahlavi*, p 17.

28 Harold Nicolson, *Curzon, The Last Phase*, p 129.

29 Mehdi Bamdad, *Tarikh Rejal Iran Quroun 12, 13, 14 (Dictionary of National Biography of Iran: Twelfth, Thirteenth, Fourteenth Centuries)*, vol. 1, pp 318–321. See also Nasrollah Entezam's excellent sketch of Mostofi in *Khaterat Nasrollah Entezam (Memoirs of Nasrollah Entezam)*, pp 81–91.

30 The practice of referring to Iranian politicians as pro-German or pro-American has been the cause of many misunderstandings by Western readers of Iranian history. Similarly use of the terms russophile or anglophile should be understood in the context of a country that was dominated in varying degrees from 1828–1917 by Britain and/or Russia. The terms pro-German or pro-French in the period when the influence of the two imperial powers was almost suffocating merely meant anti-British and anti-Russian and hopeful that a third country might ease the burden.

1

The 1919 Agreement

What saved Iran from greater destruction and loss of life during World War I was the revolution in Russia in 1917. Russian troops began withdrawing from Iran shortly after October of that year and the only area of armed conflict were parts of western Iran where British troops attempted to dislodge the Ottoman forces.

Iran at this time had a population of approximately ten million, about a quarter of which were tribal and nomadic.[1] Of these ten million very few were regarded as of any consequence. There was the Crown, a few Qajar princes who were close to the Shah and a score of public officials. Equally important were the tribal leaders who dominated almost half of the country. Whole provinces such as Fars and Khuzestan were in effect independent of Central Government. The clergy were also independent of the Central Government as they were economically self-sufficient. Through their administration of property placed under religious trusts they had control of and income from areas as large as Crown property. They also derived influence through their control and administration of education and laws. Of lesser importance but still a force to be considered were some leading merchants in the capital and the provinces who controlled the flow of money through private loans and the distribution of major domestic products. They were also a large source of funding for the clergy.

The constitutional movement had brought forth a superficial parliamentary rule with almost no foundation laid and no real leaders.

21

No coherent party system arose, such as the Congress Party in India, and no dominant figure emerged. The few politicians who had some following were too timid to stand on their own feet and depended upon foreign support.

The British Legation exercised an inordinate degree of influence over each of the power groups. This had come about through a variety of factors and over a period of almost a hundred years. A broad network of paid agents and professional sympathisers had been established. Before the 1917 revolution the Russians had their own similar network, but now the British were masters of the East and it was prudent for former Czarist sympathisers to transfer their loyalties and support to the British. More important than agents and sympathisers were prominent families who had inherited their loyalty to Britain from their fathers and forefathers. These families had prospered over the decades and been kept immune from the whims of capricious rulers. This generational and patrimonial allegiance was especially true of tribal leaders. Also to be considered were those pragmatists who knew that after the armistice Britain had become the unquestioned power in the region between the Mediterranean and India.

Britain's political and economic control of Iran was further strengthened by the presence of her army in almost all parts of the country. Russia, which from 1828 had been the ascendent power in Iran, was for the moment totally out of the picture. The Germans and the Turks were no longer of any consequence. British troops, with the help of some White Russian soldiers, became active in northern Iran and the Caspian region. Maj. Gen. Dunsterville with some 200 troops and a small flotilla controlled the Caspian Sea.[2] Other British troops and the SPR (South Persia Rifles) were already in control of the rest of the country. As early as 1905 Percy Sykes, then consul in Kerman, had suggested the creation of a mounted force in southern Iran manned by Persian soldiers under British officers to 'solve the Security Question'.[3] In 1916, after he had left Iran, the ever-helpful Naser al Molk had given the British the idea of forming the South Persia Rifles, an army of Iranian recruits, called volunteers, under British command which was a direct violation of Iran's sovereignty.[4] By 1918 Britain was the undisputed power in Iran.[5] Even the Cossack Division commanded by a pro-Czarist Russian colonel, was totally dependent upon Britain for its running expenses.

With all her rivals eliminated by war or revolution the thinking of British policy-makers from this point onwards concentrated on how best to guarantee the exclusiveness of their position. It appears that for a brief period Britain seriously thought that the simplest solution would be to seek a determination from the Peace Conference that she rule Iran as a mandate.[6] However serious the idea, it seems to have been abandoned by early 1919 partly because it was believed the United States would not acquiesce and that even France, which had imperial ambitions of her own toward the former possessions of the Ottomans, would oppose such a move. The next best and perhaps simpler alternative was to keep Iran isolated and force the Iranians to agree to and acknowledge Britain's *de facto* control. There was now a feverish attempt to work out a treaty pursuant to which Iran would cede to Britain control of its financial, military and foreign affairs. Before the details of such a treaty could be negotiated, preliminary steps had to be taken. The first was to isolate Iran diplomatically and economically. This was not difficult in late 1918 and early 1919 as Iran lay devastated and in economic ruin and Britain controlled entry and exit into and from the country. In 1919, under British pressure, a blacklist of Germans, Turks and other undesirable foreign nationals had been prepared. These people were expelled and not allowed to re-enter Iran. The list included German technicians and even orientalists and archaeologists.[7] With Britain in control of all telephone and telegraph lines, unauthorised communication with other countries was next to impossible.

It was also thought desirable to exclude Iran from the forthcoming Paris Peace Conference and any contact with other allied leaders. Iran, a non-belligerent in the war, had suffered probably more than any other neutral nation including Belgium, and intended to send a delegation to the Peace Conference to seek redress for at least the material losses suffered. Britain tried to thwart these efforts. At first an attempt was made by the British Legation to convince Ahmad Shah and the Government that such representation was unnecessary. When it seemed that the Iranians nevertheless intended to send a delegation and further overt moves to block it could embarrass the British Government, Britain tried to influence its composition. When this proved only partially successful, the Foreign Office began to make certain that the Iranian delegation would not gain admittance and be heard. John Lawrence Caldwell, the United States Minister in Tehran, informed the State Department that although Iran's grievances during the war were far greater than any other neutral country, Britain continued to object to its demands being discussed at the peace conference.[8] Mo'tamen al Molk (Hosein Pirnia), a much-respected member of parliament informed Caldwell that he intended to go to the United States to plead Iran's case. The British Legation immediately exerted pressure and the trip was cancelled.[9]

In December 1917, the Cabinet of Ain al Dowleh* fell. Hassan
Vosouq (Vosouq al Dowleh)† who as Prime Minister briefly in early
1917 had shown some initiative and forcefulness in office became
the choice of the British Legation to form a government. Vosouq was
reluctant to accept the appointment primarily because he felt the
economic and political situation in Iran made it a hopeless task.
Vosouq also knew that the young Shah was cool if not hostile toward
him. Ahmad Shah, who had never cared for Vosouq (for reasons
which will be discussed later), appointed the Bakhtiari tribal leader
Samsam al Saltaneh as Prime Minister.#

By the spring of 1918 the British were firmer in their belief that
only Vosouq could create a stronger yet pliable Persia, and became

---

*   Soltan Abdol Majid Mirza Ain al Dowleh, c.1846–1927, was a grandson
of Fath Ali Shah. He was close to Mozaffar al Din Mirza when the latter
was heir to the throne. He became a powerful Prime Minister in 1903
and lasted until the end of 1905 when his autocratic ways and opposition to constitutionalist demands led to civil disturbance and the Shah
was forced to remove him. He became Prime Minister again for brief
periods in 1915 and 1917.[10]

†   Hassan Vosouq (Vosouq al Dowleh), 1868–1951, came from one of the
most prominent Iranian families of the last 200 years. His ancestors had
served Qajar kings from the beginning of the nineteenth century. From
his father's family Vosouq could count three prime ministers, Mostofi
and later Matin Daftari and Mosaddeq; and on his mother's side another
Prime Minister, Mirza Ali Khan Amin al Dowleh. Vosouq was raised by
the latter as his mother died when he was still a youngster and his father
was in the provinces as a finance administrator. He received a solid
Persian education in his youth, and became fluent in French during his
many trips abroad and conversant with English. At an early age he
became an assistant to his father and soon became the financial administrator of Azarbaijan province. He was elected to the founding session of
parliament and served as one of the Deputy Speakers. He became
Minister of Finance in 1911; Minister of Foreign Affairs in 1913 and
again 1914; Minister of Finance in 1915; Prime Minister and Minister of
Foreign Affairs from August 1916 to May 1917; and again Prime Minister
from August 1918 to June 1920, after which he left Iran not to return
until 1926. Under Reza Shah he was appointed Minister of Finance in
June 1926 and later Minister of Justice. He resigned in November of the
same year as he had been elected member of parliament. He was re-
elected to parliament's seventh session in 1928 after which he retired.
He was occasionally consulted by Reza Shah on financial matters and
was appointed chairman of the Iranian Academy of Culture in 1936.
Vosouq was a person of exceptional ability, brave, direct and fearless,
who took risks. He was learned in Persian history and literature and is
regarded as a competent minor poet. He was also interested in accumu-
lating wealth to support his life-style and was often unconcerned about
the means by which this was done.[11]

more adamant. Vosouq was still hesitant and set several conditions for his acceptance. He wanted the assurance that the Shah would not interfere with his government and programme. In discussions with Sir Charles Marling, the British Minister in Tehran, he set forth further conditions: the withdrawal of all foreign troops; an end to extra-territorial rights by foreign powers, or at least a revision of such prior agreements; the disbanding of the SPR; the enlargement of the Cossack Division under neutral and Iranian officers; representation at the Peace Conference and an assurance that Iran would be compensated for material damage suffered during the war; and the abrogation of the 1907 and 1915 conventions. In the meantime Vosouq wanted an interim arrangement whereby Britain would finance the running expenses of the Cossack Division in the amount of 300,000 tomans monthly.

In 1918 the new Government in Russia renounced all Czarist privileges in Iran including the 1907 and 1915 conventions and in order to embarrass Britain made public the provisions of the then secret 1915 Constantinople Convention.[12] As a result Marling appears to have responded favourably to some of Vosouq's proposals. The Foreign Office, while still toying with the idea of some sort of a mandate arrangement, supported Marling in his choice of Vosouq. Marling again began discussions with Ahmad Shah to secure a pledge that he would appoint and support Vosouq as Prime Minister.

Ahmad Shah was now twenty-one years old and had become a pre-eminent force in the country. He had passed through a difficult childhood. When he was twelve he had witnessed the overthrow and exile of his father to whom he was closely attached. Mohammad Ali Shah had also greatly loved his young son and when forced to leave the country had proposed to take his son with him into exile with the promise that he would be sent back to rule the country when he had attained majority. In the interim the country would be ruled by a regent. After some hard bargaining with the victorious leaders of the uprising the son was forced to remain behind. The first regent,

---

\# Najaf Qoli Khan Samsam al Saltaneh, c.1850–1930, was the son of the Chieftain (Ilkhani) Hosein Qoli Khan Bakhtiari (murdered by Zell al Soltan) and the older brother of Ali Qoli Khan Bakhtiari (Sardar As'ad II). It was at the urging of Sardar As'ad that Najaf Qoli Khan joined in the march to liberate Tehran. He had held various ministerial posts in numerous cabinets and was Prime Minister on seven occasions. He was simple and uneducated, raised in the tribal environment and devoid of any political acumen. It was his tribal standing and the exigencies of the day which made him a leading political figure.[13]

the elderly and respectable Azd al Molk, had been aloof and exercised no influence on the young boy. The second regent, the self-centred Naser al Molk, also showed no interest in his education. Ahmad Shah was later exposed to several tutors, including the learned Mohammad Ali Foroughi (Zoka al Molk), but with no discernible effect.

From all available evidence Ahmad Shah's traumatic childhood memories and his father's dethronement and expulsion turned him into a confirmed cynic with no real interest in his native land. His primary preoccupation became the gathering of wealth. His father had advised him to beware of the fickleness of his countrymen and that he too could be discarded. He should therefore enrich himself and lay aside money for any eventuality. In his teens he was already hoarding grain. By early 1919 he began to play the Paris stock market. Before his first trip to Europe in 1919 his agent was an Iranian financier, Toumanians. Later when his path to Europe was opened he secured the services of various French Bourse agents. Marling had said of him, 'Ahmad Shah always hoped to make a killing on the Paris Bourse'[14] and that he had 'few of the Persian virtues and their vices in a highly depraved form'.[15]

When in May 1918 Marling approached the Shah again on the question of his consent and support of Vosouq's premiership, the Shah used the opportunity to strike a bargain and to extract as much money as possible. He reminded Marling that when his father had been banished, it had been agreed by the Iranian Government, with the guarantee of the Czarist regime, that a monthly pension be paid to his father. He was therefore willing to appoint Vosouq on the condition that he would be guaranteed a pension of 75,000 tomans a month (£25,000) if he were forced to leave Iran at any time. He also asked for a monthly sum of 20,000 tomans while he was on the throne. Marling advised the Foreign Office to leave the issue of a life pension silent but recommended a monthly payment of 15,000 tomans (£5000).

In a later dispatch dated 29 July 1919,[16] the entire history of the financial arrangements reached with Ahmad Shah in the spring of 1918 is set out: payment of 15,000 tomans monthly was approved and paid from August 1918 (the same month Vosouq was appointed Prime Minister) 'for as long as he retains and supports Vosouq ed Dowleh loyally'. In December 1918, Ahmad Shah began showing opposition to Vosouq and the Legation threatened to stop payments; in April 1919 Ahmad Shah further requested a life subsidy of 20,000 tomans a month. Sir Percy Cox (who at the time of this dispatch had succeeded Marling as Minister to Tehran) had recommended, 'We should agree because Ahmad Shah can't live very long due to his obesity'. The Foreign Office opposed the additional scheme and Cox then recommended 'that we agree for at least 10 years because Ahmad Shah cannot live much beyond that period'. Curzon, the new Foreign Secretary, rejected any additional payments and the reason advanced was that such an arrangement needed British parliamentary approval, which was unlikely.

Cox's 'medical' prognosis of Ahmad Shah was not far off the mark. Ahmad Shah was to die in exile in Paris in 1930 within 11 years of Cox's telegram. John Caldwell, the United States Minister in Tehran, commented on Ahmad Shah's frequent crash diets and ventured that the Shah probably had lost and regained some 200 pounds (90 kilograms) between 1919 and 1921. In 1919, within a four-month period, the Shah lost some seventy pounds (30 kilograms).[17]

During the summer of 1918 Marling continued to press Vosouq's candidacy. Ahmad Shah, who had not enjoyed the best of relations with Vosouq during the latter's brief premiership in 1917, was even more apprehensive now. Vosouq was a self-assured, confident man whose ancestors had served several Qajar kings. He was not willing to countenance the whims and greed of a twenty-one year old. The Shah was especially envious of Vosouq's closeness to the British Legation which he saw as a threat to his own direct access.[18] Marling's persistent pressure and the agreement of the Foreign Office to the monthly payment finally yielded results. In late July 1918 Samsam al Saltaneh resigned and on 5 August Vosouq became Prime Minister. The Foreign Office agreed to continue the moratorium on repayment of prior loans and also began payment of a 350,000 toman monthly subsidy for the Government to function.[19] However, Vosouq's other pre-conditions, such as the disbanding of the SPR, the creation of a unified military force and the employment of a few advisers from neutral countries at the Ministry of Justice were rejected or deferred for later discussions.

Marling left Iran in early September and was replaced by Sir Percy Cox, who arrived in Tehran shortly thereafter on 15 September 1918.[20] It is not clear why Marling left. He may have felt that his primary task of the appointment of Vosouq was accomplished. However, there is lingering doubt. Some £25,000 was spent to induce certain members of the ulama and merchants to start a demonstration to induce Ahmad Shah to appoint Vosouq. It led to a riot and there were arrests. This bungled attempt may have contributed to Marling's recall but there is no supporting evidence for the supposition.

Marling and Cox came from different backgrounds. Whereas Marling was a member of a prominent family, Cox came from a more

modest background. After Harrow and Sandhurst Cox had begun
his career as an India Office civil servant and in 1899 Curzon
had appointed him Consul in Muscat. In 1903 he and his wife
had travelled by boat with Curzon, who was then Viceroy of India
(1899–1905), and Sir Arthur Hardinge, British Minister in Tehran
(1900–1905), up the Persian Gulf on a leisurely inspection trip
and had gained the further confidence of Curzon. Cox had been
appointed in 1915 Britain's Resident in the Persian Gulf, a post he
held until his appointment to Tehran. The Resident was in effect the
supreme authority concerning British interests in the Gulf region
including all the Sheikhdoms. The Resident's seat was in Bushehr
in southern Iran which flew the British flag and was treated by
Britain as part of her territory. Cox had extensive dealings with
Iranian officials during this period and was regarded as an expert in
Iranian affairs.[21]

A far more important development in Anglo-Iranian relations was
the appointment of Lord Curzon as Foreign Secretary after Lord
Balfour's[22] resignation on 24 October 1919. Although Curzon did
not officially secure his post until that date, he in effect ran the
Foreign Office from September 1918 and became acting Foreign
Secretary from January 1919 when Balfour went to the Paris Peace
Conference. Curzon had always believed that people from the India
Office were better suited to deal with 'easterners' and Cox was in
Curzon's eyes the ideal envoy to implement his policy.

What made Curzon the architect of British policy towards Iran
even before his appointment as Foreign Secretary was his chairman-
ship of the key committee dealing with Iran. The total dependence of
the British Navy on Iranian oil during the First World War as well as
the perennial issue of the defence of India compelled the British
Government to establish a Persia Committee in late 1917. Its purpose
was to 'solve the Persian question once and for all' by extending
Britain's control over the country.[23] In March 1918 an Eastern
Committee was created, its purview being the Arab territories east of
Suez, Persia, the Caucasus, Turkestan and Afghanistan. Its membership was composed of Field Marshall Sir Henry Wilson, Chief of
the Imperial General Staff, Lord Balfour, the Foreign Secretary,
Robert Cecil, his deputy, Edwin Montague, the Secretary of the War
Cabinet, and the ranking officials of the relevant ministries. Curzon
became chairman of the committee as a senior member of the War
Cabinet.[24] As an expert Curzon dominated the formulation and execution of policy insofar as Iran was concerned. Curzon knew the
country better than any diplomat in the West. He had been drawn
to it much earlier from his arduous journey of 1889–1890 which had

provided him with material for the most important of his books, *Persia and the Persian Question.*[25]

The 1919 Agreement had several authors but the conceptual father and driving force was Curzon. Curzon's life-long preoccupation was the protection of India and the elimination, once and for all, of any possible future threat. Whether the potential aggressor were to be Russia, as it had long been, or Germany as in the last war, made no difference to his thinking. The most effective way was to create a chain of vassal states stretching from the western borders of India to the Mediterranean. In this chain of buffers, Iran was the key. Most of the neighbouring states east and west of Iran were already securely under British control. Iran still had pretentions of being an independent country and could cause trouble. Curzon conceived the grand scheme, but it was left to others to devise the most feasible and expeditious route and to work out the details.

Meanwhile Vosouq had formed his first Cabinet, which was composed of nonentities. Vosouq had, however, promised Marling that soon he would bring into his Cabinet two well-known anglophiles who enjoyed the confidence of the Legation and the Foreign Office, namely Sarem al Dowleh (Mas'oud) and Nosrat al Dowleh (Firouz).[26] Sarem al Dowleh and Nosrat al Dowleh became respectively Ministers of Finance and Justice in February 1919. In August 1919 Firouz replaced Moshaver al Mamalek as Minister of Foreign Affairs. Even before his appointment as Foreign Minister, Nosrat al Dowleh was consulted by Vosouq on all foreign policy matters.

Cox was much more of an activist than Marling and from his first days in Tehran began searching for the appropriate framework to implement Curzon's master plan. At the outset Cox seriously entertained the idea of a mandate 'in the interest of world civilisation and neighbouring states'.[27] The idea did not get far. In addition to the apprehension that the US and France may openly oppose such a scheme, the Government of India thought it impractical.[28] It is not certain what finally persuaded Curzon and Cox to give up the thought of a mandate, but in discussions among Vosouq, Firouz and Cox the structure of the 1919 Agreement between Iran and Britain began to take shape. Cox soon realised that an agreement whereby Britain would control Iran's military and finances would be tantamount to her control of every aspect of Persia's domestic and foreign affairs. The ultimate aim of Britain could be more easily accomplished by a bilateral agreement between two sovereign nations. No third party could object, including the United States which was critical of any colonial arrangement.

Under the Agreement Britain would send a team of financial advisers including a Treasurer General, who would control any disbursement of funds. The military advisers would effectively control the armed forces. There would be advisers in other ministries, including Interior, Education, Justice, Public Works and Agriculture. Although there would remain the legislative and judicial branches of government, all decisions vital to British interests would be taken by the advisers. The arrangement essentially would operate as a mandate. As the proposed agreement would be open-ended with no fixed duration, for all practical purposes only Britain at its sole discretion could terminate it.

The only significant dissent came from the Viceroy of India, who thought that Cox had gone too far and that soon there would be an outcry from the Iranians. The Viceroy was especially concerned that the principal sponsors of the plan, the so-called triumverate of Vosouq, Nosrat al Dowleh and Sarem al Dowleh, had been too closely associated with British interests and did not enjoy public confidence.[29] Additionally, Edwin Montague, Secretary of State for India, argued that Britain should take control of the affairs of Iran only at the invitation of the Paris Peace Conference or the Iranians themselves. Curzon knew the Peace Conference would not grant a mandate and would see the bilateral agreement as a disguised attempt to create a mandate in fact if not in name. An agreement with the Iranian Government without its submission to the Peace Conference was the only feasible route. Montague further believed that the Government of India should handle the 'Persian question'.[30] This jurisdictional conflict combined with personal antipathies sustained continuing friction between Curzon and Montague. Curzon, who by January 1919 was the acting Foreign Secretary, had become an even more enthusiastic supporter of this bilateral approach and paid no attention to the few dissenting voices. He believed the key to a successful conclusion of the agreement lay in isolating Iran and its representatives at the Peace Conference and in convincing all who mattered in Iran that Britain was the only country which could resolve Iran's problems and fulfill the demands it wished to present at the Peace Conference.[31] Cox continued to assure Curzon, 'We should be able to achieve a position which will be unchallengeable for generations to come'.[32]

Vosouq now began to press Cox to implement the pre-conditions he had set when he accepted office. Cox argued that the proposed agreement would embody all of Vosouq's realistic aims. On the issue of the creation of a unified military force, Cox attempted to convince Vosouq that the employment of British military advisers would bring about the same result. Cox, like Marling, readily agreed to repudiate the 1907 Convention as it no longer had any significance. As for the financial issues, i.e. new loans, subsidies, moratorium on past loans and new tariffs, Cox promised some immediate financial assistance but left the other issues to be resolved over the years by the British team of financial advisers.[33] On the issue of Iran's representation at the Peace Conference and reparations for war damages Cox would not acquiesce and Vosouq had to yield.[34] Nor did Cox budge on the question of ending extra-territorial rights. Iran had to wait almost nine years before Reza Shah had these preferential rights repealed.

Vosouq was to protest over the years that he was a nationalist whose sole aim in sponsoring the 1919 Agreement was to protect the territorial integrity of Iran and preserve her cohesion. He argued that as a realist he took the only practical approach possible. He later claimed that as early as 1916 he knew Iran was bankrupt and her salvation lay only in close co-operation with Britain. All customs receipts were going toward repayment of debts incurred by capricious Qajar kings, and the treasury had no other source of income. Vosouq also argued that when his second chance as Prime Minister came in 1918 the outcome of the war seemed more certain and that Britain would emerge as the unchallenged ruler of all adjacent lands. A deal had to be struck with her.[35]

In his first months as Prime Minister Vosouq did indeed show initiative and strength. He reinforced the Gendarmerie and arrested and executed a gang of terrorists in Tehran. He forced merchants who had hoarded grain and other commodities to open up and offer their hoarded stock to the people at fair prices. Most important, he captured a band of armed bandits which had controlled all the roads south of Tehran. Na'eb Hosein Kashi and his son Mashallah Khan were leaders of a gang of ruthless bandits operating in the Qom, Saveh and Kashan area. By 1918 they controlled all access roads from Tehran to Esfahan. Vosouq mobilised the Gendarmes and gradually decimated the bandit forces. Na'eb Hosein, his son and 20 bandits were hanged in Tehran in September 1919. All together some 200 bandits were captured and executed between May 1919 and April 1920. This was the high point of Vosouq's popularity among the populace.[36]

Vosouq may have had patriotic convictions but there are disturbing factors which have led commentators to express grave doubts about his motivation in sponsoring the proposed agreement. Foremost is the composition of the triumverate and the fact that each benefitted and enriched himself by the conclusion of the agreement.

Sarem al Dowleh* was the second surviving son of Mas'oud Mirza Zell al Soltan, the eldest surviving son of Naser al Din Shah. Zell al Soltan, 1850–1918, could not inherit the throne because his mother was a commoner and not of the Qajar tribe. He was made the powerful Governor of Esfahan and 14 other provinces. Curzon estimated that in 1890 two-fifths of Iran was under his control. Zell al Soltan was forever hopeful of the partition of Iran for, as a profound anglophile, he expected to be allowed to rule a portion of the country. He was one of the cruelest princes of the nineteenth century and his excesses are legendary. Zell al Soltan will also be remembered for his defacement and destruction of Safavid palaces, frescoes and paintings.[37] Sarem al Dowleh was also a professional anglophile with few convictions and continued to enrich himself in the tradition of his father by improprieties and coercion.

The third member of the triumvirate is a more complex character. Firouz Mirza Nosrat al Dowleh (Firouz Firouz)† was the eldest son of

---

*   Akbar Mirza Sarem al Dowleh (Akbar Mas'oud), c.1885–c.1975, was the eighth and favourite son of Mas'oud Mirza Zell al Soltan, and inherited the major part of his father's fortune. Like his father he was particularly close to the British, serving their interests at crucial times. With Britain's increasing influence during World War I he was appointed Minister of Public Works in 1915; Minister of Foreign Affairs in 1916; Governor of Esfahan in 1917; Minister of Finance in 1919; Governor of Kerman and Hamadan in November 1920; Governor of Fars between 1920 and 1923, and again under Reza Shah in 1929. He was arrested in 1929 for inciting tribes and kept under surveillance for several months, but in 1932 was allowed to return to his vast properties in and around Esfahan. It is generally accepted that 'Sarem al Dowleh shot and killed his mother on the instructions of his father on a point of honour'.[38]

†   Firouz Mirza Nosrat al Dowleh (Firouz Firouz), 1889–1938, was the eldest son of Abdol Hosein Mirza Farmanfarma and Ezat al Dowleh, the daughter of Mozaffar al Din Shah. In 1906 at the age of eighteen when his father as Governor of Kerman had to return to Tehran, he replaced him briefly as an unpopular Governor. Between 1908 and 1914 he studied law in Beirut and Paris. He spoke good French and some English and made numerous friends during his stay in France in political and even literary circles. On his return from Paris he became Under Secretary then Minister of Justice between 1914 and 1916; again Minister of Justice in 1918; Minister of Foreign Affairs in 1919; was elected to the fourth, fifth and sixth sessions of parliament; was Governor of Fars from 1923–1924; Minister of Justice August–December 1925; Minister of Finance in 1927, dismissed by Reza Shah in 1929. He was kept under house surveillance for a year, tried and convicted of corruption in 1930 and arrested again 1936 and imprisoned. After a transfer to prison in Semnan, he was murdered in January 1938.[39]

Abdol Hosein Mirza Farmanfarma. He, like his father, was held in the highest esteem by the British Government, and King George V personally awarded him the GCMG in 1919. Firouz was highly intelligent and outshone other Iranian princes. More will be heard of him as he became one of the dominant politicians of the twenties.

With these three, Curzon and Cox intended to conclude an agreement which would last 'for generations'. The Government of India continued to have its doubts. 'You cannot have as your sponsors the sons of Zell al Soltan and Farmanfarma... It would raise a public outcry'.[40] Furthermore, how could Iranian nationalist elements accept a treaty with Britain when only 12 years earlier Britain had been the signatory to the 1907 convention which had divided Iran into spheres between Britain and Russia. The new agreement titled 'Friendship and Assistance' would now give all of the country to Britain.

Vosouq continued attempts to strike a balance in the final formulation of the agreement. Previous Iranian governments had occasionally employed French nationals to serve as advisers to the Ministry of Justice. In late 1918 Vosouq attempted to employ two French nationals as legal and financial advisers. Curzon curtly refused and so informed the French Ambassador in London.[41] In March 1919 during negotiations Vosouq again raised the issue of employment of a legal adviser arguing that French Civil Law was closer to Iranian practices than English Common Law. An attempt was also made to employ some 14 French professors to teach at various schools. Curzon immediately telegraphed Cox and stated he was 'astonished at Vosouq ed Dowleh attempting to hire 14 French professors... it is an attempt to evade our agreement... it is incredible that Vosouq ed Dowleh argues they are instructional and not executive... It indeed argues bad faith on the part of the Persian Government which justifies a strong protest... I will not fail to make strong protest to the French Ambassador here'.[42] Vosouq later requested a joint Anglo-American declaration on Iranian independence and an international guarantee of Iran's territorial integrity. Curzon acidly replied, 'Britain had no desire to be associated with other countries in such an undertaking'.[43]

There is some evidence that Vosouq attempted to obtain the best terms for Iran within the confines and limitations of the proposed agreement but soon gave up and managed to convince himself that Cox and Curzon were indeed sincere in their desire for the 'regeneration of Persia'. He had been promised that if he refrained from pressing Iran's claim at the Peace Conference, Britain would assist the country in obtaining some compensation for war damages and a fair review of the issue of rectification of frontiers. In fact in July 1919 Vosouq asked Cox for written confirmation from Britain concerning these undertakings. There is a body of evidence which show an element of bad faith on the part of Britain during negotiations. There appears no serious intent by Britain to have any effective obligation toward Iran once she took control of the financial and military machinery of government. An example was the fact that the agreement was silent on the military defence of Iran if she were attacked by a third country. Another indication of bad faith is Cox's insistance upon a letter to be signed by both parties to the effect that Britain would not claim costs for the maintenance of British troops 'which his Majesty's Government were obliged to send to Persia owing to Persia's want of power to defend her neutrality and on the other hand the Persian Government will not claim from the British Government an indemnity for any damages which may have been caused by the said troops during their presence in Persian territory'. The proposed letter ends with the following paragraph: 'It is to be understood, however, that this agreement of the two parties does not in any way affect the claims of individuals and private institutions, which will be dealt independently'.[44] Not only does this letter (marked note 4 to the Agreement) show the utmost hypocrisy in stating that Britain sent troops to Iran to defend her neutrality, and not only does it close the door on Iran's claiming any compensation for war damages, but it leaves the door open for British nationals and legal entities to press claims and sue for losses incurred in Iran during the war. There were in fact claims by Britain and the Anglo-Persian Oil Company for such losses. Furthermore, as we shall see later, Britain never intended to do much on the issue of claims for reparations by Iran against third countries and rectification of borders. Curzon was on a holy mission and wanted to go down in history as the saviour and guarantor of the British Empire. It has been said that 'Mr Curzon seems to be under the impression that he discovered Persia and that having discovered it he now, in some mysterious way, owns it'.[45]

Meanwhile, against the wishes of Vosouq, the Shah sent a five-man delegation to the Peace Conference in Paris. The unheeded choice of the British Legation to head any possible Iranian representation at the Peace Conference had been Naser al Molk.[46] The delegation in fact included two experienced and reputable diplomats in the persons of Moshaver al Mamalek and Zoka al Molk Foroughi who made valid and legitimate claims: 'Membership and participation in the Peace Conference; abolition of treaties and agreements which violated the territorial integrity and independence of Iran;

payment for damages caused by the belligerents in the last war; the economic freedom of the Persian Government; reconsideration and abrogation of all capitulation treaties; freedom to make new commercial treaties and revise tariffs; assistance in reconsideration and rectification of any boundary treaties'.[47]

In Tehran Vosouq's allies made personal attacks on members of the delegation. One Seyyed Zia al Din (of whom a great deal will be heard later), the owner and editor of *Ra'ad* – the most fervent of the pro-British newspapers in Tehran, inspired and probably financed by Vosouq and the British Legation – did not lose any opportunity to ridicule individual members of the Iranian delegation in Paris and their 'extravagant demands'.[48] The newspaper had also stated that the Iranian delegation had made outlandish demands on rectification of borders, asking for the frontiers to be extended to the Caucasus, the Oxus and Euphrates. There probably was some element of truth in the newspaper's assertion. At one time or another a member or members of the Iranian delegation had stated that the frontiers of Iran be extended to its Safavid Empire boundaries. However, on the issue of reparations, the demands were very modest: 1,000,000 tomans from Russia; 500,000 tomans from Turkey and 20,000 tomans (about £7,000) from Germany.

As expected, the delegation was refused admittance to the conference and denied permission to state its case. The head of the mission, the Foreign Minister Moshaver al Mamalek,* an elderly and respected public servant repeatedly attempted to see Balfour in Paris and Curzon in London. Curzon refused to see him or any other

---

*   Aliqoli Khan Mas'oud Ansari (Moshaver al Mamalek), c.1868–1940, was the grandson of Mirza Mas'oud Moshaver al Mamalek who had been Foreign Minister under Mohammad Shah. Aliqoli Khan joined the Foreign Ministry and rose through the ranks to become Foreign Minister in 1915. He was appointed Foreign Minister again in 1917 and in Vosouq's second Cabinet of August 1918. He was sent by the Shah as Iran's main representative to the Paris Peace Conference, but was recalled and made Ambassador to Turkey. He was sent to Moscow in June 1920 to negotiate a treaty for the withdrawal of Russian troops from northern Iran (culminating in the Perso-Soviet Agreement in February 1921). He served briefly in Moscow again in 1926 and in late 1926–1927, served again as Foreign Minister and negotiated the Perso-Polish commercial treaty in 1927. He was sent for a brief time as an emissary to Prague and Berlin; as Ambassador to Moscow again in 1928; Minister to London between May 1931 and December 1932. He was effectively retired from 1933. He was considered an anglophile although he was always well received in Moscow. He spoke Russian and French fluently and had a pleasant demeanour, although somewhat lethargic.[49]

member of the Iranian delegation until 'they realised no one in the Peace Conference could do anything for them'.[50] Curzon had made certain that the delegation would neither be admitted to the conference nor be heard, though there was apprehension that the United States delegation would meet with them and hear their case. Curzon's efforts to shut off the Iranian delegation in Paris and effectively isolate Iran was beginning to work. The next step was to enfold the country in a treaty of submission to British hegemony.

NOTES ON CHAPTER 1
Further details of publications and documents in Bibliography

1 Donald N. Wilber, *Riza Shah Pahlavi*, p 17. James Bassett, an American Presbyterian missionary estimated the population of Iran in 1872 at between five and ten million. James Bassett, *The Land of Imams*, p 255. Lord Curzon estimates the population in 1889 at nine million.

2 Maj. Gen. Dunsterville, *The Adventures of Dunsterforce*, p 108.

3 FO 60/698, Dispatch No. 2, Sykes to Hardinge, 27 February 1905.

4 The SPR lingered on until after the 1921 coup when it was disbanded and merged into the regular army. Florida Safiri, *Police Jonoub Iran – SPR (The Southern Police of Iran – SPR)*, pp 25–40.

5 In 1918 Maj. Gen. Dunsterville headed British troops in northern Iran (Norperforce); the South Persia Rifles (SPR) was headed by Brig. Gen. Sir Percy Sykes; The East Persia Cordon Troops in Sistan manned by Indian soldiers were under the command of Brig. Gen. R.H. Dyer; Maj. Gen. Sir Wilfrid Malleson commanded a small contingent of troops in north-east Iran. Florida Safiri, *Police Jonoub Iran – SPR (The Southern Police of Iran – SPR)*, pp 143–173 and 209.

6 William J. Olson, *Anglo-Iranian Relations During World War I*, p 223. Also see references in exchange of telegrams between India Office and Foreign Office: FO 371/3263, Viceroy's dispatch, 26 November 1918; FO 371/3263, Cox to Curzon, 14 November 1918; FO 371/3263, 27 November 1918.

7 Yair P. Hirschfeld, 'German Iranian Relations 1921–1941', PhD Thesis. Eminent orientalists such as Fredrich Sarre were among those deported.

8 DoS, Caldwell to Secretary of State, 12 September and 1 October 1919.

9 DoS, Caldwell to Secretary of State, 1 October 1919.

10 Mehdi Bamdad, *Tarikh Rejal Iran Quroun 12, 13, 14 (Dictionary of National Biography of Iran: Twelfth, Thirteenth, Fourteenth Centuries)*, vol. 2, pp 93–102.

11 *Ibid.*, vol. 1, pp 348–352.

Vosouq had eight accomplished daughters and two sons. In an astute display of political acumen, the daughters were married off to the cream of the Iranian establishment. The sons-in-law included a European-trained physician who became the doctor of Reza Shah and his immediate family; one of the largest landowners of western Iran; the great-grandson of a Qajar Shah who would become minister of Foreign Affairs; the son of an important clerical leader from Azarbaijan; another European trained physician and landed grandee of western Iran; a future prime minister whose mother was the daughter of another Qajar Shah; the grandson of one of the most revered nineteenth century clerical leaders; and yet another Western-trained physician who had a distinguished career in international organisations.

12 DoS, Quarterly Report No. 3, US Legation in Tehran to Secretary of State, 1 April 1919; FO 371/3266, Marling to Balfour, 21 December 1917; FO 371/3266, Marling to Balfour, 14 June 1918.

13 Mehdi Bamdad, *Tarikh Rejal Iran Quroun 12, 13, 14 (Dictionary of National Biography of Iran: Twelfth, Thirteenth, Fourteenth Centuries)*, vol. 4, pp 330–332.

14 Melvin Hall, *Journey to the End of an Era*, p 208.
15 FO 371/3260, Marling to Balfour, 27 June 1918.
16 FO 371/2862, George P. Churchill to Curzon, 29 July 1919.
17 DoS, Quarterly Report No. 10, Caldwell to Secretary of State, 15 January 1921. The repeated crash diets and the loss of 70 pounds within a mere four months on a person who was no taller than five feet four inches was bound to have tragic effects.
18 FO 371/3260, Marling to Foreign Office, 27 June 1918.
19 During World War I the Iranian Government became bankrupt and was unable to repay the installments on its debts to Britain and Russia. With Anglo-Russian co-operation in Iran at its highest point, the two powers devised a scheme, calling it a moratorium on previous loans and advances. They additionally advanced Iran £30,000 monthly, secured by customs revenues. The repayment of previous loans and advances were deferred indefinitely until the country was on a sounder financial footing: L/PS/10/550/4968 and L/PS/10/872/7698, 12 and 21 October 1915.
20 FO 371/3260, Marling to Balfour, 26 June 1918; FO 371/3273, Marling to Balfour, 16 July 1918.
21 Percy Cox, 1864–1937, later became High Commissioner in Iraq with Gertrude Bell as his Oriental Secretary and Arnold Wilson as senior assistant, both of whom had long associations with Iran and later remained as advisers to the Foreign Office on Iranian issues. See Philip Graves, *The Life of Sir Percy Cox*.
22 Arthur James Balfour, 1849–1930: Prime Minister 1902–05, Foreign Secretary 1911–1918.
23 F/112/271 (F designates the Curzon Papers), 20 December 1917: quoted by Houshang Sabahi, *British Policy in Persia 1918–1925*, pp 2–4.
24 L/PS 10/734/1270, Memo by Field Marshal Wilson, 7 March 1918: quoted by Houshang Sabahi, *British Policy in Persia 1918–1925*, p 2.
25 *Persia and the Persian Question* was published in 1892 in two volumes totalling almost 1300 pages. Curzon describes his work as 'compendious... dealing with every aspect of public life in Persia, with its inhabitants, provinces, cities, lines of communication, antiquities, government, institutions, resources, trade, finance, policy and present and future development – in a word, with all that has made or continues to make it a nation'. With Curzon's extraordinary powers of observation and analysis, the book amply lives up to his own description. George Nathaniel Curzon, 1859–1925, was a prolific writer and a great traveller with wide-ranging interests.
26 FO 371/3266, Marling to Balfour, 5 November 1918
27 FO 371/3263, Cox to Curzon, 14 November 1918 and 27 November 1918.
28 FO 371/3263, Viceroy's Dispatch, 26 November 1918.
29 FO 371/3860, Viceroy's Dispatch, 28 January 1919.
30 CAB/27/24 (CAB designates Cabinet Committee), Eastern Committee, 45th Meeting, 19 December 1918.
31 FO 371/3859, Minutes of Foreign Office Meeting, 20 February 1919.
32 FO 371/3859, Cox to Curzon, 25 February 1919.
33 FO 371/3859, Cox to Curzon, 25 February 1919.
34 *Ibid.*

35 Parliamentary Debates, Iranian Parliament, 29 Shahrivar 1305 (1926).
    Hosein Makki, *Tarikh Bist Saleh Iran* (*A Twenty Year History of Iran*),
    vol. 4, pp 178–189.
36 WO 106/942 (WO designates War Office), For further information see
    Report on minor military operations in Persia, No. 16, 30 October 1919.
37 Mehdi Bamdad, *Tarikh Rejal Iran Quroun 12, 13, 14* (*Dictionary of
    National Biography of Iran: Twelfth, Thirteenth, Fourteenth Centuries*),
    vol. 4, pp 78–100; For further information see Treacher E. Collins, *In the
    Kingdom of the Shah*; Wilfred Sparroy, *Persian Children of the Royal
    Family*. George Churchill, *Biographical Notices of Persian Statesmen and
    Notables*.
38 FO 371/7906, R.H. Hoare to John Simon, 26 July 1934; FO 416/98, 7
    February 1940. See also Claremont Skrine, *World War in Iran*, p 60,
    where he differentiates among anglophiles. FO 371/4909, Sidney
    Armitage Smith, report to Foreign Office, 22 November 1920; James M.
    Balfour, *Recent Happenings in Persia*, London, 1922, p 123.
39 Firouz Mirza Firouz (Nosrat al Dowleh), *Majmoueh Mokatebat, Asnad,
    Khaterat va Asar-e-Firouz Mirza Firouz* (*Collected Documents, Correspon-
    dence, Memoirs and Works of Firouz Mirza Firouz*), vols 1 and 2.
40 FO 371/3860, Viceroy's Dispatch, 28 January 1919.
41 FO 371/3859, Curzon to Cambon, 11 March 1918.
42 FO 371/3860, Curzon to Cox, 1 June 1919.
43 FO 371/3859, Curzon to Cox, March 1919.
44 FO 371/3802, Cox to Curzon, 23 July 1919.
45 Lord Ronaldshay, *The Life of Lord Curzon*, vol. 1, p 156, quoting the
    Sunday Sun, 5 June 1892.
46 Hosein Makki, *Zendegi Siaasi Ahmad Shah* (*The Political Life of Ahmad
    Shah*), p 86.
47 DoS, Decimal File 891, August, September and 15 November 1918;
    Decimal File 763, 30 January 1919, Persian Foreign Minister, Moshaver
    al Mamalek to John Caldwell, United State Minister in Tehran,
    November 1918 and relayed to the American Mission at the Peace
    Conference in Paris on January 1919.
48 DoS, Quarterly Report, John L. Caldwell to Secretary of State, 1 October
    1919.
49 Mehdi Bamdad, *Tarikh Rejal Iran Quroun 12, 13, 14* (*Dictionary of
    National Biography of Iran: Twelfth, Thirteenth, Fourteenth Centuries*),
    vol. 2, pp 459–461.
50 FO 371/3859, Foreign Office Minutes, 20 February 1919.

2

Declining Prospects of the Agreement

By April 1919 there was general consensus at the Foreign Office on the basic terms of the proposed agreement. Britain reiterated past pledges with respect to the integrity and independence of Iran and agreed to a loan of £2,000,000 as an additional incentive repayable over 20 years at a relatively high 7 percent interest. In those early months of 1919 everything seemed to be going well for Britain. The Agreement was near conclusion and would accomplish Curzon's

---

* Ahmad Qavam (Qavam al Saltaneh) c.1875–1955, was younger brother of Vosouq and rose rapidly after 1909. He became Minister of Interior in 1911. The Gendarmerie were formed during his term as Minister of Interior and he acquired a reputation as a capable administrator. Between 1914 and 1918 he held two more ministerial positions, Finance and again Interior. He was appointed Governor of Khorasan between 1918 and 1921 and Prime Minister twice for short periods in 1921 and 1922–1923. He was accused of plotting to oust Reza Khan, then Minister of War, and exiled abroad in October 1923. He returned in March 1930 and settled on his properties in northern Iran. He became Prime Minister again in 1942 and 1946 and for a few days in 1952. He was variously described by the British Legation in Tehran as 'sly, an intriguer and unreliable' and as 'energetic and capable' and having the friendliest feelings for Great Britain 'but unfitted to preside over relatively honest government'.[1] Qavam was one of the finest calligraphers of his day.

dream of protection for India in perpetuity. In the haste to conclude an agreement an atmosphere of optimism had clouded experienced eyes. Trouble had already started which should have been foreseen at least by the older hands at the Legation and Foreign Office. The key Iranian players in this intricate mosaic had additional expectations and made some unanticipated demands.

From the outset Ahmad Shah had been bitterly opposed to the appointment of Vosouq and had delayed it as long as possible, to be appeased only by the granting of a monthly stipend by the British Government. It was merely a matter of time before a serious clash between the two would occur. The first trouble began in late 1918 when the Shah attempted to remove Vosouq's younger brother Ahmad Qavam (Qavam al Saltaneh)* as Governor General of Khorasan. Ahmad Shah's primary interest had always been the acquisition of wealth and as soon as he had reached the legal age of eighteen[2] he continued the practice of his predecessors of selling titles and offices.[3] He sold the postal concession of Mashhad, the capital of Khorasan province, to his uncle Nosrat al Saltaneh. Ahmad Qavam had been an effective Governor. He had brought calm and stability to a vast region and was not about to submit to the Shah on this matter. The postal service at that time was one of the primary sources of revenue for the Governor. Salaries of the Governor himself, his administrative staff and local troops were partially paid from this source. After several acrimonious sessions with Vosouq the Shah was forced to yield but the animosity between the two was intensified.

Cox had to warn Ahmad Shah that any further efforts to undermine Vosouq would force Britain to stop the Shah's monthly payments. By 15 January 1919 Cox reported that all was fine, the Shah had realised Vosouq's indispensibility and was on a 'straight path'. Cox warned, however, that the head of the Cossack Division, Col. Starosselsky, who had great influence over the Shah, was 'instigating against us and Vosouq'. On 18 January Cox sent another telegram informing Curzon that Vosouq had had a meeting with the Shah with a frank exchange of views. Vosouq had assured the Shah that he had no designs against him as the Shah may have imagined.[4] Another direct clash occured, however, regarding the decision by Ahmad Shah to send a relatively high level delegation to the Paris Peace Conference. Vosouq resented the Shah's unexpected unilateral decision and thereafter attempted to withhold funds needed by the delegation and generally create difficulties for its effective functioning.[5]

As early as 6 February 1919 the Shah decided to go to Europe ostensibly for health reasons but more probably for pleasure and closer proximity to the Paris Bourse. Cox immediately informed

Curzon who, being afraid of 'possible intrigue in Paris between the
Shah and the Persian delegation', flatly objected to the trip. Curzon
was also afraid that the Shah's departure from Tehran would delay
finalising the Agreement. The Shah argued that he had had a very
difficult time during the war years and now needed a respite. He also
stated the need to have a medical examination. Cox of course knew
the main reason was that the Shah wanted 'to put his finances in
order', estimating that since his accession he had accumulated
about £1 million. The Shah assured Cox that he would fully back
any Anglo-Persian arrangement but since an agreement with a foreign power needed the approval of parliament and a new parliament
could not possibly be convened for several months he would prefer
to spend that time in Europe. Cox further informed Curzon that
since the Shah wanted to take the land route (Baghdad-Alleppo-
Istanbul-Vienna-Paris), Vosouq believed 'he will be in our hands
until he reaches Paris and by then the Agreement would have been
signed and we will present him with a practical *fait accompli* merely
requiring his acquiescence'.

On 22 February Cox told Curzon that Vosouq believed the Shah
should be allowed to leave. If he 'remains here in a disgruntled frame
of mind he will be a source of constant difficulty'. Furthermore, as
the Shah wanted to take either Firouz or Sarem al Dowleh with him,
Britain could be 'assured he would not fall into bad hands'. Cox
pressed Curzon, arguing that the Shah's trip to Paris may also
include London and British hospitality would make him beholden to
Britain. Curzon was still adamant that the Shah could leave only
when the Agreement was signed. Vosouq may have influenced the
decision to let the Shah go abroad since he felt he could work more
effectively with the Shah out of the country. Curzon finally agreed
on 28 March.

On the same day the Shah told Vosouq that if he were permitted
to travel he would recall Moshaver al Mamalek from Paris and allow
Vosouq to enter into full negotiations with Britain to work out a satisfactory agreement. On 5 April the Shah informed Cox that he had
decided to postpone his journey until the autumn as it would be too
hot to travel at that time. The Shah meanwhile had changed his
mind and stated that he would not dismiss or recall Moshaver al
Mamalek as it was bound to create difficulties. On 9 April Cox
telegraphed Curzon that the triumverate felt they could shortly conclude an agreement. Moshaver al Mamalek could be told that Iran
intended to enter into a definitive agreement with Britain and that
his continued presence in Paris would serve no purpose. If, however, he wished to stay in Paris his work would be confined to tasks

related to the establishment of the League of Nations and not the Peace Conference.[6]

The next demand came from the triumverate of Vosouq and the two trusted Ministers. They informed Cox that there was serious opposition to the Agreement and the only way to deal with it would be either through coersion or bribery. On 11 April the triumverate became more direct. They asked for 500,000 tomans 'paid down and no questions asked'. They also asked guarantees for their personal safety and property and an assurance of asylum should the need arise.[7] At almost the same time the Shah also asked for guarantees for his personal safety and continuity on the throne.

These requests for money should not have come as a surprise to either Curzon or Cox. As early as 30 December 1918 when asked how he intended to overcome possible Iranian opposition to his policy, Curzon had replied, 'The case will be settled by cash'.[8] Curzon's remark was neither rash nor flippant. There was a good measure of history behind the use and power of cash in Britain's dealings with Iran. Czarist Russia's means of achieving policy goals were frank and too obvious. It was the use of raw power and force by massing troops at the borders, the shelling of parliament in 1907, the execution of civilians in 1911–1912, and the brutal conduct of her soldiers during the World War I occupation of northern Iran. British policy in Iran, on the other hand, though acquisitive, was seldom accompanied by military agression. Until World War I, Britain sought to maintain the status quo while always striving for economic advantages and, if the situation allowed, for economic supremacy. There was the presence and occasional use of gun-boats and the landing of soldiers from India but the most successful way was, as Curzon had said, 'cash', which could take one of two forms.

Firstly the Iranian Government would be encouraged to borrow or be placed in a situation where it became necessary to borrow. In 1903, Arthur Hardinge, the British Minister in Tehran, in a dispatch to Lord Landsdowne, the British Foreign Minister, wrote, 'The more we get her [Persia] into our debt the greater will be our hold and our political influence over her Government'.[9] To induce the Iranian Government to borrow was not very difficult. The Shah consumed money for his pleasure trips abroad and the chronic budget deficits forced the Government to find funds elsewhere. The Foreign Office on numerous occasions discouraged commercial and merchant banks in London from lending to Iran, invariably forcing the Iranian Government to look to the Foreign Office.[10]

The second route was much older and time-tested. It consisted of the payment of monthly or yearly stipends to Iranian officials for past and future services. Money had indeed been given by Britain to Iranian notables for almost a century. One of the earliest prominent Iranians to be bribed was Mirza Abol Hassan Shirazi, c.1775–1845, a nephew of the First Minister of Fath Ali Shah who was sent to London as envoy in 1809. (He was accompanied by James Morier whose character of Haji Baba was partially based on Abol Hassan). He was made envoy to Russia in 1813 and again to England in 1817. He returned to Iran in 1820 having secured a life pension of 1500 tomans per annum from the East India Company. British military officers travelling through Iran commented on his wealth, his pension, and his loyalty and usefulness to the empire, all with the knowledge and approval of the Shah.[11]

By August 1918 Ahmad Shah was receiving his 15,000 tomans monthly. Sardar Zaffar, a Bakhtiari leader, had received 1500 tomans monthly until the end of the war provided he 'remained chief and conformed to our wishes in every way'. There were monthly payments of 6000 tomans to Farmanfarma 'as long as he remained the Governor of Fars and friendly to us'. Similar allowances were being made to others, including Qavam al Molk, the head of the Khamseh tribe.[12] Mozaffar al Din Shah and Ahmad Shah had set the example and the governing elite had learned that foreign powers would pay to achieve their aims. In January 1919 Robert Cecil, at a meeting of the Eastern Committee had suggested that the British Minister in Tehran be allowed 'to bribe persons whom he thinks worth bribing'.[13] It is against this background that the triumverate felt entitled to ask for 500,000 tomans, and there was no doubt in anyone's mind that it was a request for bribes.

Theodore Rothstein, the Soviet Minister in Tehran in 1921, who while in exile before the October Revolution had lived in Britain and had been an editor of the *Manchester Guardian*, made a sardonic comment to Vincent Sheean, a noted American journalist travelling to Iran:

> Persia is fundamentally sound. They will take money from everybody. From the British today from the Russians tomorrow or from the French or the Germans or anyone else. But they will never do anything for the money. You may buy their country from them six times over but you will never get it. I say Persia can never go under. Persia is fundamentally sound.

Sheean himself comments that the British believe they no longer need agents in Tehran as 'bribery is more civilised'.[14]

Curzon's response concerning guarantees and pledges of personal safety was swift and favourable. To Ahmad Shah there was a pledge of friendly support. To the members of the triumverate a 'secret' letter was issued and individual assurances were given that 'His Majesty's Government are prepared to extend to their Highnesses [the triumverate] their good offices and support in case of need, and further to afford them asylum in the British Empire should the necessity arise'. Another letter was issued to Ahmad Shah as follows:

> ... His Majesty Sultan Ahmad Shah and his successors will enjoy the friendly support of His Majesty's Government so long as they act in accord with our policy and advice'.

With respect to the letter to the Shah, Cox had suggested that it be worded 'to Ahmad Shah and his heirs'. Curzon had changed it to 'Ahmad Shah and his successors'.[15] This change of one word rendered the 'guarantee' meaningless and freed the British Government to acquiesce to the change of dynasty in 1925. It is also indicative of the erosion of confidence by Britain in the Shah. Curzon even then may have believed the Shah's days were numbered.

Curzon was disappointed in the triumverate, 'in their following the Shah's example in opening their mouths wide'.[16] Ronald Graham of the Foreign Office commented,

> I hesitate to advocate reinvestment of 500,000 tomans for persuasion purposes... [however] greasing the wheels is regarded as perfectly natural and the only question is the scale.

Knatchbull Hugesson, also of the Foreign Office, who became British Minister in Tehran in the mid thirties stated, 'the matter should be kept secret... the Triumverate cannot last forever and one day the transaction is bound to come to light'.[17] In order to disguise the transaction, Cox suggested a solution acceptable to both Curzon and the triumverate. He recommended, 'the money [the bribe] be paid as an advance on the loan to Persia'. Cox argued that this method of payment would be more palatable for Britain because 'it will appear in the accounts and it would be inconvenient to parties whose palms were greased' to disclaim receipt or responsibility. The triumverate then made a further demand. They asked that the other members of the Iranian Cabinet be instructed 'not to probe too excessively'. Curzon finally told Cox, 'I leave it to you to make the most suitable terms you can'. After lengthy haggling, Cox persuaded the triumverate to reduce the amount to 400,000 tomans (£131,000) and so informed Curzon adding that 'Vosouq did not insist much... it was the other two who tried my patience'.[18] On the day the Agreement was signed Cox opened a letter of credit with the Imperial Bank of Persia in the name of Sarem al Dowleh for 400,000 tomans as the first instalment on the loan of £2,000,000. The Imperial Bank had been established in 1889. For almost 40 years it functioned not only as the major commercial bank but also as the state bank. Although foreign owned, foreign based, with foreign directors and subject to the regulatory control of the British Treasury, it served as the Central Bank of Iran with the sole right to issue currency. The issue of the bribe at this time was known by only a handful of British officials at the Legation, the Foreign Office and the senior managers of the Imperial Bank. As we shall see, it took only a little over a year before knowledge of the bribe became more widespread.

With all the pieces in place and everyone worth persuading or bribing having been attended to, the Agreement was signed on 9 August 1919, and Vosouq issued a proclamation on 10 August published in a Tehran newspaper. The Government of India, which had been sceptical about the Agreement and its virtues throughout the negotiations insisted that their criticism and reservations be recorded.[19]

Shortly before the signing of the Agreement Firouz was moved from the Ministry of Justice to Foreign Affairs replacing Moshaver al Mamalek who was still at the Peace Conference in Paris. Vosouq planned to send the latter as the chief delegate to the League of Nations which was in the process of being formed. The Shah meanwhile finalised his travel plans to go to Europe at the end of the summer. Firouz informed Cox that the Shah 'in order to retain our confidence' had asked him (Firouz) to accompany him to Europe. Firouz also informed Cox that the French Government, having learnt that the Shah planned to visit Paris, had offered to put a French warship at his disposal from Batum onwards. The Shah had thanked the French Minister but had said Britain was arranging his travel route.[20]

Although the Agreement had been signed, Cox remained uncertain about its reception by other countries and was concerned about the French 'threat'. On 13 August he informed Curzon that the French Minister to Tehran, M. Bonin, was working against British interests and was engaged in an 'undisguised and unfriendly rivalry'. Cox went so far as to appeal to Curzon to have the French envoy transfered from Tehran.[21] Prior to Firouz's departure for Europe Cox had informed Curzon that he felt sure:

[Firouz] may be relied upon to be loyal to us in connection with the agreement but owing to his private tastes and upbringing he has strong French sympathies and in view of the attitude of the French, I think it would be well if you asked him to come straight to London for a day or two before he becomes anchored in Paris. You could give him advice which would help him to withstand the blandishments and intrigues to which he may be exposed.[22]

Firouz was indeed a shaken man when he first called at the Foreign Office on 16 September. Curzon, who was out of London, had arranged for his private secretary to meet him. Firouz stated that he had stayed in Paris only a few days and had avoided meeting any French officials. However, at a gathering of old friends he had met 'a great international lawyer' who had criticised the Anglo-Persian Agreement and had said its provisions openly flouted the statutes of the League of Nations. Curzon's private secretary reported that Firouz was 'highly upset'[23] and his support for the Agreement appeared shaken. At this time Firouz enjoyed the best of relations with Curzon, who valued his advice. Curzon held an elaborate dinner for Firouz at the Carlton Club on 18 September and was most anxious that it be well attended.[24] On the recommendation of Curzon, Firouz was awarded the GCMG by King George V. Firouz left for Paris after the reception at the Carlton Club and later returned to London to await the Shah's arrival.

Ahmad Shah also left Iran shortly after the signing of the Agreement via Tabriz and Russia. After a few weeks in Paris he arrived in London on 31 October 1919 for a stay of eight days. He was met at Dover by Prince Albert and stayed at Buckingham Palace. Curzon arranged two dinners for the Shah, one at Guild Hall and the other at Buckingham Palace. Iranian writers have perpetuated a myth that Ahmad Shah had been opposed to the Agreement from its inception and his refusal to endorse it led to his fall from grace and the subsequent British revenge of having him removed from the throne. There is no credible evidence to support this thesis. The simple fact is that Ahmad Shah had no firm beliefs. He was forever trying to determine what he personally could gain from any situation. What we have on record is Ahmad Shah's enthusiastic support of the Agreement at both dinners. The only person who claims to have been present in London when Ahmad Shah was presumably pressured into issuing a categorical statement supporting the Agreement was Hosein Qoli Mirza Mozaffari (Nosrat al Saltaneh) who had became close to his nephew Ahmad Shah. Nosrat al Saltaneh has told the story to several people that prior to the second dinner Firouz and Naser al Molk, the former regent, had sought an audience with the Shah to convince him to emphatically state that he was a firm advocate of the Agreement and that to do otherwise would cost him his throne. There is no corroboration to support his story.[25]

Prior to the Shah's arrival in London Firouz had again called on Curzon ostensibly with regard to the status of the opposition to the

Agreement in Tehran. Firouz mentioned that a primary source of difficulty was the Commander of the Cossack Division, Col. Starosselsky, who still hoped that Russia would one day 'come into her own in Persia' and exert her former influence. Firouz suggested all the Russian officers should be dismissed as they were against the Agreement. Lastly, Firouz 'with marked trepidation' raised the question of the possible granting of the Garter to the Shah on the occasion of his approaching visit to England. He argued that the Shah, whose grandfather and great-grandfather (Mozaffar al Din Shah and Naser al Din Shah) had received the same decoration, 'would be placed in an invidious and humiliating position if he were not similarly honoured, particularly on the morrow of the conclusion of the Anglo-Persian Agreement'. Firouz added that his own position would be gravely jeopardised if he did not succeed in obtaining the Garter for the Shah. Curzon lamely explained that the grant of the Garter was the sole prerogative of the King and he could have no opinion on the matter until he consulted the court. The two previous Shahs had obtained the Garter with great difficulty and in any event Naser al Din Shah had been on the throne almost 50 years. The present Shah was only 21 years old and had inherited the crown by the accident of his father's expulsion. Furthermore, it was the Shah's first visit to Europe. The matter could be entertained on his next visits when the Anglo-Persian Agreement had proved to be successful with his loyal support.[26] The request for granting of the Garter achieved nothing. However the eagerness of the Shah to receive the decoration on the occasion of the conclusion of the Agreement also belies his alleged lack of enthusiasm and support of the Agreement. The Shah visited Manchester on 4 November and on 8 November returned to Paris.

Firouz stayed almost 16 months in Europe. He did not return to Iran until late December 1920 and did not reach Tehran until 16 February 1921 as he stayed at one of his estates in western Iran for almost two months. It is not clear why he chose to stay away this long when his presence in Tehran would have helped a beleaguered Vosouq. This long absence also prevented Firouz from playing any part in the crucial events leading to the coup of 21 February 1921.

Curzon was elated by the visits of Firouz and the Shah. His differences with the Secretary of State for India, Montague, had been resolved temporarily. Montague had gone on record that he did not endorse the Government of India's objection to the Agreement. Curzon also had the full blessing of Balfour who was in Paris then. Ronaldshay, Curzon's official biographer has written:

A Persian delegation reached Paris, knocked boldly but vainly at the door of the Peace Conference, and disappointed of any hope of success which they may have cherished in this direction, turned a chastened ear to the suggestions which Great Britain had to offer. In Tehran itself with an Anglophile ministry in power under the control of a leading Persian statesman of conservative views, Vosouq ed Dowleh, and with the representation of British interests in the capable hands of Sir Percy Cox, the officer who nearly twenty years before had been specially selected by Lord Curzon himself to take charge of matters in the Persian Gulf, negotiations proceeded with gratifying success.[27]

Curzon and Cox had miscalculated. Looking back they even seem naive. One can go down a list of the main reasons for which the Agreement was doomed.

Everyone seems to have underestimated nationalist sentiments. How could Britain, one of the two signatories of the 1907 and 1915 conventions, be looked upon with a benign eye? The country that had negotiated spheres of influence and carved Iran into zones now wanted Iranians to accept the proposition that it intended to save that very country from bankruptcy out of humanitarian motives. A country whose neutrality had been violated and was devastated by war and famine was expected willingly to become a prize of war and fall under British rule.

Too much secrecy had surrounded the negotiations. When Vosouq issued his declaration on 10 August, stating that Iran had entered into an agreement with Britain for financial and military assistance few believed, and rightly so, that the Agreement was that simple. Even fewer believed that Iran was to be saved by Britain and that a bright future lay ahead of her. The secrecy fed wild rumours that Iranian culture and social structure would be altered, the Persian language itself would have to be modified, and Iran would be overrun by the sheer number of British advisers. Cox and the triumverate had been too confident and arrogant. Most of the Cabinet, including Moshaver al Mamalek who had been Minister of Foreign Affairs when the Agreement was being negotiated, were kept totally out of the picture. Either by oversight or deliberately there was no expressed requirement that the agreement be deposited in the archives of the League of Nations. The provisions of the agreement therefore were to be kept secret from all third parties.

The most glaring example of haste was the ignorance of or indifference to the Iranian Constitution. Article 24 of which expressly stated that the conclusion of treaties and international agreements must be approved by parliament. It is difficult to understand how this provision was overlooked. The Iranian parliament had not met since it had been disbanded in 1915. Preparations for new elections had begun in late 1918 and in some districts elections had been held. By August 1919 about half of the deputies had been elected. Almost all of them had been hand-picked by Vosouq and the British Legation. If elections had been completed and parliament convened, the subservient parliament probably would have ratified the Agreement. Most writers on the period believe the Foreign Office, the British Legation in Tehran and the triumverate were unaware of Article 24. But the facts indicate otherwise. As already mentioned, the Shah told Cox on 6 February, six months before the signing of the Agreement, that parliamentary approval was required. Even if Cox had been ignorant of the requirement, upon hearing the Shah's comment he certainly would have informed the Foreign Office and the triumverate of the matter. It is therefore safe to assume that the triumverate and Cox were aware of the provision in the constitution but may have thought it could be bypassed. It is also possible that the parties intended to seek parliamentary approval only when they were certain that parliament was packed in their favour. The most likely explanation still seems to be the sheer indifference and arrogance of Cox and the triumverate.

There was public antipathy towards the Government. Vosouq's two ministers, Nosrat al Dowleh (Firouz) and Sarem al Dowleh (Mas'oud) were extremely unpopular. The reputations of their fathers, Farmanfarma and Zell al Soltan, as tools of British interests had not been forgotten. Sarem al Dowleh in his short tenure as Minister of Finance had acquired further notoriety. He had shown 'insatiable greed... the exchequer was his private purse... he robbed his brothers... his evil as Finance Minister will long live after...'[28] Vosouq himself by mid 1919 had become unpopular. People had forgotten the relative security he had established in central Iran. Most commentators consider him to have become 'arrogant and unapproachable'.[29] His treatment of politicians opposed to the Agreement was often harsh and violent. He exiled some respected Iranians to remote regions, the most prominent among whom were Mostashar al Dowleh (Sadeq Sadeq), Mohtashem al Saltaneh (Hassan Esfandiari) and Momtaz al Dowleh (Esma'il Momtaz). He would have arrested more were it not for fear of an uprising. Some of those exiled had been active during the constitutional turmoil and enjoyed good reputations and support among the merchant class and other segments of the population.

There was discord and dissent in the Cabinet. Sepahdar (Fathollah Akbar), who had become Minister of War in February 1919 felt left out of Vosouq's inner cabinet and slighted at not being privy to negotiations with Cox. He thereafter worked to topple Vosouq and

1. Aḥmad Shāh. The last Qajar monarch was a venal and weak king, who preferred the comforts of Europe to the complexities of leadership.

2. Reza Khan 1917. From humble beginnings this colonel from the Cossack brigade was already one of the top Iranian military commanders by his early forties.

organised an unsuccessful demonstration in Shah Abdul Azim outside Tehran during late March 1919. He was forced to retire from
the Cabinet but did not stop trying to undermine Vosouq. Vosouq
was also unhappy with Sarem al Dowleh's conduct at the Ministry
of Finance and suspected him of corruption and bribery. Although
Sarem al Dowleh remained in the Cabinet until after the signing of
the Agreement (solely it appears with the expectation of receiving his
share of the bribe) he continued to intrigue against Vosouq.[30]

The choice of Cox as the British envoy was a mistake. Cox had
been used to dealing with the Sheikhs in Arabia and the Persian
Gulf. 'Cox's love was Arabia' [31] and he cared little for nor understood
Iranians. He was insensitive to the 20-year history of turmoil and
struggle in Iran and the growing nationalist sentiments. He was
used to buying nomadic loyalty in Arabia and the Persian Gulf and
he confused the tribal loyalty of Arabs with the greater Iranian sense
of national identity. Cox misled Curzon as well as the triumverate.
He did not serve Curzon well with his optimistic reports or by down-
playing the magnitude of the opposition. He packed the Iranian
Cabinet with less-than-respected anglophiles and made Vosouq's
task more difficult in the long run. He can be blamed for bringing
Sarem al Dowleh into the Cabinet and for being more than ready
to accede to payment of the bribe. His solution to have the bribe
as part of the loan to Iran is a further indication of his cynicism.
He misled Vosouq and Firouz into expecting a resolution of matters relating to border disputes and reparation for war damages.
When Vosouq sought some minor rectification of borders, e.g. the
status of Arablar near Maku, Cox and Curzon postponed these
matters to a later date. Once the Agreement was signed Vosouq's
requests were ignored.[32] Cox and Curzon had no intention to indem-
nify Iran for war losses and damages, but had led Vosouq to believe
that Britain would look after Iran's claim if only she stopped trying
to be heard at the Peace Conference. Instead Iran was coerced into
signing a waiver of claim for any losses suffered during the war and
Britain waived her spurious claims of indemnity against Iran for
having sent troops for the purpose of 'defending Persian neutrality'.
Additionally, the door was left open for any British national or
juridical entity to press claims against Iran for losses incurred
during the war even if caused by the belligerents themselves. Thus
the Anglo-Persian Oil Company could claim damages against Iran,
a non-belligerent in the war, for destruction of pipelines instead of
proceeding against Turkey or Germany.[33] By pressing her advantage
and superior bargaining power against a devastated and bankrupt
country Britain weakened her moral influence in the eyes of

Iranians and gave further ammunition to the opponents of the Agreement.

Ahmad Shah played both sides of the fence. He expressed differing sentiments to different parties and foremost in his mind were personal financial considerations. He wanted British protection to ensure continuity of his rule and his powers but he also wanted a subservient Prime Minister. Moreover, he expected Britain to finance his desired life-style and believed Britain would pay him what he asked were it not for Vosouq's influence with the Legation and Foreign Office. Despite his repeated protestations to the contrary his relations with Vosouq were described as 'dislike of Vosouq ed Dowleh for the Shah which is quite as violent as the Shah for him'.[34]

Vosouq underestimated emerging Soviet influence and the growing role she was playing in Iran. He did not believe the Russian Revolution would be successful and did not send an envoy to Russia during his entire term as Prime Minister. He even had the Iranian Legation in Moscow closed.[35] In November 1917 the Bolsheviks published the terms of the secret Anglo-Russian accord of 18 March 1915, in which Britain was to have control of the 'neutral zone' and Russia to have 'full freedom of action in northern Persia'. Throughout 1918 and 1919 Vosouq refused to respond to Moscow's diplomatic overtures. In January 1918 Trotsky had sent a formal note abrogating the 1907 Convention. The first Soviet envoy Karl Bravin invited Iran 'to join Russia to fight against the most rapacious imperialist government [Britain] on earth'.[36] In the summer of 1918 the Soviets' second envoy I. Kolomitsev reached Tehran, but Vosouq refused to see him. In June 1919 the Soviets sent another note renouncing all prior Iranian debts to Czarist Russia. Leo Karakhan of the Soviet Foreign Ministry made a more formal representation to Iranian authorities. All loans made by Czarist Russia to Iran, all concessions granted by Iran, capitulation (extra-territorial rights), the Discount Bank and railway rights were declared null and void. Russian loans by 1914 were substantial by the standards of the time as specified earlier.[37] The lack of response to any of these Russian overtures intensified the Russian campaign against the Agreement and British dominance.

The French Government and her Legation in Tehran never fully supported British aims in Iran. Although the Legation was officially silent on the merits of the Agreement it was known by many Iranians that France had serious reservations. Cox was forced to ask Curzon on 13 August 1919 to make the French Government keep quiet and be reminded that France had territorial ambitions of her own in Lebanon and Syria.[38] Curzon lodged several protests to Paul Cambon, France's Ambassador in London, against Bonin, the French Minister in Tehran, for the latter's 'unfriendly remarks' about the Agreement and 'marked hostility towards Britain'. The Foreign Office even requested Bonin's recall from Tehran, which went unheeded.[39]

The United States, however, was not easily silenced. As early as April 1919 Robert Lansing, the United States Secretary of State, informed Balfour that the US may raise the issue of Persia at the Peace Conference, prompting Eyre Crowe, the Permanent Under-Secretary of the Foreign Office to urge:

> Why not take the bull by the horns and tell the Americans that Persia for us is covered by what is our equivalent in Asia to the Monroe Doctrine...'[40]

The US Minister in Tehran, John Laurence Caldwell, let it be known that the US was opposed to the Agreement. Caldwell informed the State Department of the intense degree of opposition to the Agreement and mentioned that numerous Iranians had sought asylum at the US Legation for fear of arrest. Caldwell published a letter in an Iranian newspaper answering Seyyed Zia and his newspaper *Ra'ad* which had accused the United States of not helping Iran at the Peace Conference. In the same letter Caldwell stated that the United States had never been a supporter of the Agreement.[41]

On 1 October 1919 Caldwell informed the State Department that the parliamentary elections being held were a farce as Britain dictated the choice of candidates. These reports resulted in Secretary of State Lansing instructing John Davis, the US Ambassador to Britain, to let Curzon personally know that the United States was displeased with British policy in Iran.[42] Curzon was forced to write a lengthy letter to Davis and explain that the United States had not been kept in ignorance of the negotiations and Col. Edward House, President Wilson's Chief Adviser at the Peace Conference, had been informed and the United States had never even hinted its disapproval. Curzon therefore expected the State Department to inform the Iranian Government that the United States did not oppose the Agreement.[43] Lansing prepared a reply for Davis. The State Department stressed the argument that Col. House had been made cognisant of the negotiations only in conversations 'too casual to be taken seriously'. Lansing concluded by saying that the United States was not:

> ... in a position at the present time to give approval to the Anglo-Persian Agreement until and unless it is clear that the Government and people of Persia are united in their approval and support of this undertaking'.[44]

The revelation of the bribes was to be another blow to the implementation of the Agreement. By late 1919 there were widespread rumours of Vosouq and other members of his Cabinet having been bribed. The matter became more public soon after Vosouq's resignation in June 1920. On 30 November 1920 Lancelot Oliphant, in charge of Near Eastern Affairs at the Foreign Office sent a memorandum to Curzon stating the following:

> Vosouq ed Dowleh called on me very disturbed. He said that Sepahdar [Fathollah Akbar,* the Prime Minister at the time] had sent him a telegram saying he has been told that he [Vosouq] had received £150,000 [from Britain]. Vosouq ed Dowleh had replied that it must have been in connection with the supply of arms [by the British Government] and that Sepahdar should ascertain the details from Nosrat ed Dowleh [who was in Paris at the time] and Sarem ed Dowleh [who was in Esfahan]... Vosouq ed Dowleh gave the following version: ...[just before the signing of the Agreement] Nosrat ed Dowleh had suggested a *douceur* [a sweet-ener] for the conclusion [of the Agreement]... Vosouq ed Dowleh had opposed the idea but was afraid that Nosrat ed Dowleh and Sarem ed Dowleh may refuse [to conclude the Agreement]. He had therefore allowed them to take something.

Sarem ed Dowleh received the entire sum of 400,000 tomans (£131,000) from Cox and 'kept 100,000 for himself and Nosrat ed Dowleh received 100,000'. Sarem ed Dowleh advised Vosouq 'to take the remaining 200,000 but Vosouq ed Dowleh refused'. Vosouq maintained that he later decided to use the idle 200,000 tomans to assist the firm of Toumanians which was nearly bankrupt. Toumanians was an Iranian businessman who also dealt in currency as money changer and adviser on investments. He and his brother acted as personal bankers to numerous prominent Iranians and had been for a time financial agents of Ahmad Shah. Vosouq stated that he gave them the money and as security took the deeds of property owned by Toumanians in the northern region of Iran. Unfortunately

---

*   Fathollah Akbar (Sardar Mansour, later Sepahdar, later Sepahsalar), c.1860–c.1947, came from a landowning family in Gilan. His uncle, Akbar Khan Beeglar Begi, who had received the concession of customs col-lection for northern ports, was the largest and wealthiest landowner in Gilan. After his uncle's death Sepahdar married his widow and inherited his uncle's wealth. In return for payments to Mozaffar al Din Shah, he be-came titled and continued as administrator of customs receipts of Gilan. He supported the constitutionalist cause and after 1911 served in several cabinets, including Vosouq's second as Minister of War. He became Prime Minister in 1920 until removed by the Coup of February 1921, when he re-tired to his estates. He was well-meaning and curteous but ineffectual and out of his depth as Minister and Prime Minister. Sepahdar was a trusted confidant of the British Legation and for services rendered he had received the KCMG in 1903 from the British Crown. He died in his late eighties.[45]

Toumanians' business failed and 'Vosouq assumes the 200,000 tomans were lost. Vosouq is willing to give the title deeds and other securities he had received to our Legation in Tehran. As an alternative, he is willing to give back the 200,000 tomans'.

Oliphant added that 'our records show that payments were made on 11 and 13 September 1919; £30,000 to Sarem ed Dowleh and £30,000 to Nosrat ed Dowleh and the rest to Vosouq ed Dowleh'. Oliphant went on to say that 'there appears some possibility of truth in Vosouq ed Dowleh's story'. On Curzon's instructions Oliphant sent a cable to Herman Norman, the British Minister in Tehran who had replaced Cox, instructing him 'to tell Sepahdar that the amount in question was £130,000 and not £150,000 or £250,000'.[46] On 8 December 1920 the British High Commissioner's Office in Baghdad sent a telegram to the Foreign Office stating that at the time of signing £131,000 was given to Vosouq for 'Secret services purposes' but the only document on the subject is a receipt by Sarem al Dowleh at the Legation. 'The receipt has been shown to Sepahdar who has shown it to other Ministers. Sepahdar has asked Sarem ed Dowleh for explanation'.[47]

By now, if not earlier, the Prime Minister, Sepahdar, and at least some members of the cabinet knew of the bribe. Members of the British financial and military teams certainly knew. J.M. Balfour, the Chief Assistant to Sidney Armitage Smith, the Financial Adviser to the Iranian Government, mentioned the bribe in his book 'Recent Happenings in Persia' which became the subject of libel proceedings in London.[48] More than a few members of the Imperial Bank of Persia also knew. A letter dated 17 February 1920 from J. McMurray, the Chief Officer of the Bank to S. Rogers, another officer of the Bank based in London states the following:

> Tell Wood [a former Chief Officer of the Bank] the advance made in August last, the secret one, very nearly caused a split in the Cabinet and it had to be accounted for by Akbar [Akbar Mas'oud, Sarem al Dowleh]. I was asked by the Legation to confer with A [Akbar] and help him out of the hole. A's [Akbar's] proposal was that a big slice of the 2 million [loan] should be given at once and that I should make false entries in our books in order to account for the whole of the advance in the difference between the correct rate and a false one. I rejected this proposal indignantly. After a long talk I found that what he wanted was an excuse to bring up the question in the Cabinet before someone else did... I said he would receive from me a letter... in which I would give him an opportunity

What Sarem al Dowleh wanted was for the Bank to state that due to fluctuations in the rate of exchange, the £2 million advanced by Britain was £2 million minus £130,000 when converted into tomans.

With that letter he [Akbar] turns to his colleagues in the cabinet and says that this is a matter which he had not mentioned before as at the time the advance was made he had hopes that the rate might go up... How Akbar accounted for it is no concern of ours... However, the Cabinet was preserved and that is what was required and what we must still endeavour to do for a few months more if possible... But again I say, walk warily. Persia is the dominant factor in world politics today, not Russia, not Poland and not Germany, if one will read between the lines and read the right stuff.[49]

This letter together with Foreign Office documents clearly establishes Sarem al Dowleh as an avaricious and unprincipled character in the mould of his father, Zell al Soltan. Sarem al Dowleh inherited his intimacy with the British from his father and British interests were always uppermost in his mind.[50]

The Foreign office did not regard the revelation of the bribes as an impediment to implementation of the Agreement and did not give up hope. Britain began to implement its provisions in the autumn of 1919 and to assemble a team of financial and military personnel to be sent to Iran. In November 1919 Brig. Gen. William E.R. Dickson was chosen as the head of a seven-man military mission whose task was to create a Persian army by integrating the Cossacks, Gendarmerie and the smaller provincial units. Dickson had been selected because he knew 'Persia, its language and people'. He was considered 'most tactful and popular with the people of the country' and possessed 'decided diplomatic instincts'.[51] He arrived in Tehran in mid December 1919 and soon began negotiations with the Assistant War Minister Abbas Mirza Salar Lashkar (the second eldest surviving son of Far-manfarma). The arrival of the Military Mission led to public outcries, and opposition newspapers intensified their attacks on Vosouq. Public anger reached higher pitch with the suicide of Col. Fazlollah Aqevli, a respected Gendarme officer and the ranking Iranian military officer assigned to the Dickson Commission. Fazlollah Aqevli, 1886–1920, had studied in France and joined the Gendarmerie on his return. He acquired a reputation as a nationalist while serving as a military officer for Shuster in 1911.[52] He had been in several military campaigns to quell tribal uprisings in western Iran. As he was conversant in English and French he was selected to work with Dickson.[53] Some in the opposition to the Goverment and the agreement maintained that Aqevli committed suicide because he had been censured by Sepahdar, the War Minister, for refusing to countersign a report by Dickson. Most Iranians went further. They interpreted his suicide as an act of protest against Britain taking over the Iranian armed forces. It has been argued also that since Dickson had decided that senior ranks in the British-proposed unified Iranian army be restricted to British officers, Iranian officers could be promoted only to the rank of major. Aqevli's suicide was over this humiliation of his fellow Iranian officers.[54] The British Military Attaché in Tehran attributed the suicide to 'over work and a love affair'.[55] In any event Dickson began his work on an inauspicious note.

By early spring of 1920, a financial team headed by Sidney Armitage Smith had also arrived in Tehran. Armitage Smith was a Treasury official whom Nicolson considered 'scholarly... much respected by Persians' and maintained that Armitage Smith would have been retained by the government of Moshir al Dowleh and his successors were he not part of the 1919 Anglo-Persian arrangements.[56] Britain appeared to believe and acted as if the Agreement had come into effect and parliamentary approval were a mere formality which would soon be forthcoming once parliament was called into session. Vosouq probably knew better. He had hand-picked candidates for parliament whom he believed would vote in favour of the Agreement and by May 1920 more than half of the deputies had been elected. Although most of them were nominally supporters of Vosouq and had the blessing of the British Legation, Vosouq still dared not call parliament into session to submit the Agreement for their consideration.

The payment to the triumverate was not the end of dispensing bribes. Some newly-elected members of parliament as well as some important members of the clergy were asking for money for their support of the Agreement and some in fact were being paid off. This led Armitage Smith to contradict the triumverate's contention that they had spent all or part of the £131,000 bribe towards calming the opposition and report: 'These payoffs did not come from the pockets of Vosouq or his Finance Minister but directly from the Iranian Treasury'.[57]

The Shah, who had been in Europe for over seven months now decided to return. Both Vosouq and Cox prefered the Shah to stay away at least until the autumn. They were of the opinion that his return would prejudice the situation in Tehran. Vosouq, now weakened, was even afraid that he would not be able to remain in office if the Shah returned and began to interfere in matters of state. The question of the Shah's return and its timing ultimately turned, as often before, on the Shah's remaining supply of funds. Cox reported that the Shah 'had taken 120,000 tomans of government money with him and been sent an additional FF50,000 since but has been continually pressing for more and the Persian Government has not had it to give'. Cox finally advised the Foreign Office:

> It would be much in our common interests if he remained away, until autumn and both Prime Minister [Vosouq] and I would be relieved if

His Majesty's Government could suggest or get his medical adviser to suggest that Caucasus being unsafe, and the Persian Gulf route being dangerously hot at this season, it might be better for him to remain until the autumn. He will then raise the question of funds and we can see what is the best bargain that can be made with him...[58]

The Shah apparently could not be persuaded to delay his return but immediately realised that the time was ripe to make another demand on Britain and the Government in Tehran for more money. Lord Derby, Britain's Ambassador to Paris, informed Curzon on 30 March 1920 that Ahmad Shah had visited him and wanted at least FF40,000 to return from Paris to Tehran via the northern route. 'The Shah says he has two routes to travel; either through the Caucacus or Basra/Baghdad. He believes the second route is speedier. In any event he wants Britain to guarantee his personal safety and safe voyage. The Shah claims that unless he gets the money in two weeks it may be difficult to travel via either route. The Bolsheviks may have occupied the northern part of Persia and the southern route may be too hot to travel. He would then be forced to delay his trip for six months'. If he takes the second route he needs 400,000 tomans. He stated that 'when his great grand-father Naser ed in Shah had made a pilgrimage to the holy sites in Mesopotamia he had spent 10 million tomans'. He wants 'nothing like that amount' but he must have at least FF1,000,000 for prestige reasons when he makes the trip. The Shah also told Derby that 'he is unhappy with the Government in Tehran... The Government is acting unfriendly towards him... he only keeps Vosouq ed Dowleh as Prime Minister for Britain's sake.[59]

Further Foreign Office attempts to make the Shah delay his trip proved unsuccessful and the matter acquired some 'urgency' when Derby telephoned Curzon that Firouz reported:

The Shah is still obstinately set upon returning to Persia... [the Shah] declares that if the British Government put obstacles in the way it will be proof to him that they want to get rid of him. He alternately says he will abdicate and that he will ask French or Americans to convey him home. Prince Firouz's decided view is that it would be better to let the Shah go as arranged [by him] about May first... The Shah pays no heed to account of difficulties of such a journey at this season.[60]

On 18 April 1920 Derby again informed the Foreign Office that he saw 'the Shah in the presence of Prince Firouz... The Shah gave me the most categorical assurance that he would support the present Persian Prime Minister and would also loyally adhere to the Anglo-Persian Agreement'.[61]

Ahmad Shah returned to Iran on 2 June 1920. During his visit to the Shi'ite shrines in Iraq he had met with several senior members of the clergy who had expressed their opposition to the Agreement.[62] It took only a few days in Tehran for the Shah to realise the enormity of the opposition and that Vosouq could not last long in office. The Shah, who had never lent any real support to Vosouq, now made his antagonism overt.

More important than the Shah's continuing feud with Vosouq was the appointment of a new British Minister to Tehran. Curzon had been more than satisfied with Cox's work in Iran and believing that the Anglo-Persian Agreement had been finalised and was ready for implementation, rewarded Cox with the post of *de facto* ruler of a new country. As one of the spoils of the First World War Britain secured a League of Nations mandate over Iraq, formerly a province of the Ottoman Empire. Britain intended to install Amir Faisal of Arabia as the King of the new country to rule under an administrative staff furnished by Britain. Cox whose ambition had been to hold a high post in the Arab world, received the prized position of High Commissioner. Herman Norman,* a career Foreign Office diplomat who had distinguished himself as the senior member of Balfour's secretariat at the Paris Peace Conference, was chosen as the replacement for Cox. Norman was sent to Iran despite Eyre Crow's insistence that he was invaluable at the Peace Conference.[64] This independent-minded diplomat 'of intelligence and vision'[65] not only proved to be a thorn in the side of Curzon but set in motion a chain of events the logical outcome of which was to be the coup of February 1921.

---

* Herman Cameron Norman, 1872–1955, was educated at Eton and Trinity College, Cambridge. He joined the Foreign Office in 1894 and between 1896 and 1916 served in various capacities in Cairo, Constantinople, Washington DC, St Petersburg, Buenos Aires and Tokyo. With the rank of Minister he was attached to the British Delegation to the Paris Peace Conference of 1918–1919. He was conversant with six languages, including Arabic, Turkish and Russian. He arrived in Tehran as Minister in May 1920 and left in October 1921, Curzon refusing to see him on his return to London. Norman was offered the post of Minister to Santiago, but declined and retired in 1924.[63]

NOTES ON CHAPTER 2
Further details of publications and documents in Bibliography

1   FO 416/98, Bullard to Halifax, 7 February 1940; FO 371/9406, December 1934; Mehdi Bamdad, *Tarikh Rejal Iran Quroun 12, 13, 14 (Dictionary of National Biography of Iran: Twelfth, Thirteenth, Fourteenth Centuries)*, vol. 1, pp 94–99.

2   The legal age for ascending the throne was then 18. It was raised to 20 under the Pahlavis.

3   Melvin Hall, *Journey to the End of an Era*, pp 204–209.

4   FO 371/3860, Cox to Curzon, 15 and 18 January 1919.

5   DoS, Quarterly Report No. 2, US Legation in Tehran to Secretary of State, 10 January 1919; FO 371/3860, Cox to Curzon, 10 May 1919.

6   FO 371/3858, Cox to Curzon, 13 February 1919; FO 371/3258, Curzon to Cox, 22 February 1919; FO 371/3860, Cox to Curzon, 15 January, 6 and 22 February, 20 and 28 March, 5 and 9 April 1919.

7   FO 371/3860, Cox to Curzon, 11 April 1919.

8   CAB 27/24, Eastern Committee, 30 December 1918. Houshang Sabahi, *British Policy in Persia 1918–1925*, p 11.

9   Hardinge to Landsdowne, 18 July 1903: quoted in D. McLean, 'Finance and Informal Empire Before the First World War', *Economic History Review*, 29 (1976). Houshang Sabahi, *British Policy in Persia 1918–1925*, p13.

10 *Ibid.*

11 See Lt Col. John Johnson, *A Journey from India to England*, p 154; Capt. George Keppel, *Personal Narrative of a Journey from India to England*, vol. 2 pp 126–27; Capt. Richard Wilberham, *Travels in the Trans Caucasian Provinces of Russia*, p 417; Mirza Abul Hassan Khan, *The Journal of Mirza Abul Hassan Khan 1809–1810*.

12 CAB 27/24, Eastern Committee, 10th meeting 28 May 1918 and 15th meeting, 21 June 1918; Houshang Sabahi, *British Policy in Persia 1918–1925*, p 11. See also Denis Wright, *The English Amongst the Persians*, p 175.

13 Cecil to Balfour, 8 January 1918: quoted in B.C. Busch, *Madras to Lausanne*, p 11.

14 Vincent Sheean, *The New Persia*, pp 27–28.

15 FO 371/3802, Cox to Curzon, 23 July 1919.

16 FO 371/3862, Curzon to Cox, 30 July 1919.

17 *Ibid.*

18 FO 371/3862, Cox to Curzon, 19 April 1919.

19 FO 371/3871, C 199.

20 FO 371/3802, Cox to Curzon, 20 July 1919.

21 FO 371/3802, Cox to Curzon, 13 August 1919.

22 FO 371/3863, Cox to Curzon, 28 August 1919.

23 FO 371/3864, Curzon to Cox, 24 September 1919.

24 Letter by Curzon to Lord Lemington, September 13, 1919: quoted by Lord Ronaldshay, *The Life of Lord Curzon*, vol. 3, p 219.

25 Hosein Qoli Mirza Mozaffari (Nosrat al Saltaneh),the fifth son of Mozaffar al Din Shah, is the source for both Makki and Golsha'yan: Hosein Makki, *Tarikh Bist Saleh Iran (A Twenty Year History of Iran)*, pp 22, 67–74; Abbas Rafa'at, article in *Ayandeh*, Tehran, Azar and Day 1360 (winter 1981). Recollections of Abbasqoli Golsha'yan, from Ghasem

Ghani, *Yaddasht ha-e-Dr Ghasem Ghani* (*Memoirs of Dr Ghasem Ghani*), vol. 11, pp 638–647. See also the definitive study of Ahmad Shah by Dr Javad Sheikh ol Eslami, *Simay-e-Ahmad Shah Qajar* (*A Portrait of Ahmad Shah Qajar*), in which he documents and refutes all prior written material that support the versions put forth by Nosrat al Saltaneh and others. After Reza Shah was crowned, Nosrat al Saltaneh periodically bought space in Tehran newspapers to state he was overjoyed with Reza Shah as the new king. FO 371/17908, 26 July 1934.

26 FO 371/3865, Curzon to Cox, 21 October 1919. There had been a furore in 1903 over the grant of the Garter to Mazaffar al Din Shah, and Britain's Foreign Minister had threatened to resign if the award were not made. Thereafter an unwritten policy had been adopted that the decoration should be awarded only to Christian monarchs unless there were special circumstances.

27 Lord Ronaldshay, *The Life of Lord Curzon*, Vol. 3, p 217.

28 FO 371/4909, Sidney Armitage Smith, Chief British Financial Envoy to Tehran under the provisions of the 1919 Agreement, to the Foreign Office, 22 November 1920.

29 *Ibid.*

30 FO 371/3870, Cox to Curzon, 1 April 1920.

31 Claremont Skrine, *World War in Iran*, p 58.

32 FO 371/3860, Cox to Curzon, 8 May 1919.

33 L.P. Elwell-Sutton, *Modern Iran*, p 26. Furthermore, a practice was begun early this century that the Iranian Government would receive the bill for losses sustained by any non-Iranian national who was robbed in Iran.

34 FO 371/4909, Norman to Curzon, 6 July 1920.

35 M. Reza Ghods, *Iran in the Twentieth Century*, p 69. See also Rouhollah Ramazani, *The Foreign Policy of Iran 1500–1941*, pp 141, 146 and 150.

36 FO 371/3874/205742.

37 James M. Balfour, *Recent Happenings in Persia*, pp 157–158.

38 FO 371/3802, Cox to Curzon, 13 August 1919.

39 DBFP, doc. no. 448, Curzon to G. Graham, Britain's Minister to Paris, 31 May 1920.

40 Minutes by E. Crowe, 18 April 1919: quoted by Houshang Sabahi, *British Policy in Persia 1918–1925*, p 141.

41 DoS, Caldwell to Lansing, 9 and 12 September 1919.

42 DoS, vol. 2, Lansing to Davis, 4 October 1919.

43 FO 371/3863, Curzon to Davis, 13 September 1919.

44 DoS, 4 and 6 October 1919.

45 Mehdi Bamdad, *Tarikh Rejal Iran Quroun 12, 13, 14* (*Dictionary of National Biography of Iran: Twelfth, Thirteenth, Fourteenth Centuries*), vol. 3, pp 51–53.

46 FO 371/4909, Oliphant to Curzon and Norman, 30 November and 1 December 1920.

47 FO 371/4910, telegram from Baghdad, 8 December 1920. The telegram is unsigned but probably was sent by Cox who was then High Commissioner in Baghdad.

48 James M. Balfour, *Recent Happenings in Persia*, p 256. In 1922 Vosouq initiated libel proceedings against Balfour. The Foreign Office refused to release any documents pertaining to the 1919 Agreement. Balfour's defence collapsed and the publisher was forced to withdraw the book from further circulation. Gordon Waterfield, *Professional Diplomat*, p 65.

See also Alexander Powell, *The Struggle for Power in Moslem Asia*, pp 297–298.

49 From the files of the Imperial Bank of Persia. Given to the author by Ms Francis Bostock who had researched the history of the Imperial Bank of Persia.

50 Sir Reader Bullard, *Persia in Two World Wars* and *Royal Central Asian Journal*, Vol. I, Pt 1; It is a mystery why someone who had committed matricide, and, as several British officials have attested, was by far the most corrupt and useless member of the triumverate retained such close relations with high-ranking British officials. Sir Reader Bullard, one of the longest-serving British envoys to Tehran, held Sarem al Dowleh in high regard and praised him repeatedly. Throughout his life he remained an invitee to the annual British Embassy garden party in honour of the King's or Queen's birthday. FO 371/7906, R.H. Hoare to J. Simon, 26 July 1934. In a recent book based on interviews with the late Mohsen Foroughi, a noted architect and the eldest son of Mohammad Ali Foroughi, one of the most important Iranian politicians between 1921 and 1942, the author maintains that Soleiman Behboodi, a trusted valet and factotum of Reza Shah, received 250,000 tomans (50,000 tomans more than Vosouq is alleged to have received) from Vosouq and supposedly gave it to Reza Shah. Baqer Aqeli, *Zoka al Molk Foroughi va Shahrivar 1320 (Zoka al Molk Foroughi and August 1941)*, p 74; Hassan Taqizadeh, an important politician active from 1905–1965, maintains that Akbar Mas'oud (Sarem al Dowleh) gave back his 100,000 tomans in four installments. Vosouq returned his 200,000 tomans while Nosrat al Dowleh first maintaining that he had no money ultimately paid back his 100,000 tomans. Taqizadeh claims Foroughi was the intermediary sent to collect the 100,000 from Nosrat al Dowleh. Hassan Taqizadeh, *Khaterat Seyyed Hassan Taqizadeh (Memoirs of Seyyed Hassan Taqizadeh)*, pp 194–196. Neither account has been verified. No dates or particulars are given in this or the above account and they are allegedly based on second- and third- hand reports. The first source is what the writer Baqer Aqeli heard from Mohsen Foroughi, who heard from his father, who allegedly heard it from Behboodi. Taqizadeh's interview was given when he was advanced in age and his recollections were often faulty and self-serving.

51 L/PS/10/859/5036, Cox to Curzon, 17 August 1919.

52 Mehdi Bamdad, *Tarikh Rejal Iran Quroun 12, 13, 14 (Dictionary of National Biography of Iran: Twelfth, Thirteenth, Fourteenth Centuries)*, vol. 5, pp 176–178.

53 Gen. Arfa, *Under Five Shahs*, pp 91–92.

54 Mehdi Bamdad, *Tarikh Rejal Iran Quroun 12, 13, 14 (Dictionary of National Biography of Iran: Twelfth, Thirteenth, Fourteenth Centuries)*, vol. 5, pp 176–178. See also Ali Granmayeh's 'Introduction' in Brian Pearce and Ali Granmayeh, *The Staroselsky Problem 1918–1920*, p 21.

55 L/PS/10/859/5460, Military Attaché to W/O, 9 April 1920.

56 Harold Nicolson, *Curzon, The Last Phase*, p 141.

57 FO 371/4909, Sidney Armitage Smith Report to the Exchequer or the Foreign Office, 22 November 1920.

58 DBFP, doc. no. 401, Cox to Curzon, 5 April 1920.

59 FO 371/3870, Derby to Curzon, 30 March 1920.

60 FO 371/3870, Derby to Foreign Office, 18 April 1920. The shrines Ahmad Shah mentions are in Karbela and Najaf.
61 *Ibid.*
62 Dr Mohammad Javad Sheikh ol Eslami, *Simaye Ahmad Shah Qajar* (*The Profile of Ahmad Shah Qajar*), vol. I; DBFP, doc. no. 456, Cox to Curzon, 8 June 1920.
63 The Foreign Office List, 1956; *Who Was Who*, vol. V.
64 Gordon Waterfield, *Professional Diplomat: Sir Percy Loraine*, p 47. Sir Eyre Crowe had succeeded Lord Hardinge as Permanent Under-Secretary at the Foreign Office.
65 Harold Nicolson, *Curzon, The Last Phase*, p 114.

3

The Resignation of Vosouq al Dowleh

After the signing of the Treaty of Brest Litovsk of 3 March 1918 Russia pulled out of the war and her troops withdrew from Iran. This left north-west Iran and the Caucasus-Caspian route open to Turkish troops. In February 1918 the British Command in Mesopotamia despatched a small unit of troops through Iran commanded by Maj. Gen. Lionel Dunsterville with the objective of uniting White Russians fighting the Red Army in the Caucasus and taking control of the oil fields in Baku. Dunsterville had difficulty from the start in making any advance north of Qazvin. The road between Qazvin and Anzali on the south-western shore of the Caspian Sea was controlled by the forces of Kouchek Khan, a nationalist guerilla leader of contradictory and confused ideals. Dunsterville finally reached the Iranian port of Anzali, but no further. A Russian revolutionary committee controlled the port and Dunsterville was forced to withdraw. In April of the same year Dunsterville, with a larger ground force and aerial bombardment, opened the Qazvin-Anzali road and drove out Kouchek Khan's Jangali forces from Rasht, the provincial capital of Gilan. A tacit agreement was reached with Kouchek Khan whereby he undertook to keep the road open and Dunsterville agreed to allow Kouchek Khan's forces to operate in other parts of the province.[1] Britain further increased its forces in north-west Iran by the addition of 2000 men and heavy artillery.[2]

The Jangalis derived their name from the word 'jangal', or forest, which borders the south-central coast of the Caspian Sea. Kouchek Khan, 1880–1921, was born Younes, son of a small land-owner in Rasht. He had studied theology in Tehran with the intention of becoming a clergyman but became drawn to the constitutional movement. When Mohammad Ali Shah invaded Iran in 1911 to reclaim his throne, Kouchek Khan volunteered as a soldier to repel the invasion and was wounded in one of the skirmishes in the north. Early in World War I he returned to Rasht and formed an organisation called 'Islamic Unity' with the aim of restoring parliamentary rule and driving Russian and British soldiers out of Iran. Soon the Jangali forces were receiving military training from the Ottoman Turks. At their height, Kouchek Khan commanded some 2,000 guerrillas operating in Gilan and Mazandaran. After the Bolshevik revolution he formed a coalition with Azarbaijani Marxists led by Haidar Khan and received military support from the Bolsheviks. By the end of 1917 the Jangalis were a major force in the north and controlled most of Gilan. They published a newspaper which called for economic assistance to small farmers; administrative autonomy for Gilan; the re-birth of Islam; cancellation of all unequal treaties; and the evacuation of British troops from Iran.[3] In robbing the rich and feeding the poor, Kouchek Khan became known to some as the Robin Hood of the Caspian region.[4] Iranian writers depict Kouchek Khan either as a national hero exploiting the Russian Revolution to advance his cause or as a naive and innocent nationalist betrayed by Communist agents and infiltrators.[5] Kouckek Khan soon became a serious threat to the central Government as he controlled two of Iran's richest provinces. He also became a threat to the British through his control of the Manjeel Pass through the Alborz Mountains into the thickly wooded areas of Gilan.

British forces remained active in north-west Iran during the balance of 1918. There was a change of command in that year and Maj. Gen. H.B. Champain replaced Dunsterville. At the end of February 1919 Vosouq ordered the Cossack Division to attack and dislodge the insurgent forces of Kouchek Khan from Gilan. Champain was ordered by the military command in Baghdad to support the operation with the use of British troops and planes. He expressed reluctance, arguing that there was a pact with the Jangalis and as the Qazvin-Anzali road was now open British intervention was unnecessary. Champain was overruled and the pact with Kouchek Khan, which had become bothersome to Vosouq was in effect abrogated. Kouchek Khan was offered an amnesty and asylum in Mesopotamia. He refused and the Cossack troops with heavy air support forced him and his men to withdraw to the inner forest.[6] Several leaders of the movement were captured and executed by the Cossacks. Kouchek Khan was not to emerge from the forest until a year later when the British troops were forced to withdraw from Anzali and Rasht.[7]

By the end of 1919 the anti-Bolshevik forces had been driven out of almost all of Russia proper, and had retreated to the borders of the Czarist empire: the borders of Poland, Turkey, Turkestan and Russian Azarbaijan. The interventionist British and American forces had also withdrawn from Archangel in north-west Russia. There was only sporadic fighting in eastern Siberia. By late March 1920 Gen. Anton Denikin, the last remaining leader of the anti-Bolshevik forces, had been routed. An anti-Bolshevik flotilla consisting of some 18 vessels took refuge in the harbor of Anzali. The Soviet forces captured Baku and strengthened their fleet on the Caspian. On 6 May the Soviets told an Iranian official that they had no design on Iran but 'intended to advance against English forces by land and sea'.[8] This message had been communicated to the British Legation but no measures were taken as Curzon and Cox wanted to retain troops in northern Iran as leverage in having the Anglo-Persian Agreement implemented. Curzon had always maintained that force was an adjunct of diplomacy. He had 'refused to believe that anyone who was not prepared to contemplate the employment of force in the last resort could possibly have a policy worth the name'.[9] His predecessor Balfour's thinking had been no different. He had written some two years earlier, 'Our experience of the last two years shows that the only thing that keeps the Persians straight is force'.[10]

The India Office, as always, was dubious of the prospect of success for Curzon's policy and worried that if British troops remained in Iran it would become progressively harder to withdraw them. They believed Curzon's Persian policy 'would stand as long as it had the support of British bayonets'.[11] The Treasury was now also exerting pressure on the War Office to withdraw troops from north-west and north-east Iran. By the end of 1918 Britain's expenditure in Iran was about £30,000,000 a year including the monthly subsidy to the Iranian Government, the Cossack Division and the payments to the Shah.[12] Curzon could only argue for a delay and to be given more time, admitting that without the British military presence in Persia, 'the Anglo-Persian Agreement would crumble'.[13]

On 18 May 1920, Gen. Champain was visiting Anzali to report on the condition of his troops and to witness the test-firing of newly-installed shore batteries. Instead, the only firing came from 13 Soviet warships which had sailed down the Caspian from Baku. Soon afterwards some 2,000 Soviet soldiers landed at the harbour.

Champain knew he was out-gunned and immediately began negotiations with the Russian Commander, Feodore Raskalnikov, who
agreed to allow the British forces to withdraw from Anzali if he could
have the White Russian vessels which were in the harbour. Champain
withdrew his troops to Rasht and a few days later all British forces
withdrew from Gilan province. He left a small garrison at Manjeel
Pass and the main body of his troops relocated to Qazvin.[14]

The landing of Soviet troops and the forced withdrawal of British
troops sent shock-waves through every department of the British
Government. Field Marshal Henry Wilson wrote in his diary, 'For
months I have been begging the Cabinet to allow [troops] to withdraw from Persia and the Caucasus'. (A small contingent of British
forces were still stationed near Baku.) He wrote to Curzon the following day, 'perhaps the regrettable incident at Anzali which has
now occured and which will be followed by others may lead you to
change your mind and even trust a little in the advice of responsible
advisers'.[15]

As expected there was a full-scale debate in the Cabinet. Wilson
and Winston Churchill, the War Office Secretary, advocated total
withdrawal from northern Iran. On the other hand Lord Milner, the
Colonial Secretary, threatened to resign if withdrawal took place.[16]
There was also disagreement over the motives of Moscow. The consensus was that Russia was merely securing its borders and was too
involved in its own domestic affairs to launch a full-scale invasion of
Iran. The India Office felt that since Britain was not prepared to
defend Persia, Curzon should allow the Iranians to negotiate directly
with the Russians. The smouldering antipathy betweeen Curzon and
Montague surfaced again. Montague believed, 'The best way for
Persia to handle the Russian threat would be to declare the Anglo-
Persian Agreement as inoperable'.[17] In a later telegram which is
indicative of the thinking of the Indian Government, Lord
Chelmsford argued, 'Cut the ground from under Bolshevism by
scrapping the Anglo-Persian Agreement'.[18] The Cabinet failed to
reach a decision and the matter was deferred to a later meeting. For
the time being a compromise was reached to keep troops at
Qazvin.[19]

On 20 May 1920 the Lord Privy Seal, Andrew Bonar Law, in
answer to a question in the House of Lords, declared that His
Majesty's Government 'are under no obigation' to defend Persia
against a Soviet invasion.[20] On 28 May David Lloyd George in reply
to another parliamentary question repeated that the British
Government did not have any naval or military obligation towards
Iran.[21] These pronouncements further dissipated whatever Iranian

support was left for the perceived advantages of the Agreement, especially among the landed gentry. One of Vosouq's main arguments had been that Iran was too weak and helpless to defend herself and needed Britain to protect her territorial integrity. With British withdrawal from the north and Bonar Law's statement it appeared to most Iranians that Britain's only interest in Iran was to control the government for the sole purpose of protecting its oil fields in the south and its economic and strategic interests in India.

On 3 June Soviet forces occupied Rasht and on 4 June Kouchek Khan declared an Iranian Soviet Socialist Republic in Gilan with himself as chief commissar.[22] With this latest move it became clearer that some elements in the Soviet hierarchy had a more ambitious goal than merely driving British troops out of northern Iran. Raskalnikov had maintained that Moscow had no knowledge of his operation at Anzali and he had carried it out on his own initiative simply to retrieve the naval vessels. However, after the declaration of the Soviet Republic in Gilan it became apparent that Moscow, with the co-operation of the Caucasian and Soviet Azarbaijani Communists, must have backed the entire operation and probably hand-picked Kouchek Khan's lieutenants to govern Gilan. These lieutenants were Azarbaijani Communists led by Haidar Khan and Ja'far Peeshevari who took their orders from Baku. It took a while for Kouchek Khan to realise he was a mere figurehead. He resigned in July and withdrew to the forest. There were several skirmishes between the forces of Haidar Khan and Kouchek Khan. The Communist forces were defeated and Haidar Khan was killed. Kouchek Khan remained in the forest, attacking Rasht sporadically. Meanwhile the British Prime Minister, Lloyd George, concluded that, 'troops should be maintained at their present level... until the Persian parliament votes on the Anglo-Persian agreement'.[23]

Herman Norman had the misfortune of being appointed Minister to Tehran at the worst possible time. The exact date of Norman's arrival is not certain. He may have arrived in late May. Cox left Tehran on 13 June and Norman had been at the British Legation for at least a few days before Cox's departure. Norman's first report from the Legation in Tehran is dated 11 June 1920. By early June Britain's unpopularity had reached its highest point and not only was Curzon's dream of hegemony in Iran rapidly fading, but the Soviets were threatening the British presence in the northern half of the country. There were misgivings even amongst established anglophiles. What use was there in handing over the administration of the country to Britain if she would not even defend it against Bolshevik encroachment. Bonar Law's statement and the troop withdrawals had left Norman with a very weak hand. Yet Curzon's instructions to Norman were no different to previous ones. It was as if nothing had changed. Norman was to keep Vosouq in power, have the Agreement ratified and begin its implementation as soon as possible.

Norman and Cox differed greatly. Norman had served in the Near East, in Cairo and Constantinople, but he had also served in the Far East, the United States, Latin America and Europe. Norman had seen a wider changing world and witnessed the rising tide of nationalism. Cox had spent all his career dealing with hereditary sheikhs and tribal leaders. Additionally Norman, as someone not involved in the murky background to the Agreement, was able to view the matter with less passion. As he was fully aware of the background and the corruption and bribery surrounding the Agreement, he could not have had much respect for those involved, especially the Shah and the triumverate. Norman was soon to know for himself the leading players on whom the success of Curzon's policy rested.

Norman shared the early part of his trip from Europe with the Shah who was returning to Tehran. Norman and the Shah had boarded the same boat on the journey from Marseilles to Alexandria. Their paths parted in Egypt. The Shah went to the shrines in Mesopotamia while Norman, after brief visits to Cairo and Baghdad came to Tehran. The Shah arrived in Tehran on 2 June, was met by Vosouq and 'drove in state slowly through town. They had extraordinary good receptions throughout except at one spot where a handful of students chanted 'long life to Shah, death to the English and the Agreement'.[24] Norman's first communication with Curzon is on 7 May, when he reported from Cairo that 'the Shah gave me the most categorical assurances of his complete loyalty to the Agreement'. The Shah had also assured Norman that on his return he would transfer control of the Cossack Division to British officers and 'would maintain the present government [Vosouq] as long as we want it'.[25] Despite the Shah's protestations of fidelity, Norman must have been aware of the history of antagonism between the Shah and Vosouq and how the Shah had used his support for Vosouq to receive a monthly stipend from Britain. By the time the Shah reached Tehran his declaration of support for Vosouq had become qualified. Norman's initial report from Iran concerned his first audience with the Shah on 11 June 1920. The Shah informed Norman that when he had left Iran Vosouq had been 'comparatively popular', but since his return he had found growing animosity to Vosouq mainly for his arrest and exile of prominent Iranians opposed to the Agreement. The Shah again assured Norman, however, that he was prepared to support and keep Vosouq in office 'if that was the desire of the British Government'.[26]

On 13 June Norman had his first recorded meeting with Vosouq. Norman reported that he found him 'extremely depressed'. Vosouq dismissed any assurances of support by the Shah and believed the Shah was plotting against him and was 'in communication with his enemies'. Vosouq also informed Norman that his relationship with the Shah had deteriorated since the latter's return primarily because the Shah demanded reimbursement by the Government for 'sums he had spent from his private means to defray expenses of his recent journey'. The Shah had insisted on reimbursement at every meeting with Vosouq 'who had tried unsuccessfully to convince the Shah that the treasury was empty'. Vosouq had suggested 'payment in installments but the Shah wants immediate payment'. Vosouq also informed Norman that he had asked the Shah to be given powers to arrest and deport persons who 'with the aid of the Russians, Americans and French' were working against the implementation of the Agreement. Norman added that the Shah believed a policy of repression would only increase the prevailing discontent and ultimately 'the resentment could turn towards himself [the Shah] and put his life in danger'. At the end of the meeting Vosouq raised the issue of resignation and mentioned that 'he cannot carry the load all by himself and that his health has suffered after a prolonged illness'. Norman suggested bringing new people into the Cabinet and Vosouq answered that people of stature such as Moshir al Dowleh and Mostofi al Mamalek 'had no personal objections to him but would refuse to serve in the Cabinet because they lacked courage'.[27] As early as 1 April 1920 Vosouq had told Cox he contemplated resigning. At that time he had given as reasons the 'intrigues of Sarem al Dowleh and Sepahdar'. Cox, however, had talked him out of it.[28]

Norman concluded his report by saying that Vosouq was unpopular because he had been in office too long and refused to share power with anyone. Since the resignation of Sarem al Dowleh and Firouz's lengthy stay in Europe, Vosouq had to oversee both the Ministries of Finance and Foreign Affairs. The Cabinet was comprised of 'his relatives and dependents' who were worthless.[29] It is interesting to note that Norman gave no encouragement to Vosouq to remain in office. Norman had already sensed that his instructions from London were unrealistic and carrying out Curzon's mandate was impossible, at least for as long as Vosouq remained in office. He must have discovered soon after arrival the prevailing hostility towards the Agreement and the immense unpopularity of the triumverate who had negotiated it. Furthermore, he could not have been much impressed with the Vosouq he saw, who was by now a spent and exhausted man. This was not the Vosouq about whom Marling and Cox had written so glowingly and upon whom Curzon had relied for the success of his policy. At his first meeting Norman saw a tired and isolated man whose only option had narrowed down to the arrest and exile of more opponents. His early encounters with the Shah were not encouraging either. The Shah's only concern was reimbursement for a bogus claim concerning his European travel expenses including his speculations on the Paris Bourse.

What made it even more difficult for Norman to manoeuver was the decision by the British Cabinet to terminate the 350,000 toman monthly subsidy to the Iranian Government at the end of June. The Treasury had also recommended cutting off the 100,000 toman monthly subsidy to the Cossacks and the 6,000 toman annual subsidy to Iranian troops in Khorasan. Before leaving Iran, Cox had insisted that payments should continue at least until September. Norman, on reviewing the situation, also pleaded with Curzon that the subsidies continue. He argued that if the subsidies were cut off the Government of Vosouq would surely fall and even the Shah could be deposed, 'not in itself regretable but there could be Soviet Republics established in other northern provinces'.[30] Norman received no answer from Curzon and was forced to wait for events to unfold.

Norman and Curzon's perspectives were quite different. Curzon was more concerned about Russia again becoming dominant in Iran and believed that Iran under British administration was the only way to thwart Russian schemes. Norman, as a direct observer on the scene, saw the internal threat as far more serious than the external one. The province of Gilan had already declared itself a republic and severed its ties with the Central Government. Mazandaran and Azarbaijan were in a state of rebellion and could join Gilan. Withdrawal of British troops from the north, the decision to have further troop cuts and now the decision to end the subsidies robbed Norman of the clout which Cox had in appointing and removing Prime Ministers. Since Soviet troop landings the Cossack Division under its Russian officers was also acting independently of the Central Government and appeared to have an agenda of its own. Norman realised that it would be harder to make Curzon aware of the seriousness of the British position in Iran as long as Vosouq remained in power. When Norman saw the Shah on 14 June he was told that Vosouq was close to resigning. Norman made no response and merely enquired the reasons for Vosouq's decision. The Shah did not elaborate but hinted that it would be better for all concerned because 'public discontent could soon be directed at him and against the throne'.[31] Norman realised that Vosouq could be nudged towards resigning if he were denied encouragement to remain in office, but Curzon would again insist on another 'reactionary' Prime Minister who would use force to have the Agreement implemented. Norman felt that none of the discredited anglophiles would be able to have the Agreement ratified even with force. He had come around to the thinking of the India office, that if there were any hope for British political supremacy in Iran, Britain must accept and work with popular politicians more in tune with nationalist sentiments.

Norman telegraphed Curzon on 15 June and argued that Vosouq had outlived his usefulness and that British policy would have a better chance of success with a new Government in office. 'What is required is a Prime Minister who would be able to win over honest opponents of the Agreement whose objections are due to the imperfect comprehension of its purposes.' A compromise could be worked out. For example the Agreement could be limited in its duration to 'say 20 years'. Now that Norman had opened the door to the possibility of Vosouq's resignation he began to suggest possible successors. At the outset he mentioned and then cleverly dismissed the two people he knew would be most acceptable to Curzon. He quoted Vosouq as saying that 'were it not for his relative young age' a logical successor would be Firouz, or alternatively, Firouz's father Farmanfarma 'who may be too old and would not be acceptable to the opposition'. Having eliminated from contention the two people who may have been on Curzon's mind, Norman raised the names of Moshir al Dowleh and Mostofi al Mamalek as possible Prime Ministers. He again quoted Vosouq as saying that both 'would be suitable but [that he] doubts either would accept'.[32]

In earlier telegrams to Curzon when Norman spoke vaguely of 'honest opponents of the agreement' he was referring to these same men, Mostofi al Mamalek and Moshir al Dowleh. Norman believed that if there were any hope of salvaging the Agreement, it could be done only by these two who were untainted, honest and enjoyed public esteem and respect. It did not take long for Curzon to reply. He must have immediately understood that his envoy was contemplating the abandonment of Vosouq. Curzon insisted that Vosouq should stay and asked Norman to tell Vosouq 'to expect a personal message from me'. Curzon also instructed Norman to tell the Shah that if Vosouq resigned his subsidy of 15,000 tomans monthly would cease.[33] Curzon's position was weakened, however, by a report from the War Office the same day that highlighted the hopelessness of Vosouq's situation. 'The Persian Cabinet is a one man concern... The acting Minister of Foreign Affairs [Rajab Ali Mansour] is an obscure clerk... [Vosouq] can be kept in power only by money and British troops,' which the 'Treasury finds difficult to fund'.[34]

Now that the possibility of Vosouq's removal had been seriously raised, Norman, in a series of telegrams to Curzon, intensified his attempts to bring him around to accept a more popular figure as Prime Minister. Norman's most telling communication was on 18 June in which he argued that although he is new to the country and 'does not know Persia well' he knows of the popularity Britain enjoyed during and after the constitutional movement. 'They owe the Constitution to us.' Now we are 'becoming intensely unpopular... partly as a result of our withdrawal from Gilan and Azarbaijan... which have made the worst impression... I cannot convince Persians that we can defend them...'. Norman continued:

> We are replacing the hated Russians [and] His Majesty's Government must decide whether they will allow all the money sunk in Persia to be lost, our commerce destroyed... our interests and position in the country ruined... our policy represented by the Anglo-Persian Agreement to be scrapped, Mesopotamia rendered intolerable, our hold over India jeopardised... it is true that by the Agreement we give no specific undertaking to defend Persia [but] surely we are under a moral obligation to make an effort to do so... failure would inflict a heavy blow to her [Britain's] prestige throughout the East and increase her difficulties almost as much as would our ignominious expulsion from the country.[35]

In order to reinforce his arguments Norman also sent Armitage Smith's opinion which painted as gloomy a picture as Norman's. Armitage Smith's report reads in part as follows: that the Persian Government has a chronic deficit of 250,000 tomans a month.

> They have no budget; they live from hand to mouth... corruption and nepotism are universal and there are few honest and capable officials... The Central Government cannot control the provinces or collect taxes... three of the richest provinces are out of its control.[36]

Although Norman sent at least one report daily to Curzon from 13 June to the end of that month, it does not appear that he made much of an impression. Curzon's few replies during the period are magisterial edicts which reiterate his past position that Vosouq should remain in office at all costs. What finally compelled Curzon to accept the reality of Vosouq's departure and the necessity of considering a successor had little to do with Norman's feverish telegrams.

Vosouq's own choice of successor, with the concurrence of Cox and Curzon, was Firouz, who was travelling between London and Paris. The first ten months of Firouz's lengthy stay in Europe from September 1919 to late June 1920 (when Vosouq resigned) may have been at Vosouq's request. His functions abroad were initially to act as a 'minder' to the Shah[37] and later to be a participant in the selection and seconding of British personnel to serve in Iran under the Agreement. These functions came to an end by the close of 1919 and Firouz's further stay does not appear to have had a definite purpose or justification, although it may have had at least the tacit approval of Vosouq. From the beginning of 1920, Firouz had only occasional meetings with British officials, including Curzon, with no definitive results. One of the more interesting meetings took place on 10 April 1920 when Firouz called on Curzon. He raised the advisability of US participation in the financial and economic recovery of Iran. Firouz suggested the employment of US advisers on agriculture, railways and oil. Curzon 'warns him strongly against introducing the Standard Oil Company to Iran... that will mean competition which will be a source of trouble in the future'. Firouz was no more successful when he raised the issue of direct negotiations with Russia which Curzon also strongly disapproved. Firouz then brought up the question of parliamentary approval of the Agreement and the mechanism of its submission to parliament.[38] Subsequent substantive contacts concerned the Soviet landing of troops at Anzali and Firouz's plea for arms and more British troops.[39] There was also an urgent plea by Firouz to Balfour (now Britain's chief representative at the Council of League of Nations) to have the League take up the issue of Bolshevik aggression against Iran. Balfour rejected the proposal 'as a difficult issue' because 'the French are jealous of us and maintain the Agreement has reduced Persia to the status of a dependent state and hardly deserves to be counted as a member of the League of Nations', and the French representative on the Council 'may raise the issue to embarrass us'.[40]

On 21 June G.P. Churchill, the senior member of the Persian Department at the Foreign Office, reported that he had seen Firouz who informed him that he had received a telegram from Vosouq asking him to become the new Prime Minister. Firouz however, told Churchill that 'his acceptance was out of the question' as he could not, for personal reasons, return to Tehran any earlier than two months hence. Firouz recommended that Vosouq be kept in office and the Shah be threatened with the loss of his subsidy and the further threat of Bolshevik rule over Iran if Vosouq were removed.[41] Firouz knew he was as unpopular as Vosouq, and even if Britain forced his premiership, his government would not last more than a few months. Firouz was an ambitious politician and was clever enough to calculate that it was best to have one or two 'weak interim' Prime Ministers in office after which there would be clamour for a strong autocratic government which he would lead.[42] As we shall see his calculations were to have a profound effect on the important events of 21 February 1921 and his subsequent relationship with Britain.

Firouz's withdrawal from the race made it easier for Norman to propel his own 'nationalist' candidate. Another element which strengthened Norman's position was the status of the command of the Cossack Division which had been led from its establishment by Czarist Russian officers. In 1917, the reformist Government of Kerensky recalled the Czarist commander of the Division, Baron Moadel, and replaced him with a liberal-minded Col. Clerge. Clerge, while passing through Tiflis *en route* to Iran to assume command, met a former colleague, Col. Starosselsky, who was not in any post at the time. Starosselsky had served with a Tartar regiment which had been recently disbanded. Clerge offered him the post of second-in-command and took him to Tehran. Either for personal or ideological reasons Starosselsky accused Clerge of pro-Bolshevik sympathies and asked the Shah to have him dismissed. When the Shah refused to intervene, Starosselsky turned to senior Iranian officers in the Division and, with the help of Col. Reza Khan (later Reza Shah) and other officers, executed a bloodless mutiny resulting in Clerge's removal in 1918.[43] On assuming command Starosselsky, who took orders only from the Shah, soon became a dominant force on the political scene and opposed Britain's attempts to reorganise the Iranian armed forces which he saw as a threat to his own future. Starosselsky also had his doubts about the success of the Russian Revolution and believed that sooner or later Russia would again become the dominant power in northern Iran. Before leaving for Europe the Shah had instructed Starosselsky 'to refuse obedience to any order given to him by the Persian Government during the Shah's absence... and if the Persian Government tried to compel him to obey he was to resist by force'. Pursuant to these instructions Starosselsky refused to take any orders from Vosouq.[44]

In November 1919 Brig. Gen. W.E.R. Dickson was appointed to head the seven-man British military mission in Tehran to organise a unified Iranian army absorbing the Cossacks, Gendarmes, SPR and the smaller local units. He had served as the Inspector General of the East Persia Cordon under Gen. Malleson, was considered a soldier-diplomat and was conversant in several languages. Dickson was seconded from the War Office to the Foreign Office for the duration of his mission and he arrived in mid December of that year. He was faced from the outset with the overt hostility of Starosselsky who knew he would lose his position if the British succeeded in their mission. Dickson's task was not made easier by the resentment and

anger generated over the previously discussed suicide of Col.
Fazlollah Khan (Aqevli), a respected Iranian Gendarme officer.

The British military team found it impossible to pursue and
accomplish their plans for a unified military force as long as Russian
officers, and especially Starosselsky, commanded the Cossack
Divison. Starosselsky refused to accept the merger of the Cossack
Division with the proposed new army. He argued that 'he could not
compromise Russian interests and take action' in the absence of the
approval of the Russian Government in exile under Sazanov in
Paris. Equally disturbing to the British was that Starosselsky's overt
opposition to Dickson had gained him a degree of popularity among
the opponents of Vosouq and the Agreement.[45] Probably at the urging
of Cox, Vosouq had tried to remove Starosselsky in early 1920. He
was forced to abandon the effort pending the Shah's return. The
Shah, who considered the Cossacks essential to his protection and
safety, again flatly refused.[46] On 17 June 1920 Norman reported to
Curzon that Starosselsky was in 'communication with Bolshevik
officers' in the Soviet army and 'tells his own Russian officers that
after all we are all Russians' and that 'the common enemy are the
British'.[47] Norman, quoting Gen. Dickson, went as far as saying that
'there is even fear that Starosselsky may defect to the Bolsheviks.'
The matter was brought to the attention of the Shah who told
Norman that if any of the Russian officers were to go over to the
Bolsheviks he would then dismiss the rest, but as long as they continued to prove loyal to him he would do nothing. Norman, in the
same telegram, strongly hinted that Vosouq had lost his nerve and
was unwilling to intervene or take any steps that might incur the
displeasure of the Shah.[48]

The cumulative result of Vosouq's ineffectiveness coupled with
the insurgency in Gilan and other potential secessionist movements
in Azarbaijan and Mazandaran further diminished Vosouq's stature
at the Foreign Office. The final blow to his standing was the total
deterioration of relations between Vosouq and the Shah. On 20 June
Norman saw the Shah who told him that he had rejected Vosouq's
demand for additional powers to curb the opposition to the
Agreement and that Vosouq had therefore definitely decided to
resign. Norman explained that 'there was an intense dislike' between
the Shah and Vosouq. Norman next called on Vosouq who confirmed
that he had told the Shah that he had decided to resign. Vosouq
added, however, that a delegation of merchants from the bazaar had
called on him and 'begged him to stay' and therefore he may delay
his resignation. Norman, in the bluntest terms he had used so far,
commented that the delegation that had called on Vosouq 'was

probably organised by (Vosouq) himself'. Norman added: 'I suspect one motive is to retain control of means of making money which [the] office provides' and concluded that, 'my task is more difficult... There must be change if Persia is to be saved'.[49] What had largely been unsaid until now was openly said by Norman, and later others, that Vosouq was enriching himself while in office.[50] (Some six months earlier Armitage Smith had reported that Vosouq was making money from the Government opium monopoly).[51] Curzon ignored Norman's reasoning and gave his standard reply that Vosouq 'is the best person to safeguard the Agreement', but for the first time asked Norman who he had in mind as a possible successor. Knowing that Moshir al Dowleh was Norman's main choice, Curzon pre-empted Norman by saying that 'Moshir ed Dowleh is a weak character and inspires no confidence'.[52]

Vosouq's desperate attempts to stay in power were further illustrated by his acceding to the Shah's continuing demand to be reimbursed for the alleged expenses he had incurred in Europe. Vosouq sent Rajab Ali Mansour, the Acting Minister of Foreign Affairs, to see Norman to inform him that he, Vosouq, had had a very unpleasant meeting with the Shah who had insisted on the immediate payment of 150,000 tomans. Vosouq had been forced to suggest the payment of only half of the amount from the subsidy of 350,000 tomans for the month of June with the balance to be paid in ten days.[53] Once the Shah had sensed that Vosouq had lost his resolve and would buckle under pressure, he continued to insist upon the entire sum. Later in the day the Minister of Interior called on Norman at Vosouq's request and said the Shah had raised his demands and now insisted that the civil list (the expenses for operating the royal household) be increased. Specifically the Shah had demanded that the salary of the Crown Prince, Mohammad Hassan Mirza,* be increased from six to eleven thousand tomans a month. The Shah had also demanded that his two uncles who had accompanied him to Europe be reimbursed for their expenses, and 'he wanted something further for his immediate family'. Norman added that Vosouq had

---

* Mohammad Hassan Mirza Qajar, 1899–1943, was the third son of Mohammad Ali Shah and full brother of Ahmad Shah. He was exiled abroad in 1925 when the Qajar dynasty came to an end. In 1930 after Ahmad Shah's death, he issued a declaration in Paris that he was the legitimate successor to the throne. He lived in Paris briefly and then settled in England and Wales where he died in 1943. In August 1941, after the abdication of Reza Shah, he campaigned to put on the throne his son, Hamid Qajar, who spoke no Persian and was an officer in Britain's Merchant Navy.[55]

'begged me not to mention any of this to the Shah himself, otherwise his relationship with the Shah would become untenable'.[54]

Norman made no attempt to hide his disappointment over Vosouq's weakness and concessions. He wanted Curzon to know how ineffective and despondent Vosouq had become and to know of Vosouq's inability to control the Shah. Norman stated that one could not deal with the Shah through concessions and added that in the past Vosouq would have stood up to the Shah and not acceded to his demands merely to assure his own continuation in office. At the end of his report Norman pleaded with Curzon to authorise the payment of subsidies for the month of June and assured Curzon that he would attempt to dissuade the Shah from demanding immediate payment.[56]

Norman next called on the Shah and informed him that he was doing his best to induce the Foreign Office to authorise payment of the subsidy for the month of June. He reminded the Shah that the subsidy was intended for the administrative expenses of the country and could not be used for any other purpose. 'I begged his majesty not to lend any countenance to attempts to divert money for other purposes'. The Shah was not 'impressed' and said 'he knew nothing of finances of his country but would certainly comply with the request... but there was however one sum which ought legitimately to come out of the subsidy and which the Prime Minister had approved... the amount necessary to repay him for his journey'. The Shah asked whether Vosouq had mentioned this request for reimbursement and Norman replied in the negative. The Shah then gave a summary of how the expenses were incurred. Since the Government had promised to defray all of his expenses while in

---

*   Moshir al Dowleh (Hassan Pirnia), c.1872–1935, was the eldest son of Nasrollah Khan Moshir al Dowleh who rose from simple scribe (i.e. he received a marginal amount writing letters for the illiterate) to become Prime Minister and acquire great wealth. Nasrollah Khan slowly gained access to the rich and influential and married the daughter of a well-to-do politician/merchant. He became a private secretary to the Minister of Foreign Affairs and his rise thereafter was rapid. Hassan Pirnia was educated in Russia, spoke French fluently and became Minister to St Petersburg in 1902. He was one of the drafters of the Iranian Constitution of 1906. (He later identified and published various European sources for the constitution). He received the title of Moshir al Dowleh after his father's death in 1907. At the end of 1907 and beginning of 1908, he was briefly Minister of Foreign Affairs and in 1908 Minister of Justice. He was Prime Minister in 1915 for one month; in 1920 for four months; in 1922 for six months; and in 1923 for five months. He then retired and wrote a history of pre-Islamic Iran. Pirnia's last years were lived in near-isolation and he continued to be held in high esteem by his contemporaries.[62]

Europe he had not reduced his entourage or the length of his stay. Now, therefore, he needed the money 'not for himself but to repay the debts he had incurred in Europe... his small private fortune cannot meet these obligations'. Norman further reported, 'I begged him to delay for several months... if he insisted there would be grave consequences for his country and I could not answer for that'. Norman concluded that his admonition had no visible affect on the Shah.[57]

Feeling more confident now, Norman answered Curzon's earlier query on a successor to Vosouq and said, 'my choice is Moshir ed Dowleh (Hassan Pirnia)* whom I have deliberately not seen' since my arrival in Tehran. In a conciliatory gesture to Curzon, Norman quickly added that of course 'Nosrat ed Dowleh [Firouz] should be retained in the Cabinet'. Norman concluded that he could not act forcefully unless 'I have the moral and financial support of His Majesty's Government'.[58] Norman saw the Shah later in the day ostensibly to ascertain his choice of a successor to Vosouq. The Shah offered no names and merely said that he 'disliked and distrusted Vosouq ed Dowleh so extremely that he would never be able to work with him... but if I insist he would keep him'.[59] Norman then called on Vosouq who, realising his hopeless position, had decided to resign. 'He asked me to beg the Shah to accept his resignation which I did by letter to the Shah at Vosouq ed Dowleh's request... He told me he did not intend to stay in Tehran because his successor would feel uncomfortable'.

Norman informed Vosouq that he meant to see Moshir al Dowleh and Vosouq responded that he thought Moshir al Dowleh would refuse. Norman then asked who he should consider if Moshir al Dowleh did in fact refuse and Vosouq named Sepahdar and Mostofi, 'but would not say whom he preferred'. Vosouq added that the former would be more ready to accept but 'is an ill-educated man'. The latter would be more popular 'but lacked energy (and) His Majesty's Government would not look favourably on him'. In parting Vosouq warned Norman that without financial assistance from Britain 'no government can succeed'.[60] Curzon in reply merely advised Norman 'to do the best you can', and added that Firouz had told him he would support Moshir al Dowleh or anyone else if the new premier supported the Agreement. Curzon warned Norman not to make any financial commitment to the Shah or the new prime minister 'until you have fully informed us of the situation'.[61]

Vosouq's resignation was accepted by the Shah on 25 June. His second tenure as Prime Minister had lasted almost two years. He is vociferously damned by Iranian writers for his sponsorship of the Anglo-Persian Agreement although with less intensity than the other two members of the triumverate. He came to power when the country, devastated by war, was falling apart. The few supporters of Vosouq argue that he had no alternative other than to conclude an agreement with Britain and seek her protection. Vosouq reasoned that the Agreement gave the country some breathing space and held it together. There is some evidence that Vosouq may have sincerely believed in the necessity for the Agreement and saw it as the only way to save and free Iran from a cycle of tyranical and incompetent rulers. He also believed that under British protection a better class of civil servant would emerge. He will, of course, be tainted with having received a bribe and his motives will continue to be questioned.

Vosouq underestimated the resurgence of nationalism in Iran and ironically his premiership gave greater impetus to its rise. The Coup of 1921 and the emergence of Reza Khan can be traced to Britain having been too eager to pursue a policy that was not compatible with the realities of post-war Iran. Vosouq went into self-exile soon after his resignation not to return to Iran for some six years. He reappeared on the political scene briefly in the late twenties, then retired completely from politics.

NOTES ON CHAPTER 3
Further details of publications and documents in Bibliography

1   WO 157/854, Summary of Dunsterforce, no. 15 for week ending 14 June 1918.
2   CAB 27/24, 11 July 1918: quoted by Houshang Sabahi, *British Policy in Persia 1918–1925*, p 40.
3   Ervand Abrahamian, *Iran Between Two Revolutions*, p 112.
4   M.H. Donohoe, *With the Persian Expedition*, pp 72–73.
5   Sepehr Zabih, *The Communist Movement in Iran*, p 14.
6   FO 371/1248, Cox to Curzon, 24 March 1919.
7   FO/371/1244, Report of Vice Consul in Rasht: quoted by Houshang Sabahi, *British Policy in Persia 1918–1925*, p 43.
8   FO/371/3872, Cox to Curzon, 9 May 1920.
9   Lord Ronaldshay, *The Life of Lord Curzon*, vol. 2, p 206.
10 L/PS/10/712/5146, Balfour to Marling, 25 December 1917.
11 The Viceroy (Lord Chelmsford) to Montague, 12 February 1920: quoted by Houshang Sabahi, *British Policy in Persia 1918–1925*, p 43.
12 Denis Wright, *The Persians Amongst the English*, p 205.
13 F/112/275, Curzon's Papers, Quoted by Houshang Sabahi, *British Policy in Persia 1918–1925*, p 44.
14 Richard H. Ullman, *The Anglo-Soviet Accord*, vol. 3, p 362. In this excellent work Ullmann was the first historian to reproduce portions of the Ironside Diaries, and he analyses Ironside's dilemma during his posting in Iran.
15 Field Marshal Wilson, diary entry for 19 May 1920; F/112/218, Curzon papers, box 65, Wilson to Curzon, 20 May 1920.
16 CAB 23/21, 21 May 1920: quoted by Houshang Sabahi, *British Policy in Persia 1918–1925*, p 75.
17 Richard H. Ullman, *The Anglo-Soviet Accord*; vol. 3, p 331.
18 DBFP, vol. XIII, doc. nos 662 and 624, Chelmsford to Montague, 22 January 1921.
19 CAB 23/21, 21 May 1920.
20 FO 371/3872, Cox to Curzon, 25 May 1920.
21 FO 371/3874, Cox to Curzon, 28 May 1920.
22 FO 371/3872, Cox to Curzon, 6 and 10 June 1920.
23 CAB 27/21, 12 August 1920.
24 DBFP, doc. no. 449, Cox to Curzon, 3 June 1920.
25 FO 371/3873, Norman to Curzon, 7 May 1920.
26 FO 371/3873, Norman to Curzon, 11 June 1920.
27 FO 371/3873, Norman to Curzon, 13 June 1920.
28 FO 371/3870, Cox to Curzon, 1 April 1920.
29 FO 371/3873, Norman to Curzon, 13 June 1920.
30 FO 371/3874, Policy Paper, 14 June 1920.
31 *Ibid.*
32 FO 371/3873, Norman to Curzon, 15 June 1920.
33 FO 371/3873, Curzon to Norman, 16 June 1920.
34 FO 371/3873, War Office to Curzon, 16 June 1920.
35 FO 371/3873, Norman to Curzon, 18 June 1920.
36 FO 371/3873, Armitage Smith to Foreign Office, 18 June 1920.
37 FO 371/3863, Cox to Curzon, 28 August 1919.
38 FO 371/3870, Curzon to Cox, 10 April 1920.

39 FO 371/3872, Derby (British Ambassador to Paris) to Curzon, 20 May 1920.
40 FO 371/3872, Balfour minutes, 2 June 1920.
41 FO 371/3874, Churchill to Curzon, 21 June 1920.
42 FO 371/6399, Norman to Curzon, 23 January 1921.
43 Hassan Arfa, *Under Five Shahs*, pp 90–91. In some sources Moadel is spelled 'Meidel' and Clerge as 'Clereget' or 'Clerize' and the date of Clerge's dismissal is given as November 1917 or February 1918.
44 DBFP, doc. no. 461, Norman to Curzon, 13 June 1920.
45 DBFP, vol. 13, doc. no. 415, Cox to Curzon, 13 March 1920: quoted in Granmayeh's 'Introduction' in Brian Pearce and Ali Granmayeh, *The Staroselsky Problem 1918–1920*, p 21.
46 FO 371/4908, Norman to Curzon, 7 August 1920.
47 FO 371/4908, Norman to Curzon, 13 July 1920.
48 FO 371/3875, Norman to Curzon, 17 June 1920.
49 FO 371/3874, Norman to Curzon, 20 June 1920.
50 *Ibid.*
51 FO 371/4909, Sidney Armitage Smith to Foreign Office, 22 November 1920.
52 FO 371/3874, Curzon to Norman, 23 June 1920
53 FO 371/3873, Norman to Curzon, 23 June 1920.
54 FO 371/3873, Norman to Curzon, 23 June 1920.
55 FO 416/98, Bullard to Halifax, 7 February 1940. See also Denis Wright, *The Persians Amongst the English*, pp 212–215; Prince Hamid Kadjar, *Memoirs of Prince Hamid Kadjar*, ed. Habib Ladjevardi.
56 FO 416/3873, Norman to Curzon, 23 June 1920.
57 FO 371/3874, Norman to Curzon, 23 June 1920.
58 FO 371/3874, Norman to Curzon, 24 June 1920 (first telegram).
59 FO 371/3874, Norman to Curzon, 24 June 1920 (second telegram).
60 FO 371/3874, Norman to Curzon, 25 June 1920.
61 FO 371/3874, Curzon to Norman, 25 June 1920.
62 Mehdi Bamdad, *Tarikh Rejal Iran Quroun 12, 13, 14* (*Dictionary of National Biography of Iran: Twelfth, Thirteenth, Fourteenth Centuries*), vol. 1, pp 323–325.

3. Reza Khan as Minister of War. He was the real power in Iran following the British-inspired 1921 coup which removed the government in Tehran.

4. Reza Shah. In his coronation, the former Cossack colonel broke with tradition to crown himself King of Kings.

4

The Premiership of Moshir al Dowleh (Hassan Pirnia)

On 25 June, following Vosouq's resignation, Norman saw the Shah. The Shah had already summoned Hassan Pirnia[1] (Moshir al Dowleh) and asked him to form a government. The Shah informed Norman that the Prime Minister designate had made his acceptance of office conditional and contingent upon several factors: first, in his acceptance declaration Pirnia intended to state that the Agreement was deemed inoperative until ratified by parliament; second, he would be willing to allow the British financial advisers to continue their work but his Cabinet would reserve the right to accept or reject their recommendations; third, Britain would continue to subsidise the Cossack Division for at least a month or two longer, and any further subsidies by the British Government would be used only for purposes for which they were intended. Lastly he intended to include his brother Hosein Mo'tamen al Molk (Pirnia)* and Mehdi

---

* Mo'tamen al Molk (Hosein Pirnia), c.1875–1948, was the second son of Nasrollah Khan Moshir al Dowleh. He was educated in Iran and France and spoke French and some English. He began his career as secretary to
CONTINUED OVER PAGE

Qoli Mokhber al Saltaneh (Hedayat)* in his cabinet. In order to avoid future misunderstanding, Pirnia also had informed the Shah that he would not and could not dismiss any of the Russian officers of the Cossack Division until the secessionist movement in the north had been dealt with.

What Pirnia was in effect saying was that the British military team would have to work with the Cossacks for the time being and defer the reorganisation of the army to a later date. Another issue important to the Foreign Office was the status of the £2 million loan by Britain to Iran. Britain wanted the Iranian Government to draw down on the loan and use the proceeds in lieu of the monthly subsidies. Pirnia was aware that if the loan or any part thereof were

---

Mo'tamen al Molk CONTINUED FROM PREVIOUS PAGE
his father, the then Foreign Minister; became Minister of Education in 1918; Minister without portfolio in 1920; was elected to every session of parliament from 1906 and was president of the third, fourth, part of fifth and sixth sessions. He was elected to the seventh session but declined to serve. Years later in 1943 he was elected from Tehran to the 14th session but again declined. One of the most respected politicians of 20th century Iran, he lived his last years in isolation and saw but few friends.[2]

* Mokhber al Saltaneh (Mehdi Qoli Hedayat), c.1864–1955, came from a prominent family of public servants. His grandfather, Reza Qoli Khan, one of the learned men of his day and poet laureate of the land, served as a capable administrator and ambassador. His father, uncles and brothers all held important offices. Hedayat was educated in Tehran and Berlin, began his career at the Telegraph Office, and was appointed Special Chamberlain to Naser al Din Shah. Between 1903 and 1905 he travelled extensively in Europe, the United States, Russia, Japan, China, India and completed his travels with a pilgrimage to Mecca. On his return he supported the constitutionalist cause and collaborated in drafting the first election laws. In 1907 he was Minister for Public Instruction; 1908, Minister of Justice; later the same year Governor General of Azarbaijan, but removed from the post for pro-constitutionalist sentiments. After Mohammad Ali Shah was deposed he was again appointed Governor of Azarbaijan, where he aroused the enmity of the Russians. He resigned and went to Berlin for over a year, but returned in 1912 and held ministerial portfolios several times. He was appointed Governor of Fars with Britain's blessing because he was thought to be anti-Russian, hence pro-British. He proved to be an honest and capable governor. British officials, including Sykes, accused him of pro-German sympathies and of aiding German agents in the area. He was recalled in 1915, became Minister of Justice in Mostofi's Cabinet, and was appointed Minister of Interior in Mostofi's short-lived cabinet of April–July 1918. Hedayat was to play an important role in Iranian politics for the next 15 years. A well-read and learned man, he wrote a good autobiography, *Khaterat va Khatarat* as well as two other books relating to his travels.[3]

used, it would amount to a tacit admission by the Iranian Government that the entire Agreement had come into effect. For this reason Pirnia made it clear to the Shah that he should tell Norman that he could not touch the loan until parliament had voted on the Agreement. Norman knew he had to discuss these 'conditions' with the Prime Minister designate and that it would be a waste of time discussing them with the Shah. At his meeting with the Shah on 26 June Norman therefore confined his discussion to the Shah's monetary claims and asked whether he had reflected on the matter. Norman refered to the condition set by the prospective Prime Minister to use the subsidies only for matters for which they were earmarked. 'I knew I could not ask him to waive his demands... ' The Shah gave the following breakdown of his claims: 'FF800,000 for the unexpected prolongation of his journey; £7,000 which he had lent to Firouz in Paris to cover the expenses of the Persian delegation at the Paris Peace Conference'; and 46,000 tomans 'he had deposited with the Toumanians[5] brothers which has been lost'. (At an earlier meeting with Cox the Shah had given an entirely different set of numbers.[4]) The Shah concluded by telling Norman he would agree to reimbursement in three monthly installments. Norman sounded horrified and said Britain could not accept such sums as part of the subsidy. Later that day Vosouq told Norman that the Government had promised the Shah the total sum of FF200,000 for the expenses of the journey and he should not be paid more.[5]

On the same day Norman sent another telegram to Curzon to prepare him for Pirnia's conditions:

> I regret to have been obliged to act without instruction in the matter of change of government... and force the hand of His Majesty's Government... but I had no choice. Indeed I should have done better to act earlier for situation in revolting provinces of the north has become worse. There is a rumour that... Azarbaijan has declared itself a republic independent of Iran. Moshir ed Dowleh's government, if he succeeds in forming one, will not be ideal but the best that can be found.

Norman also tried to dampen the expectations of Curzon by adding, 'One must not expect them to sing the praises of the Anglo-Persian Agreement'. Norman also questioned his predecessor's optimistic assessment of Britain's ascendency in Iran and the dream of hegemony over the East by concluding:

> The Agreement has never been really popular because it was concluded secretly by a statesman even then deeply distrusted, who persistently postponed submitting it to parliament and never explained it to the public.[6]

Any criticism of the Agreement and denigration of Vosouq was bound to upset Curzon. Norman was not only deprecating a chosen favourite of Curzon and Cox but bringing their whole policy into question.

Norman called on Pirnia at the latter's request and had a lengthy conversation. Pirnia stated that he had not yet accepted the Shah's call to form a government and needed time to reflect. Pirnia then reiterated what he had told the Shah. He intended to hold new elections as the previous elections by Vosouq were held under pressure and the members of parliament chosen were discredited. When he had a quorum he would convene parliament and submit the Agreement for consideration. Until then, the provisions of the Agreement would be suspended. Norman objected and said the Agreement should form the basis of the new Government's policy. Pirnia repeated that the Agreement would remain inoperative until parliament met. He then named several people he must have in his cabinet: his brother Hosein Pirnia, Mostofi and Hedayat. Norman commented that the last two probably had a 'bad record' at the Foreign Office, but Pirnia insisted he must have them in his cabinet if he were to succeed.[7]

On the subject of the command of the Cossacks, Pirnia stated that it was not opportune at this time to dismiss the Russian officers. He could do it when calm was restored in the northern provinces. Lastly Pirnia revealed that he intended to send a mission to Moscow to seek an accord for Bolshevik troop withdrawal. Norman denigrated the plan as fruitless since Moscow would maintain that the forces in northern Iran were acting without its consent. In parting, Norman suggested that Firouz be retained as Foreign Minister. Pirnia answered that he felt disposed to keep Firouz in his present post but needed to consult his colleagues on the subject.[8]

Norman was convinced that the inclusion in the cabinet of Mostofi and Hedayat would greatly enhance the status of the new Government, gain the support of the nationalists and mollify the rebels in the north, especially Azarbaijanis. To win over Curzon, Norman sent him another dispatch on 27 June in which he stated:

> I am absolutely convinced that the time has come when His Majesty's Government should agree to forget the past and allow all personal grievances to be set aside'.

Norman defended Mostofi and Hedayat and went on to say:

> ... their policy in the past was mainly directed against [the] Russians... and they only opposed Great Britain on account of her Russian association... Mokhber al Saltaneh [Hedayat] was perhaps not so directly and personally responsible for the turn of events in Fars as has generally been supposed'.[9]

Hedayat's greatest sin in British eyes stemmed from his days as Governor of Fars (1913–1915) and his attempts to maintain Iran's neutrality during the war. He believed the creation of the SPR violated Iran's sovereignty and refused to co-operate with the British consul in Shiraz.[10] He was also accused of being anti-British for not having been helpful to Gen. Dunsterville's campaign against Bolsheviks in the Caucasus. It is against this background that he became anathema to Britain's Foreign Office. He was a nationalist of the old school, probably better understood by the British Consul in Shiraz who wrote:

> [He had] perfect manners and a good command of French and German... but in his heart he detested the whole lot of us Europeans.[11]

A report by the British Legation in November 1920 stated:

> [He is] one of the few capable governors produced by Persia in recent years... He has a reputation for patriotism and honesty and unlike most governors has not become a rich man... However, he is suspicious of British motives...'[12]

The next day Pirnia made things even more difficult for Norman as he informed him that he could not keep Firouz much longer as Foreign Minister. 'The effect on public opinion would be very bad. Both he [Firouz] and his family were very unpopular and much distrusted'. Norman had hoped to arrange a trade by letting in Mostofi and Hedayat in return for retaining Firouz in the proposed cabinet and thereby winning over Curzon. He pleaded with Pirnia to keep Firouz. Pirnia was unmoved and stated that perhaps Firouz could later be appointed Minister of Justice or Finance, but he could not keep him at Foreign Affairs. Ironically, Armitage Smith had let it be known that he could not work with Firouz as Minister of Finance. Firouz was deemed haughty and impervious to any suggestions. Armitage Smith, knowing of the bribe, must also have questioned Firouz's honesty and integrity. Norman was forced to seek guidance from Curzon and asked:

> What am I to do? Shall I insist on his [Firouz's] retention... which is difficult to force on a new Prime Minister... or shall I just say he should be treated with consideration... so he [Firouz] does not feel humiliated'.[13]

Norman received no answer to his previous five telegrams and on 28 June he wrote to Curzon to warn him that Iran was still without a Government and Pirnia would not accept his post until the Foreign Office considered his conditions satisfactory. Norman repeated the same message on the twenty-ninth and thirtieth and added:

> ... situation in Tehran is most dangerous... anarchy [reigns] in various
> government departments... Lurs [a tribe in western Iran] have staged an
> uprising and were attacking [neighbouring towns]; Kouchek Khan is pre-
> paring for an eventual attack on Tehran; and Moshir ed Dowleh refuses
> to accept office and name his cabinet because he believes there is lack of
> confidence on your part in not answering... The Shah is frightened for his
> life and contemplates moving to another palace outside of Tehran.

Norman again argued for the inclusion of Mostofi and Hedayat in the
cabinet and went further to plead the case of several Iranian politicians exiled by Vosouq. He especially espoused the cause of
Mosteshar al Dowleh (Sadeq Sadeq)[14] who 'is still in exile in Kashan
but I imagine the time has come which will see his exile terminated
and I think that he has been punished sufficiently for the past and
that in future he may be trusted to work for the real good of the
country'.[15] Pirnia must have raised the issue of exiles with Norman
arguing that their return would enhance his credibility with the
public.

Curzon, disappointed at the turn of events, could not bring himself to comment on Pirnia's pre-conditions. There was almost a
sense of despair in his tone. He wanted Vosouq back but knew that
was not possible.

> I cannot regard the entrance into power of Moshir ed Dowleh without con-
> siderable misgivings in view of the fact that the names of individuals whom
> he proposes to include in his cabinet appear to be of very mediocre capa-
> city. This view taken in conjunction with his own character throw serious
> doubt upon the likelihood of his passing the Agreement through the
> Majliss... The question of exiles does not appear so easy of solution as you
> imply. While some of the culprits may have been doubtful of the eventual
> issue of the war, actions by Mokhber ed Saltaneh were such as to inspire
> us with the most profound suspicion of his loyalty... and his appointment
> now could only aggravate the apprehension that we already entertain.

Curzon also opposed the plan to send a mission to Moscow as fore-
doomed to failure. He was willing, however, to go along with
Norman's choice of Prime Minister and continue the monthly subsidy of 350,000 tomans for a period of only four months, pending
the outcome of parliament's vote. He emphasised that the Shah's
allowance would cease as of the end of June since it was contingent
upon the retention of Vosouq in power. Furthermore, 'we cannot be
responsible for any expenses incurred by His Majesty in Europe'.
Curzon also told Norman of a personal message he had sent to
Vosouq for 'eminent services to his country and our joint interests...
[hoping] his health will benefit by the rest he so much deserves and
I am sure he will assist His Majesty's Legation whenever required by
his valuable advice and guidance... '[16]

Norman, buoyed by the implied acceptance of Pirnia by Curzon, saw Pirnia the following day and merely transmitted the sense of Curzon's telegram without dwelling on Curzon's foreboding tone or his objections to the composition of the Cabinet. Their conversation was limited to the severance of the Shah's allowance and rejection of reimbursment of the Shah's expenses in Europe. Pirnia said he had no prior knowledge of any financial arrangement with the Shah and was not greatly concerned, adding however that the cessation of the allowance would 'annoy His Majesty'. Norman agreed and in order to maintain his cordial relations with the Shah he would say nothing to the Shah on either subject for the time being.[17]

There was one last serious discussion with the Shah concerning his allowance. The Shah protested that he was not responsible for the fall of Vosouq and that in any event the arrangement with Cox was that he would receive his allowance 'as long as he maintained an attitude friendly to His Majesty's Government, irrespective of who was in power'. The total sum thus far paid to the Shah was £132,568 (about 345,000 tomans). Norman attempted to persuade the Shah that payments may resume 'when reforms are in place'.[18] (Ironically, the £132,568 thus far paid to the Shah by the British Government was almost the same as the £131,000 bribe paid to the triumverate).

On 3 July Norman sent three telegrams to Curzon, none of which would enhance Curzon's mood or lift the gloom surrounding him. He reported that Pirnia, after consulting colleagues, had decided to leave Firouz out of his cabinet. Norman's protestations had no effect and Pirnia had merely suggested that perhaps Firouz could be appointed as the Iranian representative to the League of Nations.[19] To compound the bad news, Pirnia had restated his decision not to use any portion of the £2 million loan until parliament was convened and had approved the Agreement. Pirnia had also decided to appoint Hedayat as Minister of Finance as he needed the support of nationalists if he were to succeed. Norman, who had hoped that Hedayat would be given one of the lesser ministries now had to inform Curzon that the British financial mission would have to work under one of its antagonists. Norman lamely promised that Hedayat 'and the other suspects will honestly work with us if only because they see that Pirnia's sole hope lies in that direction. Moreover he [Pirnia] would not tolerate amongst his colleagues the slightest disloyalty to Great Britain'.[20] As it happened, Hedayat left the Ministry within a fortnight to be sent as Governor to Azarbaijan to quell the secessionist movement.

Without the official blessing of Curzon, Pirnia formed his Government and named members of his Cabinet. Furthermore, despite Curzon's forebodings he decided to send a mission to Moscow headed by Moshaver al Mamalek (Mas'oud Ansari) who had recently left Paris and had been appointed Ambassador to Constantinople. Pirnia had decided to reverse the policy of Vosouq who, heavily influenced by Curzon, had all but ignored the Russian Revolution and the new rulers of Russia. Vosouq had closed the Iranian Legation in Moscow and had refused to receive or acknowledge two Soviet envoys, Karl Bravin in the summer of 1918 and I. Kolomitsev in June of 1919. Russian overtures renouncing past Czarist concessions in Iran had gone unacknowledged and Vosouq had altered a century-old policy of maintaining an equilibrium of relations with Britain and Russia.

Curzon's continued objection to any contact between Iran and the Soviets forced Edwin Montague, Secretary of State for India, to write to Curzon:

> You take an enormous responsibility in dissuading Persia from entering into a state of peace with the Soviet Government. Persia looks to us under the Agreement to prevent an invasion of that country by foreign forces. You know we have not the forces with which to discharge this responsibility. By preventing Persia from entering into relations with Russia... you emphasise our liability which we cannot perform.[21]

Pirnia had also decided to send a secret mission to the Shi'ite holy cities in Mesopotamia to induce the religious authorities to issue a fatwa (religious decree) condemning Bolshevism as contrary to Islam. An assembly of clergymen had also been summoned in Tehran to preach and campaign against Bolshevism.[22]

As expected, Norman's difficulties with Curzon were to persist. Norman argued for the continuance of the subsidy to the Cossacks to enable them to mount an offensive against the rebels in the north and for the restoration of the Shah's allowance as it would enable Norman to have an easier working relationship with him. Curzon, still upset over the inclusion of 'nationalists'[23] in the Cabinet, ignored the first request and on the issue of the Shah's allowance categorically told Norman not to raise the matter again.

> The Shah is not such a pauper as to be dependent on us for subsistence and ought not require payment for a loyalty which is even more to his own interest than to ours...[24]

Generally the internal situation began to improve under Pirnia. Several of the people exiled by Vosouq to Kashan were allowed to return to Tehran. Some tribal leaders had agreed to join in a military campaign against the rebels in Mazandaran and Azarbaijan. In Lurestan the rebels had been temporarily subdued. Martial law had been declared in Tehran and communist agitation had decreased. parliamentary elections were being held in some of the tranquil parts of the country. The Foreign Office, however, remained dissatisfied and the return of the exiles from Kashan to Tehran did not please Curzon.[25] There were also Iranian politicians in exile in Constantinople who wanted to return. Pirnia and Norman were urging Curzon that they too be allowed to come back.[26] The most notable of the exiles in Turkey were Reza Qoli Khan Nezam al Saltaneh (Ma'afi)* and Soleiman Mirza Eskandari.

There were a number of other on-going British concerns. Although the Cossack Division started to move north to engage the rebels, the status of its commander still posed a dilemma for the Legation. If Starosselsky failed in his campaign in the north, disaster would follow because the rebels could move south and attack Tehran. If the expedition were successful Starosselsky would shine brighter and dominate Tehran and the Government. He would then have a virtual veto power over any British plan to reorganise the armed forces. There was equal dismay over the fact that the financial adviser and his staff were not entirely welcome at the Ministry of Finance and their plans of reform would have to wait until parliament met.[27] Of further concern to the Foreign Office was the decision to send Moshaver al Mamalek as special envoy to Moscow. In the course of their advance on Rasht in mid August the Cossack Divison had captured some official documents from Bolshevik officers which gave proof that the Bolshevik invasion of Gilan was planned by the Soviet Government of Azarbaijan. The captured documents also showed that Moscow, despite its repeated denials, was supporting or at least acquiescing in the dispatch of troops to Iran and revealed that the Russian soldiers in Gilan were part of the Russian Soviet Forces.[28] Moshaver al Mamalek's instructions were to demand that the Soviet Government abstain from interference in Iranian domestic affairs, withdraw troops from all parts of Iran and withdraw all moral and material support from rebels and insurgents. If these demands were met, Iran would be prepared to sign a treaty of friendship with the Soviets. Britain was afraid that such a treaty would be

---

* Reza Qoli Khan Nezam al Saltaneh II (Ma'afi), c.1867–1924, a scion of a Kurdish tribe in western Iran, served in minor positions early in life and received his title after the death of his uncle, a former prime minister. In 1915, while in his last position as Governor of Lurestan and Khuzistan, he formed a government in exile committed to fight on the German-Turkish side. Several prominent Iranians joined his government, but when Russian troops occupied Kermanshah he fled to Constantinople. He returned to Iran in late 1920 and soon retired from public life.[29]

tantamount to recognition of the Soviet regime which Britain herself had not yet granted. Pirnia, under pressure from Norman, agreed that if Iranian demands were met the proposed treaty would be limited to the establishment of commercial relations and negotiations for postal and telegraphic conventions.[30]

Every act and assertion of independence by the Iranian Government ran counter to Curzon's master-plan of total control over its domestic and foreign policy. To Curzon, the sending of an envoy to Moscow, the pardon and release of political exiles and holding the Agreement in a state of suspension were just the first signs of Britain losing control. Curzon's directives over the previous 30 days had been simplistic: keep Vosouq in power, threaten the Shah with severance of his allowance, keep Firouz in the cabinet, and press for the earliest ratification of the Agreement. It appeared to Norman that Curzon was out of touch with the Iran of post Soviet troop landings, rebellions in almost all northern provinces and near anarchy in Tehran. Curzon had given the Government of Pirnia a mere four months to hold elections, convene parliament and have the Agreement approved. Curzon's dispatches carried an implied threat that unless Pirnia had the Agreement approved by the middle of October there would be a reversion to a 'reactionary' government that would seek to enforce the Agreement by force if necessary.

Norman decided to make another attempt to impress upon Curzon the realities of the situation and in a lengthy telegram of over 2,000 words reported:

> Situation is indeed unsatisfactory but it is the inevitable result of events of past two years... [There is] widespread though probably mistaken belief that existence of Anglo-Persian Agreement and presence of British troops and advisers in Persia... have brought Bolshevik danger on the country... Prime Minister is well aware that His Majesty's Government regard the Agreement as fully in force... A nationalist and constitutional government like the present cannot however consistent with their principles and with the conditions on which, with our consent, took office, and which have gained for them the support of moderate people, at once impose the Agreement on the country... we must for a time put up with this state of things... and suffer perhaps, in the eyes of the ignorant, a temporary loss of prestige... Chief advantages of working with present government are that they are relatively, and the most important amongst them, absolutely honest in money matters... and they alone are likely to be able to obtain wide approval for the Agreement and secure its acceptance by the Madjliss... [31] Their retention of power offers the only chance of preserving Azarbaijan by peaceful means... and the best prospects of reconciling Gilan and Mazandaran... Moreover till they are proved to have violated the conditions on which they took office we appear bound to support them. As a more radical cabinet would be altogether hostile to

the Agreement we could only call into power a more conservative one. Such a government would doubtless undertake to do what we want but it is uncertain whether, without any military support from us, they would be able to fulfill their engagements any better than did the cabinet of Vosouq ed Dowleh who for lack of such support could keep theirs only on paper. They would certainly be more corrupt than present government and financial adviser is so convinced that even if schemes of reform were sanctioned their unfortunate quality would defeat his efforts to carry them out, that he has already categorically stated that he could not work with them. Support of a conservative government of the old type would also entail loss of confidence of enlightened and progressive elements in the country which we are, I hope, beginning to regain... two further alternatives present themselves. One is to denounce present Agreement on our own initiative and negotiate another one which would be free from unpleasant association of present one and thus be more agreeable to Persian public opinion... The sole remaining course... is to shut down our enterprises, withdraw our commissions and troops and probably also our diplomatic and consular establishments from northern Persia and make other arrangements for defence of Mesopotamia and India, leaving this region to anarchy and Bolshevism.[32]

In conclusion Norman asks Curzon to press APOC to pay the Persian Government 1,500,000 tomans due as royalty for the past several years since British Government subsidies and advances have been cut back.

This was the bleakest picture of Iran ever painted for Curzon during his entire term as Foreign Secretary and one can imagine his annoyance and anger. Curzon could not care less for the 'progressive and enlightened' elements in Iran whose cause and arguments Norman advanced. The centrepiece of his policy lay in near-ruin and his envoy, who was expected to be the principle implementor of that policy, was questioning its efficacy. Curzon would never forgive Norman and would hold him singularly responsible for his policy's failure.

Curzon did not comment on Norman's telegram but in subsequent dispatches he rejected requests for the British Government to send arms and munitions in anticipation of the proposed campaign in the north against Kouchek Khan.[33] He also rejected the plea for the return to Iran of Nezam al Saltaneh and Soleiman Mirza,[34] though he later reluctantly agreed. What finally prompted Curzon to reply to the 24 July telegram was Norman's dispatch of 29 July in which he reported that Pirnia had concluded that he could not annul the elections already held because only parliament itself could rule on the validity of each member's election. Pirnia had therefore decided to hold a plebiscite in each of the constituencies where an election had been held to enable the voters to declare whether the election had been fair and the candidate chosen was acceptable. Norman hastened to add that the plebiscite should not take long. In order to soften the bad news, Norman reported that the Government had purged 'some notorious thieves' from several ministries; that Hedayat would soon resign from the Ministry of Finance and be appointed Governor of Azarbaijan to cope with the rebels; Mazandaran had been cleansed of rebels; and a secret mission would depart for the shrines in Mesopotamia within a week to obtain the desired Fatwa against Bolshevism.[35]

The delay in convening parliament had already upset Curzon and now with talk of a plebiscite, Curzon exploded:

> Prior to your arrival and return of the Shah, the policy pursued by British and Persian Governments... was in support of Vosouq and execution of Anglo-Persian Agreement, which was already in effective operation. Since then there has been complete revulsion, in circumstances over which His Majesty's Government have been powerless to exercise control. Vosouq has disappeared; a nationalist minority has been installed; prominent Persians who had distinguished themselves by unfriendliness to Great Britain and the Agreement have been recalled. Starosselsky whom it had been decided to dismiss, is master of the situation. As regards Agreement, the position is one which it is impossible to defend and position occupied by Great Britain appears to be one of no small humiliation... At the very moment when Persian territory is being invaded, and efforts of British Military Commission are pre-eminently required for organisation of national forces, its doors are closed... and capable British officers are left with nothing to do... The financial adviser who had commenced to function and was rendering valuable service, is not permitted to work... Moshir ed Dowleh cannot play fast and loose with international obligations or expect us to give unmurmuring support to a government which treats the power upon whom it depends for its continuance with such scant respect.[36]

Before Norman could recover from Curzon's harsh indictment, Curzon sent another telegram telling Norman that unless the Government of Pirnia began to consider the Agreement operative and in full force and started its implementation:

> ... there is little that he [Pirnia] or his country can hope from us... we cannot consent to be put off by vague prospects of what Madjliss may or may not do three months hence or acquiesce in a policy of do-nothing in interim'.[37]

Norman must have felt that Curzon was grossly unfair to Pirnia, who had taken office on the basic premise that he would treat the Agreement as being in abeyance until parliament had met. The Prime Minister was now asked to put his principles aside and ignore the conditions he had set prior to assuming office. Norman had used all the arguments he could conjure in favour of Pirnia, and Curzon had been unmoved. He therefore decided to let the Foreign Office know that he was not alone in believing that Curzon's Iranian policy had no chance of success. Armitage Smith's assessments of past and present situations, very similar to his own, had been transmitted to London. Norman now decided to let Curzon and the Cabinet know the military's analysis of conditions. On 6 August Norman sent the following report from Gen. Dickson:

> It does not appear to be realised at home how intensely unpopular Agreement was in Persia and how hostile public opinion had become to Vosouq ed Dowleh's Cabinet before it fell. It was believed in Persia that notwithstanding pledges given Agreement really aimed at destruction of her independence and that Vosouq and those acting with him had sold their country to the British, for fact that money had been received by them for signing Agreement could not be kept a secret. Secrecy with which the Agreement had been concluded, fact that Madjliss was not summoned and attempt made to create a packed Madjliss by resorting to most dishonest methods in carrying out elections, all added to conviction that Great Britain whom all nationalists and constitutionalists had hitherto regarded as friendly to Persia... was in reality no better than their hereditary foe, Russia... The Vosouq policy was running the country into a sea of anarchy and revolution and any attempt to revive that policy now would certainly lead to same result. The only way to save policy underlying the Agreement [would be to] admit past errors, summon an honest Madjliss and lay the matter frankly before it ... The only men who could get Agreement ratified by Madjliss are those at head of present cabinet. They wield great influence in the country because of their reputation for honesty and because they are regarded as men who would not sell their country... If in present circumstances British officers were allowed to function suspicion would be created in the country that cabinet had been bought as Vosouq's was. Cabinet would thus lose confidence of the country and with it possibility of getting Agreement ratified by Madjliss. Disagreeable as it is for British officers to be in position which they now occupy and for no one more so than for myself, I fully realise the necessity for line taken by [the Pirnia] cabinet...

At the end of Dickson's report Norman added, 'I am in entire agreement with [Dickson's report]... I venture to submit that his views are worthy of serious consideration'.[38] Cox, who was in London at the time briefing the Eastern Committee, commented that 'such views by Gen. Dickson show a complete volte-face...'[39]

Curzon, who must have been embarrassed in the Cabinet by Norman's reports, and now Dickson's affirmation of Norman's views, responded:

> I think you ought to know that length and frequency of your telegraphs are a source of unfavourable comment in Cabinet... it would facilitate our task by observing greater proportion and conciseness in your messages...[40]

Unfazed by Curzon's admonition, and as if newly inspired, Norman sent his own reply to Curzon's 31 July dispatch. He wrote:

> Until Persia is delivered from external dangers which threaten her, no cabinet can attempt... internal reform... Once Agreement is approved British troops can withdraw... Present Government is not acting disloyally... They were allowed by His Majesty's Government four months... They have not moved fast enough because of external situation... They are trying to complete elections... They ask financial support in the same manner as they did when Cox was Minister here. Unless His Majesty's Government are prepared to use force, they are not in a position to dictate to Persia. Co-operation with a Constitutional administration is therefore the only course open to them unless they prefer to cut their losses... and abandon Persia to her fate.[41]

Norman refused to stay silent and in a second telegram of the same date openly challenged Curzon and his instructions and demanded to know what Curzon really had in mind.

> If you are instructing me to seek the resignation of the Government [I will do so quickly]. The Shah is so dependent on Great Britain that he would name anybody I ask to become the Prime Minister... [but] it would be unwise because at the moment [Pirnia has planned] an expedition to the north to dislodge Bolsheviks and rebels.

A change of Government would only strengthen Kouchek Khan in Gilan and Khiabani* in Tabriz. Norman then methodically refuted Curzon's assumptions. He defended Mostofi and Hedayat as never having been hostile to Britain. 'They were against Russia and turned to countries who could help them.' He defended the newly-pardoned political exiles. 'Former Prime Minister [Vosouq] pursued a policy of vengeance against them.' With reference to Starosselsky's 'ascendancy' in Tehran Norman responded that the British military position and status were weakened by British troop withdrawals from

---

*   Sheikh Mohammad Khiabani, c.1879–1920, was born in Tabriz and studied to become a clergyman, became an affective preacher and gave sermons in both Persian and Azari Turkish. He joined the constitutionalist cause and fought against the authoritarian regime. In 1909 he was elected a member of parliament and in 1911, during the debate on the removal of Shuster and the Russian ultimatum, gained prominence by delivering an eloquent speech. Upon dissolution of parliament he went back to Tabriz and started a newspaper, *Tajadod* (*Renewal*). The 1907 supplement to the constitution provided for the establishment of provincial councils and a measure of local autonomy which he espoused. He soon took this a step further and agitated for total autonomy for Azarbaijan, later demanding independence for the province. He was killed in September 1920 in a skirmish with Government troops.[42]

Anzali and Rasht and now that the Cossacks were planning to mount a campaign in the north, British troops had to co-operate with Starosselsky, otherwise his prestige and power would be further enhanced. 'His dismissal will take place at the appropriate time'. Norman could not resist reminding Curzon that Vosouq and Cox were also unable to get rid of Starosselsky.

Norman then turned to financial matters and drew the conclusion that the only 'bonus' for the Persians was the £2 million loan which Pirnia would not touch. He went on to explain that the Persian Government was going ahead with elections and the only amendment they sought to the Agreement was a fixed duration and the elimination of its preamble which talks of Britain respecting Persia's sovereignty, reminding Persians of the 'detested' 1907 Anglo-Russian accord, which used the same hypocritical wording.[43] Very little was left unsaid by Norman. Curzon, faced with the choice of recalling Norman or remaining silent, chose the latter. Curzon appeared to have conceded this round of acrimonious exchanges as Norman received no serious admonition for the next two months. But Norman was left in a quandary. Should he take steps to remove Pirnia from office and bring in a more pliable prime minister? In the course of five days between 8 and 11 August Norman sent three further dispatches[44] all basically aimed at drawing out Curzon to give him more specific instructions. In these dispatches Norman restated his argument that Pirnia, for the moment, was the only viable choice as prime minister; that Pirnia and members of his Cabinet were men of principle who if in the past had demonstrated anti-British sentiments in words or deeds, had done so for what they considered justifying causes. Concerning the dismissal of Starosselski, Norman again argued that the Persian Government felt the Cossacks were the only disciplined force and constituted the sole defence against insurgents, and if their Russian officers were to be dismissed the Division could collapse. He pleaded for more time before attempting to force the dismissal of Starosselski. Norman also disputed Curzon's statement that Britain had been humiliated and said that the Persian Government still relied on Britain to defend it against the Bolsheviks, although they question 'why our troops remain here doing nothing'.

Receiving no answer, Norman again on 9 August[45] pleaded with Curzon to tell him plainly what he was expected to do. If Curzon simply wanted Pirnia dismissed he could accomplish that very easily. If, however, Pirnia were to stay in office, 'we cannot dictate our policy' and expect him to carry it out blindly. Pirnia was sympathetic to British policy but the route he had taken would take time to accomplish results. Britain could not have a Prime Minister who enjoyed the confidence of 'enlightened Persians' and yet appeared as her stooge. Norman concluded by urging Curzon to 'banish his suspicions and lend the Persian Government ungrudging support'.

Curzon, either moved by Norman's pleas or feeling that he had no alternative but to support the course his envoy had embarked upon, responded with the warmest dispatch Norman was to receive during his entire tenure in Tehran. Curzon complimented Norman for the sincerity with which he had often explained his views and positions. He went on to say that he had no desire 'to upset the present Government or to install another in its place...'

> On the contrary when we accepted it, upon your advice, we meant to give it a fair chance... All we desire is that Moshir ed Dowleh's Government should, with least possible delay fulfill its obligations, put the Anglo-Persian Agreement with the consent of Medjliss into effective operation and thus enable reduction of British forces in Persia... or alternatively, by rejection of Agreement show that Persia does not want our assistance and so release His Majesty's Government from all responsibility and justify complete withdrawal.

Curzon went on to say it was of no use to revive bygone history and discuss the virtues and vices of Vosouq al Dowleh's administration. As to suggested modifications of the Agreement it was premature to discuss changes. When it came before the Iranian Parliament 'we shall be quite willing to meet the views of the Persian Government'. Curzon ended his dispatch by saying that he had never agreed to have the Agreement placed in abeyance. All he had promised was that the monthly subsidy would be continued for four months until the end of October hoping that Pirnia could complete the elections and have the Agreement ratified by that time.[46] Norman must have been pleased by the partial endorsement from Curzon and he probably conveyed the more encouraging aspects of Curzon's telegram to Pirnia.

As for the military situation in the north, Gen. Champain's 'occupation' of the Manjeel Pass did not last long. At the beginning of August Champain, fearful of an attack by rebel forces, panicked and withdrew his troops from the pass and retreated to Qazvin. He did not think his force could defend the Pass. The War Office, preoccupied with an uprising in Mesopotamia, began to consider moving several battalions from Qazvin to Baghdad. At Norman's urging and the intervention of Curzon the War Office rescinded its orders and decided to keep the forces at Qazvin, 'unless the situation in Baghdad [became] so critical as to render their return to Mesopotamia absolutely indispensible'.[47]

Despite Gen. Champains refusal to engage the rebel forces, in early August the Persian Cossacks began their advance towards Gilan and reoccupied Manjeel.[48] After brief skirmishes the Cossacks were able to take Rasht by mid August. Starosselsky, taking his success too seriously, overplayed his hand and decided to attack and retake Anzali. On 25 August the Cossacks were repulsed about eight miles from Anzali suffering heavy casualties.[49] With this defeat the Cossacks' momentum radically diminished and Starosselsky was forced to evacuate Rasht. Pirnia's policy also suffered a severe blow. He had pursued a two-pronged policy of sending a mission to Moscow while pressing a military option in the north to dislodge the insurgent forces. Now any hope of scoring even a limited victory in Gilan had vanished and his hand was considerably weakened in negotiations with the Soviet Government.

Norman, greatly disturbed by these reversals, immediately informed Curzon:

> In view of the disaster of Starosselsky's force before Anzali, it is imperative that British troops in North Persia should prevent Bolsheviks moving south... through Manjeel and that the British forces should form screen behind which Persian troops can be reorganised and reinforced preparatory to fresh attempt to clear Gilan of enemy. Fate of Persia and of all British interests there depends upon North Persian Force doing this...[50]

The reversals of Starosselsky were a mixed blessing to the Foreign Office. Only a month earlier no one could have disputed his authority. Now his defeat at Anzali and hurried withdrawal from Rasht and Manjeel had thrown the Cossack Division into disarray and seriously damaged his reputation. Norman, who had been chided for his inability to have Starosselsky removed, saw an opportunity to bring the matter to a head. The Shah could be forced to accept his dismissal but Pirnia would be more difficult to convince. Pirnia was still unsure of reaching an accord with the Soviets and therefore the Cossacks represented the only force to cope with disturbances and insurgency. The question of Starosselsky began a new round of acrimonious exchanges between Norman and Curzon and their relationship which only a few weeks earlier had stabilised once again became strained.

Norman arranged a meeting with Starosselsky on 8 September and reported that Starosselsky was still defiant and had protested:

> ... [his force] was now defending British interests in Persia with the knowledge that as soon as the danger of Bolshevik invasion was over, [Britain] intended to destroy it [the Cossack Division] as an independent organisation... This knowledge... made [Russian] officers reluctant to

fight, while in the minds of [the Persian] soldiers Bolshevism simply meant opposition to England and was consequently popular.

Starosselsky had further argued that 'it would greatly facilitate his task of co-operation with [Britain] if he were able to give the Division some assurance that its destruction was not intended...' Starosselsky had warned Norman that he was 'prepared to resist by force any measure intended to destroy the Cossack Division'.[51]

Curzon on 13 September responded that it might be too soon to decide on the ultimate fate of the Cossacks but in the interim he should inform the Shah and Pirnia that the comments of Starosselsky were totally uncalled for and were against the interests of Britain and Persia.

> If, as has been contended more than once, the primary role of the Division is that of bodyguard to the Shah, it must be apparent [to the Shah] that any hostility on the part of the Cossacks toward British forces, who are fighting in the joint interests of Persia and Great Britain, must inevitably be opposed to Persian interests... Persian Government cannot expect active assistance from us in defence of their capital if they give countenance or support to any disintegrating action by Russian Commander.[52]

Norman informed Pirnia of the substance of Curzon's telegram and showed him examples of the harsh language used by Col. Starosselsky. Although Pirnia was 'considerably impressed' by the information furnished by Norman he did not appear to have altered his belief that the time had not come to dismiss the Russian officers.[53] It also appears that Curzon, who only weeks earlier had chided Norman over Starosselsky's continued command, reconsidered and now informed Norman, '... it is too soon to decide on the fate of the Cossack Division'. As we shall see, Gen. Champain had decided to retire from service and the War Office was seeking a replacement. It was probably for this reason that Curzon believed that the removal of Starosselsky should be delayed until the successor to Champain was in place.

The necessity to organise military expeditions to northern Iran and general lack of funds had prevented Pirnia from completing parliamentary elections. Pirnia's highest priority had been to quell the rebellions and restore a degree of calm before elections were held. He believed that unless there were fair and honest elections the public would not accept any decision of parliament, especially a decision concerning ratification of the Agreement. Pirnia had originally contemplated the annulment of the elections held by Vosouq, but faced with the hostility of deputies already elected abandoned the idea and substituted a plan akin to a plebiscite to ascertain the views of the electorate in each constituency as to whether the election held had been fair. Although the plan was made public amid much fanfare, it was never implemented due to its impracticality. Furthermore, deputies already elected banded together and announced they would take their seats irrespective of the results of the plebiscite and only parliament could rule on the validity of their election. By mid September about 80 out of 137 deputies had been elected, the majority being those elected during Vosouq's tenure. Although technically a quorum could be reached, Pirnia was not willing to convene parliament until the majority of deputies were those elected during his term of office.[54]

Curzon, already irritated by the delay in the opening of the parliament and Pirnia's obscure legalistic approach, sent a harsh dispatch to Norman accusing him of having wasted valuable time by having agreed with Pirnia's scheme of a plebiscite.[55] Norman had in fact supported the idea and could not answer Curzon's criticism without again recounting the circumstances in which he had found himself when he arrived in Tehran. He responded forcefully:

> On my arrival I found in power a Government universally detested and entirely subservient to a Prime Minister to whom ill-health had left only energy required to increase his private fortune at the public expense. His policy had caused Azarbaijan practically to separate itself from Persia and had driven Mazandaran into rebellion. Gilan was in the possession of Kuchek Khan and his followers were allied with Bolsheviks. [Tehran] was seething with Bolshevik intrigue. Had Bolsheviks responded in time they could have marched into Tehran and received a welcome from a large section of population.

The Anglo-Persian Agreement was nominally in force but in practice it was a 'dead letter'. The Agreement was widely condemned not so much for of its terms but for:

> ... the manner of its conclusion and personalities of its Persian signatories. Had I been able to keep Government in office... I am convinced a Bolshevik revolution would long since have broken out in capital, Azarbaijan become separate Soviet Republic and Bolshevism spread from Gilan to Mazandaran... whole of northern Persia, with possible exception of Khorasan, which was still garrisoned by British troops, would have fallen into power of Soviets. I had therefore no choice but to install a cabinet chiefly consisting of moderate nationalists... your telegram [of 13 August] which appeared to me to indicate marked change in attitude... encouraged me to hope that I had pleaded cause of present Government with some success but I see from your telegram under reply that this is not the case.[56]

Again Norman not only challenged Curzon's policy but informed him
he intended to pursue his own path.

> As however there is as yet in my opinion no combination which would
> enjoy the same support in the country as this one or have so good a
> chance of piloting Agreement through Medjliss, I propose to do my best
> to keep them [Pirnia's Grovernment] in power until they have had chance
> of fulfilling their promise... If policy your Lordship deprecates should
> now break down, as in default of any encouragement from His Majesty's
> Government it probably will, I am convinced that I have at least prolonged
> for three months existance of Persia in her present form and perhaps
> even have removed permanently danger of her dissolution and ruin of all
> British interests in the country...[57]

By this telegram Norman left little room for reconcilliation or mending
of relations with Curzon. He was telling his Foreign Secretary that
his policy from its inception was misguided. Norman, in essence,
accused Curzon of having selected the most disreputable Persians to
carry out British policy. He was implying that Curzon's envoy (Cox)
had not served him well and misinformed him about the true situation in Tehran. The triumverate was no more than a pack of
crooked politicians whose unpopularity tainted Britain's reputation.
In any event, Norman was saying that he knew better how to secure
and enhance British interests in Persia. However, since Curzon was
the chief architect of British foreign policy he would pursue Curzon's
policy aims in Persia but only with the people he himself had selected
since they were the only ones who had a chance to have that policy
implemented.

It is astonishing that the proud and autocratic Curzon did not
recall Norman right then. (It was another year and three Iranian
governments later before Norman was recalled and Curzon exacted
his revenge when Norman returned to London.) Curzon, however,
either to protect his reputation at the Foreign Office or for the sake
of posterity sent a reply on 29 September:

> With regard to the contention that owing to the absence of instructions
> from me you had inevitably to install present Government... On 23
> June... I instructed you to support Vosouq ed Dowleh unless and until it
> becomes apparent that even our help cannot save him. On the same day
> I received nine telegrams from you regarding the Cabinet crisis from
> which it was apparent that His Highness [Vosouq] had already resigned,
> and that you had acquiesced in the appointment of Moshir ed Dowleh....
> I acquiesced perforce in the new situation...[58]

Relations between the two were never to be restored and Norman
began to act more independently than ever.

An important development during this period was the elimination of Sheikh Mohammad Khiabani from Azarbaijan. Khiabani had effectively taken control of Tabriz, the capital, by early April 1920. He had changed the name of the province to Azadisetan ('Province that took back her freedom'). The British political officer at Norperforce (North Persian Forces), Maj. C.J. Edmonds, had travelled to Tabriz on April 26 to assess the situation. Edmonds had a lengthy meeting with Khiabani and reported that Khiabani's movement had started as a genuine political attempt to topple Vosouq's Government and restore constitutional rule. Edmonds had concluded that there was nothing 'separatist or Bolshevik [about Khiabani's agitation]. It is of course impossible to foresee the result of mishandling by the Government'.[59] Two governors had been recalled from Azarbaijan as they could do little about the growing discontent and agitation against the Agreement, the Government in Tehran and British influence in the country. The two governors sent by Vosouq were two highly unpopular former Prime Ministers, Mohammad Vali Khan Tonokaboni (Sepahsalar) and Soltan Abdol Majid Mirza Ain al Dowleh. The former was never allowed to take up his post and the latter was literally driven out of Tabriz. Norman soon after his arrival in Tehran realised that the movements in Azarbaijan and Gilan were basically a revolt against the landed class who were supported by Vosouq and Britain.

The sending of a delegation to Moscow and the appointment of Hedayat (Mokhber al Saltaneh) as Governor of Azarbaijan were the two most astute moves made by Pirnia. The opening to Moscow, long delayed, proved to be not only the beginning of the end of insurgency movements in Gilan but also ushered in the final demise of the 1919 Agreement. The choice of Hedayat, who as a leading member of the Democrat Party enjoyed a high reputation in Azarbaijan, was another inspired move. Khiabani and most of his followers had been affiliated with the Democrat party and the appointment of Hedayat was bound to create tensions and perhaps defections within Khiabani's ranks. Hedayat was the first governor in over a year whose entry into Tabriz was not impeded; in fact he received a sympathetic albeit muted welcome. Hedayat's attempts to hold talks with Khiabani proved fruitless. At meetings with local notables[60] Hedayat was advised that support for Khiabani had eroded over the past two months and he had suffered defections. Hedayat decided on a show-down and on 13 September ordered the local contingent of Cossacks and Gendarmes to seize the public buildings Khiabani and his followers had occupied. After some four hours of fighting, the insurgents surrendered and Khiabani himself fled and hid in the cellar of a house. He was found that evening and it was reported that he had been killed while attempting to flee. Norman informed Curzon of the event,[61] but Curzon, who had so harshly castigated Norman over the inclusion of Hedayat in Pirnia's Cabinet, never acknowledged or credited Pirnia with the restoration of calm in Azarbaijan.

Amidst all the difficulties Curzon's policy was facing in Iran, another irritant began to surface. A major tenet of his policy had been to prevent any power from gaining either a political or economic foothold in Iran. France's colonial ambitions had been satisfied by the restoration of its former colonial possessions in Africa, the Middle East and South East Asia, and posed no threat to British interests in Egypt, Mesopotamia, Iran or India. Although the United States had no territorial ambitions in Britain's spheres of influence, it was beginning to seek an economic foothold in the Middle and Near East. The United States could get nowhere in Mesopotamia or the Persian Gulf sheikhdoms which were tightly and effectively ruled by Britain. Iran therefore appeared the most promising region. The United States could possibly obtain oil concessions in areas excluded from the 1901 concession to APOC. After World War I Curzon had always considered an American economic thrust into Iran a possibility and had tried to shut the door on such incursions. The Foreign Office was fearful that US involvement could provide Iran with new sources from which to raise money and to employ advisers which were bound to loosen Britain's grip on Iran's finances. During negotiations surrounding the 1919 Agreement Cox had wanted to insert a clause whereby Iran would be prohibited from going anywhere but to Britain for loans and advisers. Vosouq had strenuously objected as 'it reminded him of the Czarist ultimatum of 1911'. The Russian ultimatum concerning the dismissal of Shuster had contained an undertaking by Iran not to employ any adviser without the express approval of Russia and Great Britain.[62] This background of limiting Iranian governments' freedom to employ foreign nationals of their own choosing was one of the main reasons for Iranians reacting so negatively to the 1919 Agreement and in particular to the employment of British financial and military advisers which they regarded as a threat to their independence.[63]

Relations between the Foreign Office and US Department of State were strained over Iran during and after the Peace Conference. For the Wilson administration the 1919 Agreement could not have come at a worse time. Wilson, who was fighting to convince the Republican controlled Senate of the necessity of the United States joining the League of Nations, had the ground cut from under him by Britain's pre-emptive thrust to take over Iran. The opponents of

the League soon seized on the 1919 Agreement as another example
of Britain and France's deviousness. In several speeches US senators
accused Britain of essentially getting a mandate over Iran through
the back door asserting that the 1919 Agreement made Iran a
protectorate of Great Britain.[64] Senator Henry Cabot Lodge of
Massachusetts, leader of the anti-League faction, had the 1919
Agreement printed in the Congressional Record enabling senators
and congressmen to examine for themselves evidence of 'Britain's
perfidy'. Senator William E. Borah of Idaho, in a speech on the
Senate floor, argued that the 1919 Agreement was evidence of
Britain having annexed Iran, and the United States, if it were to join
the League, 'would have to go to war against Persia if she one day
wanted her freedom from Britain'.[65]

The American oil companies' desires for inroads into Iran further
strained Anglo-American relations. Foremost among the US companies seeking oil concessions in Iran was Standard Oil, which had
begun to show interest in Iran soon after the war. As early as 8 April
1920 Firouz had raised the possibility of US economic involvement
in Iran and Curzon had warned him to dismiss the idea from his
mind.[66] The Republican victory in the 1920 US presidential election
intensified British concern over plans of the American oil companies
as the Republicans were even more amenable to Standard Oil
Company's interests.[67]

In January 1916 Akaky Medfdievich Khoshtaria had been
awarded a 25-year concession to drill for oil in Gilan, Mazandaran,
Astarabad (Gorgan), Khorasan and Azarbaijan. The award was made
by coercion and threat of force when these regions were occupied
by Czarist forces and the Prime Minister Sepahsalar Tonokaboni,
a Russian protegé, had dissolved parliament and most deputies
had fled Tehran in fear of their lives. In 1918 the Government
of Samsam al Saltaneh annulled the concession. The Iranian
Government had declared the concession null and void, having
been forcibly acquired under duress by the Czarist Government.
In 1920 Khoshtaria sold his interest to APOC for £200,000. APOC,
fully aware of the Iranian position, nevertheless purchased the
Khoshtaria concession with the support of the British Government
which promised to contest Iran's contention. After the Perso-Soviet
Treaty of February 1921, under which Russia renounced all concessions and privileges in Iran, Britain advanced the notion that
Khoshtaria was not a Russian but a citizen of the Free State
of Georgia. This argument fell when Georgia was incorporated into
the Soviet Union in 1922.[68] Britain then argued that irrespective
of the background of the original award of the concession, the

subsequent sale by Khoshtaria to APOC was a valid and *bona fide* transaction.[69]

On 18 August 1920 Norman informed Curzon that his 'sure sources' had told him that US oil companies had approached the Persian representative in Washington with a view to acquiring the Khoshtaria concession. Pirnia had told his Minister in Washington that any award of concessions would have to wait until parliament had met[70] Curzon on 21 August telegraphed Norman to say that his 'most reliable informant' had told him that the Persian Government and its Minister in Washington would in fact prefer to see the United States rather than any other nation acquire oil concessions in northern Persia and instructed Norman to inform the Persian Government 'categorically that we contest their view as to cancellation of Khoshtaria concession for oil and minerals and that we support APOC in their purchase of the former which we believe to have been legally carried out'. In reply to Norman's protestations, Pirnia informed him that the Iranian Government considered any concession obtained in the absence of parliamentary approval in whatever circumstances invalid. Norman, in turn, merely responded that 'the British Government could not acquiesce to this point of view'.[71] This controversy further weakened Pirnia's Government and even Norman began to lose confidence in him.

The matter of a northern oil concession was perforce put in abeyance by the interested parties. However, it remained a divisive issue for the next three decades, unresolved until 1946. What was significant in this initial phase was the degree of cynicism and hypocricy shown again by Curzon. The Khoshtaria concession was clearly invalid. Britain had already been forced to acknowledge that the Iranian Constitution required parliamentary approval for the validity of any agreement, treaty or award of concession with or to any country or foreign national. Additionally in this instance the new Soviet Government had renounced all award of concessions to the former Czarist regime and Russian nationals.

In late August 1920 Maj. Gen. Champain decided to retire. He had been an officer in the India army with little experience of war and none of independent command. He had mishandled the Russian assault at Anzali and had not realised what a prize it was for the Bolsheviks to have seized the ships harboured there. His actions had greatly dismayed the War Office in London and his superior in Baghdad, Lt Gen. J.A.L. Haldane, yet no decision was taken to remove him from active command. As Bolshevik infiltration in northern Iran increased it became obvious that Britain had no policy to counter the continued Soviet presence. British parliamentary and financial pressure required the earliest possible troop withdrawal from Iran and forced the British Cabinet to decide on the withdrawal of all British troops from northern Iran as soon as the weather improved and the passes were opened.[72]

Norman, who by now must have given up any hope of the Agreement coming into force, soon began thinking of plans to abandon Tehran if rebel and Soviet troops advanced any further south. Others at the Foreign Office began to think of using Bakhtiari tribesmen to take control of central Iran while British troops concentrated on preserving Britain's primary area of interest in the oil fields of western and south western Iran. It was against this gloomy background that the War Office decided on 26 September to appoint Maj. Gen. Sir Edmund Ironside* as Commander of Norperforce. Norperforce then consisted of some 6,000 British and Indian troops. Its main body was at Manjeel holding the head of the Pass, preventing entry and exit. A battalion was stationed at Zanjan, some troops were partrolling the Manjeel-Qazvin Road and the remainder were in Qazvin.

Ironside had been engaged in the withdrawal of British troops from Archangel and Ismid and had acquired a reputation as being proficient in risky withdrawals. Now that Britain had decided to withdraw her troops from Iran by the spring of 1921 Ironside was considered the best prospect to effect the plan with minimum difficulty and casualties. He was also an officer with wide command experience and more important he had combat experience against Soviet troops. Field Marshal Wilson, in recommending Ironside to Haldane, described him as 'beyond question one of the most rising... of the young officers in the army... a wonderful linguist, great physical strength and... infinite courage and resources'.[73] Ironside's orders from his superiors were 'to hold the fort until decision by the Cabinet to withdraw all the troops... not to get troops embroiled in the country [Persia]... to use his influence to subdue Starosselsky...

---

* Edmund Ironside, 1880–1959, was the youngest Major General in the British army up to that time and had received his knighthood at the relatively early age of 39, all of which indicated the high esteem in which he was held by his superiors. His first major assignment had been to supervise the withdrawal of British troops from the ill-fated campaign at Archangel, October 1918–September 1919. He then supervised the withdrawal of Greek and British troops from Ismid (Turkey) between July and August 1920. After command of Norperforce he was appointed Commander of the Staff College (1922–1926). Ironside became a Field Marshal and in 1940 was appointed head of CGIC. He was retired by Winston Churchill later that year and made a peer. Ironside kept a diary, later published by his son.[74]

and other Persian forces [inimical to] the political authorities in London'.[75]

What had been a routine appointment of yet another general with orders merely to extricate British troops from northern Iran with minimum risk turned out to have far-reaching consequences. As will become evident, Ironside came to Iran with his own ideas of British interests and how best to serve them. After only a few weeks in his new post he started to form and adopt policies at variance with those of the British Cabinet and Foreign Office. Through sheer force of character he began to dominate the scene and imposed his will on his subordinate officers as well as his political counterpart, Norman. Ironside's experience following World War I led him to believe that Britain was involved in too many unpopular causes and he sought to reverse Great Britain's declining popularity. He wrote in his diaries, 'This was the third time since the armistice in 1918 that I had found myself commanding unpopular military forces in widely separated parts of the world. I was rapidly becoming an ill omen'.[76]

The debate over the general direction of British policy in the East had been fairly predictable, with the defence of India being the central issue. Curzon and Lord Hardinge, the Under Secretary at the Foreign Office, argued against the War Office plan to withdraw British troops from northern Iran. They maintained that Iran must be controlled by Britain and that troop withdrawals would lead to a chain reaction; in the Caucasus there would be Bolshevik rule, then Iran would fall, Afghanistan would be destablised and the threat to India would be magnified.[77] Field Marshal Wilson argued that the debate was somewhat academic as three or more divisions would be necessary to stop the Communists in the Caucasus and northern Iran and such a number of troops was simply not available. Ironside, while siding with the War Office, refined the argument somewhat.

India should be defended behind her own frontiers and not in advance of them... there is no doubt that the question of invasion of Persia was always held up as a bogey in order to ensure that a proper army in India [was maintained]... Gradual penetration of Persia and Afghanistan certainly [is a possibility] but that is another thing to an invasion of India.[78]

In an earlier entry in his diary Ironside had written:

I personally cannot see that we should gain very much from controlling Persia... we do not want an extension of our military committment but rather a reduction if possible... why deliberately make a frontier with the Soviets?...The defense of Persia is not our job. We must defend only the Karun Valley and the Anglo-Persian oil... we must liquidate in the spring... The menace will grow but it will not be a military menace.[79]

Ironside was in effect arguing that Bolshevism posed a political not a military threat and money should not be wasted on an imaginary military foe.

The Soviet-Iranian talks spelled the end of Britain's supremacy in Iran. Esmond Ovey of the Eastern Section of the Foreign Office wrote in a memorandum:

> It will be difficult for us to prevent the Persians from accepting from the Bolsheviks [a] treaty guaranteeing no trespass by them on Persia... unless we are prepared indefinitely to afford military support. Everything points to this being financially and politically impossible. If however, we do not do so we shall have lost our prepondering influence in Persia.[80]

Norman on 7 October wrote to Curzon that Moshaver al Mamalek had obtained from the Bolsheviks the following concessions:

1 All Persian officials who were imprisoned [by the Soviets] have been released and apologies have been tendered.
2 A commission has been formed to compensate Persians for property seized or destroyed.
3 Troops on the Caspian coast of Persia have been recalled and Anzali is to be evacuated.[81]

There were to be more concessions from the Bolsheviks before the agreement between the two countries was finally signed in February 1921.

Pursuant to a decision by the British Cabinet to maintain the existing level of Norperforce troops in Iran until the coming spring, the War Office in a memorandum to Gen. Haldane, commander of British troops in the Middle East stationed in Baghdad, set out the following instructions and general guideline:

> Norperforce depends for its existence on Mesopotamia. The whole of Norperforce may be withdrawn in case of extreme emergency in order to save the situation in Mesopotamia, [There had been several revolts against Britain's mandate and the British garrison at Samawa on the lower Euphrates had been besieged by rebel forces since 13 August. It was relieved on 14 October] but this should not be done until after the War Office has been consulted and their approval has been obtained... You should impress on General Ironside that we are not in a position to reinforce him in the event of a serious military invasion of North Persia by the Russians.

The memorandum also dealt with the status of Starosselsky. Although the War Office gave latitude to Ironside in dealing with him it forewarned him:

> It must be remembered that Starosselsky is before all else a Russian and considers himself the guardian of Russian interests in Northern Persia

although he has been fighting against the Bolsheviks. He also, in common with all Russians, considers that the British have profited unfairly from the internal dissentions in Russia by ousting them from their pre-war sphere of influence in Persia and establishing British influence in its place.[82]

Ironside entered Iran on 1 October 1920, Champain having left via Baghdad to Britain before he arrived. On 4 October he reviewed the position of British troops at Qazvin and then proceeded to Tehran where he met Norman for the first time. Norman painted a gloomy picture of the situation and told Ironside that he saw little chance of the Agreement ever being ratified and put into force. Norman added that the Cossacks were poorly commanded and not fighting well and all the funds advanced to the Persian Government had been dissipated. Most of the funds given to the Cossacks had gone into the pockets of Starosselsky and the Shah, and the Persian Government had no source of income other than the sale of provincial and district governorships and other positions. The appointed officials, eager to recoup the money they had given for their appointments, resorted to the imposition of unfair taxes and levies and squeezed the populace for as much money as they could extract. Col. Starosselsky and the other Russian officers were openly contemptuous of Britain's efforts to create and organise a national army and attempted to belittle and abuse Britain at every turn. The Shah, who regarded the Cossacks as his personal bodyguards, supported them and refused to dismiss Starosselsky.

Ironside, still groping his way, said little to Norman. He spent the following week inspecting British troops in the north and becoming acquainted with the terrain. He was assured by his senior officers that unless the Bolsheviks attacked with a large force Manjeel Pass could be held. Ironside then travelled by plane to Baghdad to report on his preliminary observations. He returned to Tehran on 12 October and spent the following few days in seeing and appraising the principal players on the scene. Ironside was scarcely impressed.[83]

With the reversals Starosselsky had suffered in the North, Ironside began to believe that time was ripe to make the final move to dislodge the Russian officers. He had already set in motion the machinery for the dismissal of Starosselsky. He had instructed British officers stationed at Manjeel not to assist Starosselsky in his withdrawal: 'It would be advantageous to us to leave Col. Starosselsky to make [a mess] of things as it would then be more easy for me to get rid of him'.[84]

Ironside knew he had to have Norman's support and began to urge Norman to join him in forcing the dismissal of Starosselsky.

Norman had pinned his entire hope on Pirnia and had gambled on the latter's success in restoring calm in the north, enabling him to hold elections and convene parliament. Although the chances for the approval of the Agreement were slim without substantive modifications, Norman believed that having the Agreement approved in whatever modified form would still tie Iran to Britain and accomplish long-term British policy aims. Norman must also have known that Pirnia did not think the time was opportune to dismiss Starosselsky before a definitive agreement was reached with the Bolsheviks and that Pirnia in all likelihood would resign if undue pressure were put upon him.

There had always existed an inherent contradiction in Norman's thinking and in his decision to have Vosouq step aside and bring in Pirnia as prime minister. One couild not have a 'moderate' nationalist who believed in constitutional rule and expect him to carry out a British policy essentially designed to dominate and rule Iran in order to safeguard her oil and other commercial interests. Other than the forcefulness of Ironside's arguments, there is little indication of why Norman so abruptly changed his views and became prepared to sacrifice Pirnia, on whom he had staked his reputation and career. Norman was willing to take an additional risk. He had already selected and talked to Pirnia's successor, Sepahdar (Fathollah Akbar) without the knowledge of the Foreign Office or Curzon. Norman may have been influenced ultimately by the view of the Foreign Office that the only way the Agreement could be salvaged was to have a 'strong reactionary' prime minister who by sheer force would compel the parliamentary deputies to approve the Agreement. Firouz fitted the part and was the candidate of Cox who, although in Baghdad, still exercised great influence over Curzon. Firouz had further enhanced his position by promising to campaign against and derail the ongoing negotiations between Moscow and Tehran.[85] Norman, however, was opposed to any member of the triumverate becoming prime minister and probably had approached Sepahdar in order to pre-empt the Foreign Office supporters of Firouz.

On 25 October Norman sent the following message to Curzon:

[The Cossack] Division have evacuated Rasht for the second time owing according to their officer commanding, to bad morale... Ironside here assures me this has been done without military reason...Cossacks who [were] in superior force [had] not been seriously attacked and suffered no casualties. This new retreat appears to [Gen. Ironside] and me completely to change the situation of Colonel Starosselsky and his Russian officers ... [the Colonel] has shown himself to be an incompetent officer of doubtful courage... [who] has appropriated a large portion of the money given to him... situation is also profoundly affected by recent change in command of North Persia Force for whereas the general officer commanding [Gen. Champain] considered himself unable with the troops at his disposal to guarantee the defence of the Capital against a hostile advance from North his successor is perfectly confident of his ability to do so... General Ironside and I therefore explained situation to Prime Minister... and urged him at once to dismiss Colonel Starosselsky and put a Persian in command of the Division...with British officers to assist him... the Prime Minister said that he personally concurred in the opinion that the moment had come to dismiss the Colonel but as I foresaw he demurred to appoint British officers to the Division as being certain to weaken position of government. The Prime Minister said he would have to consult the Shah and some of his colleagues... I am confirmed in this opinion by hope that improvement in our position will enable us to find what we could not have found four months ago, viz. another government at once popular and willing to work with us and able to steer Agreement through Medjliss while free from pedantry which characterises present one.[86]

Norman later the same day saw Pirnia who told him that the Shah would not agree to the dismissal of the Colonel although the Colonel himself was willing to resign. Pirnia asked Norman whether he would agree to another Russian officer presently serving in the Division to take command, or an officer from a neutral country. 'I said no to both... and the Prime Minister said if I persisted he would resign'.[87]

This was indeed a strange turnaround for Norman, who had forced Pirnia on Curzon and had categorically assured him that Pirnia was the only person who could get the Agreement approved. Norman surely knew that Pirnia would not accept any action which would indicate even a tacit acceptance of the Agreement by the Iranian Government. Pirnia might agree to the dismissal of Starosselsky even though he believed the time was not right and could lead to destabilising the Division, but to allow the Cossacks to be commanded by British officers was tantamount to acceptance of the 'military advisory' clause of the Agreement. The appointment of an Iranian figurehead to act as the nominal commander while British officers ran the show did not sit well with Pirnia who saw through the proposed scheme.

Ironside's own account of their meeting with Pirnia varies in some aspects from Norman's. To begin with, Ironside seems to have formed a somewhat low opinion of Norman. He unfairly described him as 'an indeterminate little man'.[88] Ironside recounted the crucial meeting with Pirnia as follows:

An ultimatum was delivered by us both to the [Prime Minister]. I insisted on his [Starosselsky] being recalled, dismissed and called up to render an account of the money he had spent in the so-called campaign. I told the [Prime] Minister that he had asked me not to interfere and I had refrained but now the Persian Cossacks had collapsed and we could waste no more money on them. The wretched man was up against it. He wriggled in his chair like an eel at the end of a line... he said that his head would be chopped off if he went to the Shah and asked for his [Starosselsky's] dismissal... I was told that to institute British control in the Cossacks now would make the Agreement impossible...I told him that I had no intention of instituting British control. I merely refused to have British money embezzled and wasted by Russians...the Prime Minister resigned two days later...the new Prime Minister [Sepahdar] did what we told him... and the Shah would do whatever we asked him... now the British would be the sole support and he (the Shah) pleaded that they should not abandon him.[89]

Norman saw the Shah the next day and related the charges of 'incompetence, corruption and anti-British propaganda by the Russian officers'. The Shah told Norman that the Prime Minister had already informed him of Norman's demand for the dismissal of the commander of the Division. The Prime Minister was willing to dismiss the corrupt officers and those of doubtful loyalty but the time was not opportune to make mass dismissals. The Prime Minister feared that if he took any steps in that direction:

... it would have a bad effect on public opinion. Everyone would believe Great Britain was putting the Anglo-Persian Agreement in force without consent of Medjliss and trying to possess Persia... sympathy for Bolshevism would at once attain proportions which it had reached in time of late Government and he himself would become as much hated as Vosouq ed Dowleh.

Norman argued that unless Starosselsky were removed all funding by Britain would cease and all British troops would be withdrawn. These last two threats turned the Shah around and he asked Norman who he would recommend as the new Prime Minister if Pirnia were to resign. Norman mentioned Sepahdar and the Shah welcomed the proposal. They then discussed the composition of the new cabinet. Norman at the end of his telegram informed Curzon that 'I had previously caused Sepahdar to be sounded and had ascertained that he is prepared to carry out policy which I propose'.[90]

On 27 October Norman again saw the Shah. He was informed that the Shah had seen Pirnia the day before and had told Pirnia that he had made up his mind to dismiss Starosselsky. The Prime Minister had said he had therefore no alternative but to resign. The Shah further stated that he had summoned Sepahdar to form a new government. The Shah, who believed he [had] again rendered an important service to His Majesty's Government', immediately wanted a *quid pro quo* and asked if his monthly subsidy of 15,000 tomans could be reinstated with arrears from June and be paid at least until

such time as parliament was convened. Norman promised to recommend that the Shah's request be met. The Shah, finding the
atmosphere congenial, next asked if he could go to Europe in early
April. Norman answered that April was a long way off and his trip
could be discussed later. He observed that the Shah 'prefers the life
in foreign capitals' where there is less fatigue and stress. Norman
then added that Starosselsky should be forced to give back 'the
money he had stolen and should then leave Persia as soon as possible'. The Shah argued that this was an unfair demand on someone
who had rendered valuable services to Iran and 'such a request
would appear as an act of ingratitude'. Norman reminded Curzon
that the Shah had shared in Starosselsky's proceeds of embezzlement. On the very last payment to Starosselsky for 'refitting the
Cossacks for the campaign in the North, the Colonel had asked [of
the Imperial Bank] to be paid 50,000 tomans all in large notes,
'which had attracted the attention of the bank officials as large notes
are difficult to change in the provinces'. A few days later an emmis-
sary of the Shah had deposited 40,000 tomans in large notes in the
Shah's account, 'the very similar notes given to Starosselsky'.
Norman concluded, with some relish, that his sources further had
informed him that a necklace worth about 35,000 tomans also had
been given recently by Starosselsky to the Shah.[91]

A Russian presence had been eliminated, the Foreign Office was
expected to be appeased, and a principled prime minister had been
sacrificed. If Norman had believed that by the removal of Starosselsky the implementation of the Agreement would be any easier he
was to be sadly disappointed. Ironside's search for an Iranian officer
to head the Cossasks was to gather a momentum of its own.

NOTES ON CHAPTER 4
Further details of publications and documents in Bibliography

1   For the sake of brevity and uniformity from this point onward I have chosen to refer to Iranians who lived and were active beyond the 1925 Law of Identity and Status under their chosen family names. Vosouq for Vosouq al Dowleh, Firouz for Nosrat al Dowleh and now Hassan Pirnia for Moshir al Dowleh.

2   FO 416/71, Bullard to Halifax, 7 February 1940; Mehdi Bamdad, *Tarikh Rejal Iran Quroun 12, 13, 14* (*Dictionary of National Biography of Iran: Twelfth, Thirteenth, Fourteenth Centuries*), vol. 1, pp 388–389.

3   Mehdi Bamdad, *Tarikh Rejal Iran Quroun 12, 13, 14* (*Dictionary of National Biography of Iran: Twelfth, Thirteenth, Fourteenth Centuries*), vol. 4, pp 184–187; FO 416/78, Bullard to Halifax, 7 February 1940.

4   DBFP, doc. no. 456, Cox to Curzon, 8 June 1920.

5   FO 371/3874, Norman to Curzon, 26 June 1920 (first telegram).

6   FO 371/3874, Norman to Curzon, 26 June 1920 (second telegram).

7   FO 371/3874, Norman to Curzon, 26 June 1920.

8   *Ibid.*

9   FO 371/3874, Norman to Curzon, 27 June 1920.

10 Christopher Sykes, *Wassmuss, the German Lawrence*; Percy Sykes, *A History of Persia*, vol. 2, pp. 444–445.

11 Lt Col. Frederick O'Connor, *Things Mortal*, p 122.

12 FO 248/1300, November 1920.

13 FO 371/3874, Norman to Curzon, 28 June 1920.

14 For biographical material refer to Chapter IX.

15 FO 371/3874, Norman to Curzon, 28, 29, 30 June and 1 July 1920. DBFP, doc. nos 494, 495 and 496 of same dates.

16 DBFP, doc. no. 497, Curzon to Norman, 1 July 1920.

17 DBFP, doc. no. 499, Norman to Curzon, 3 July 1920.

18 FO 371/4904, Norman to Curzon, 22 July 1920.

19 DBFP, doc. no. 497, Norman to Curzon, 3 July 1920.

20 DBFP, doc. no. 500; FO 371/4908, Norman to Curzon, 3 July 1920.

21 F 112/217B, Curzon papers, Montague to Curzon, 14 April 1920: quoted by Houshang Sabahi, *British Policy in Persia 1918–1925*, p 70.

22 DBFP, doc. no. 503; Norman to Curzon; 7 July 1920.

23 DBFP, doc. no. 500, Norman to Curzon, 3 July 1920 and doc no. 507, G.P. Churchill memo of 9 July 1920. The term 'nationalist' begins to lose its meaning in these exchanges of telegrams between Curzon and Norman. Curzon applies the term to anyone who had not been a supporter of the Agreement and the triumverate. Beginning in 1920, the term is invariably used by the Foreign Office in a highly pejorative sense. Members of Pirnia's Cabinet are referred to as 'notorious nationalists' and more than once as 'suspects'.

24 DBFP, doc. no. 508, Curzon to Norman, 10 July 1920.

25 DBFP, doc. no. 515, Norman to Curzon, 20 July 1920.

26 DBFP, doc. no. 518, Norman to Curzon, 22 July 1920.

27 DBFP, doc. no. 516, Norman to Curzon, 21 July 1920.

28 DBFP, doc. no. 543, Norman to Curzon, 26 August 1920.

29 Mehdi Bamdad, *Tarikh Rejal Iran Quroun 12, 13, 14* (*Dictionary of National Biography of Iran: Twelfth, Thirteenth, Fourteenth Centuries*), vol. 2, pp 31–34.

30 DBFP, doc. no. 521, Norman to Curzon, 23 July 1920.
31 'Madjliss' or 'Majles' is the Persian (Arabic origin) word for parliament.
32 DBFP, doc. nos 522, 523 and 524; FO 371/4908, Norman to Curzon, 24 July 1920.
33 DBFP, doc. no. 527, Curzon to Norman, 27 July 1920.
34 DBFP, doc. no. 527, Curzon to Norman, 27 July 1920.
35 FO 371/4908, Norman to Curzon, 29 July 1920. The sheer number and volume of telegrams during the months of June and July between London and Tehran indicate the preoccupation or rather obsession of Curzon to construct an Iran that would serve as an external buffer zone in the protection of India.
36 DBFP, doc. no. 531; FO 371/4908, Curzon to Norman, 31 July 1920.
37 DBFP, doc. no. 533, Curzon to Norman, 5 August 1920.
38 DBFP, doc. no. 534, Norman to Curzon and Dickson's dispatch, 6 August 1920.
39 DBFP, doc. no. 534, Minute prepared by Lancelot Oliphant, 8 August 1920.
40 Note to doc. no. 535, Curzon to Norman, 6 August 1920.
41 FO 371/4908, Norman to Curzon, 7 August 1920.
42 Mehdi Bamdad, *Tarikh Rejal Iran Quroun 12, 13, 14* (*Dictionary of National Biography of Iran: Twelfth, Thirteenth, Fourteenth Centuries*), vol. 6, pp 196–198.
43 FO 371/4908, Norman to Curzon, 7 August 1920.
44 DBFP, doc. no. 537, Norman to Curzon, 8 August 1920.
45 DBFP, doc. no. 538, Norman to Curzon, 9 August 1920.
46 DBFP, doc. no. 540, Curzon to Norman, 13 August 1920.
47 DBFP, doc. no. 558, Norman to Curzon, 7 August 1920; doc. no. 411, Curzon to Norman, 7 August 1920.
48 British officers later told Ironside that 'the British troops sulkily withdrew [and] the Persian Cossacks going forward jeered at them'. Ironside was disturbed enough to comment in his Diaries, 'What a thing to happen'. Richard H. Ullman, *The Anglo-Soviet Accord*, vol. 3, p 379, from the unpublished manuscript of the Diaries of Maj. Gen. Sir Edmund Ironside.
49 DBFP, doc. no. 599, Norman to Curzon, 28 August 1920.
50 DBFP, doc. no. 544, Norman to Curzon, 29 August 1920.
51 DBFP, doc. no. 618, Norman to Curzon, 8 September 1920.
52 DBFP, doc. no. 550, Curzon to Norman, 13 September 1920.
53 DBFP, doc. no. 640, Norman to Curzon, 18 September 1920.
54 DBFP, doc. no. 552, Norman to Curzon, 16 September 1920.
55 DBFP, doc. no. 553, Curzon to Norman, 20 September 1920.
56 DBFP, doc. no. 556, Norman to Curzon, 25 September 1920.
57 DBFP, doc. no. 556, Norman to Curzon, 29 September 1920.
58 DBFP, doc. no. 557, Curzon to Norman, 29 September 1920.
59 FO 248/1292, Edmonds to British Legation in Tehran, 4 June 1920.
60 Mehdi Qoli Hedayat (Mokhber al Saltaneh), *Khaterat va Khatarat* (*Memoirs and Hazards*), pp 405–408. 'Khaterat' is an artful word and could be translated as 'challenges'.
61 FO 371/4914, Norman to Curzon, 13 October 1920.
62 L/PS/10/736/2000, Cox to Curzon, 10 April 1919.
63 DBFP, doc. no. 516, Norman to Curzon, 21 July 1920.

64 Congressional Record, 66th Congress, first session 58-5216-5217-6080-6087 and 6089: quoted by Abraham Yesselson, *United States-Persian Diplomatic Relations, 1883–1921*, p 158.
65 *Ibid.*, p 159.
66 FO 371/4587, Curzon to Norman, 26 November 1920.
67 President Harding's Cabinet included Albert B. Fall, Secretary of the Interior who was later convicted of having received a bribe from independent oil producers Edward Doheny and Harry Sinclair. Sinclair Oil Company later became a rival of Standard Oil and APOC in Iran.
68 Nasrollah Saifpour Fatemi, *Oil Diplomacy*, pp 73–74 and 106. See also Alan Ford, *The Anglo-Iranian Oil Dispute of 1951–1952*, pp 20–21 and R.W. Ferrier, *The History of the British Petroleum Company*, vol. 1, p 27.
69 DBFP, doc. no. 546, Curzon to Sir Auckland Geddes, Washington DC, 30 August 1920.
70 DBFP, doc. no. 541, Norman to Curzon, 18 August 1920.
71 DBFP, doc. no. 542, Curzon to Norman, 21 August 1920.
72 CAB 67 (20), 8 December 1920, CAB 23/23.
73 Wilson Papers, 55, no. 2, Wilson to Haldane, 24 August 1920.
74 Maj. Gen. Sir Edmund Ironside, *High Road to Command*, pp 1–4.
75 FO 371/4906, War Office to GOC Mesopotamia, 10 October 1920.
76 Maj. Gen. Sir Edmund Ironside, *High Road to Command*, p 163
77 FO 800/156, Hardinge to Curzon, 20 May 1920: quoted by Richard H. Ullman, *The Anglo-Soviet Accord*, vol. 3, p 327.
78 Richard H. Ullman, *The Anglo-Soviet Accord*, vol. 3, p 327. See also Elizabeth Monroe, *Britain's Moment in the Middle East 1914–1918*, p 11.
79 Richard H. Ullman, *The Anglo-Soviet Accord*, vol. 3, p 328.
80 FO 371/4907, Minutes by Esmond Ovey, 4 December 1920.
81 DBFP, doc. no. 562; Norman to Curzon; 7 October 1920.
82 DBFP, doc. no. 561; War Office to Lt Gen. A.L. Haldane; 6 October 1920.
83 Maj. Gen. Sir Edmund Ironside, *High Road to Command*, p 141–142.
84 WO 158/697, Ironside to Manjeel Command, 22 October 1920: quoted by Houshang Sabahi, *British Policy in Persia 1918–1925*, p 51.
85 FO 371/6399, Cox to Curzon, 9 January 1921; FO 371/6401/2144, Norman to Curzon, 23 January 1921.
86 DBFP, doc. no. 556, Norman to Curzon, 25 October 1920.
87 FO 371/4914, Norman to Curzon, 25 October 1920.
88 Maj. Gen. Sir Edmund Ironside, *High Road to Command*, p 138. The question of height was of some importance in Ironside's appraisal of men he met in Iran and influenced his judgement. Ironside himself, variously described as 6 feet 4 inches or 6 feet 6 inches, weighing some 270–280 pounds, had been given the nickname of 'Tiny'. We see several entries in the Diaries where he refered to the height of others, Iranian and British.
89 Richard H. Ullman, *The Anglo-Soviet Accord*, vol. 3, p 381–382; from the unpublished Ironside Diaries manuscript.
90 DBFP, doc. no. 569, Norman to Curzon, 26 October 1920.
91 FO 371/4914, Norman to Curzon, 27 October 1920; DBFP, doc. no. 570 of the same date.

5

Sepahdar as Prime Minister

In getting rid of Starosselsky, Ironside had taken another calculated step towards fulfilling his agenda. But what had Norman hoped to accomplish by joining Ironside? He had gambled and chosen Pirnia, a democratically-oriented and principled politician, as Prime Minister despite his superior's displeasure, with every hope that his candidate would prove successful and accomplish what Norman's predecessor, Cox, had failed to do with an unpopular and authoritarian Vosouq. Norman had hoped that Pirnia would hold new parliamentary elections and his honesty and good name would ensure the passage of the Agreement, albeit with some modifications and ornamental changes. Norman had resisted Curzon's attempts to install another authoritarian politician as prime minister because he knew that imprisonment and exile of opponents was not the way to have the Agreement ratified.

Pirnia gave a good account of himself, served his country well and remained true to his principles. It is interesting to note that even in early 1920 when an Iranian was prepared to stand up to the British he could have his way up to a point, a lesson seldom, if ever, learned by Pirnia's contemporaries. He refused to have anything to do with the Agreement without parliamentary approval. He took no action which would allow even a part of the Agreement to be deemed to have come into operation. The military clause to reorganise the army, intended to assert total British military control and the financial clause, designed basically to isolate Iran economically, had been placed in abeyance. He refused to touch the £2 million loan lest it be interpreted that Iran had benefitted under the terms of the Agreement. However, by having pushed Pirnia a step too far Norman had lost his chosen premier and any hope of returning to a consti- tutional government. In fairness to Norman, it must be said that Pirnia might have worked out well. Certainly he had a better chance than his predecessor at least partially to implement Curzon's policy, that is to tie Iran to Britain irrevocably, with or without an agree- ment. No-one had foreseen the extent of Bolshevik penetration in the northern provinces nor their material support of the insurgents. Furthermore no-one, including Curzon, had counted on the British Cabinet bowing to public pressure to withdraw all her troops from northern Iran.

What made little sense was that Norman's new candidate, Sepahdar, was probably the weakest and most servile Prime Minister since the beginning of the constitutional era. He had been subservient to British and Russian interests in Iran from the outset of his public career and had followed their dictates without question. As a man of great wealth and the largest landowner in Gilan he had a great deal to lose if British influence diminished or the Bolsheviks became ascendant. He had already suffered losses in the turmoil caused by the insurgency in Gilan.[1]

Despite his European-style attire Sepahdar spoke not a word of a foreign language and his Persian is said to have been wanting. Accounts abound of his slowness of mind and lack of education. Though he was slow and timid, his asset in British eyes was his being a devout and tested member of the anglophile clique who had already been awarded the KCMG in 1903 by the British Crown. In 1907, having taken a marginal part in the constitutional movement, he had been arrested by Mohammad Ali Shah. At the intervention of the British Legation he had been released from jail and exiled to Mazandaran. He returned to Tehran in December 1908 and, fearing arrest again, took refuge at the Russian Legation until July 1909. In early 1910 he went to Europe and returned later the same year. He had served as Minister of War during Vosouq's second term as Prime Minister. He had not been entirely loyal to Vosouq and had under- mined him by organising protests in the Bazaar.[2] When found out, he had been forced to resign. Sepahdar's motives for intriguing against Vosouq are uncertain. They probably had to do with his having been left out of Vosouq's inner circle and his long-harboured ambition to become Prime Minister.

What had now become important to Norman was the fact that Sepahdar 'would do as he was told'. Equally important was the fact that Sepahdar had laid down no conditions in accepting office other than continued financial assistance and a promise by Britain to strengthen the fighting capabilities of the Cossacks. Sepahdar found no difficulty in having British officers in command of the Cossacks. The bogeyman Starosselsky, who had proved a primary obstacle to Britain's implementing the military clause of the Agreement, had been removed. Britain could now move ahead. Sepahdar had promised to convene parliament and to get the Agreement through once he had a quorum. The cabinet he was to form would not include anyone objectionable to the Foreign Office. Surely Norman believed that Curzon would be pleased with the change and the new Prime Minister.

Ironside appears intemperate in having described Norman as 'indeterminate'. The harassed Norman may have appeared so to Ironside, who had never dealt with Curzon. He did not know of Norman's daily struggle with Curzon nor that Norman had staked his reputation and career in standing up to the master of British diplomacy and his impossible and 'insane policy'.[3] What probably induced Norman to agree with Ironside in the removal of Starosselsky was Norman's having come around to believing that the Cossack Division under British command could hold off the insurgents a while longer. Additionally, in any possible battle with Bolshevik forces British troops would be more likely to aid the Cossacks with arms and logistical assistance instead of standing aloof as they had while the Division was under Russian command. There would be at least some breathing space and things could take a turn for the better in Tehran. Norman had every reason to think that Curzon would be pacified by the removal of Starosselsky, the tacit implementation of the military clause of the Agreement and the resignation of Pirnia, who had seemed anathema to him.

In a euphoric telegram on 28 October Norman informed Curzon that Sepahdar had agreed to form a government. He is 'totally in our hands' and has promised to call parliament into session and have a vote on the ratification of the Agreement. Norman, as in previous instances, warned that no-one would accept office with the knowledge that there were no funds in the treasury. He argued that the monthly subsidy of 350,000 tomans should be extended for at least a month or two. The last of these payments had been made on 24 October 1920. The Imperial Bank had been ready to advance funds by way of commercial loans but Curzon had objected. The bank had argued that the Iranian Government had to stay afloat if it were to continue doing business in the country. If the Bolsheviks took over, it would be forced to close all branches in northern Iran.[4] The Bank persisted in its argument and finally succeeded in being allowed to advance credit, but the monthly subsidy remained blocked.[5]

Norman also urged that the expense for the reorganisation and upkeep of the Cossack Division should be borne by Britain pending a financial adjustment later with the Iranian Government. To strengthen his demand Norman argued that the expulsion of the Russian officers 'and virtual control by British officers of the only regular military force in Persia would make us practically independent... and ensure gradual execution of the Agreement'. Norman, as was his custom, followed with the disheartening news that Sepahdar did not want to use any advances from the £2 million loan prior to ratification because it would excite 'popular opposition especially as [Sepahdar] would inaugurate term of office by installing British officers in Persian army, a measure contrary to policy of fallen Cabinet' of Pirnia.[6]

Against the wishes of the British Legation, Starosselsky came to Tehran on 29 October ostensibly to pay his respects and bid farewell to the Shah. He may have hoped to convince the Shah to reverse his dismissal. Norman, fearing that Starosselsky could be successful or could provoke the Cossack contingent in Tehran to stage a mutiny, sent an agitated message to the Shah to reprimand Starosselsky for his disobedience, order him to reliquish his command to the designated Persian officer and return to Qazvin. Norman warned that otherwise Starosselsky would be sent back to Qazvin under arrest. At the intervention of the former Czarist envoy to Iran who had remained in Tehran after the Russian Revolution, it was agreed that Starosselsky would return to Qazvin the same evening and the British Legation would give him a written guarantee that he and his family could travel to Paris by way of Mesopotamia free from interference or molestation. According to the Czarist envoy, Starosselsky had demanded a written guarantee of safe passage because he feared Norman would have him assassinated.[7] Starosselsky returned to Qazvin and left the country on 6 November. A major impediment to British plans in Iran had departed from the scene. After a brief stay in Paris Starosselsky left for the United States where he settled. He left no papers or diaries.

There are conflicting views concerning the misappropriation of funds by Starosselsky. Lt Col. Henry Smyth, the British officer who worked with the Cossacks, had discovered the total number of Cossack troops at the Qazvin camp to be about 3,000 with another 500 on leave and accounted for. Starosselsky had a ledger sheet that showed 4,500 troops and collected provisions and pay for 4,500. These 1,000 'blank files' enabled him and the other Russian officers to pocket the difference.[8] On the other hand the United States Minister to Tehran, John Caldwell, reported to the State Department,

'I cannot believe a man of Moshir ed Dowleh's character would acquiesce in any crooked deal or offer himself up as a martyr on a political throne. if he believed the charge of dishonesty made against the Russian officers were well founded. The proof of the charge has never been made public... '. Caldwell then added, 'People have no faith in the Soviet Treaty but they welcome anything in order to be freed from the British and think not of how much worse the future may be... The British policy in Persia of force and money has proven as disastrous to themselves as it has to the Persians... Persia always seems to be between the devil and the deep sea, but somehow lives in spite thereof'.[9]

All thoughts that Curzon would now be pacified by the removal of Starosselsky and the resignation of Pirnia were soon dispelled. Curzon left no doubt about his reaction to these events in the opening paragraph of his telegram to Norman on 29 October:

> I find some difficulty in forming or expressing an opinion on a situation in which there appears to have been a complete volte face in Persian policy, and in which I am again presented in this case without the slightest warning with a fait accompli. Till a week ago I had been led by you to believe that success of British policy in Persia was inseparable from Premiership of Mushir ed Dowleh [Pirnia], summons of Medjliss by him, suspension of Anglo-Persian Agreement in interim and toleration and support of Starosselsky... In these circumsances I must leave it to you and General Ironside to deal with a situation which appears suddenly to have developed since arrival of latter and which no instructions from this end can avail to control. In deciding upon new policy... you will doubtless recognise that General Ironside and yourself have assumed no slight responsibility which will require the justification of success'.

Curzon also rejected demands made by the Shah for the restoration of his monthly subsidy and permission to travel to Europe.[10]

A few days later, once Curzon had had time to overcome the shock of the new developments engineered by his envoy, he instructed Norman to press the new Government to convene parliament as soon as possible and decide on the fate of the Agreement. Curzon rejected the continuance of the monthly government subsidy and advised Norman to tell Sepahdar to seek needed funds from APOC.[11] Curzon however, agreed to pay for the cost of reorganisation and maintenance of the Cossack Division for the time being, since British officers were to assume command. In late September the Iranian Government represented by Sidney Armitage Smith had already reached agreement with APOC for partial payment of royalty arrears.

As in the past Norman did not allow Curzon's sarcasm to go unanswered. He dismissed the charge of *volte face* by arguing that the change of government was a natural consequence of inevitable events. In any case he had believed Curzon would view with satisfaction the resignation of a prime minister in whom he had frequently expressed distrust. More important, Norman, obviously disturbed by the intimation that he acted under the influence and prodding of Ironside, wrote:

> The coincidence of his [Ironside's] arrival with the dismissal of Russian officers should not induce belief that he is solely responsible in the matter, though he has co-operated with me most whole-heartedly and efficiently throughout and continues to do so. I am, of course, fully prepared to assume responsibility of step which I have taken, and if it fails, to accept its consequences insofar as they affect myself. I can safely leave General Ironside to present his own case to the War Office.[12]

Sepahdar, who had been so eager to become Prime Minister and had waited long to achieve his ambition, had not known what awaited him. He had believed that Vosouq was too unbending and uncompromising towards his opponents. With some flexibility and the spreading of more money amongst elements in the clergy and the hand-picked newly-elected members of parliament he felt he could complete elections and have the Agreement approved. It also appeared to Sepahdar that Pirnia had been too legalistic in pursuing unattainable goals. Had Pirnia been a realist he would have bowed to British pressure, dismissed the Russian officers, allowed the British financial team more freedom at the Ministry of Finance, and more importantly he would have excluded from his Cabinet people who were objectionable to Britain. Finally Sepahdar believed that the timing of British troop withdrawals was negotiable. If he did as the Legation instructed him, Britain would be more likely to keep her troops longer in Iran.

Things began going badly for Sepahdar soon after assuming office. The first tremour came when a British Junior Minister at the Treasury, in answer to a routine question by a member of parliament as to the status of the £2 million loan to Iran, inadvertently revealed that 'except for a small fraction of the loan which had been disbursed at the time of the execution of the agreement, the balance had not been withdrawn by the Persian government'. The news was telegraphed by Reuters to the British Legation in Tehran but escaped the notice of censors at the Legation. Sepahdar, although a member of Vosouq's Cabinet, had not known of the bribe paid to the triumverate and asked Norman to issue a flat denial that any fraction of the loan had been used. Norman had to explain to Sepahdar that he could not do so because the statement was in fact true. He suggested that Sepahdar let his colleagues and the press know that 'a small sum had been deducted from the loan for commissions and to defray the expenses for underwriting'. Soon thereafter Norman had to admit to Sepahdar that in fact £131,147,11s had been paid to and divided among the triumverate. Sepahdar, whose reputation was now at stake, knew that people would assume that as a member of Vosouq's Cabinet he at least had known of the bribe, if not benefitted from it. He told Norman that he had to make the matter public and demand restitution from the three offending parties. Norman, faced with a difficult situation, asked Curzon for guidance and suggested naively that the best solution would be that the British Government somehow 'make up the loan to the original sum', enabling Sepahdar to state that the British Government had decided to bear the 'incidental expenses for underwriting' and thus the £2 million loan was intact and 'nothing has been deducted from the original sum'.[13]

Curzon's haughty reply was laced with his customary piety:

> This phase of the Agreement was, as you know, extremely repugnant to me, and I only gave way on the urgent and repeated insistence of Sir Percy Cox. Present [Persian] Prime Minister was at the time a member of the Cabinet and continued in office for eight months afterwards. We must therefore hold him jointly responsible with his colleagues for the official act of the Cabinet, and you should speak to him very strongly in this sense... We can on no account consider the suggestion made in your telegram.[14]

Norman passed on Curzon's pronouncement on joint and several responsibility of Vosouq's ministers to Sepahdar who repeated that he knew nothing of the bribe and intended to pursue the matter and collect the money from the recipients. Sepahdar begged Norman to assist him in this pursuit. Norman answered that the British Government had no information as to how the money had been divided and pleaded with Sepahdar to delay his inquiries 'as more important matters lie ahead'.[15] Norman of course knew the exact division of the bribe among the triumverate. His primary concern was that these revelations would make it much harder, if not impossible, for a number of deputies to vote for ratification of the Agreement. Any member who supported it would be presumed to have been bribed. Norman also felt that members of Sepahdar's Cabinet would be wary of supporting the Agreement.

Sepahdar's Cabinet was mostly made up of harmless nonentities with a background of pro-British sympathies. The Cabinet was more noteworthy for those omitted than for those included. Norman would have liked to include Ahmad Qavam (Qavam al Saltaneh), Governor of Khorasan and younger brother of Vosouq, and also the rising politician Abdol Hosein Teimurtash (Sardar Mo'azam), but was unsuccessful on both counts. The Cabinet was comprised of Amir Nezam (Hosein Qoli Qaragozlou), Minister of War; Abbas Mirza Salar Lashkar, Public Works; two members of the Hedayat family, Nasr al Molk and Fahim al Dowleh. Sepahdar kept the portfolios of the Ministries of Foreign Affairs and Interior for himself. The only person objectionable to Curzon was Soleiman Mirza (Eskandari), a returned exile, as Minister of Justice.

Norman provided Curzon with some revealing insight into the new Cabinet: Amir Nezam, one of the largest landowners of Western Iran, was in the Cabinet merely as the elder brother of Sardar Akram, Vosouq's son-in-law. Salar Lashkar, the second-eldest surviving son of Farmanfarma, was included because Sepahdar had calculated that Farmanfarma would be unlikely to intrigue against the Cabinet if one of his sons were included. Norman added that although Farmanfarma was 'extremely unpopular, [Sepahdar] had to have a Farmanfarma in the Cabinet for tactical reasons... [The sons of Farmanfarma] often visit me and always allude to their attachment to Great Britain... We therefore owe them something'. The appointment of Soleiman Mirza, whose return to Iran Curzon had strenuously objected to some five months earlier, was explained by the fact that Soleiman Mirza was a friend of the respected Mostofi, and his inclusion in the Cabinet might help wavering members of parliament (soon to be convened) to climb aboard and support the Agreement.[16]

When some two weeks later Sepahdar asked Norman for funds to be disbursed amongst the newly-elected members of parliament and Norman routinely asked Curzon for approval, Curzon responded with indignation, probably prompted by the recent revelation of the bribe and his prior assent to it. He wrote to Norman:

> Sepahdar [who] prided his government on repudiation of venality which he severely condemned in some of his predecessors now contemplates adoption of similar methods of support for Anglo-Persian Agreement. You should emphatically dissociate yourself from any such suggestion.[17]

This is the same Curzon who some fifteen months earlier had approved the bribe to the triumverate and a monthly retainer for the Shah. Now sensing that the Agreement had little chance of ratification he acted offended and morally outraged.

Norman, already irritated with Curzon for disassociating himself from the bribery episode and now portraying himself as a paragon of virtue, could not help but indicate the contrast between the practices of Sepahdar and those of Vosouq and Cox:

> Sepahdar is personally honest and his request does not appear to afford
> evidence to the contrary any more than use of Secret Service Funds by
> European statesmen reflects on the integrity of the latter... Sepahdar
> never flattered himself that he was certain of getting Anglo-Persian
> Agreement accepted by the Medjliss without expenditure of money... Till
> late this question would have presented no difficulties since [Persian]
> Government could always dispose of revenue according to their pleasure.
> For example when I arrived I found a great part of monthly subsidy of
> 350,000 tomans being used to silence the opposition.

Norman explained that the practice stopped when Pirnia introduced
a monthly budget which excluded any provision for 'Secret Services'.
Sepahdar was unwilling to revive the old practice, for it would be
obvious to all what any payment above and beyond the confines of
the budget was intended for. Norman asked Curzon to reconsider
the matter and reassured him that Sepahdar 'is in our hands to a
much greater extent than was his predecessor and if he can be sure
that His Majesty's Government will support him adequately will do
practically anything they wish'.[18] Norman's telegram is also interesting in that it indicates that Vosouq paid off politicians from the
Iranian Treasury and not from his personal funds or from proceeds
of the bribe as Vosouq claimed years later. Lest Curzon still believed
Vosouq had never used his share of the bribe for personal use,
Norman in another dispatch reported, 'I have been told by an unim-
peachable authority that Vosouq ed Dowleh did not give 200,000
tomans, as he claims to Tomanians to help the latter [out of bank-
ruptcy] but paid it to him as the purchase price of a dozen villages
in Mazandaran'.[19]

The failure to have the Agreement approved was beginning to
cost Curzon dearly and he began to lose support in the British
Cabinet. Confronted with uprisings in Mesopotamia, Egypt and
Ireland, and industrial strife in mainland Britain itself, the need for
troops became acute. These events, coupled with budgetary con-
straints, made the Cabinet unwilling to delay the recall of troops
from northern Iran any longer than early spring of 1921, whatever
the consequences. Curzon reluctantly accepted, hoping that before
withdrawal the Iranian Parliament would meet and approve the Agreement.[20] Curzon, who until now had assented to the appointment of
a weak and servile Prime Minister as the answer to his problems,
soon despaired and in a series of telegrams to Norman voiced suspicions about Sepahdar. He warned Norman that the Iranian
Government, having exhausted all financial resources of the British
Government, had turned to APOC and the Imperial Bank and somehow had eked enough money to carry on for a few months longer.
APOC had agreed to pay the Iranian Government one million tomans

in settlement of all royalties for the period ending 31 March 1919. The payments were staggered over eight-to-nine months. Curzon was fearful that once the Soviets reached an agreement with the Iranians and renounced concessions acquired during the Czarist regime, the Iranian Government could well turn around and offer the same concessions (such as the Khoshtaria oil concession) to the Soviets and/or other countries.[21]

By the end of December gloom had descended upon the British Cabinet and the Government sought expert advice as how best to deal with the deteriorating situation in Iran. G.P. Churchill, a former Oriental Counselor at the Legation in Tehran familiar with Iranian affairs for over a quarter of a century, submitted one of the first memoranda. Churchill predicted that Bolshevik troops with their Iranian allies would attack Qazvin and then Tehran as soon as British forces withdrew. Iranian military forces were unreliable and would offer no resistance. The Government in Tehran would collapse and the Shah would escape to Europe. The Bolshevik forces would stop short of actually occupying Tehran but with the help of their agents and sympathisers would control the capital and install a pro-Bolshevik government. The Cossack Division could not be reorganised by British officers in time, hence no military equipment should be given to them as they would fall into enemy hands. The Gendarmes, the Tehran police and other Iranian local forces would either return to their homes or take arms and turn into highway robbers. Churchill warned of dire consequences not only in southern Iran but the likelihood of a similar process in Afghanistan and Mesopotamia. He further predicted that in such circumstances the India Office would contend that the best place to defend India was on the Indian frontiers and Iran should be left to her fate. Churchill argued that this attitude was unacceptable as British commercial interests, including the Imperial Bank and APOC, would suffer. The debt to Britain amounting to several million pounds would have to be written off and the expenditures incurred in Iran over the past five years would have been wasted. Churchill felt that it was too late to think of acceptance of the Agreement by the Iranian parliament. Even if ratified at the last moment none of its provisions could be put into effect. He then proposed measures to minimise British losses. He suggested that the Legation be moved to Esfahan. Britain should conclude a military and financial assistance arrangement with the Bakhtiari leaders under which the latter would support a government to be formed in central and southern Iran. Britain should then send selected officers with a large contingent of SPR to Esfahan to strengthen Bakhtiari forces. This plan Churchill contended would lay the groundwork for an eventual attempt to re-establish the Shah's authority in the north while continuing to protect the oil fields in the South. Churchill concluded his report with an obvious jibe at Norman and the India Office:

> All idea of governing Persia with and through a Medjliss or by employing democrats should, at this dangerous stage in Persia's affairs be abandoned. A government might be composed of strong men whose names are known and feared by the great tribes. These men, it is true, are usually corrupt and rapacious, but they are the only people who can deal with the tribal chiefs who will not move for democratic leaders whom they despise. Ain al Dowleh is perhaps the best of this class.[22]

(Ain al Dowleh, an old-line autocrat, had been Prime Minister three times: 1904–1906, 1915 and 1916.)

In a well-reasoned memorandum Montague, the Secretary of State for India and Curzon's chief adversary in the Cabinet, also voiced his recommendations. He argued that the Anglo-Persian Agreement would never be accepted as it presently stood. Iran, within the near future, would not be able to raise an army fit to oppose an external enemy. Any involvement on Britian's part whether military or financial would eventually impede the growth of a nationalist spirit which was, in the long run, Britain's real defence against Bolshevism. Montague suggested the following: Britain should forestall rejection of the Agreement by scaling it down to a point acceptable to Iran.

> [Iran] merely expects a sufficient flow of revenue to carry out her miserable administration... The Shuster experiment showed that expert foreign control of finance would not only be welcome but bring in large increase of revenue.

Montague stopped short of recommending a British team of financial advisers and suggested the retention of only one or two experts. The Cossack Division and the SPR should be handed over to Iran:

> ... to be officered by her as she likes. If she chooses to bring in a foreign element one should not object, although we shall endeavour to guide her choice into unobjectionable channels.

Persia should look after her own external defence.

> Our disappearance will rob Bolshevism of her one valid excuse and possibly even remove temptation for open aggression... These are not the most attractive proposals but they are designed to square with the facts.[23]

Other expert advice was sought later and by the beginning of 1921 detailed plans for the evacuation of Tehran were seriously considered.

Ahmad Shah, more agitated than the seasoned politicians, began to press once more for permission to go to Europe. He began to complain to Norman that 'the state of his nerves were getting worse' and described the symptoms of his imaginary malady at great length to whomever had an audience with him. Norman sympathised with the Shah but vigorously argued against his departure ,comparing it to a soldier deserting his post, and reproached him for wanting to 'enjoy himself on the money he has been able to remit abroad'. The Shah appealed to Norman for a trip of no more than two months for the sole purpose of consulting a neurologist in Paris. Norman concluded the discussion by saying that he had to have the approval of Curzon before the Shah could be allowed to leave. In his report to Curzon, Norman lamented:

> If the Shah had shown more interest in affairs of state and less in increasing his private fortune and remitting it abroad he might have become popular, but as it is his indifference to everything save his own interest has disgusted all classes of his subjects, and if he left the country it is unlikely that he would ever be able to return... A change of the Shah in itself would doubtless not be an unmixed evil if it were easy to find a satisfactory substitute for His Majesty, but in the present circumstances his deposition will impart new elements of instability into a situation which already contains more than enough of them, and might well hasten a revolution, which I believe in any case to be inevitable if British protection to Persia is not continued in some form.[24]

Curzon advised Norman to begin planning for the evacuation to Baghdad of women, children and other members of the British Colony whose presence was not essential by no later than the beginning of spring.

> [Members of the Legation] should remain in Tehran as long as possible... if and when you consider the capital to be untenable you should withdraw to Ispahan. Much will depend on whether the Shah and the Persian Government decide to leave Tehran and set up a Government in another city, or whether they feel themselves strong enough to remain in the North.

Curzon for the first time saw merit in the talks in progress in Moscow and ended by saying that 'assuming the conclusion of a Perso-Soviet Agreement, there may be no need to withdraw at all'.[25] In a later dispatch Curzon instructed Norman to tell the Shah that under no circumstances would he approve a trip abroad, even for two months.

> [His departure would be] interpreted as an act of cowardice. Were he to decide to run away he could in no circumstances expect the slightest support or help from us. I agree with you that few alternative candidates for the throne could be worse. If however, any Government is to

exist in Persia, it is essential that such a destabilising factor as flight of sovereign should if possible be avoided.[26]

Pursuant to Curzon's instructions Norman told the Shah that his departure from Iran at this time was out of the question. The Shah, further alarmed by reports of intended evacuation of Europeans, kept Norman for over two hours to induce him to agree to his leaving immediately. Sensing that Norman was unmoved the Shah threatened to abdicate if his request were denied. He asserted that 'if he were caught by the Bolsheviks he would invevitably lose his life. On the other hand he would fare no better if he fell into the power of the Bakhtiaris.' In no event would he move to Esfahan, the seat of the Bakhtiari Khans, even if the Iranian Government transferred there. The Shah admitted that his support of British policy had made him unpopular and if he waited to leave just before the departure of British troops, he would be even more unpopular and it would be said 'he was a mere servant of Britain'. Norman reported that the Shah was in a hopeless state and if his departure would not cause 'immediate revolution and his brother would prove a more popular and energetic ruler, I propose he should go sooner'. Norman added that he would consult the Prime Minister to obtain his views.[27] The following day Norman wrote to Curzon that there was not much more that could be done. 'The Shah mad with fear is dead to shame and inaccessible to reason.'[28]

At their next meeting a few days later the Shah informed Norman that he had considered the matter more carefully and definitely decided 'to leave the country as a private individual'. But before leaving he would consult a 'small assembly of notables' and then announce his decision. He had talked to his brother Mohammad Hassan Mirza, the Crown Prince, who had emphatically told him that he would not accept the succession and wanted nothing to do with the Throne. The Shah casually informed Norman that Iran would then become a republic and 'there is nothing wrong with having a republic'.[29]

Some three days later the Shah, in a complete turn-around, informed Norman that he had met with the notables who had pressed him to stay. He had also met with representatives of 'various classes who also begged him not to go'. Now that the Shah apparently had been convinced to remain in the country, the question of moving the Government to Esfahan was seriously revived. Sepahdar had been in favour of the move to Esfahan as opposed to Shiraz which had also been under consideration. It was the Shah who, fearing the Bakhtiaris, had ruled out Esfahan.[30] Curzon urged Norman to persuade the Shah as well as other members of the

Cabinet who had contemplated a move to another city to accept Esfahan as the interim capital. From the first thoughts of evacuation of Tehran, Curzon had been a proponent of Esfahan, a former capital from the late sixteenth century to the first quarter of the eighteenth century. Additionally Curzon felt Shiraz was further away and isolated.[31]

On 19 January Norman and Ironside met with representatives of the United States, Belgium, France and the old Czarist Russian regime. Ironside gave an appraisal of the military situation and arrangements for the evacuation of the foreign community. He stated that his intelligence sources believed the withdrawal of his force would be followed immediately by an advance on Qazvin and Tehran by Bolshevik troops now in Gilan calling themselves the 'Persian National Army' but including some 400 Soviet troops. With or without the approval of Moscow they would march southward and as they advanced 'a revolution will break out in Tehran either before or after the arrival of these troops'.[32] Ironside's dire warnings were echoed by Norman who added that there were a further 30,000 Bolshevik troops concentrated at Baku who might take part in the campaign against Tehran.

Norman suggested to Curzon that an assurance to Moscow that British troops were on their way out of Iran might dissuade the Bolsheviks from their invasion plans.[33] To discourage a premature abandonment of Tehran by the foreign community Curzon wrote to Norman: 'The Shah who is the most timid man in Persia has decided to stay... Persia has concluded or is on the verge of concluding a treaty with the Bolsheviks. Why then should the latter invade Persia or attack the Capital? Why should there be a general scuttle from Tehran?' Curzon warned that great damage would be done to Britain's prestige by a 'precipitate retreat and abandonment of whole of Northern Persia to an enemy whose advance is by no means certain, and a revolution which can probably still be avoided'.[34]

Another compelling voice against evacuation and change of capital came from the Viceroy of India, Lord Chelmsford, who wrote to Montague on 22 January, 'The pivot of the situation and the immediate danger is any hasty action to abandon Tehran before withdrawal of British troops'. The Iranian Government, the British Legation and the Imperial Bank should remain in Tehran. The Iranian Government should gamble on the sincerity of Bolshevik assurances that they will not invade Iran in the event of British troop withdrawals. 'Any action to abandon Tehran is tantamount to suicide'. As an intermediate step Chelmsford advocated the withdrawal of the Anglo-Persian Agreement unilaterally 'with good grace'.[35]

Norman also had been opposed to abandonment of Tehran all along. His position was strengthened by the Viceroy's comments and now by extraordinary demands being made by the Bakhtiari Khans. The Bakhtiaris had asked for transfer of sovereignty of large parts of Iran to themselves with a Qajar Prince as a puppet Shah. They demanded that henceforth all oil royalties be paid to them directly. In return for British agreement they would undertake to protect Esfahan and the south together with the forces of Qavam al Molk* who they insisted should receive a separate British financial subsidy. Faced with these demands Norman questioned whether it was worthwhile to have any alliance with the Bakhtiaris. Their request:

> ... entails condemning a great part if not the whole of Persia to most rapacious rule which it would ever have experienced. Already Bakhtiari governors wherever they exist, are hated for their oppression and if country is delivered into their hands... it is to be feared that their exactions will everywhere incline the people to welcome Bolsheviks in which case... we shall again be confronted in the South with problem which will have baffled us in the North.

Norman also argued that Bakhtiari rule would mean the end of all attempts at any type of reform in Persia. He made the further point that the Bakhtiaris were disunited. The younger Khans would not take orders from their seniors and only would be anxious to get a share of the spoils.[36]

To round out the circle, the opinion of Sir Percy Cox, an old colonial hand, at that time a king-maker in Mesopotamia and formerly the chief executor of Curzon's policy in Iran, was also sought. Cox strongly supported close co-operation with the Bakhtiari Khans and suggested that if the Bolsheviks occupied Tehran and the Khans felt more comfortable with a new Shah, the British Government should seriously entertain their proposal. In such a case the British Government should encourage the Sheikh of Mohammereh (Sheikh Khaz'al) and Wali of Posht-e-Kouh to declare their respective territories, Arabistan (Khuzestan) and Lurestan, independent states. These two new states, together with the area under Bakhtiari control should form a confederation which would offer 'a very formidable bulwark against

---

*   Ebrahim Qavam (Qavam al Molk), 1888–c.1972, was titular head of a confederation of five 'Khamseh' tribes in Fars. The position was inherited by him from his father (Habibollah Khan) and forefathers who had been loyal to the British for over a century. He was one of the wealthiest landowners in Iran. Elected to several sessions of parliament, he was forced by Reza Shah to live in Tehran from 1923–1941, away from the tribes. Reza Shah's third eldest daughter Princess Ashraf married Qavam's eldest son, Ali.[37]

Bolshevik aggression'.[38] Cox's proposals were similar to the threatening scenario which had been put forward by some British officials
to justify their effort to obtain a mandate from the Paris Peace
Conference to rule Iran as a protectorate. They also cast doubt upon
declarations by Curzon and Cox that the 1919 Agreement was
designed to maintain and protect the independence and territorial
integrity of Iran.

From the outset the Government of Sepahdar had little chance
of success. He had counted on two factors when he had formed
it. First, he had hoped the Perso-Soviet talks initiated by Pirnia
would produce a full-fledged treaty whereby Soviet troops would
evacuate the north and cease their assistance to the insurgents
in the region. Second, he had counted on Britain to assume the
reorganisation, supervision and funding of the Cossack Division to
make it battle-ready to deal with insurgency movements. Sepahdar
was frustrated on both counts. The talks in Moscow dragged on
longer than anticipated mainly because the Soviets wanted to be
certain there would be a prior withdrawal of British troops from
northern Iran.

By late December 1920 the Iranian delegation in Moscow was
getting nearer to the final draft of a treaty. There was tentative
agreement on most issues: abrogation of all existing treaties
between Czarist Russia and Iran as well as treaties and agreements
between Russia and other countries concerning Iran; cancellation of
Iran's debts to Russia as well as all mortgages, pledges and securities given by Iran; the transfer to Iran of the Russian Bank with
all of its immovable properties; the surrender of Russian-built roads
and telegraph lines on Iranian soil; surrender of all Russian Government real property except the Legation and Consulate buildings;
equal rights of navigation on the Caspian Sea; abolition of extra-
territorial rights and privileges (capitulations); the establishment of
a mixed commission to fix tariffs on goods imported and exported by
either country to the other; and consular representation in various
provincial cities.[39]

It was remarkable that the draft contained no demand for the
abrogation of the 1919 Anglo-Persian Agreement nor any mention of
withdrawal of British troops from Iran. The Soviets' only demand
was that Iran receive their special envoy, Theodor Rothstein, as
the Soviet Minister in Tehran before a treaty was concluded.[40] The
question of withdrawal of Soviet troops and an undertaking to desist
from giving assistance to Iranian insurgents remained unresolved.
The Soviets argued that they had no troops in Iran. In reality
Moscow was waiting for British troop withdrawals.[41]

The reorganisation of the Cossack Division by Britain did not take place in the way Sepahdar had hoped. From the outset his colleagues in the Cabinet admonished Sepahdar that to have British officers command the Division was tantamount to acceptance of the military clause of the Agreement without parliamentary approval, something Pirnia had persistently refused to do. Gen. Ironside, without the express approval of his superiors, in fact somewhat surreptitiously assigned British officers to reorganise, train and command the division. These initiatives set in motion a series of events which were not anticipated by the Foreign Office and probably not even by Norman.

Sepahdar soon became regarded as a stop-gap Prime Minister not to be taken seriously by the Shah, the Legation, nor even by most of his colleagues, which allowed Ironside to pursue his own plans with respect to the Cossack Division. Sepahdar had been sincere in promising to convene parliament and to place the Agreement before it. He began to hesitate, however, because he was not sure of the loyalties of even pro-Government deputies. He was also apprehensive of the effect it might have on the talks in Moscow. The revelation of the bribe gave him further pause. Sepahdar's pursuit of Mas'oud (Sarem al Dowleh) to retrieve a portion of the bribe could not have endeared him to pro-Vosouq factions in his own Cabinet nor to the Foreign Office. Norman believed Vosouq, who was in London, had turned Curzon against Sepahdar and asked Lancelot Oliphant, the new head of the Eastern Department and formerly Curzon's Private Secretary, to ascertain the reasons for Curzon's distrust of Sepahdar.[42] Oliphant replied that Vosouq had had little to do with it. It was Curzon's own belief that Sepahdar was an 'extremely weak man with no courage'.[43]

The first signs that even Norman was losing patience with Sepahdar came in early January. Norman wrote to Curzon:

> Sepahdar's moderate capacity is unequal to the situation produced by the approaching departure of British troops. The withdrawal of the country's sole protection against Bolsheviks has totally driven him to seek support of demagogues who profess to see Persia's salvation in an agreement with the Russian Soviet Government... He has gained a high reputation for the negotiations now in progress in Moscow amongst these people but has lost the confidence of the upper and official classes.

Members of his Cabinet complained of a lack of consultation and hence some have turned against him and want him out of office. 'He honestly means to open the Parliament, but is doubtful the deputies will have the courage to attend in face of intimidation. He refuses to silence or exile vocal opponents of the Agreement.' At the end

Norman elicited the reaction of Curzon as to whether he would have any objection to Sepahdar being forced out of office and a 'strong reactionary prime minister' installed in his place.[44]

Curzon supported the idea to revert to a 'strong reactionary prime minister' and instructed Norman to consult Firouz. 'The advent of a strong Cabinet would be welcome, either for the purpose of conducting the affairs of the country from Tehran, or, should evacuation of the Capital become necessay, to provide a rallying point at Ispahan'.[45] Norman in desperation also suggested an incongruous cabinet including Farmanfarma, whom he had deprecated since arrival but nevertheless credited with possessing 'energy and experience', and Mostofi, who was 'popular and respected'.[46] Curzon must have been amused by the suggestion. There is no record of his having commented to Norman on his proposal but at a subsequent Cabinet meeting he caustically had remarked, 'Mr Norman has now accomplished the complete circle, having come back to one of the corrupt triumvirate, Firouz, of Sir Percy Cox's days'.[47]

Cox was an early admirer of Firouz, having known Farmanfarma and Firouz since 1906 when each, father and son, alternately had served as Governor of Kerman. He wrote to Curzon from Baghdad on 9 January that Firouz while in Mesopotamia had made a pilgrimage to Kazemain, Karbela and Najaf and had obtained a 'valuable fatwa proclaiming Bolshevism incompatible with Islam'. He added, 'Firouz is ready to continue his support of British policy and aims in Persia. His pluck and ability may be of much help to Norman and Sepahdar's Cabinet'.[48]

As mentioned earlier, Firouz with the support of Curzon and Cox might have become a key player in the events of early 1921 had he not overstayed in Europe and further delayed his arrival in Tehran by lengthy visits to his various properties in Kangavar and Hamadan. His month-long stay at his lands in western Iran may have had a two-fold purpose. Firouz was a lavish spender and probably had exhausted his funds in Paris and London.[49] These stops may therefore have been attempts to raise money. Firouz was also making certain he would be elected as member of parliament from the region. The exchange of telegrams with Norman indicates that he had a political timetable of his own. He probably and rightly believed that his involvement in the negotiations and conclusion of the 1919 Agreement and the bribery episode had made him so unpopular that for the time being he had little chance even of joining Sepahdar's Cabinet, let alone becoming Prime Minister. A seat in parliament would be more prudent and serve as the beginning of a political come-back.

Norman wrote to Curzon on 23 January that Firouz had telegraphed on 13 Janauary with the request to 'prevent the situation [in Tehran] from developing until he can talk it over with me', that is to keep Sepahdar in office a while longer. Norman had replied that events were moving too rapidly and doubted his ability to control them. Norman urged Firouz to hasten his arrival and wrote to Curzon that Firouz had twice before postponed his departure but now promised to start on 24 January. 'It shows how impossible it is to make even the most political Persian realise the value of time.' Norman had later seen Salar Lashkar, Firouz's younger brother, who had elaborated on Firouz's future plans. Firouz did not intend to enter the Cabinet of Sepahdar. He preferred that Sepahdar stay in office for some two or three months longer 'until he himself [Firouz] has overcome the dislike long felt for him by the public' because of his rapid rise in politics. 'He intends to establish his personal ascendancy in Parliament which he is confident of his ability to do'. He would then try for the premiership.[50]

On 15 January the Shah informed Norman that he intended to seek a replacement for Sepahdar and Norman had replied that the Shah was free to do what he wished. The Shah further informed Norman that he intended to ask Mostofi to form a cabinet which would include Farmanfarma and Ain al Dowleh.[51] Mostofi, before accepting the post, sent a message to Norman that if he undertook to form a government he would be unable to submit the Agreement to parliament. The Shah, informed of Mostofi's condition, withdrew the offer and asked Norman to whom he should turn. Norman replied that since Britain was 'no longer in a position to afford material help to keep any Prime Minister in office he would be unwilling to accept the responsibility of recommending anyone'. Faced with Norman's feigned or real indifference the Shah finally decided to ask Sepahdar to remain in office and to form a new Government 'with a strengthened Cabinet'. To Justify his indifference Norman informed Curzon that anyone he might recommend would be regarded as the nominee of the Legation and if he were to fail or be removed Britain's prestige would suffer.[52]

Norman's actions during this period are puzzling. The same activist Norman, who only two weeks earlier had sought a change of prime minister now appeared to resign himself to the continued do-nothing Government of Sepahdar. He could have persuaded Curzon to accept Mostofi as Prime Minister, a candidate Norman had thought of from the first day he arrived in Tehran. Faced with the events of the previous three months Curzon had nothing to lose.[53] It is difficult to accept at face value Norman's explanation that with the impending departure of British troops he had lost his clout. A more persuasive reason would be that Norman was privy to and working with Gen. Ironside on other plans which would reveal themselves shortly.

Curzon, apparently alarmed by Norman's new hands-off policy, wrote that although the Legation was now in a difficult position the Persian Government should not think 'Britain is indifferent to their future'. Norman was instructed to convey the message to the Shah and Sepahdar.[54] Norman accordingly called on Sepahdar on 24 January and reassured him that Britain was still 'vitally interested in Persia, her Government and Prime Minister'. Norman then pressed Sepahdar to call parliament into session and ascertain what changes in the Agreement were necessary to have it accepted. He further suggested that Sepahdar act swiftly to 'arrest and deport trouble-makers who are standing in the way of approval...' Sepahdar recounted the difficulties he had faced in forming a new Government and stated that he was roundly criticised for allowing British officers to take over command of the Cossacks, even on an unofficial basis. He suggested that his path would be easier if he could substitute Belgian for British officers. Curzon responded that the engagement of Belgian officers should not be encourged and it was useless at this late hour to talk of delaying the departure of British troops. He also deprecated any attempt to modify the terms of the Agreement.[55]

Undeterred and somewhat naively, Norman urged Curzon to accept modifications to the Agreement. No government would be willing to submit the Agreement to parliament in its present form and it was even more doubtful whether any prime minister would attempt to defend it. Norman further pressed that without modifications 'it would revive suspicion that ... we wish to rob Persia of her independence'.[56] It was useless to argue any further with Curzon, who had given up all hope of salvaging his policy. In private minutes prepared after a Cabinet meeting he had written:

> The responsibility for all the catastrophes that impend in Persia is that of the War Office to begin with, the India Office in the second place and the Cabinet in the third. No doubt when the debacle comes the Foreign Office will receive the entire blame.[57]

In another set of minutes he had confided:

> Everyone, Mr Norman, the Government of India, Sir Percy Cox, favours us with independent views. But as any one of them who wants anything done postulates the expenditure of money, which no one is prepared to find, the discussion is rather futile. Of course Sir Percy Cox is much nearer the mark than any of the others.[58]

Curzon's espousal of Cox's plan to divide Iran into at least four parts renders meaningless the high-sounding declaration by him and others concerning the territorial integrity of Iran. Curzon blamed everyone for failure of his policy except himself who had introduced a nineteenth century format to the post World War I era. He had taken Iranian acquiescence for granted. His comment that Sir Percy Cox was 'nearer the mark' indicates the old colonial streak in his thinking. Carve up Iran into several autonomous regions, play one faction against the other, then it would be easier to control. The despair of Curzon and his throwing up his hands gave even more freedom to any plans Ironside might devise, and to a lesser degree freed Norman to work on an *ad hoc* basis.

There had been no government in Iran now for nearly a month. Sepahdar had been unable to form a second cabinet acceptable to the Shah and it seemed unlikely that anyone else would be able to put together a government as long as the official British position was that any prime minister must immediately upon taking office convene parliament and put the Agreement before it. The Shah now had become amenable to having a 'reactionary' prime minister who would force the Agreement through parliament but only if British troops agreed to remain in northern Iran and use force to silence the opposition. As matters stood some 50 deputies had already declared themselves opposed to the Agreement in order to rebut charges that they might have been bribed. These 50, together with an entrenched opposition of some 30 other deputies, deprived the Legation of any chance of having the Agreement ratified. Since Curzon was adamantly opposed to any modification, the only option to salvage at least some prestige would have been for the British Government unilaterally to renounce the Agreement and use the delay on the part of Iran as a valid excuse. Another alternative would have been to bring into power a new Iranian government which would repudiate the Agreement.[59] Faced with these unpalatable alternatives, Curzon sulkily advised Norman that he was indifferent as to whether the Iranian parliament would ever be convened and denied ever having instructed Norman that the pre-condition for the appointment of Sepahdar had been that he convene parliament as soon as he took office. Curzon also sternly informed Norman that the British Government would never renounce the Agreement 'allowing the Persians to deny responsibility for having rejected' what could have been the salvation of Persia. Curzon had lowered his sights and his only hope now was 'to find a decent Government... deprecating the panic with which everyone at Tehran appeared to be unreasonably overwhelmed'.[60]

On the very day of Curzon's telegram, Sepahdar was finally successful in putting together a Cabinet acceptable to the Shah
although not much change of personnel had taken place. The
Cabinet was basically the same with several ministers moving later-
ally. The only significant change was the appointment of Hassan
Esfandiari (Mohtashem al Saltaneh) as Foreign Minister. Sepahdar
intended to issue a proclamation stating that as it was impossible to
accept the Anglo-Persian Agreement as drafted he planned to begin
negotiations with the British Government with a view to concluding
'a new and more advantageous agreement to Persia'.[61] The intended
declaration was a mere gesture. The Government of Sepahdar was
in no position to renegotiate the Agreement and Britain had no
desire to do so.

Firouz was left out of the new Cabinet. Relations between Firouz
and Norman had never been cordial and Norman's references to
Firouz in his dispatches are frosty. Firouz had been Cox's man and
had been involved in the bribery episode, neither of which would
have recommended him to Norman. Upon his return to Tehran at
his first meeting with Norman, Firouz in a complete turn-around
had stated that he had come to believe that Britain's interests would
be served better if Britain itself unilaterally renounced the
Agreement. He also expressed dissatisfaction with the terms of the
proposed Perso-Soviet Treaty and told Norman that he intended to
campaign against that treaty shortly. Firouz suggested that the
British Legation should let Sepahdar take office again. He predicted
the new Government would not last long and when it fell he himself
would be ready to assume office since the public by then would
demand a strong government.[62] Firouz was unaware that the leading
player on the Iranian stage was neither Curzon nor Norman but a
newcomer, Gen. Ironside, whom Firouz barely knew.

Ironside appears to have had a full schedule from the very first
day of his arrival in Iran on 1 October. Within the first two weeks he
had reviewed the condition of British troops in Qazvin, travelled
north to Manjeel, held numerous meetings with his subordinate officers, conferred with Norman in Tehran and flown back to Baghdad
to report personally to his superior, Gen. Haldane. During these two
weeks his first priority had been to improve the 'deplorable' condition of British troops. He had sent the sick and infirm soldiers to
Mesopotamia and the remaining troops had been relocated and
housed in better living quarters. Despite the condition and small
number of troops manning the defences at the Manjeel Pass he had
concluded very early that unless the Bolsheviks attacked in great
force the pass could be defended and held. Ironside had found

Norman extremely worried about the presence and influence of
Russian officers commanding the Cossack Division. By working with
Norman and reinforcing his resolve they had been able to force the
Shah to dismiss all the Russian officers. The Shah had appointed a
nonentity in the person of Sardar Homayoun (Qasem Khan Vali) as
the new commander of the Cossacks. With the tacit approval of
the Shah and the new Prime Minister, Ironside and Norman had
delegated the powers of command to a British officer, Lt Col.
Henry Smyth.

In these manoeuvres Ironside completely ignored Gen. William
Dickson who had been sent to Tehran for the express purpose of
heading the British team designated to reorganise the Iranian armed
forces. Ironside, who would brook no interference with his plans,
described Dickson as 'not a man of outstanding ability [and] not a
soldier. He has commanded nothing [and now] he has got involved
in politics... He ought to go away'.[63] Ironside, unaware that he himself was becoming involved in politics, had contempt for political
military men. The fact that Dickson was seconded from the military
to the Foreign Office and received his orders from the Foreign Office
probably further strained relations between them. Dickson's having
been born in Iran and having spent most of his life in the East
meant little to Ironside. Furthermore, Ironside himself being presumably something of a linguist was not overly impressed by
Dickson's knowledge of Persian and other Eastern languages. More
important, the Foreign Office had wanted Dickson to assume the
responsibility of organising the Cossacks,[64] which did not sit well
with Ironside who tolerated no intrusion and wanted his subordinates to be answerable only to him. Norman appears to have had
difficulties with Dickson as well and aligned himself with Ironside.
Dickson was effectively rendered useless from early November and
his counsel was not sought for the brief remainder of his stay in
Iran. Relations between Norman and Dickson worsened and
Norman was forced to ask for Dickson's recall.[65] Dickson believed
that it was in Britain's interest to support and work with Iranian
nationalist elements and was disappointed in Norman's turn
around. He appears to have been against the forced resignation of
Pirnia and the appointment of Sepahdar. Dickson returned to
England in late February thoroughly embittered and received a cool
reception at the Foreign Office.[66]

Col. Smyth had been one of several British officers employed by
Vosouq to organise the Azarbaijan Gendarmerie. When that province
almost seceded from Iran, Vosouq gave up the idea of an independent Gendarmerie and decided to merge all its units to become part

of the unified force as envisaged in the 1919 Agreement. Smyth remained in Iran hoping to become a member of the British military advisery force. There is no evidence as to whether he had known Ironside before the latter's arrival in Iran but he soon caught Ironside's attention and became his most trusted military officer. Smyth's acquaintance with the Persian language also recommended him to Ironside and though outranked by other officers he was selected as the senior British officer with the duty of reorganising the Cossacks and converting the Division into a more efficient force. He became privy to whatever plans Ironside and Norman had and saw both frequently, often acting as a go-between.[67] The first mention of Smyth in a report to Curzon is on 25 January when Norman introduced him as 'the British officer who for the past two months or so has been unofficially and almost secretly working amongst the Cossacks [in the Qazvin area] with the result that their working efficiency has been greatly increased'.[68]

Although Ironside had been given enough leeway to deal with Starosselsky and other contingencies as he saw fit,[69] his activities soon began to worry the War Office. Field Marshall Wilson wrote in his diary 'Tiny [Ironside] wants to take over the whole thing and kick out Dickson and kick out Starosselsky ... I don't want to get involved in that beastly country.'[70] In addition to the reservations of the War Office, Ironside was mindful of Curzon's admonition to both Norman and himself that success was imperative and they would be held responsible for the failure of any action they had initiated.[71] Both Ironside and Norman knew they had assumed a risk in forcing the resignation of Pirnia, a popular Prime Minister. They were elated of course by the removal of Starosselsky, one of the major irritants to British policy in Iran, but they had gambled that the Cossacks now would become a more effective force to withstand the threat of Bolshevik rebels and guarantee the safe evacuation of British troops scheduled for early spring. An additional gamble was the assumption that the new Prime Minister would support any plans Norman and Ironside might devise.

NOTES ON CHAPTER 5
Further details of publications and documents in Bibliography

1   Mehdi Bamdad, *Tarikh Rejal Iran Quroun 12, 13, 14* (*Dictionary of National Biography of Iran: Twelfth, Thirteenth, Fourteenth Centuries*), vol. 3, pp 51–53.
2   FO 371/3873, Norman to Curzon, 13 June 1920.
3   FO 1011/126, note from Norman to Loraine, 25 December 1923.
4   FO 371/6415, Imperial Bank of Persia to Foreign Office, September 1921.
5   FO 371/6416, Imperial Bank of Persia to Foreign Office, 6 October 1921.
6   DBFP, doc. no. 571, Norman to Curzon, 28 October 1920.
7   DBFP, doc. no. 574, Norman to Curzon, 1 November 1920.
8   Maj. Gen. Sir Edmund Ironside, *High Road to Command*, pp 147 and 148.
9   DoS, Quarterly Report, No. 10, Caldwell to Secretary of State, 15 January 1921.
10 DBFP, doc. no. 573, Curzon to Norman, 29 October 1920.
11 DBFP, doc. no. 576, Curzon to Norman, 5 November 1920.
12 DBFP, doc. no. 577, Norman to Curzon, 5 November 1920.
13 DBFP, doc. no. 582, Norman to Curzon, 19 November 1920.
14 DBFP, doc. no. 585, Curzon to Norman, 25 November 1920.
15 DBFP, doc. no. 587, Norman to Curzon, 25 November 1920. Refer to Chapter 2 for the genesis of the bribe and whether any part of it was returned.
16 FO 371/6424, Norman to Curzon, 16 November 1920.
17 DBFP, doc. no. 604, Curzon to Norman, 8 December 1920; FO 371/4910 of same date.
18 DBFP, doc. no. 610, Norman to Curzon, 12 December 1920 and FO 371/4910 of same date.
19 FO 371/4910, Norman to Curzon, 15 December 1920.
20 CAB/23/23, 3 November 1920.
21 DBFP, doc. no. 603, Curzon to Norman, 8 December 1920; DBFP, doc. no. 625, Curzon to Norman, 1 January 1921.
22 DBFP, doc. no. 616, Memorandum by G.P. Churchill, 20 December 1920.
23 DBFP, doc. no. 624, Memorandum by Montague, 31 December 1920.
24 DBFP, doc. no. 626, Norman to Curzon, 3 January 1921.
25 DBFP, doc. no. 628, Curzon to Norman, 3 January 1921.
26 DBFP, doc. no. 636, Curzon to Norman, 6 January 1921.
27 DBFP, doc. no. 638, Norman to Curzon, 7 January 1921.
28 DBFP, doc. no. 641, Norman to Curzon, 8 January 1921.
29 DBFP, doc. no. 644, Norman to Curzon, 12 January 1921.
30 DBFP, doc. no. 651, Norman to Curzon, 19 January 1921.
31 DBFP, doc. no. 654, Curzon to Norman, 20 January 1921.
32 DBFP, doc. no. 656, Norman to Curzon, 15 January 1921.
33 DBFP, doc. no. 658, Norman to Curzon, 20 January 1921.
34 DBFP, doc. no. 660, Curzon to Norman, 21 January 1921 and FO 416/68 of same date.
35 DBFP, doc. no. 662, Lord Chelmsford to Montague, 22 January 1921.
36 DBFP, doc. no. 667, Norman to Curzon, 28 January 1921.

37 FO 416/98, Bullard to Halifax, 7 February 1940.

38 DBFP, doc. no. 668, Sir Percy Cox to Montague, 29 January 1921.

39 DBFP, doc. no. 621, Norman to Curzon, 27 December 1920.

40 DBFP, doc. no. 635, Norman to Curzon, 6 January 1921.

41 DBFP, doc. no. 674, Norman to Curzon, 10 February 1921.

42 DBFP, doc. no. 620, Norman to Oliphant, 27 December 1920.

43 DBFP, doc. no. 623, Oliphant to Norman, 29 December 1920.

44 DBFP, doc. no. 648, Norman to Curzon, 13 January 1921.

45 DBFP, doc. no. 652, Curzon to Norman, 15 January 1921.

46 FO 371/6399; Norman to Curzon, 13 January 1921.

47 CAB/14/1, Minutes by Curzon, 15 January 1921.

48 FO 371/6399, Cox to Curzon, 9 January 1921.

49 Firouz was in debt upon his return to Tehran and his father had to come to his assistance on several occasions. He had accumulated unpaid bills in London, including those from his tailor and for the purchase of a Rolls Royce: FO 371/14542, Clive to Henderson, 19 March 1930.

50 FO 371/6399, Norman to Curzon, 23 January 1921.

51 Ibid. and DBFP, doc. no. 655 of same date.

52 Ibid.

53 FO 416/68, Norman to Curzon, 23 January 1921.

54 FO 371/6399, Curzon to Norman, 21 January 1921.

55 FO 371/6400, Norman to Curzon, 25 January 1921.

56 DBFP, doc. no. 669, Norman to Curzon, 25 January 1921.

57 Ibid.; CAB/2/2, Minutes by Curzon; 25 January 1921.

58 Ibid.; CAB/10/2.

59 DBFP, doc. no. 676, Norman to Curzon, 11 February 1921.

60 DBFP, doc. no. 678, Curzon to Norman, 17 February 1921.

61 DBFP, doc. no. 679, Norman to Curzon, 17 February 1921.

62 FO 371/6401, Norman to Curzon, 16 February 1921.

63 Houshang Sabahi, British Policy in Persia 1918–1925, p 50; quoting from the unpublished Ironside Diaries.

64 FO 371/4914, M. Hankey to Foreign Office, 4 November 1920.

65 FO 371/6427, Norman to Curzon, 19 January 1921.

66 Donald N. Wilber, Riza Shah Pahlavi, pp 50–51.

67 FO 371/6403, Norman to Curzon, 1 March 1921.

68 FO 371/6400, Norman to Curzon, 25 January 1921. In at least one Foreign Office dispatch Smyth is refered to as Colonel R.C. Smyth. On another occasion, Smyth is spelt 'Smythe'. Peter Avery, in his book Modern Iran, refers to 'Smythe'.

69 DBFP, doc. no. 561, War Office to Haldane, 6 October 1920.

70 Houshang Sabahi, British Policy in Persia 1918–1925, p 51: quoting from Wilson's Diary, 27 October 1920.

71 DBFP, doc. no. 573, Curzon to Norman, 29 October 1920.

6

Prelude to
the Coup

The term 'success', as used by Curzon, appears to have had varying connotations for the major personalities involved. For Curzon himself success had come to mean the speedy ratification of the Agreement with no modifications, tying Iran irrevocably to Britain, creating yet another buffer zone for the defence of India.

For Norman success was more modest. It meant the elimination of any prospect of a Bolshevik Iran and the continued preponderance of British influence in the region. To accomplish this the Iranian armed forces, especially the Cossacks, had to be strengthened. Concurrent with the build-up of the Cossacks the government of the day had to have some support amongst the populace and not be burdened with the odium of the Agreement. If this meant modification and amendment of the Agreement or even its renunciation by either Iran or Britain, so be it. Britain would not suffer from it. Norman had toyed with a nationalist Prime Minister in the person of Pirnia and things had not worked out well for several reasons: the poisoned atmosphere left behind by Vosouq, the secessionist movements, and Pirnia's refusal to sacrifice his principles, which to Norman may have appeared mere obstinacy. With Sepahdar things were bound to be smoother. Sepahdar had not been tainted as Vosouq had and unlike Pirnia 'would do as he is told'. Equally important in Norman's mind was the replacement of the lethargic Gen. Champain with the active and forceful Ironside who would take care of the strengthening of the Cossacks.

For Ironside success primarily meant the unhampered and safe withdrawal of British troops from northern Iran, a reorganised Cossack Division, ultimately commanded by Iranian officers and not hostile to Britain, which would deal with insurgency, and a strong central government able to restore calm and maintain order. Ironside had also realised that the introduction of the 1919 Agreement had tilted the balance against Britain and the best that could be hoped for was a return to the *status quo ante*. He wrote in his Diary on 2 November 1920:

> The more I consider this show, the more I think, one ought to get out of it. The state of affairs which allow us to be opposed in a state of actual war to a greatly inferior Bolshevik army, without being able to deal with it, is unsatisfactory... The Bolshevik says that he is only helping the would-be Soviet element in Persia while we are helping the old corrupt capitalist system. We cannot complain his helping Kouchek Khan if we back the Shah. We are both mixing up in the internal politics of Persia. We want a status quo ante and they want a revolution.[1]

The fact that Ironside felt the Bolshevik forces in Iran were inferior and that Moscow had its hands full on other fronts and could not reinforce or upgrade them was crucial to his thinking. If Starosselsky were able to score a victory here and there against the rebels, a reinforced and better-led Cossack Division surely could do as well. What worried Ironside were reports from Tehran of internal dissention and the paralysis of the Central Government. Col. Folkstone, the British Military Attaché at the Legation in Tehran, sent a report in early January:

> Among the professional intriguers there is a tendency to combine and work together on socialist lines. Hitherto these intriguers worked against each other. At the same time the upper classes who have a stake in the country are busily engaged in competing for government posts and show no sign of combination to combat the Bolshevik peril.

In a later report he added:

> Discontent is rife amongst the men of the Central Brigade and the Cossacks stationed in Tehran owing to non-receipt of pay and the work of propagandists. Yesterday men of the Central Brigade beat a battalion commander, and this morning the carriage of the Cossack Division Commander was held up by men who showered abuse on him.[2]

Two weeks later Smyth submitted an equally disturbing report to Ironside:

> The Persian Government had for the last two months been terrorised by Bolshevik Committees. On these Committees numerous Persian officers are serving, in fact there is actually a Committee of officers. These Committees prevent the Majlis meeting, stop all effective government and are simply a preparation for actual Bolshevism.

Smyth had discussed with Sardar Homayoun, the new Commander of the Cossacks, the necessity to move against and 'put down' these committees. Although Sardar Homayoun had promised to take action Smyth was gloomy and reported that 'the Government lacked the courage to carry the thing through'.[3]

Even before receiving these alarming reports Ironside had realised that a forceful Iranian commander at the head of the Cossacks was essential. In a situation report to the War Office dated 8 December 1920 he had written that a capable Persian officer must command the Cossacks and 'that would solve many difficulties and enable us to depart in peace and honour'.[4] The Shah, however, remained an obstacle. Norman knew the Shah counted heavily on the loyalty of the Cossacks for protection and was sensitive as to who would command them. While urging Starosselsky's dismissal Norman had advised the Shah to appoint his favourite uncle Nosrat al Saltaneh Commander of the Cossacks.[5] Norman's recommendation served a two-fold purpose. The Shah would be assured as to the loyalty of the Cossacks by having a close and trusted relative as its commander. Additionally having an Iranian figurehead in charge of the Cossacks would make it easier for Ironside to place British officers in effective control. For reasons not entirely clear the Shah appointed Sardar Homayoun, a little-known courtier with no record of any combat or command experience. His duties had merely consisted of comanding troops which escorted the Shah at various ceremonial functions. The Shah probably chose not to appoint his uncle in the aftermath of the financial irregularities in the Cossack Division. It is also possible that his uncle was not interested in the position. Nosrat al Saltaneh was known to be seeking positions that provided a lucrative income. The Shah's appointment of Sardar Homayoun was not objected to by either Norman or Ironside who for their purposes saw no difference between Sardar Homayoun and Nosrat al Saltaneh.

The first recorded meeting between Ironside and Sardar Homayoun took place at the end of October. Sardar Homayoun confessed to Ironside that 'he was not a soldier... He had been appointed head of the Cossacks to ensure loyalty to the Shah'. He was ill-at-ease and asked to be introduced to the officers of the Division. Ironside answered that he would introduce him to Col. Smyth who in turn would introduce him to the officers.

Sardar was hopeless. He did not shake hands with any of the Persian officers and barely said a word to them. They all bowed to him. He did not thank them for what they had done at Rasht nor did he tell them a better future awaited them now that they would be under their own officers. He had no intention of living in Camps or near them.

5. *Abdol Hosein Mirza Farmanfarmaian (Farmanfarma)*. The former prime minister was one of the most influential politicians of his time. His acquiescence to the accession of Reza Shah helped to make for a smooth transition of power.

6. Hassan Mostofi (Mostofi al Mamalek III). Prime minister on numerous occasions during the period before and after Reza Shah's accession, Mostofi was a decent and much loved politician who nevertheless failed to provide a strong leadership.

7. Hassan Vosouq (Vosouq al Dowleh). As prime minister between 1918 and 1920 he was the leader of the 'triumvirate' which, through the 1919 Agreement with the British, wanted to manoeuvre Iran into the British Empire.

Ironside walked with Smyth and Sardar Homayoun amongst the troops and it was evident that the soldiers had no winter clothes. Even the officers had lightweight clothing not suitable for the severe winter months ahead. 'They were all shivering. Many of them had no boots.' Sardar Homayoun had no suggestions or comments. Smyth assured Ironside that within a week all the troops would have new clothing. He was 'concentrating the next month on good feeding and physical exercise'.[6]

It did not take long for Ironside to realise that Sardar Homayoun was 'a useless little creature' and he decided to find a deputy for him at once. On previous tours Ironside had noticed that the 'Tabriz battalion had looked better and more cheery'. Furthermore, he was advised by Smyth that the Tabriz battalion had given a good account of itself and beaten off a Bolshevik attack north of Manjeel. They had then withdrawn to Qazvin for 'refitting'. Ironside enquired about their commanding officer, who was subsequently introduced to him. The officer, Reza Khan, 'was well over 6 feet tall, broad shoulders and a most distinguished face. His hooked nose and sparkling eyes gave him a look of animation.' Reza Khan was 'shivering from a bout of malaria but handled himself well and never went on sick leave'. Ironside, sufficiently impressed, immediately 'decided to make him Commander of the Cossack Brigade at least temporarily and at once'. Smyth was given the task to 'control the administration and finances of the Cossacks and Reza Khan the duty to reorganise them and concentrate on their training'.[7]

Ironside by now also had prepared a full-length report on his observations in Iran and 'not wishing to commit my report to a cipher telegram' decided to go to Baghdad to report personally to Gen. Haldane. On his return Ironside saw the Shah for the first time. He described this memorable meeting as follows:

I saw a fat young man in a grey frock suit wriggling and nervous at my words. I thought it painful to see such a wretched specimen of a man in so great a position. He was sad to see the Russian officers leave. He would never allow flagrant embezzlement as had occurred under Russian officers...

We should not replace them with British officers. Persia won't accept it. He then changed the subject. The only safe roads were those under British control... therefore could we help him. He wanted to transfer some money to his bank in Bombay. The only safe way would be by British convoy to Baghdad. At first I hardly understood what he required me to do but gradually I elicited the fact that he had some Persian tomans in large silver coins the size of French five Frank pieces. The value of this enormous weight of silver amounted to about £500,000. Did he understand the weight, the number of trucks? I told him we needed Persian money for our troops. Why not sell it to the Imperial Bank. He

brushed it aside. I said I think what he is doing is not right... He looked
at me with a wry smile, while he said, 'Peut etre que oui, mon general,
mais n'oubliez pas qu'au fond tout le monde est egoiste'... what could
Persia do with such a ruler? Was it a wonder that she had sunk so low.
She needed a strong man to bring her through... It had been a continued
mystery to me how she had been able to preserve her independence.[8]

Ironside returned to Tehran again on 31 December and spent the
evening with James McMurray, the Manager of the Imperial Bank.
On New Year's Day he took a long walk in the streets of Tehran and
saw only dejected faces and despondent people. Once again Ironside
confided in his Diaries, 'When would the strong man come to rule
Persia?' On 14 January he visited the Cossack camp again and was
pleased that the Iranian troops appeared efficient and disciplined.
He was especially heartened by reports from Smyth that Reza Khan
had fulfilled all of his expectations. 'The real life and soul of the
show was Reza Khan, a colonel, the man I liked much before. Smyth
says he is a good man.' Together with Smyth it was decided that
Sardar Homayoun's continued presence in the camp served no purpose and could be a disruptive influence. Ironside instructed Smyth
to 'give Homayoun leave to visit his estates'. This decision effectively
gave complete control of the Cossacks to Reza Khan.[9]

In mid January Bolshevik forces bore heavy losses in Poland. In
the Caucasus they also suffered reverses at the hands of the Turks.
Ironside became convinced that with these defeats the Bolsheviks
were in no position to mount any large operation in Iran in the near
future. 'If we left the Persian Cossacks in sufficiently good shape to
deal with the disintegrating forces of Kouchek Khan there would
be little danger to the Persian state for a long time to come.' At the
end of January the forces of Kouchek Khan, having heard of the
impending departure of British troops, decided to test them as well
as the Cossacks in the area. In a minor skirmish near Manjeel pro-
Bolshevik forces lost some 30 men and 20 prisoners were taken.[10]

Beginning in January there are recurrent references in the
Diaries to the need of a strong man as saviour of Iran. It appears
that Ironside from about this time began to expand his outlook. He
was not merely thinking of a safe and orderly departure of British
troops from northern Iran but also the installation of a strong leader
at the head of the Iranian Government. Ironside believed he had
found such a leader in the person of Reza Khan.

The southern strategy advocated by Cox, G.P. Churchill and
tacitly endorsed by Curzon whereby southern Iran would be ruled
by regional kings or tribal chieftains was rebuffed by the India Office
and turned down by the Treasury which refused to finance the

scheme. Additionally, APOC was not sure that the Bakhtiari Khans could control their tribesmen sufficiently to ensure the safety of the oil regions. The shifting loyalties of the Bakhtiaris during World War I gave them further doubts. Curzon, who until very recently had involved himself with every detail in Iran, gradually began to lose interest. Norman had a freer hand in devising day-to-day policy. Curzon had initially agreed to bear the cost of reorganisation and training of the Cossacks once Starosselsky was removed but soon changed his mind and forced Norman and Ironside to improvise and obtain the needed funds from other sources. Norman telegraphed Curzon on 25 November, 'Your telegram of 5 November gave me the assurance that His Majesty's Government were prepared to assume the entire cost of reorganisation of the Cossacks. I cannot blame [the Persian Government] if they accuse me of a breach of faith.' Norman pleaded in vain with Curzon to abide by his promise and quoted Generals Ironside and Dickson to the effect that the Cossack Division had been reduced to a dangerous state of indiscipline and inefficiency. The only remedy was 'to put British officers in command and have complete financial control'. Norman strongly hinted that he and Ironside would go ahead with their plan whether or not funding by the Foreign Office was approved.[11]

Even with his strengthened resolve Norman knew he was still in a difficult position. He had acted without express instructions in forcing out two successive Prime Ministers, and neither move had had the desired result. His present choice as Prime Minister, the submissive Sepahdar, had not worked out any better. The Bolshevik threat still existed and the Cossacks' capabilities had not improved. Therefore, from late November Norman became receptive to any proposal to combat the Bolsheviks and install a more forceful individual in place of Sepahdar. An opportunity presented itself in early December when Sepahdar refused to place British officers in command of the Cossacks for fear that it would lead to the fall of his Government. Norman met with two newcomers to the scene, Seyyed Zia al Din (Tabataba'i) and Abdol Hosein Khan Sardar Mo'azam (Teimurtash), who proposed the creation of a new military unit numbering 15,000 to counter any attack by Bolshevik forces on Tehran. They further suggested the reorganisation of the Gendarmerie and police, putting these troops under the nominal control of the Ministry of War but effectively under the command of British officers. The plan could be implemented at a cost of £1 million. Norman recommended the scheme to Curzon and suggested that the money could come out of the £2 million loan.[12] At later meetings Teimurtash pursued the plan and argued that the first step should be to stop terrorists in Tehran who prevent recently-elected deputies from opening the new parliament.[13] Curzon, in his newly-assumed hands-off and aloof attitude, summarily rejected the proposal. 'There will be no new expenditure of money until Parliament meets and either accepts or rejects the Agreement.'[14]

The names of Seyyed Zia and Teimurtash will be heard often. Seyyed Zia's prominence would last a mere three months and Teimurtash's for over 12 years. Seyyed Zia has been mentioned before as the editor of the newspaper *Ra'ad*, one of only two Tehran newspapers[15] which consistently and without any reservations supported Britain and Czarist Russia in World War I, the Government of Vosouq and the 1919 Agreement. He would soon assume an importance that probably no-one in Iran or the Foreign Office ever visualised. Teimurtash's rise would be less meteoric but by 1926 he would become the alter ego and the voice of the new ruler of the country.

Seyyed Zia* came to the fore by virtue of his unquestioned and unequivical support of Vosouq and the 1919 Anglo-Persian Agreement. As a reward for his support Vosouq sent him to Baku in early 1920 as the Iranian representative at the Conference of Caucasia and Azarbaijan to conclude a commercial treaty. He returned in May 1920 when the Bolsheviks were about to overrun Baku. On his return Vosouq's Government had gradually weakened and Vosouq

---

* Seyyed Zia al Din, who later adopted the surname of Tabataba'i, was born in Shiraz in 1888 (British Foreign Office records give Seyyed Zia's birth date as 1891) and died in 1969. His father Seyyed Ali Yazdi was an itinerent clergyman who had fathered over 30 children from 15 wives. Seyyed Ali was a good pulpit speaker and had initially supported the cause of Mohammad Ali Shah and the absolutists. He soon converted to the constitutionalist side and after the fall of Mohammad Ali Shah was elected to the second session of parliament from Shiraz as the representative of the clergy. For reasons unknown he never took his seat and continued his activities on the pulpit circuit. Seyyed Zia was taken as an infant to Tabriz and had some schooling there. At the age of fifteen he moved with his family to Tehran, and in his early twenties began publishing the newspaper *Sharq*. The publication was critical of almost every prime minister of the day, and it was not long before he was accused of sedition. To escape imprisonment he sought refuge at the British and Ottoman Legations. Denied entry by both he was given asylum by the Austrian Legation. After a general amnesty he travelled to Paris ostensibly to further his education. He visited London briefly in 1911 and returned to Iran in 1913. In 1914 he began publishing a new newspaper *Ra'ad* which was in complete sympathy with the Allies in World War I. Between 1914 and 1918 he married and had two sons and a daughter of whom very little is known.[16]

was forced to resign. Seyyed Zia was friendless and could not establish any relationship with Pirnia's Government.[17] Toward the end of Pirnia's premiership Seyyed Zia began to think of himself as a potential cabinet member and even prime minister. More than six years of unquestioned loyalty to British interests in Iran had made him well known to some members of the British Legation but still he was not taken entirely seriously and had his detractors. Lt Col. Meade, who had known Seyyed Zia from his days in Shiraz, would later report to Lancelot Oliphant of the Eastern Department of the Foreign Office that he had been a 'mere mountebank in Shiraz'.[18] Even Norman, though appreciative of Seyyed Zia's services, had kept his distance and did not consider him ministerial material, if for no other reason than the fact that he was too closely identified with Britain and was generally known as 'a notorious Anglophile'.[19]

In the summer of 1920 Seyyed Zia was given the opportunity he had been looking for. The Imperial Bank insisted that drafts and cheques drawn on it by the Iranian Government should be examined and approved by the British Legation before they were honoured and negotiated. Somehow Seyyed Zia was chosen as one of the intermediaries for this task and as a result became acquainted with most members of the Legation. As a facilitator for these financial transactions he gained direct access to Sepahdar and members of his Cabinet. The appointment to Baku, his access to the Legation and now his contacts with the top levels of the Iranian Government gave him a status he had long sought.[20]

At about the same time he formed the Tehran branch of the 'Iron Committee' (Komiteh Ahan), a social/political group originally established in Esfahan under British auspices. The group met at regular intervals at his house in Zargandeh in northern Tehran, very close to the summer residences of the British and Russian envoys. Some eight or nine individuals attended the gatherings with regularity with five or six others making occasional visits. Most of the members were fairly prominent in political and social circles and had ambitions of higher office. Almost all were trusted anglophiles and greatly apprehensive of the growing Bolshevik influence. The regulars were Hosein Khan Adl al Molk (Dadgar) who was Under Secretary of the Ministry of Interior in Sepahdar's Cabinet and a former member of parliament; Mansour al Saltaneh (Adl) and Mo'azez al Dowleh (Nabavi), both high-ranking members of the Ministry of Foreign Affairs; Epikian, an Iranian Armenian who was a leader in the Armenian community; Karim Khan Rashti, an influential and wealthy land-owner from Gilan; Mo'adab al Dowleh (Nafisi), a French-trained physician with an extensive clientele; and Seyyed Mohammad (Taddayon), who had been elected to the yet-to-be convened Fourth Parliament. Occasional participants were Mahmoud Khan Modir al Molk (Jam), a future Prime Minister; Mohammad Taqi Bahar (Malek al Sho'ara), a well-known essayist, literary critic and an important widely-read poet.[21]

Amongst the regular and devoted members of the group were also two Gendarme officers, Col. Kazem Khan Sayyah and Maj. Mas'oud Khan Keyhan. Kazem Khan had served in the Ottoman army during the war and had been captured by British forces on the southern front in Mesopotamia. As a prisoner of war he had been exiled to and imprisoned in India. Seyyed Zia had known Kazem Khan as a youngster in Tabriz and later from his days in Paris, and had used his influence for Kazem Khan's release and return to Iran. Maj. Mas'oud Khan had studied in France and compiled a distinguished record of service in the Gendarmerie. More significantly both officers had served under Smyth in the Gendarmerie in Tabriz and were held in high regard by him. This contact with Smyth was to serve Seyyed Zia well.[22]

After his return from Baku Seyyed Zia had presented the Legation with some far-fetched proposals. In late June 1920 he had proposed that he be appointed Governor General of the Caspian provinces in order to conduct a propaganda campaign against the Bolsheviks. Pirnia had summarily rejected the proposal although some members of the British Legation and the British Military Advisory Team had backed it.[23] Soon afterwards Seyyed Zia, in collaboration with two British officers, Col. Wickham and Maj. Edmonds, came up with a plan to assist British troops in dislodging Kouchek Khan in Gilan.[24] As mentioned before, in December 1920 he had advanced plans to defend Tehran against the Bolsheviks by the creation of a new army.[25] In a memorandum by G.P. Churchill, Seyyed Zia is described as 'a young man who had occasionally unfolded the most fantastic projects with himself as dictator'.[26] These plans, although dismissed by the Foreign Office and described as 'fantastic', enhanced Seyyed Zia's reputation as one of the very few Iranians who were willing to do something to forestall a Bolshevik takeover of his country. Although he held no office he could be ignored no longer by the Legation. Norman in fact had recommended the last of Seyyed Zia's plans to Curzon. Probably by the end of 1920 Norman began to consider Seyyed Zia as the possible 'reactionary Prime Minister' he had been searching for.

Norman's newly-acquired admiration for Seyyed Zia should come as no surprise. From the exchange of telegrams with the Foreign Office it is clear Norman was once again sadly disappointed in his choice of prime minister. Sepahdar was getting nowhere and Norman's stock with Curzon had plumetted to a new low. From late December Sepahdar was kept in office only because no consensus on a replacement could be reached. The search for a 'strong reactionary leader' was now a serious proposition. Much to Curzon's amusement Norman had come full circle, from the autocratic but effective Vosouq to the servile but useless Sepahdar and now again searching for a strong reactionary prime minister. It was doubtful, however, that Curzon would accept a newcomer such as Seyyed Zia. Norman hoped that Vosouq, who was in London and still enjoyed the confidence of Curzon, would put in a good word for Seyyed Zia for the support he had given him over the years. Norman began to lay the groundwork by having numerous conversations with Seyyed Zia, who probably told him of his plans to reform the finances and administration of Iran. Seyyed Zia had never hidden the fact that he was a steadfast supporter of British policy in Iran and intended to continue his support. He also must have told Norman that he would have no choice but to conclude the Perso-Soviet treaty and if he were going to be an effective premier he must renounce the 1919 Agreement. Neither of these proposed steps posed a serious problem for Norman. Curzon had surely given up hope of ever realising the ratification of the Agreement, and a renunciation by Seyyed Zia would put an end to everyone's misery. Norman later would reason that whether the Agreement were ratified or renounced, Seyyed Zia intended to bring its provisions into practical effect. British personnel would be employed, independent of the Agreement, to reorganise the army and the country's finances. It would be of no importance if Iran were to employ a few nationals of countries friendly to Britain such as Belgians. Iran under Seyyed Zia would remain firmly in Britain's orbit with all British economic and other interests intact.

On a parallel track Ironside was following an agenda in the Iranian military which sat well with Norman's. The two plans appeared to complement each other, which in fact they later did. Ironside made periodic visits to both the British camp in Qazvin and the Cossacks stationed at Aqa Baba some 15 miles west of Qazvin. In early January he saw Reza Khan again and commented that his troops had gained in efficiency and discipline. Smyth told Ironside that good nutrition, good supervision and intensive training had enabled the Cossacks to stand on their own feet and British officers soon could be withdrawn. Ironside began to ponder the date on which the Cossacks could be 'released from our control. It has to be a month before the withdrawal of our troops to Baghdad'. Ironside, remained uneasy about their 'release' and decided to confront Reza Khan directly about the terms and conditions for ceding control of the Cossack Division. Ironside set two conditions. Reza Khan had to give his word 'not to take any offensive action [against withdrawing British troops] or we would turn on him'. Secondly, whatever plans Reza Khan may have, Ironside told him he must also pledge 'not to take any action or use force to depose the Shah'.

> To both my requests he gave a solemn promise that he would do as I wished. He talked very openly to me, expressing his dislike of politicians who controlled the Medjliss for their own benefit. He was a soldier and came from a family of soldiers... He seemed to me a fearless man who had his country's good at heart.

This conversation with Reza Khan confirmed Ironside's initial view that he had found the right man who would ensure the safe withdrawal of British troops and prevent a Bolshevik takeover of Tehran. Ironside concluded the entry in his diary with, 'Persia needed a leader in difficult times ahead and here was undoubtedly a man of outstanding value'.[27]

It is clear from the Diaries that Ironside had become convinced that Iran needed a military strongman who would impose order on the country even if this required a forcible takeover of the government. The several entries in his diary relating to 'release' of the Cossacks from British control meant in effect that Reza Khan could move against Tehran to impose his will in the selection of a new government. Ironside had attempted to make Reza Khan's actions bloodless by trying to convince the Shah to appoint him officially as the commander of the armed forces. The Shah had refused to appoint someone unknown and with no proven loyalty to him to command forces which had traditionally served as his personal bodyguards.[28] In mid February Ironside made another attempt and confided in his diary: 'I have only seen one man [Reza Khan] who could save Persia. Would the Shah have the sense to put his trust in this man?'[29]

On 2 February Ironside was instructed by Gen. Haldane to be in Baghdad no later than 20 February to continue on to Cairo for a meeting called by Winston Churchill, newly-appointed Colonial Secretary, to review the British position in the Middle East. The last recorded meeting between Ironside and Reza Khan is on 17 February, the day before his departure from Iran. Ironside wrote in his diary:

> I have interviewed Reza Khan and have put him definitely in charge of the Cossacks. He is a man and the straightest... I wondered whether I ought to have anything in writing but I decided in the end that writing would be no good. If Reza wants to play false he will and he will merely say that any promises he made were made under duress and that he wouldn't fulfill them. I made two things clear to Reza when I agreed to let him go: 1– That

he mustn't shoot me from behind as he goes or as I go. That would lead to his humiliation and good to nobody except the revolutionary party. 2– That the Shah on no account must be deposed. Reza promised glibly enough and I shook hands with him. I have told Smyth to let him go gradually.[30]

The term 'to let him go' in this context can have two meanings. It could mean merely that Reza Khan would soon be released from control and supervision by British officers and could run the Cossack Division in any manner he deemed appropriate. If one were to accept this interpretation it would naturally follow that Ironside had no idea that Reza Khan was planning a coup or some drastic action to topple the Government in Tehran. The other interpretation is that Ironside had been aware from early January that Reza entertained taking drastic action which could entail a military coup. There are several clues that lead one to accept the latter. To begin with there are repeated entries in the Diary in which Ironside sees Reza Khan not just as the new head of the Cossacks but as a 'leader', one 'who could save Persia'. Ironside knew Reza Khan believed the politicians in Tehran to be selfish and corrupt and had to be removed from office. Furthermore, Ironside himself believed Iran needed a leader to initiate reforms and bring stability to the country. If the term 'to let him go' merely meant release from supervision of British officers why did Ironside make Reza Khan promise not to take any action against or depose the Shah? Ironside must have known and in fact, may even have encouraged Reza Khan in the belief that the time had come to throw the ineffectual and corrupt Tehran Government out of office. The request for a promise not to depose the Shah, which probably came from Norman, reinforces the argument that Ironside knew Reza Khan was thinking of a coup d'etat. Both Ironside and Norman were well aware of the Shah's uselessness but knew there were no alternatives and deposition of a king when the country was in danger of disintegrating was dangerous.

Meanwhile in the search for a new 'strong' prime minister members of the Legation talked to a number of prominent Iranians. Britain's official documents of this period are silent as to these contacts and conversations, but a number of Iranian commentators have related personal accounts. The most reliable of these is by the poet, essayist and political figure Mohammad Taqi Bahar (Malek al Sho'ara).* Bahar mentions that he himself was visited by W.A. Smart of the Legation to sound him out on the desirability of a 'strong reactionary Prime Minister'.[31] He further relates that Brig. Mohammad

---

*   Mohammad Taqi Bahar (Malek al Sho'ara) SEE NEXT PAGE

Nakhjavan (Amir Movassaq)† had been contacted by Seyyed Zia to lead the military component of a coup. It is likely that Seyyed Zia, who did not know Reza Khan and initially had been unaware of Ironside's efforts to promote Reza Khan, approached high-ranking officers of the Cossacks and Gendarmerie to assist him in his plans. Bahar also mentions Seyyed Hassan Moddares,# a leading cleric, who had told him that in late 1920 he had been approached by Reza Khan to join forces in toppling the Government. Moddares shared with Reza Khan a fear of a Bolshevik government in Iran but it is highly unlikely that Reza Khan, who at that time knew very few Iranian notables would have known or trusted Moddares well enough to confide in him and seek his co-operation. Furthermore, in any attempt to seize power by force a cleric's help would not have been vital in the initial stage. Yahya Dowlatabadi has stated that Maj. Gen. Abdollah Amir Tahmasebi, then in charge of troops protecting the palace and the Shah, had been contacted by members of the Legation to lead a coup.[32] Hosein Makki who has written extensively on the Reza Shah era, also mentions Brig. Gen. Mohammad

---

* Mohammad Taqi Bahar (Malek al Sho'ara), 1886–1951, in addition to his vast literary output was active in politics (member of parliament in the third, fourth and fifth sessions from Mashhad and in the sixth from Tehran). He had supported Vosouq although his sympathies lay with Germany and Turkey in World War I. He fell out with Reza Shah and was exiled, but made his peace and returned to Tehran in 1935. He will best be remembered as one of the major poets of twentieth-century Iran.[33]

† Mohammad Nakhjavan (Amir Movassaq), c.1882–c.1970, was the son of a Cossack officer, studied at military school in Teflis and knew Russian and French. He became Brigadier General in 1920; in 1922 became head of the newly-formed military school; Army Chief of Staff in 1928; Minister of War in 1934; promoted to Major General and relieved in 1936. After Soviet-British invasion of Iran in 1941 he was again appointed as Minister of War for a short period. British dispatches are extremely derogatory about his capabilities.[34]

Seyyed Hassan Moddares, 1870–1938, a highly popular cleric, became a well-known parliamentarian, having been elected to the second through the sixth sessions. He was known as a fearless foe of Russian and British imperialism, outspoken, brave and always willing to take risks. He chose to throw his lot with the Iranian Government in exile during World War I and lived in self-imposed exile in Syria and Turkey. He enjoyed an excellent reputation and was revered by the masses. Although living the simple life of an ascetic he wanted to be counsellor to kings, princes and prime ministers. An opponent of Reza Khan, he was exiled and subsequently murdered. His simple life-style cloaked an arrogant and vain interior.[35]

Nakhjavan (Amir Movasseq).[36] There is no supporting evidence that either Tahmasebi or Nakhjavan were ever considered.

Of those mentioned by various Iranian writers as candidates to succeed Sepahdar as Prime Minister and as likely under certain circumstances to have been capable of executing a coup, Firouz (Nosrat al Dowleh) is the only person who may have had a chance. His primary asset was his being the son of Farmanfarma with established loyalties to Britain. He had proven to be an unwavering ally as steadfast as Vosouq himself. He had accompanied the Shah to Europe, making sure the Shah remained bound to the implementation of the Agreement. He had advised Curzon on how best to put the Agreement into operation and had gained Curzon's respect. His ties to Sir Percy Cox remained intact even after the latter's new posting to Baghdad. The matter of the bribe had not bothered Cox, nor had it demeaned him in Curzon's eyes. They probably thought Firouz would feel even more indebted to Britain by having been compensated for his efforts. Had the Agreement gone into effect there is little doubt that sooner or later he would have become prime minister. The paternal tone Cox used in his telegrams showed the degree of affection he had for him. Additionally, Firouz was a highly intelligent man with a superior political temperament. He could be charming and command loyalty, but once the bribe had been inadvertently revealed in December 1920, Firouz's stature suffered a heavy blow. Norman, a better judge of the prevailing mood in Tehran, knew Firouz was tarnished and it would be a while before he would be thought of seriously and become acceptable as a prime minister. When in January and February 1921 Norman was advised by Curzon to seek counsel from Firouz he mechanically followed orders but his dispatches show no warmth or respect toward Firouz and by inference tried to tell Curzon that Firouz had become a liability for the time being. When Norman denigrated Vosouq in his telegrams he basically was telling Curzon what he also thought of Firouz. In any event, Firouz kept delaying his return to Tehran for reasons mentioned earlier. He did not arrive until 6 February, barely two weeks before the coup. Prior to his arrival Firouz had asked his brother, Salar Lashkar, to tell Norman that he did not think the time was ripe for him to make a move to become Prime Minister. Firouz was too clever not to know that he must wait and rebuild his base of support before attempting to reach higher office.

Based on numerous reliable accounts[37] Firouz, on his trip to Tehran, had to leave his car behind in Hamadan due to a severe snowstorm in the mountain passes on the road to Tehran. He somehow managed to reach Qazvin by alternate means on the evening of

6 February. He had the bad fortune of meeting Ironside, who was visiting the British camp that day. Ironside recorded in his diary:

> [Firouz] had just returned from Europe, held up at Aveh [Avaj] Pass and abandoned his car... He was wearing a sport coat and very baggy knickerbockers, finished off with gaudy coloured stockings. On his head was an astrakhan hat. He was afraid that there would be a revolution a few days after the departure of British troops. He was in a terrible state about our withdrawal. He begged me to give him a car to go to Tehran to see the Shah. I packed him to see Norman but I had little hope that he would be of any more help than Sardar Homayoun.[38]

Ironside was somewhat unfair to Firouz. He would not have commented in such derogatory detail on Firouz's attire, however gaudy, were it not for Ironside's great annoyance at having the favourite of Cox make an unexpected appearance. Norman and Ironside's planning had progressed too far and neither wanted to contend with a wild card who could upset their calculations. Doubtless Ironside was aware of the high esteem in which Firouz was held by Curzon and Cox but this chance encounter dispelled whatever myths had surrounded Firouz. In a dispatch dated 11 February Norman informed Curzon that 'Nosrat ed Dowleh has at long last reached Tehran'.[39] After the coup Firouz and his allies propagated the myth that had he not been held up in Hamadan by a snow storm, he would have been the leader of the coup.[40]

On 15 February 1921, less than a week before the coup, Ironside saw Norman and then the Shah. Ironside's Diary entries are of significance in considering how much Norman and Ironside knew of each other's plans, particularly in light of Norman's later denials of his role in the coup. Ironside wrote: 'I told Norman of my talks with Reza Khan and arranged with him to settle the actual date when the Persian Cossacks would be released from our custody. I recommended [not later than] a month before the North Persian Force left Qazvin'.[41] Later the same day Ironside saw the Shah in the latter's private apartments (andarun) where the Shah's family and personal entourage lived. The Shah bestowed on Ironside the Order of the Lion and the Sun, the highest Iranian award for meritorious services, and expressed his dismay and sorrow over the impending departure of British troops 'not for the sake of Persia... but the British Empire and India'. Ironside seized the opportunity and urged the Shah to appoint Reza Khan as commander of the Cossacks but met with silence.[42] Ironside left Tehran for Qazvin on 16 February and on the seventeenth departed by plane for Baghdad, never to return. On leaving Iran his last words were, 'I have seen one man in the country who was capable of leading the nation, and that is Reza Khan'.[43]

NOTES ON CHAPTER 6
Further details of publications and documents in Bibliography

1   Richard H. Ullman, *The Anglo-Soviet Accord*, vol. 3, p 384: quoting from
    the unpublished Ironside Diaries. Ullman had access to the complete
    unpublished manuscript of Ironside's Diaries and makes several refer-
    ences to them in this excellent work.
2   WO 158/687, Military Attaché, Tehran, to Gen. Ironside, Headquarters
    Norperforce, Kasvin, 6 January 1921.
3   WO 156/687, Appreciation of Tehran Situation by H. Smyth, 19
    January 1921.
4   Richard H. Ullman, *The Anglo-Soviet Accord*, vol. 3, p 384: quoting from
    the unpublished Ironside Diaries.
5   DBFP, doc. no. 569; Norman to Curzon; 26 October 1920.
6   Maj. Gen. Sir Edmund Ironside, *High Road to Command*, p 148. The date
    of Starosselsky's dismissal is not certain. It is variously stated as 22, 24
    and 25 October (most of the entries in Ironside's Diaries do not mention
    days but merely months).
7   *Ibid.*, p 149.
8   *Ibid.*, pp 151–153.
9   *Ibid.*, pp 148–149.
10 *Ibid.*, p 162.
11 DBFP, doc. no. 576, Curzon to Norman, 5 November 1920; DBFP, doc.
    no. 586, Norman to Curzon, 25 November 1920.
12 DBFP, doc. no. 599, Norman to Curzon, 7 December 1920.
13 DBFP, doc. no. 605, Norman to Curzon, 8 December 1920.
14 DBFP, doc. no. 614, Curzon to Norman, 19 December 1920.
15 The other newspaper was *Asr-e-Jadid*, a less known publication edited
    by Matin al Saltaneh: Mohamad Taqi Bahar, *Tarikh Mokhtasar Ahzab
    Siasi (A Short History of Political Parties)*, vol. 1, p 56.
16 Ja'far Mehdi Nia, *Zendegi Siasi Seyyed Zia al Din Tabataba'i (The
    Political Life of Seyyed Zia al Din Tabataba'i)*. James A. Bill, 'Interview
    with Seyyed Zia', unpublished.
17 Hosein Makki, *Tarikh Bist Saleh Iran (A Twenty Year History of Iran)*, vol.
    1, p 186.
18 FO 371/6404, Oliphant Memorandum of Conversation with Lt Col.
    Meade, 6 June 1921.
19 FO 371/6403, Norman to Curzon, 23 April 1921.
20 Peter Avery, *Modern Iran*, pp 222–223; see also Donald N. Wilber, *Riza
    Shah Pahlavi*, pp 39–41.
21 R.N. Boston, *Rahavard* magazine, Los Angeles, 30 November 1992.
22 Peter Avery, *Modern Iran*, p 225.
23 FO 158/697, Minute by Champain, July 1920.
24 FO 248/1320, Edmonds to Norperforce, 5 July 1920.
25 DBFP, doc. no. 599, Norman to Curzon, 7 December 1920.
26 FO 371/4915, Memorandum by Churchill, 8 December 1920.
27 Maj. Gen. Sir Edmund Ironside, *High Road to Command*, p 161.
28 Richard H. Ullman, *The Anglo-Soviet Accord*, vol. 3, p 387: quoting from
    the unpublished Ironside Diaries.
29 Maj. Gen. Sir Edmund Ironside, *High Road to Command*, p 178.
30 *Ibid.*, p. 161.

31 Mohamad Taqi Bahar, *Tarikh Mokhtasar Ahzab Siasi* (*A Short History of Political Parties*), vol. 1, p 61.
32 Yahya Dowlatabadi, *Hayat Yahya* (*The Life of Yahya*), vol. 4, p 223.
33 Ghasem Ghani, *Yaddasht ha-e-Dr Ghasem Ghani* (*Memoirs of Dr Ghasem Ghani*), vol. 11, pp 417–418.
34 FO 416/98, Bullard to Halifax, 7 February 1940.
35 Mehdi Bamdad, *Tarikh Rejal Iran Quroun 12, 13, 14* (*Dictionary of National Biography of Iran: Twelfth, Thirteenth, Fourteenth Centuries*), vol. 1, pp 343–345. Hosein Makki, *Tarikh Bist Saleh Iran* (*A Twenty Year History of Iran*), vol. 1, pp 432–440. Mehdi Qoli Hedayat (Mokhber al Saltaneh), *Khaterat va Khatarat* (*Memoirs and Hazards*), pp 450, 452, 461, 469, 473.
36 Hosein Makki, *Tarikh Bist Saleh Iran* (*A Twenty Year History of Iran*), vol. 1, p 199.
37 Gen. Hassan Arfa, *Under Five Shahs*; Amanollah Jahanbani, *Reza Shah Kabir Dar Ayeneh Khaterat* (*Reza Shah in Reflective Memory*), ed. Ebrahim Safa'i.
38 Maj. Gen. Sir Edmund Ironside, *High Road to Command*, p 164.
39 FO 371/6401, Norman to Curzon, 11 February 1921.
40 Donald N. Wilber, *Riza Shah Pahlavi*, p 44.
    Just prior to the anniversary of the coup, 16 February 1922, a Tehran newspaper, *Setareh Iran*, identified Firouz as the author of the coup, with British connivance, to establish a republic. The article continued that Seyyed Zia found out and enlisted the help of Reza Khan and the Crown Prince and thwarted the plot. On 21 February 1922 Reza Khan felt compelled to publish a declaration that he was the author and leader of the coup and that no foreigners were involved. Iranian writers, not having had access to reliable documents and relying on heresay, have given varying accounts of Firouz's arrival in Tehran. Mohamad Taqi Bahar, in *Tarikh Mokhtasar Ahzab Siasi* (*A Short History of Political Parties*), stated that Firouz was stopped by a snow storm at Hamadan and reached Tehran the day after the coup, when his father and brother had been arrested (22 February 1921). He further added that if Cox had been in Tehran, Firouz would have pulled off the coup. Hosein Makki, *Tarikh Bist Saleh Iran* (*A Twenty Year History of Iran*), repeated the same version. In a subsequent edition of his book, he acknowledged that Firouz arrived in Tehran 15 days before the coup but he was de-selected as its leader because he disagreed with Norman on post-coup policy, especially the necessity to imprison certain prominent Iranians. Ja'far Mehdinia, in his biography of Seyyed Zia, puts forth the absurd proposition that Firouz was stopped at Qazvin on the orders of Seyyed Zia and was not allowed to reach Tehran.
41 Maj. Gen. Sir Edmund Ironside, *High Road to Command*, p 166.
42 Richard H. Ullman, *The Anglo-Soviet Accord*, vol. 3, p 387.
43 Maj. Gen. Sir Edmund Ironside, *High Road to Command*, pp 177–178.

7

Reza Khan and the Coup d'Etat of 21 February 1921

Little is known about Reza Khan prior to the coup. He was born in the village of Alasht in the region of Savad Kouh in the province of Mazandaran. Alasht was an isolated village some 6,000 feet above sea level and at the turn of the century its population did not exceed 1,000. Reza Khan's grandfather, Morad Ali Khan, had been an officer in the local provincial army regiment and had been killed about 1848 in the siege of Herat.[1] A geneological chart prepared by the descendants of Morad Ali Khan, the Pahlavan family, traces the lineage to the late seventeenth century and cites a Mohammad Khan as the first known member of this family, with Jahan Bakhsh Khan the elder as his son, Jahan Bakhsh the younger as grandson and Haji Mohammad Hassan as the great grandson and father of Morad Ali. The chart lists some 300 living descendants of Morad Ali Khan. In a recently published book on Reza Shah, Reza Niazmand, having conducted the definitive research on Reza Khan's ancestry believes that it is difficult to ascertain his forbearers beyond his grandfather Morad Ali Khan.[2] Morad Ali had seven sons. The eldest, Cheraq Ali, was also an officer in the provincial army and apparently reached the rank equivalent to colonel. The youngest, Abbas Ali Khan also

161

known as Dadash Beik, was in the same regiment and probably reached the rank equivalent to major. The other known sons were Nasrollah, Fazlollah and Abbasqoli. The remaining two cannot be identified with certainty.[3] The family were members of the small clan of Palani of the Savad Kouh region. Although small in numbers the clan has been mentioned in the history of the region as having furnished soldiers to the local armies.[4] Several writers, among them Arfa and Wilber, state that the family came from the much larger Bavand clan of the region. This is apparently an error. The Bavand clan was in fact a rival and relations between the Bavand and Palani clans were often strained.[5]

Abbas Ali, the youngest of Morad Ali's children was born around 1815. As a member of the Savad Kouh regiment he took part in the third Afghan War in 1856 as a junior officer.[6] Abbas Ali's background and military record has been substantiated by the recent surfacing of a letter he had written to Ali Reza Khan Azd al Molk, an elder of the Qajar tribe and later regent, who at one time as Governor of Mazandaran had been the honorary commander of the Savad Kouh regiment. In the letter, dated around 1877, Abbas Ali refers to his past military service and seeks financial assistance from Azd al Molk.[7] Abbas Ali Khan married at least twice and had four children who survived infancy: three daughters from his first marriage and a son, Reza, from the second. He married his second wife, Noush Afarin, around 1877. She was a girl of Persian-speaking stock whose father had come to Iran from Erivan. The following year 1878 a son, Reza, was born.[8] Abbas Ali died some three to six months after Reza's birth. The new wife had not had a good relationship with Abbas Ali's other wife and children and shortly after Abbas Ali's death, Noush Afarin, at the urging of her youngest brother, decided to leave Alasht and settle in Tehran.[9] Noush Afarin had three known brothers. The eldest, Ali, was one of the many physicians at Naser al Din Shah's court. The second brother, Abol Qasem, who had done some soldiering in Erivan, had enlisted in the Cossack Brigade. The third brother, Hosein, had accompanied Noush Afarin to Alasht and on her return to Tehran.[10] There is an often-told story that the infant Reza almost froze to death on the journey. It was thought the child was dead but the heat inside a caravanserai revived him.[11] Probably at the urging of his uncle, Abol Qasem, and because of his meagre circumstances, Reza joined the Cossacks in 1893-94 at about the age of fifteen. Most of the volunteers and recruits in the Cossack Brigade came from humble backgrounds. There is no existing or available record of Reza's service until 1911. There are references by several Iranian writers to Reza Khan having served as a guard at either the Dutch, Belgian or German Legation.[12] Although there is no convincing evidence of such service it should not be entirely discounted.

In 1911, serving under the overall command of Farmanfarma, Reza Khan took part in battles against Salar al Dowleh who was attempting to topple the Government in Tehran and reinstate his brother Mohammad Ali on the throne. Reza gave a good account of himself in that campaign and was promoted to First Lieutenant. His proficiency in handling machine guns elevated him to the rank equivalent to captain in 1912. By 1915 he had come to be regarded as a brave and fearless soldier and was hand-picked by successive senior commanders to accompany them on expeditions to quell tribal uprisings.[13] Reza Khan's military reputation, his native intelligence and professionalism served him well and he was soon known by some prominent Iranians in Tehran and the provinces. By 1915 various sources refer to him as Col. Reza Khan.[14] In 1918 Reza Khan is referred to as a Brigadier General (Sartip) in the campaign of Cossacks in the Kashan area against the bandit Na'eb Hosein and his sons.[15]

About 1903 Reza Khan married Tajmah, a girl from Hamadan, from whom a daughter Fatemeh, later known as Hamdam al Saltaneh, was born. He divorced Tajmah soon after the birth of Fatemeh and her name was rarely mentioned thereafter.[16] In 1916 he married Nimtaj (Taj al Molouk), the eldest daughter of Teimour Khan (Ayromlou), a Brigadier General in the regular army whose family had come to Iran from the Caucasus. (Many Iranian families left the Caucasus and emigrated to Iran proper in 1828, after the Russo-Persian War). Taj al Molouk gave birth to four children including the Crown Prince, Mohammad Reza Pahlavi.[17] In 1922 Reza Khan married a third time to Turan (Qamar al Molouk) Amir Soleymani, the daughter of Issa Majd al Saltaneh and grand-daughter of Mehdi Qoli Majd al Dowleh, one of the most respected and prominent men of his day. From this marriage a son was born.[18] Reza Khan divorced her in 1923. Reza Khan's last wife was Esmat Dowlatshahi, the daughter of a Qajar Prince Mojalal al Dowleh, whom he married in 1923. From this marriage four sons and a daughter were born.[19]

From early 1918 we have more information about Reza Khan. In that year he rose from an obscure military officer to catch the attention of the higher levels of the Iranian Government and the British Legation. Probably the most important contributing factor was his role in the removal of Col. Clerge, the commander of the Cossack Division recently appointed by Kerensky. Reza Khan joined the conspiracy organised by Starosselsky, the deputy commander, to oust Clerge from his command. Clerge was accused, probably falsely, of pro-Bolshevik sympathies by his subordinate Russian officers. Reza Khan's motives in this episode are not entirely clear. As a patriot he was surely disturbed by the rebellions and secessionist movements in northern Iran openly supported by the Bolsheviks. He was therefore amenable to accepting Starosselsky's accusations against Clerge. More importantly, as an ambitious officer Reza Khan was probably promised advancement if he threw in his lot with Starosselsky. That Reza Khan played a prominent, if not the decisive, role in the ousting of Clerge is unquestioned. The newspaper *Ra'ad* in January 1918 refered to a Col. Reza Khan as having been one of the major participants in the events surrounding the removal of Clerge. The article stated that a Col. Filartov, the Commander of the Cossacks in Hamadan, together with Col. Reza Khan, the ranking Iranian officer in the Hamadan Cossack Brigade, ousted Clerge from his command.[20] Bahar has stated that at the time his own newspaper referred to Reza Khan's role in the incident.[21] British Foreign Office documents also mention Reza Khan's involvement. Other British sources confirm this and even speak of Reza Khan having been involved in 'other plots' in addition to the Clerge affair. There is, however, no elaboration of the 'other plots'.[22]

The immediate reward for having supported Starosselsky to become the new commander of the Cossacks appears to have been Reza Khan's promotion to the rank of Brigadier General in mid 1918. The matter of Reza Khan's rank and promotions from 1918 to the eve of the coup in February 1921 is cloudy. Arfa states that Reza Khan was promoted to Brigadier General immediately after the removal of Clerge as part of the bargain with Starosselsky. Bahar maintains that in September 1920 Reza Khan signed documents as Reza Sartip (Brig. Gen. Reza). The very few British Foreign Office and War Office documents that make mention of Reza Khan before the coup do so mostly as Colonel. Ironside in his Diaries is indifferent to the rank of Reza Khan and refers to him by various ranks but never as a Brigadier General.

The ancillary benefits which Reza Khan gained from this episode far outweighed his promotion. In July 1918 and in several subsequent campaigns Reza Khan led troops in the north, enhancing his reputation as a courageous leader. As he became more prominent his relations with the Russian officers, and especially Starosselsky, deteriorated. By 1919 he came to the attention of senior British officers who had been employed either directly by Vosouq or sent to Tehran by the War Office as part of the military advisery team. It is at this time that it appears Reza Khan came to the direct attention of Gen. Dickson, who soon formed a high opinion of him.[23] There are other complimentary references to Reza Khan in this period. He is described as 'handsome and distinguished and a first rate soldier who grasped things quickly'.[24] Furthermore, his hostility towards the Russian Cossack officers had not gone unnoticed by the British.

Reza Khan rose through the ranks on merit enduring hardships which included recurrent bouts of malaria which plagued him to the end of his life. He had a disciplined and austere mode of living with few material pleasures, a regimen he maintained throughout his life. This is substantially the extent of reliable information.

There are references to Reza Khan having worked with the British military advisery mission in 1920 and having declared himself ready to take steps to oust Starosselsky from command.[25] The question of his having worked with British officers prior to the 1921 coup and his introduction to Ironside have been the subject of several commentaries in the last 25 years. There is no doubt that Reza Khan was known to the British military establishment in Iran prior to the coup because of his rank, distinguished military record, his work with Gen. Dickson's officers who had been sent to Iran as part of the 1919 Agreement and, of course, his prominent role in the removal of Clerge and his later conflict with Starosselsky. However, the question of who introduced Reza Khan to Ironside has produced conflicting claims and self-serving accounts some of which are absurd.[26] The first and most reliable account is in the Diaries of Ironside himself in which he unequivocally states that it was Col. Smyth who first introduced Reza Khan to him. The weight of reliable evidence indicates that Reza Khan had been hand-picked by an adventurous British General who had seen in him courage, determination and patriotism.

There are very few accounts left to us of the events of 20 and 21 February 1921 by Iranian participants and witnesses. Few had a grasp of the larger picture. Only years after the fact did they realise the significance of what had taken place. The following appear the most reliable.

ACCOUNTS BY IRANIAN OBSERVERS
Morteza Yazdanpanah*

In 1919 he [Reza Khan] became the head of my brigade. He was then a
Brigadier. I had the rank of Colonel and became his deputy. It was during
the war with the Bolsheviks in Gilan. From the beginning he was a dignified and thoughtful person. He had been in Farmanfarma's circle,
during which time he had eventually become a Major... Reza Khan must
have been green in those days but because of his proximity to
Farmanfarma he was soon introduced to politics and politicians. Later
he got to know Nosrat al Dowleh, from whom he learned even more about
politics... Later Reza Khan joined the plot to oust Clerge which resulted
in Starosselsky becoming the head of the Cossacks. However, Starosselsky soon turned against Reza Khan and wanted to discredit him. The
British did not trust the Russian officers who commanded the Cossacks.
They wanted to eliminate the Cossack Division and create a unified
armed force. During Vosouq al Dowleh's Government Reza Khan became
close to the British military mission through Nosrat al Dowleh. He told
the head of the mission [Gen. Dickson] that he was willing to take steps
toward the removal of the Russian officers. He assured Dickson that it
was an easy task and he was willing to take the risk. Soon thereafter all
the Russian officers were ousted.

Later Reza Khan returned to Gilan [to the campaign against Kouchek
Khan] and I was with him. After a while we started back towards Tehran
and stayed in a village belonging to Ahmad Shah about 30 kilometres
from Qazvin. One day Reza Khan prepared a telegram and gave it to one
of our trusted sergeants to take to Qazvin for transmission to Tehran...
A few days later the sergeant returned with the reply. Reza Khan read it
and was joyous... He began dancing and whistling and snapping his fin-
gers and kept saying everything will be all right now. He must have said
in his telegram that he was ready and prepared to move and the time was
propitious. The reply telegram was a confirmation that he could do so.
We then moved closer to Tehran and camped at another village. It was
there that two people whom I did not know called on him one day. They
were introduced as Major Mas'oud Khan and Colonel Kazem Khan
Sayyah. He introduced me to them and added that I was like his son and

---

*   Lt Gen. Morteza Yazdanpanah, c.1884–c.1970, was born in Tehran. His
     father was a colonel in the regular army. In 1907 he attended the Cossack
     Cadet School where he learned some Russian, and by 1921 had risen to
     Brigadier General. He was loyal to Reza Khan throughout the latter's
     career and served in various military posts. He was briefly out of favour
     and unposted, but regained favour and in 1928 was promoted to Major
     General and Chief Inspector of the Army. In 1929 he became Chief Com-
     mander of the Gendarmerie. He remained equally loyal to Mohammad
     Reza Shah and was promoted to Lieutenant General in 1942; Minister of
     War and later head of the Imperial Inspectorate; appointed to the Senate.
     In 1967 he was nominally in charge of coronation ceremonies which,
     unlike other public celebrations of the late Pahlavi period, were handled
     with tact and good taste.[27]

that he kept no secrets from me. Reza Khan was the consummate political artist. All one saw was the surface layer but there were a hundred layers beneath...

I first met Seyyed Zia a few days later. Reza Khan introduced him as His Excellency Seyyed Zia, the future Prime Minister of Iran. Seyyed Zia asked Reza Khan what he needed. Reza Khan said first and foremost clothes. Seyyed Zia said they would shortly arrive. 'Anything else?' asked Seyyed Zia. Reza Khan said the salary of the men and officers had not been paid for three months. Seyyed Zia said the money would reach us that very day. The clothes arrived with English-made shoes, and bags of money in silver coins arrived, with which everyone was given back pay.

Reza Khan told me to tell my men to have lunch and an early dinner and be ready by sunset. We did it all. After dinner the men were assembled. Reza Khan climbed on a stool and addressed them: 'Dear comrades-in-arms, you were eyewitnesses to our situation in Gilan. We were neck deep in mud and filth. They gave us no clothes, did not pay our salary and we were forgotten. We must put an end to this state of affairs. I have been inspired by God to rectify this intolerable situation.' The soldiers applauded. He dismissed the soldiers and when everyone had left only Seyyed Zia and I remained. Reza Khan seemed a little embarrassed. He insisted that he had had no intention of invoking the name of God in his talk to the men. Seyyed Zia said no harm was done and in any event it was a good omen. He hoped God would inspire us all and help us to succeed in our mission to save and reform our country.

We started at midnight. There were 600 of us. Tehran was undefended. The Tehran contingent of the Cossacks had been instructed to stay put in their barracks and lock all the gates. Habibollah Khan Sheibani with a few Gendarmes was in charge of maintaining order in the city. We entered Tehran. A few shots were fired and two people were accidentally killed. We took control of the city. The gates of the Tehran Cossack barracks were opened and the coup became a fact. We took over the entire machinery of government. It did not take long for misunderstandings with Seyyed Zia to develop.[28]

Hassan Arfa[†]

On the morning of 20 February 1921, Major [Habibollah] Sheibani called me and said that about 1000 Cossacks had rebelled at Qazvin, as they

---

[†]   Maj. Gen. Hassan Arfa, 1890–1975, was the eldest son of Reza Arfa (Arfa al Dowleh). Reza Arfa was an undistinguished notable of the late nineteenth and early twentieth centuries. He had been close to Atabak and was appointed Minister to St Petersburg and Ambassador to Constantinople during the years 1900–1910. He had an insatiable appetite for self aggrandisement and received some eight titles from successive Qajar Shahs, including the pseudo-title of 'Prince'. He retired to Monte Carlo. Hassan Arfa was educated in Russia and France, and began his career at the Ministry of Foreign Affairs in 1907, serving in
CONTINUED OVER PAGE

had not received their pay for several months and were marching on Tehran to get their salaries. They would probably reach the city in the evening. He ordered me to take command of a battalion for that evening and to occupy the western approaches to the city... I had to prevent the Cossacks from entering and ensure that the several hundred Bolshevik prisoners in a camp near Baghe-e-Shah did not escape. I was astonished at these instructions and remarked that there were four other captains senior to me in the regiment. Under the circumstances how could I take command? Major Sheibani replied that he had already disposed of this difficulty by giving two days leave to the senior captains. I asked him if I should fire on the Cossacks if they tried to force my barrage [position]. 'You can fire on them if they open fire on you,' he answered.

At 8pm the telephone rang and it was the Shah enquiring about the situation. The Shah told Arfa he was at the Farahabad hunting lodge some five miles east of Tehran and instructed Arfa to report if anything happened. At 9pm a Cossack Colonel with a few men tried to enter one of the city's gates but were stopped by Arfa and his men. Arfa then tried to reach the Shah and Sheibani by telephone but was unsuccessful.

At 11 o'clock Arfa returned to Bagh-e-Shah and heard gunshots coming from the centre of the city. He was finally able to contact Sheibani who informed him that the Cossacks 'numbering perhaps 1500 men had entered the town and three policemen had been killed'. Arfa was ordered to guard the prisoners camp and to shoot anyone trying to enter, but to take no notice if the Cossacks merely pass in front of the barracks.

> The next day Major Sheibani came to Baghe-e-Shah and told me the Cossacks had occupied the town and installed a new government headed by Seyyed Zia al Din Tabataba'i, that the new military commander was General Reza Khan of the Cossack Division and that many important people had been arrested. He allowed me to go home and rest for 24 hours... Reza Khan received the title of Sardar Sepah and a jewel studded golden sword from the Shah. All his officers and soldiers received pecuniary rewards and most of his officers received promotions.[29]

Maj. Gen. Hassan Arfa CONTINUED FROM PREVIOUS PAGE
consulates in Teflis and St Petersburg. He joined the Gendarmerie in 1911 and the regular army after the coup and later commanded the elite Pahlavi Regiment of the Imperial Guard. In 1931 he became Military Attaché to London, accompanied Reza Shah on his trip to Turkey in 1934 and attended Ataturk's funeral in 1938. He became Brigadier General in 1939; Chief of Staff of the Tehran Defence Forces in 1941; Chief of Staff of Armed Forces in 1944; dismissed in 1946; Minister of Roads in 1951; Ambassador to Turkey 1955–1961; Ambassador to Pakistan 1961–62. Arfa wrote a readable and useful autobiography.[30]

Amanollah Jahanbani*

I first met Reza Khan in 1916. He had been promoted to the rank of Brigadier General and was the Commander of the Kermanshah Brigade... After the First World War, I was sent as a military attaché to the Paris Peace Conference... on my return to Iran I ran into the Cossack forces by chance in Karaj on 19 February [1921]. They were poised to enter Tehran and topple the Government. I felt obliged to present myself to the Commander, Brigadier General Reza Khan, who instructed me to remain the night in Karaj and accompany the forces to Tehran the following day. Reza Khan told me of the chaos in Tehran and he was hopeful his action would save the country. The next day we started towards Tehran and met no resistance. Reza Khan assumed command of all the armed units and I was appointed Commander of the artillery forces of the Cossack Division.[31]

Ahmad Amir Ahmadi†

When it was decided to send a large number of the Cossack forces to the Qazvin area, Brigadier General Reza Khan also came to Qazvin with his troops... I called on him... and he told me he was going to Tehran to have discussions with certain influential people to ascertain whether we could seize the Cossack barracks in Tehran... He then left for Tehran. A few

---

*   Lt Gen. Amanollah Jahanbani, c.1890–c.1972, was the son of Amanollah Mirza Zia al Dowleh, a grandson of Fath Ali Shah. In protest against Russian cruelty toward the civilian population in Azarbaijan, and more probably in fear of his life, Zia al Dowleh sought refuge at the British Legation in Tabriz where, for reasons not entirely clear, he committed suicide in 1911. His son was educated at St Petersburg and Moscow military academies and returned to Iran in 1913 where he was attached to the Royal Guards. In 1916 he joined the Cossack Division with the rank of Captain. He soon distinguished himself in campaigns against insurgents in Azarbaijan. After the coup he was briefly Chief of General Staff in 1922; Commander of the Eastern Division in 1926; promoted to Major General in 1928; received successive appointments in the military as well as Director General of Industry in 1936 and Senator in 1950. Jahanbani was regarded as a competent officer.[32]

†   Ahmad Amir Ahmadi, 1884–c.1974, joined the Cossacks in 1899. His father was a Colonel in the regular army. In 1916 he reached the rank of Major; in 1919 Colonel; in 1921 Brigadier General; in 1923 commander of the Western Division, where he ruthlessly put down revolts by Lurs; Lieutenant General in 1929 (first officer to obtain that rank). He fell out of favour and was given mundane positions. After 1941 he was appointed Military Governor of Tehran on numerous occasions at signs of unrest. He was Minister of War and later Senator and had an insatiable appetite for wealth.[33]

days later he sent me a letter asking me to meet him. I immediately left my camp and saw him again in Qazvin. He told me he had discussed his plans with several people who had agreed to his becoming the Commander of the Cossacks, provided other officers who had seniority over him did not object. It was agreed he would write a letter to the two most senior officers in the Division including Major General Mohammad Tofiqi [Sardar Azim] my father-in-law.

Amir Ahmadi took the letters to Tehran and at a meeting of the then most senior officers obtained their written consent to support Reza Khan in his attempt to oust Sardar Homayoun and become the Commander of the Cossacks.

A letter by the Ministry of War in Tehran addressed to an officer senior to Reza Khan was intercepted. The letter authorised a small contingent of the Qazvin Brigade to come to Tehran to restore order. Amir Ahmadi states that somehow Reza Khan's name was substituted for the intended officer. Reza Khan now armed with the support of the highest level Cossack officers and a government authorisation to bring troops into Tehran could claim legitimacy and demand support from the junior officers. It was agreed to move to Tehran for the ostensible purpose of restoring order.

On 12 February a force of some 1000 men moved from their camps around Qazvin. However, the Shah and the Government changed their minds and wanted the troops to stop. The Minister of War ordered Reza Khan by telegraph to return to Qazvin. Through threats and bribery the head of the telegraph station was forced to report to Tehran that he had been unable to reach Reza Khan. With these new developments it was decided to expedite the troop movement towards Tehran. Amir Ahmadi mentions that by 20 February, Maj. Jahanbani and Col. Kazem Khan Sayyah had joined them. A car carrying Sardar Homayoun who had been told, probably by the Shah, to order Reza Khan to stop the movement toward Tehran was intercepted on the road. Soon after another car from Tehran arrived. The passengers were Seyyed Zia and Maj. Mas'oud Khan Keyhan. They had come to see Reza Khan, who arrived within an hour. Seyyed Zia produced a Qoran which was sworn on by five people, Reza Khan, Seyyed Zia, Kazem Khan, Mas'oud Khan and Amir Ahmadi to protect the independence of Iran. Amir Ahmadi took a further oath on the holy book to remain faithful to Reza Khan.

On 20 February the infantry reached the outskirts of Tehran. Reza Khan urged caution as he anticipated resistance by Gendarmes. 'On the afternoon of 20th February several people from Tehran came to our temporary camp and asked Reza Khan to halt.' The delegation was comprised of Moin al Molk, Private Secretary to the Shah; Adib al Saltaneh (Hosein Samii), Vice Premier; Col. T.W. Haig, the acting British Counsellor; and Col. Huddleston, a senior military officer sent to Iran as a member of the British military team under the 1919 Agreement. Reza Khan rejected their plea and stated that his purpose in coming to Tehran was merely 'to see his family'.

> We set out for Tehran. Seyyed Zia accompanied us on horseback. The few troops guarding the gates of Tehran offered no resistance and we took over the police stations. Martial law was declared with Kazem Khan as Military Governor. Many prominent people were arrested...

In connection with those considered to lead a coup, Amir Ahmadi states that there were 'statesmen' who wanted the troop movement to Tehran to culminate in a coup.[34]

Adib al Saltaneh Samii (Hosein Samii)*

Samii begins by recounting that he had known Sepahdar for some time and they had been friends. At Sepahdar's insistence he had accepted the post of Vice Premier. A few days before the coup the Government learned that a large contingent of Cossacks commanded by Reza Khan, the head of the Hamadan Brigade, was marching on Tehran from Qazvin with the intention of toppling the Government and seizing power. The news created fear and panic at all levels of the Government and Sardar Homayoun had been sent to Qazvin to dissuade the Cossacks. In the meantime orders had been given for the defence of Tehran. On Sunday 20 February Sardar Homayoun returned and reported that he had failed in his mission. His report dashed whatever hopes there had been of averting the crisis. The Ministers dispersed in gloom but about an hour later Sepahdar telephoned Samii and asked him to accompany Moin al Molk, the

---

*   Adib al Saltaneh Samii (Hosein Samii), c.1879–1954, was born in Rasht the son of Hassan Adib al Saltaneh, a landowner in Gilan and prominent public official. He received a solid traditional Persian education and entered government service in 1898 at the Ministry of Foreign Affairs. In 1915 he joined the government in exile as Minister of Interior, was in self-exile in Syria, returning in 1918. He held several ministerial posts between 1922 and 1927, including Minister of Justice; several governorships; was acting head of Reza Shah's court from 1935–1938; held similar position in early reign of Mohammad Reza Shah. Samii, a learned man, wrote several books on Persian grammar and prose, a short memoir of his years of self-exile and a book of poetry. He was a highly respected public servant whose services and counsel were often sought.[35]

Private Secretary to the Shah, to Mehrabad to convince the Cossacks to abandon their plans. He was instructed to go to the British Legation, join Moin al Molk and head for Mehrabad. Samii was irritated and wanted to know what the British Legation had to do with this mission

Samii went to the Legation in late afternoon and was ushered into a room where Moin al Molk had been waiting. A few minutes later Col. Haig, whom Samii had met before, and Col. Huddleston, entered the room. Samii describes Haig as highly intelligent and fluent in Persian. He always gave the impression of not being serious and mocking everything. Haig stated that the Minister (Norman) had taken a long walk that afternoon and had not yet returned. The Minister had to be briefed on the situation and he might want to give specific instructions. Samii added that for the first time he realised that Haig and Huddleston would be accompanying him to Mehrabad. It was soon reported that Norman had returned and they all went to his office. Haig then began a lengthy report on how the Cossacks had unexpectedly marched from Qazvin towards Tehran. Samii observed that 'Haig's manner of presentation and Norman listening to him with such intensity, surprise and astonishment were obviously intended to make us think that the Minister had not known anything of the matter until that moment'. Haig then concluded that the four of them intended to go to Mehrabad and dissuade the Cossacks from entering Tehran. Norman approved the plan, bade them farewell and left the room. Haig suggested that they first call on the Prime Minister for possible instructions. Sepahdar had nothing new to say beyond that the four should convince the Cossacks to turn back.

The party left in two cars and reached Mehrabad about 8pm. They were directed to a dilapidated tea house and told to wait. Soon Reza Khan and Seyyed Zia appeared. Seyyed Zia had abandoned his turban and was wearing an astrakhan hat. Reza Khan enquired about their purpose. Samii stated that he and Moin al Molk were bearers of messages from the Shah and the Government and suggested to Moin al Molk that he, as the representative of the Shah, should speak first. Moin al Molk briefly stated that the movement of the Cossacks had created panic in Tehran and the Shah requested that the Cossacks return to Qazvin. Reza Khan, in an angry and harsh tone, expressed surprise at the message. 'Doesn't the Shah know what hardship the Cossacks have suffered? They have borne heavy casualties in their fight against the rebels and Bolsheviks. Now that they need a respite to come to Tehran and see members of their families the Shah prohibits them from doing so. Is this the

gratitude due to the Cossacks?' Reza Khan concluded by saying that
it was too late to turn back. A decision had been reached and it was
irreversible. After Reza Khan finished speaking, Samii in a conciliatory tone essentially repeated what Moin al Molk had said but
emphasised that the Shah and the Government were fully cognisant
of the sacrifices the Cossacks had made. He also made the argument
that the Bolsheviks might mount an offensive in the north at any
moment and the Cossacks needed to return to Qazvin to prepare for
a defence of their position. They could come to Tehran later. Seyyed
Zia in an even harsher tone attacked the Government and the
Ministers in Tehran, calling them traitors and saying nothing would
stop them from entering Tehran to 'remove these traitors... and
clean up the place'.

When Seyyed Zia had finished, Samii asked Haig to say something. Haig 'in his usual mocking and sardonic' manner and with no
conviction merely repeated that the Prime Minister had requested
the Cossacks to change direction and return to Qazvin. After some
moments of silence, Reza Khan and Seyyed Zia left the room, shortly
followed by Haig and Huddleston without saying anything to Samii
or Moin al Molk.

The rest of the account concerns Samii and Moin al Molk's desperate attempts to return to Tehran on their own finally arriving at
4am on 21 February when the coup had been accomplished.[36]

ACCOUNTS FROM BRITISH LEGATION REPORTS

The first report from Norman on the coup was sent at 5.30pm on 21
February. It stated:

> Kazvin and Hamadan detachments of Cossack Brigade, numbering from
> 2,500 to 3,000 men with eight field guns and 18 machine guns under
> Command of Colonel Riza Khan marched from Kazvin on Tehran and
> entered the town 21st February shortly after midnight.

The report related that while the Cossacks were still encamped outside the city the representatives of the Shah and the Government
and two members of Norman's staff went out to ascertain their
intentions and dissuade them from entering Tehran. The delegation
was unsuccessful. Reza Khan told the deputation that the Cossacks
had experience of the Bolsheviks and knew of their intention to
march into Tehran after British troops had withdrawn. They were
tired of a succession of incompetent governments failing to prepare

defences against the Bolsheviks and hence had decided to come to Tehran to install a strong government. Norman added that the Cossacks had professed loyalty and devotion to the Shah but were determined to remove the 'evil' counsellors who had surrounded him. Norman then stated there were no forces to oppose the Cossacks' entry but owing to a misunderstanding some seven policemen were killed.[37]

In this telegram as well as one sent on 22 February, Norman informed Curzon that Sepahdar had taken refuge at the Legation and had sought assurance that he would not be molested. Norman continued that he had seen the Shah and advised him to 'enter into relations with the leaders of the coup and acquiesce in their demands'. The Shah was frightened and seemed frozen and incapable of any action. Norman also reported the arrests of Farmanfarma and his two eldest sons, Firouz and Salar Lashkar, 'on whose behalf I am exerting my influence'.[38] On 26 February Norman reported that he had been given assurances that 'the lives of Farmanfarma and his two sons will be spared, as Farmanfarma and Firouz hold His Majesty's decorations and have guarantees from His Majesty's Government of 9 August 1919'. Norman, however, seemed resigned to their imprisonment for at least a short while as 'all three owe back taxes which I cannot stop from being collected'.[39]

A further and lengthier report on the coup was sent a week later on 1 March. Norman at the outset reintroduced Col. Smyth to Curzon as the officer appointed by Ironside to reorganise the Cossacks. 'Smyth had done an efficient job and made them disciplined.' Norman added that he had been in touch with Smyth on the latter's trips to Tehran. He also explained that the condition of the Cossacks in Tehran had been miserable. Smyth had suggested that these troops be sent to Qazvin for refitting and training and be replaced by Cossacks from Qazvin. Smyth had suggested that Reza Khan, one of his best officers, 'be sent to Tehran with these reliefs'. On 18 February, Moin al Molk, the Shah's secretary, had informed Norman that Sardar Homayoun, at the suggestion of Col. Smyth, had sent a telegram to Qazvin ordering the whole of the Tehran and Hamadan detachments, numbering 2,200 men and quartered in Qazvin, to come to Tehran. Moin al Molk told Norman that the Shah now did not want these instructions to take effect because he did not consider that so large a force was needed in Tehran, where order could be maintained effectively by the Gendarmerie and the police. Norman responded that he had no objections to countermanding these orders except as regards the troops, which were already on their way and were to take the place of the undisciplined and discontented

Cossacks in Tehran. Norman added that he prepared a telegram to the commanding officer of Norperforce 'asking him to ascertain from Col. Smyth the facts regarding his interview with Sardar Homayoun'. On 19 February Moin al Molk returned with a further message from the Shah to the effect that although the counter-order prepared by Norman had been sent it had either not been received or had been disobeyed because the Cossacks were continuing their advance. The Shah wanted to send Sardar Homayoun personally to meet the Cossacks and induce them to return to Qazvin. Norman replied that he had no objection. 'On the same day Smyth answered my telegram that he had nothing to do with the order for the Cossacks to come to Tehran and Sardar Homayoun was solely responsible for issuing the initial orders.' Norman then contacted Sepahdar, with whom he had not spoken since the formation of his new cabinet, and pressed for the immediate dismissal of Sardar Homayoun.

Sardar Homayoun returned from his mission on Sunday 20 February and informed the Cabinet that he had met the advance guard of the Cossacks on the road between Qazvin and Karaj and had obtained from their leaders a promise that they would return to Qazvin. However, during the night of the nineteenth Sardar Homayoun had become aware that in spite of the promise, the Cossacks were continuing their march to Tehran.

Norman concluded:

> ... the part played by Sardar Homayoun in this affair was somewhat mysterious. He appeared to have favoured the movement at least in its initial stages... [since he] on his own initiative dispatched the original telegram which summoned the whole two detachments of Cossacks to Tehran... The most probable explanation of this action is therefore that he was merely the unconscious tool of the conspirators and that he was induced to send the telegrams by some of the officers surrounding him without realising the significance of what he was doing... In view of Sardar Homayoun's equivocal behaviour and of the fact that his general reputation for veracity is not high, I am reluctant to guarantee the accuracy of his version of what passed between him and the Cossacks.

Norman then mentioned that W.A. Smart, a Counsellor at the Legation, had been in touch with Sepahdar, who had been 'thoroughly alarmed over the resignation of Sardar Homayoun'. Sepahdar had proposed to send Col. Gleerup, the head of the Gendarmerie, with some men to intercept the Cossacks and ask them not to come to Tehran. Smart had suggested this would be inadvisable as there may be a fight and the Gendarmes would suffer heavy casualties. It had then been agreed that Sepahdar would send his deputy, Adib al

Saltaneh, to see the leaders of the Cossacks and enquire about their plans and demands. The Shah having been unable to reach Norman on the twentieth (Norman had decided to take a long walk that day), had instead contacted Smart at Sepahdar's house. Smart met the Shah at the latter's hunting lodge. The Shah had appeared 'agitated and wanted to flee' but Smart had been able to calm him. The Legation then decided to send Lt Col. Haig and Col. Huddleston to see the Cossack leaders. The Shah had added his secretary Moin al Molk to the group. The deputation, together with Adib al Saltaneh met Reza Khan's advance guard of Cossacks at Mehrabad (four miles from Tehran). In addition to Reza Khan the group met Maj. Mas'oud Khan, Col. Kazem Khan and one civilian, Seyyed Zia, 'who was probably the originator of the whole movement'. Norman explained that the two officers (Mas'oud Khan and Kazem Khan) 'were the two Persian officers attached to Smyth for the organisation of the Gendarmerie in Azarbaijan and Smyth had formed a high opinion of the capabilities of both'. He had enlisted their help in his work among the Cossacks and this was the reason for their presence at Qazvin. Reza Khan, as the spokesman for the group, had told the delegation:

> The Cossacks who had experience of the Bolsheviks and knew what to expect from them if they advanced further into Persia are tired of successive Persian Governments who failed to take any steps for the organisation of a force to oppose the invasion which might follow the withdrawal of British troops. They were therefore resolved to come to Tehran to establish a strong government which would remedy this state of affairs.

Norman added that in the interim he had telephoned Gen. Westdahl, the Chief of Police of Tehran, and cautioned him not to resist the Cossacks when they entered Tehran. He now reported that only 'two policemen were wounded when due to mixed signals they fired on the Cossacks'.

Norman dwelt no further on the origins of the coup or how the leaders came together and whether the Legation or British military advisers were privy to their plan. He again took up the case of the Farmanfarma family and reported that at 8.30am on 21 February Firouz had sent him a letter informing him that his father had been arrested and that he was expecting the same fate (Firouz was arrested at noon the same day). Norman protested that there was little he could do but he had received assurances that neither Firouz nor his family would be harmed. Norman then added:

> I have since learned that Farmanfarma had been arrested at 3am outside his house on his way to seek asylum at the US Legation. If indeed

he sought refuge there instead of this Legation, it would seem to show that he suspected we organised the Coup.

The Shah had not been able to reach Norman until the morning of the twenty-first when the coup had taken place and enquired what the British position was. Norman assured the Shah of his safety and advised him to support Seyyed Zia and Reza Khan. It was not, however, until the afternoon of the next day that the Shah received Seyyed Zia who asked that he be given the title of 'dictator'. The Shah refused this request but acquiesced in his premiership. Norman went on to say:

> All foreigners believe we organised [the coup] and my denials have no effect. But I am embarrassed over the arrest of pro-British Persians, especially Farmanfarma and his two sons. They have decorations and assurances in [Curzon's] telegram of 9 August 1919 [to Cox]... Several former Prime Ministers have been arrested... [Even] some opponents of the 1919 Agreement have been arrested.[40]

The former Prime Ministers arrested were Sepahsalar Tonokaboni, Sa'ad al Dowleh, Ain al Dowleh and Farmanfarma. The prominent opponents of the Agreement arrested were Mohtashem al Saltaneh, Momtaz al Dowleh and Seyyed Hassan Moddares. It can be safely said that almost all politicians of note and large landowners were arrested. The exceptions were less than a dozen: Mostofi; Hassan and Hosein Pirnia; Samsam al Saltaneh, the Bakhtiari leader and former Prime Minister; Saheb Ekhtiar (Gholam Hosein Ghaffari), a highly respected adviser to several Shahs; Maghrour Mirza (Movasaq al Dowleh), Minister of Court to Ahmad Shah; and Sepahdar, Prime Minister at the time of the coup. Within a month of the coup the number of detainees reached about 200.[41]

This is about the extent of available information from the Foreign Office and War Office records concerning reports and communications between Norman and Curzon. The lack of diligence by Norman and the apparent lack of interest by Curzon about the origins, details and sponsors of the coup are most puzzling. Norman, who kept Curzon informed of every significant development in Iran sometimes by as many as four dispatches a day, appears to have believed the coup was not important enough to have delved into its details and keep Curzon informed. There is no comment on the role of the British military personnel in Iran, not even a mention of Gen. Ironside and only a fleeting reference to Col. Smyth. These questions will be dealt with later.

COMMUNICATIONS BY VARIOUS BRITISH OFFICIALS

There are also some letters, memoranda and commentaries by British officials other than Norman which should be considered before the details of the coup can be discussed and its authorship ascertained. The material below will shed some light on these matters.

In a memorandum 'minuted for the files' dated 3 March 1921 G.P. Churchill wrote, 'The whole thing is evidently the result of a plot and Seyyed Zia ed Din the probable new Prime Minister is no doubt at the bottom of it'.[42]

In a memorandum prepared by Pierson Dixon of the Foreign Office and sent to Curzon on 14 May 1921, Dixon stated that 'Colonel Smyth had prior knowledge of the Coup and co-operated with the principals'.[43]

In a letter from Gen. Dickson, who had been recalled to London, to a member of the US Legation in Tehran dated 6 June 1921 he stated:

> I saw Colonel Smyth at Kazvin when I passed through and he admitted what we had all suspected, that it was he who had organised the Cossack Coup in Tehran. He also told me that he had done it with the knowledge of the Legation in Tehran. He did not say Mr Norman had a hand in it but admitted that W.A. Smart had. I am rather inclined to think that Smart, Haig and company ran the business without letting Norman in on the secret.[44]

In a letter from Gen. Dickson to Gen. Radcliffe (Ministry of War) dated 8 October 1921, Dickson stated that he advocated co-operation with nationalist elements in Persia, especially the former constitutionalists, in order to enlist public opinion on the side of Britain. Norman and others, however, 'believed in a forceful policy. They believed Persians would more readily submit to force and better results could be obtained.'[45]

In a letter from Maj. C.J. Edmonds, who had known Seyyed Zia from 1919 and had worked with him in preparing several plans to roll back the Bolsheviks, he stated: 'I did form a pretty shrewd idea what was in mind... [but] I did not probe too deeply... Seyyed Zia's fears were well founded and he thought too much knowledge would be embarrassing to me'.[46]

Another British officer in Iran at the time of the coup wrote: 'A little while after the Coup we were passing Kazvin and I asked Colonel Smyth whether in his opinion his participation in political movements in the country was not a little strange. He answered '... they asked my advice on military affairs and I as a military adviser had the duty to give my views'.[47]

8. Firouz Mirza Firouz (Nosrat al Dowleh III). Foreign minister when the 1919 Agreement with the British was concluded, he was highly ambitious and intelligent. But his vanity and extravagance eventually led under Reza Shah to his imprisonment and murder for suspicion of treachery.

9. Akbar Mirza Mas'oud (Sarem al Dowleh). The minister of finance in Vosouq's cabinet was the chief financial arm of the 'triumvirate's' schemes.

10. Lord Curzon. The British Foreign Secretary effectively controlled the politics of Iran between 1918 and 1923, ostensibly in the defence of India. But according to the British press, having discovered Persia in his travels as a younger man, Curzon thought he owned the country.

11. Sir Percy Cox. As British minister in Tehran between 1918 and 1920, Cox was to implement the 1919 Agreement. But his background in Mesopotamia and the Persian Gulf sheikhdoms failed to equip him to understand the emerging nationalism in Iran.

Lancelot Oliphant called the coup 'astounding' and observed that 'the large body of men can not have passed through Tehran or near Kazvin without Gen. Ironside having some inkling of their presence,' Curzon appears to have agreed with Oliphant regarding Ironside's complicity and believed Norman was also involved. He had added, 'Mr Norman has at last found a worthy rival in the art of creating Persian governments and Prime Ministers'.[48]

J.M. Balfour, the highest-ranking Treasury official in Iran, (Armitage Smith had gone to London to negotiate with APOC on behalf of the Iranian Government concerning royalty payments) had been a witness to the events of 20-21 February. In his book *Recent Happenings in Persia* there is a brief chapter on these events and what he relates is substantially the same as Norman's reports. He believed that the Legation had no hand in staging the coup. His conclusion was that although Britain gave moral support, 'the Coup was the result of the conjunction of two separate movements'. He did not specify, however, what these movements were.[49]

The primary force and motivator in this drama, Ironside, also made several specific references to an imminent coup. The earliest reference was on 14 February. 'Better a Coup d'etat than anything else... I'll bounce old Norman'. On 15 February his entry in the Diaries reads: 'I told him [Norman] about Reza and he was very fearful that the Shah would be done in. I told him I believed in Reza... I had to let the Cossacks go sometime or other'.[50] After the coup, Ironside reported to his superior, Gen. Haldane, that the Cossacks went to Tehran 'to arrest turbulant Cossack officers by the order of the Shah and with the knowledge of Norman'.[51] In the Diaries Ironside was less modest. In an entry after the coup written on 23 or 24 February he stated, 'I fancy that all the people think that I engineered the Coup d'etat, I supposed I did strictly speaking'.[52]

ACCOUNTS FROM US LEGATION REPORTS

In an early report on the immediate consequences of the coup dated 11 March 1921 Caldwell, the Minister to Tehran, reported:

> Seyyed Zia issued a proclamation on 26 February that he has assumed... the premiership with plenary and dictatorial powers and is now by direction of the Shah conducting governmental affairs with hourly advice from the British Legation... The Premier is a British protegé whose purpose, character and antecedents are not above suspicion, in fact he is known to have received while editor of the official newspaper *Ra'ad*, a regular stipend from the British...

He has now announced the abrogation of the Anglo-Persian
Agreement of 1919.

> The present Premier was one of its principal protagonists since its very
> inception and up to his taking office. He is known to be simply a tool for
> British politics and his announcement of the abrogation of a treaty not
> yet ratified by the Persian Parliament, as provided by the Persian
> Constitution is at best a misnomer, even though an attempt was made to
> put the Agreement into effect without such ratification... It is perfectly
> apparent that the whole movement [the coup] is of British origin and
> support, in furtherance of the scheme of forceful control of the country.[53]

The first detailed report of the US Legation in Tehran on the coup is
in a quarterly report sent by Caldwell to the US Secretary of State
dated 5 April 1921. Caldwell had waited some five weeks to be able
to assemble all the available information. The report begins with the
state of Cossack troops and reports on their 'miserable condition.
They had no clothing and their food was bad... They grumbled a lot
and were near revolt'. British military personnel were making an effort
to improve their lot and train the contingent that was stationed in
Qazvin.

> On the morning of Sunday 20th February we heard a force of about 1500
> Cossacks had marched from Kazvin and were at that moment only a few
> miles from the capital, but the full scope of their purpose was then
> unknown. That afternoon the British Minister had gone out of the city for
> a walk and did not return until about 5pm. But a few hours before that
> time the Counsellor of the British Legation, Colonel Haig, together with
> Seyed Zia, had gone out to meet the Cossacks. The purpose of these two
> was stated to be to ascertain the intentions of the invading Cossacks, but
> the Cossacks themselves made no secret of the fact that each one of
> them had been given five toumans (about five dollars), by the British just
> before entering the city.
>   It should be remembered in connection with this invasion that
> these Cossacks were under the direct control of Colonel Smyth, an
> Englishman in the employ of the Persian Government who was some
> months ago in charge of the intelligence office at Kazvin, and who for
> some time past [had] been actually at the head of the Cossacks... He
> made frequent trips to Tehran and it is known that he spent a good part
> of his time during these trips in the presence of Seyed Zia. It is also
> known that just previous to the Cossacks' departure from Kazvin,
> Colonel Smyth received the money to pay this force, but it seemed that
> he preferred that they wait for their money until their arrival in Tehran
> and soon after their arrival here they were paid and the money was
> drawn from the bank under Colonel Smyth's signature. But the strange
> point is that although this force was kept in Kazvin [the headquarters of
> the British forces in Persia] under British control, they left that city with
> British supplies, marched the distance of approximately 100 miles in
> four days, there being both telephone and telegraph along the whole

route, as well as wireless stations in the hands of the British at both Kazvin and Tehran and that neither the Persian Government nor the British Legation here seem to have known that the Cossacks were marching on the capital with the intention of capturing it until the afternoon of the fourth day after the troops had left Kazvin and when they were only a few miles outside of Tehran. The whole thing was so well ordered and well arranged that it would have been impossible for it to have been carried out as it was, without collusion.

The British Minister denies that he had any fore-knowledge of the affair and the facts seem to bear out his statement, but it is well known that the London Foreign Office has been dissatisfied with the accomplishment of their Minister in Tehran and the things he has failed to do, and it is therefore not to be wondered at that this movement was carried out without his knowledge.

A little after midnight on the night of the 20th the Cossacks entered Tehran. They were joined by the Gendarmes who are supposed to protect the capital and the interior of Persia and when the Shah sent a Swedish officer to take charge of the Persian militia [regular army] in an effort to keep the Cossacks out of Tehran, that officer found that the regular army had joined the Cossacks. Three canon shots were fired in the air as well as numerous rifle shots. The only resistance encountered was that of the police at their central office. Two men were killed and the rest surrendered. Otherwise the Coup seems to have been accomplished without bloodshed.

It was learned that practically all the principal players in the movement were men who had before been intimately connected with the British. Major Massoud Khan who has since been made Minister of War, has for several months past been the personal assistant of Colonel Smyth at Kazvin. Colonel Reza Khan who has assumed the Commandership of the Cossacks served on the Anglo-Persian Mission, being practically a spy working for the Chief of that Mission, and for some months past has been working in close co-operation with the British in Kazvin.[54]

Caldwell concludes his report by implying that the Foreign Office had been behind the coup, saying Curzon 'reiterates that he is a true friend of Persia. It is very evident that he feels what is to India's interest is for Persia's good.' Curzon feels that Great Britain would 'be doing Persia the greatest kindness if it assumed the white man's burden... but the Persians resent being put in the same position as the Indians'. Caldwell then adds:

It seems the [British] Legation here had begun to feel that [Gen. Dickson] was no longer in entire accord with the policy it wished to pursue. The General was born at the British Legation in Tehran and was strongly in sympathy with nationalists... Several days after the Coup d'etat... the General was called by the British Legation and told that he should leave immediately as his continued presence here was considered detrimental to the British cause, and he was specifically accused of having given reports on the present situation and late happenings to the American

Legation. This false accusation he, of course, denied but immediately left the city...[55]

The most telling report by the US Legation was sent some four years later in which the Chargé d'Affaires states:

Colonel Gleerup of the Gendarmerie and Colonel Westdahl in charge of Tehran police issued summary instructions to their units to keep to their quarters during the nights of February 20 and 21 and both subsequently were awarded GCMG for their loyalty to British interests in Iran.[56]

* * *

The two principal actors, Reza Khan and Seyyed Zia, have left no written record of their versions of these events.[57] Several generations after the coup there is still a lack of unanimity as to how it came about and what role Britain played in its genesis and execution. Even assuming the coup was the result of the conjunction of 'two separate movements',[58] one headed by Reza Khan and the other by Seyyed Zia, many questions of detail remain unanswered. When and how did these two principals meet? Who put them in touch and who financed the operation? It is nearly certain that Ironside was the godfather of the coup. Together with Smyth they narrowed down the choice of candidates to lead the coup and settled on Reza Khan. It is less certain how and by whom Seyyed Zia was chosen. Was it Norman and/or other members of the Legation? Did Smyth, as the representative of Ironside, also have a hand in Seyyed Zia's selection? Also unanswered is whether the Foreign Office in London was aware of the coming coup and whether Curzon gave his blessing to the enterprise? Although there is a paucity of material in the files of the British Public Record Office, enough ancillary and circumstantial evidence exists for a well-rounded picture to emerge and allow the reconstruction of the event from its inception to conclusion.

The chief instigator of the coup, Gen. Ironside, left behind a written record of his thoughts and actions during his short stay in Iran. He wrote soon after his arrival that Curzon's policy was unworkable and should be abandoned. His policy had made it more difficult to effect the orderly and safe withdrawal of British troops. There had to be a strong government in Iran to ensure a safe withdrawal and enable the Iranian forces to withstand the looming Bolshevik threat. The most often repeated refrain in Ironside's Diaries is that 'Persia needs a leader'. Soon after the removal of Russian officers from their command of the Cossacks, Ironside was introduced by Col. Smyth to a relatively obscure Iranian officer, Reza Khan, and appointed him as the deputy Commander of the Cossacks stationed in the Qazvin area. On evidence of Reza Khan's previous command Ironside believed he could train and reorganise the Cossacks into a fighting unit. The progress reports Ironside received from Smyth concerning Reza Khan were reassuring and Ironside became convinced that Reza Khan could extract loyalty from his soldiers and fellow officers. By mid December Ironside had met the Shah and some members of the Iranian Government and considered them useless. He became even more convinced that Iran needed new leadership and by late December he began to view Reza Khan as more than merely the leader of the Cossacks. Reza Khan could be the leader he had been hoping for. He found additional reasons to strengthen his judgement in Reza Khan's humble background and absence of ties to the decadent governing class.

Ironside soon realised that he may have exaggerated Reza Khan's strengths. His candidate was a fine soldier and commander but he had no political base and was relatively unknown to the Legation. Reza Khan could not possibly assume the post of Prime Minister. He had to have a civilian counterpart who was better known and had political acumen. Whether it was Norman or others who alerted him to Reza Khan's shortcomings, Ironside knew he must have Norman's co-operation. It should not have been difficult to convince Norman that a general shake-up was the only answer. Sepahdar had proven weak and had not been able to form a new Cabinet. He had remained in office only because others had declined or were unacceptable to the Shah or the Legation. Ironside and Norman also concurred that Curzon's insistence on ratification of the agreement was futile. There are more than five entries in the Diaries that indicate Ironside discussed with Norman the substance of his plans. We also know from Norman's own dispatches that he had been in contact with Smyth.

One reputable commentator has argued that Ironside believed security arrangements at the Legation were lax and hence he would have been loathe to trust Norman with confidential matters.[59] The writer then cites the example of Ironside having gone to Baghdad to personally report to Gen. Haldane instead of informing the latter by telegraph. There is no mention in the Diaries about 'laxness' of security or any indication that Ironside did not trust Norman. Ironside's report to Gen. Haldane concerned the condition and deployment of British troops at Manjeel Pass and the road from Manjeel to Qazvin and it would have been prudent to impart the information to Haldane in person. Flight time between Hamadan and Baghdad was only five hours. On the other hand we have three entries in the Diaries in which Ironside confides his decision to 'release' Reza Khan and the Cossacks.

As discussed before, the term 'release' as used by Ironside, could only mean the Cossacks would march on Tehran to topple the Government and replace it with one more to their liking. If 'release' simply meant that Reza Khan would be authorised to lead his troops to Tehran to discipline their fellow soldiers, why does Ironside extract a promise from Reza Khan that he must not take any action against the Shah? There is a final entry of 15 February in which Ironside again spoke of Reza Khan to Norman and added that Norman 'was very fearful that the Shah would be done in'. Ironside was forced to reassure Norman that 'he believed in Reza' and no harm would come to the Shah. Ironside concluded that in any event he had 'to let the Cossacks go sometime or other', regardless of the consequences. This last conversation with Norman, only six days before the coup, makes it clear that Norman understood the full implication of the term 'letting the Cossacks go'. The Cossacks had actually started their march towards Tehran on 12 February and Norman probably had been convinced much earlier that something drastic had to be done. It is clear from the Diary entries that Ironside did or ultimately had to trust Norman to further implement his plans.

Norman had had a difficult time in Iran. He had previously acted without the approval and knowledge of the Foreign Office on several occasions and the results had not been satisfactory. He had offended Curzon, who still blamed him for failure to support Vosouq. Curzon continued to believe that Britain's difficulties in Iran began with the departure of Vosouq. Norman now had the timid Sepahdar on his hands. Sepahdar's promises to implement the Agreement either by parliamentary approval or tacitly by utilising British military and financial advisers had been unfulfilled. Since Sepahdar could not even form a government, Norman was probably justified in thinking that the removal of Sepahdar would be welcome in London, even if effected by a coup. Norman believed his new candidate, Seyyed Zia, would be able to accomplish what his predecessors had been unable to do. Norman always had been over-enthusiastic about the prime ministers he had chosen. Pirnia was 'honest and respected' and the only person who could complete parliamentary elections, convene parliament and have the Agreement ratified. Sepahdar was decent and harmless and would do 'what he is told'. He would effectively put the Agreement into operation. Yet neither of his candidates lived up to expectations and the situation worsened. In Seyyed Zia Norman had a person who had proven his loyalty to Britain during the war years and had remained a steadfast supporter of Vosouq during the latter's most difficult period. He had proved resourceful and had prepared plans to defeat the insurgents in the North. Several members of the Legation had worked with Seyyed Zia and had found him trustworthy. Furthermore, Seyyed Zia was ready to assume office. He had a ready cabinet from the membership of his 'Iron Committee'. Upon becoming Prime Minister, Seyyed Zia in fact appointed four members of his 'Iron Committee' as ministers with important portfolios, and another as the Military Governor of Tehran.[60]

Norman was later to deny his involvement in the coup and the selection of Seyyed Zia as Prime Minister but these denials are negated by his ringing endorsement of Seyyed Zia immediately following it. From the very first reports Norman defended Seyyed Zia with an intensity and fervour not shown even when Pirnia or Sepahdar assumed office. The reports also indicate that Norman had had many conversations with Seyyed Zia and had been privy to his thoughts and plans. On 25 February, a few days before the actual renunciation of the Agreement by Seyyed Zia, Norman assured Curzon that 'Renunciation of Agreement should not mean anything as Seyyed Zia would carry out contents of the Agreement with British officers and financial advisers and would reorganise the Cossacks with British officers'.[61]

On 3 March 1921, Norman wrote to Curzon:

The new Prime Minister is the first person who has ever seriously attempted to introduce reforms and thus put Persia in a position to help herself and I trust the fact that he has assumed office by somewhat drastic methods will not prejudice His Majesty's Government against him... Power could not have been wrested otherwise than by force from small gang of men either corrupt or incapable, or both who have hitherto monopolised it and well nigh ruined the country, and imprisonment and exile provide the only means of preventing them from regaining their former positions and completing their evil work... [Even] some of the old corrupt governing class welcome Coup d'etat and its results as Persia's last hope of salvation from the Bolsheviks.

In a later telegram Norman made the ludicrous comparison that Seyyed Zia 'after Mirza Taqi Khan [Amir Kabir] is the first person to attempt serious changes'.[62]

Seyyed Zia's supporters were not limited to Norman and the civilian members of the Legation. By the middle of 1920, he was known to members of the British military. As mentioned before, Col. Sayyah and Maj. Keyhan who had served with Smyth were on close terms with Seyyed Zia. It is very likely that Smyth's first introduction to Seyyed Zia came through Sayyah and Keyhan. Maj. Edmonds and his colleagues had worked with Seyyed Zia in preparing military plans to oust the insurgents from their strongholds in the North. Norman, after reviewing the plan, had recommended it to Curzon.[63] Ironside must have heard about Seyyed Zia from Smyth although it is most unlikely that the two ever met.

There are further indications of Norman's knowledge of or complicity in the coup. The number of exchanges between Norman and Curzon during previous changes of prime ministers was considerable. In the five days preceeding the resignation of Vosouq in June 1920 and the appointment of Pirnia, the telegraphic traffic between Tehran and London averaged four telegrams each day. Roughly the same is true of the period beginning with the dismissal of Starosselsky, leading to the resignation of Pirnia and the installation of Sepahdar as Prime Minister. During the period between 19 February and 1 March communications were limited to about one telegram a day dealing mainly with the arrest and imprisonment of Iranian politicians who held decorations and had been given guarantees of protection by the British Crown and Government. It took a week before Norman sent his first report on the details of the coup itself. It is surprising that Curzon, who had literally gambled his political fortune on his plan to reconstitute Anglo-Persian relations, should now become a disinterested observer and indifferent to the genesis and outcome of a military coup unprecedented in Iran for over 130 years.[64] It is quite probable that certain exchanges of incriminating correspondence and telegrams have been removed at least for the time being from the active files of Britain's Public Record Office.

However highly Seyyed Zia was regarded by Norman and his staff Reza Khan initially appears to have been somewhat unknown to them and they appear to have been indifferent to his role in the coming events. Norman was counting on Seyyed Zia to carry the load as the future Prime Minister. Other than a passing reference to Reza Khan as an 'honest and capable officer without political ambitions',[65] there is hardly any mention of him in Norman's early reports to Curzon. Later, when Reza Khan proved to be an obstacle in the path of Seyyed Zia's employing British officers, and especially when Seyyed Zia was forced to appoint him Minister of War, Norman turned against Reza Khan. In his remaining days in Tehran Norman denigrated him and accused him of being sympathetic to the new Soviet envoy Rothstein and the Soviet Military Attaché. After Seyyed Zia was ousted on 25 May 1921 Norman's enmity towards Reza Khan increased. It was reported that 'Reza Khan is openly anti-British and working in close touch with Rothstein'.[66] Later he was accused of having frequent meetings with Rothstein and having 'two meetings daily with the Soviet Millitary Attaché'.[67]

From Ironside's Diaries and earlier accounts by others, as well as Norman's course of conduct before and after the coup, one reaches the inescapable conclusion that Norman was aware of and collaborated with Ironside in laying the groundwork. The highly theatrical episode related by Samii on the eve of the coup when Col. Haig briefed Norman on the march of the Cossacks to the outskirts of Tehran was transparent even at the time. Norman's feigned ignorance of the movement and its purpose was solely to protect himself later viz-a-viz the Shah and Sepahdar. As early as 18 February Norman, in a dispatch to Norperforce Headquarters in Qazvin, had stated that 'a few hundred Cossacks are on the way to Tehran to replace unruly Cossacks'.[68] Norman could not deny on the twentieth what he knew already on the eighteenth and his protestation to Curzon that Col. Haig was also in the dark about the movement of the Cossacks is equally difficult to believe.

Haig's demeanour at the meeting with Norman and later at the Cossack camp in Mehrabad was also a charade to convince the representatives of the Shah and Sepahdar that the Legation was as ignorant as they were about the possibility of a coup. The distance from the Cossack Camp at Aqa Baba to Tehran is about 140km. There were at least four telegraph stations along the way in addition to mobile wireless sets and telephones. We are asked to believe that the Cossacks started out from their camp on 12 February and no-one knew or became aware of the movement of between 600 and 1500 men marching towards Tehran until 20 February.[69]

The long walk of Norman on the twentieth is equally suspect.[70] His hosting a dinner that evening borders on the absurd.[71] How could Britain's envoy, who was running every vital facet of the Iranian Government, act so nonchalantly on the eve of a significant day? Even if we were to believe that Norman thought that only 600 Cossacks were entering Tehran to punish and disarm their unruly brethren, his indifference and detachment are surprising. There could have been fighting amongst the two groups with serious consequences. There could have been a mass escape by imprisoned Bolshevik sympathisers and agents. The situation called for more involvement from Norman and Legation staff. The explanation for Norman's activities on the twentieth is simply his reluctance to be accessible to the Shah and Sepahdar that day and evening.

The telegram of 1 March from Norman to Curzon which intended to explain the reasons for the movement of troops to Tehran, is unconvincing. If Smyth's entire purpose was to discipline a few unruly

Cossacks in Tehran, why did he request a force of 2200 men? Even if it were an exercise for the Cossacks stationed in Tehran to be sent to Qazvin for refitting and training and to be replaced by Cossacks from Qazvin, several questions still remain. First, why the mass displacement of the Cossacks in one operation? Would it not have been militarily prudent to accomplish the replacement in stages? There were Bolshevik troops and local insurgent forces in the north that could attack British and Cossack positions. Second, why should Reza Khan have been sent to Tehran with these reliefs? He would have been more needed in Qazvin to discipline the arriving unruly Cossacks and attend to their training. Norman does not explain why he readily concurred with Smyth's initial request without questioning the advisability of sending such a large force to Tehran in one movement. Furthermore, if Norman believed in the necessity for the replacement of troops as requested by Smyth, why did he without question accept the Shah's request to countermand the initial order? Finally, why was the task of implementing the countermanding orders entrusted to Sardar Homayoun who Norman described as 'distinguished neither for intelligence nor for discretion'.[72] Despite Norman's arguments that he made a genuine effort to countermand the orders, it appears that he had no intention of doing so when the wheels of the coup had been set in motion.

A compelling reason for Norman's readiness to acquiesce to Ironside's plans was the hopelessness of Sepahdar's situation. Sepahdar had been unable to call parliament into session to vote on the Agreement. He became unwilling to take any further steps that could be interpreted as a tacit acceptance of the Agreement; there was no draw down on the loan; British financial advisers were still hampered from doing their work; and the plans for the creation of unified armed forces was held in abeyance. From early January Sepahdar had been unable to form a cabinet acceptable to the Shah. The Shah had approached Mostofi and Ain al Dowleh on the possibility of a new government but both had declined. Sepahdar had resigned on 19 January 1921. On 23 January he assumed office again but was unable to form a cabinet until 3 February. He was forced to tender his resignation again on 6 February. He headed a caretaker government until he was finally able to constitute a cabinet on 17 February. After nearly two months of delay the new Cabinet remained basically the same, with five ministers simply changing portfolios and only one newcomer.

The idea of the division of Iran into regions to be ruled by sectional kings and rulers, as advanced by G.P. Churchill and Cox, was unworkable and risky. It was not difficult for Norman to reason that the only alternative would be a combination of the eager and ready Seyyed Zia and Reza Khan, even if they had to come into power by extraordinary means. Curzon surely would be realistic enough to know there were no other alternatives. Curzon had always wanted an authoritarian prime minister and Seyyed Zia appeared to fit that description. Reza Khan had given his word to Ironside that the monarchy would be unaffected and the Qajars would remain on the throne. Order would soon be restored and Curzon's anger would be only temporary. Seyyed Zia and Reza Khan complimented each other perfectly. One would attend to political and administrative reforms and the other would revitalise the military to withstand the threat of Bolshevism. More important to Curzon, the primary aims of the 1919 Agreement would be realised as Seyyed Zia had promised the employement of British financial and military advisers. As a final argument Norman could maintain that the Cossacks in Tehran were in a state of open revolt and something had to be done. Since British troops could not enter Tehran to quell the Cossack uprising without the approval of the British command in Mesopotamia, the Qazvin contingent of the Cossacks had to inter-vene to avert a state of anarchy.[73]

The recounting of events by Iranian military officers who took part in the march to Tehran all refer to or strongly hint at the par-ticipation of other unnamed conspirators in the coup. Yazdanpanah indicates collusion with certain unnamed parties who gave Reza Khan the green light to begin his march. Amir Ahmadi refers to unspecified 'statesmen' who were behind the coup. Arfa strongly hints that the conspiracy had reached the Gendarmerie and its senior officers had been told not to resist the Cossacks. Samii's account clearly shows that there was no serious attempt by the Legation to dissuade the Cossacks from entering Tehran. Ironside's Diaries makes it clear that he told Norman of his plans to elevate Reza Khan to the dominant military position in Iran and to allow and even encourage him to march on Tehran. There is every indi-cation that it was understood by both Ironside and Norman that the march to Tehran would culminate in the forceful overthrow of the Government.

The involvement of the War Office is difficult to ascertain on the basis of available documents. There is the possibility that Ironside acted without letting his superiors know of his plans. But Ironside was too disciplined a soldier not to have given some explanation in order to obtain at least their tacit approval. Furthermore, as the safety and orderly withdrawal of British troops from Iran was of paramount importance, Ironside had to let his superiors know at least the broad outline of his plan. It should be remembered that within two weeks of his coming to Iran he found Bolshevik insurgent forces poised to enter Tehran. The Foreign Office and the Iranian Government were planning to abandon the northern part of the country and establish a temporary capital several hundreds of kilometres from Tehran. Iranian soldiers and officers had not been paid for months and were close to mutiny. The Government was headed by ineffectual and useless men. What choice was there other than to install a strong man to avoid chaos, even by a coup d' etat.

If the coup failed there could have been serious consquences for British troops stationed in Qazvin and the Manjeel Pass. It appears likely that Ironside informed and convinced Gen. Haldane of the necessity for a coup and that it posed no risks. Haldane, in turn, would have informed Field Marshal Wilson who continued to have the highest regard for Ironside's judgement. It was Wilson who had personally selected Ironside for the risky troop withdrawal from Iran. Whether Wilson or Haldane knew the details of Ironside's plans is open to conjecture but they at least must have been aware of Ironside's intention to groom Reza Khan as leader of the Iranian forces with all the consequences that such an appointment might entail. The only relevant communication among available British documents is a very matter-of-fact telegram that 'They [Cossacks] originally went to Tehran to avert turbulent Cossack officers by the order of the Shah and with the knowledge of Norman'.[74] In the end the matter became somewhat academic as the coup was a complete success, posing no risks and even facilitating British troop withdrawal two months later.

As to Colonels Haig, Huddleston and Folkstone, it should be noted that all three were under the command of the War Office, although Haig had been temporarily seconded to the Foreign Office serving as acting Counsellor of the Legation and Huddleston was serving as acting Military Attaché with Folkstone under him. The loyalty of all three unltimately lay with the War Office and the military chain of command. Ironside, the ranking British military man in Iran, was effectively their superior and they would follow his orders. Besides, as Norman, their nominal superior, was drawn in on the plan the three had nothing to lose. It was irrelevant as far as they were concerned whether Norman had the approval of the Foreign Office and it was not their responsibility to inform the Foreign Office of any plans Norman and Ironside may have had.

The US Legation's reports accept Norman's protestations of innocence and instead point the finger at the Foreign Office (Curzon) as having organised the coup. To support his argument, the US Minister refers to the deteriorating relations between Curzon and Norman. But the involvement of the Foreign Office is open to doubt. What the US Legation is unaware of is that Norman had a long history of acting without Foreign Office instructions. He failed to support Vosouq, he selected Pirnia for the premiership and then he brought in Sepahdar. In each of these instances Curzon was faced with a *fait accompli*. Even the timing of Starosselsky's dismissal was done without consulting the Foreign Office. With the arrival of a wild card in the person of Gen. Ironside, Norman would become even more daring. In the absence of any contradictory documents it appears that Norman, contrary to US suppositions, was an active participant in the events leading to the coup but did not keep the Foreign Office fully informed. Norman of course paid a price for his independence and insubordination. His fate was sealed when his last candidate as Prime Minister, Seyyed Zia, fell from power in late May 1921. He was soon afterwards recalled from Tehran and on his return to London was not even received by Curzon. He was offered a meaningless post in South America which he declined and resigned from the Diplomatic Service.[75]

From available evidence it appears that the coup-makers, Ironside and Norman, each only knew one of the two Iranian principals. Norman probably never even met Reza Khan until the latter became the commander of forces. Norman was of course briefed by Ironside and Smyth that Reza Khan was an honest, fearless and patriotic soldier. In the same way Ironside probably had never met Seyyed Zia but heard accounts from Norman and Smyth of his trustworthyness and pro-British sentiments. In all likelihood Ironside did not want to know the political component of the coup and Norman did not want to be involved in its military aspects.

Another consequence of the coup was that Ironside never returned to Iran. He had been sent there to accomplish an orderly and safe withdrawal of British troops. The troops were to remain for another two months after the coup. Ironside's task was unfinished and yet he was kept in Baghdad and assigned to units in Mesopotamia. As quoted earlier, Ironside commented after the coup, 'I fancy that all the people think that I engineered the Coup d'etat. I suppose I did strictly speaking'.[76] Did this boastful admission prevent him from returning to Iran to complete his mission? What Ironside confided in his diary was probably suspected by others and the military did not want to be embarrassed further.[77]

Despite official British protestations over the years that Britain did not have anything to do with the coup, it is worth noting that when it suited Britain's purpose British Information Services in

August 1941 issued statements admitting and even exaggerating Britain's role in the coup. This was when the continued rule of Reza Shah was deemed detrimental to British interests and pressure was being exerted to discredit Reza Shah and force him to abdicate and go into exile.[78] It is also interesting to note that the publication by Gen. Ironside's son of his father's Diaries and the appearance of the so-called 'last will and testament' of Ardeshir Reporter were both in the 1972–1973 period when Mohammad Reza Shah had reached the zenith of his power and enjoyed worldwide success. The correspondence between Ironside's heirs and the Iranian court makes one wonder about the timing.[79] With the increase of Iranian oil revenues, Britain was most anxious to enlarge her share of exports to Iran. How advantageous now to be associated with the coming to power of the Pahlavi dynasty and the creation of the new Iran, although one might think that this would have been an embarrassment to the ruling Pahlavi monarch.

In discussing the speedy success of the coup it should be pointed out that beyond whatever assistance the British may have given, Iranians had become tired of the succession of incompetent and weak politicians who were ruling the country and wanted a strong central government. Even in 1921 Iran was not a country that could have been taken over by 600 or even 3,000 Cossacks. The coup had to have had the support of large segments of the bureaucracy, merchants, the intelligentsia and the overwhelming support of the various branches of the armed services. Iran was ripe for a strong and autocratic leader and desperately yearned for a saviour.

NOTES ON CHAPTER 7
Further details of publications and documents in Bibliography

1   Gen. Hassan Arfa, *Under Five Shahs*, p 90.
2   Reza Niazmand, *Reza Shah az Tavalod ta Saltanat* (*Reza Shah From Birth to Throne*), p 7; see also Gen. Arfa, *Under Five Shahs*, pp 90–91 and Donald N. Wilber, *Riza Shah Pahlavi*, pp 4–5.
3   Reza Niazmand, *Reza Shah az Tavalod ta Saltanat* (*Reza Shah From Birth to Throne*), p 9.
4   The Palani clan is mentioned in *Tarikh Khani*, a history of Gilan and Mazandaran by Ali Larijani originially published in 922 of the Lunar Year (1535AD) and republished in St Petersburg in 1857: quoted in Mohamad Taqi Bahar, *Tarikh Mokhtasar Ahzab Siasi* (*A Short History of Political Parties*), vol. 1, p 69.
5   Interviews with members of Pahlavan family, descendants of Cheraq Ali Khan, Los Angeles, January 1995.
6   Reza Niazmand, *Reza Shah az Tavalod ta Saltanat* (*Reza Shah From Birth to Throne*), p 13.
7   Letter from Abbas Ali Dadash Beik Savad Kouhi to Azd al Molk: *Tarikh Mo'aser Iran* (*History of Contemporary Iran*), vol. 6, p 227.
8   Reza Shah's birth is variously given as 1877 (Reza Niazmand, *Reza Shah az Tavalod ta Saltanat* [*Reza Shah From Birth to Throne*], p 16) and 1878 (Donald N. Wilber, *Riza Shah Pahlavi*, p 5). In an official document issued by the Iranian Birth Registrar some 44 years after Reza's birth, the date is 1875: doc. no. 5963, 1298 (1919). Noush Afarin's death was probably in 1884 when Reza was six or seven years old: Reza Niazmand, *Reza Shah az Tavalod ta Saltanat* (*Reza Shah From Birth to Throne*), p 26.
9   Donald N. Wilber, *Riza Shah Pahlavi*, p 5.
10 Reza Niazmand, *Reza Shah az Tavalod ta Saltanat* (*Reza Shah From Birth to Throne*), p 16.
11 According to Mohamad Taqi Bahar, *Tarikh Mokhtasar Ahzab Siasi* (*A Short History of Political Parties*), vol. 1, p 69–70, Reza Khan had personally related this story to him and had repeated the story to several other people. Reza Niazmand, *Reza Shah az Tavalod ta Saltanat* (*Reza Shah From Birth to Throne*), pp 17–18.
12 Reza Niazmand, *Reza Shah az Tavalod ta Saltanat* (*Reza Shah From Birth to Throne*), p 58. The historian Ahmad Kasravi mentions that Reza Khan, then a junior Cossack officer, took part in the siege of Tabriz in 1909. Ahmad Kasravi, *Tarikh-e-Mashrouteh Iran* (*The History of the Constitutional Movement of Iran*), pp 825, 855.
13 Vincent Sheean, 'Rival Imperialism in Persia', *Asia*, 1927, p 35, mentions that Reza Khan may have served as a guard or adjutant for Farmanfarma and Sardar As'ad III during this period. Bahar states that Reza Khan served under Sardar As'ad in a military campaign in Ardabil in Northwest Iran: Mohamad Taqi Bahar, *Tarikh Mokhtasar Ahzab Siasi* (*A Short History of Political Parties*), vol. 1, p 71.
14 Mohamad Taqi Bahar, *Tarikh Mokhtasar Ahzab Siasi* (*A Short History of Political Parties*), vol. 1, p 73: see also Gen. Hassan Arfa, *Under Five Shahs*, pp 91, 106; Donald N. Wilber, *Riza Shah Pahlavi*, pp 11–12.
15 Hassan Naraqi, *Tarikh-e-Ejtema'i Kashan* (*The Social History of Kashan*), p 309; Hassan Naraqi, *Kashan dar Jonbesh Mashrouteh Iran* (*Kashan in*

the Constitutional Movement of Iran) p 159: see also Seyyed Assadollah Montakheb al Sadat Yaghma'i, *Hamaseh Fath Nameh Naibi* (*The Epic of the Victorious Naibi*), pp 186–189. It recounts that the Cossacks in the campaign against the bandits in 1911–1913 were led by Reza Khan who held the rank equivalent to Captain.

16 Hamdam al Saltaneh, 1904–1992, married Hadi Atabai in 1924 and had three children: Reza Niazmand, *Reza Shah az Tavalod ta Saltanat* (*Reza Shah From Birth to Throne*), p 109 maintains that Reza Khan married a girl (Safieh) from Hamadan in 1913 whom he divorced soon after.

17 Taj al Molouk, 1897–1981, was the official Queen of Iran during Reza Shah's reign. Her children are Shams, 1917–1996; Ashraf, b. 1919; Mohammad Reza Pahlavi, also b. 1919, became Crown Prince on 1 January 1926, second Pahlavi monarch in September 1941 and he died in 1980; the last offspring from this marriage was Ali Reza, 1922–1955.

18 Gholam Reza, b. 1923. Reza Khan divorced Turan within a year for reasons not entirely clear. He probably resented the fact that her father and grandfather were Qajar grandees. Conversation with Gholam Reza Pahlavi, the only offspring of that marriage, New York, November 1996.

19 Abdol Reza, b.1924; Ahmad Reza, 1925 to c.1981; Mahmoud Reza, b. 1926; Fatemeh, 1930–1989; Hamid Reza, 1932–1992.

20 *Ra'ad*, no. 280, Bahman 1296 (January 1918).

21 Mohamad Taqi Bahar, *Tarikh Mokhtasar Ahzab Siasi* (*A Short History of Political Parties*), vol. 1, p 75–78.

22 FO 371/6427, Dixon to Curzon, 14 May 1921.
    In a recently published work it is alleged that in early 1918 Reza Khan, then a Brigadier General, dismayed over the Anglo-Russian occupation of Iran contacted the German Legation in Tehran and proposed that with German financial support he could dislodge the Russian officers commanding the Cossack Division. He could thereafter oust the Tehran Government and bring a nationalist government into power. Reza Khan's proposals were relayed to Berlin but by the time Germany decided to support Reza Khan, German forces had been defeated on the western front and Germany had sued for an armistice. The account is not further substantiated: Abolqasem Kahalzadeh, *Dideh ha va Shenideh ha* (*Things Seen and Heard*), pp 299–308, 387–388, 397. Kahalzadeh was the secretary of the German Legation in Tehran.

23 Gen. Hassan Arfa, *Under Five Shahs*, p 91.

24 F.A.C. Forbes Leith, *Checkmate: Fighting Tradition in Central Asia*, p 22. Forbes Leith had been an officer in Dunsterville's expeditionary force against the Bolsheviks in 1917–1918. He had resigned his commission to work as the administrator of the vast estates of Sardar Akram, the son-in-law of Vosouq. In an interesting book he describes the famine of 1917–1918 in Iran, the condition of the country on the eve of the coup and Ahmad Shah's unpopularity for hoarding grain during the war, having acquired the name Ahmad Alaf (Ahmad the grain dealer): *ibid.*, pp 150–152.

25 Gen. Hassan Arfa, *Under Five Shahs*, p 91.

26 Shortly after the publication of the Ironside Diaries, Ardeshir Reporter's 'Last Will and Testament' surfaced. It was allegedly written in November 1931 and was brought to the attention of the late Mohmmad Reza Shah

in about 1972 by Ardeshir Reporter's son Shahpour. Ardeshir Reporter, an Indian Parsee who served at the British Legation in Tehran for some 30 years in unspecified capacities maintained that he groomed Reza Khan for promotion and was the first person to introduce him to Ironside. Reporter gives no dates or details. The 'Will' was first published in *Khaterat Arteshbod Sabeq Hosein Fardoost* vol. 2, pp 146–159.

Since the Revolution of 1979 other accounts have emerged in Iranian publications. These accounts are often of questionable authenticity and are a conscious effort to demean Reza Shah. For the sake of rounding out the picture brief references are in order. There is a preposterous account by one Mohammad Reza Ashtianizadeh published in *The Comtemporary History of Iran*, vol. 3, pp 106–108, a publication of an agency of the Islamic Government of Iran. The writer maintained that Habibollah Rashidian, a lackey and minor go-between for the British Legation, had told him that he had been present when Ardeshir Reporter had sought the assistance of Ain al Molk (Habibollah Hoveyda), a middle-ranking Ministry of Foreign Affairs official but a high-ranking Freemason and prominent Baha'i leader, to find an Iranian officer 'who is tall and well built' and who need not be a 'real Shi'ite Moslem' to lead the coup. After a search Ain al Molk recommended Reza Khan, who had all the atributes Britain sought. This account was doubtless published to tarnish Reza Shah's origins. By showing that he was hand-picked by the Freemason and Baha'i hierarchy, the legitimacy of the founder of the Pahlavi dynasty is called into question. As a non-Shi'ite, Reza Khan would not have qualified under the Iranian Constitution to assume the throne. Ain al Molk was the father of the late Amir Abbas Hoveyda, Prime Minister of Iran 1965–1977. A further motive in implicating him in the rise to power of Reza Shah would be to drive one more nail in the coffin of his son.

Another highly dubious 'document' to emerge recently in the same government publication, *The Contemporary History of Iran* (pp 270–274), is a purported interview by an unnamed individual with Mostafa Fateh, the highest ranked Iranian employee of APOC and its successor companies. Fateh had related that some time between 1928 and 1930 he had visited Col. Smyth, who was then retired from the military and running a farm in Scotland. Smyth had told Fateh that 'Britain had some 30 candidates to lead the coup'. Reza Khan had finally been selected because he was 'brave, willing to take risks and handsome... he came from a poor family and had no connection with the aristocracy and the well-to-do' and he would accept Britain's directives without question. Smyth also told him of two negative traits. Reza Khan was uneducated and addicted to opium. Smyth had related further that Reza Khan had lost his nerve during the coup and Smyth had been forced to sooth and reassure him. Smyth had also told Fateh that Reza Khan had pocketed the money given to him to pay the Cossack soldiers.

The document contains a mass of contradictions and is factually inaccurate. The initial reasons stated by Smyth for Reza Khan's selection are negated at the end of the interview. Furthermore, we know from all accounts of the coup, including Foreign Office documents, that Smyth did not accompany either Seyyed Zia or Reza Khan into Tehran on the eve of the coup. It is possible that the entire interview is spuriously attributed or never took place. Because of Fateh's association with British interests he was profoundly distrusted by most Iranians and came to be *persona non grata* to the Pahlavis. Toward the end of his life he was a deeply embittered man and made highly derogatory remarks and offered unsubstantiated reports of his own role in a number of events.

27   FO 416/98, Bullard to Halifax, 7 February 1940.
28   Ghasem Ghani, *Yaddasht ha-e-Dr Ghasem Ghani (Memoirs of Dr Ghasem Ghani)*, vol. 11, pp 365–367. Conversation between Ghasem Ghani and Gen. Yazdanpanah, Friday 16 February 1951, edited and translated from Persian by Cyrus Ghani.
29   Gen. Hassan Arfa, *Under Five Shahs*, p 108.
30   FO 416/98, Bullard to Halifax, 7 February 1940.
31   Amanollah Jahanbani, *Reza Shah dar Ayeneh Khaterat (Reza Shah in Reflective Memory)*, ed. Ebrahim Safa'i, pp 88–89.
32   FO 416/98, Bullard to Halifax, 7 February 1940
33   FO 416/98, Bullard to Halifax, 7 February 1940.
34   Ahmad Amir Ahmadi, *Khaterat Nakhostin Sepahbod Iran Ahmad Amir Ahmadi (The Memoirs of the First Lieutenant General of Iran, Ahmad Amir Ahmadi)*, pp 164–171, edited and translated by Cyrus Ghani.
35   Hosein Samii, autobiographical sketch published in *Rahavard*, vol. 11 no. 43, winter 1997, pp 280–283.
36   Adib al Saltaneh Samii, 'Shab Sevom Hout 1299', *Ayandeh* magazine, Esfand 1360 (February-March 1982), translated by Cyrus Ghani.
37   DBFP, doc. no. 681, Norman to Curzon, 21 February 1921.
38   FO 371/6401, Norman to Curzon, 21 and 22 February 1921.
39   FO 371/6401, Norman to Curzon, 26 February 1921.
40   FO 371/6403, Norman to Curzon, 1 March 1921 (the document has been wrongly dated 1920).
41   Hosein Makki, *Tarikh Bist Saleh Iran (A Twenty Year History of Iran)*, vol. 1, pp 236–244.
42   FO 371/6401, Minute prepared by G.P. Churchill, 3 March 1921.
43   FO 371/6427, Pierson Dixon to Curzon, 14 May 1921.
44   US National Archives, Washington DC, American Delegation Dispatch, dated 25 August 1921: quoted by Donald N. Wilber, *Riza Shah Pahlavi*, p 48.
45   FO 371/6427, Gen. Dickson to Gen. Radcliffe, 8 October 1921.
46   Edmonds papers, Box no. XII, file 6, Edmonds to Lt Col. G.E. Wheeler, Tehran Embassy, 14 January 1949: quoted by Houshang Sabahi, *British Policy in Persia 1918–1925*, p 229.
47   Lt Col. Grey, 'Persia', *Journal of Central Asian Society*, vol. 3, 1926, pt 2: quoted in Ali Asghar Zargarpour, *The History of Diplomatic Relations Between Iran and Britain in the Reza Shah Period*, p 70 of the Persian translation.
48   FO 371/6401, Memorandum prepared by Lancelot Oliphant for Curzon, 22 February 1921.
49   James M. Balfour, *Recent Happenings in Persia*, London, 1922, p 218.
50   Denis Wright, *The English Amongst the Persians*, p 184, quoting from the unpublished Ironside Diaries, entries for 14 and 15 December 1920.
51   FO 371/6409, Haldane to War Office, 23 February 1921.
52   Richard H. Ullman, *The Anglo-Soviet Accord*, vol. 3, p 388: quoting from the unpublished Ironside Diaries.

In 1994 a book was published in Tehran under the title of *Khaterat Serri Ironside* (*The Secret Diaries of Ironside*). The book comprises a Persian translation of *High Road to Com-mand*, but with 57 new pages. There is no question of the authenticity of these new pages, but they contain no significant new information. They do not throw further light on the coup. There is still no mention of Seyyed Zia and how and when Reza Khan and Seyyed Zia met. The 57 pages are the same unpublished pages referred to by Ullman. Mohammad Reza Shah Pahlavi probably had been given a copy of these pages by Lord Ironside's son. After the revolution the new government gained access to them.

53 DoS doc. no. 646, Caldwell to Secretary of State, 11 March 1921. Emile Lesueur, a French law professor who was in Tehran at the time of the coup had called Seyyed Zia 'The damned soul of the British Legation': *Des Anglais en Perse*, Paris, 1923: quoted by Rouhollah Ramazani, *The Foreign Policy of Iran 1500–1941*, p 177.

54 DoS, Quarterly Report No. 11, Caldwell to Secretary of State, 5 April 1921.

55 *Ibid.*

56 DoS doc. no. 891/00/1346, Wallace Murray to Secretary of State, 6 March 1925.

57 In Seyyed Zia's case there are a few third-hand accounts that have found their way into the writings of Iranian commentators, one more questionable than the other. Bahar quotes an unnamed Iranian as the source of a conversation with Seyyed Zia in Palestine some ten years after the event. Seyyed Zia had maintained that he was the force and impetus behind the coup and Reza Khan was a reluctant participant. It was Seyyed Zia who had obtained the necessary funds. Sensing that Reza Khan was hesitant to undertake the march to Tehran, Seyyed Zia had given 2,000 tomans to Reza Khan personally. According to this alleged conversation, Reza Khan had lost his nerve and was close to abandoning the plot on three occasions. One occasion was the arrival of the deputation from Tehran to Mehrabad, which the narrator names as Samii, Moin al Molk and Gen. Dickson. Seyyed Zia had hidden behind a door to see how Reza Khan would handle the situation. When Seyyed Zia realised that Reza Khan was losing his nerve and succumbing to the entreaties of the emissaries, he appeared, admonished the group and had them arrested. The lame account goes on to say that on the same evening, after occupying the army barracks in Tehran, Seyyed Zia was told that Farmanfarma was waiting outside to see Reza Khan. Sensing Reza Khan was close to losing his nerve again Seyyed Zia prevented the meeting and had Farmanfarma arrested. Mohamad Taqi Bahar, *Tarikh Mokhtasar Ahzab Siasi* (*A Short History of Political Parties*), vol. 1, pp 112–115.

There are so many inaccuracies in this tale as to render the whole account a self-serving fabrication. To begin with the narrator confuses Gen. Dickson with Col. Haig. Dickson at that point was on the verge of being recalled from Tehran and was not among the deputation sent by the Legation to Mehrabad. Samii's account makes no mention of Seyyed Zia hiding behind a door, or any hesitation by Reza Khan in his reply to the deputation. There are no reports or mention of the arrests of Samii, Moin al Molk or Colonels Haig and Huddleston. From the US Legation's and Norman's reports we know that Farmanfarma had been arrested at his house on the twenty-first at 3am. Finally, the idea of Seyyed Zia acting as a nursemaid to Reza Khan and giving him courage runs counter to everything we know of Reza Khan at that time. It appears that either Seyyed Zia in exile wanted to recapture his moment of glory and magnified his role or the purported interviewer gave a false account to Bahar.

58 James M. Balfour, *Recent Happenings in Persia*, p 218.
59 Richard H. Ullman, *The Anglo-Soviet Accord*, vol. 3, p 388.
60 The 'Iron Committee' is sometimes referred to as the 'Steel Committee'.
61 FO/371/6402, Norman to Curzon, 25 February 1921.
62 FO 371/6403, Norman to Curzon, 3 March 1921. Mirza Taqi Khan Amir Kabir, a visionary and an outstanding administrator, is generally regarded as the greatest first minister of nineteenth-century Iran (see Introduction for biographical information).
63 FO 371/6406, Norman to Curzon, 21 April 1921.
64 The closest analogy would be in 1789 when the last of the Zand dynasty rulers lost his capital, Shiraz, due to his senior commanders having deserted him. Aqa Mohammad Khan, the first Qajar Shah, then captured Shiraz with ease.
65 DBFP, doc. no. 688, Norman to Curzon, 3 March 1921.
66 FO 371/6403, Intelligence Summary, Military Attaché Tehran, No. 10 to week ending 9 July 1921.
67 FO 371/6405, Norman to Curzon, 5 July 1921.
68 FO 158/687, Norman to Norperforce Headquarters, 18 February 1921.
69 DoS, Quarterly Report No. 11, Caldwell to Secretary of State, 5 April 1921.
70 *Ibid.*
71 Peter Avery, *Modern Iran*, p 227.
72 FO 371/6403, Norman to Curzon, 1 March 1921.
73 FO 371/3873, Norman to Curzon, 3 June 1920, contains War Office directive concerning the position of British troops in Persia.
74 FO 371/6409, Haldane to War Office, 23 February 1921.
75 Gordon Waterfield, *Professional Diplomat – Sir Percy Loraine*, p 56.
76 Richard H. Ullman, *The Anglo-Soviet Accord*, vol. 3, p 388: quoting from the unpublished Ironside Diaries.
77 Maj. Gen. Sir George Cory replaced Ironside as Commander of British troops in Iran. Cory, however, did not arrive until three weeks after Ironside's departure on 18 February: L.P. Elwell-Sutton, 'Reza Shah the Great' in George Lenczowski (ed.), *Iran Under the Pahlavis*, p 17.
78 Peter Avery, *Modern Iran*, p 228.
79 *Khaterat Serri Ironside*, (*The Secret Memoirs of Ironside*), pp 27 and 28. Two extremely flattering letters were sent by Ironside's son to Amir Assadollah Alam, the then Minister of Court, both dated 5 December 1973.

8

Seyyed Zia's 100 Days

By 21 February Tehran was under control of the perpetrators of the coup. The people of Tehran woke up that Monday to discover that Cossack troops had occupied all the ministries, government buildings, police stations, post and telegraph offices, and with soldiers stationed at key intersections their hold on the capital was complete. Martial law had been in effect since the previous midnight. Exit from and entrance into the city was subject to the approval of the newly-appointed Military Governor of Tehran, Col. Kazem Khan Sayyah.

Seyyed Zia was master of the political situation, at least in the capital, and Reza Khan was the unquestioned leader of the Cossacks, the only effective military force in the country. Not only was the coup the most jolting political event to have occurred in Iran for several generations, but the mere advent of Seyyed Zia introduced a new element into Iranian politics. Here was a self-made man with no affiliation with any political party, the landed gentry or the court. He was to be the first untitled Iranian Prime Minister since the beginning of the nineteenth century. At his first meeting with the Shah on Tuesday 22 February, when he received his written confirmation as Prime Minister, the Shah offered him a title of his own choosing. Seyyed Zia declined a conventional title and instead requested to be designated as 'dictator' in the Shah's public declaration of his appointment. The Shah, surprised and not comfortable with the ramifications of a Roman title and its contemporary connotations of extra-constitutional powers, refused 'because this would constitute a humiliation of the position and dignity of the Sovereign'.[1]

Seyyed Zia appears never to have pressed the issue any further. The Shah in his declaration of appointment of Seyyed Zia as Prime Minister merely stated that because of past failures, it had been 'decided to appoint a capable person as Prime Minister'. Reza Khan was confirmed by the Shah as commander of the Cossacks and was given the title of Sardar Sepah (Commander of the Army).

Even before having an audience with the Shah, and while waiting for his formal appointment as the new Prime Minister, Seyyed Zia had already issued a proclamation on the first day of the coup. It departed radically from those of former prime ministers. There was no praise or homage to the Shah nor any stated intention to govern the country under the Shah's guidance. His declaration in effect said that it had been 15 years since the granting of the constitution yet nothing had changed. Iran was still ruled by an oligarchy of certain notables who controlled the wealth of the country as if it were their birthright. He then laid out an ambitious programme which included the reorganisation of the Ministry of Justice to allow ordinary citizens to seek redress for wrongs; improvement of the lot of workers and peasants; more schools and teachers; and allocation of greater resources towards improvement of commerce and industry. He also announced a programme for the beautification of the capital and other municipal centres. In foreign policy he intended to have friendly relations with all countries. Most importantly, he argued that the circumstances for which the 1919 Agreement was designed had changed and hence he sought its abrogation on amicable terms. In conclusion he made only a passing reference to the Shah and stated that he had been granted complete powers to administer the country with Iran's 'own money and resources'.[2]

Reza Khan's official appointment was equally unprecedented. An unknown soldier risen through the ranks with no connection to any prominent family or to the court had seized the capital and was now the *de facto* head of all armed forces. His initial declaration also exuded confidence and authority. With no introduction it began with the words 'I hereby order' and set out regulations for the duration of martial law: all publications were suspended and resumption was subject to later approval by the Government on an individual basis; all gatherings and rights of assembly were suspended; all cinemas, theatres, gambling clubs and shops selling alcoholic beverages were closed; all government offices other than those concerned with the distribution of food stuffs were closed. The population of Tehran was warned that to disobey the edicts of the Military Governor would result in severe penalties.[3] Some five days later Reza Khan issued a second declaration giving an account of the sacrifices the Cossack soldiers had made in fighting the Bolsheviks in the North. Although his soldiers had received no support from the previous Central Government they had fought to save the northern provinces and prevented the establishment of autonomous governments in the region. Reza Khan concluded that he would continue to protect the people of all provinces from enemies within and without.[4]

The first Cabinet of Seyyed Zia, with one exception, Reza Qoli Khan Hedayat, Nayer al Molk, was composed of people who had never previously held ministerial rank. They were officials and functionaries rather than politicians and were untainted by allegations of corruption. The key ministries were held by Mahmoud Jam* as Foreign Minister; Issa Fayz,† Minister of Finance; Reza Qoli Hedayat,# Minister

---

* Mahmoud Jam (Modir al Molk), c.1884–1969. His ancestors were from Kerman but his father had settled in Tabriz, where Jam was born. He began his career as an apprentice pharmacist to a Frenchman in Tabriz. Having learned some French he came to Tehran and for the next eight years worked at the French Legation as a translator and secretary. A fortuitous marriage into the Navab family brought him to the attention of Vosouq and in 1919 he became the administrator of food and grain storage and distribution. Hassan Pirnia appointed him Treasurer General in September 1920, and in 1921 Seyyed Zia made him Foreign Minister. When Reza Khan became Prime Minister he served as Minister of Finance. Under Reza Shah Jam was appointed Governor of Kerman and twice Governor of Khorasan; Minister of Interior in September 1933; Prime Minister between December 1935 and October 1939; Minister of Court until September 1941 when he became ambassador to Egypt; Minister of Court again in 1948; Ambassador to Italy. Thereafter he was a Senator until his death. Loyal and trustworthy, he was a dedicated public servant.[5]

† Issa Fayz, long an employee of the Ministry of Finance, had some education in England and remained close to succeeding British Legations in Tehran. He especially enjoyed the confidence of Armitage Smith. He left Seyyed Zia's Cabinet in April 1921 due to illness, travelled to England and spent the last years of his public career as Iranian High Commissioner for Petroleum in London.[6]

Reza Qoli Hedayat (Nayer al Molk II), 1872–1945, a grandee of the Hedayat family and cousin of Mokhber al Saltaneh, established a reputation as an impartial jurist. He was a member of the Iranian Supreme Court from 1927 and Chief Justice from 1928–1936. He refused to preside over the trial of several people accused of corruption in transactions with the Ministry of Roads; incurred the displeasure of Reza Shah and resigned. In 1943, after Seyyed Zia's return to Iran, he served as Chairman of Seyyed Zia's newly-formed party. Some British Foreign Office Documents mistakenly refer to him as Ja'far Qoli Hedayat, who in fact was Reza Qoli's father.[7]

of Education; Mostafa Adl,* Minister of Justice; Hossein Dadgar,†
Deputy Minister of Interior (with Seyyed Zia keeping the ministerial
portfolio for himself); Ali Asghar Nafisi,# head of the Department of
Health and Hygiene; Maj. Mas'oud Keyhan,§ Minister of War;
Mahmoud Khan Movaqar al Dowleh, Minister of Public Works and
Commerce and Taqi Khan Moshir A'zam (Khajavi), Minister of Post
and Telegraph.[8]

The composition and membership of the Cabinet was to matter
very little. Seyyed Zia, although denied the title of 'dictator', con-

---

*   Mostafa Adl (Mansour al Saltaneh), c.1885–1950, was born in Tabriz and
     studied in Egypt and France. He joined the Ministry of Foreign Affairs
     and served as secretary at the Iranian Consulate in Teflis at the turn of
     the century. From 1919 he alternately served in Ministries of Foreign
     Affairs and Justice and acted as adviser in drafting of laws in the late
     1920s and early 1930s. He was Professor of Law at Tehran University
     and wrote a valuable commentary on the Iranian civil code. As the most
     senior ex-minister, he was head of the Iranian delegation to the founding
     session of the United Nations in San Francisco in 1945.[9]

†   Hosein Dadgar (Adl al Molk), c.1881–1970, supported the constitutional
     movement and served in parliament from the third to ninth sessions. He
     was adept at allying himself with various and sometimes opposing fac-
     tions and served as Under Secretary of Ministry of Interior under
     Sepahdar in 1920, being appointed to same position by Seyyed Zia in
     1921. He served briefly as assistant to Reza Khan during the latter's pre-
     miership; as Minister of Interior in 1925; as President of parliament from
     the seventh to the ninth sessions. He left Iran in the summer of 1935
     after having been suspected of receiving bribes, and did not return until
     the abdication of Reza Shah. He was appointed/elected to the Senate for
     three consecutive terms. Most Iranian commentators as well as the
     British Foreign Office consider him vain and an intriguer of question-
     able honesty.[10]

Ali Asghar Nafisi (Moadeb al Dowleh), c.1870–c.1942, was the eldest son
     of Nazem al Ataba, court physician to Mozaffar al Din Shah. He studied
     medicine in France and upon his return established himself with an
     extensive clientele. He was appointed special physician to the Crown
     Prince during the latter's schooling in Switzerland. Several Iranian com-
     mentators have questioned his intellectual suitability as special tutor to
     the young prince.[11]

§   Mas'oud Khan Keyhan, 1886–c.1961, studied at military shools in
     France and took some courses at St Cyr. He joined the Gendarmerie in
     1913 and came to the attention of Col. Smyth. He never recovered from
     his removal from the post of Minister of War to be succeeded by Reza
     Khan, and left the military in 1924. He taught at secondary schools,
     teachers' college and later at the University of Tehran, and wrote a valu-
     able three-volume geography of Iran.[12]

ducted his Government as a one-man enterprise. Others who wielded power were Kazem Khan as Military Governor of Tehran and Maj. Habibollah Khan Shaibani, the effective head of the Gendarmes in Tehran, who had offered no resistance to the Cossacks on their entry into the city and allied himself with the perpetrators of the coup. Shaibani, a highly respected professional soldier, subsquently played a prominent part in Reza Khan's build-up of the new army. But the overwhelming military power was in the hands of Reza Khan. In the first few weeks after the coup he appears to have had some shared goals with Seyyed Zia as both agreed to the immediate build-up of the Cossacks for reasons of internal security and countering the revolutionaries in the North.

Although the coup had the support of the great landlords, the Bazaar merchants and even elements among the intelligensia (journalists, pamphleteers, teachers and civil servants) and though there had been no overt resistance in the provinces, most of the country was far from under the secure control of the central Government. In addition to Kouchek Khan and his band of revolutionaries and Soviet soldiers in Gilan, there were the Turkaman chiefs in Astarabad; Eqbal al Saltaneh Makoui who ruled in northwest Azarbaijan; the Shahsavan tribe in Ardabil and the Moghan plains; Kurds led by Sardar Rashid who ruled parts of western Iran; and the Sanjabi and Kalhor tribal leaders who ruled in Kermanshah. Further south the Qashqa'i held sway; south-east Iran was under the control of the Baluchi tribal leaders, Bahram Khan and Doost Mohammad Khan; Sheikh Khaz'al ruled supreme and unhindered in Khuzestan; and central Iran was the domain of the Bakhtiaris. Even Tehran and its immediate environs were not totally secure. There were bands of criminals who controlled the streets at night.

The initial blow to Seyyed Zia's prestige was dealt in the very first few days after the coup when two prominent governors of large provinces refused to endorse the coup and his premiership. The Shah had sent a routine telegram to all provincial governors informing them of the appointment of Seyyed Zia. Mohammad Mosaddeq,** the

---

** Dr Mohammad Mosaddeq (Mosaddeq al Saltaneh), 1882–1967, is amongst the three or four most important political figures in 20th century Iranian history. His influence was felt in the early fifties in every major capital of the world and even with the passing years his legacy in Iran is undiminished. Descended from one of the most notable families of public servants, he was educated in Iran and Switzerland. He held various positions of importance including the Prime Ministership from April 1951 to August 1953. A full length biography and a study of his era would require several volumes.[13]

highly popular governor of Fars, refused to accept or publicly proclaim the premiership of Seyyed Zia. In a telegram to the Shah on
24 February Mosaddeq informed him that a public announcement
would cause disturbances in the province and requested that he be
allowed to defer the announcement until such time as he thought
appropriate. On 27 February Seyyed Zia sent a harsh telegram to
Mosaddeq urging him to proclaim publicly his premiership.
Mosaddeq tendered his resignation on 5 March and fearing for his
safety left Shiraz and sought refuge near Esfahan with Bakhtiari
leaders. Mosaddeq was replaced as Governor of Fars by the Shah's
favourite uncle, Nosrat al Saltaneh.[14]

Ahmad Qavam, the Governor of Khorasan also refused to accept
the premiership of Seyyed Zia. Qavam had answered Seyyed Zia's
telegram by addressing it 'to Mr Seyyed Zia al Din, publisher of
Ra'ad'. After this overt insult, Seyyed Zia felt forced to remove and
arrest Qavam.[15] Col. Mohammad Taqi Khan, the commanding officer of the Gendarmerie in Khorasan, arrested him on Seyyed Zia's
orders. Soon after the Colonel was appointed Military Governor of
the province. Qavam was sent to Tehran under arrest to face trial.[16]

After an inflamatory inaugural speech accusing the notables of
having ruled the country for the past 15 years and having 'sucked
the blood of the nation like leeches', Seyyed Zia had little choice but
to order the arrest of a large number of prominent politicians. He
was also making a show of strength by arresting these grandees
since few of them had ever taken him seriously. Despite his own background of pronounced association with British policy and interests
in Iran, he was not in a position to spare those politicians who had
the support of the British Legation. Seyyed Zia also calculated that
the arrest of people who theretofore had been immune from judicial
authority would bolster his support amongst the less privileged.

Seyyed Zia had probably prepared a list of those to be arrested
some days before the coup. From the early morning of 21 February,
Cossacks assisted by Gendarmes and the police began to round
people up. Within the first four days over 80 were arrested. Seventy
or more were politicians of one stripe or another and 10 to 15 were
journalists, teachers and writers. By the end of his first month in
power, Seyyed Zia had ordered the arrest of some 50 to 60 others.
Some people were exiled or placed under house arrest. Bahar was
under house arrest in north-west Tehran, Teimurtash was exiled to
Kashan and Moddares to Qazvin. The houses of some of the
detainees were searched.[17] The pattern of those who were exempt
from arrest soon became clear. Grandees who had armed men in
their employ enjoyed immunity. Mohammad Vali Khan Tonokaboni

(Sepahsalar), who had a private militia, was spared. All three senior Bakhtiari leaders, Samsam al Saltaneh, Sardar Jang and Sardar Zafar, went untouched. Nor were the elders of other tribes arrested, all of whom had private militias.

Seyyed Zia then set a condition for the release of the imprisoned grandees. He demanded varying sums from the prisoners for their release. In some instances he demanded the extraordinary sum of four million tomans per family, the alternative being trial and possible sentence of death. Norman, who was supporting Seyyed Zia with ever-increasing fervour, informed Curzon on 10 March that the Prime Minister intended to 'set up special tribunals to hear charges against those arrested who will be allowed counsel'. Against Farmanfarma and his eldest two sons, Firouz and Salar Lashkar, Seyyed Zia alleged 'that not only there is overwhelming evidence of fraud and robbery but also of oppression, violence and murder... Thus if they are tried they could be convicted of murder and sentenced to death.' Norman gave no details of Seyyed Zia's accusations but asked for guidance as to how he should handle the situation. He wrote, 'on the one hand if we intervene, the Government will be weakened and we will be even more unpopular'. Norman again recited the fact that both Farmanfarma and Firouz had oral and written guarantees of immunity from prosecution and both held awards granted by the British Crown. Norman concluded that Seyyed Zia had asked the family for four million tomans for their release and safe conduct out of the country. He added that the high-ranking prisoners were well lodged and well treated and attended by their own servants and cooks.[18] Firouz himself sent a telegram to Curzon via Norman stating that Seyyed Zia had set a deadline of five days for them to raise the money. Firouz pleaded that the family had no such sums and reminded Curzon of what the 'family has done for Anglo-Persian relations for the past seven years' and of awards bestowed on them and written guarantees from Britain.[19]

Curzon on 14 March answered that the British Government 'cannot interfere in carrying out just claims', but he instructed Norman to tell the Prime Minister that 'if Farmanfarma and his family are treated unfairly they [Seyyed Zia's Government] would lose our support... The trial must be fair, public and with the presence of a suitable representative of your Legation'.[20] Norman reported on 8 April that the Prime Minister had reduced the amount in question from 4 million to 2 million tomans but Farmanfarma would not budge.[21] Akbar Mas'oud (Sarem al Dowleh), while serving as Governor of Kermanshah, was also arrested. Seyyed Zia had asked him to repay to the Government his portion of the £131,000 bribe and he then could leave the country under British protection. Curzon appears to have taken a more active interest in this case since the matter of the bribe had surfaced again. He instructed Norman to tell Seyyed Zia that Sarem al Dowleh 'is under our protection'.[22] Sarem al Dowleh, however, was kept imprisoned and was not released until 24 May 1921, together with the other prisoners.

In the event none of the grandees made payment for his release except for Hosein Ali Qaragozlou (Amir Nezam), probably the largest land-owner in the Kermanshah and Hamadan regions, who paid 25,000 tomans. As the main prison began to overflow with new prisoners the most notable of the detainees were gradually moved to somewhat better quarters in the outskirts of Tehran.[23] Two of Reza Khan's trusted officers were placed in charge. Maj. Jan Mohammad Khan Ala'i (Davallou) was the warden and Captain Karim Aqa Khan (Bouzarjomehri) was assigned to see that Farmanfarma and his sons were treated with deference.[24]

Seyyed Zia was to pay a heavy price for the imprisonment of the notables. Their relatives began a systematic campaign against the Government and undermined it in any way they could. Rumours spread that the arrests had been made solely for extortion and not to cleanse the Government of undesirable elements as Seyyed Zia had proclaimed. The public soon wearied of the spectacle when they witnessed no trials. Seyyed Zia's mediocre and inexperienced colleagues were of no help in preparing or documenting charges. He had to attend personally to all the pleadings lodged by the relatives of the detainees. Recently released documents relating to the Prime Minister's office from 21 February to 25 March 1921 indicate that between 24 February and 14 March over 50 telegrams were received from relatives of the imprisoned. In addition there are over 20 letters by others requesting permission to travel to the provinces. In almost all of these instances Seyyed Zia had to intervene personally and instruct his subordinates.[25] He was faced with a dilemma: he could put no-one on trial as he was not able to prepare specific charges for past misdeeds and yet he could not release anyone for fear of loss of prestige. More importantly, if his enemies were released his Government stood little chance of survival. Almost all of those arrested were to linger in jail until 24 May, the day after Seyyed Zia's forced resignation. On 21 March during the Shah's traditional New Year reception when the senior members of the nobility and officialdom attend the palace, the assemblage was unusually small in protest over the imprisonments. Respected and popular politicians such as the two Pirnias and Mostofi made a strong point by their absence.[26]

The lofty programme of Seyyed Zia was also floundering. The pronouncement that the Ministry of Justice would be totally revamped came to nought except for the appointment of some jurists charged with the enormous task of revising existing laws. Those appointed were: Mostafa Adl, Mohammad Ali Foroughi, Nasrollah Taqavi, Mohammad Boroujerdi, Mohammad Qomi and Ali Qomi. There is no record of the committee having met even once.[27] Iran was to wait another six years before a serious and comprehensive effort was made under Reza Shah. The reorganisation of the Ministry of Finance did not get off the ground either. Its closing made the public and especially its employees wary and impeded the day-to-day work of the Government. There was no coherent plan for improvement of commerce and lack of funds forced the abandonment of any plans to improve transportation. Another much talked about promise had been the cancellation of the odious system of capitulations through the creation of special judicial bodies that would attend to offences and trial of foreign nationals in Iran. It too never came about. The unrealistic plan to distribute land to the peasants was never pursued. Seyyed Zia's plan for the beautification of Tehran ended merely with his appointment of a *de facto* head of the municipality. The only fulfilled promises were the enforced ban on alcohol and the closing of shops on Fridays and religious holidays. Even these moves had their detractors among the Christian minority, shopkeepers and small merchants.

Seyyed Zia's foreign policy met with even greater scepticism. He had to please and satisfy three diverse elements. In addition to the British and Soviet Governments, Seyyed Zia had the difficult task of convincing his countrymen that by cancelling the 1919 Agreement he intended to treat Britain no better than any other friendly country and would not grant her any further privileges. This was extremely difficult given his reputation as a 'notorious anglophile' and his background of having supported almost blindly every British initiative in Iran for the past seven years. This suspicion was soon confirmed as he began to unfold his policy of employing foreign 'advisers'. It became apparent after the first month in office that he intended to grant Britain the right to control the military and finances of the country. He was to face an equally difficult road in his dealings with the Soviets who continued to regard him as a mere British pawn.

Seyyed Zia may have anticipated his difficulties with the Soviets and less than warm support from his countrymen, but he had been certain of and strongly counted on unqualified support from Britain. Although Curzon must have known for more than six months that the Agreement had no chance of being ratified he took Seyyed Zia's announcement to cancel it with little grace. Norman pleaded continuously with Curzon to no avail, that it was 'useless to object' and Britain's acceptance of its demise 'would at least enhance our popularity'.[28] Nevertheless, Curzon took the news almost personally and thereafter he gave Seyyed Zia only half-hearted support. Seyyed Zia's repeated pledges that nothing would change and Britain would be assured control of finances and the military did not soothe the Foreign Office. Curzon still failed to appreciate the changing times and how little Britain was trusted. Britain had established a protecterate over Iraq and her aggresive policy towards Afghanistan and Turkey made it appear to Iranians that Britain sought dominion over all Middle-East nations.

British policy in Iran, which had always been aggressive and acquisitive, had not changed much even with the anticipated rejection of the 1919 Agreement. It remained aggressive in its attempt to keep all powers out of the country and acquisitive in seeking further financial rewards. Seyyed Zia was offering Curzon what he really had been after, economic and military supremacy in Iran with a few morsels to other powers to keep them quiet. To Curzon this was unacceptable. All other powers still had to be prevented from gaining even the slightest political or economic foothold. The Foreign Office on 18 April informed Norman that they had been alerted that the Iranian Government intended to employ US financial advisers. Specifically, Morgan Shuster had been asked to head an agricultural bank to form the basis of a national bank in the future. Additionally it intended to employ one or two US technicians to work at the Ministry of Post and Telegraph. Curzon warned Norman that the matter was of great consequence to British interests. The creation of a new bank would undermine the Imperial Bank, and the employment of US nationals at the Ministry of Post and Telegraph would be prejudicial to British interests which owned the Indo-European telegraph line. Curzon concluded that the 'intention of the Prime Minister... gives ground for utmost distrust for his protestation of an Anglophile'.[29]

Norman continued to defend the Prime Minister. On 22 April he wrote to Curzon,

[You] misunderstood Seyyed Zia. He has consulted me on everything. Once in a while he has to say and do things to make it appear he is not a pawn.[30]

The next day he wrote to Curzon again:

... the Prime Minister's policy is based on friendship and support for Great Britain and that policy is unfortunately misinterpreted. The reactionary governments of last year gave promises but did not do anything [but the] Prime Minister owing to his reputation as a notorious Anglophile and as owner of newspaper *Ra'ad* long regarded by all as organ of this Legation, has to be specially careful to avoid this charge... That is why he appears friendly to the US and France. He intends to flatter France but give her as little as possible'. With the Soviets he had to be careful and wanted to 'deprive [them] from complaining.[31]

Curzon was unconvinced by these arguments and wrote to Norman that he may accept Seyyed Zia's assurances of being an anglophile but there should be no employment of French or American nationals.

The cosmopolitan policy pursued by the Prime Minister is doomed to failure. An army under officers of a single nationality, preferably British has always impressed me to be in Persia's interest.

Seyyed Zia wished to hire other nationals for other purposes they 'should be Belgians or possibly Swedish'.[32] In a later telegram Curzon instructed Norman to tell Seyyed Zia categorically that there should be no new bank and no Americans at the Ministry of Post and Telegraph.[33]

Norman was forced to inform Curzon bluntly that the 'Prime Minister regrets his inability to reverse' his decision concerning employment of American advisers, but 'repeats his assurances of safeguarding British interests'. Furthermore the Prime Minister would employ an Englishman at Post and Telegraph for technical control and the new bank would be formed with British capital.[34]

Relations with the neighbouring power were even more difficult for Seyyed Zia to navigate. The Perso-Soviet agreement was concluded on 26 February despite earlier British objections. Pirnia (Moshir al Dowleh) had set in motion a course which could not be reversed. Much of this agreement covered the re-statement of previous Soviet declarations renouncing every vestige of the Czarist special position and interests in Iran. It pledged non-interference in Iranian affairs with one exception which had been initially conceded by Pirnia, which Sepahdar had had to go along with, and which Seyyed Zia could not have reversed. This sole exception stated:

In the event a third party should attempt to carry out a policy of usurpation by means of armed intervention in Persia, or if such power should desire to use Persian territory as a basis of operation against Russia and if the Persians were not strong enough to prevent it, then Russia shall have the right to advance her troops into Persia's interior for the purpose of carrying out military operations necessary for its defences'.[35]

Britain had additional reasons to be apprehensive over the ramifications of the Perso-Soviet treaty. The Soviets by renouncing the Treaty of Turkamanchai, whereby Russia had obtained a 'most-favoured-nation clause' and the right of capitulation, had in effect given up that right. Britain, which had obtained the same right in Article 9 of the 1857 Treaty of Paris, feared that the Iranians also would ask Britain to renounce the privileges.[36] Britain could do little to halt the conclusion of the Perso-Soviet agreement as she herself was concurrently holding discussions with the Soviets in London and Moscow for a bilateral trade agreement, concluded on 16 March 1921.

The conclusion of the treaty did not resolve the immediate difficulty Iran had with the Soviets, whose troops remained in the country and were actively assisting the rebels in Gilan. A small force of Iranian Cossacks had been unsuccessful in dislodging rebels from their positions near the Manjeel Pass and had been shelled by Soviet troops.[37] The situation was tense enough for Seyyed Zia to telegraph Rothstein, the first officially accredited Soviet envoy, who was in Mashhad on his way to Tehran, to delay his arrival until the Soviet troops ceased firing on the Cossacks.[38] Although Soviet troops remained in northern Iran, a temporary cessation of hostilities was effected as a face-saving device for Rothstein's arrival in Tehran on 5 May and the presentation of his credentials to the Shah and the Government.

From the time of the conclusion of the treaty, and especially after the arrival of Rothstein, Russia's hand strengthened considerably in Iran. Rothstein, an old Bolshevik, was close to both Lenin and Trotsky and his voice carried weight in the highest quarters of the Soviet heirarchy. Only a few months after Rothstein's arrival the Soviet Legation had expanded to a 100-man staff with consulates in almost all the major cities.[39] The Legation began a systematic campaign against the Government of Seyyed Zia, who became fearful enough to ask the British Legation to exert pressure on the Soviets on his behalf.[40]

The Foreign Office had initially instructed Norman that he should have no relations with the Soviet Minister. Later he was advised not to initiate but to return courtesies and was authorised only 'to transact official business'.[41] On 9 May Norman had his first meeting with Rothstein at the British Legation. Norman informed him that all British troops had left Qazvin and were on their way out of Iran. Rothstein expressed satisfaction and stated that Soviet troops were also leaving northern Iran.[42] At a meeting on 19 May, the Soviet Military Attaché, Col. Boris Rogachov, told the British Military Attaché, Col. Saunders, that Soviet troops had begun their withdrawal and would not intervene 'in any action the Persian Government may take to deal with the rebels such as Kouchek Khan'.[43]

Despite Soviet troop withdrawals, Rothstein was to remain a thorn in the side of the British. He was received by several prominent Iranian politicians and later made calls on all the released prisoners with the exception of Farmanfarma and his two eldest sons. Even the Shah found him to be 'mild and reasonable'.[44] By 23 May all British troops except for a contingent in south-west Iran had left. Upon hearing the news, Rothstein told Norman, 'What a relief. Now ours will be able to begin to move. Our people have been suspicious as to whether yours would definitely leave.' He mentioned that most of the Russian troops in northern Persia had been Soviet Azarbaijanis but they had been induced to leave.'[45]

Seyyed Zia's public image was being undermined by Curzon's obstinacy and refusal to accept the new realities. The Iranian Government's request that departing British troops sell their field guns and ammunition to the Iranian forces was rejected by Curzon, who argued that the weapons would ultimately fall into Bolshevik hands. Norman's pleadings were ignored.[46] Seyyed Zia, who had been certain that the Legation would meet this request lost prestige by the British refusal. The Government of Seyyed Zia was further embarrassed by APOC's refusal to settle and pay royalties due to Iran for the preceeding three years. Armitage Smith, who had been entrusted by the Governments of Pirnia and Sepahdar to review the accounting procedures of APOC, submitted a report which clearly showed that two subsidiaries of APOC, Bakhtiari Oil Company and First Exploration Oil Company, had sold Iranian produced oil to APOC below world prices. Armitage Smith concluded that these subsidaries had no right to sell at such prices before consulting the Iranian Government and condemned these self-dealing practices. Curzon not only ignored the report but instructed Norman to see whether Armitage Smith could either withdraw or amend it.[47] In a subsequent telegram Curzon again raised the issue of the defunct Khoshtaria oil concession and told Norman to inform the Iranian Government that APOC would be willing to make payment of arrears and cease further self-dealing practices if the Iranian Government recognised APOC's title to the concession.[48] The Government of India wrote to Curzon that the position of APOC was untenable. Curzon merely acknowledged receipt of the letter but ignored their views.[49]

Seyyed Zia was bound to fail. The Soviets continued to distrust him. His countrymen saw no difference between the policies of Seyyed Zia and Vosouq. More importantly, Curzon never gave Seyyed Zia the support he expected. Some Western writers have called Seyyed Zia a visionary and an intellectual.[50] His preoccupation with municipalities was the furthest extent of his vision. He was an impaired intellectual who had been exposed to the prevalent ideas of the West without having assimilated them, and when it came to governing he was out of his depth. He organised and took part in the coup solely to attain power. In Yazd and Fars, where he had grown up, Britain had been the dominant power and young Seyyed Zia had been awed by her omnipotence. It was quite in character for the opportunistic Seyyed Zia to throw his lot in defending British interests in Iran. This view would have seemed justified when after the World War he witnessed British hegemony stretching from Egypt to India. He probably thought Vosouq could have rammed the Agreement through a hand-picked parliament if he had cracked down on the opposition earlier. Now that he was in power he believed he could accomplish the same aims, tying Iran irrevocably to Britain by giving Britain the authority to administer and run the finances and the military. That was the extent of his idealism. He, no less than Curzon, Cox and Vosouq, failed to realise a change in the times and the expectations of the Iranians.

Seyed Zia was also an incompetent administrator. He selected his priorities clumsily and set an impossible and grandiose agenda such as the reorganisation of ministries and grants of land to peasants, neither of which came to fruition. He was hampered by lack of funds but did nothing to create or tap new sources of revenue. To gain mass support he proclaimed the grandees traitors and had them indiscriminately arrested, but with no specific plan to bring them to justice. It was a confused and incoherent move.[51] His only concrete accomplishments were the closing of shops on Fridays and holidays, the prohibiting of the consumption and sale of alcohol and providing for calls to prayer from public buildings at noontime to gain the broader support of the ulama.

None of the people close to Seyyed Zia, including Maj. Keyhan and Col. Kazem Sayyah, showed any courage or tenacity. Later, as they faced pressure from Reza Khan, they easily gave up their posts.[52] His Cabinet was made up of novices and when Issa Fayz, his Minister of Finance, fell ill and had to leave the Cabinet he was deprived of the only official experienced in financial matters. Seyyed Zia's Cabinet resembled Vosouq's last one. Both were staffed with nonentities and the Prime Minister had to shoulder most of the work and the entire burden of decision-making. J.M. Balfour said of the Cabinet:

> with the exception of two ex-officials, they were entirely amateurs with the consequence that it was publicly liable to commit errors in administration... with the closing of ministries pending reorganisation, the Government was, upon the civil side, a one man affair... Seyyed Zia attended to every detail'.[53]

Seyyed Zia could never shake off his reputation as a mouthpiece of the British Legation and as the 'damn soul of the British in Persia'. As word of his plan to employ British nationals for the army and Ministry of Finance spread, he began to lose whatever support he had from the intelligentsia, the clergy and the civil service bureaucracy. Curzon was slow to appreciate that Seyyed Zia was trying to bring in the Agreement through the back door. Norman had written to him only four days after the coup that Seyyed Zia intended to place 'the two essential administrations in British hands... this policy would in the end gain for Great Britain most of the advantages she had expected to obtain from an impractical Agreement'. In the same telegram Norman had warned Curzon that 'it is of utmost importance that the pro-British character of the new administration should, for the moment, as far as possible be disguised'.[54]

Despite these assurances by Norman, Curzon remained hostile to any plan to hire nationals of any country other than Britain. The proposed employment of one or two Americans and French nationals to advise on an agricultural programme or to teach law was not taken seriously even by the Iranians who knew these were token gestures intended as a cover for the employment of a large number of British nationals in the Finance Ministry and the military. Nevertheless, Curzon was suspicious of the 'internationalisation of Persia' and it was not until late April that the Foreign Office realised the advantages Seyyed Zia was offering and reluctantly accepted the programme.[55]

Seyyed Zia did nothing to mollify a frightened Ahmad Shah. Instead he reduced the civil list while increasing the salary of the devious and ambitious Crown Prince, arousing the suspicions of the Shah even further. From the moment Seyyed Zia had burst upon the scene the Shah had been frightened by what appeared to be his radical tendencies. It is highly likely that the two had never even met before but the mere fact that Seyyed Zia had seized power through a coup must have aroused deep fears in the Shah. The only coup and revolution the Shah had heard about had been undertaken by the Bolsheviks in Russia. The very first request of Seyyed Zia, to be granted the title of 'dictator', must have been regarded as a foreboding sign. From the beginning the Shah had been ignored and his advice had not been sought. The arrest of the 'notables' did not sit well with him as many of those imprisoned were people he knew and who had worked for him in various capacities. Some were even related by marriage. Seyyed Zia treated the Shah 'as if he had been sent as something between the scourge of God and a modern schoolmaster'.[56] He observed no protocol in his audiences with the Shah and often visited him unannounced.[57] The Shah also began to create difficulties for Seyyed Zia and it was only a matter of time before the Shah would begin to plot his downfall.

The Shah, always thinking first of his own safety and financial independence, had at the beginning of Seyyed Zia's premiership decided to travel to Europe. In early March the Shah obtained Seyyed Zia's promise that he would be allowed to go to Europe on Iranian New Year's Day. Seyyed Zia, however, had set two conditions: that the Shah make an appearance at some official function in Tehran and publicly express confidence in the new Government and that the British Legation agree to the trip. Curzon wrote to Norman that the Shah could leave but 'we will furnish him with no means of conveyance to Europe... and he will not be welcomed in England'. Curzon added that 'knowing his reasons for the trip are purely selfish and are based on fear [the Shah had pleaded illness], personally I doubt whether, should His Majesty leave the country, he will be disposed to return'.[58] The Shah withdrew his promise and refused to attend a public function and express confidence in the Prime Minister. Seyyed Zia retaliated by informing the Shah that he could not leave as his departure could endanger the security of the country. The Shah soon changed his mind and as promised came to the city on 21 March and in a brief address at the Cossack camp expressed satisfaction and confidence in the new Government. Their relations, for a brief period, appeared outwardly cordial and the Shah postponed his trip until the end of May.[59] By the time Seyyed Zia tried to mend relations the Shah had organised a coup of his own.

There is some evidence that Seyyed Zia and the Shah each began to think seriously of removing the other. Seyyed Zia was in contact with the Crown Prince from early March. Norman informed Curzon that 'the Veli'ahd [Crown Prince] is making advances to this Legation with a view to supplant his brother'.[60] After Seyyed Zia's fall there is clearer evidence of collusion between the Vali'ahd and Seyyed Zia.[61] The Shah must have had an inkling of these moves by his brother and Seyyed Zia and ultimately played a key role in the removal of the latter.

Despite the hostility of the Shah and the grandees, and the erosion of support from other quarters, Seyyed Zia's Government could have lasted longer had he continued to have the support of Reza Khan. In the final analysis it was Reza Khan who ended Seyyed Zia's brief premiership. Their incongruous and uneasy relationship had been tenuous from the beginning and it was inevitable that their priorities and goals would diverge. Both the Legation and Seyyed Zia had badly miscalculated Reza Khan. He was not the simple soldier they had imagined. From the outset Norman, the principal advocate of Seyyed Zia, had considered Reza Khan as 'a soldier without political ambitions'[62] and continued to maintain that Reza Khan 'knows he is incapable of administration of the country' and has no choice but to support Seyyed Zia.[63] There is no record of Norman ever having met with Reza Khan for any length of time. Each appears to have kept his distance from the other. Norman slowly came to realise the potential threat Reza Khan posed to Seyyed Zia and began to disparage him frequently in his reports. 'Norman calls Reza Khan a peasant. One with whom no upper class foreigner would associate.'[64]

Neither Norman nor Seyyed Zia ever credited Reza Khan with having an independent vision for Iran and distinct priorities and agenda. Whereas Seyyed Zia advocated a revival of agriculture and individual crafts for the future prosperity of the country, Reza Khan believed Iran's regeneration lay in industry, roads and railroads. In order to accomplish these goals Iran needed a strong central government to ensure internal security. The buildup of the military was the first step in that direction. Seyyed Zia, fearful of the Bolshevik threat, had initially supported Reza Khan's agenda. Reza Khan also had left the running of civilian government to Seyyed Zia and continued single-mindedly to bolster the military. He initially concerned himself solely with the strengthening of the Cossack Division and the welfare of its men. He knew that in order to have a united country all rebels had to be suppressed and the authority of the Central Government had to be established throughout the land. Seyyed Zia and Reza Khan may both have thought the Shah was useless and shared a contempt for politicians, but there was nothing personal in Reza Khan's attitude. Seyyed Zia's imprisonment of the grandees contained a personal element, not merely prompted by his humble background but the fact that he had been on the periphery of politics so long and had not been taken seriously. Reza Khan wanted structural changes, changes which he later implemented. For Seyyed Zia the maintenance of British supremacy was of paramount importance and any changes were to take place within that framework. His attempt at a balanced foreign policy really meant keeping Britain the dominant power in Iran while dispensing morsels to the United States and France. Reza Khan wanted a merger of all the armed forces to be commanded only by Iranian officers while Seyyed Zia was still thinking of hiring British officers to command the Cossacks and Swedish officers to command the Gendarmerie.

With Reza Khan set on his own programme and Seyyed Zia still pursuing a policy of British control of the Iranian military, serious differences began to emerge. From the outset Reza Khan had been an *ex-officio* member of the Cabinet and had argued for greater allocation of resources to the military. Inevitably Reza Khan came to insist on his appointment as Minister of War. Seyyed Zia had to yield as he relied on the Cossacks for internal security. Reza Khan was appointed as Minister of War and Keyhan became Minister without portfolio. Seyyed Zia had calculated that if Reza Khan were appointed Minister of War he would relinquish his post as commander of the Cossacks, freeing Seyyed Zia to appoint someone else to replace him. Furthermore, Reza Khan would probably wear civilian clothes when attending Cabinet meetings as a minister and in so doing lose his aura of authority. Seyyed Zia appears naive in his thinking as Reza Khan did neither. After becoming Minister of War Reza Khan seldom attended Cabinet meetings and at those he did attend he was in full uniform and continued to ignore Seyyed Zia.[65] In early April Reza Khan held a reception at the Cossack camp which Seyyed Zia and his ministers attended. It was apparent to the guests, including members of the Cabinet, that it was Reza Khan who wielded the power and was the real leader.[66]

Matters came to a head with Seyyed Zia's employment of British officers. On 21 April some 20 British officers were sent to Qazvin without Reza Khan's knowledge. Reza Khan objected and openly declared that he would not agree to the employment of any further British officers and in fact would dismiss the few who were then with the Cossacks. He was willing to co-operate with the British but not if they were to run the finances and the military of the country as before. He argued that the employment of Englishmen would be looked upon by the public as another attempt to renew the discredited 1919 Agreement. For the Iranian soldiers, British officers were as much resented as their former Czarist officers. For the Iranian officers the question was, why did we risk a coup if foreign officers were to remain in control of the military?

Reza Khan from the beginning had strongly objected to 'executive command' by British officers. Now he thought the time had come to put an end to their continued employment. He believed the presence of British officers would weaken his control over the Division and would also have consequences in the reorganisation and unification of the armed forces.[67] A large number of Iranian officers encouraged by Reza Khan met and took an oath on the Qoran not to serve under British officers.[68] Reza Khan forbade the soldiers to accept any innovation in drill or procedure and demanded return to the Russian system. These orders were issued to undermine the position of British officers and weaken their control.[69] Soon the employment of

Colonels Smyth and Huddlestone, the two most senior British officers, was terminated.[70]

On 6 May, a few weeks after becoming Minister of War, Reza Khan made a further demand: that the control of the Gendarmerie, hitherto under the Ministry of Interior, be transferred to the Ministry of War. Seyyed Zia, who by now realised that Reza Khan was not the simple soldier he had imagined, again acceded to this demand. He had no choice as he had become dependent on Reza Khan from his first few days in office, relying too much on the Cossacks to whip the populace into line. He had not realised that the Cossacks, whom he regarded as mere enforcers, had become masters; Reza Khan now controlled all the armed forces.

Seyyed Zia's position had become untenable and on 23 May when Reza Khan demanded that Seyyed Zia resign and leave the country. Seyyed Zia left Tehran on that day accompanied by Maj. Keyhan, Col. Kazem Khan and Epikian, the *de facto* Mayor of Tehran.[71] On 24 May Seyyed Zia's distinguished prisoners were freed. Norman wrote to Curzon on 25 May:

> Minister of War who is also Commander of the Cossack Division and the Shah after a long struggle forced the Prime Minister out of office... All my efforts to dissuade the conspirators failed owing to the fact that since withdrawal of our troops, Minister of War no longer fears us. [British troop withdrawal had been completed on 19 May]. The Shah who was always afraid of Seyyed Zia whom he regards as a dangerous Bolshevik put his trust in Minister of War.

Norman added that the Shah played a key part in the removal of Seyyed Zia and used two people to accomplish his aim: Reza Khan and Hassan Moshar (Moshar al Molk) who had been appointed Minister of Court by the Shah on Seyyed Zia's recommendation. Moshar had been expected to keep Seyyed Zia informed of the Shah's moves and plans. 'Moshar played a double game as he was promised by the Shah to become the [next] Prime Minister.' Despite his 'double game', Moshar continued to retain the highest confidence of the British Legation.

Norman continued to make disparaging remarks about Reza Khan. He called him 'an ignorant peasant but an astute peasant... He is honestly anti-Bolshevik... but inspires me with misgivings'.[72] In a later report Norman wrote, 'Seyyed Zia could have forced Reza Khan out but lost energy from overwork'. His Cabinet was useless and of no help to him. When Seyyed Zia was weakened Reza Khan 'literally told him to resign and leave'. Reza Khan gave him 25,000 tomans to cover his travel expenses. 'But the Shah and later Reza Khan wanted to detain him at Kazvin. Our intervention saved him'.[73]

The US Legation, which at first had the lowest opinion of Seyyed Zia, revised its appraisal because during his term of office he had attempted to hire a few American advisers. A report in early July argues that Seyyed Zia could have continued in office if he had convened parliament, where he would have found enough support to survive. The report enumerates reasons for his fall and mentions the imprisonment of notables and the attempt to extract money from them 'even though they were crooks; failure to convene parliament and differences with Reza Khan'. The report concludes that Seyyed Zia was an 'independent and fearless leader... [but] once he fell he had to leave. He would have been torn to pieces by the released prisoners'.[74]

With Seyyed Zia gone, Reza Khan became the dominant figure on the scene. It is difficult to know whether at this point he saw himself as Prime Minister. In retrospect, taking into account his cautious nature and the considered and meticulous moves he was to make during the coming two years, it is safe to conclude that he felt he was not yet ready to assume control of the government. Even if he were to have forced the hand of the Shah to appoint him as prime minister, he probably would not have lasted long. Reza Khan needed an expansion of his power base and he still had to build up the army, defeat the revolutionaries in the north and quell rebellions in other parts of the country to reinforce his position and stature.

From this point Reza Khan single-mindedly pursued his own agenda with a pre-set timetable. First the dismissal of British and Swedish officers from the Cossack Divison, the Gendarmerie and the police; then the merger of all armed forces including Cossacks, Gendarmerie and the incorporation of the remnants of the SPR (which would be disbanded by Britain in September 1921).

To expand his power base, Reza Khan began to court the grandees. He had already seen to it that they had been well treated in prison and thus had acquired their good will. He reminded them that it had been Seyyed Zia who had imprisoned them and he who had released them as soon as Seyyed Zia had been forced to resign. Reza Khan knew it would not take much to bring them into his corner. He had personally witnessed the weakness they had shown in prison and how easily they had been frightened. They were primarily concerned about security and order and he could promise them that. Having tasted fear these grandees would now eat from Reza Khan's hand in order to avoid danger to themselves. Reza Khan had several more advantages over Seyyed Zia. While Seyyed Zia had dwelt on the evils and corruption of the 'ruling class', Reza Khan had merely talked of 'a handful of traitors in the Capital' without identifying anyone or any group. Reza Khan on various occasions had told notables that he had believed the Shah had authorised the coup, giving his actions a justification they could understand. 'He himself saw the Shah several times after the Coup and explained why he had to do it'.[75]

With the departure of Seyyed Zia, Reza Khan obtained an almost irrefutable right over the appointment of prime ministers and the privilege of having one or two of his own people in the cabinet. The British Legation, especially Norman, were slow to realise Reza Khan's potential. He was first seen as an apolitical soldier, then as a tool of the Russians. When Seyyed Zia fell Reza Khan was regarded merely as an interim figure.[76] Even after Reza Khan's decisive defeat of revolutionaries in Gilan, which enhanced his standing with the Foreign Office, Norman continued to have his doubts.

With the emergence of Reza Khan as a major figure, Norman's days in Iran were numbered. Not only had he missed the significance of Reza Khan but his unqualified support of Seyyed Zia had made him powerful enemies including Firouz, Moddares and Teimurtash. Norman indeed had the unusual talent of having made enemies from widely diverse groups among whom were the supporters of such disparate personalities as Vosouq, Pirnia and Sepahdar, as well as grandees who blamed him for their imprisonment. Norman's array of foes probably hastened his departure from Tehran. A report from the US Legation states:

> Mr Herman Norman, although an able and cultured man has not been known to make himself popular with the Persians. He... expresses his dislike of Persia and everything Persian rather freely. His staff is bad. Most of them are ex-Indian army men with the rank of colonel and they are derisively referred to by the Persians as 'Colonel India Company'.[77]

Britain looked forward to the arrival of a new envoy to mend fences with Reza Khan. The new envoy, Sir Percy Loraine, was quick to appreciate that Reza Khan's coup was the first step in strengthening just those forces of nationalism within Iran which the Government of India looked to as an effective bulwark against a communist revolution. Curzon appears not to have realised this. Britain's two powerful tools of enforcing its policy in Iran, Norperforce and SPR, had ceased to exist. Curzon was to comment:

> The weakness of our position is the dreaded consequence of the withdrawal of our troops from north Persia and the dismemberment of SPR. Both of these acts were the result of Cabinet decisions taken out of combined economy and ignorance at the advice of persons who knew nothing of the case.[78]

Reza Khan was to become to Iran what Mostafa Kamal (Ataturk) was to Turkey. Reza Khan, like Kamal, was more concerned about the dangers posed by the neighbour to the north. Britain was merely an avaricious and untrustworthy ally but Russia could swallow Iran. Reza Khan never confused the threatening Soviets with the British and took this distinction into account in all his dealings with Britain. Although the Iran over which Reza Khan later ruled was far removed from the client state which Curzon had envisaged, Reza Shah was always mindful of Britain's commercial interests in the country.[79]

The ascent of Reza Khan marked the beginning of a rapid decline in British influence in Iran, 'A decline which reached its nadir in 1951 under the premiership of Mohammad Mosaddeq. Mosaddeq only completed in rather more precipitate a manner a process instituted three decades earlier by Reza Khan'.[80]

NOTES ON CHAPTER 8
Further details of publications and documents in Bibliography

1 FO 371/6403, Norman to Curzon, 1 March 1921.
2 Baqer Aqeli, *Ruz Shomar Tarikh Iran* (*A Daily Calendar of the History of Iran*), vol. 1, p 146; see also Hosein Makki, *Tarikh Bist Saleh Iran* (*A Twenty Year History of Iran*), vol. 1, pp 303–305.
3 *Ibid.*
4 *Ibid.*
5 FO 416/78, Bullard to Halifax, 7 February 1940; Mehdi Bamdad, *Tarikh Rejal Iran Quroun 12, 13, 14* (*Dictionary of National Biography of Iran: Twelfth, Thirteenth, Fourteenth Centuries*), vol. 5, pp 283–285.
6 FO 416/98, Bullard to Halifax, 7 February 1940.
7 FO 416/98, Bullard to Halifax, 7 February 1940.
8 Of the other two senior ministers of Seyyed Zia, Mahmoud Khan Movaqar al Dowleh, Minister of Public Works and Commerce, died shortly after his appointment and Taqi Moshir A'zam (Khajavi) only served briefly as Minister of Post and Telegraph.
9 Mehdi Bamdad, *Tarikh Rejal Iran Quroun 12, 13, 14* (*Dictionary of National Biography of Iran: Twelfth, Thirteenth, Fourteenth Centuries*), vol. 4, pp 107–108.
10 FO 416/98, Bullard to Halifax, 7 February 1940; Mehdi Bamdad, *Tarikh Rejal Iran Quroun 12, 13, 14* (*Dictionary of National Biography of Iran: Twelfth, Thirteenth, Fourteenth Centuries*), vol. 6, pp 92-93.
11 FO 416/98, Bullard to Halifax, 7 February 1940.
12 FO 416/98, Bullard to Halifax, 7 February 1940.
13 See Homa Katouzian, *Mosaddeq and the Struggle for Power in Iran*; Mohammad Mosaddeq, *Mosaddeq Memoires*, edited and translated by Homa Katouzian.
14 Hosein Makki, *Tarikh Bist Saleh Iran* (*A Twenty Year History of Iran*), vol. 1, pp 258–263.
15 *Ibid.*, p 318.
16 FO 416/68, Norman to Curzon, 6 April 1921. Norman adds that 'Qavam [is] exceedingly corrupt although capable'.
17 Hosein Makki, *Tarikh Bist Saleh Iran* (*A Twenty Year History of Iran*), vol. 1, p 238–240, 279; Mohamad Taqi Bahar, *Tarikh Mokhtasar Ahzab Siasi* (*A Short History of Political Parties*), vol. 1, pp 88–89.
18 FO 371/6402, Norman to Curzon, 10 March 1921.
19 FO 371/6402, Norman to Curzon, 11 March 1921.
20 FO 371/6402, Curzon to Norman, 14 March 1921.
21 FO 416/69, Norman to Curzon, 8 April 1921.
22 FO 416/68, Curzon to Norman, 19 April 1921.
23 Hosein Makki, *Tarikh Bist Saleh Iran* (*A Twenty Year History of Iran*), vol. 1, pp 238–239.
24 *Ibid.*
25 Asnad-e-Cabine, *Coup d'Etat 3 Esfand 1299* (*Documents Relating to the 21 February 1921 Coup*), ed. H. Morselvand, pp 65–157.
26 Baqer Aqeli, *Zoka al Molk Foroughi va Shahrivar 1320* (*Zoka al Molk Foroughi and August–September 1941*), vol. 1, p 149.
27 Asnad-e-Cabine, *Coup d'Etat 3 Esfand 1299* (*Documents Relating to the 21 February 1921 Coup*), ed. H. Morselvand, p 235.

28 FO 371/6402, Norman to Curzon, 17 March 1921.
29 FO 371/6403, Curzon to Norman, 18 April 1921.
30 FO 416/69, Norman to Curzon, 22 April 1921.
31 FO 371/6403, Norman to Curzon, 23 April 1921.
32 FO 416/68, Curzon to Norman, 25 April 1921.
33 FO 371/6403, Curzon to Norman, 28 April 1921.
34 FO 371/6403, Norman to Curzon, 30 April 1921.
35 Richard H. Ullman, *The Anglo-Soviet Accord*, pp 390–391.
36 FO 416/66, Curzon to Norman, 5 April 1921.
37 FO 416/68, Norman to Curzon, 21 April 1921.
38 *Ibid.*
39 DoS, Quarterly Report, US Legation, Tehran, to Secretary of State, 12 October 1921.
40 FO 371/6405, Norman to Curzon, 23 April 1921.
41 FO 371/6401, Foreign Office to Norman, 21 April 1921.
42 FO 371/6435, Norman to Curzon, 3 May 1921.
43 FO 371/6435, Intelligence summary for week ending 21 May 1921.
44 FO 371/6404, Norman to Curzon, 8 May 1921.
45 FO 416/69, Norman to Curzon, 23 May 1921.
46 FO 416/69, Norman to Curzon, 26 March 1921.
47 FO 416/68, Curzon to Norman, 16 April 1921.
48 FO 416/68, Curzon to Norman, 19 April 1921.
49 FO 371/6435 Government of India to Curzon, 6 May 1921.
50 Peter Avery, *Modern Iran*, p 222; L.P. Elwell-Sutton, 'Reza Shah the Great' in George Lenczowski (ed.), *Iran Under the Pahlavis*, p 14.
51 Mohamad Taqi Bahar, *Tarikh Mokhtasar Ahzab Siasi* (*A Short History of Political Parties*), vol. 1, p 101.
52 *Ibid*, p 94.
53 James M. Balfour, *Recent Happenings in Persia*, pp 231–232.
54 FO 371/6401, Norman to Curzon, 25 February 1921.
55 FO 371/6403, Curzon to Norman, 28 April 1921.
56 Peter Avery, *Mordern Iran*, p 252.
57 Hosein Makki, *Tarikh Bist Saleh Iran* (*A Twenty Year History of Iran*), vol. 1, p 299; Mohamad Taqi Bahar, *Tarikh Mokhtasar Ahzab Siasi* (*A Short History of Political Parties*), vol. 1, p 102.
58 DBFP, No. 692, Curzon to Norman, 8 March 1921.
59 FO 416/68, Norman to Curzon, 25 March 1921.
60 *Ibid.*
61 FO 371/6446, Seyyed Zia to Norman and L. Oliphant, note, 8 April 1921.
62 FO 416/68, Norman to Curzon, 3 March 1921.
63 FO 371/6106, Norman to Curzon, 3 March 1921.
64 DoS, Quarterly Report No. 12, US Legation, Tehran, to Secretary of State, 1 April to 30 June 1921.
65 Mohamad Taqi Bahar, *Tarikh Mokhtasar Ahzab Siasi* (*A Short History of Political Parties*), vol. 1, p 101.
66 Yahya Dowlatabadi, *Hayat Yahya* (*The Life of Yahya*), vol. 4, p 246.
67 FO 371/6435, Intelligence summary for week ending 21 May 1921.
68 FO 371/6435, Intelligence summary for week ending 18 June 1921; see also James M. Balfour, *Recent Happenings in Persia*, p 235.
69 FO 371/6435, Intelligence summary for week ending 28 May 1921.
70 DoS, Caldwell, US Legation, Tehran, to Secretary of State, 6 June 1921.

71 Mohamad Taqi Bahar, *Tarikh Mokhtasar Ahzab Siasi* (*A Short History of Political Parties*), vol. 1, p 100. Epikian is sometimes referred to as Epakchian.
72 FO 371/6404, Norman to Curzon, 25 May 1921.
73 FO 371/6404, Norman to Curzon, 6 June 1921.
74 DoS, Quarterly Report No. 12, US Legation, Tehran, to Secretary of State, 1 April to 30 June 1921.
75 FO 416/69, Norman to Curzon, 26 March 1921.
76 FO 371/6404, Minute by G.P. Churchill, 26 May 1921.
77 DoS, US Legation, Tehran, to Department of State, 6 June 1921.
78 FO 371/6407, Minute by Curzon, November 1921.
79 Richard H. Ullman, *The Anglo-Soviet Accord*, vol. 3, p 394.
80 *Ibid.*

9

Qavam's First Government

Seyyed Zia disappeared from the political stage as abruptly as he had entered. After his exile he was to remain in Baghdad for some four months before going on to Paris briefly, and then settling in Switzerland and later Palestine. Initially he chose to remain as near to Iran as possible, for he could not accept his premature political demise. It was during his brief stay in Baghdad that he made one last attempt to return to Iran and regain power.

The Vali'ahd (Crown Prince), Mohammad Hassan Mirza, had remained an inconsequential figure even after being proclaimed heir to the throne. He was ignored by most Iranian notables and even his brother, Ahmad Shah, rarely bothered to pay much attention to him. While the Shah continued to enrich himself by selling offices and titles, the Vali'ahd had to content himself merely with his annual salary and, when his brother would allow, occasional bribes from public officials seeking minor appointments. Resentment toward his brother had been building steadily when in early March 1921 he approached the British Legation with proposals to supplant Ahmad Shah.[1] Seyyed Zia appears to have been privy to and may even have encouraged the Vali'ahd in the pursuit of this enterprise. Despite the extremely low opinion in which the Shah was held by Norman and the Foreign Office, the Vali'ahd's advances were ignored for many reasons, one of of which was that the Vali'ahd himself was held in even lower esteem by the Legation.

When Seyyed Zia came to power both brothers had begun their usual clamour to go to Europe for 'health' reasons. As mentioned previously, the Shah was denied permission by Seyyed Zia, backed by Norman.[2] The Crown Prince also decided to defer his trip after Seyyed Zia raised his salary. But barely two weeks after the fall and ouster of Seyyed Zia the Crown Prince unexpectedly left Iran, ostensibly for Europe, via Baghdad where Seyyed Zia had settled temporarily. On 10 July 1921 the High Commissioner's office in Baghdad informed Norman:

> [Seyyed Zia has] told us the Vali'ahd is very dissatisfied with the Shah and fears for safety of Persia from Bolsheviks. If Tehran falls he is prepared to head new Government in South Persia separated from North Persia and even if the Bolshevik threat does not eventuate he is prepared to form new Government as he considers the Shah useless... Crown Prince wishes to go to London to arrange meeting with Lord Curzon through Vosouq ed Dowleh... I dissuaded him... to await further developments.[3]

Norman sent the following message to Seyyed Zia via Cox. He confirmed that he too was fearful of a Bolshevik attack now that British troops had been withdrawn:

> ... but as representative accredited to the Shah [I am prevented] from encouraging any movement which has for its object, dethronement of His Majesty. It is also my duty to do my best to preserve the unity of Persia as long as possible and I am therefore precluded from listening to proposal of His Royal Highness.

Norman asked Seyyed Zia to convey this message to the Vali'ahd who had since travelled to Bombay and added, 'While I agree with you [Seyyed Zia] that the Shah is useless and even harmful to the country, I am not sure that the Vali'ahd is not in some respects still worse and I have always understood that to be also your opinion'. As Seyyed Zia was planning to travel to India to join the Vali'ahd, Norman advised Seyyed Zia to remain in touch with him through the Govenment of India 'but to avoid sending telegrams from Dehli and Simla as they may arouse suspicions in Persia'.[4]

Cox, who had been one of the early and foremost supporters of a separate government in southern Iran, appears to have seen some merit in the Crown Prince's proposal. Norman, who had not favoured the 1920 schemes for a multi-government Iran, dismissed the idea of the Crown Prince as a successor or alternate to the Shah, although, still appeared hopeful that Seyyed Zia could stage a comeback and encouraged him to remain in touch. Whatever may have been in the minds of the Crown Prince, Seyyed Zia, Cox and Norman came to naught as both Curzon and the Government of India strongly objected to any plot being hatched or developed in India.

On 18 July Curzon informed the Government of India that 'it was a mistake to allow either [Seyyed Zia or the Vali'ahd] to go to India', and expressed surprise that the Vali'ahd had been able to change travel plans without it having been reported and stopped. Now that Seyyed Zia had completed part of his journey he should be admitted entry to India but 'he must be prevented from using India as a base for political manoeuvres'. As far as the Vali'ahd was concerned he should be persuaded to leave India as soon as possible. The Viceroy of India expressed his embarrassment at being caught unaware and assured Curzon that he would find an appropriate excuse to cut short their visits.[5]

Seyyed Zia was not to be heard of again until his return to Iran in 1943 after the 1941 Anglo-Russian invasion and subsequent occupation, when British influence once again became ascendant. For the next ten years he was regarded as a potential prime minister by his band of ardent anglophiles. After the coup of 1953 he retired to a farm in north-west Tehran and oblivion. He was seen publicly only at large official receptions at the British Embassy. He was also invited to some functions at court and lunched privately with Mohammad Reza Shah several times a year.

Even before Seyyed Zia was out of the country the Shah with unaccustomed haste approached Hassan Pirnia (Moshir al Dowleh), twice before a Prime Minister, and offered him the premiership.[6] Pirnia declined and the Shah, following the familiar ritual, next offered the post to Mostofi who also declined.[7] Hassan Moshar (Moshar al Molk)* who had been appointed Minister of Court by Seyyed Zia expected the position to be offered to him. Moshar had collaborated with the Shah in the ouster of Seyyed Zia and had every

---

*   Hassan Moshar (Moshar al Molk), c.1864–1948, was trained as an accountant and began his career at the Ministry of Foreign Affairs supervising its finances. He was elected to the founding session of parliament, served twice as Minister of Finance during Vosouq's first and second terms as Prime Minister and became a partner with Vosouq and Toumanians in the opium monopoly company and acquired great wealth. He was appointed Minister of Court at Seyyed Zia's urging; denied the premiership; and elected to the fourth session of parliament. Accused of plotting the murder of Qavam, his parliamentary immunity was lifted and he was exiled abroad, returning in 1924, his innocence established. He became Minister of Foreign Affairs, then Minister of Finance, again in 1929, resigning in 1930. He remained close to the British Legation and on occasions imparted useful and sensitive confidential information to them. He left Iran around 1937 and settled in Monte Carlo for the rest of his life. A cautious man and a survivor, he lived an undistinguished life.[8]

reason to expect his reward. For reasons not entirely clear, but probably because Moshar's duplicitous role in the fall of Seyyed Zia had made him untrustworthy both to the Shah and Reza Khan, the premiership was denied him. Although Moshar had been close to the British Legation, Norman, equally angered by Moshar's role in the abrupt downfall of Seyyed Zia, probably made no attempt to recommend him. Soon the Shah was running out of candidates. Next to be considered was Ahmad Qavam, the energetic and capable Governor of Khorasan, presently languishing in prison. Although Qavam had been tainted with corruption, his governorship of Khorasan had enhanced his reputation as an effective administrator. He had restored calm to a province sharing borders with the newly established Soviet republics to the north and a turbulent Afghanistan to the east. The fact that Qavam had stood up to Seyyed Zia and had not recognised his forced assumption of power for which he was imprisoned, now recommended him to the Shah. Being the brother of Vosouq also may have worked in his favour as the Shah was eager for resumption of British financial assistance. Equally significant was the fact that Reza Khan had raised no objections to Qavam's proposed appointment. There was even to be a nascent community of interest between Qavam and Reza Khan. In addition to having to deal with Kouchek Khan in Gilan, Reza Khan knew that sooner or later he must cope with the autonomous rule of Col. Mohammad Taqi Khan in Khorasan. The Colonel, head of the Gendarmerie in Khorasan, had removed Qavam from the governorship and sent him to Tehran to face trial for disobedience in not having recognised Seyyed Zia as Prime Minister. Given their mutual antagonism it was highly unlikely that the Colonel would obey Qavam's directives as Prime Minister.

Norman appears to have stayed aloof from the selection process. He saw the Shah a few days after Seyyed Zia's fall and refused to name his preference for prime minister. He wrote to Curzon, 'The Shah says he could not keep Seyyed Zia in office despite my recommendation [but] as he is anxious as ever for support from Great Britain he would only appoint someone as Prime Minister of my choosing'. Norman had declined to choose and merely answered that the future Prime Minister should be 'an honest man free of political bias [with] the same type of cabinet'.[9] Norman had been deeply disappointed by the removal of Seyyed Zia. However, by now it also must have dawned on him that his activism in choosing prime ministers had not produced the desired results. Neither Pirnia nor Sepahdar had lived up to his expectations and in bringing Seyyed Zia to the foreground he had taken an even greater gamble.

A period of distancing himself from the volatile Iranian scene could be beneficial.

Additionally, Norman's dislike and distrust of Reza Khan had remained unaltered. Norman knew he would be the key person in any future government and that regardless of who was Prime Minister, Reza Khan would dominate the scene and pay scant heed to the Legation's priorities. Norman, who had never sympathised with Reza Khan's agenda and plans, expressesd the harshest criticism of Reza Khan's role in the abrupt dismissal of Seyyed Zia. In the same telegram Norman wrote:

> Sardar Sepah [Reza Khan] is still in a position to dictate his terms and remains as Minister of War and Commander in Chief of the army... Sardar Sepah's attitude towards the British officers serving with the Cossack Division becomes daily more unsatisfactory. Not only does he appear determined to refuse them executive authority, but he also shows signs of opposing the signature of their contract...[10]

He later informed Curzon:

> The Minister of War who remains virtually a dictator appears unwilling that contracts with individual British officers be signed... Col. Huddlestone has resigned and I am going to call on the Prime Minister.[11]

The Shah's choice being limited, on 28 May he sent his Chief of Protocol, Asadollah Shams Molk Ara (Shahab al Dowleh),* to the prison in Eshratabad to bring Qavam directly to the court. Qavam and the Shah had a long conversation lasting several hours and the Shah offered him the premiership, which Qavam accepted without reservations. Norman of course had deep reservations about Qavam because of repeated allegations of corruption. He wrote to Curzon:

> ... though the new Prime Minister besides being energetic and capable, is animated by the friendliest feelings towards Great Britain, I foresee no good results from his assumption of power, because he is totally unfitted by training and association to preside over a reforming government or even a relatively honest one.[12]

---

* Assadollah Shams Molk Ara (Shahab al Dowleh), c.1880 to c.1955, was the great grandson of Fath Ali Shah; educated in Iran; for many years employed at the Telegraph Department; Governor of Yazd in 1911; accused of financial irregularities; Minister of Post and Telegraph 1914–1915; accompanied Ahmad Shah to London in 1919; Minister of Public Works; Chief of Protocol under Ahmad Shah 1922–1925; between 1929 and 1936 Governor of Kermanshah and later Kurdestan; appointed to the Senate in 1949 where he served for two terms.[13]

Qavam's past history of plunder and dishonest government had caught up with him. Norman, however, warned the Shah to tell Qavam that there should be no vengeance by the new Government against members and supporters of the Government of Seyyed Zia.[14]

It took Qavam some five days to put together a Cabinet, announced on 3 June. Qavam assumed the Ministry of Interior himself; Sadeq Sadeq (Mosteshar al Dowleh)[†] Minister without portfolio; Reza Khan (Sardar Sepah) Minister of War; Hassan Esfandiary (Mohtashem al Saltaneh)[#] Minister of Foreign Affairs; Mohammad Mosaddeq (Mosaddeq al Saltaneh) Minister of Finance; Hosein Samii (Adib al Saltaneh) Minister of Public Works and Commerce; and Esma'il Momtaz (Momtaz al Dowleh)[§] Minister of Education. There were three

---

† Sadeq Sadeq (Mosteshar al Dowleh), 1865–1952, came from a prominent family in Tabriz. His uncle, Mohsen Khan Moshir al Dowleh, was Ambassador in Constantinople. Sadeq served at the Embassy there for many years before being elected to the founding session of parliament in 1906 and the second session in 1909. An ardent constitutionalist he was arrested and imprisoned by Mohammad Ali Shah from 1908–1909. In 1911 he became Minister of Interior; between 1914 and 1915 and again in 1917 Minister of Post and Telegraph. He expressed pro-German sympathies and at the insistence of the British Legation was exiled to an outlying province. He was Chairman of Constituent Assembly in 1925 and served as Ambassador to Turkey 1931–1935. His last Government post was Minister without portfolio in Qavam's Cabinet of 1942.[15]

Hassan Esfandiary (Mohtashem al Saltaneh), c.1867–1944, came from a prominent family. His father was the equivalent of Permanent Under Secretary at the Ministry of Foreign Affairs for almost two decades. Esfandiary began his career at the Ministry of Foreign Affairs and in 1897 became Under Secretary. He travelled with Mozafar al Din Shah to Europe, held various cabinet positions, including Justice in 1910, Foreign Affairs in 1911, Finance in 1912, 1914 and 1915. From 1921–1927 he again served in various ministerial posts, and was President of parliament from 1935–1942. He was a decent and respected gentleman of the old school, helpful to his constituents, and author of several books on Islamic law and a book on ethics. He was also a good calligrapher.[16]

§ Esma'il Momtaz (Momtaz al Dowleh), 1879–1933, began his career at the Ministry of Foreign Affairs where his father was a middle-ranking official. His first assignment was to Constantinople where he spent some ten years. He was a member of parliament at its founding session in 1906 and became its presiding officer. With the shelling of parliament he sought and was granted assylum at the French Legation. After Mohammad Ali Shah was ousted he was re-elected to Second Parliament in 1909. He served in several cabinets and translated several Turkish legal codes.[17]

newcomers who soon disappeared from the political scene: Moshar al Saltaneh as Minister of Post and Telegraph; Amid al Saltaneh,* a close ally of Qavam as Minister of Justice; and Hakim al Dowleh as Minister of Health and Public Charities. Norman wrote:

> Amid al Saltaneh as Minister of Justice is very friendly towards us. The rest are demagogues. Only honest person is Mosaddeq at Finance. All the thieves Seyyed Zia kicked out are back. Qavam made his brother, Motamed al Saltaneh, number two at Finance... Motamed al Saltaneh whose depredations were notorious when he occupied the same position under Sarem ed Dowleh in the Government of Vosouq ed Dowleh.[18]

In announcing his Cabinet, Qavam issued a proclamation making the usual promises of reforms, including amelioration of the lot of workers and peasants, employment of experts, exploration of natural resources, a new judicial system and abolition of capitulations. The Russian bank was to be reopened as an Iranian entity with the capital to be raised internally. In a private interview with Norman, Qavam made it known at the outset that in view of public hostility he could not grant British financial advisers any meaningful powers unless Great Britain were willing to make substantial financial advances. As to the role of British military advisers, Qavam being aware of Reza Khan's attitude, made no promises.[19]

Qavam got off to a good start. Although the Cabinet was devoid of anyone of energy or initiative it included several established constitutionalists and three prominent foes of the 1919 Agreement. This overall composition stood him well with the public. Qavam's opposition to Seyyed Zia had also gained him many supporters, especially amongst the released prisoners and notables. The opening of the Fourth Parliament after nearly six years enabled the new Government to rely on the support of a hard core of adherents. The Fourth Parliament was more assertive than its predecessors and its members more experienced, many having served in the previous two parliaments. From the very first session they made their presence felt. The respected Hosein Pirnia (Mo'tamen al Molk) was elected

---

* Ebrahim Amid Semnani (Amid al Hokama, later Amid al Saltaneh), 1874–c.1949, was the son of a medical practitioner and took up his father's practice after the latter's death. He was elected to the founding session of parliament from Semnan, and became close to Vosouq, soon becoming Under Secretary at the Ministry of Finance. He later became Deputy Governor in Qavam's governorship of Khorasan and a fixture in Qavam's four Cabinets between 1921 and 1922 as Minister of Justice or Public Works. Amid could only function as a satelite of Vosouq and Qavam, and was soon forgotten.[20]

Speaker with Moddares and Ebrahim Hakimi (Hakim al Molk) as Vice Presidents.

The Fourth Parliament was divided into several factions. The two which had the largest number of fairly constant supporters were the Socialists and the Moderates. Some who in the Third Parliament had called themselves Democrats now reassembled as Socialists. They could count on about 29 deputies and had competent speakers in the persons of Soleiman Mirza Eskandari and Mohammad Sadeq Tabataba'i, the eldest son of a deceased senior cleric who had been in the forefront of the constitutional cause. They advocated nation-alisation of means of production, centralisation of the government and welfare rights for workers. They also emphasised egalitarian principles. The other principal faction called themselves Moderates and sometimes Reformists, and totalled 32 deputies. They had much greater talent in their midst and two excellent and persuasive speakers in Moddares and Abdol Hosein Teimurtash (Sardar Mo'azam). They had support from bazaar merchants, lower ranking clergy and a number of notables who were seeking higher office. They were in general wary of political centralisation and sought more diffusion of power. They were basically secularist reformers within a constitutional framework. Their allies included Firouz, a good parliamentarian and debater who often joined the Moderates, and Seyyed Mohammad Taddayon who could reach the other side of the aisle and influence other factions (he later became one of the key advocates of Reza Khan). Reza Khan also had his hard core of sup-porters who functioned under various names such as the Renewal Party and the Radical Party. They advocated the creation of a modern army, strong central government, rapid industrialisation, expansion of educational facilities and the separation of religion and state. The rest of the deputies were the so-called non-aligned who more often voted with the Moderates on key issues. Their ranks included such respected notables as the Pirnia brothers, Moshir al Dowleh and Mo'tamen al Molk.

One of the first acts of the Fourth Parliament was to reject the credentials of three close allies of Seyyed Zia, Hosein Dadgar (Adl al Molk), Soltan Mohammad Ameri and Moshir Mo'azam. Firouz's cre-dentials were also challenged and only a vigorous defence by Moddares enabled him to take his seat. Firouz's credentials were objected to by Eskandari and Tabataba'i, who charged that he had been elected by bribing local officials. Firouz was also accused of 'selling' his country in his sponsorship and advocacy of the 1919 Agreement. Firouz argued in his own defence that he had been no worse than the pro-German 'democrats' who had organised an emigration of notables from Tehran with the help of the German and Turkish envoys and had nearly succeeded in placing Iran on the side of the Central Powers in the war. His support of Britain in 1919 had been legitimate and in the best interests of Iran. Firouz's arguments were pure sophistry but with Moddares's help they influenced enough deputies to have him seated.[21]

The Fourth Parliament asserted itself time and again in the selection of prime ministers and the length of their tenure. It was no longer at the whim and pleasure of the Shah alone. Equally important were the policy initiatives adopted by parliament often culminating in legislation. For the next two years parliament was to be equal with other branches of government. The Fourth Parliament also was to espouse the most legitimate nationalistic sentiments to date. Although a large number of its members had gained their seats in elections held under Vosouq's premiership they began to manifest strong anti-British sentiments and for the first time began to challenge Britain's economic and political supremacy in Iran. Elections under Vosouq had been so corrupt that if serious investigations had been held probably more than half of the deputies would have been diqualified from taking their seats. As it was the credentials of only a few were challenged. Yet these same men who had been elected through bribery and coercion in return for promises to support and ratify the 1919 Agreement were now asserting independence and exuding nationalist sentiments. The initiatives taken by Reza Khan in dismissing foreign officers from the military was partly responsible for having emboldened them. The Government of Qavam was an echo of these nationalist feelings and gave further impetus to them. Although his Government was soon to be mired in corruption and would fall under the pressure of British and Soviet disapproval, in its first few months it was to demonstrate initiative and energy. From the day it convened, parliament expressed its bitter opposition to the employment of the British financial advisers. If Qavam had not intervened, parliament probably would have passed a law prohibiting the employment of any British national. As Norman was to write to Curzon, 'The only way for advisers to stay would have been for Parliament to have been shut down'.[22]

With Reza Khan already refusing to sign employment contracts with British military officers it followed that the Qavam Government would begin to search for new sources of funds and financial advisers. Even before parliament was to open officially on 22 June 1921, the US Chargé d'Affaires, Cornelius van H. Engert (Caldwell having left in early June) wrote to the US Secretary of State that he had had a meeting with the Shah and Esfandiary, the Minister of

Foreign Affairs. Both had specifically asked for agricultural experts and financial advisers to form and head an Iranian bank. They had both intimated that Persia would in turn consider advantageous concessions for oil, railroads, mines, etc.' Engert had added, 'Britain appears reconciled to the fact they cannot have exclusive privileges in North Persia'.[23] At about the same time the Iranian envoy to Spain, Hosein Ala (Mo'in al Vezareh),* had met with the Counsellor of the US Legation in Madrid. Ala, who had been nominated to become the Iranian Minister to Washington, had stated that because of the unpopularity of the 1919 Agreement, its failure to be ratified, and because of the traditional rivalry between Britain and the Soviets, the Iranian Government had decided to employ US advisers. Ala had also mentioned the formation of a national bank and had asked whether the US would be prepared to make a loan of $5 million to Iran to be guaranteed by the proceeds of the APOC concession.[24]

Later in July Qavam telegraphed his brother Vosouq in London to enquire about the possibility of loans from US oil companies.[25] On 20 July Vosouq, on behalf of his brother but acting in a private capacity, called on Lancelot Oliphant at the Foreign office and 'complained about Britain's refusal to make funds available to the Persian Government'. Oliphant in turn mentioned 'the treatment of British officers and curtailment of the powers of the financial advisers and the general attitude towards SPR' by Reza Khan. Vosouq argued that support by Britain for Seyyed Zia had alienated many people. After these preliminary exchanges Vosouq explored Britain's attitude towards the possibility and advisability of loans from other

---

*   Hosein Ala, formerly Ala'i, (Mo'in al Vezareh), 1884–1965, was the son of Mohammad Ali Ala al Saltaneh, Minister to London, Minister of Foreign Affairs and Prime Minister. He was educated at Westminster School in London and awarded C.M.G. in 1905 while accompanying his father bearing gifts from Mozzafar al Din Shah to King Edward VII. He joined the Ministry of Foreign Affairs in 1906 when his father was Foreign Minister and served as private secretary to successive Foreign Ministers until 1915. He was Minister of Public Works in the Cabinets of Mostofi and Samsam al Saltaneh in 1918, delegate to the Paris Peace Conference 1918–1919 and Minister to Madrid in 1919 and Washington in 1921. He was a member of the fifth session of parliament in 1925; Minister of Public Works in 1927; Minister to Paris in 1929; London in 1934; Minister of Commerce in 1937, Head of National Bank; Ambassador to Washington 1945–1950; Minister of Foreign Affairs, Prime Minister (twice) and Minister of Court; was forced to resign in late 1963 having displeased Mohammad Reza Shah with his views on riots in June 1963; and was appointed to the Senate. A decent, well-meaning public servant, he was fluent in English and French, but wanting in substance.[26]

countries, specifically the US. Qavam's telegram to Vosouq had been
intercepted by the Foreign Office and Oliphant, having been alerted,
declined to give his views and was non-committal.[27]

By early September the employment contracts of Armitage Smith
and his assistants had been terminated[28] and on 10 November
Hosein Ala, the Iranian envoy to Washington, called on the Assistant
Secretary of State, Dearing, and 'urgently requested the US to name
its finacial adviser'. Ala also stated 'unequivocally that US Oil
Companies will be granted a concession for northern oil as the
Khoshtaria Concession defenitely will not be given to APOC'.[29] On 9
November Rabbi Joseph Saul Kornfeld was appointed as US Minister
to Tehran to succeed Caldwell, although, the appointment of a US
financial adviser was delayed pending Kornfeld's recommendation
after arrival in Tehran.[30]

Britain now began to use all her resources to keep the United
States out of Iran. The Foreign Office feared that the US Government
might be drawn into Iran in the wake of American investors and
once again reverted to the argument that Iran was covered by their
equivalent in Asia of the Monroe Doctrine.[31] Moreover, US investment would provide the Iranian Government with new sources of
funds, reducing Britain's control of Iranian finances. On 7 October
Sir Aukland Geddes, Britain's Ambassador to the United States, wrote
to the US Secretary of State Charles Evans Hughes that the northern
Iranian oil concession (Khoshtaria) of 9 March 1916 was still valid
and the property of APOC.[32] A week later, Hughes wrote Geddes that
he had determined after lengthy enquiries that there is reasonable
doubt as to the validity of the Khoshtaria concession, the most
glaring defect being that it was not submitted to the Iranian Parliament. Hughes concluded that in light of its invalidity Britain 'should
not prevent US citizens to apply for the same Concession'.[33] A few
days later Qavam, at a session of parliament in answer to a deputy's
question about the status of the Khoshtaria concession, unequivocally stated that the Khoshtaria concession had been granted
illegally and was therefore null and void.[34] On 22 November the
Iranian parliament by a unanimous vote passed a bill granting
Standard Oil a 50-year concession in northern Iran.[35]

Britain's next move was to instruct its Ambassador in Washington
and the Chargé in Tehran to make it publicly known that APOC
would not allow its royalties to Iran to constitute security for any
loans the Government of Iran may obtain, thus killing any chance of
loans from the United States or other sources. Furthermore, the
British Government asked for immediate repayment of all its prior
'loans', at a time when the Iranian Government was insolvent and

could not even pay its employees. Loraine wrote to Curzon 'All Government public schools are closed for lack of funds... Cossacks, public servants and Gendarmes have not been paid...'[36] In order to make Iran's financial condition publicly known, Curzon on 20 December 1921 instructed Geddes in Washington to inform the US Government that 'Persia owed over £1,200,000, excluding claims by various British subjects and excluding other claims of Great Britain'. Reginald Bridgeman, the Chargé in Tehran, was instructed to inform all other foreign legations of the amount of Iran's indebtedness.[37]

The Soviets also lodged a protest. On 24 November Rothstein argued that since the Perso-Soviet treaty had not yet been ratified by the Iranian Parliament the waiver of any rights by the Soviets had not taken effect and Iran had no right to grant a former Czarist concession to a US company. The answer of the Iranian Government was straightforward. The Khoshtaria concession was never valid and neither Russia nor any of its nationals ever had any rights to forego, hence it was not subject to the Perso-Soviet treaty. Qavam wasted no time and wrote to Engert, 'I wish to reiterate to you that the Government and Parliament are firmly resolved to stand by their decision'. Engert further informed the US Secretary of State that the 'Minister of War who is virtually a dictator was orally even more emphatic'.[38] Engert transmitted the views of the Iranian Government to the State Department and to Bridgeman who 'formally informed [Engert] that Britain will continue to uphold prior right of the British group'.[39]

Standard Oil did not respond to the Iranian move. It still had doubts as to whether Iran had clear title and could grant a valid concession without the British Government and APOC contesting it in court. Morgan Shuster, whom Ala had employed to advise and represent Iranian financial interests in the United States,[40] continued to press Standard to make up its mind and specifically to make an advance of $1 million (as part of a proposed $5 million loan) as soon as possible lest the Government of Qavam, faced with an acute financial crisis, fall and all hopes for the award of a concession to US oil interests disappear.[41]

Meanwhile the picture became cloudier with the arrival in Iran of the representative of another US company, Sinclair Consolidated Oil, apparently unaware that the Iranian Parliament had awarded the northern concession to Standard Oil. Engert suggested that the two US companies join forces as any rivalry between them would doom the outcome of the concession.[42] The US Department of State immediately instructed Engert to avoid taking sides and to act impartially.[43]

With Standard still insecure over the validity of title and possibility of a court battle, its apprehension increased with the entry of a rival US company. APOC in turn was convinced that the Iranians were determined to award a concession to a US company. It did not take long before Standard and APOC agreed to join forces. Their representatives met in Washington and agreed on a joint venture.[44] The Foreign Office was beginning to acknowledge that Britain could no longer entirely monopolise Iran and grudgingly accepted the joint venture. As Curzon was to write, 'better Americans than the Bolsheviks',[45] although he remained concerned over a US company becoming a lender, giving Iran a financial source other than Britain. Curzon wrote to Geddes:

> The only thing I worry about is the advance Standard wants to make to [the Government of Persia]. It will make the Persian Government more intractible than ever... Therefore, it is better if both parties Standard and APOC make the loan.[46]

The award of an oil concession to a US company ran into further difficulties and ultimately did not materialise. The State Department had always been fearful that any diminution of British influence in Iran would lead to chaos. The United States was also concerned about Bolshevism and that any decrease in British influence would enhance that of the Soviets. The Iranian Parliament confused the question of a US oil concession further. Disappointed with the proposed joint venture between Standard and APOC, parliament decided to favour the entry of Sinclair Oil, which also yielded no results.

The secondment of US advisers was to take another six months, partly because the United States was hesitant to interfere in Britain's preserve. The ongoing debates in the Iranian Parliament on the advisability of employing financial advisers from foreign countries also gave pause. After lengthy debates, at the end of 1921 an overwhelming number of deputies voted to encourage the Government to proceed with its programme of hiring foreign advisers in various fields. Deputies opposed to the employment of foreign nationals argued that it was better to send Iranians abroad for training and to increase the salaries of present government employees. Two key speeches turned the tide in favour of the deputies who argued for employment of advisers from the United States, France and Sweden. Hassan Pirnia, representing the secular element in parliament, argued that the employment of foreign advisers was not incompatible with sending Iranians abroad for education and training. The cleric Moddares swung many deputies with religious inclinations when he argued that the Prophet himself had encouraged learning from people of other lands and had said 'seek ye knowledge even in China'.[47]

The US State Department nevertheless ignored the Iranian Government's request to designate a financial adviser until the British Foreign Office had waived its objections. Moreover, the State Department was careful to select an individual acceptable to Britain, and rejected the names of several people who had 'pronounced antipathies against the British'.[48]

The decision by Qavam to terminate the contract of British financial advisers and Reza Khan's refusal to sign the employment contracts of military advisers, relegating them to mere observers, was disturbing to both Curzon and Norman. Within the first few weeks of the Qavam Government, Curzon had instructed the Imperial Bank to cease making any further advances to the Iranian Government.[49] Several months later Curzon again wrote Reginald Bridgeman, the Chargé d'Affaires after Norman's departure:

> We have no confidence in the Prime Minister. A Persian Government that dispenses with the services of the British military and financial advisers seeking to replace them with Americans and Swedish and is making every effort to secure US aid and offering [them] railroad and oil concessions has lost our trust and the Imperial Bank has been advised not to make any advances regardless of their pleas.[50]

Curzon also overruled Norman and later Bridgeman on the recommendations that some 3,000 rifles and 20 machine-guns from the SPR be sold to the Iranian Government.[51]

Norman in turn wrote to Curzon that he was distressed over Armitage Smith authorising advances to the Iranian Government ostensibly earmarked for the British controlled SPR. Norman argued that the funds would be taken over 'by Reza Khan for other military purposes and none would be given to the SPR'. Norman's relations with Reza Khan progressively worsened and he continued to warn Curzon about Reza Khan's alleged pro-Bolshevik sympathies. He wrote that 'the Minister of War is in close and constant touch with the Russian Minister and wants a Cabinet hostile to us'.[52] There is no record of Reza Khan ever having called on Norman or even having had a formal meeting with him. It appears that part of the hostility shown by Norman may have been due to his having been ignored by Reza Khan. Having lost the confidence of Curzon, being ignored by Reza Khan and ostracised by Iranian notables, Norman's position was becoming untenable.

In late June a manifesto called a 'Statement of Truth' was published in a Tehran newspaper signed by some 60 people. It stated that the British Legation had been behind the coup that brought Seyyed Zia to power and specifically named Col. Smyth as the organiser. It concluded that Seyyed Zia should be brought back and stand trial for illegal acts committed during his term of office and his arrest of 'innocent people' on false charges. The statement urged parliament to reject the 1919 Agreement even though the matter was academic by this time as Seyyed Zia had annulled the Agreement some four months earlier. The signatories to the statement were mostly those arrested by Seyyed Zia and included Moddares; three former Prime Ministers, Ain al Dowleh, Sa'ad al Dowleh and Sepahsalar Tonokaboni; some prominent friends of Britain, Sarem al Dowleh, Farmanfarma (also a former Prime Minister) and his eldest two sons, Firouz and Salar Lashkar. Other less prominent pro-British notables signing the manifesto were: Abdol Hossein Teimurtash, Mohammad Hosein Mahdavi (Amin al Zarb), Shokrallah Sadri (Qavam al Dowleh), Seyyed Mohammad Taddayon, Malek al Sho'ara Bahar, Seyyed Mehdi Fatemi (Emad al Saltaneh) and Morteza Qoli Bayat (Saham al Soltan). Over 30 of the signatories were newly elected members of parliament.[53] The publication of the 'Manifesto' was to influence the thinking of the Foreign Office in the coming several years. It forced Britain's Eastern policy-makers to reassess the special relationships she had created with a handful of Iranian families from the end of the nineteenth century. What must have been especially galling to the Foreign Office was the inclusion of the names of Farmanfarma, Firouz and Sarem al Dowleh. These people had benefitted financially and politically from British support. If they could be turned by the prevailing wind Britain could hardly count on the support of many others. Firouz was thought to be the leader of this 'new rage' against Britain. Some of the signatories had complained to the British Legation that Firouz had coerced them into signing. Norman wrote to Curzon on 16 July:

> Firouz is now against us. He has lots of money and subsidises mullahs and agitators. He has asked the Foreign Ministry to lodge a complaint against me driven only by self interest. When Britain was on top he was with us... Farmanfarma probably feels the same way...'

Norman concluded his report by suggesting that Britain 'no longer owes any obligation to his family'. Esfandiari (Mohtashem al Saltaneh), the Minister of Foreign Affairs, had in fact sent a telegram to Meftah al Saltaneh, Chargé d'Affaires in London, that the British Legation was responsible for the deterioration of Anglo-Iranian relations, implying that Norman should be recalled.[54] Norman had not been appeased when Firouz, on his release from prison sent him:

> ... an obsequious message protesting his unchanged devotion and soliciting my [Norman's] support to obtain power... He has become the head

of anti-British party and has since spared no effort to injure us... [Firouz] now professes socialism and wants to get close to Soviet Minister... but latter won't have anything to do with him.[55]

Norman had previously reported that 'Rothstein has personally called on most of the released prisoners except Farmanfarma, Nosrat ed Dowleh and Salar Lashkar'. Firouz, once regarded by Cox and later Curzon almost as a prodigal son, the natural successor to Vosouq and the best hope of Britian's continued ascendency in Iran, was to be disparaged in later dispatches in the harshest terms. Norman's telegram further inflamed Curzon and the breach with Firouz was to become irreconcilable. There is a mention that Firouz's 'rage against the British... almost amounted to mania' and Curzon replied 'What a contemptible man'.[56]

Some three months later Bridgeman was to report to Curzon:

Farmanfarma sent for Oriental Secretary [Smart] and wanted to know whether he and his family could resume their former relations with the Legation... Russian Legation will not have anything to do with them... Smart replied that if Farmanfarma wants resumption, Nosrat ed Dowleh should stop anti-British comments.

Bridgeman added that the family 'blames us for Seyyed Zia and their arrests. But we should resume relations, although nothing preferential, since they are still important'.[57]

Farmanfarma was to withdraw quietly and gradually from the political scene but Firouz was yet to play a key part in Reza Khan's rise to power and the implementation of Reza Shah's plans early in his rule. Firouz would never be forgiven by the Foreign Office, and something akin to a personal grudge would be held against him by successive British envoys. In his later hours of need, not only would he receive no comfort from Britain but their animosity would hasten his downfall.

A review of the British Legation dispatches indicate that Norman, even before his arrival in Tehran, had little sympathy for Vosouq and members of his Cabinet. In fact, it appears he had a low regard for most of the Iranian grandees, including Farmanfarma and his sons. His support of Seyyed Zia partially stemmed from his dislike of the 'old order' in Iran. For the moment Firouz gained satisfaction in Norman's hastened departure from Tehran on 1 October. The Legation would be headed by Reginald Bridgeman until the arrival of the new envoy Sir Percy Loraine.

Qavam's Government was labouring to stay in office. British financial and military advisers had left Iran but Qavam had been unable to hire nationals of other countries. The granting of an oil concession to a US company had stalled and procurement of funds from alternative sources had not materialised. In addition to the separatist movement in Gilan there were sporadic uprisings in Mazandaran, the adjacent province.[58] There was also the full-scale revolt in Khorasan started by Col. Mohammad Taqi Khan.

Mohammad Taqi (his descendants later adopted the family name Pesyan) had undergone a course of military instruction in Germany and later had been given a command in the Iranian Gendarmerie which joined the Turks and Germans on the Kermanshah front during World War I. After the war he had been appointed head of the Khorasan Gendarmerie with the rank of Colonel. His relations with Qavam, the Governor of Khorasan, had never been amicable and Col. Mohammad Taqi Khan had thrown in his lot with Seyyed Zia. On 2 April 1921 the Colonel on his own initiative mounted a coup in Mashhad, the capital of Khorasan province. He had Qavam and his close associates arrested for having ignored Seyyed Zia's appointment as Prime Minister and declared martial law. He also took over the administration of the Shrine in Mashhad and dismissed virtually all of Qavam's appointees. Seyyed Zia, in turn, appointed the Colonel Military Governor of the entire province. Qavam was sent to Tehran where he remained imprisoned until Seyyed Zia's fall. When Qavam became Prime Minister he appointed one of his former subordinates in Mashhad as Deputy Governor of the province, who was promptly arrested by the Colonel. The subsequent appointment of the Bakhtiari leader and former Prime Minister, Samsam al Saltaneh, as Governor also went unrecognised and the Colonel refused him entry into Mashhad. The Colonel now decided to print new currency in Khorasan and threatened to attack Tehran with some 4,000 men, possibly with help from Kouchek Khan with whom he was in contact. The Colonel also made overtures to Bolsheviks in Central Asian republics and sought their help. His animosity towards Qavam had made any compromise impossible and all offers of monetary compensation, safe passage out of the country and general amnesty for himself and his supporters were rejected. At the instigation of the Central Government, the local tribes (Birjandi, Bakherzi, Afghan Barbari and Teimuri) united to topple the Colonel. With the addition of Quchan Kurdish tribesmen the balance shifted and the Colonel's Gendarmes were badly defeated at Quchan. The Colonel escaped but was killed in a skirmish with the tribes soon afterwards and some of his supporters were later executed. Reza Qoli Khan Nezam Ma'afi (Nezam al Saltaneh) was appointed Governor of Khorasan.[59]

The other lingering and more serious threat facing the Central Government was also coming to an end. The Soviet troop withdrawals and the Perso-Soviet accord of 26 February 1921 (although not yet ratified by the Iranian parliament) spelled the end of Kouchek Khan's separatist movement. After the initial Soviet withdrawal Kouchek Khan recruited more men and there was fear he could even attack Tehran.[60] In early July, when the Soviets for unexplained reasons once again landed some troops at Anzeli, Kouchek Khan was emboldened and threatened Qazvin anew. As suddenly as they had landed, Soviet troops withdrew on 17 July, probably at the intervention and urging of Rothstein, who had argued that Iran was far from ready for a Soviet-style revolution.[61] Kouchek Khan again stopped short of Qazvin and the Cossacks, in a counter-attack inflicted heavy losses on the rebel forces.[62] In early August Reza Khan launched a more concentrated attack and captured Rudsar and Langaroud, important rebel bases. By 15 October Government troops had occupied Rasht and Reza Khan pursued Kouchek Khan to the edge of the forest. In fighting on 20 October the Cossacks, at the cost of over 600 men, inflicted even heavier losses on the rebels. Anzali was taken without opposition on 24 October. Some of the rebels came over to the Government side and the pro-Soviet elements escaped to Baku. Kouchek Khan having lost most of his men, escaped to the interior of the forest and froze to death in a severe blizzard on 6 December 1921.

Qavam and Reza Khan, although an unlikely combination, worked well together for the first six months. The patrician Qavam and the plebeian Reza Khan appear to have respected one another and each allowed the other to pursue his agenda. Qavam was desparately trying to raise revenue and keep the Government afloat even if only from month to month. Although he had not been particularly successful his compliance with parliament's desire to terminate the services of British financial advisers and his support for Reza Khan's dismissal of British military advisers had created an amicable working relationship with Reza Khan and parliament. Reza Khan had been given a free hand to build up and reorganise the military forces and Qavam had given Reza Khan's efforts priority in allocation of the scarce funds the Government had at its disposal. By the end of 1921 Reza Khan's position had been made even stronger by the deaths of Kouchek Khan and Col. Mohammad Taqi Khan. For Qavam, the Colonel had been an almost personal enemy who had been intent on driving him from office and destroying him. For Reza Khan the Colonel had also represented a serious threat. If the commander of a provincial Gendarmerie garrison could lead a rebellion against the authority of the Central Government, other commanders of military units could also declare autonomy. Ironically, the elimination of the Colonel was the end of an important element in the co-operation and mutuality of interest between Qavam and Reza Khan and their relationship thereafter became strained.

The elimination of Kouchek Khan stregthened the authority of the Central Government and also dispelled the notion propagated by Norman that Reza Khan was a Bolshevik sympathiser if not a Soviet stooge. In a meeting with the British Military Attaché on 11 August Reza Khan had expressed anger and indignation at Rothstein's attempts to prevent the destruction of Kouchek Khan's forces. Reza Khan had also 'reiterated his dislike of Bolsheviks and said for political reasons he is on good terms and close touch with Russians but he would never accept assistance from them either in money or war materials, although the army was badly in need of money'.[63] At a later meeting with the Military Attaché after Norman's departure, Reza Khan had stated:

> ... Persians are capable of administrating their own armed forces without assistance of foreign advisers, [hence] the removal of Swedes from executive command of the Gendarmes... [although] he may use foreign military advisers at military schools he intends to establish... He also said his next military campaign will be against the renegade Kurd Simko in Azarbaijan... the Cossacks now number 34,000 men and Reza Khan desperately needs an advance on oil royalties, otherwise he may have to take over the revenue-making machinary of the Government.[64]

By late January 1922, just before Qavam's Government was to fall, Reza Khan had issued decrees eliminating the terms 'Gendarmes' and 'Cossacks': the two forces would henceforth be members of a single armed force. The SPR had already been disbanded in late December. Qajar terms for military ranks were abolished and new ones equivalent to Western ranks were created. As an early act under the new organisation, Reza Khan promoted seven senior officers of the former Cossack Division to the highest newly-established rank of Major General (Amir Lashkar). These officers were to play a minimal role in the new armed forces. Their promotions were merely an act of solidarity and respect by Reza Khan towards his former superior officers. Two officers who had been helpful to Reza Khan in the February 1921 coup were amongst those promoted: Mohammad Tofiqi (Sardar Azim), Amir Ahmadi's father-in-law, and Qasem Vali (Sardar Homayoun), the last commander of the Cossack Division before the coup who had conveniently absented himself during the events leading to the entry of the Cossacks into Tehran. He also promoted five active officers to the rank of Major General: Abdollah Amir Tahmasebi, Ahmad Amir Ahmadi, Hosein Khaza'i, Mahmoud Ayrom and Mahmoud Ansari (Amir Eqtedar). Three other officers

12. Hassan Pirnia (Moshir al Dowleh VI). Prime minister four times between 1917 and 1923, he was a scholar and a man of integrity who prevented the implementation of the 1919 Agreement.

13. Mehdi Qoli Khan Hedayat (Mokhber al Saltaneh). A competent and honest former cabinet minister and provincial governor, he was to become Reza Shah's longest serving prime minister.

were promoted to the rank of Brigadier General (Sartip): Khodayar Khan Khodayar, Esma'il Amir Fazli and Morteza Yazdanpanah. The forces were also reorganised on the basis of divisions, brigades, battalions, companies and platoons. Each division would have not only infantry soldiers but also a cavalry and artillery unit.[65] In addition to the Ministry of War, an army High Command Centre was established which would oversee the disposition of troops in times of peace and war. Plans were also made for creating a military academy to function as the equivalent of a secondary school for career army personnel. Most of these projects were still in a planning stage and their realisation would be several years hence.

By September Qavam had lost his Minister of Foreign Affairs in the aftermath of the so-called Azerlinko incident.[66] In the ensuing Cabinet reshuffle Moshar al Saltaneh, who was acceptable to the Soviets, was appointed as Minister of Foreign Affairs. Moshar al Saltaneh had been the head of the Russian section at the Ministry of Foreign Affairs for several years and had briefly served in one of Moshir al Dowleh's Cabinets as Minister of Foreign Affairs.[67] Qavam's reshuffled Cabinet survived for some four months, mostly due to Rothstein's insistance. In conversations with the Shah, Rothstein requested that Qavam's Government remain at least until the ratification of the Perso-Soviet treaty.[68] The new Cabinet of Qavam demonstrated even less energy than his first one.

Earlier in July Hassan Moshar (Moshar al Molk), the former Minister of Court and recently elected member of the Fourth Parliament, was accused (by Qavam) of plotting to assassinate Qavam and Reza Khan. Moshar was arrested after having been made to resign from parliament so as to neutralise his parliamentary immunity. At the Shah's intervention Moshar was allowed to leave the country. The alleged plot was most doubtful and did little to enhance Qavam's standing in parliament.[69] One of the leading members of parliament, Mohammad Taddayon, made a bitter attack on Qavam over the arrest and deportation of Moshar and exhorted his resignation as Prime Minister. The Moshar incident inflamed other members of parliament and Qavam was not able to count on their support in his second term of office.[70] Soon accusations of corruption began to be made against his Government. Several Deputy Ministers including Qavam's younger brother Mo'tamed al Saltaneh (Abdollah Vosouq), were involved in graft and receiving bribes. Loraine was to report to Curzon, 'By all accounts there has never been a more corrupt Persian Government than this one... Qavam is astute and energetic but corrupt'.[71]

With the financial situation of the country still perilous there were few opportunities for the Shah to increase his private fortune.

His personal subsidy by Britain had been terminated and he could expect very little from the Government of Qavam other than his salary and the civil list. The emergence of a dominant Reza Khan further inhibited him. He had no say in the appointment and promotion of favourites to higher ranks in the military. The Shah, however, was by now financially secure, with most of his funds transferred abroad. He had come to prefer living in Europe. In addition to his concern for personal safety he was fearful that he could be deposed. The British Legation had come to regard him as politically irrelevant, but it was believed he should be kept on the throne or the country could be factionalised with the Soviets as the only beneficiary.

The Shah had wanted to go abroad from early March, only to be held back by Seyyed Zia. After the latter's fall he changed his mind as he believed new financial opportunities would arise from the award of concessions to US companies and loans from US sources. By the middle of the summer he again reversed his thinking and began pressing to leave the country. Norman saw the Shah several times in August and September and on each occasion the Shah complained about the lack of confidence in him by the British Government.[72] By October the Shah once more decided to go to Europe but changed his mind when Qavam's Government looked about to fall.[73] When Qavam survived by reshuffling his Cabinet the Shah again began to clamour to go abroad. Norman left Iran on 10 October and the Shah in his first meeting with Bridgeman, the Chargé d'Affaires, gave full vent to his true feelings and told Bridgeman that 'he preferred Paris and London to the monotony and incessant political worry here'. Bridgeman in his report added: 'The Shah embarrassed me by suddenly enquiring, 'Est-ce que vous ne trouvez pas la vie terriblement desagreeable ici?'.[74] 'Finally, with the fall of Qavam on 24 January 1922 and the appointment of Hassan Pirnia (Moshir al Dowleh), the Shah felt safer to leave the country and publicly announced he would leave on 25 January for six months for 'medical treatment'. The Crown Prince, who was in Paris at the time was summoned to act as regent in his absence.[75] Until the arrival of the Vali'ahd from Paris, Ahmad Shah's oldest brother, Etezad al Saltaneh (who had been by-passed as successor to the throne as his mother was not a Qajar) ,was appointed regent.

Qavam would be called back to form a second Government in less than six months. By then, however, he had become just another politician lingering and filling the political void until Reza Khan was ready to make his move. In retrospect his first Government fared well compared with the succeeding three Iranian Governments. The opening to the United States and the attempts to employ financial advisers from that country (which would take place at the end of 1922) were greatly responsible for making Iran solvent, and the training of accountants and tax collectors later enabled the Pahlavi regime to pursue its ambitious plans. The award of the northern oil concession never came to fruition, but it jolted and awakened APOC to the realities of post World War I Iran and at least hereafter APOC would make the meagre royalty payments on due dates. The ratification by parliament of the Perso-Soviet treaty enabled the Iranian Government to put an end to insurgency movements in the northern provinces. Also amongst the Qavam Government's important achievements was the conclusion of a treaty of amity and friendship with a turbulent neighbouring Afghanistan.

It will soon be apparent with the fall of Qavam that Reza Khan had become the unquestioned leading political and military figure in Iran. A conversation he held with the British Military Attaché a day before Qavam's formal resignation clearly shows that he had reached the stage where he could speak with authority about the future of his country:

> Sardar Sepah [Reza Khan] expressed strong disapproval of the Shah's departure merely for his convenience, adding that except for his oath of fealty he would consider steps for establishing another form of government. He abused Qavam al Saltaneh and said his whole Cabinet was unscrupulous and working merely for personal gain. He was determined to break [the present] Government but could not find a man both honest and capable to be prime minister. He was unwilling to assume that office himself, believing that he could serve his country better in his present post. He applauds the policy of His Majesty's Government in withholding funds because he believes that when Persians realise their inability to get money for the asking they would be compelled to work themselves and put their house in order.[76]

NOTES ON CHAPTER 9
Further details of publications and documents in Bibliography

1   FO 416/68, Norman to Curzon, 25 March 1921.
2   *Ibid.*; DBFP doc. no. 692, Curzon to Norman, 8 March 1921.
3   FO 371/6446, Cox to Norman, Foreign Office and the Government of India, 10 July 1921.
4   *Ibid.*, Norman's answer to Cox, same date.
5   FO 371/6446, Curzon to Government of India and Viceroy's reply, 18 July 1921.
6   FO 371/9406, Norman to Curzon, 9 June 1921.
7   *Ibid.*
8   Mehdi Bamdad, *Tarikh Rejal Iran Quroun 12, 13, 14 (Dictionary of National Biography of Iran: Twelfth, Thirteenth, Fourteenth Centuries)*, vol. 1, pp 345–347; FO 416/98, Bullard to Halifax, 7 February 1940.
9   FO 371/6406, Norman to Curzon, 9 June 1921.
10 FO 416/68, Norman to Curzon, 2 June 1921.
11 FO 416/68, Norman to Curzon, 9 June 1921.
12 FO 371/6404, Norman to Curzon, 9 June 1921.
13 Mehdi Bamdad, *Tarikh Rejal Iran Quroun 12, 13, 14 (Dictionary of National Biography of Iran: Twelfth, Thirteenth, Fourteenth Centuries)*, vol. 1, pp 114–115; FO 416/98, Bullard to Halifax, 7 February 1940.
14 FO 371/6406, Norman to Curzon, 9 June 1921.
15 Mehdi Bamdad, *Tarikh Rejal Iran Quroun 12, 13, 14 (Dictionary of National Biography of Iran: Twelfth, Thirteenth, Fourteenth Centuries)*, vol. 2, pp 166–168; FO 416/98, Bullard to Halifax, 7 February 1940.
16 Mehdi Bamdad, *Tarikh Rejal Iran Quroun 12, 13, 14 (Dictionary of National Biography of Iran: Twelfth, Thirteenth, Fourteenth Centuries)*, vol. 1, pp 321–322; FO 416/98, Bullard to Halifax, 7 February 1940.
17 Mehdi Bamdad, *Tarikh Rejal Iran Quroun 12, 13, 14 (Dictionary of National Biography of Iran: Twelfth, Thirteenth, Fourteenth Centuries)*, vol. 1, pp 140–141.
18 FO 371/6406, Norman to Curzon, 9 June 1921.
19 FO 416/68, Norman to Curzon, 11 June 1921.
20 Mehdi Bamdad, *Tarikh Rejal Iran Quroun 12, 13, 14 (Dictionary of National Biography of Iran: Twelfth, Thirteenth, Fourteenth Centuries)*, vol. 1, p 19.
21 FO 371/6401, Norman to Curzon, 29 August 1921; DoS Quarterly Report no. 13, 1 July to 30 September 1921.
22 FO 371/6407, Norman to Curzon, 11 September 1921.
23 DoS vol. II, 711.91, Cornelius Van H. Engert to Charles Evans Hughes, US Secretary of State, 21 June 1921.
24 DoS vol. II, 711.91, Engert to Charles Evans Hughes, US Secretary of State; 21 June 1921.
25 Houshang Sabahi, *British Policy in Persia 1918–1925*, p 147.
26 Nasrollah Entezam, *Khaterat Nasrollah Entezam (Memoirs of Nasrollah Entezam)*, p 125; FO 416/98, Bullard to Halifax, 7 February 1940.
27 FO 371/6405, Memorandum prepared by Lancelot Oliphant, 20 July 1921.
28 DoS 891.01A/22, Engert to US Secretary of State, 10 November 1921; FO 416/69, Norman to Curzon, 4 September 1921.

29 DoS 891/51A/9, Memorandum by Assistant Secretary of State, 10 November 1921.

30 DoS 891/51AA/159, Memorandum by Under Secretary of State, 29 November 1921.

31 Minute by E. Crowe, 18 April 1919: quoted by Houshang Sabahi, *British Policy in Persia 1918–1925*, p 141.

32 DoS 891/6363, Standard Oil/39, Geddes to Hughes, 7 October 1921.

33 DoS 891/6363, Standard Oil/37, Hughes to Geddes, 15 October 1921.

34 DoS, 891/6363, Oil/42, Engert to Secretary of State, 16 November 1921.

35 DoS, 891/6363, 22 November 1921. Standard Oil was later to become Exxon.

36 FO 416/69, Loraine to Curzon, 26 December 1921.

37 FO 416/69, Curzon to Geddes, 20 December 1921.

38 DoS, 891/6363, Oil 47, Engert to Secretary of State, 26 November 1921.

39 *Ibid.*, 891/6363, Oil/56, Engert to Secretary of State, 3 December 1921.

40 *Ibid.*, 891/5AA/159, 29 November 1921.

41 FO 416/69, Geddes to Curzon, 23 December 1921.

42 DoS 891/6363, Oil/64, Engert to Secretary of State, 9 December 1921. Sinclair Oil was later to merge into Arco.

43 DoS 891/6363, Oil/73, Secretary of State to Engert, 20 December 1921.

44 The talks in Washington were held between A.H. Bedford of Standard Oil and Sir John Cadman of APOC. (Cadman, later to become the chief operating officer of APOC, was the crucial player in the negotiations between APOC and the Iranian Government in the oil dispute of 1931–1933): FO 415/69, Geddes to Curzon, 26 December 1921.

45 FO 371/6417, Minutes by Curzon, 23 November 1921.

46 FO 416/70, Curzon to Geddes, 18 January 1922.

47 DoS, Quarterly Report No. 14, Engert to US Secretary of State, 1 October to 31 December 1921.

48 Houshang Sabahi, *British Policy in Persia 1918–1925*, pp 149–150.

49 FO 416/68, Curzon to Norman, 14 June 1921.

50 FO 416/68, Curzon to Bridgeman, 18 October 1921.

51 Ultimately only 700 rifles (and no machine-guns) were sold, and what remained was destroyed: FO 371/6407, Bridgeman to Curzon, 12 October 1921.

52 FO 371/6405, Norman to Curzon, 1 July 1921.

53 FO 416/69, Norman to Curzon, 16 July 1921.

54 FO 416/69, Norman to Curzon, 16 July 1921.

55 FO 371/6405, Norman to Curzon, 19 July 1921.

56 FO 371/7802, Minute by Curzon, undated.

57 FO 416/69, Norman to Curzon, 16 July 1921; FO 416/7802, Bridgeman to Curzon, 21 October 1921.

58 In early July 1921, Sa'ed al Dowleh, the eldest son of Sepahsalar Tonokaboni, had attacked and seized several towns in Mazandaran. Only after the intervention of his father had he withdrawn and submitted to the authority of the Central Government. In late July of the same year, a local grandee, Amir Mo'ayed Savad Kouhi had attacked and

pillaged small towns and villages in central Mazandaran. Under threat of reprisals from the Central Government and the dispatch of some Cossacks he agreed to withdraw. Hosein Makki, *Tarikh Bist Saleh Iran* (*A Twenty Year History of Iran*), vol. 2, p 400.

59 FO 371/7802, Bridgeman to Curzon, 26 November 1921; *Majmoueh Asnad va Madarek dar 1300* (*Documents Pertaining to the Khorasan Revolt in 1921*), ed. Kave Bayat.

60 FO 371/6435, Intelligence Summary no. 13, 30 July 1921.

61 FO 371/6405, Norman to Curzon, 23 May 1921.

62 FO 371/6435, Intelligence Summary no. 13, 30 July 1921.

63 FO 371/6405, Military Attaché, Tehran, to Baghdad, India and Foreign Office, 15 August 1921.

64 FO 371/6407, Bridgeman's report of Military Attaché to Curzon, 8 December 1921.

65 By this time the number of soldiers had increased by another 50 percent to almost 50,000, Reza Khan having inducted into the new army many rebel troops who had surrendered or had been captured. Some '$100,000 [in US currency] were collected from the defeated forces and supporters of various insurgents in the north'. These funds were used to settle the back pay of soldiers and officers. This practice of extracting funds from supporters of insurgents was Reza Khan's primary way of financing these early military expeditions: FO 416/69, Loraine to Curzon, 21 December 1921.

66 Azerlinko, a Polish national who had escaped to Russia and then to Iran, was accused by Soviet authorities of having embezzled Soviet funds. Azerlinko was granted asylum by the French Legation which was looking after Polish interests in Iran. Rothstein insisted that Azerlinko was a Russian national and issued an ultimatum for his hand-over to Soviet authorities. The matter was finally settled when the French and Soviet Legations agreed to be bound by the findings of an enquiry by the Belgian Legation which declared Azerlinko to be a Polish national and exonerated him of the charges. A consequence of the affair was the resignation of the respected Hassan Esfandiari who had refused to bow to Soviet pressure to hand over Azerlinko. Esfandiari had been one of the primary advocates of approaches to the United States for advisers and granting of oil concessions. Rothstein also lost prestige over the incident and for reasons not entirely clear he too left Iran soon after, subsequently to return briefly: FO 416/68, Loraine to Curzon, 21 December 1921.

67 *Ibid.*

68 FO 416/69, Bridgeman to Curzon, 1 October 1921.

69 FO 416/69, Norman to Curzon, 16 July 1921.

70 FO 416/70, Loraine to Curzon, 11 April 1922.

71 FO 416/69, Loraine to Curzon, 22 December 1921.

72 FO 371/6404, Norman to Curzon, 29 August 1921. At a meeting in September the Shah, intending to impress Norman with his resolve and relevance, told Norman, '... he wants to do something drastic... either dismiss the Prime Minister and/or the Minister of War and/or dissolve Parliament'. Norman, who must have had an equally heavy heart towards Qavam, Reza Khan and parliament refused to comment. He later wrote to Curzon that he did not comment on the Shah's remarks

'as the Shah is indiscreet'. A year earlier, Norman would readily have given his opinion.

73   FO 371/6407, Norman to Curzon, 11 September 1921.
74   FO 416/70, Bridgeman to Curzon, 25 October 1921.
75   FO 416/70, Loraine to Curzon, 15 January 1922.
76   FO 416/70, Loraine to Curzon, Military Attaché's report, 22 January 1922.

10

The Rotating Premiership

Hassan Pirnia (Moshir al Dowleh) put together his Cabinet in a short time. He assumed the Ministry of the Interior himself with Reza Khan, now a fixture, at the Ministry of War. Ebrahim Hakimi (Hakim al Molk)* was given the portfolio of the Foreign Ministry; two former ministers in the Cabinet of Seyyed Zia, Mahmoud Jam and Reza Qoli Khan Hedayat, were given the Ministries of Finance and Education respectively; and Hosein Samii was to serve as Minister of Public Works. The appointment of Jam and Reza Qoli Hedayat caused Pirnia some initial difficulties as a number of deputies objected to having associates of Seyyed Zia in the Cabinet. Hakimi, whose knowledge of general foreign policy issues was limited, was not to prove useful but as he was regarded a friend of Britain, Pirnia had

---

* Ebrahim Hakimi (Hakim al Molk), 1871–1958, the son of a court physician and nephew of the personal physician and Minister of Court of Mozaffar al Din Shah. He studied medicine in France and on his return became one of the many physicians who surrounded the Shah. After Mozaffar al Din Shah died he abandoned medicine and was elected to the first and second sessions of parliament. With no special qualifications he served in various cabinets and in his lifetime he held some 18 ministerial posts including Finance, Foreign Affairs, Justice and Education. An early member of the French-based masonic lodge, he gained seniority and became one of the three most senior Freemasons in Iran. This seniority became his most important asset. Prime Minister for a short period in 1945 and later Minister of Court, he was honest and decent, but had an undistinguished life and public career.[1]

considered his inclusion in the Cabinet an asset. Loraine believed Hakimi to be 'ignorant on foreign policy matters' but regarded him as sympathetic to Britain and preferred to 'deal with him than other Persians'.[2] The only noteworthy newcomer was Abdol Hosein Teimurtash (Sardar Mo'azam),[†] the Minister of Justice, who was to have a profound effect upon subsequent governments of his time.

One of the principal items on the new Government's agenda was legal reform. Pirnia had studied law in Russia and was to remain interested in law all his life. He had translated the constitutions of several countries into Persian and had written a treatise on the European sources of the Iranian Constitution. When he himself had served as a Minister of Justice he had attempted, with little success, to introduce some aspects of the French court structure into the Iranian legal system. Now he expected Teimurtash to institute reforms in the judiciary. Teimurtash did in fact obtain parliamentary approval to suspend the operation of some courts and administrative bodies.

---

† Abdol Hosein Teimurtash, 1879–1933, was born in Khorasan the son of a minor tribal chieftain, Karimdad Khan Nardini (Mo'azas al Molk). Teimurtash was sent as a child to Czarist Russia (Eshqabad) to a preparatory school and later to the military college at St Petersburg. He became fluent in Russian and French. On his return he immersed himself in Persian literature and history which more than compensated for his lack of a formal Persian education. His first employement was with the Ministry of Foreign Affairs, where he served as a Russian translator. A fortuitous marriage to the niece of the regent, Azd al Molk, and the close relative and ward of the then governor of Khorasan, Nayer al Dowleh, served him well. From the second to the sixth sessions of parliament he was elected from Neishabur, Khorasan. He declined to serve in the sixth session as he had been appointed Minister of Court by Reza Shah in 1926. By the time of his entry into parliament he had become an effective public speaker. He was forceful, quick-witted and always had presence of mind. It was inevitable that Teimurtash would be propelled to prominence and a successful public career. He was appointed Governor of Gilan by Vosouq in 1919 during the Cossack Division's expedition against the insurgent forces of Kouchek Khan. After his brief service as Minister of Justice he was appointed Governor of Kerman between September 1923 and April 1924. When Reza Khan became Prime Minister he served twice as Minister of Public Works. After Reza Khan's accession to the throne Teimurtash was appointed Minister of Court, where he became virtually the Shah's alter ego. Reza Shah is alleged to have said, 'Teimurtash's word is my word'. Teimurtash came closer than anyone else to sharing power with Reza Shah. Never before or since Teimurtash's fall was Reza Shah to delegate so much authority to any one person. He fell from grace and was removed as Minister of Court in December 1932. He was accused and convicted of corruption, bribery and misuse of foreign currency regulations. Teimurtash was murdered while in prison in September 1933.[3]

He also dismissed some 90 judges and magistrates on charges of corruption and gross incompetence. The life of Pirnia's Government was so short and beset by other far more important problems that Teimurtash never had a chance to make a lasting impression on the judicial system. Pirnia's programme was basically the continuation of Qavam's policies, that is to say the employment of US financial advisers and granting of the northern oil concession to a US company avoiding, if possible, the participation of APOC. Pirnia attempted to accomplish the same goals but to soften the blow to Britain. On the question of employment of US advisers Pirnia told Loraine he intended to press forward but it would be done in such 'a manner as to create solidarity between Persian, British, and American interests'. Loraine was obviously not impressed by these perfunctory remarks. On the issue of northern oil Pirnia suggested that whatever arrangement Standard Oil and APOC had reached would be no great matter as long as the name of the joint venture company to be awarded the concession excluded any reference to APOC. Pirnia naively assured Loraine that in such a case he could probably obtain parliamentary approval for the joint venture. Loraine had rejected the proposal out of hand.[4] Other less pressing matters also got nowhere. Under its mandate Britain had created the state of Iraq and was eager to have the new Hashemite Kingdom recognised by its neighbours, Turkey and Iran. Pirnia believed the matter could not be resolved presently, and further time was needed. In turn Pirnia's request that Britain transfer its telegraph stations in the south to the Iranian Government also achieved no results.[5]

The Government of Pirnia would have fallen within the first months of coming to office were it not for the dearth of willing and acceptable successors. Pirnia had assumed office simply because Mostofi had declined the premiership; the Shah felt comfortable with him and Reza Khan had shown no outward interest in the office. On 13 May Pirnia tendered his resignation, which was turned down by the Shah who was in Paris.[6] The Shah lost no time in drawing out the Foreign Office on their preferred replacement candidates. The Iranian Minister in London, at the instruction of the Shah, called on the Foreign Office and told Lancelot Oliphant, head of the Eastern Department, that the Shah had instructed him to inform the Foreign Office that although Pirnia was close to resigning he would not appoint 'anyone as Prime Minister who was unfriendly to Great Britain'. The Iranian Minister had then enquired what the Foreign Office thought of Reza Khan as Prime Minister. Oliphant had replied 'seldom a military officer makes a good politician'.[7] It is highly improbable that the Shah had any intention of appointing Reza

Khan as Prime Minister. It was merely an attempt by the Shah to ascertain the British attitude towards Reza Khan. At the urging of the Shah, Pirnia continued in office for a few days more, but the tension between Pirnia and Reza Khan grew over the latter's demand for increased allocation of funds for the military. Matters came to a head when a newspaper attacked Reza Khan bitterly, accusing him of being a dictator usurping the authority of other ministries. Reza Khan demanded that Pirnia close the newspaper and arrest the editor. Pirnia temporised and argued that he could not do anything until parliament passed a pending bill regulating the conduct of the press. Reza Khan then informed Pirnia that henceforth he would not attend Cabinet meetings. Pirnia tendered his resignation on 25 May and despite telegrams from the Shah and pleas from a number of deputies refused to alter his decision. Parliament, mostly through the efforts of Moddares, proposed Qavam as the new Prime Minister.[8] There are indications that Qavam had strongly lobbied the British Legation to make a comeback and be re-appointed Prime Minister. Loraine reported 'Qavam has contacted me many times and professes he would be friend of Great Britain'.[9]

The Cabinet of Qavam included many familiar faces and its programme consisted of the conclusion of the northern oil concession, passing of a bill regulating the conduct of the press and defeat of a new and serious insurgency in Azarbaijan.[10] Qavam was not to be the assertive premier he was in his first term. Reza Khan, continuing as Minister of War, completely overshadowed him; Qavam was totally dependent on him. Ironically Qavam's supporters in parliament had voted for him in the belief that if there were anyone who could curb the growing power of Reza Khan it would be Qavam. Moddares, who was emerging as the leading opponent of Reza Khan and the principal proponent of Qavam, is alleged to have said: 'Mostofi is a well carved, bejeweled sword useful to be exhibited at ceremonial occasions. Qavam, on the other hand is a sharp and cutting sabre that should be used in critical times'.[11]

A singular important event which was to have a profound effect on the course of events from 1922 onwards was the appointment of Sir Percy Loraine* as the new British Minister to Tehran to succeed Herman Norman who had been recalled in August 1921 and had left in October. Just as the introduction of a wild card in the person of

---

* Percy Loraine, 1880–1961, was born in northern England. He attended Eton in 1893 and New College, Oxford in 1899. He had interrupted his education by enlisting in the army to fight in the Boer War, in which he
CONTINUED OVER PAGE

Gen. Ironside had shaken traditional Iranian politics and left policy-makers in London with new realities to which they had to adjust, Loraine's four years in Iran were to have a similarly jolting effect. Once again the Foreign Office was faced with unexpected choices and decisions. Loraine began to have doubts about established British policy in Iran and it took some time before his immediate superiors realised that he was questioning the fundamental premises of British policy.

Loraine arrived in Tehran on 18 December 1921 and saw the Shah on the twentieth.[12] Four days after his arrival he sent Curzon his first appraisal of the 'outstanding personalities of Persian politics'. Qavam, who was in the last days of his first term as Prime Minister, was described as 'astute and energetic but corrupt'. Reza Khan was presented as:

> ... [a] resolute but ignorant soldier of fortune... but is downright straight and it might be possible to have dealings with him. He has contempt for civil authorities. Trial of strength between him and the Prime Minister [Qavam] seems probable. If this happens I shall stand aloof...

Loraine also commented, 'There is a far more effective and coherent public opinion that I formerly knew in this country' (referring to his

---

Percy Loraine CONTINUED FROM PREVIOUS PAGE
was wounded. After completing Oxford he lived some two years in France, where he perfected his French. He joined the Foreign Office in 1904 and was posted to Turkey for three years. He came to Tehran in 1907 as third secretary and stayed for two years, serving under Cecil Spring Rice with Charles Marling as Counsellor and Robert Vansitart as a third secretary. In September 1920 Curzon wanted to send Loraine to Tehran to serve as Counsellor under Norman. Loraine, through the help of his friend Robert Vansitart, who was then Private Secretary to Curzon and Lancelot Oliphant, his first cousin, somehow avoided it. Instead he was posted to Poland for a brief term. On his return he was appointed to the number two position at the Eastern Department. Loraine had been one of Curzon's favourites and in July 1921 Curzon offered him the highest diplomatic position in Tehran. At forty he was one of the youngest appointees to a sensitive post. After Tehran he became Minister to Athens and then High Commissioner in Egypt between 1929 and 1934. He achieved his greatest success in Turkey, where he served from 1934–1939. He was close to Ataturk and kept Turkey friendly to Great Britain despite British military intervention in Turkey after World War I. In May 1939 he became Ambassador to Italy. When Italy entered the war in June 1940 on the side of Germany, Loraine returned to England and retired. Loraine is one of Britain's legendary diplomatic envoys, having served under seven Foreign Ministers: Balfour, Curzon, Austin Chamberlain, Henderson, Simon, Eden and Halifax.[13]

service at the Legation in Tehran as third secretary between 1907 and 1909).

> [Public opinion] is intensely nationalistic. It has mistakenly become con-
> vinced that in our attitude towards Persia we have stepped into the shoes
> of Imperial Russia and are bent on subjecting Persia to our political dom-
> ination.[14]

Despite the events between 1919 and 1922, Curzon's thinking towards Iran had changed very little. When the Foreign Office and Curzon in particular spoke of an independent Persia with a strong Central Government, they excluded southern Persia from the suzerainty and control of the Central Government. The southern provinces were the centres of their strategic and economic interests and had to be ruled by British surrogate tribal chieftains free from interference by the Central Government. Curzon's first written instruction to Loraine upon reaching Tehran was:

> ... consolidate your influence on the Khans to check the south-west
> thrust of Cossacks whose presence in the oil fields should be avoided at
> all costs... Armitage Smith has seen and talked to the Khans... who have
> assured him they would resist to utmost if their power is encroached by
> the Central Government on their territories... They are not asking for
> money but for moral support and possibly arms from His Majesty's
> Government'.[15]

Loraine contacted senior Bakhtiari Khans the following day. The Khans asked Loraine to instruct the Imperial Bank to continue to withhold funds from the Central Government, otherwise Bakhtiari in-fluence in the region would be destroyed. Loraine did not commit himself and merely told the chiefs that 'both they and the Govern-ment of Persia were friends of Great Britain'. Loraine reported to Curzon that he 'did not want to leave the impression that we are neutral and therefore [the Bakhtiaris] could take it as an invitation to attack Cossacks in Esfahan'.[16]

When Loraine arrived in Tehran he found the British Legation virtually boycotted by Iranians. The cumulative effect of the pro-posed 1919 Agreement, continued British domination, Seyyed Zia's arrest of notables and continuous attacks on Britain by newspapers subsidised by the Soviet Legation had taken their toll.[17] By early January, with Qavam on his way out, Loraine realised he must make contact with Reza Khan. He wrote to Curzon on 11 January 1922:

> The Shah is determined to leave Persia as soon as possible. Reza Khan
> is capable of seizing power whether the Shah stays or goes as soon as he
> gets the principal provincial centres under his control through detach-
> ment of army. He may be only a shooting star in the Persian firmament,

but some speak of him as the new Nader [Shah]. His popularity is based on: his non-identification with any foreign power; the energetic and for Persia remarkable efficiency with which he is reviving the army; the aloofness from politics; his judicious choice of Lieutenants... If suppression of [Semitqu] be added to his previous success in Khorasan and Gilan his share will go up and he may well be the hero of Persia. I have no relation with him as he has not called.[18]

Curzon had received numerous reports on Reza Khan and, now that his trusted envoy also confirmed Reza Khan's significance on the political stage, instructed Loraine to make contact. 'If opportunity presents itself of getting in touch with him without loss of dignity, I feel you will do so.' Curzon justified Reza Khan's non-observance of diplomatic protocol by his 'humble origins'.[19]

The first time the two met was at an official dinner at the residence of Engert, the US Chargé d'Affaires. Their conversation was brief. Loraine enquired about rumours concerning Pirnia's imminent premiership. Reza Khan stated that he would support Pirnia 'because he considers him honest'.[20] In the course of the next three weeks they met twice more, once at the residence of the British Military Attaché on 22 January. Loraine wrote:

> It is only natural that having regard to his origin and humble upbringing [Reza Khan] should be an ignorant and uneducated man. Nonetheless he betrays no awkwardness of manner nor self consciousness. He has considerable natural dignity and neither his speech or features reveal any absence of self control... He gets straight to what he has to say and does not waste time in exchanging the delicately phrased but perfectly futile compliments so dear to the Persian heart... I need not recapitulate them but it will suffice to say that, having been selected as an instrument, he has proved himself a master... The rich and the aristocrats are jealous.

He could have been prime minister after Qavam but he felt he would be getting far out of his depth. 'He genuinely wants reforms but looks at Mejles with contempt.' Loraine ended his description of Reza Khan by saying, '... he is a patriot above all else'. Despite his favourable impression of Reza Khan, Loraine recommended that 'we should not offer him our support. We should instead convince him that England is the only real and disinterested friend of Persia.'[21]

At a later meeting when the two began to discuss specifics Loraine was disappointed to find that Reza Khan agreed with Pirnia that northern oil should go solely to the United States without APOC having a share. Reza Khan later compromised and added that British investment in the US oil company would be acceptable if 'it is kept in the background'. Reza Khan again expressed his support for Pirnia. 'Whatever [Pirnia] did, even if wrong would be accepted by the people'. Reza Khan then advised Loraine to 'let Americans in before Russia becomes strong and drives away both England and the US'. Loraine was impressed that 'Reza Khan was not without knowledge of the oil question in its world aspects'. At the end of the meeting Reza Khan told Loraine that certain people had accused him of having pro-Bolshevik sentiments because he frequented their Legation. He stated emphatically that his only purpose was to get them out of the Caspian provinces and that he was:

> ... as anti-Bolshevik as the British... He would do with Persian hands what the British wished to do with British hands... create a strong army, restore order and consolidate a strong and independent Persia.[22]

Loraine was impressed with Reza Khan's forcefulness, singleness of purpose and general understanding of current problems, but more important he was becoming convinced that Reza Khan could be a winner in the long run. Although still advising caution and harbouring personal doubts, Loraine's dispatches after the initial meetings are generally complimentary towards Reza Khan as a political figure, for example:

> [Reza Khan] could be an asset to us because he was the only man who today because of his prestige... is preventing the machinations and intrigues of pro-Bolshevik elements.[23]
>
> As things are now [Reza Khan] calls the tune in Persia and is the best guarantee of protection of our legitimate interests... and we should realise the advantage of [his] being on good terms with us.[24]
>
> If he [Reza Khan] goes, stability will go.

Loraine also recommended that the financial embargo imposed on Iran should be lifted. Finally, at his repeated urging, the Foreign Office allowed the Imperial Bank to lend funds to Iran against oil royalties.[25]

Reza Khan continued his campaign against the remaining and newly-arisen insurgencies. Operations against a Kurdish tribal leader, Semitqu,* had not been successful principally because the main government forces in the area were manned by recently recruited

---

* Esma'il Semitqu, c.1890–1930, was the son of a minor Kurdish tribal leader. He began raiding towns and villages in western Azarbaijan and attempted to unite other Kurdish tribes with the plan to create an independent state out of parts of Azarbaijan and Kurdestan. He was supported and armed by the new Turkish Government and elements in Soviet Azarbaijan. The Turkish Government, which had objections to previous boundary agreements with Iran and had ambitions to annex parts of western Azarbaijan, furnished the tribe with artillery and safe haven in Turkey following raids into Iran. He was killed in 1930 following a minor skirmish.[26]

raw soldiers. Government reverses had enabled Semitqu to increase his manpower, and to defeat him Reza Khan needed a much larger and better-trained force. Another drawback was that Reza Khan had few officers with combat experience.

After a lapse of three months, in June 1922 Reza Khan was able to assemble a detachment of 5,000 to go after Semitqu. After a few minor skirmishes, Semitqu's forces were badly defeated in a major confrontation. He fled to Turkey and the rebellion ended, a significant victory for government troops. 'If Semitqu had scored one more victory, he would have been the chieftain of all western [Kurdish] tribes and would have established a Republic.'[27] Order had also been restored in Lurestan, where Lur tribesmen had continued to raid and loot villages. In Gilan a new insurgency movement headed by a Seyyed Jalal had also been defeated, Seyyed Jalal escaping to the forests.

Reza Khan's first aim from the time he became Minister of War in early 1921 had been to bring the provincial centres under the control of the Iranian national army. With the northern campaign almost complete he had to tame the Qashqa'i in Fars, the Bakhtiari in central and south-western Iran and the Arab tribes in Khuzestan. Beginning at the turn of the century the British Government had concluded various agreements with almost all the major tribes in the south. Some of the agreements were oral declarations of support and monetary compensation if the tribes caused no problems to British interests in the region. With the Bakhtiaris, it went further. They had been given shares in one of the APOC subsidiaries and loans with no immediate expectation of repayment. They were also periodically furnished with light arms. With the virtual ruler of Khuzestan, Sheikh Khaz'al,* Britain had assumed a much more serious and binding undertaking. In 1910 in a unilateral written declaration signed by Percy Cox, Britain's chief political officer in the Persian Gulf, and Arnold Wilson, chief of security and later manager of APOC at Abadan, Britain assumed the following undertaking:

---

*   Sheikh Khaz'al, 1860–1936, was the son of the chieftain of a small Arab tribe. He murdered his brother who had succeeded his father as chieftain and became the ruler of the tribe. He had blinded numerous other rivals who stood in his path. With Britain's help he became Governor of Khuzestan where he ruled for almost 20 years and gradually gained dominion over all the other Arab tribes in the province. He accumulated great wealth, was the recipient of some nine titles from Qajar Shahs and was awarded the KCSI knighthood by the British Crown. A dispute with the Ministry of Finance gave Reza Khan the excuse to bring him to Tehran under house arrest, where he lived out his days.[28]

> His Majesty's Government will be prepared to afford you [Sheikh Khaz'al]
> the support necessary for obtaining a satisfactory solution in the event
> of encroachment by the Persian Government on your jurisdiction and
> recognised right or your property in Persia.[29]

An important qualifying clause had been added, that the support of
the British Government was given on the understanding that the
Sheikh and his descendants observed their obligation to the Central
Government of Persia and were guided by the advice of the British
Government. The Iranian Government had not been informed of
these undertakings by Britain. Thereafter, the Sheikh had acted as
a virtual independent head of state and from the beginning of World
War I had paid no taxes nor transmitted levies collected at southern
ports. Now that Tehran was pressing him to settle his accounts, he
had approached the British authorities and wanted Britain to support his scheme for the partition of Iran, with himself as the ruler of
Southern Persia.[30]

Less than a month after his arrival in Tehran Loraine had travelled to Mohammareh (the present Khorramshahr) in the province of
what was then called Arabestan (Khuzestan)[31] to see Sheikh Khaz'al,
whom he had seen during his first posting to Tehran in 1907 and
also on his way to Tehran in early December 1921. Since his arrival
in Tehran Loraine had sought to calm and reassure the Sheikh of
continued British support, but had had to report that the Sheikh
was disappointed in Britain. For the services he had rendered to
Britain the Sheikh had expected he would be made king of Iraq but
had been bypassed. He admitted he had not paid any taxes to the
Central Government since 1913 but he alleged that he had spent
more than what was claimed in safeguarding southern Persia. He
had asked Loraine to have him appointed Governor of all southern
ports with ten percent of all receipts at the port of Mohammareh
paid directly to him. The Sheikh had also requested a gift of 10,000
rifles. Loraine further informed Curzon that the Bakhtiari Khans
had contacted him and they too wanted arms and financial assistance.[32] Soon after Loraine's visit APOC representatives concluded a
loan agreement with the Khans secured by their shares in APOC
subsidiaries.

From the last days of the Government of Pirnia to the re-appoint-
ment of Qavam as Prime Minister, Reza Khan had acted as a one-man
caretaker government, even attending to non-military matters. With
Qavam's appointment Reza Khan again was able to concentrate on
military affairs. Now that the northern provinces were secure he
planned to send troops to other parts of the country, and so
informed the British Military Attaché.[33] Loraine, sensing danger,

planned a two-pronged response. He advised the British consul in
Bushehr to see Sheikh Khaz'al and tell the Sheikh to settle his
accounts before the US financial advisers came to Tehran and formally determined the exact amount owed. Loraine's hand would
then be strengthened and he could argue against sending troops to
Khuzestan. Next Loraine asked Godfrey Havard, the Oriental
Counsellor, to see Reza Khan and advise him to delay the dispatch
of troops to the south. On 18 July Reza Khan informed Havard that
the troops had already left Esfahan and could not be recalled. Reza
Khan further stated that he had informed the Cabinet of his decision and had obtained their approval for the expedition. Later, in
conversation with Qavam, Loraine was informed that the plan was
for the troops to stop half way before they reached Bakhtiari territory.
Qavam had then added gratuitously that government troops passing
close to oil installations would be beneficial to and further ensure the
safety of APOC employees. On 23 July Reza Khan casually remarked
to Loraine that troops were now in Bakhtiari territory. Loraine protested that the Prime Minister had assured him the troops would
stop half way. Reza Khan stated that Qavam and the full Cabinet had
approved the expedition and they knew the destination was the borders of Khuzestan. At a subsequent meeting arranged by Loraine with
Qavam and Reza Khan, Qavam denied having said anything to Loraine
concerning the expedition and had left the meeting somewhat
embarrassed.[34] Reza Khan 'not wanting to see the Prime Minister
further humiliated' also left. Less than ten days after this meeting
government troops were attacked near Shalil in Kuh-e-Morvarid by
Kuhgelu Lurs. Government troops suffered heavy casualties, 35–40
killed and 20 wounded. They lost their machine-guns and some
soldiers even lost their rifles and clothes. The remaining troops returning to Esfahan identified some Bakhtiari tribesmen among the
attacking forces. Reza Khan from the outset suspected the Bakhtiari
had organised the ambush but took no immediate action.[35]

The attack on government troops was to have important consequences. It became apparent to Loraine that Reza Khan would send
troops to the oil region to exercise dominion over the territory and
Sheikh Khaz'al's days as an independent ruler were numbered.
Loraine also knew that sooner or later Reza Khan would mount a
punitive campaign against the Bakhtiaris, whom he considered the
instigators of the ambush. Loraine had at least an inkling of who
had been behind the ambush. In a telegram to Curzon, Loraine had
unequivocally stated that 'intrigue by Sheikh Khaz'al had caused the
attack on government forces'.[36] In a separate dispatch he informed
Curzon that Samsam al Saltaneh, the senior Bakhtiari chieftain,

had hinted at a plan by the Bakhtiaris to ambush government forces 'which he [Loraine] had deprecated'.[37]

Another fallout from the incident was the disgracing of Qavam, who had now totally lost the respect and confidence of Loraine and Reza Khan. Loraine wrote:

> Qavam wants Sardar Sepah [Reza Khan] removed but cannot do it. He is waiting for an opportunity... The opinion I have formed of Qavam is that his duplicity and resourcefulness are unusual even for a Persian, that in all of his doublings and turnings and intrigues there is remarkable streak of tenacity and that it is this tenacity which has raised him to his high position.[38]

Qavam had calculated he would be a winner no matter how the southern troop movements fared. If troops passed without incident he could claim credit and tell Reza Khan he had placated Loraine. If troops were attacked and men were lost, Reza Khan would be blamed and would have his hands full trying to organise a punitive expedition. Reza Khan had been contemptuous of Qavam even earlier, and relations had been tense during Qavam's entire second term. This latest incident strained their relationship beyond any hope of repair.

One of the weapons Reza Khan had come to use was threat of resignation when he met opposition either in the Cabinet or Majles. It was to be a semi-annual event as Reza Khan used it again and again until he had attained absolute power. After the ambush of troops he had asked for more funds for the military. Hesitancy by the Cabinet gave him the opportunity to use this weapon. He tendered his resignation on 23 September because of 'obstruction and lack of complete support by the Cabinet'. This tactical resignation gave Loraine an occasion to re-think his earlier appraisal of Reza Khan. Loraine became apprehensive and realised that Reza Khan intended to deal with the southern tribes in the same manner he had dealt with northern insurgents despite Britain's 'special relationship' with its southern surrogates and allies. Nevertheless he wrote to Curzon, 'We should let events take their course'. Loraine foresaw that whether or not Reza Khan were serious about his resignation he would sooner or later come into conflict with the US financial advisers over the extent and control of military expenditure (The US financial advisers were to arrive in December 1922). Loraine expressed grave doubts:

> [about Reza Khan's] ultimate intentions towards British interests in Persia. With Sardar Sepah out of the picture, the risk of conflict with the Bakhtiaris and Sheikh Khazal would disappear... [and his plan] to dominate the south will disappear.

Even in a report that sounded despairing of Reza Khan, Loraine included a cautionary note: 'Sardar Sepah's disappearance will enhance Soviet interests in Persia'.[39] It took Loraine another six months to resolve the conflict in his thinking.

Southern Iran had always loomed large in the minds of British policy-makers. The control of southern Iran also meant control of the Persian Gulf, the Sheikdoms and Mesopotamia which were considered the gateway to India and points east. With the discovery of oil the region also acquired economic importance. When British statesmen spoke of a stronger Persia they really meant a stronger province of Arabestan. When Britain talked of Persian independence it meant support for a central government that would in effect leave the administration, finance and defence of the southern provinces to Britain and her tribal allies. Nomads should be loyal only to their chiefs who in turn should be loyal to Britain. Their control, punishment and reward should rest with British authorities. With this line of reasoning, the Iranian Central Government should concern itself only with the northern and western provinces. Its military should merely act as a barrier to Soviet ambitions. Britian would look after the defence of the rest of the country.

These established principles of British foreign policy were what had begun to trouble Loraine, who within a short time of his arrival knew there were flaws and contradictions in the premises. Loraine believed 'there had been no coherent Persian policy' after the coup of 1921. 'We do not seem to know what we want.'[40] In September 1922 Loraine wrote to Curzon:

> It must, I think, be perpetually born in mind that Tehran is the ultimate criterion of our relations with Persia and that the cohesion of the Persian Empire as a whole is more important to British interests generally and in the long run than the local supremacy of any of our particular protegés.[41]

Loraine began to develop and refine his arguments as time went on. In reporting an incident where a tribal leader had been arrested by Reza Khan,[42] Loraine explained that since Semitqu's defeat Reza Khan intended to bring the whole country under direct control of the army. The military hegemony to which Reza Khan aspired sooner or later had to involve a showdown with southern tribes, especially the Bakhtiaris, and in such a fight Reza Khan ultimately would win. The tribes would undoubtedly seek help from Britain. Britain therefore had to review its relationship with local tribal leaders and 'loosen our ties' to them. In arguing Reza Khan's case, Loraine hastened to add:

I do not maintain that Sardar Sepah is pro-British in the sense which that expression has been commonly used and understood in the past. He is a nationalist through and through, though of a more level-headed and less chauvinistic type than the Tehran politicians, and is essentially pro-Persian.

Loraine concluded:

[Reza Khan] is the one comparatively stable element in the general situation here and that his disappearance would almost certainly be the prelude to the spread of certain influences which are hostile to the British Empire and to an encroachment of an undesirable nature capable of raising the whole Persian question afresh in an acute form.[43]

What Loraine was arguing came down to the fact that a stable, centralised and orderly Iran could never be a danger to British interests. A weak and divided Iran influenced by Moscow could be a menace. In a later report Loraine wrote to Curzon:

We have to decide now whether we are going to support or oppose extension of the authority of the Central Government throughout the entire country and in either case by what means. I do not think we can afford any longer to remain neutral... To support the Minister of War means the almost certain lapse of our local friendships of which the most difficult and important case is of course the Sheikh of Mohammareh. But support might enable us to control Sardar Sepah to some extent and perhaps to tie him down to definite assurances as regards the Sheikh's position. Support would also strengthen the bulwark against Russia. To oppose him means 1– Prospect of these local friendships crumbling under visible force when our friends are successfully attacked by the central power as they certainly will be. 2– Collapse of our position and influence unless we uphold them and our friends by force. 3– Thwarting the one chance that has appeared for decades of stability of Persia under Persian control. 4– A period of intense friction with the Persian Government almost certainly leading to a rupture. 5– Playing into the hands of Russia.[44]

By early May 1923 Loraine had reached a conclusion and had come down firmly on the side of Reza Khan and the authority of the Central Government. In a lengthy report Loraine summarised his experience in Iran since he arrived some 17 months earlier. He related that he had witnessed the crushing of revolts of Col. Mohammad Taqi Khan, Kouchek Khan and Semitqu.

If any of these revolts had succeeded there would have been independent republics established in the region... The Shahsavan tribes in eastern Azerbaijan, who were looting at will, have been subdued and delivered 40,000 rifles to the Government. The Turkamans who accepted no authority have been made silent. In the south and southwest, Lurs, Bakhtiaris, Qashqais, Khamse and Sheikh Khazal were really independent fiefdoms.

Loraine continued to explain that most southern tribes were now quiet, despite the fact that Reza Khan intended to bring them all under the control of the Central Government. He concluded that these developments had benefitted British interests and the Bolshevik threat in northern Iran had receded. These changes all had been brought about through the efforts of one man, Reza Khan, 'who is handicapped by a chronically empty treasury and an impotent civil Government'. If Reza Khan decided to send forces to the south either to collect back taxes or just to assert government authority there would be only two courses open to the British Government if it wished to oppose them; to stir up local tribes to oppose the passage of Government troops or to tell the Iranian Govenment it cannot send troops to the south. 'Once we are pledged to this course we should have to see it through to the end and its consequences are not easy to forsee.'

> [It is in the power of Reza Khan] to become Prime Minister, to close the Mejles and rule as a dictator, even to overthrow the Qajar dynasty. Any one of these would diminish the difficulties which beset his path but the fact that he has abstained from all of them, pretty well dismisses of any idea that he is solely attracted by personal ambition. The three Prime Ministers Persia has had since my arrival, Qavam al Saltaneh, Moshir ed Dowleh and Mostofi al Mamalek, were all insignificant. Qavam was the best of the three but his activities were so perverse and tortuous that he cannot be relied on to pursue a clear line of policy unless it be demonstrably in his personal interest to do so...[45]

Another element that strengthened Loraine's advocacy of Reza Khan's position was the gradual dissillusionment of the Foreign Office and Curzon in particular with old allies and the great families of Iran on whom Britain had relied for several decades. The Shah had come to be viewed as 'an inconsequential figure' by three successive British envoys.[46] Curzon had come to despair of all Iranian politicians and had written a year earlier about 'the incomparable, incurable and inconceivable rottenness of Persian politicians'.[47] When in May 1922 Pirnia had been close to resigning and no successor other than Qavam or Mostofi could be found Curzon had written, 'I consider these political crises irresistable... we should let them succeed each other with mathematical regularity without showing the slightest concern'.[48] Loraine was astute in reinforcing the mood and outlook of his mentor towards old allies and commented, 'Qavam al Saltaneh, Moshir ed Dowleh and Mostofi are of no use to us and never will be. As you say we must let them come and go and perform their rather stale tricks without emotion or surprise.'[49] Loraine, who had informed Curzon a few weeks after arrival that public opinion was now a factor in Iranian political life, wrote to Curzon again:

> The vast majority of Molks, Saltanehs and Dowlehs are avaricious self seekers with no God but Mammon and no incentive but greed for money and power... part of our difficulty in Persia during and immediately after the war has been our association with, in the popular mind, [these] reactionaries who are profoundly distrusted and cordially disliked.[50]

The next day he wrote:

> The whole country is in the hands of an upper class numbering a few thousands, mostly ravenous Molks, Saltanehs and Dowlehs. There is practically no middle class and the mass of the population takes no interest in what happens and sells its vote for 5 or 6 Krans and merely asks not to starve. Among the upper classes there are certainly a handful of decent and enlightened men but they seem incapable of bonding together. For the moment any chance of improvements centres around Reza Khan and the American advisers.[51]

Relations with Firouz, one of the favourites of Cox and Curzon and heir apparant of Vosouq, had worsened despite attempts by Farmanfarma to mend them. On the occasions that Farmanfarma and Loraine had met the former had pleaded for Firouz to be forgiven and justified his son's bitterness over his imprisonment by Seyyed Zia. When Farmanfarma had asked if he could arrange a meeting between his son and Loraine, Loraine had replied he 'would be pleased to receive Firouz but would not make a call on him'. Farmanfarma had also stated that, 'he was always at my [Loraine's] disposal to give any information in regard to political movements and thoughts among his fellow countrymen with which he kept in close touch'. Farmanfarma had then asked if Loraine could use his influence on behalf of Farmanfarma himself to become governor of Fars or Azarbaijan. Loraine had replied 'he did not interfere in these matters'. Loraine wrote to Curzon that 'relations are beyond repair. Pressure should be put on Nosrat ed Dowleh [Firouz] to settle his debts with the military authorities and other British creditors, such as Rolls Royce to show that we have weapons of retaliation'.[52] The matter of Firouz's unpaid bills in London and Baghdad was to haunt him until his death and the Legation made the matter public to discredit him. When in October 1922 Firouz planned a trip to Paris via Baghdad, there were some ten exchanges of telegrams between Loraine and Cox in Baghdad over whether to issue him transit permits to travel through Iraq. As it happened, Firouz decided against the trip, although he had received transit papers to travel via Baku and Moscow.[53]

Loraine and Firouz finally met as pre-arranged at the residence of a third party. Firouz later called on Loraine at the Legation and Loraine reciprocated. Their relations remained frosty on the surface and on Loraine's part fundamentally hostile. In the only lengthy meeting the two had Firouz complained that despite his 'past services to the British crown' he had been humiliated when he and his father had been imprisoned. Firouz 'was certain that the Coup was organised by Col. Smyth and it was impossible for him to believe that Norman and the Legation were not cognisant of what was taking place'. Therefore, once released he decided to take 'his own line and form his own judgement on all questions that arose'. As to the future, Firouz believed that the British Government 'should not have a monopoly on all economic and political matters in Persia... and APOC has become too powerful which is not desirable'.[54]

Farmanfarma's efforts to maintain cordial relations with the Legation yielded no better results and when he called at the Legation to enquire 'what value were now attached to the letters of guarantee for himself and family given by Sir Charles Marling', British Minister to Tehran during the war, Loraine at first attempted to avoid a direct answer and stated he needed to consult the Foreign Office. Later Loraine bluntly told Farmanfarma:

> Anti-British activities of Nosrat ed Dowleh have made a most disagreeable impression on His Majesty's Government and the question of cancelling of these letters altogether had actually been considered... If His Highness's life were in danger I would intervene to save him, but I advised him not to insist too much on possession of [these] letters and to keep out of politics. His Highness said he did not wish to be a burden or embarrassment to us and accepted my assurances as a fair one.[55]

Curzon and Loraine came to agree on the 'rottenness of Persian politicians' and abandoning old favourites in Tehran, but on the question of abandoning tribal leaders they were still far apart. Curzon was to remain wary and could not emotionally accept Loraine's recommendation to place his trust in an unknown newcomer, Reza Khan, to uphold Britain's economic and strategic interests in Iran. In his state of near melancholia he wrote Loraine a private letter and recited all his efforts over the years to protect the integrity of the British Empire.

> We have spent, or rather wasted millions upon [Persia] in the last ten years... Here also you have a British Minister who has devoted more years of labour in the last 35 years to the cause of Persian integrity and freedom than most other people have devoted days or hours. And what is the result of it all? A complete collapse of British prestige and influence in [that] country... Now from what does it come?. 1– I have

wondered whether Sir Percy Cox for whom I have the warmest esteem, Vosouq ed Dowleh and the Farmanfarma family consciously deceived us when the Agreement was under discussion. Cox always answers that had he stayed none of the evil consequences would have ensued... 2– Then came Norman's regime about which I can scarcely speak with equanimity and seems to have rattled the bricks out of a perhaps none too stable structure with a remorseless and tireless rapidity surely unequalled in diplomatic history. 3– Next came the Cabinet at home... and their decision to withdraw troops... 4– The arrival of Sovietism in the north and the propaganda and payments by Rothstein. 5– The latent and now full hostility of the Mejles. 6– The incomparable and incurable rottenness of Persian politicians. 7– The desperate and collosal incapacity of the Shah...

At the end of the letter Curzon paternally advised Loraine:

> Do not jump into the arms of any one Persian politician. They come and go these puppets... like performing dogs on a music hall stage. They don't count... Never release or slacken our hold on the [Persian] Gulf... Some day give a good smash between the eyes to that traitor Firouz.[56]

Curzon continued to urge Loraine to maintain alliances with southern tribes[57] and remained at best dubious of Reza Khan's intentions. He did not agree with Loraine that Reza Khan's actions had been 'favourable to us'.[58] Curzon was influenced by reports from British consular officials in southern Iran who were mostly recruited from the Indian Political Service. They looked at Iranian southern tribal chieftains in the same way they regarded the semi-independent Indian Princes who protected British interests in India. For example Arnold Wilson, now the head of the Abadan refinery, reported on 4 February 1923 that 'Sardar Sepah is bitterly opposed to any Khan who is friendly to the British' and argued that Reza Khan could be stopped as Sheikh Khaz'al, the Bakhtiari, Khamse and Boir Ahmadi tribes could raise 15,000 men.[59] Curzon was to write to Loraine and warn him that Reza Khan's 'national army was built to eliminate our friends'.[60] At times Curzon appears exasperated by Loraine's defence of Reza Khan's position and reminded Loraine that Britain had done most, if not all the things asked by Reza Khan, with no reciprocity. Britain had closed its post offices, removed troops from the Bushehr area and surrendered the Duzdab railway in southeast Iran. At the end of the dispatch Curzon reminded Loraine that 'Bakhtiaris are important to our oil interests... [and] we have no intention to abandon [Sheikh Khaz'al] as we are bound to him by special obligation'.[61]

Reza Khan knew he must continue and even accelerate his campaign to assert the authority of the Central Government in all parts

of Iran or he would lose his newly-gained power. The test case was
the dispatch of troops south which could enhance his status or
break him. It was a gamble he had to take. Yet Reza Khan was by
nature a cautious man, especially when it came to a possible confrontation with either the Soviets or the British. He had to wait for
an opportune time. His continued fencing with Loraine was one indication of his deliberate moves while waiting for an opening. Reza
Khan also knew Britain's options were limited. If he moved south
what could Britain do? The financial leverage it had exercised in the
years following World War I had lessened. Cutting off advances on
oil royalties would not be totally effective since the arrival of US financial advisers who had established some fiscal order. The country
was slowly becoming solvent and further, how long could APOC
withhold payment of royalties? If Britain decided to send troops, she
had to know that the Russians might send troops as well, at least to
the northern provinces. Would Britain want to see the disintegration
of Iran?

Loraine also knew that arming the southern tribes was not the
answer. On the other hand, the logical extension of Reza Khan's
policy would sooner or later place it in conflict with British interests.
The only answer was to seek an accommodation with Reza Khan and
explore compromises to avoid a direct clash. For almost two years
Loraine and Reza Khan had continued sparring and getting a measure of each other. Loraine was hoping to find a compromise and
Reza Khan was waiting either for the tacit acquiescence of Britain or
for an opening to allow him to bring the south under the control of
the Central Government with minimum risk and danger of conflict
with Britain. Since the ambush of troops at Shalil, Reza Khan had
avoided meeting Loraine. When by chance they met at a diplomatic
function Reza Khan with some charm and guile told Loraine, 'We do
not see each other because Persians think I am hand in glove with
the British... He then laughed and said we would be in touch.'[62] Some
three weeks later when they met again, Reza Khan told Loraine that
he was still trying to determine who had been behind the attack on
his troops in the south and he would take no action against the
Bakhtiaris until his enquiry was completed. He also assured Loraine
that he had no personal animosity towards Sheikh Khaz'al and
would treat him impartially.[63]

After a lapse of six months Reza Khan informed Loraine that his
enquiry had yielded results and he had documentary evidence of
Bakhtiari involvement in the incident. He had therefore demanded
the sum of 48,000 tomans from their chiefs as compensation for loss
of equipment. Since they had not responded he was considering a

military expedition against them. Loraine lamely commented that the demand was inequitable as the Bakhtiaris were not responsible. Loraine, realising the urgency of the situation, wrote to Curzon:

> ... the moment for dealing one way or another with Reza Khan's centralised policy has passed... I think our major interests indicate an alliance with Sardar Sepah [Reza Khan].[64]

In a later interview with the British Military Attaché Reza Khan was more blunt. He insisted that the Bakhtiaris had been given a reasonable grace period and they had to pay. 'He wished to avoid to send an expeditionary force against them but it is essential that the Bakhtiaris carry out the terms of his demand. He could not allow the tribe to defy him.' He added that he had no respect for Bakhtiari fighting abilities. 'They could put 10,000 soldiers in the field but they cannot fight. One Shahsavan is worth 10 Bakhtiari.' Reza Khan further stated that the Bakhtiaris could not count on support from neighbouring tribes. The Qashqa'i and Arab tribes of Khamse would stay out of the conflict.[65] Loraine informed of the assertive language used by Reza Khan and his exuding confidence, wrote to Curzon:

> We are now face to face with the Minister of War. If he forces us into opposition we shall doubtless break [him] in the end by power of the purse. We [would] probably break Persia in the process. [Reza Khan] would be an inconvenient opponent; he might be a useful friend. He is too much of a patriot to be a subservient instrument. I will attempt, as you say, to have a frank discussion with him.[66]

In a lengthy meeting with Reza Khan and Mostofi (who had been Prime Minister since February 1923) Loraine took the lead to set forth British policy in Iran. Loraine represented it as benign and interested only in protecting its legitimate interests. Reza Khan, without disagreeing with Loraine, explained how foreign powers had interfered in Iranian affairs for 'as long as he could remember' but that things had changed in the last years.

> The emergence of a national army and the authority of the Central Government have changed many things. He therefore hoped I would convince London, Dehli and Baghdad of the great difference between the present and the past state of the country... The army will reduce all sections of the nation to submission to the Central Government... which will maintain a neutral attitude towards foreigners in Persia. To complete this process it would be necessary to disarm the entire civilian population and keep all physical power in the hands of the state.

Loraine continued his report saying, 'the above was Sardar Sepah's internal policy. His foreign policy was to keep friendly relations with Great Britain and any other neighbouring state whose institutions rested on firm foundations.' Loraine added that Reza Khan did not include Russia among such neighbouring states.

Loraine thanked Reza Khan for his frank explanation and said that Great Britain had no objection to these aims but the question was the practical method of achievement. If the pursuit of Reza Khan's policy

> ... were to result in a collision with important British interests the results could be most unfortunate... whatever steps the Prime Minister and the Minister of War had in mind should not disturb the tranquility of Arabestan or endanger the operations of APOC... The British Government did not deny the right of the Persian Government to send troops to any point in Persian territory but did ask the Persian Government to consider with utmost care the possible results of sending them to Arabestan and to refrain from doing so if there was any danger of unfortunate consequence.

Loraine then dealt with the status of Sheikh Khaz'al and repeated that the Sheikh had been consistently friendly to Britain. The Sheikh had rendered valuable service during the war and Britain owed him a debt of gratitude.

> He was not under British protection but His Majesty's Government did have a special relationship with him. Of course he must fulfill his proper obligation to the Persian Government... It was also true that we had a long standing relationship, for instance with the Bakhtiari Khans and it had been a friendship which had been essential for the protection of the interests of APOC... Britain's relationship with the Sheikh was however, of a closer nature than those with the Bakhtiari Khans.

Reza Khan made no comment on the Sheikh and again said he hoped:

> [Britain] would see no objection to encourage internal security in Persia and to entrust the protection of British interests to Persian authorities... He felt bound to continue his policy of centralisation and disarmament but in view of what [Loraine had said] he realised it would be necessary to move slower... and [Britain] might rest assured that he would take no precipitate steps likely to endanger the situation.[67]

Curzon still living in another era, wrote to Loraine:

> It would be better if we had the Minister of War's assurances in writing, countersigned by Mostofi.[68]

Both sides left the meeting fully understanding what the other was saying. Loraine would accept the Iranian Government's policy of extending its dominion to all parts of Iran except Arabestan. The Central Government could even punish the Bakhtiaris and exercise authority over their territory. But the Sheikh's terrain was out of bounds. Reza Khan had said in turn he would continue his centralisation policy one way or another. As far as the Sheikh was concerned he could wait longer and see if he could bring him down without having to send troops. In any event he would ensure the continued safeguarding of British intersts in the region. Reza Khan's opening statement that the Iranian Government intended to pursue its own course and Britain and other countries should adjust to new realities was tantamount to a declaration of independence which had not been uttered by an Iranian in high office for several decades.

At a later meeting with the same participants Reza Khan used a new argument to sway Loraine. He argued that his prestige was at stake and he had to move southward. If he were unable to send forces to the south because of British opposition he would not be able to answer his critics and detractors. Mostofi supported Reza Khan's arguments vehemently and Loraine reported to Curzon that he was 'struck by the sincerity shown by the two'.[69] Loraine summarised Reza Khan's arguments for Curzon as follows:

> The Minister of War basically says you [Britain] would prefer my not sending troops to Arabestan... I understand your reasons and I don't want a quarrel between us. Indeed I very much want to be friends. But I do really feel it necessary and if I can not send Government troops there as elsewhere in Persia I am stultified for I could not disguise capitulation to your views. Can we not reconcile our two points of view? I do not want to threaten or collide with your interests.[70]

The last of these meetings arranged by Loraine at the urging of Curzon to ascertain further the intentions of Reza Khan towards Arabestan and the Sheikh was held a week later. Loraine again began by probing for any immediate plans Reza Khan may have formulated regarding the south. At the outset Loraine stated that he had asked for the meeting to see how relations between the two countries could be improved. Reza Khan instantly responded by sharply asking what reason Britain had to keep several hundred soldiers in Bushehr 'on Persian soil? What proof do you require of the ability of the Persian army to maintain order?' Loraine having no answer, reverted to the proposition that if the 1919 Agreement had been put into effect relations between the two countries now would be excellent. Sensing that if the conversation continued along these lines Reza Khan would make further demands, Loraine shifted the conversation to Arabestan and was forced to ask Reza Khan plainly what his intentions were. Reza Khan simply repeated that he needed to conclude what he had started. He had sent troops to every part of Iran except Arabestan. 'People want to know why.' They ask doesn't Persian sovereignty extend there? 'I know you have a special relationship with the Sheikh and that is why I intend to send only a few hundred troops. But they must go.' Loraine answered that this course of action would 'cause serious anxiety to Britain'. Reza Khan gave his word that as far as British interests were concerned there would be no trouble. 'He will not change the status quo without assurances to His Majesty's Government and APOC. As for the Sheikh 'the anxiety only existed in the Sheikh's imagination'.[71]

The status of the Sheikh remained in serious contention and would not be resolved for more than a year. A relatively small incident highlighted the untenability of the British position with regard to the security of their economic interests in Iran. In early September 1923 some APOC employees travelling in the south-eastern province of Fars were fired on by Qashqa'i tribesmen. APOC immediately demanded the dispatch of Indian troops to the area to punish the Qashqa'i.[72] Arnold Wilson, General Manager of the Abadan refinery, also demanded that the Iranian Government be held responsible and should make monetary amends. Loraine felt both requests were unjustified.[73] Nevertheless APOC, which had opposed Reza Khan's centralisation policy and his efforts to disarm the tribesmen, now held the Iranian Government responsible for compensation. A few years earlier an Indian merchant who had been robbed by tribesmen on Iranian territory had also claimed compensation. At Curzon's urging Loraine had interceded with the Iranian Government, arguing that Iran was responsible and its Government should have suppressed brigandage in Iranian territory. Curzon further argued that Iran had the burden of proof to show that it had done everything to prevent the robbery. The victims had been robbed in south-east Iran which was occupied then by British troops.[74] Although there is no record of Loraine's views on these matters apart from those implied by his disapproval of the request for compensation from the Iranian Government it is safe to assume that his arguments in support of an Iranian national army and the disarming of tribes as beneficial for the protection of Britain's economic interests were strengthened.

Two more unrelated incidents further strengthened Loraine's position for a strong Iranian army. In the same month as the APOC employee incident, as a result of a dispute regarding the precise location of the Iranian-Soviet frontiers in the north-west, Soviet troops killed the entire Iranian border garrison of six men. Almost simultaneous with this occurence a small number of Soviet sailors landed at Anzali and occupied the fisheries buildings. The Russians wanted to force the Iranian Govenment to give up the fisheries concession which Russia had renounced only two years earlier in accordance with the Perso-Soviet accord.[75]

Another cause of friction which further clouded relations between Britain and Iran was the expulsion in October of three senior Shi'a ulama from the holy cities in Iraq. The three Mojtaheds had signed a declaration (fatwa) proclaiming it unlawful to assist the Iraqi Government in its dispute with Turkey. They had also called for the boycott of Iraqi parliamentary elections. Cox had supported their expulsion. Loraine, who had his hands full with Reza Khan and his planned southern campaign, strongly objected and knew there would be added pressure from the ulama on Reza Khan to attack the Bakhtiaris, who were the handmaidens of the British. Pirnia, then Prime Minister, warned Loraine of grave consequences in the Shi'a world but Cox informed Loraine there was little he could do. It took almost six months before the matter was settled by compromises on both sides. Some of the clerics who had accompanied the Mojtaheds returned to Iraq and the representatives of King Faisal and the Iranian Government ultimately worked out a settlement that allowed the other senior clerics also to return. With public opinion firmly behind Reza Khan's desire to punish the Bakhtiaris, and now the expulsion matter having inflamed the public, Reza Khan could have undertaken an expedition to the south. He chose to bide his time and instead attempted with some success to create divisions and rifts amongst Bakhtiari tribal leaders.[76]

The Shah returned from his journey to Europe in December 1922 after an absence of almost 11 months. Reza Khan went to Bushehr to welcome the Shah personally and escort him to Tehran. He had arranged an elaborate welcome on the route to Tehran as well as in all provincial centres. Relations between the two remained cordial, at least outwardly, for several months. Shortly after the Shah's arrival, Reza Khan arranged a parade of troops for his personal viewing and inspection. The army showed itself to be well disciplined and the Shah was visibly impressed.[77] Soon afterwards, Reza Khan asked to be given the title Commander in Chief of the Army. He argued that he had been appointed by the Shah as commander of the Cossack Division with the title of Sardar Sepah (Commander of the Army), a title he continued to hold contemporaneous with his appointment as Minister of War. Now that the armed forces were reorganised and expanded he should exercise the same authority over the new army as he had previously exercised over the Cossack Division. The Shah was reluctant and argued that in accordance with the constitution the title and the power rested only with himself.[78] An event which further highlighted growing tensions between Reza Khan and the Shah was the former's blocking the Vali'ahd from taking his customary seat in Tabriz as previous heirs to the throne had done. Reza

Khan argued that Azarbaijan was not entirely safe and the matter should be deferred.[79]

Qavam had been able to remain in office but by the end of 1922 his Government was moribund and could have collapsed at any time. His main support still centred on Moddares and his followers. Another source of support, Rothstein, had been recalled in May 1922 and replaced by a party functionary, Shumyatsky, who had none of Rothstein's talent for public relations. Shumyatsky had ignored and alienated a great number of Iranian notables. He had chosen not to call on the Shah and the relationship established by Rothstein with the Shah had disappeared.[80] Qavam's failure to come to an agreement with the Soviets on commercial and economic matters, especially a new tariff, hastened his fall. He finally resigned on 26 January 1923. It was obviously the turn of Mostofi, who had not been Prime Minister since 1918. It would have been somewhat ludicrous to bring in Pirnia (Moshir al Dowleh) who had immediately preceded Qavam. The revolving chair practice dictated it should be someone other than Pirnia. Mostofi had kept aloof from politics and was living the life of a country gentleman, hunting in the company of a few intimate friends. He was a member of parliament and although he had attended no more than one or two sessions he was still extremely popular among the deputies.

Mostofi's attempts to reach an agreement with the Soviets on new trade tariffs were to be more successful, and during his brief time in office there was a lift in the economy, mostly due to expanded trade with the Russians and the reforms introduced by the American economic advisers who had arrived in December 1922 and had begun work almost immediately. Mostofi formed his Cabinet on 14 February. The prominent members were Mohammad Ali Foroughi as Minister of Foreign Affairs, Hassan Esfandiari at Education, Mehdi Qoli Hedayat at Public Works and Hosein Samii as acting Minister of the Interior. The members of the Cabinet were all respected and enjoyed reputations for probity. Equally important was Mostofi's relations with Reza Khan. The two got along well and Reza Khan had enormous respect for him.

The matter of employment of US financial advisers had dragged on until parliament in late August 1922 had finally passed the relevant bill. The US Government announced the appointment of Arthur C. Millspaugh, a thirty-nine-year-old native of Michigan with a PhD in economics, as the Head of the Mission. Millspaugh had been an adviser to the Office of Foreign Trade at the Department of State. In his new position he was given the title of Administrator General of Finance, a title held by Morgan Shuster a decade earlier. When the

14. Fathollah Akbar (Sepahdar). This ineffective politician happened to be interim prime minister at the time of the 1921 coup which removed him.

15. Seyyed Zia al Din Tabataba'i. An overly ambitious schemer, he partnered Reza Khan in the 1921 coup to become prime minister before being deposed by his co-putschist after one hundred days.

16. General Edmund Ironside. Britain's specialist on risky military ventures became commander of British forces in Iran in 1920. He took initiatives at variance with established British Foreign Office policy and effectively engineered the 1921 coup.

Iranian Government had made its initial request it had in mind the re-employment of Shuster, who had become a legendary figure for his unqualified support of Iran in 1911. The Department of State under Charles Evans Hughes decided that Shuster would be unacceptable to the British Government and hence could be detrimental to the interests of US oil companies, particularly Standard Oil, which had entered into a joint venture agreement with APOC. In any event, Millspaugh benefitted greatly simply by being an American and by the high esteem in which Shuster had been held. He was welcomed by almost all segments of Iranian political life and was treated most deferentially. Shuster had been criticised for not having called on the Czarist and British envoys in Tehran. Millspaugh exercised unusual tact. He called on Ahmad Shah in Paris on his way to Tehran and called on Reza Khan immediatley after arrival in December 1922 as well as the usual courtesy calls on all heads of foreign legations. He applauded Reza Khan 'for his courtesy, cordiality and common sense'. He saw Reza Khan 'as one of the most significant and encouraging phenomenons in Persia. He seemed to be the leader the country needed. He had shown constructive genius... and had taken all the preliminary steps necessary for the making of a modern nation.'[81]

Millspaugh's first two years in Iran were an unqualified success. The only taxes in Iran at the time of his arrival were on agricultural produce, crops and livestock. Shopkeepers, craftsmen and artisans paid a nominal sum to the state through their guilds or group organisations and there were occasional levies on tribes and lease of public lands. Millspaugh introduced a host of taxes. There were to be taxes on the issuance and execution of commercial documents, on non-rented or idle real estate, on sales and on inheritance. Equally important, and perhaps revolutionary, he cancelled all tax exemptions formerly granted by Qajar Shahs going back almost 70 years. A sizeable number of notables and grandees had been granted exemptions from all levies and assessments by the Shah as reward for services to the state. In some cases the exemptions devolved upon their heirs. Also exempted were favourites of the Shah and some provincial governors who had claimed misfortune from forces beyond their control such as fire, famine and storm. These exemptions were all cancelled. Millspaugh also publicly identified those guilty of gross delinquency in payment of taxes, most notably Sheikh Khaz'al, who personally owned half a province, and Sepahsalar Tonokaboni who also owned part of a province and the largest citrus groves in the north. Delinquent Bakhtiari Khans and other tribal leaders were also identified by name. Through control

and audit Millspaugh almost eradicated embezzlement by government officials, although he could do nothing about bribery which
continued, albeit on a lesser scale, even during the rule of Reza
Shah despite serious and punitive measures. Another important contribution of Millspaugh was the training of competent tax assessors
and collectors who formed the professional core of the Ministry of
Finance long after his first mission left. Were it not for Millspaugh's
reforms Reza Khan would not have been able to continue his campaign to pacify the tribes. Above all, Millspaugh was instrumental in
making Iran a solvent nation and increasing by bounds the revenue
of the government.[82] He was to encounter difficulties after his first
three years which led to the non-renewal of his five-year contract. A
contributing factor was the disappointment by leading Iranians over
lack of any US investment in Iran which initially had been one of the
main reasons for his employment.[83]

The question of the northern oil concession, which had constituted the other major attempt to involve the United States in Iran,
had remained unresolved. After the formation of the joint venture
between Standard Oil and APOC and their arrangement whereby
half of the proposed $10 million loan would be raised by US banks
and half by British banks, the Iranians realised that their primary
aim of granting the concession solely to a US oil company was
being thwarted. APOC, with its 50 percent interest in northern oil,
would become an even greater economic force in Iran. In view of the
impartiality of the US Government between Standard and Sinclair,
parliament had passed a law on 10 June 1923 'empowering the
Government of Iran to negotiate an oil concession in North Persia
with any independent and responsible American company', conditional upon the company providing the entire $10 million loan. The
law also included a provision that the concessionaire could not assign
or transfer the concession to any non-US company or national. The
latter condition eliminated APOC from any liklihood of becoming an
assignee of the concession or a joint venturer. Standard Oil dropped
out of the picture and Sinclair accepted the offer. The concession was
to be for 50 years with a royalty of 20 percent for the initial period
of operation and an increase on a sliding scale to 28 percent as production rose.[84] From the outset Sinclair had difficulty in raising the
required loan. The primary difficulty was that Sinclair had to come
to terms with the Soviet Government since the only way to export
the oil would have been through the Caucasus and the Russians
had to agree to a pipleline running through their territory. Sinclair
entered into negotiations with the Soviets but after lengthy talks
realised that an agreement would not be forthcoming. Other factors

also dissuaded Sinclair from pursuing the project. Harry Sinclair, Chairman of the company, had been close to President Harding and his Secretary of Interior Albert Fall and Attorney General Harry Daugherty. With Harding's death, the presidency of Coolidge and the disgracing of Daugherty and Fall in the Teapot Dome Scandal, Sinclair lost all of his key sponsors. The rivalry between Charles Evans Hughes, the Secretary of State who had supported Standard Oil, and Herbert Hoover, Secretary of Commerce who had encouraged Sinclair to compete against Standard Oil, hampered the efforts of both companies. The murder of the American Maj. Imbrie, which will be discussed later, also played a part in the Sinclair withdrawal.[85] The project was dead for all practical purposes.

The expectation was that Mostofi's Government would last longer than its predecessors but from the beginning Mostofi had great difficulties with parliament, notably with Moddares, who began an anti-Mostofi campaign almost from the very first day. When Mostofi was barely able to have the budget for the fiscal year ending March 1924 approved, it was obvious that he could not remain in office much longer.[86] Moddares had wanted several of his favourites, including Firouz, in the Cabinet, a proposal which Mostofi had rejected.[87] Shortly other disappointed deputies started criticising him in parliament. Elections for the fifth session of parliament had begun early in the summer of 1923. A number of deputies believed their chances of re-election would be better under a new government.[88] The Shah also failed to support Mostofi and after another attack on him by a number of deputies, Mostofi made a memorable farewell address to parliament in which he said he had never been in the habit of doing favours for deputies in return for their support. He left parliament and resigned.[89]

The Shah had no-one to turn to but Pirnia again. Reza Khan, who might have had the office had he wished to pursue it, chose to stay out of contention. His support in parliament was slim and in a contest with Pirnia at this time he was assured only of the votes of the leaders of the Socialists. The Moderates and Independents swayed by Moddares would vote overwhelmingly for anyone other than Reza Khan. More importantly, the Shah by now mortally afraid of Reza Khan, had made it clear that he would be unacceptable. Probably the most important calculation by Reza Khan was that with parliament's term expiring soon he would have a better chance with the new parliament scheduled to convene in the autumn. Reza Khan may also have calculated that if Pirnia were to resign before the new parliament was convened he could force the Shah to appoint him Prime Minister with no need for an immediate parliamentary vote.

Pirnia received the approval of parliament and formed his Cabinet on 16 June. It was apparent to most observers that this was the last attempt to deny Reza Khan the premiership and Pirnia began to be viewed as merely an interim Prime Minister. By the end of the summer it was clear that the Government of Pirnia could not last much longer.

Reza Khan began his serious campaign for the office of prime minister in early September. He made at least his supporters know he wanted the position and was 'tired of the Shah's intrigues, self-ishness and lack of genuine interest in the country'.[90] Reza Khan himself told Loraine that 'there was a popular desire for a more efficient government'.[91] He also argued that the grandees had come and gone with no results and the finances and civil administration of the country were still in shambles. He had organised the military and brought order and security, and he deserved a chance to organise the civil departments of government and provide for the economic development of the country.

The Shah had been back in Iran for almost nine months, and that was the extent of his tolerance for remaining in his own country. He had been telling his entourage that he intended to go to Europe by the end of the summer. He told Loraine on 3 September that he believed Reza Khan was close to staging a coup d'etat and he wished to be out of the country if the coup were to take place. He had decided to stay in Europe longer on his last trip and had returned because Reza Khan had told him he would be loyal to the throne. 'He now thinks Sardar Sepah has become the Persian Kamal [Ataturk]'. Loraine reported that the Shah 'is thoroughly frightened and intends to leave as soon as the new Mejles meets, if not before. He asked if Britain could send a plane in case of an emergency to take him out of the country.' The Shah further said that his brother, the Vali'ahd was also frightened and had warned him to leave the country because 'Sardar Sepah could chain both of us when it suited him'.[92] Curzon immediately answered:

> ... if the Shah wants to desert his kingdom, it would be the end of his dynasty, although such a contingency may be regarded with perfect composure... Were he in danger of physical violence and take bast [asylum] at the Legation... his removal to a place of safety is possible... but placing an aeroplane at his disposal is out.[93]

Loraine reported that the Shah had no intention of putting up a fight for his throne and there was nothing he could do to change the Shah's mind.[94] He was prepared to leave at the end of autumn and if there were no coup in his absence he would return.[95]

An intervening event which sealed the impending premiership of Reza Khan was the elimination of Qavam from any future consideration as Prime Minister. Qavam was arrested on 8 October for plotting the murder of Reza Khan during his second term as Prime Minister in the winter of 1922. It was alleged that four men who had been employed by Qavam had been arrested and confessed to the plot. At the intercession of the Shah and Reza Khan, who had waived his personal rights against Qavam under Islamic law, Qavam was allowed to leave the country for Europe. Loraine was convinced of the existence of the plot and Qavam's role as the organiser.[96] Kornfeld, the US Minister, was doubtful. He reported that with Qavam's arrest and exile and Pirnia's impending resignation, the path was cleared for Reza Khan.[97] Loraine later reported that after Reza Khan had become Prime Minister, he had asked him about the plot. Reza Khan's version of the events as related by Loraine were as follows: Qavam had confided in Sardar Entesar (Mozaffar A'lam), a former Gendarmerie officer.

> Qavam had argued that Reza Khan was a great danger to the state and must be eliminated. Since the Gendarmes were upset over their merger with the Cossacks, Qavam asked Sardar Entesar to round up dissatisfied gendarmes and wield them into an effective opposition to Reza Khan and to arrest him at a cabinet meeting and force him to resign. Sardar Entesar had wanted a written order but Qavam had declined and the plot was abandoned.

Later Qavam 'found four Caucasian terrorists recommended by a gendarme officer. They had committed two murders in Tehran, then they disbanded. One of them was arrested as a petty thief in Qazvin and confessed to the plot. All four were now in jail.' Reza Khan also told Loraine there had been another plot to kill him when he went to Bushehr to greet the Shah in November 1922.[98]

Pirnia formally tendered his resignation on 23 October. The Shah saw Reza Khan the next day and said he intended to persuade Pirnia to remain in office with a revised cabinet but with Reza Khan remaining as Minister of War and that immediately thereafter he would depart for Europe. Reza Khan informed the Shah that in that case he 'too will resign and accompany the Shah to Europe'. The Shah 'had commented that the two of them could not both be away from the country at the same time'. Reza Khan then said very plainly that he would stay only if he were appointed Prime Minister.[99]

Pirnia refused to remain in office and the Shah told Loraine that if Reza Khan insisted on becoming Prime Minister he would leave the country sooner than planned, within no more than a fortnight.[100] The Shah asked Loraine to dissuade Reza Khan. Loraine met Reza

Khan the next day and advised him of the risks he would face if 'he descended into the political arena'.[101] Reza Khan was undeterred and Loraine saw the Shah again and told him Reza Khan persisted in becoming Prime Minister. The Shah replied that 'he cannot resist any further and will appoint Sardar Sepah as Prime Minister but he himself cannot remain in Persia'. Loraine added that the Shah intended 'to get guarantees from Reza Khan for his safe departure to the frontier for which he wants me to be a witness. He will leave on November 7th via Baghdad, Damascus, Beirut to Marseilles. The Vali'ahd would act as Regent.'[102] In fact Loraine had grave doubts about the wisdom of a military man in the position of Prime Minister and he had 'personally warned Sardar Sepah against it'.[103] Loraine had also told the US Minister that 'he had more confidence in Sardar Sepah as Minister of War than as Prime Minister'. Kornfeld had added that 'Reza Khan has even higher ambitions' and the Vali'ahd had told him 'the Royal family knows its days are numbered'.[104]

On 28 October the Shah received Reza Khan with Loraine present. Loraine reported that the 'Shah behaved lamentably and the Minister of War sensibly'. The Shah formally stated he would appoint Reza Khan Prime Minister.[105] Later Reza Khan privately told Loraine that he had respect for the Shah but had lost it for the man. Reza Khan had also told Loraine, 'he still wants the Shah to remain'. Loraine, in his report to Curzon concluded:

> What will happen is difficult to say. The Government even if it is constitutional in form, is certainly a dictatorship in character and it remains to be seen whether Sardar Sepah possesses the capacity and resourcefulness needed to wield justly, with moderation and with benefit for his country the enormous powers which are now concentrated in his single hands. I myself am inclined to take the optimistic view.[106]

On 31 October Loraine saw the Shah, who put forward the following conditions for Reza Khan's appointment: Loraine was to obtain written assurances from Reza Khan concerning the Shah's safety which Loraine would transmit to the Shah in writing. The Shah would then announce publicly that he was leaving the country for health reasons and two days later he would issue a royal decree appointing Reza Khan as Prime Minister. Loraine did his part and wrote his letter and delivered it with Reza Khan's letter to the Shah. In his letter Loraine added that 'he was acting as a mere intermediary'.[107]

The Shah, in his anxiety, left five days earlier than planned, on 2 November. Ahmad Shah's departure coincided with the abdication of the Ottoman Sulatan Mohammad VI and the declaration of a republic in Turkey. 'Neither Ahmad Shah nor Reza Khan could have been aware of the symbolism and it could have hardly been mere coincidence that a few months later in March 1924 the establishment of a republic was advocated in Iran.'[108] Reza Khan returned to Tehran on 11 November after escorting the Shah to the frontier and was honoured as Prime Minister by the Tehran merchants guild at a large reception.

There is enough evidence to suggest that Reza Khan saw himself as the natural leader of his country even before the anniversary of the February 1921 coup. In January 1922, a few weeks before Qavam's first Government was to fall, he had told the British Military Attaché that he had lost confidence in the Shah and had been considering steps for the establishment of a republic (presumably with himself as the president).[109] On the anniversary of the coup he had issued a communiqué in a Tehran newspaper assuming total responsibility for the coup. He had stated: 'I am responsible both for its conception and execution'.[110] The declaration was in response to a lengthy article published a few days earlier claiming that Firouz had been the real instigator of the coup but that Seyyed Zia had pre-empted him. Reza Khan's counter-statement was not an expression of vanity. It was the expression of total self-confidence by a man who knew where he was heading but, being cautious and patient, had waited. The country had seen a parade of popular but ineffective politicians come and go. His reputation meanwhile was enhanced by his efficiency in building up the army and his elimination of insurgents in the north. By remaining as Minister of War and concerning himself with military matters he had avoided the usual fate of politicians, being identified with a foreign power. When he was certain he had no rivals he had stepped forward and demanded to be appointed Prime Minister.

Instinct can be a great matter and Reza Khan had known all along that what his countrymen wanted was internal security and stability. In his very first proclamation on assuming the premiership he hit upon this note. 'No country can advance or make progress until security is prevalent in all of its regions.' Furthermore, he had become identified with the emerging mood of the country which was concerned with national identity and freedom from foreign influence and domination.

When Reza Khan came on the scene a considerable segment of the population owed its fealty to tribes or regions and, through years of subservience or exigency to a foreign country. The tribes in the south and the south-west were even rivals in seeking British support. Reza Khan had told Loraine some five months before becoming Prime Minister that Iran would never be orderly or independent until the whole country was brought under a single and unquestioned authority which must be that of the national government, and until the civilian population had been disarmed so that physical power rested in the hands of the state. The state and not local chieftains must assume responsibility for protecting its citizens.

> Foreign influences when they are not obviously [detrimental] but actually beneficial to Persia must be respected. Foreign influences to the extent that they make Persian subjects dependent on a foreign government rather than the Persian Government must be eradicated.[111]

This attitude was not merely directed against Britain. Much earlier, when a number of deputies had advocated the hiring of US military advisers, Reza Khan had firmly stated that he would not employ any foreign nationals as military advisers.[112] From the moment Reza Khan became Minister of War he had focused on the single theme that Iran must be an independent country and its citizens give allegiance to no other country.

Reza Khan made no pretence to intellect or learning, but he knew early what his goals were. He was the hedgehog in the saying, 'The fox knows many things, the hedgehog knows only one thing but knows that one thing well'.[113] The one thing was that tribal power first must be eradicated. Only then could an independant state be constructed. There was, however, a great deal of fox in Reza Khan as well. It was this singleness of purpose and exceptional will that had turned an ordinary soldier into a leader. He had complete confidence in himself and had been willing to take enormous risks. From the beginning, he ruled while he seemed to serve: his part in the coup; his ascendency over Seyyed Zia barely a month after their association; maintaining his independence and dignity when dealing with Qavam, Pirnia and Mostofi; ignoring Norman and yet establishing a fairly close relationship with Loraine; his confrontation with Sheikh Khaz'al which, as we shall see, almost provoked an armed conflict with Britain; his relationship with the Soviet envoys, all the while making them aware that he was 'too much of a partriot ever to be a subservient instrument'.[114]

Reza Khan's physical attributes also served him well. He was a big-boned man, probably 6'3' (1.90m), a commanding height at any time but even more so for Iran of the 1920s, where he towered over everyone around him. His simplicity and natural dignity is commented on by many observers of the period.[115] At gatherings he often appeared aloof and detached, confirming that power demands a certain detachment. Reza Khan did not have a commanding voice and was never known as a captivating speaker. He exuded power but was by no means charismatic. He was a man of few words and seldom made long speeches. When he had to make a speech he was brief and to the point. At the ceremony for the laying of the first stone in construction of the University of Tehran his speech was confined to two sentences: 'The establishment of a university should have taken place earlier. Now that it has been started all efforts must be made for its speedy conclusion.'[116]

Almost all great men have great weaknesses, and Reza Khan was no exception. There were flaws in his character which would be accentuated as he aged and gathered greater power. By far the most serious of these flaws was his insatiable appetite for wealth. It was an anachronism which will be more fully discussed later. A simple man with simple tastes and a simple and austere life-style, he lived almost as an ascetic. He required no worldly possessions and had no time to enjoy them, yet there was a hunger and acquisitive urge to accumulate land. It is difficult to know the origins of this hunger. Qajar kings shared this insatiable appetite. Was it that from time immemorial land had symbolised power? Was Reza Shah merely following in the path of past rulers? Was it his own humble background and the years spent in near poverty? Was it that he felt it his due for services rendered to save a disintegrating country? The very first evidence of this inclination is an admission in October 1923 which on the surface appears innocent and even justifiable.

Loraine reported to Curzon:

> I saw Sardar Sepah on 24 October [a few days before his appointment as Prime Minister]. Spontaneously he made the following comments about his personal accounts and those of Ministry of War... [he said] he had been criticised in many quarters firstly for refusing to submit the Ministry's accounts for tax examination and secondly for amassing a personal fortune.

The reason he had declined was:

> ... he did not believe any of his compatriots were better qualified to undertake the task or to be superior in financial morality. He had been given a fixed yearly budget for the Ministry of War to maintain troops at a certain level of strength. He had been able to reduce expenditure in various ways and added 4,500 more troops. Since he became Minister of War he had saved the State 5 million tomans. The accusation that he had pocketed any money is false. He had however on two occasions taken money not as bribes but by force from wealthy families. 70,000 tomans from sons of Zell al Soltan and of this sum he had spent 30,000 tomans on the military school and had deposited the remainder in the bank... 30,000 tomans from Farmanfarma and had deposited it in another bank... these two sums to provide for the future of his six children... His

own modest expenses have been paid by the State. The accounts of the
Ministry of War are in perfect order.

Loraine added his own views:

> It reveals the difference between the character of Sardar Sepah and that
> of the vast majority of his compatriots. I am strongly disposed to accept
> it as true.[117]

In less than three years this relatively unknown soldier was about
to come to the centre of the political stage, dominate it for almost 20
years and even establish a new dynasty. The world he was entering
was totally alien to him and one for which he had no training or
experience. His military background hardly could have prepared
him for the labyrinthian world of Iranian politics with its intrigue,
ceaseless negotiating, deal making and ultimately, at best an unsatis-
factory compromise. As a Cossack officer, he had learned to give
concise orders and expect prompt compliance without question or
appeal. As will become evident he rose to the occasion.

NOTES ON CHAPTER 10
Further details of publications and documents in Bibliography

1   Mehdi Bamdad, *Tarikh Rejal Iran Quroun 12, 13, 14 (Dictionary of National Biography of Iran: Twelfth, Thirteenth, Fourteenth Centuries)*, vol. 1, pp 8–10; FO 416/98, Bullard to Halifax, 7 February 1940.
2   FO 371/7805, Loraine to Curzon, 30 March 1922.
3   Ghasem Ghani, *Yaddasht ha-e-Dr Ghasem Ghani (Memoirs of Dr Ghasem Ghani)*, vol. 1, pp 226–229; Mehdi Qoli Hedayat (Mokhber al Saltaneh), *Khaterat va Khatarat (Memoirs and Hazards)*, p 512. A great deal has been written about Teimurtash. Refer to Aqeli and Khajenouri in the Bibliography.
4   FO 371/7802, Loraine to Curzon, 30 January 1922.
5   FO 416/70, Loraine to Curzon, 7 March 1922.
6   FO 416/70, Loraine to Curzon, 13 May 1922.
7   FO 371/7805, Memorandum by Oliphant, 9 May 1922.
8   FO 416/70; Loraine to Curzon; 13 May 1922.
9   FO 371/7807, Loraine to Acting Secretary of State (Balfour), 18 June 1922.
10   *Ibid.*
11   Hosein Makki, *Tarikh Bist Saleh Iran (A Twenty Year History of Iran)*, vol. 2, p 235.
12   FO 416/69, Loraine to Curzon, 18 December 1921.
13   Gordon Waterfield, *Professional Diplomat: Sir Percy Loraine.*
14   FO 416/69, Loraine to Curzon, 22 December 1921.
15   FO 371/7802, Curzon to Loraine; 3 January 1922. The appearance of Armitage Smith in Bakhtiari territory is intriguing. Three months earlier he had been employed by the Government of Iran as Chief Financial Adviser. His contract had been cancelled and he had been given 41,000 tomans as severence pay. As a person of many talents he reappears now as a political emissary of APOC.
16   FO 371/7802, Loraine to Curzon, 4 January 1922.
17   *Ibid.*
18   FO 416/70, Loraine to Curzon, 11 January 1922.
19   FO 416/70, Curzon to Loraine, 18 January 1922.
20   FO 416/70, Loraine to Curzon, 23 January 1922.
21   FO 371/7804, Loraine to Curzon, 31 January 1922.
22   FO 371/7805, Loraine to Curzon, 20 February 1922.
23   FO 371/7806, Loraine to Curzon, 21 April 1922; Houshang Sabahi, *British Policy in Persia 1918–1925*, p. 162.
24   FO 371/7813, Loraine to Curzon, 24 June 1922.
25   FO 371/7816, Loraine to Curzon, 27 May 1922.
26   Mehdi Bamdad, *Tarikh Rejal Iran Quroun 12, 13, 14 (Dictionary of National Biography of Iran: Twelfth, Thirteenth, Fourteenth Centuries)*, vol. 1, pp 136–137.
27   FO 371/9024, Loraine to Curzon, 21 May 1923.
28   Mehdi Bamdad, *Tarikh Rejal Iran Quroun 12, 13, 14 (Dictionary of National Biography of Iran: Twelfth, Thirteenth, Fourteenth Centuries)*, vol. 1, p 476–479; Lord Hardinge, *Old Diplomacy*, p 65.
29   FO 371/10843, 15 October 1910 and November 1914.
30   FO 416/71, Loraine to Curzon, 20 September 1922.

31   The province was known as Khuzestan at least until the late Safavid period. From the beginning of the nineteenth century it gradually acquired the name Arabestan. It reverted to its ancient name in early 1925.
32   FO 416/70, Loraine to Curzon, 26 January 1922.
33   FO 371/7808, Loraine to Balfour, 3 July 1922.
34   FO 416/71, Loraine to Curzon, 20 September 1922.
35   FO 371/7809, Loraine to Curzon, 17 August 1922.
36   FO 416/71, Loraine to Curzon, 20 September 1922.
37   FO 371/7810, Loraine to Curzon, 21 September 1922.
38   FO 371/7810, Loraine to Curzon, 21 September 1922.
39   FO 371/7810, Loraine to Curzon, 24 September 1922.
40   FO 371/7830, Loraine to Curzon, 4 September 1922.
41   *Ibid.*
42   FO 371/9024, Loraine to Curzon, 10 January 1923. Allah Khan was the 'son of Haidar Khan of Hayat Davoud, a chieftain who for many years had had close and friendly relations with the British authorities and rendered notable assistance to the allied cause during the war'. Allah Khan had been arrested in Bushehr for discourtesy to an Iranian official who had accompanied Reza Khan in welcoming the return of Ahmad Shah from Europe. At the intercession of Loraine, Reza Khan released the son but inducted him into the army with the rank of captain provided Allah Khan could bring 100 men from his tribe into the army and promise never to show any discourtesy to any superior officer. Loraine convinced Allah Khan's father of the justice of the solution.
43   *Ibid.*
44   FO 416/72, Loraine to Curzon, 5 May 1923.
45   FO 371/9024, Loraine to Curzon, 21 May 1923.
46   FO 371/7802, Loraine to Curzon, 11 January 1922.
47   FO 1011/49, Loraine papers, Curzon to Loraine, 30 May 1922.
48   FO 416/70, Curzon to Loraine, 29 May 1922.
49   F 112/226A, Loraine to Curzon, 8 August 1922.
50   FO 371/9024, Loraine to Curzon, 19 and 23 May 1923.
51   FO 416/73, Loraine to Curzon, 24 May 1923.
52   FO 371/7807, Loraine to Curzon, 7 July 1922.
53   FO 371/7810 and 7811, Loraine to Cox and Cox to Loraine, 12, 13, 16, 17, 19 and 24 October 1922.
54   FO 371/9025, Loraine to Curzon, 30 August 1923.
55   FO 371/9025, Loraine to Curzon, 26 October 1923.
56   FO 1011/49, Loraine papers, Curzon to Loraine, 30 May 1922.
57   FO 1011/50, Loraine papers, Curzon to Loraine, 12 April 1923.
58   FO 371/9043, Minute by Curzon, 5 June 1923.
59   FO 371/9094, Loraine to Curzon, 4 February 1923.
60   FO 371/9043, Curzon to Loraine, 7 May 1923.
61   FO 416/72, Curzon to Loraine, 10 May 1923. Curzon adds, 'I am beginning to become tired of Persian suspicions... Persia is not the hub of the universe'. This from someone who was obsessed with Persia most of his life.
62   FO 371/7805, Loraine to Curzon, 15 April 1922.
63   FO 416/71, Loraine to Curzon, 11 October 1922.
64   FO 416/72, Loraine to Curzon, 2 April 1923.

65   FO 371/9052, Military Attaché report, 8 May 1923.

66   FO 371/9024, Loraine to Curzon, 17 May 1923.

67   FO 416/73, Loraine to Curzon, 28 May 1923.

68   FO 416/73, Curzon to Loraine, 5 June 1923.

69   FO 416/72, Loraine to Curzon, 1 June 1923.

70   FO 416/73, Loraine to Curzon, 4 June 1923.

71   FO 371/9024, Loraine to Curzon, 20 June 1923.

72   FO 416/73, Loraine to Curzon, 23 September 1923.

73   FO 416/73, Loraine to Curzon, 2 October 1923.

74   FO 371/9024, Loraine to Mosaddeq, Minister of Finance, 23 June 1923; FO 416/73, Curzon to Loraine, 22 June 1923.

75   FO 371/9052, Military Attaché to the War Office, 22 September 1923.

76   FO 371/7809, Cox to Loraine, 6 October 1922; FO 371/9046, Cox to Secretary for the Colonies, 13 April 1923; FO 371/9053, Loraine to Cox, 13 July 1923.

77   FO 416/72, Loraine to Curzon, 23 January 1923.

78   FO 416/112, Loraine to Curzon, Review of the year in 1923, January 1924.

79   FO/ 416/80, Bullard to Halifax, 7 February 1940.

80   FO 416/112, Loraine to Curzon, Review of the year 1922, January 1923.

81   A.C. Millspaugh, *The American Task Force in Persia*, pp 43, 200–201.

82   The first budget prepared by Millspaugh for the fiscal year 22 March 1923 to 21 March 1924 is as follows (in tomans): Shah, Vali'ahd and the court 675,000; salary of Mohammad Ali Shah, former king and father of Ahmad Shah, 75,000; the Cabinet and ministers 68,236; members of parliament, including the upkeep of the parliament building and employees 300,520; Ministry of Finance (excluding salaries and emoluments of the US team of advisers) 3,328,025; Ministry of Interior, including police other than Tehran police, 2,982,420; Tehran police 456,000; Ministry of War 9,000,000; Posts 1,066,300; Telegraph 812,638; Ministry of Foreign Affairs (excluding officials abroad) 699,220; Justice 455,230; Education 378,400; Trade and Public Works 1,136,869. When the budget was passed the monthly deficit was about 900,000 tomans. By the end of 1923, the deficit was reduced to 200,000 tomans and disappeared in 1924: FO 416/72, Loraine to Curzon, 4 April 1923.

83   A.C. Millspaugh published a second book after his second mission in the forties, *Americans in Persia*, wherein he literally retracts everything complimentary he had said in his earlier book about a number of Iranians, including Reza Shah. It is ironic that Millspaugh, who vents his rage against Reza Shah's autocracy, admits that he could not function properly in the relative open society of occupied Iran in the early forties where there were diverse factions and interest groups. Millspaugh's second mission 1943–1945 was an utter failure.

84   DoS 891.6363, Standard Oil 293, Tehran Legation to Secretary of State, 27 June 1923.

85   Michael A. Rubin, 'Open Door – The US In Persia and the Standard-Sinclair Oil Dispute', *Iranian Studies*, vol. 28, no. 3–4, Summer/Fall 1995, pp 203–229.

86   FO 371/9024, Loraine to Curzon, 24 February 1923.

87   FO 371/9024, Loraine to Curzon, 12 June 1923.

88   DoS, Kornfeld to Secretary of State, 30 June 1923.
89   Mohamad Taqi Bahar, *Tarikh Mokhtasar Ahzab Siasi* (*A Short History of Political Parties*), vol. 1, p 333. Mehdi Qoli Hedayat (Mokhber al Saltaneh), *Khaterat va Khatarat* (*Memoirs and Hazards*), p 453. Hosein Makki, *Tarikh Bist Saleh Iran* (*A Twenty Year History of Iran*), vol. 2, p 305. See also Baqer Aqeli, *Ruz Shomar Tarikh Iran* (*A Daily Calendar of the History of Iran*), vol. 1, p 178.
90   FO 416/73, Loraine to Curzon, 7 October 1923.
91   *Ibid.*
92   FO 371/9024, Loraine to Curzon, 3 September 1923.
93   FO 371/9024, Curzon to Loraine, 6 September 1923.
94   FO 371/9025, Loraine to Curzon, 8 September 1923.
95   FO 371/9025, Loraine to Curzon, 6 October 1923.
96   FO 416/73, Loraine to Curzon, 24 October 1923.
97   DoS no. 295, Kornfeld to US Secretary of State, 31 October 1923.
98   FO 416/73, Loraine to Curzon, 15 November 1923.
99   FO 416/73, Loraine to Curzon, 20 November 1923.
100   FO 371/9025, Loraine to Curzon, 23 October 1923.
101   FO 416/73, Loraine to Curzon, 24 October 1923.
102   FO 371/9025, Loraine to Curzon, 27 October 1923.
103   FO 416/73, Loraine to Curzon, 20 November 1923.
104   DoS, Quarterly Report, Kornfeld to Secretary of State, 20 January 1924.
105   FO 416/73, Loraine to Curzon, 28 October 1923.
106   FO 416/73, Loraine to Curzon, 30 October 1923.
107   FO 416/73, Loraine to Curzon, 31 October 1923.
108   L.P. Elwell-Sutton, 'Reza Shah the Great' in George Lenczowski (ed.), *Iran Under the Pahlavis*, p 23.
109   FO 416/70, Military Attaché to the Foreign Office, 22 January 1922.
110   FO 416/70, Loraine to Curzon, 2 March 1922.
111   FO 371/9024 Loraine to Curzon, 21 May 1923.
112   FO 371/7808, Loraine to Balfour, 3 July 1922.
113   Isaiah Berlin, *The Hedgehog and the Fox*.
114   FO 371/9024, Loraine to Curzon, 17 May 1923.
115   F.A.C. Forbes-Leith, Alexander Powell, Ironside, Loraine and Vincent Sheean.
116   Amin Banani, *The Modernisation of Iran*, p 40.
117   FO 416/73, Loraine to Curzon, 15 November 1923.

11

Reza Khan as Prime Minister and the Movement for a Republic

From early 1922 Reza Khan had been regarded as the Prime Minister-in-waiting. It is also fairly clear that Reza Khan saw himself in the same light at least as early as the first anniversary of the coup in February 1922. For someone who had more than 18 months to contemplate the composition of his cabinet Reza Khan's selection of ministers was less than inspired. Most were of mediocre talent and were not to add much lustre to his reputation. Four of the ministers were selected purely in settlement of political debts. These four were members of the Socialist faction in parliament who had supported Reza Khan's build-up of the armed forces and attempts to establish internal security. The *de facto* leader of this group, Soleiman Mirza (Eskandari), was to serve as Minister of Education. He genuinely believed in social and economic reform but was hampered by a meagre education and being poorly read. He was also burdened with the unreasonably low budget of 378,400 tomans for the fiscal year 1923–1924. Soleiman Mirza* was obstinate, dictatorial and difficult to work with and accomplished nothing in his brief tenure. Abol Hassan Mo'azed al Saltaneh (Pirnia)† became Minister of Justice. Mo'azed al Saltaneh had become a close ally of Reza Khan and as the cousin of Hassan and Hosein Pirnia commanded a certain amount of respect, though he never attained the stature of his cousins, nor was he an able administrator. Amanollah Ez al Mamalek (Ardalan),# Minister of Public Works, was selected because he was close to Soleiman Mirza and was a tribal grandee of bygone days

---

* Soleiman Mirza (Soleiman Mohsen Eskandari), c.1870–1943, was the great grandson of Abbas Mirza, son of Fath Ali Shah. He began his career at the Police Department in Tehran and later transfered to Customs Administration. In 1909 he was elected to the Second Parliament and gained prominence when he voted to reject the Russian ultimatum that Shuster be removed, for which he was arrested and exiled to Qom by the regent Naser al Molk. He was re-elected to the Third Parliament, but was forced to flee to Baghdad and later to Constantinople as he sided with the German-Ottoman axis. He returned to western Iran in 1917 to incite tribes to hamper British war efforts; was arrested by British forces and exiled to India. He was allowed to return in 1920 and was elected to the Fourth and Fifth Parliaments. After a brief tenure at the Ministry of Education between October 1923 and April 1924, for which he was ill-suited, he effectively retired from politics. In October 1927, on the tenth anniversary of the Russian Revolution he went to Moscow in a semi-official capacity after which he remained in Europe until 1930. In the late 1930s in order to make a living he opened a grocery shop in Tehran. In September 1941, after Reza Shah's abdication, he was elected Chairman of the newly-formed Communist (Tudeh) Party in Iran.[1]

† Abol Hassan Khan Mo'azed al Saltaneh (Pirnia), c.1878–c.1939, was the nephew of Nasrollah Khan Moshir al Dowleh, former Minister of Foreign Affairs and Prime Minister. He served at the Iranian Consulate in Baku between 1901 and 1906, returned to Iran and was active in the constitutional struggle. After the shelling of parliament in 1908 he took refuge at the British Legation. He travelled to Europe, was elected to the Second Parliament in 1909, allied himself with the Democrat faction and later was close to the Socialists. In 1911 he was Minister of Post and Telegraph, and after a brief term as Minister of Justice in Reza Khan's first Cabinet served as Governor of Yazd, Kerman and Fars. He retired in 1936.[2]

Haji Amanollah Khan Ez al Mamalek (Ardalan), c.1888–c.1977, was the son of a Kurdish grandee. He was elected to the Second Parliament. Close to Soleiman Mirza, he left Iran in 1915 and remained in Turkey for the duration of the war. He was elected to the Fifth Parliament, and after his short tenure as Minister of Public Works he became Governor of Astarabad (Gorgan) in 1928, Governor of Lurestan in 1932, Gilan in 1933, Lurestan in 1934 and Bushehr and the Persian Gulf ports in 1935. His last posting during Reza Shah's rule was Governor of Kerman. From 1942 he held several Cabinet posts and later was appointed to the Senate.[3]

with a dignified demeanour. His administrative skills, however, were limited. Lastly, Qasem Sur Esrafeel,[§] Acting Minister of Interior, had secure Socialist credentials as well as a constitutionalist pedigree.

Reza Khan owed a great deal to the Socialists. They were the only organised faction which had supported him from the very beginning of the Fourth Parliament. They had stood in opposition to Moddares who had by then become the leader of the anti-Reza Khan faction. He had to reward the Socialists or it would have discouraged their crucial support in the coming struggles to consolidate his power. In demonstrating his loyalty Reza Khan compromised the standards of his Cabinet. Political compromise at this stage of his career was a necessity.

Reza Khan's difficulties with his first Cabinet were not merely the elevation of the four Socialists to cabinet rank. Two other appointments were also potential risks. Mahmoud Jam, who had served in Seyyed Zia's Cabinet, was designated Minister of Finance. Feelings still ran high against Seyyed Zia, and Jam's collaboration with him did not sit well with those whom Seyyed Zia had imprisoned. Fortunately for Reza Khan the Fifth Parliament was not to convene until February and by then Jam's pleasing demeanour and geniality enabled him to overcome any lingering bitterness. More hostility was to be expected by the appointment of Hosein Adl al Molk (Dadgar) as Assistant Prime Minister. Dadgar had served as Acting Minister of Interior in Seyyed Zia's Cabinet and had been closely involved in the arrest and detention of notables. He was roundly disliked and after Seyyed Zia's fall there had been a serious move to arrest him. Dadgar had fled to Qom where he was given asylum at the holy shrine. On his return to Tehran his credentials were rejected by the Fourth Parliament, to which he had been elected and he was denied his seat. As in Jam's case there was a passage of some four months between Dadgar's cabinet appointment and the opening of parliament, and his efforts during that period to ingratiate himself with newly-elected members of parliament bore fruit and made him less

---

§ Qasem Sur Esrafeel (Sur), c.1880–c.1940, was born in Tabriz the son of Mirza Hassan Khan, a minor court official who was the founder of the influential journal *Sur Esrafeel* of decidedly pro-constitutionalist sympathy with socialist leanings. The journal was soon suppressed by Mohammad Ali Shah in 1909 and its editor hanged. The young Qasem was elected to the Second and Third Parliaments. During the war he settled in Turkey. Upon return he became an active member of the Socialist Party. He served in several government posts during Reza Shah's rule: Minister of Post and Telegraph 1928–1932; Governor of Gilan and later Esfahan, 1933–1937; acting head of Tehran municipality, 1938–1939.[4]

objectionable. Jam and Dadgar were to serve Reza Khan for 18 and 12 years respectively and both rose to greater heights. Jam was to become Prime Minister and Dadgar President of parliament from the seventh to the ninth sessions. Dadgar left Iran in 1935 amidst rumours of bribery in the sale of government lands in Gilan.

The most laudable and significant appointment was the selection of Mohammad Ali Zoka al Molk (Foroughi)* as Minister of Foreign Affairs. Foroughi had held several previous cabinet posts. He had served in the Second Parliament briefly as its President and had acquired a reputation for probity and sagacity. He was also a cultured

---

* Mohammad Ali Foroughi (Zoka al Molk), 1873–1942, was the son of the learned Mohammad Hosein (Zoka al Molk) who had served as the head of the Translation Bureau of the State Printing Office under Naser al Din Shah. He had dabbled in writing poetry using the pen name Foroughi (which his son adopted as the family name). In 1907 after the death of his father the title Zoka al Molk was conferred on Mohammad Ali. The young Foroughi had intended to study medicine, abandoned it in favour of physics but soon became the editor of Tarbiyat (Education), a journal his father had founded. Tarbiyat was one of the foremost journals of the later Qajar period and enjoyed considerable influence amongst a select group of educated Iranians. In 1906 he joined the semi-secret society of Jame-e-Adamiyat (Humanist Society) which had been active in the constitutional movement since Naser al Din Shah's death. It was modelled after a masonic lodge, complete with secret oaths and rituals. The society was disbanded with the shelling of parliament in 1908. Soon afterwards Foroughi, together with several Iranian notables and some French expatriates working in Iran, formed the first official Freemason's Lodge in Iran, Reveil de l'Iran (the Awakening of Iran). The Lodge continued to support the constitutional cause and soon had as members many of the learned elite. Between 1910 and 1911 Foroughi served as a special tutor to the minor Ahmad Shah with little discernable result. Foroughi was elected a member of the Second Parliament (1909–1911). Through the influence of his masonic brethren he served briefly as President of parliament. After the forced closing of parliament over the Shuster affair Foroughi was appointed Minister of Justice in various cabinets between 1911 and 1915 while teaching a course at the Political Science College. Between ministerial positions he served on the Court of Appeals, the highest court in Iran. In 1919 he was the ranking member of the Iranian delegation to the Paris Peace Conference headed by Moshaver al Mamalek. On his return he served several times as Minister of Foreign Affairs between 1923 and 1924; Minister of Finance, 1924–1925; Acting Prime Minister, 1925; Prime Minister 1925–1926; Minister of War, 1927; Ambassador to Turkey, 1928, where he negotiated a binding settlement of Iranian-Turkish frontiers; Minister of National Economy, 1930; Foreign Minister, 1931; Prime Minister, 1932 until forced to resign on 3 December 1935.

CONTINUED OVER PAGE

man of letters who had made considerable contributions to learning. As Minister of Post and Telegraph Reza Khan appointed Brig. Khodayar Khan (Khodayar),† an intimate and comrade from his early days in the Cossack Brigade. The appointment was a manifestation of Reza Khan's recognition and reward to the army officer cadre. Khodayar Khan remained close to Reza Khan during his entire rule and continued to serve him in various capacities. Other than blind loyalty to his master, Khodayar had no special qualifications for a ministerial post.

The lack of any political ideology or specific economic and social agenda would haunt Reza Khan in the months ahead. In time the blueprint for rebuilding Iran would come from outside the Cabinet. Since the end of the war there was a small but articulate class who understood Western culture and the tremendous advances made in the West. They also had a political conscience and wrote articles and

---

Mohammad Ali Foroughi CONTINUED FROM PREVIOUS PAGE
Foroughi was one of the founders and Chairman of the Farhangestan (Academy of Iranian Culture) until he fell foul of Reza Khan in 1935, when he resigned. Between 1936 and August 1941 Foroughi devoted his time to literary pursuits. On 25 August 1941, with the invasion of Iran by Russian and British forces, Reza Shah had to turn once again to Foroughi, who became Prime Minister on 28 August. Foroughi played a key role in maintaining stability and continuity after Reza Shah's abdication and the passing of the Crown to Mohammad Reza Shah, and in the conclusion of the tripartite agreement among Great Britain, the Soviet Union and Iran which ensured the evacuation of foreign troops from Iranian soil at the war's end. He resigned as Prime Minister and briefly served as Mohammad Reza Shah's second Minister of Court. He was Ambassador designate to Washington DC in 1942, when he died of a heart attack.[5]

† Khodayar Khan Khodayar (also referred to as Khodayari), c.1873–c.1950, joined the Cossacks in 1892–93, attained the rank of Major in 1906, acquired some popularity by his resignation from the Cossack Brigade over the shelling of parliament in 1908 but was reemployed in 1909. By 1917 he had been promoted to the rank of Colonel, but was forced to retire by Starosselsky for alleged financial malfeasance. He joined Reza Khan in the coup of February 1921, rejoined the Cossacks and was promoted to the rank of Brigadier General in the unified army. Reza Khan was also instrumental in his appointment as Governor of Qazvin. After heading the Ministry of Post and Telegraph he was appointed Director of Military Conscription, 1929–1930 and Director of the Army Bank (later Bank Sepah). Thereafter he served as the principal administrator of Reza Shah's ever-growing estate, becoming a large landowner himself in the process. One of the few intimates of Reza Khan who remained in favour. He acted as an intermediary in 1923, asking for the hand of Esmat Dowlatshahi on behalf of Reza Khan.[6]

pamphlets arguing against social injustice and the deplorable economic conditions in Iran. The most influential among them was Ali
Akbar Davar,* who had returned to Iran a few months after the
coup in June 1921 after almost 11 years in Switzerland. His return

---

* Ali Akbar Davar, 1885–1937, was the son of a minor court official,
  Kalbali Khan Khazen al Khalvat, who served as the custodian of the
  family quarters of Mozaffar al Din Shah and had been able to enroll his
  son at the prestigious Dar al Fonoun (polytechnic) in 1900 to study medicine. Davar changed his field of study to law, graduating in 1908. He
  joined the Ministry of Justice in 1909 as a judge in the Provincial Court;
  received quick promotions and by 1910 had become the Public
  Prosecutor of Tehran. While a government employee he began writing in
  a newly-published newspaper, *Sharq* (*The East*), edited by Seyyed Zia.
  His articles were generally unfavourable to the government of the day,
  critical of some cabinet ministers and for the most part approving of
  Democrat Party members in parliament.
      In late 1910 Davar volunteered to be minder and supervisor to two
  young sons of a wealthy Tabriz merchant, Haji Ebrahim (Panahi), who
  were being sent to study in Switzerland. After perfecting his French he
  entered the University of Geneva, where he received a graduate degree
  on the eve of World War I. Davar never completed his doctoral thesis but
  immersed himself in the study of Western literature, philosophy and
  especially the writings of contemporary social commentators. While in
  Geneva he campaigned for Iran's representation at the Paris Peace
  Conference and the right of its representatives to be heard. He also
  formed an activist committee of Iranians campaigning against the 1919
  Agreement.
      He returned to Iran in 1921. In January 1923 he started the news-
  paper *Mard-e-Azad* (*The Free Man*). Soon thereafter he formed the Radical
  Party which attracted several hundred members. Davar had the major
  role in the constituent assembly of December 1925 which amended the
  constitution, allowing the passage of the Crown to Reza Khan. He wrote
  the relevant amendments and argued for their approval in open session
  of the assembly. He was appointed Minister of Public Works, December
  1925–June 1926 and resigned his seat in parliament. He demonstrated
  his skills by drafting laws for the construction of railways and establishment of a school of commerce. In February 1927 he was appointed
  Minister of Justice, where he showed immense organisational abilities
  and feverish energy. He revamped the Ministry and the Judicial system
  and established several committees composed of the most learned jurists
  of the day to draft a new civil code. The outcome after five years (1927–
  1932) was a masterpiece of draftsmanship. In March 1933 he headed the
  Iranian delegation to the League of Nations in Geneva where he defended
  Iran's cancellation of the 1901 oil agreement. Davar was appointed Minister of Finance in September 1933. Reza Shah was demanding miracles
  and was oblivious to the toll it was taking on the exhausted and nearly
  spent Davar. The sheer strain of 12 years of overwork and Reza Shah's
  ever more autocratic demands and taunts led Davar to commit suicide
  on 10 February 1937.[7]

shortly followed Seyyed Zia's fall. Soon afterwards he was employed at the Ministry of Education as Director General, the third highest position in the ministry. A fortuitous marriage to the widowed daughter of a grandee, Mohsen Khan Moshir al Dowleh, former Ambassador and Foreign Minister, enabled Davar to be elected to the Fourth Parliament and reelected to the fifth and sixth. His meticulous preparation for parliamentary debates, reliance on logic and presence of mind soon made him one of the most effective and prominent deputies.

Davar had begun a newspaper in early 1923 called *Mard-e-Azad* (*The Free Man*), borrowing the name from the Paris newspaper started by Georges Clemenceau. From 28 January to November 1923 he wrote a daily column wherein he expounded his political, social and economic principles, which greatly influenced key political figures, most notably Teimurtash and Firouz. His simple language, lucid style and clear logic made his writings popular, and they soon came to the attention of Reza Khan and his circle of advisers. Davar was one of the few people of the era with fully developed ideas and specific programmes. He had great resilience of thought and probably one of the keenest minds of the time. His vision for Iran appears to have been based on the humanist traditions of Western Europe. His main thesis was that the economic regeneration of the country must be the first item on a government's agenda. Eradicating poverty and lifting the standard of living should take precedence over other reforms. One of the first steps should be the construction of railways linking villages and remote areas with commercial and population centres so that the peasant and labourer could sell his produce or receive a decent wage.

A sample of Davar's line of reasoning, loosely translated would be: Iran is no worse-off than it was 50 years ago. It is the outside world which has progressed. When people worked with their hands and used animals for transportation there was not much difference between Europe and Iran. The advent in the West of the industrial revolution and the building of roads and railways condemned Iran to a hopeless state of affairs. While this revolution was taking place Iranians were asleep. When we opened our eyes we saw two able-bodied uninvited Europeans on either side of our bed. We recognised the intrusion but did nothing. We only have a few years before Britain and Russia will again carve up Iran into zones of influence and relegate us to abject poverty. What did Japan do some 40 years ago? Did they write odes or sonnets? Did they use their prayer beads to fortell what awaited them? Did they curse their rulers and shout that foreigners were an obstacle to putting their house in order?

They understood that they had to build a railway system and then schools, universities and hospitals.

In later editorials Davar wrote:

> Until we dedicate ourselves to an economic revolution nothing will move or change. We shall remain a nation of beggars, hungry and in ragged clothing, and we shall continue to suffer. We have 6,000 years of history, but that will not translate into factories, railroads, hospitals or schools. Schools alone without economic reforms will change nothing as long as the environment outside the schools continues to reek of poverty. There must be some elements of prosperity before universities and libraries can fulfill their functions. When we have at least 5,000 kilometres of railways, 50 factories, 50 roads linking east and west, dams on the Karun river, and have eradicated locusts, we can attend to the graduation of 1,000 students from institutions of higher learning.[8]

In subsequent writings Davar strongly endorsed Reza Khan as the leader who could fulfill the aspirations of Iranians and effect a material change in the welfare of the masses. He lauded Reza Khan for his attempts to create a strong central government which was a prerequisite for the realisation of the reforms he advocated.

In early 1923 Davar formed the Radical Party, which soon attracted some 300 members, almost all of whom were considered educated by the standards of the day and a few of whom had received higher education abroad. Many were later to hold leading positions in government. In May 1923 Davar published a manifesto setting out the programme of the party. It was the first attempt by an Iranian political party to articulate a detailed programme. The manifesto had 32 clauses, the most important of which were: strengthening the constitutional form of government; elections by secret ballot; separation of religion and politics; abolition of capitulations; all citizens to be equal and protected under the law; effecting an economic revival of Iran by an industrial and agricultural revolution, substituting newly-manufactured machinery for the obsolete tools presently in use; enactment of laws with respect to agriculture, industry and commerce in keeping with a developing economy.[9]

There were also voices from Iranians abroad. Their common theme was the attempt to awaken national consciousness amongst Iranians. Foremost among them was Hosein Kazemzadeh, a journalist from Tabriz with a clerical background who was prominent among the Iranian nationalist expatriates in Europe. He had settled in Berlin at the end of the First World War and from 1922–1927 published a journal called 'Iranshahr' (a Sassanian name for Iran). It exerted a powerful influence on the formulation and propagation of nationalist themes. The front page of the journal usually had an illustration of a pre-Islamic site such as Darius's tomb, Persepolis or Sarvestan. The journal was distributed in Iran and had a relatively large readership. Kazemzadeh argued that Iranians, irrespective of what part of the country they came from, must identify themselves only as Iranians and the practice of identification with regions and cities should be discouraged. Local dialects and customs must be eliminated and only the Persian language should be taught in schools. In one of the articles he argued:

> The problem of communalism is so serious that whenever an Iranian travelling abroad is asked his nationality, he will give his locality, not the proud name of his country. We must eliminate local sects, local dialects, local clothes, local customs and local sentiments.[10]

Kazemzadeh advocated an emphasis on secular education, elevating the status of women and the importation of Western technology. He further argued that Iran's backwardness originated from the Arab invasions of the seventh century and 'the country could not progress until it had freed itself from the shackles of superstition and reactionary clergy'.[11] In another article he asserted that 'clerical dogmatism, political despotism and foreign imperialism, especially early Arab imperialism had retarded the creative abilities of Iranians'.[12]

In an important and lengthy article, Kazemzadeh argued that Iranians needed an ideology if they were to overcome the backward state of their country. Religion cannot and should not be the ideal social motivator. Religion is a divine, sacred and personal matter and once it interferes in matters of state, it will be deprived of its sacredness. In later articles Kazemzadeh advocated a nationalist ideology of patriotism and secularism as the sole means of salvation for Iran.[13]

Earlier, in Germany, Seyyed Hassan Taqizadeh and a group of students had published a journal *Kaveh* named after the legendary blacksmith who had overthrown a despotic Shah. *Kaveh* had printed articles on the history of the constitutional movement in Iran and the development of socialism in Europe, including the growth of Marxism. Its principal focus, however, was on the need for national independence and internal reform. As one typical editorial had stressed, 'the only way Iran could leave behind the dark middle ages was to follow the Western experience of separating religion from politics and introducing scientific rational knowledge into public education...'[14]

There were nationalist publications in Tehran as well, most notably *Ayandeh* (*The Future*), which was founded by Mahmoud Afshar, a literary critic and poet later to be educated in Europe as a political scientist. He advocated the elimination of local dialects, emphasising a common language and universal free education.[15] Some political parties also stressed the same issues. The Socialist Party published literary journals, established literacy classes and groups to advance the education of women. In addition to pursuing its policy of an egalitarian society and nationalisation of means of production, the party was in favour of a strong central government, secular education, emancipation of women and uniting the people into a nationally conscious population.[16]

In April 1921 a cultural society under the name of Iran Javan (Young Iran) had been formed by some Iranians from prominent families, most of whom had received some form of Western education. Their manifesto emphasised the following for the advancement of Iran: the abrogation of capitulation; construction of a railway system; an independent policy on customs tariffs; emancipation of women; sending students, both men and women, abroad; revision of criminal laws; expansion of educational facilities with special attention to secondary, technical and industrial schools; depriving the illiterate of the right to vote; establishment of museums, libraries and theatres; adopting the useful and compatible aspects of European culture.[17]

These writers, publications and organisations had a common theme. Iran had been on a steady decline since the Arab invasion. Russia and Britain, motivated by greed, had subsequently exacerbated this decline. After 100 years of retrogression and humiliation by the imperialist powers the only remedy was to awaken and strengthen nationalist sentiments and ideology. Iranians had to be made aware of their ancient heritage. The corollary of this thesis was that a strong central government was necessary. These propositions created a community of interest amongst the intelligensia. They all wanted a strong central government with a patriotic and proven leader at the helm.[18] As Taqizadeh later was to explain:

> A great leader [Reza Khan] appeared and took the destiny of his country in his hand, [to work towards] a great many of the ideals [of which] the first Constitutional Revolutionary period once dreamed.[19]

There was disagreement as to strategy, tactics and social and economic policies to best achieve the desired goal but Reza Khan was the only person on the horizon and the only name mentioned as the leader.

The population as a whole was nationalist in terms of cultural identity and of being anti-British or anti-Russian but it was hardly nationalist in the modern sense. This development would occur only with the significant social and political changes under Reza Shah, particularly with the expansion of the new professional middle class.

There was disagreement among those who were close to Reza Khan or had his attention. The Socialists, including their representatives in the Cabinet, wanted eventually an egalitarian society through nationalisation of all means of production including agriculture; a controlled economy; taxes on income, wealth and inheritence. Davar and his Radical Party members advocated a semi-welfare state. Teimurtash, who was to become close to Reza Khan by early 1924, supported a capitalist economy at least for the beginning of Reza Khan's rule. In a letter to Taqizadeh written shortly after the inclusion of Socialists in Reza Khan's first Cabinet, Teimurtash stated:

> We must adopt a capitalist economic policy for the time being. When its negative aspects emerge, that is to say when it encroaches on the rights of workers and farmers, then one can begin to consider sharing the wealth of the country in a more equitable manner and ultimately convert the nation into a socialist state. But now that Iran is impoverished, it makes no sense to distribute that poverty more widely...[20]

Reza Khan was not oblivious to the debate on the economic and social course Iran was to take. The outcry that writers were generating for a secular state and a fresh beginning with acknowledgement that Reza Khan was the only logical contender to lead the nation must have pleased him immensely. But Reza Khan was not a political theorist. He had no master plan for rebuilding Iran and no scheme by which he would dispose of the secular/religious dilemma.

> Reza Shah had two overriding goals that were for him so inseparable as to be one and the same thing. He wanted to restore some of the greatness of Iran and to establish for himself absolute power within the reconstructed nation. His pursuit of these goals was determined and ruthless; any force that stood in the way of his achievement was mercilessly attacked and, so far as possible, destroyed. Thus the independence of the tribes, the strength of the landowners, the Qajar Court... all were subject to his attacks. Inevitably clerical power, too, had to be reduced.[21]

Reza Khan was not the leader of an organised party or even a group with a given ideology. 'He was in fact the product of the failure and [what he believed to be] futility of such movements in Iran. He embodied the impatience of men of action with the endless debates of the articulate reformers.'[22] The circumstances of his rise to power and the success of his leadership of the coup in 1921 could not have made him sympathetic to theoreticians who advocated a gradualist approach to political problems. But he was totally dedicated to nationalism, which was an assertion of complete independence, free from foreign interference and influence. He could accomplish this prime goal by putting an end to tribal independence which was threatening the unity and territorial integrity of Iran. Thereafter the independence of Iran could be maintained 'by the rapid adoption of the material advances of the West and a breakdown of the traditional power of religion and a growing tendency towards secularism'.[23]

By the time Reza Khan ascended the throne in December 1925 there was a consensus that if a nation were to have long-term success, cultural continuity and historical traditions must be combined with and grafted onto new ideas, practices and technology from the West. Under the auspices of Teimurtash the membership of the Iran Javan Society had increased considerably by 1925. Their programme, which was less ambitious than the manifesto of the Radical Party, gradually became the programme of successive governments under Reza Shah and as we shall see most of its provisions were enacted into law or were implemented in practice.

For the time being Reza Khan had more immediate problems. As head of government he had to deal with a wide range of issues beyond military matters. The most vexing were outstanding questions concerning the Soviet Union and Britain. By early 1923 Moscow had begun to look more favourably on Reza Khan's rise to power. This had come about for several reasons. First it was decided that Iran was not ripe for a Communist revolution. Secondly Reza Khan was seen as the leader of a national liberation movement which would drastically reduce British influence in Iran, and as the leader of a semi-bourgeois liberation movement he represented a transitional period in Iran's historical development.[24] The foremost Soviet Party theoretician Karl Radek wrote in 1923:

> For the Soviet Government, it is completely unnecessary to create in Persia artificial Soviet Republics. Its real interests in Persia consist in the fact that Persia should not become a base for an attack on Baku... The form of government in Persia, the solution of the Persian agrarian question [the labour problem barely existed yet] will be exclusively the concern of the Persian people and the spiritual influence of the Persian Communists...[25]

During negotiations on the Anglo-Soviet trade agreement which had begun in late 1920 one of the conditions Britain had insisted upon was that the Soviet Government refrain:

> ... from any attempt by military or diplomatic or any other form of action or propaganda to encourage any of the peoples in Asia in any form of hostile action against British interests or the British Empire, especially in Asia Minor, Persia, Afghanistan and India.

The Soviets were not prepared to accept such a clause as it would have meant the virtual acceptance of British predominance in the countries mentioned for an unlimited period. The Soviets in turn asked for a similar clause whereby Britain would undertake the same obligation in these countries and also in all parts of the Russian Empire. In later discussions Moscow further insisted that the contracting parties reciprocally undertake to respect the independence and integrity of Iran, Afghanistan and the territory of the newly emerging Turkey. As a compromise it was agreed to exclude both the Soviet proposal with respect to Iran, Afghanistan and Turkey and any mention of Iran as one of the countries where British predominance and interests were to be specifically respected.[26] The agreement was finally signed on 16 March 1921.

The Soviet leaders felt somewhat relieved that Britain no longer considered Iran in its exclusive sphere of influence. They also felt free to engage in a propaganda campaign against Britain in Iran. Newspaper articles became the principal means of waging the campaign. Between 1921 and 1927 successive Soviet Ministers to Tehran financed various newspapers, and the intensity of their attacks on Britain remained one of the recurrent complaints of Loraine, who requested that the Iranian Government close these publications.[27] In the summer of 1923 the Government of Pirnia closed three newspapers. The Soviet Minister gave asylum to the editors of all three. In September of the same year the Government was forced to relent and permit the suspended newspapers to resume publication. These papers played an important part in the events of late 1924 when Reza Khan began to take decisive steps against Sheikh Khaz'al.

Reza Khan's pursuit of an independent policy of unification of the army and expulsion of British military officers further convinced the Soviet authorities that he would continue along the same lines with an independent foreign policy, and that Britain's influence would be undermined. From the very beginning of Reza Khan's premiership the Soviets began to cultivate him and give him sporadic support.

What became and remained a special concern of Reza Khan during his entire rule were economic relations between the Soviet Union and Iran. The traditional dependence of northern Iran on Russian markets which had increased considerably from 1921 was to continue as a most vexing problem. By 1925 Iran was the largest exporter of goods from Asia to the Soviet Union.[28] Despite this economic dependence a commercial treaty which had been in the process of negotiation from late 1921 had not been fully concluded. In July 1924, with a final agreement in view, Reza Khan recalled the Iranian trade delegation in Moscow. It was felt that the Russians had been uncompromising and had not eased restrictions or given enough guarantees for the development of trade between the two countries. Although an interim agreement was reached in 1925 it was not until October 1927 that trade relations were stabilised and a comprehensive agreement signed.[29]

Relations with Britain had improved but there were still many contentious issues. Most of these were to be raised by Loraine time and again but were not to be settled for another two years. However, in repeated meetings among Loraine, Reza Khan, and/or members of his Cabinet the most important and particularly volatile issue was not raised. Loraine knew that sooner or later there would be some sort of military action by Reza Khan against the Bakhtiari Khans and even more important against Sheikh Khaz'al. He realised that Reza Khan could not survive politically unless he brought the last remaining autonomous tribal leaders under the authority of the Central Government. He had not been in favour of Reza Khan becoming Prime Minister for several reasons, the ostensible one being that he doubted the wisdom of a military man as head of government.[30] Loraine's real reservation, although unspoken, was that as Prime Minister Reza Khan would have fewer restraining influences to check his plans to subdue the southern tribes.

Almost contemporaneous with Reza Khan becoming Prime Minister an important event took place in Britain. In December 1923 the Conservatives lost the general election and Ramsey MacDonald became the first Labour Prime Minister. MacDonald chose to serve as his own Foreign Secretary and Curzon effectively retired from politics. Curzon's disappearance from the political arena was an unsought prize for Reza Khan. As we shall see both he and Loraine were to have greater freedom of action in dealing with traditional British tribal protegés in Iran.

In one of the earliest telegrams to MacDonald, Loraine brought him up to date and acquainted him with existing problems. The question of Reza Khan's designs on the southern tribes concerned Loraine enough for him to complain bitterly. It had been believed that if Reza Khan came to power Britain could settle most of the outstanding problems. He was known as a decisive and fair person but had proven to be more difficult than his predecessors. Loraine accused Reza Khan of:

> ... taking advantage of our forebearance. If you give him any leeway he takes all. He must be told he cannot have everything. He does not understand any barriers to his own activity unless they are made perfectly clear to him... He has a shrewd notion of the strength of the other man's hand and will always call it rather than risk being bluffed.[31]

Loraine then enumerated the outstanding issues, foremost being: the debt supposedly owed by Iran for arms and munitions; salaries of the British military personel sent to Iran; and expenses of Britain's naval mission under the 1919 Agreement. Loraine also listed anti-British acts and policies intended to discourage British commercial enterprises, such as granting an oil concession to a US company; inviting a US company to build railways and refusing to discuss the claims of the British-owned Persian Railway Syndicate for their survey in 1913; plans to purchase wireless telegraph apparatus from the Russians and trucks from Germany; discussions with France to build wireless stations; eviction of British doctors from Iranian Government hospitals; rejecting claims of a British national for navigation rights on Lake Urumieh; appointment of an Iranian to replace a British Director General of Posts; failure to settle claims of the Imperial Bank; disclaiming responsibility for British victims of robberies on Iranian roads; failure to apply uniform tariffs on all frontiers; plans to cancel extraterritorial rights (capitulation); talk of levying taxes on foreign nationals working in Iran; non-recognition of the Government of Iraq; failure to stop anti-British 'outbursts' in the press. Loraine even complained about the Persian Cabinet's 'modification of courtesy titles when addressing foreign representatives in the Persian language'. What Loraine was disheartened by was the halting of the Qajar court's practice of using the same florid and ornamental forms of address for foreign envoys as they used for high-ranking Iranians. He concluded his report by saying that Reza Khan has been helped so far by Britain's silence and forebearance. Now that 'he is the master and central authority... he ignores British interests... we must make clear to him about our interests'.[32]

Loraine had called on Reza Khan shortly after he had become Prime Minister. On 15 November 1923 Reza Khan, accompanied by Foroughi, the Minister of Foreign Affairs, returned the call. Reza Khan had stated he wanted the best of friendly relations with Great Britain and if any difficulties were to arise, Loraine should feel free to discuss the matters with him or Foroughi.[33] Discussions with Foroughi yielded no results and another meeting was arranged with Reza Khan on 13 February 1924. Loraine raised the issue of Iran's indebtedness to Britain. He added that if Reza Khan were willing to admit that money was owed to Britain he would be willing to do everything possible to reach a settlement that was compatible with Iran's capacity to pay. Loraine next suggested the formation of a 'mixed commission' with representatives of both countries to discuss the matter. Reza Khan did not acknowledge any debt and argued that Britain had extended financial assistance to Iranian

Governments which Britain herself had brought to power, but agreed to the formation of a mixed commission. Reza Khan concluded by saying that in no event would Iran acknowledge a debt for the transfer of arms and munitions to Iran.[34]

The first meeting of the commission was on 16 February with Loraine and Reza Khan in attendance. Reza Khan opened the meeting and said he had heard Loraine was upset because Iran did not accept any claims of payment for arms and munitions, and went on to state that there had been no such sale, merely a voluntary transfer of some obsolete rifles. Loraine answered that over the past year he had invited Iranian representatives to examine the records of such sales but no one had bothered to do so. Loraine then recounted that as early as eighteen months before Reza Khan himself had promised to settle Britain's claims with respect to military expenditures in Iran. Now as Prime Minister he should be able to address himself to all matters involving Britain and Iran. Reza Khan responded that he had not sought the position and had been content to remain as Minister of War. He now had the burden of resolving matters which his predecessors had initiated. Reza Khan then shifted the conversation to the overall relationship between Britain and Iran. He asked whether the recent change of government in Britain had altered Britains's policy towards Iran. Would the policy of Britain remain the same and continue to treat the issue of Iran's indebtedness in a 'cold official manner and try to drive a hard bargain or would Britain be prepared to sit down and discuss these matters in a friendly way and take into account what the Persians have to say?' Reza Khan emphasised how Iran had changed in the past three years. He had restored internal security which should mean a great deal to Britain. These changes should be important enough for Britain to revise its policy and forego any financial claims it alleged to have. Loraine stated that the attitude of the British Government would depend on the report he was to prepare for his Prime Minister. Loraine therefore pleaded with Reza Khan to take the matter of a joint commission seriously allowing the two parties to discuss and settle outstanding claims.[35]

In an earlier meeting with the British Military Attaché, Col. M. Saunders, Reza Khan had informed him that he had sent troops to Baluchestan and talks were taking place between his Commander and the Baluchi tribal chief Doost Mohammad Khan for the latter's peaceful submission to central authority. Reza Khan had further stated that he was anxious to take over the entire responsibility for guarding the oil fields and abolish the existing arrangements under which the Bakhtiaris provided guards and received payment from

APOC. Reza Khan expressed great satisfaction at Britain's recognition of the Soviet Union. 'He believes this will hasten the collapse
of Communism and at least there will be less persistent propaganda
by Russians in Persia.' In a remark aimed directly for the attention
of Loraine Reza Khan had ended the meeting by telling Col. Saunders
that he had been warned by some people that an Anglo-Russian
friendship may result again in dividing Iran into spheres of influence
'but he does not believe in such a development in view of the
strengthened position of Persia both in the political and military
area'.[36]

These meetings allowed Reza Khan to relieve Loraine of any
doubt as to the direction Iran was to take in its foreign policy. Reza
Khan was also able to impress upon Loraine that Iran had to be
treated as an equal in all future transactions. At a meeting with
Loraine on 1 March, after Britain had agreed to Reza Khan's request
and removed her troops from the Persian Gulf ports, Reza Khan
thanked Loraine for his co-operation but added:

> ... Persia wanted her complete independence recognised... She wanted
> no money from Great Britain... In future all questions involving Persia
> should be directly addressed to Persia... Any thought of any two neigh-
> bours making an arrangement between themselves regarding Persia
> would be a great mistake... Just as if Persia were to make an arrange-
> ment with a neighbour about a third party.

Loraine wanting to draw out Reza Khan as to what kind of relationship Iran was to have with Britain mentioned four forms this future
relationship could take.

> 1– Correct, courteous and friendly relations on the usual diplomatic lines.
> 2– An unwritten understanding for mutual co-operation. 3– A written
> undertaking for mutual co-operation. 4– An alliance between the two
> nations.

Loraine himself dismissed 'the concept of an alliance as it would
arouse antagonism in neighbouring countries'. Reza Khan in turn
categorically stated that 'alternatives 2 and 3 also should be dismissed'.[37] Reza Khan was saying that Britain would be considered a
friendly country but she would be treated no better or worse than
any other friendly country.

Shortly after leaving Tehran on an extended home leave (Loraine
had been in Iran since December 1921) Loraine prepared a lengthy
memorandum on the immediate status of Iranian-British relations.
He wrote that relations with Britain had improved considerably
since early 1921. Equally important the Russians had made little

headway. France and Turkey were not even players in Iran and carried no weight. The United States was playing a marginal role, having been granted an oil concession and the possiblity of a contract to build the proposed railway. However, discontent with US financial advisers was considerable and could become worse. Loraine tacitly acknowledged that Britain's 1919 policy had been a gross failure and should be totally discarded.

> I am firmly convinced that the less we or British subjects are involved in the internal affairs of Persia, the better for us... The meetings of the mixed Commission are beginning to yield results and some issues have been settled. The handover of the telegraph lines, navigation rights on Lake Urumieh and claims for salaries of British military personnel have been settled. Persia will pay part of the bill for munitions. The only major remaining question is Persia's debt to Britain.

Loraine wrote that Persians were willing to compromise if Britain were prepared to make some concessions.

> If we maintain our claims in full and I do not myself consider that all of them are strictly fair charges on the Persian Government, I do not think we shall ever get paid unless we take forcible steps to recover the money... Persia is recovering and progressing... Majority of Persians would like to be on good terms with us again but they do not wish to be driven to a capitulation... the ground is prepared for reconcilliation with Persia...

The implication was that Britain should not press.[38]

A further concession by Britain, engineered by Loraine's persistence, was that Britain allowed the senior ulama who had been made to leave Iraq in protest over Iraqi elections to return to the holy shrines. Loraine confided this information to Reza Khan but requested that the news be kept secret for a while longer until the Iraqi officials had been duly informed. This was to be a major boost for Reza Khan's reputation among the senior clergy. As we shall see shortly Reza Khan made the news public at a critical juncture when he needed clerical support.[39]

A remaining thorny issue which Loraine had complained of as discriminatory against British firms was the preliminary steps the Government of Iran was taking towards construction of a railway system. Two American construction and engineering firms which had formed a joint venture for railway projects were invited to Tehran. The Iranian Government, which had no funds for the project, had hoped the Sinclair Oil Company could raise the $10 million loan required for the award of an oil concession in the northern provinces. The proceeds of the Sinclair loan would then finance the railway project. The representatives of the joint venture, Ulen and Company and Stone and Webster, arrived in Tehran in early 1924.[40] The Foreign Office, on being alerted, immediately notified the Persian Railway Syndicate (PRS), a British Company which had performed a partial and preliminary survey in 1913. PRS maintained that they had a valid option for the building of a railway system in Iran and the contract could be awarded to no other entity.[41] The Foreign Office instructed its envoys in Washington DC and Tehran to insist that PRS had such an option but to explain that PRS would be willing to negotiate regarding a railway project with reputable US firms.[42]

The counsel of Ulen and Company informed the Iranian Government that after studying the British claim he had reached the conclusion that PRS had no legal option or preferential rights. All PRS had done was to send a few engineers to make a preliminary survey. The Iranian Government was therefore free to award the contract to any party of its choosing.[43] Ulen and Company agreed to undertake a feasibility study and ascertain the estimated cost of a railroad line to run from Sultanabad in central western Iran to Tehran, extending north to the south-eastern shore of the Caspian Sea and then south to Mohammareh.[44] This was the first concrete step toward construction of a railway system in Iran. Within the next two years the enabling legislation and the provision of funds would be approved by parliament. In the meantime the claim of PRS was settled amicably.

Reza Khan's reputation had been on a steady rise from the very first days after the coup. His supporters had every expectation that having become Prime Minister he would be able to complete what he had started. He now would take the final steps to unify the country and advance bold plans for an economic revival. However, the first six months of his premiership were to be a severe disappointment. In fact in the period ahead, March and April 1924, he would suffer a severe setback which could have ended his political career. It was only the absolute loyalty of the army which saved him and allowed him to recover.

By far the single most crucial event during Reza Khan's first six months as Prime Minister was the abortive attempt to dismantle the Qajar dynasty and establish a republic with himself as its first president. Even before the coup of 1921 the idea of a republic had been discussed amongst a small element of the intelligensia. There was general dissatisfaction with the course the country was taking. The Qajars had proven useless and a monarchy was believed to be an obstacle to political and social reform. A republic was seen as the form of government of the future and it was believed Iran would do well to remove the discredited dynasty. When Seyyed Zia became Prime Minister, there was expectation that once he was secure in his position he would take steps to be rid of the Qajars and declare a republic. Seyyed Zia's treatment of the Shah as an irrelevance, barely mentioning him in his proclamation on becoming Prime Minister, and his insistence on being designated 'dictator' gave the impression that it was only a matter of time before the Qajar dynasty would come to an end.

Thought of a republic abated after the fall of Seyyed Zia and the solidarity shown by Reza Khan with Ahmad Shah. Far more important was the fear that the establishment of a republic would bring an even greater risk of disorder especially among the tribes, 'who at least accorded the monarchy some prestige refusing to acknowledge the sovereignty of a President'.[45] The tribes would take advantage of the situation to loot and pillage towns and the countryside and could even attempt to establish independent governments.

By 1924 Reza Khan's public standing was high and Ahmad Shah's correspondingly low. The first sign that a republican form of government was being discussed was on 20 January 1924, when, a newspaper in Constantinople came out in favour of the establishment of a republic in Iran. The article was well received in Tehran by newspapers that were supporters of Reza Khan. A Tehran journalist tried to determine what Reza Khan thought of the article. Reza Khan did not answer directly and was non-committal.[46] He was quoted as saying, 'The progress of a country depended less on their form of government than on the morale of the people. Take Greece and Great Britain. Both are monarchies. One is decadent and decayed; the other great, vibrant and prosperous.'[47] Mexico and France were similarly contrasted as republics. The press however, probably with Reza Khan's encouragement, escalated attacks on the institution of monarchy, the Shah and the Qajar dynasty.

How did Reza Khan so soon after achieving his ambition to become Prime Minister decide on a republic? To begin with, becoming president and assuming the highest position in the country was fully in keeping with the trajectory of his political ascent. He may have believed at the time that with his humble background he could not become Shah, but the abdication of the Kaiser in Germany and the overthrow of monarchies in Russia and Turkey had shown that people would accept republicanism. Probabaly the main source of inspiration for Reza Khan was Ataturk's Turkey.

When the Gilan Republic was formed even farmers and labourers in the province accepted the republic. In fact the masses in Gilan had played a much more active role in the formation of a republic than they had during the constitutional struggle. They had heard speeches about abolishing the monarchy as early as 1918 and Bolshevik soldiers had sung the praises of a republic. The Bolshevik Government in Moscow had gained great credibility by their talk of equality in an egalitarian society. In the Perso-Soviet agreement they had shown how generous the Soviet republican Government could be in renouncing every Czarist privilege in Iran, contrasted with the selfishness and greed of Britain in the 1919 Agreement. From the time talk of a republic began, the Soviets encouraged the idea. The Foreign Office believed Russian support merely indicated their larger aims in destabilising British rule in India and their ultimate aim of removing Reza Khan from power after a term or two.[48]

The idea of a republic was probably strengthened in Reza Khan's mind during the course of his negotiations with Ahmad Shah to become Prime Minister. Not only was he convinced of the uselessness and cowardice of the Shah and his indifference to the fate of the country, but also of the Shah's capacity to intrigue against him. Furthermore, the generation of politicians who had ruled Iran from 1909–1921 had proven to be incompetent and had lost all self-respect. They had been incapable of independent action and were treated as paid agents by their European sponsors. A republican form of government would change everything and the old crowd of self-seeking unpatriotic notables would be discarded. Reza Khan's principal advisers were all of the same mind and encouraged the idea of a republic.[49] The only one among them who appears to have cautioned against it was Davar who believed Iran 'was not yet ripe for a republic'.

The campaign against Ahmad Shah began to gain momentum by early February. A photograph of the Shah published in the *Times* of London showing him in Biaritz in European attire in the company of a group of European women was reprinted in several Tehran newspapers.[50] Soon articles critical of the Shah and in favour of a republic became the norm. The attacks on the monarchy were accompanied by lavish praise for Reza Khan whom the newspapers proposed as the first president of the future republic. Republican Committees were formed and telegrams from the provinces poured in. Bazaars in the provinces were closed as an act of protest against Ahmad Shah. Most of these acts were financed by the Government in Tehran and there was no doubt that Reza Khan was the inspiration behind the campaign.[51] Moscow sent a message to its legation in Tehran which was released to the newspapers congratulating the people of Iran for their support for a republic. On 24 January, following Lenin's death, Russian consulates in several cities in Iran opened their doors for condolence visits. The occasion was used to let Iranians know they were in favour of a republic.[52] Turkey also made its approval of a republic known through various journals.[53] Even important Qajar princes including Ain al Dowleh and Farmanfarma decided to ride the tide and presented a petition to Reza Khan urging him to make Iran a republic.[54]

Loraine was uneasy about a republic from the beginning of the campaign. He felt it could be destabilising and that only the Russians would benefit from it. In late January he wrote to MacDonald asking what to do.[55] Oliphant, echoing what MacDonald had in mind, cautioned Loraine 'to abstain as in the past all intervention in Persian domestic affairs'. G.P. Churchill, in a separate memorandum, stated that Britain should not involve itself in the matter and besides 'the Shah has proved himself a failure and his disappearance from the scene would be no loss'.[56] When the campaign became more vociferous Loraine felt compelled to write again to MacDonald:

> Campaign against the Shah continues and the idea of a republic encounters no opposition. Crucial test will be whether deputies after validation of their election take the usual oath of allegiance to the Constitution. In my opinion the Shah will be deposed or forced to abdicate. I am to see the Prime Minister on March 1. I must know your views. Mine are to recommend retention of the monarchy and present Constitution owing to incalculable risk at home and abroad of a violent change of government and adoption of a form for which the country is not ripe, adding that the personality of the monarch is a matter which I cannot discuss and of which Persian people are sole judge. Do you concur?[57]

MacDonald in his reply stated:

> If Persians wish to introduce a republican regime it is entirely their concern and you should not intervene in the matter or offer any advice to Persian Prime Minister for or against the project.[58]

Until late February Reza Khan had preferred to stay out of the debate publicly to make it appear that the idea of a republic was mass-inspired and that he was forced to respect the wishes of the people. On 22 February he met with a large number of recently-elected deputies to discuss the legislative agenda for the Fourth Parliament: the granting of an oil concession to Sinclair Oil Company; a military conscription bill; abolition of titles and a law for adoption of family names for all Iranians; levying of taxes on sugar and tea to raise revenue to finance the proposed Iranian railway; and the most important item of changing the Constitution to make Iran a republic.[59] Reza Khan was most anxious to have the amendment to the Constitution enacted before the advent of the Iranian New Year (the first day of spring). His thinking was that as President-in-waiting he and not the Shah or Crown Prince would preside over the customary reception for government officials and notables on New Year's Day, giving him immediate public recognition.[60]

Loraine called on Reza Khan on 1 March before taking an extended leave in early March. Since Edward Monson, the counsellor, was to be away for a short period, MacDonald felt there should be a seasoned diplomat in Tehran to serve until Loraine's return. Esmond Ovey was sent from London as Chargé d'Affaires. Loraine wanted to establish British policy regarding a republic before he left Tehran. At the outset Loraine made clear that he was not there to find out how Reza Khan felt about the republican campaign nor what his intentions were. He merely wanted Reza Khan to know that the question of form of government was 'a Persian question and one which in no way concerned Britain' and Britain would take a position of complete neutrality. Reza Khan ended the meeting by saying 'he has let the agitation be allowed a free reign since he believes the present ruler was a bar to Persian progress'.[61]

Ahmad Shah, now in Paris and believing that the British were encouraging if not even the primary force behind the republican movement, met with Col. E.T.R. Wickham (a Military Attaché at the Tehran Legation in 1919–1920) and stated that he was prepared to give Reza Khan any authority he wanted provided the monarchy were maintained.

> He was quite prepared to see Reza Khan acting the part of a Persian Mussolini as long as he remains king. He is willing to give dictatorial powers to [Reza Khan] and abstain from any sort of intrigue if [Reza Khan] would promise he would not overthrow the monarchy. He would be then prepared to return to Persia in the autumn.[62]

The key element in his message was that he was still not prepared to return to Iran any earlier than at least six months hence.

The fifth session of parliament officially convened on 11 February. The Crown Prince, Mohammad Hassan Mirza, delivered the opening address. Hosein Pirnia was elected President and his two Vice Presidents were Mohammad Taddayon* and Morteza Qoli

---

* Seyyed Mohammad Taddayon, 1881–1951, born in Birjand, Khorasan and educated as a cleric. He established a school called Taddayon and became it's principal, adopting the name of the school as his family name. He became active in the original Democrat Party and was elected to fourth, fifth and sixth sessions of parliament, serving as President of that body in the second half of the fifth and beginning of the sixth sessions. He became Minister of Education in 1927, was accused of having appropriated for himself a large part of the funds put at his disposal for the
CONTINUED OVER PAGE

Bayat (Saham al Soltan).[†] The election of the two Vice Presidents indicated the strong support Reza Khan was expected to have in parliament, as both were considered to be firmly behind him. Taddayon headed a faction called Revivalists (Tajadod) and could count on 35 to 40 deputies. The Socialists, who also supported Reza Khan and his republican agenda had between 12 and 13 members. Reza Khan could count on another 10–15 additional supporters who were not allied with any faction. The remainder of the 10–12 independents were largely against a republic. They carried greater weight than their numbers would indicate as among them were most of the deputies elected from Tehran who stood high in public esteem. Moddares, who more than anyone else was responsible for denying Reza Khan the premiership between 1922 and 1923 and had emerged as Reza Khan's principal adversary, led the main organised opposition of 12 or 13 deputies.

Moddares knew that if the issue of establishing a republic were put to a vote, the pro-republic majority would prevail. The only alternative was to delay the matter as long as possible hoping for defections and disunity among the majority and a probable shift in public opinion outside of parliament. From mid February he began to hold up the seating of newly elected deputies on charges of fraud and voting irregularities in their election districts. He also demanded a secret ballot on each procedural issue, which he knew would consume time. Moddares's strategy began to work and Taddayon fell into the trap. In retaliation he too started to question the validity of the election of deputies who were close to Moddares. He made the error of questioning the election of the popular Haji Mirza Hashem Ashtiani who had been elected from Tehran. Ashtiani was the son of a respected and venerable Shi'ite leader of the late nineteenth century whose opposition to the tobacco concession had united the country and forced the Shah to cancel it. Taddayon's tactical error caused some fraying at the edges of the pro-republic coalition resulting in

---

Seyyed Mohammad Taddayon CONTINUED FROM PREVIOUS PAGE
realisation of the republican movement and forced to resign in January 1928. In 1930 he was appointed Governor of Kerman briefly, then retired from public life for the remainder of Reza Shah's rule. In 1942 he held a ministerial position and again was accused of embezzlement.[63]

[†]   Morteza Qoli Bayat (Saham al Soltan), 1882–1955, came from a wealthy landowning family with considerable holdings in western Iran. He was a member of parliament from the fifth to the tenth sessions, holding several Cabinet positions. He was Prime Minister briefly in 1945 and head of the National Iranian Oil Company between 1953 and 1955, an affable country gentleman with an undistinguished public career.[64]

at least one defection from their ranks.[65] Moddares defended the election of Ashtiani, stressing that parliamentary elections in Tehran had been totally free from government interference. Taddayon, a relative newcomer to parliamentary in-fighting and impressed by his own importance as the *de facto* leader of a majority, made other tactical errors. He ordered a walkout by his supporters which delayed proceedings and further depleted his ranks.

Moddares then argued that the newly convened parliament had no mandate from the electorate to amend the constitution to establish a republic. In fact every member had taken an oath of allegiance on the present constitution to support the institution of monarchy. He offered three alternatives to break the deadlock: cancel the parliamentary elections recently held and dissolve parliament, holding new elections with elected deputies having the specific right to depose Ahmad Shah; Ahmad Shah to be deposed by the present sitting parliament with a Qajar minor appointed as the new king with Reza Khan as regent; hold a nation-wide plebiscite on the institution of the monarchy.[66]

The debate became more acrimonious as pro-republic deputies heaped abuse on Moddares. On 17 March Hosein Bahrami (Ahya al Saltaneh), a deputy supporting the republican movement, totally unprovoked slapped the frail Moddares. The incident caused further splits within pro-republican ranks, incensed pro-Moddares supporters in parliament and antagonised and alienated the general public. It was becoming clear that Reza Khan's desire to have the issue decided before the new year (the first day of spring) would be impossible. Word of the assault on Moddares soon spread. Between 18 and 20 March an ever-increasing mob gathered outside parliament. Shopkeepers came together in a mosque near the parliament and anti-republican sentiments were expressed. Moddares continued to pursue his strategy and objected to the accreditation of more deputies, including the President of parliament. He encouraged wavering and undecided members not to attend parliament or to go to Qom to deprive parliament of a quorum to transact business. Reza Khan had miscalculated the inherent conservatism of the people and of the clergy in particular. At his request several notables called on the Vali'ahd on the nineteenth asking him to step down as Regent and resolve the crisis and turmoil. Mohammad Hassan Mirza refused.[67]

On 19 March rumours spread that elements in the army were opposed to the establishment of a republic. Brig. Gen. Yazdanpanah, head of the Tehran Brigade, and Brig. Gen. Jan Mohammad Khan Amir Alaey (Davallou) of the Arak Brigade were said to have expressed their views to Reza Khan. Both had been rebuffed.[68]

Parliament adjourned on 20 March for lack of a quorum and met again on 22 March. A mob of some 5,000 gathered outside parliament and demanded access. The doors were opened and they were allowed in. They appeared peaceful although they carried placards and shouted anti republican slogans. Reza Khan, alerted to the presence of the mob, made his greatest mistake. He decided to take command personally. The crowds would not let his carriage pass. There was shouting and missiles were thrown, some hitting his carriage and probably his person. Troops rushed the crowds using gun butts and bayonets and several people were injured. Reza Khan's carriage finally gained entrance. It was a mistake to have made an appearance at all and once he had done so he realised that the use of military power would not quell the assembled mass.

> He lost his self control and never having the gift of oratory he failed to address the mob to stem the rising tide of opposition and turn the movement to his advantage by a direct appeal to the people. Instead he ordered the use of force with the consequence of the loss of a large measure of prestige.[69]

His appearance in parliament that day was a turning point and any chance of establishing a republic vanished.

Reza Khan was met on the steps leading to the chamber of deputies by Hosein Pirnia, who rebuked him for using force. Reza Khan answered that it was his responsibility to maintain order in the country. Pirnia responded that as President of parliament he was solely responsible for order inside parliament grounds. Pirnia then warned that he would convene parliament to decide the bounds of the authority of the Prime Minister. Were it not for the intervention of Mostofi, who came between the two and calmed both, there could have been serious immediate consequences and an ultimately different outcome. Had Pirnia taken his case to the deputies there might well have been a vote of no confidence. Reza Khan backed down and expressed regret at the military intervention but in parting stated that as he could not work with either the Shah or Vali'ahd he intended to resign his office.

The next day Reza Khan left Tehran and retired to his country house. On 26 March he went to Qom, as he had previously promised, to bid farewell to the senior ulama returning to Iraq. Reza Khan had sided completely with the clergy over their expulsion from Iraq. It was believed that it had been solely through his efforts that Britain had yielded and allowed them to return. Now his journey of farewell was seen as another indication of his fealty to Islam and respect for religious leaders. He returned to Tehran on the twenty-seventh.

Parliament had adjourned between 26 March and 3 April but the republican movement had already collapsed. The final blow was news from Turkey of the abolition of the Caliphate, the Islamic counterpart of the Holy See. The institution of the Caliphate had come into existence soon after the death of the Prophet. After the Baghdad Caliphate fell to the Mongol invader Halaku, it moved westward to the rulers of Egypt. In the early sixteenth century the Ottoman Sultan Salim conquered Egypt and the Caliphate moved to Constantinople. Later when Salim conquered Mecca and Medina all Sunni Moslems accepted him as the Caliph. When the last Sultan was removed the new Turkish Government appointed a new Caliph whose powers were solely spiritual. Soon thereafter a Turkish constituent assembly voted for Mostapha Kamal as President and the abolition of the institution of Caliph.[70] Although the Shi'a community never accepted the Caliph as their spiritual leader, the abolition of the position had struck a blow to religion and it was interpreted as the concommitant result of the establishment of a republic and the separation of religion and state. The senior clergy in Iran up to that point had disapproved the concept of a republic but had remained silent. With this development in Turkey, republicanism became equated with secularism and their disapproval turned to overt hostility.[71]

Reza Khan knew he had lost the fight for a republic. To prevent any further erosion of his prestige he issued a declaration on 1 April:

> The government of any country must not oppose public opinion... which is divided and people's thoughts are confused... In Qom I exchanged opinions... and have reached the conclusion that the idea of a republic should be dropped... I counsel all parties and supporters to desist from demanding a republic and unite with me in striving to attain that end on which we are agreed.[72]

This was Reza Khan's first defeat in the political arena and he had learned a bitter lesson. If the clergy united against an issue which they felt was inimical to their interests they could carry the masses with them and their power could be overwhelming. The experience was to have a profound effect on his later decisions to curb the power of the clergy.

During the next six days Reza Khan met with hundreds of people to exchange views and decide on his next move. Earlier in February, probably to shore up support for the planned campaign to establish a republic, he had organised an informal committee comprised of six of the better known 'independent' members of parliament with whom he would meet once or twice a week to discuss the Government's programme and matters of state. The six were the venerable Hassan

Mostofi and Hassan Pirnia together with Mohammad Mosaddeq, Yahya Dowlatabadi, Hassan Taqizadeh and Hosein Ala. Two others outside of parliament had been added, namely Mehdi Qoli Hedayat and Mohammad Ali Foroughi.[73] These meetings gave the impression that Reza Khan was acting with the benefit of the counsel of popular politicians and demonstrated to his opponents in parliament that he was in touch with the most prominent of the unaligned deputies.

From 27 March to 7 April Reza Khan received courtesy calls from the Soviet, British, French and American diplomats as well as Iranian notables, clerics and journalists.[74] What advice or comments he may have received is not recorded but in the end he resorted to his time-tested gesture of resignation. On the morning of 7 April he made it known that he had definitely decided to leave Iran and to that end had executed a power of attorney in the name of one of his subordinate officers to handle his financial and family affairs in his absence. He intended to go on a pilgrimage to the holy shrines in Iraq and then select another neighbouring Islamic country for his permanent residence.[75] As soon as the news broke a delegation called on him which included Mostofi, Hassan Pirnia and even the President of parliament, Hosein Pirnia, who less than two weeks earlier had nearly ended Reza Khan's political career. The delegation could not dissuade Reza Khan from resigning. He argued that he had to resign and force parliament to face the consequences of his possible departure from public life. After lengthy discussions Reza Khan agreed to abandon the idea of going to Iraq and instead decided to go to the small retreat he had built in Rud-e-Hen some 30 miles north of Tehran.

It was a shrewd and calculated move on his part. He had been rebuffed by parliament and therefore had to resign, but he also had to show his devotion to Islam by his proposed pilgrimage. If parliament were to ask him back he would be far stronger. Not to leave any matter to chance he alerted military commanders of his intention to leave and most probably asked them to begin a campaign to let parliament know the military needed him. On the morning of 7 April he resigned officially from all offices 'on account of extreme weariness' and announced he was leaving Tehran.[76] Despite his careful plans this resignation was not risk-free as his previous threatened resignations as Minister of War had been. It was difficult to gauge the mood of parliament. He certainly would have been dismissed if there had been a vote on his continuing in office on the day of his appearance in parliament. Despite assurances from his supporters his opponents had been active and had waited exactly for such an opportunity. A precautionary move by Reza Khan some three months earlier had been the dismissal of the last remaining Swedish officers from the Police Department and the appointment of Col. Mohammad Dargahi* as Chief of Police of Tehran.[77] His new Chief of Police kept him informed of the movements of his principal adversaries. If parliament had voted to accept his resignation, only a military coup could have brought him back to power. Reza Khan's image and stature as a man of the people would have been greatly tarnished by resorting to a coup.

The fasting month of Ramadan had started on 6 April and parliament had decided to meet only three times a week in the evenings for its duration. It was next to meet on the evening of 8 April. Ahmad Shah in Paris, alerted by a telegram from his brother that Reza Khan had resigned, sent the following telegram to the President of parliament: as Reza Khan 'had openly betrayed the government and people of Iran he is hereby dismissed. Majlis should meet and decide as to whom it favoured as the next Prime Minister'. The telegram was read by Hosein Pirnia in open session the following evening.[78] In a second telegram to Mostofi and Moddares the Shah recommended that Mostofi be appointed as the new Prime Minister, Hassan Pirnia as Minister of War with Maj. Gen. Abdollah Amir Tahmasebi as Commander of the Army and Brig. Amanollah Jahanbani as Chief of Staff.

Before his resignation Reza Khan had organised a press campaign to mitigate the damage he had suffered in pursuit of the republican cause. In a co-ordinated effort the newspapers supporting him no longer mentioned the issue of the proposed republic. Instead they dwelt on Reza Khan's past services to the country and his indispensability as a leader and beseeched him not to resign and abandon the political arena. On the day Reza Khan resigned and left Tehran the press campaign reached an even higher pitch.[79] Ali Dashti,† editor of the newspaper *Shafaq-e-sorkh* (*Red Twilight*),

---

* Mohammad Dargahi, c.1886–c.1950, was educated at Dar al Fonoun, joined the Gendarmerie in 1911 and sided with rebel Gendarmes in Shiraz in 1915 against the SPR. He was arrested and imprisoned for six months, then reinstated as head of the Gendarmerie in Qom in 1921 and late in December 1923 became chief of Tehran Police, with the rank of Colonel. In 1928 he was promoted to Brigadier General, dismissed in 1929. he was made head of conscription in 1931; head of the Census Bureau in 1935, dismissed in May 1936. Vindictive and cruel, he set the precedent as head of internal security in an increasingly dictatorial regime.[80]

† Ali Dashti, c.1896–1981, was educated at theological seminaries in Iraq. He supported and later turned against the 1919 Agreement, began editing
CONTINUED OVER PAGE

began a vituperative series of articles against the monarchy and the opponents of Reza Khan. Dashti wrote the well-known article titled 'The father of our homeland has left'. He lamented the departure of Reza Khan and foretold dire and unforeseen consequences if Reza Khan were not called back.

Next it was the turn of the army to assert itself. As if by pre-arranged signal, from the afternoon of 7 April a wave of telegrams from military officers descended upon parliament all expressing dismay at Reza Khan's withdrawal and requesting parliament to bring him back threatening to march to Tehran if their wishes were not fulfilled. By the morning of the eighth the telegrams assumed even graver and more ominous tones. From the officers of the Western Division (Hamadan) the telegram read, 'Unless in the course of the next forty-eight hours you reinstate Reza Khan as Premier we will withdraw our troops from Lurestan...' implying the rebel Lurs then would be free to pillage towns and villages. There were similar threatening telegrams from the Southern Division of Shiraz and Esfahan and from northern commanders in Rasht and Mashhad. There were pro-Reza Khan demonstrations in the provinces, and bazaars were closed in some provincial centres. The telegrams were read on the floor of parliament on the evening of the eighth. By the time parliament was called to order that evening there were few undecided votes. The communiqué from the Shah was ignored and deputies voted 94 to 6 that the presence of Reza Khan was necessary for the safety of Iran and he should be brought back into office forthwith. It was decided that parliament would send a deputation

---

Ali Dashti CONTINUED FROM PREVIOUS PAGE

a newspaper *Shafaq-e-Sorkh* (*Red Twilight*) in 1922. He became Reza Khan's primary press agent for the republican movement and later for the abolition of the Qajar dynasty. Elected to the Fifth Parliament, he was disbarred for past attempts at 'extortion and blackmail', but was elected to sixth, seventh and eighth sessions while continuing to publish his newspaper which was stopped in 1935. Back in favour in 1937, he was appointed head of the Press (Censorship) Bureau of the Ministry of Interior and elected as deputy to the thirteenth session of parliament. After the abdication of Reza Shah he was the first person to suggest Reza Shah should not be allowed to leave the country until he had given an account of his accumulated wealth. He was appointed Ambassador to Egypt in 1948 and was later Senator for several terms. He was arrested and harshly treated by Islamic regime in 1979. Dashti had an engaging pen. Although not a scholar he wrote several highly readable books on Persian poets and an autobiography. A person of 'no scruples and principles', he was also thrown out of Bushehr, his native town, for 'notorious promiscuity'.[81]

of six members to Rud-e-Hen to inform him of his reappointment and bring him to Tehran. On the following morning a prestigious deputation arrived and Reza Khan returned to his summer house in north Tehran. The next day he received scores of members of parliament and notables who congratulated him on his reappointment.[82]

On 11 April parliament officially informed Ahmad Shah by telegram of the vote of confidence and reappointment of Reza Khan as premier. Ahmad Shah, having no choice but to acquiesce, sent the following telegram:

> Although the Constitution gave us the right to express our lack of confidence in the Prime Minister, nevertheless we do not reject the decision of Parliament. We have asked the Crown Prince to inform the Prime Minister to form his new cabinet.[83]

On 13 April Reza Khan reorganised his Cabinet. For reasons not entirely clear Soleiman Mirza was removed as Minister of Education and no replacement was named. The only significant change was the appointment of Maj. Gen. Mahmoud Amir Eqtedar (Ansari)* as Minister of Post and Telegraph to replace Brig. Khodayar Khan. The programme of the new Government remained unchanged: introduction of a military conscription law; expansion of education facilities; conclusion of the award of north oil concession to Sinclair; establishment of an aerial postal service and public wireless facilities.[84]

Reza Khan had wanted to be rid of the Qajar dynasty. He had believed the most practical way would be through the establishment of a republic. His sense of Iranian history and political acumen had failed him. He had survived his most serious political crisis although much weakened. It would be a number of months before his prestige was fully restored, and over a year before he made his next attempt to achieve absolute power.

---

* Mahmoud Aqa Amir Eqtedar (Ansari), 1878–1950, was born in Esfahan, where he studied theology intending to be a cleric. He decided to join the Cossack Brigade and rose to Brigadier General earlier than Reza Khan whom he had known well. He joined the coup and became Military Governor of Tehran in late 1921 and then Governor of Esfahan, where he proved to be a competent administrator. In 1924 he became Minister of Post and Telegraph and was later Minister of Interior. He was removed and kept under house arrest in 1925 suspected of conspiracy with Sardar Mo'azez Bojnourdi, an important tribal chieftain in north-west Khorasan. Pardoned and reinstated to his former army rank, he was not offered a command position. All accounts portray him as intelligent and one of the better Cossack officers.[85]

NOTES ON CHAPTER 11
Further details of publications and documents in Bibliography

1   FO 371/12300, Clive to Chamberlain, 18 July 1927; FO 416/72,
     Loraine to Curzon, 4 April 1923; Mehdi Bamdad, *Tarikh Rejal Iran
     Quroun 12, 13, 14* (*Dictionary of National Biography of Iran: Twelfth,
     Thirteenth, Fourteenth Centuries*), vol. 2, pp 112–113.
2   Mehdi Bamdad, *Tarikh Rejal Iran Quroun 12, 13, 14* (*Dictionary of
     National Biography of Iran: Twelfth, Thirteenth, Fourteenth Centuries*),
     vol. 1, pp 38–39.
3   FO 416/98, Bullard to Halifax, 7 February 1940.
4   Mehdi Bamdad, *Tarikh Rejal Iran Quroun 12, 13, 14* (*Dictionary of
     National Biography of Iran: Twelfth, Thirteenth, Fourteenth Centuries*),
     vol. 3, p 125; FO 416/98, Bullard to Halifax, 7 February 1940.
5   Foroughi's literary output is considerable. Among his better known
     works are studies of the Iranian poets Ferdowsi, Omar Khayyam and
     Sa'di. His most important work is a two volume *The Course of Philosophy
     in Europe* published in 1922 and 1941. A person of high intelligence and
     sensibility but never considered an able administrator, he more than
     compensated for this shortcoming by his valuable insight in matters of
     state. He brought dignity to every position he held. Foroughi never
     recovered from the death of his wife at an early age and forever there-
     after appeared aloof and cold which has been critically commented on
     by his contemporaries.
         Mehdi Bamdad, *Tarikh Rejal Iran Quroun 12, 13, 14* (*Dictionary of
     National Biography of Iran: Twelfth, Thirteenth, Fourteenth Centuries*),
     vol. 3, pp 450–451; Baqer Aqeli, *Zoka al Molk Foroughi va Shahrivar 1320*
     (*Zoka al Molk Foroughi and August-September 1941*); Ahmad Varedi,
     'Mohammad Ali Foroughi, Zoka al Molk, 1877–1942: A Study in the Role
     of Intellectuals in Modern Iranian Politics,' unpublished PhD thesis.
     Mosaheb, *Da'erat al Mo'aref Farsi*, (*The Mosaheb Encyclopedia*), vol. 2.
     Conversations between Cyrus Ghani and Alinaqi Vaziri, the first and
     foremost preserver of classical Persian music, whose home Foroughi fre-
     quented: Tehran, Spring 1959.
6   FO 416/79, Bullard to Halifax, 7 February 1940; Reza Niazmand, *Reza
     Shah az Tavalod ta Saltanat* (*Reza Shah From Birth to Throne*), p 384.
7   FO 371/12300, Clive to A. Chamberlain, 13 July 1927; FO 371/20828,
     Seymour to Foreign Secretary, 27 February 1937, wherein he states
     Davar 'seemed almost the only member of the government who could and
     would give a definite reply to a question and he usually did so at once';
     Kaveh Bayat, 'Andishe Siasi Davar' ('The Political Thoughts of Davar')
     from *Goft-e-Gou* (*Dialogue*), pp 116–133; Baqer Aqeli, *Davar va Adlieh*
     (*Davar and the Ministry of Justice*); Abbas Qoli Golsha'yan 'Yaddashtha-
     i-Chand Raje be Marhoum Davar' ('Some Observations About the Late
     Davar') in Ghasem Ghani, *Yaddasht ha-e-Dr Ghasem Ghani* (*Memoirs of
     Dr Ghasem Ghani*), vol. 11, p 607–652. Conversations between Cyrus
     Ghani and Golsha'yan in Tehran over the course of the years
     1959–1964. Also see Ghasem Ghani, *Yaddasht ha-e-Dr Ghasem Ghani*
     (*Memoirs of Dr Ghasem Ghani*), vols 1, 2, 3, 8, 9, 10, 11 and 12.
8   Kaveh Bayat, 'Andishe Siasi Davar' ('The Political Thoughts of Davar') from
     Goft-e-Gou (*Dialogue*), pp 116–133. English translation by Cyrus Ghani.

9   The other provisions of the manifesto were: encouraging the establishment of joint stock companies and partnerships; establishment of industrial, commercial and agricultural banks; attraction of foreign and native capital; sale of government land to peasants through long-term credit facilities in order to increase the number of farmers; development of the mining industry; adoption of an independent tariff policy favourable to local agriculture and industry; construction of railways and roads; establishment of offices of registrars to record commercial transactions and transfer of land; prohibition of practices which encourage speculation in commodities; labour laws obliging the government to provide work for the able-bodied and protect and sustain the infirm and the sick; establishment of special judicial bodies to settle disputes between workers and management with representation by both sides; establishment of a chamber of commerce and dispatch of commercial agents to other countries; programmes intended to raise health standards; progressive taxation; universal, compulsory and free education; special programmes for the education of women; vocational schools and night classes; adoption of Persian as the language of the entire country. FO 371/9024, Loraine to Curzon, 14 May 1923; Ervand Abrahamian, *Iran Between Two Revolutions*, p 123.

10   Ervand Abrahamian, *Iran Between Two Revolutions*, p 123.

11   *Ibid.*

12   *Ibid.*, p 124.

13   Shahrokh Meskoob, *Dastan Adabiat va Sargozasht Ejtema (The Story of Literature and the Fate of Society)*, pp 14–15.

14   Ervand Abrahamian, *Iran Between Two Revolutions*, p 112. For biographical data on Taqizadeh refer to Chapter 13.

15   *Ibid.*, p 123.

16   *Ibid.*, p 127. Abrahamian makes the observation that the Socialist Party 'to forestall clerical attacks recruited into its parliamentary delegation Muhammad Sadeq Tabataba'i, the highly respected and liberal son of the Mojtahed who had led the Constitutional movement'. Tabataba'i was later appointed by Reza Shah ambassador to Turkey.

17   Shahrokh Meskoob, *Dastan Adabiat va Sargozasht Ejtema (The Story of Literature and the Fate of Society)*, pp 30 and 37.

18   *Ibid.*, pp 8 and 9: the author names disparate people such as Davar, Teimurtash, Foroughi; the poets Eshqi, Aref, Farrokhi and Bahar; scholars and historians Mohammad Qazvini, Abbas Eqbal; Ebrahim Pour Davoud, who produced a translation into modern Persian of the first part of the Avesta, 'The Gathas', the holy songs of Zoroaster (1926–1927); Hassan Pirnia, who completed *The History of Ancient Iran* (1927, 1928, 1932); and the writer Mohammad Ali Jamalzadeh, an important inovator of modern Persian prose who wrote *Yeki Bood Yeki Nabood (Once Upon a Time)*.

19   M. Reza Ghods, *Iran in the Twentieth Century*, p 94: quoting from Hassan Taqizadeh, 'Modern Persia', *Journal of the Royal Society of Arts*, no. 32, 27 July 1934, p 968.

20   Abdol Hosein Teimurtash to Seyyed Hassan Taqizadeh, in *Ayandeh (The Future)*, ed. Iraj Afshar, Azar to Esfand 1367 (December 1988 to March 1989), nos 9–12, pp 657–660: translated from Persian by Cyrus Ghani.

21 Richard W. Cottam, *Nationalism in Iran*, p 146.
22 Amin Banani, *The Modernization of Iran*, p 44.
23 *Ibid.*
24 Miron Rezun, *The Soviet Union and Iran*, p 60.
25 *Ibid.*, p 18.
26 Harish Kapur, *Soviet Russia and Asia 1917–1927*, pp 190–191.
27 *Ibid.*, p 191.
28 *Ibid.*, p 198. Out of a total of 11,000,000 roubles worth of goods imported by the Soviet Union from Asia, Iran exported 7,500,000 roubles worth.
29 *Ibid.*, p 200.
30 FO 416/73, Loraine to Curzon, 20 November 1923; DoS, Quarterly Report, Kornfeld to Secretary of State, 20 January 1924.
31 FO 371/10145, Loraine to MacDonald, 11 February 1924. Curzon died in March 1925.
32 *Ibid.*
33 FO 416/74, Loraine to Curzon, 27 December 1923.
34 FO 416/74, Loraine to MacDonald, 13 February 1923.
35 FO 416/74, Loraine to MacDonald, 16 February 1924.
36 FO 416/74, Loraine to MacDonald, Report of Military Attaché, 13 February 1924.
37 FO 371/10145, Memorandum by Loraine, 1 March 1924.
38 FO 416/74, Memorandum by Loraine, 2 April 1924. Loraine mentioned that the matter of the debt had narrowed down to Britain's demand of £1,560,000 as opposed to Iran's willingness to settle on a figure of about £600,000.
39 FO 371/10147, Memorandum of conversations between Loraine and Reza Khan, 1 March 1924.
40 DoS, 891.77 Ulen and Co./3, B. Gotlieb to Secretary of State, 22 January 1924.
41 FO 416/72, Oliphant to C. Greenway, 7 January 1924; FO 416/74, Persian Railway Syndicate (PRS) to Foreign Office, 23 January 1924.
42 FO 416/74, Foreign Office to Chilton in Washington DC and Loraine in Tehran, 12 and 13 February 1924; DoS 891.77/56, Esme Howard to Charles Evans Hughes, 21 February 1924.
43 DoS 891.77 Ulen and Co. 17, Kornfeld to Secretary of State, 30 April 1924.
44 FO 371/10145, Memorandum by Loraine, 1 March 1924.
45 FO 616/68, Norman to Curzon, 1 March 1921: quoted by Vanessa Martin, 'Mudarris, Republicanism and the Rise to Power of Riza Khan Sardar Sepah', *British Journal of Middle Eastern Studies*, vol. 21 no. 2, 1994, p 199.
46 FO 371/10145, Ovey to MacDonald, 1 April 1945.
47 FO 371/10144, Col. E.T.R. Wickham to Victor Mallet, 25 February 1924.
48 FO 371/10144, Loraine to MacDonald, 31 January 1924.
49 Golsha'yan, in Ghasem Ghani, *Yaddasht ha-e-Dr Ghasem Ghani (Memoirs of Dr Ghasem Ghani)*, vol. 11, p 637.
50 FO 416/74, Loraine to MacDonald, 27 February 1924.
51 FO 371/10145, Ovey to MacDonald, 1 April 1924.
52 FO 416/74, Military Attaché to Foreign Office, 6 March 1924; FO 416/74, Loraine to MacDonald, 13 February 1924.

53 FO 371/10145, from Constantinople to MacDonald, 31 March 1924.

54 DoS 891.01/13, Kornfeld to Secretary of State, 19 March 1924.

55 FO 371/10144, Loraine to MacDonald, 31 January 1924.

56 FO 371/40144, L. Oliphant to Loraine, 6 February 1924; FO 371/10144, Minute by G. Churchill, 1 February 1924: Houshang Sabahi, *British Policy in Persia 1918–1925*, p 177.

57 FO 371/10145, Loraine to MacDonald, 26 February 1924.

58 FO 371/10145, MacDonald to Loraine, 29 February 1924.

59 FO 416/74, Military Attaché to Foreign Office, 6 March 1924.

60 It is not known whether the election of the first president would have been by a nation-wide election or an act of parliament. The bill to establish a republic never got that far.

61 FO 371/10145, Loraine to MacDonald, 1 March 1924.

62 FO 371/10144, Col. E.T.R. Wickham to Victor Mallet, 25 February 1924.

63 FO 416/98, Bullard to Halifax, 7 February 1940. Mehdi Bamdad, *Tarikh Rejal Iran Quroun 12, 13, 14* (*Dictionary of National Biography of Iran: Twelfth, Thirteenth, Fourteenth Centuries*), vol. 3, pp 235–237.

64 FO 416/98, Bullard to Halifax, 7 February 1940.

65 FO 371/10145, Ovey to MacDonald, 1 April 1924.

66 Majid Sharif Khoda'i, 'Mas'aleh Jomhouriat Dar Dowran Reza Khan' ('The Quesiton of a Republic in the Reza Khan Era') unpublished thesis, p 257.

67 Baqer Aqeli, *Ruz Shomar Tarikh Iran* (*A Daily Calendar of the History of Iran*), vol. 1, p 184.

68 FO 416/74, Ovey to MacDonald, Military Attaché Report, 5 April 1924.

69 FO 371/10145, Ovey to MacDonald, 1 April 1924.

70 Majid Sharif Khoda'i, 'Mas'aleh Jomhouriat Dar Dowran Reza Khan' ('The Quesiton of a Republic in the Reza Khan Era') unpublished thesis, pp 213–216.

71 FO 371/10145, Ovey to MacDonald, 1 April 1924.

72 FO 416/74, Ovey to MacDonald, 7 April 1924.

73 Hosein Makki, *Tarikh Bist Saleh Iran* (*A Twenty Year History of Iran*), vol. 2, pp 430–431; Yahya Dowlatabadi, *Hayat Yahya* (*The Life of Yahya*), vol. 4, pp 324–326.

74 Soleiman Behboodi, *Khaterat Soleiman Behboodi* (*The Memoirs of Soleiman Behboodi*), pp 128–130.

75 *Ibid.*, pp 131–132: Col. Karim Bouzarjomehri was given the power of attorney by Reza Khan.

76 FO 416/74, Ovey to MacDonald, 18 April 1924.

77 Soleiman Behboodi, *Khaterat Soleiman Behboodi* (*The Memoirs of Soleiman Behboodi*), pp 132–137.

78 FO 416/74, Ovey to MacDonald, 18 April 1924.

79 Baqer Aqeli, *Ruz Shomar Tarikh Iran* (*A Daily Calendar of the History of Iran*), p 187.

80 FO 416/98, Bullard to Halifax, 7 February 1940; Mehdi Bamdad, *Tarikh Rejal Iran Quroun 12, 13, 14* (*Dictionary of National Biography of Iran: Twelfth, Thirteenth, Fourteenth Centuries*), vol. 3, pp 242–243.

81 Homa Katouzian, *The Political Economy of Modern Iran 1926–1979*, p 109; FO 416/98, Bullard to Halifax, 7 February 1940.

82 FO 416/74, Ovey to MacDonald, 18 April 1924; also see Hosein Makki, *Tarikh Bist Saleh Iran* (*A Twenty Year History of Iran*), vol. 2, pp 526–531.

83 Hosein Makki, *Tarikh Bist Saleh Iran* (*A Twenty Year History of Iran*), vol.
    2, p 546.
84 FO 416/74, Ovey to MacDonald, 18 April 1924.
85 FO 416/98, Bullard to Halifax, 7 February 1940; Hosein Makki, *Tarikh
    Bist Saleh Iran* (*A Twenty Year History of Iran*), vol. 3 pp 342–343.

12

The Unification of Iran

Reza Khan had survived the most serious threat to his methodical political rise, but at a heavy cost. His reputation was tarnished. He had appeared as a power-hungry autocrat and his adversaries were quick to emphasise his boundless ambition. His abrupt turn around in calling a halt to republican agitation had demonstrated his vulneribility and that he could be stopped if a coalition of forces were to array against him. Reza Khan must also have been unsettled since he viewed the opposition to the republican movement as a personal rejection. Turkey had abolished the monarchy and had proclaimed Ataturk President without any serious dissent. He had done no less for Iran than Ataturk had for Turkey. There were now elements of paranoia in his thinking resulting in a round of recriminations. He placed most of the blame on Britain and the Soviets. Britain had opposed the republican movement and encouraged the opposition because she did not want to disrupt the status quo. Russia had opposed a republic because she did not want Reza Khan as president. He also viewed the United States as a conspirator and believed the American business community, fearing instability under republican rule, had aided the opposition.[1]

It took him a while longer to realise that the failure of the republican movement had been due to the radical nature of the proposition, for which the country was hardly ready, and to the fact that his support base was narrow, divided and confined to a few larger cities.

Of the three groups that came together to produce the 1906 revolution, Reza Khan had the greatest success with the commercial middle classes whose interests dictated internal security, strong communication and transport infrastructure. The mercantile group did not concern itself with how Reza Khan achieved power as long as the towns and roads were secure.[2]

The second group in the 1906 coalition, the intelligentsia, had given him wavering support and only backed his nationalist creed fully. The third element, the clergy, had never supported him. They had been wary of a strong central government with nationalism and secularism as its underpinnings. During the republican crisis the senior ulama had remained silent but the middle and lower-ranking clergy had been overtly hostile.

With this fragile support, any idea of deposing the Qajars, whether through a republic or by ascending the throne himself as the founder of a new dynasty, had to be discarded for the time being. If he had been rejected as president why should his path to becoming king be any easier? He had to broaden his base of support among the clergy and soften the image of a secular state. He also had to assure the intelligentsia and the merchant class that he would complete what he had started. He would complete the unification of Iran and bring the southern part of the country under the authority of the Central Government. As part of his long-range strategy he had to convince foreign legations that the failure of the republican movement had neither eroded his stature nor dented his resolve to modernise Iran.

From late April 1924 Reza Khan began what can be called a feverish public relations campaign. He attended most receptions at foreign legations. These included not only the Soviet and British but the Belgian, German, Italian and US Legations as well. He set aside Wednesdays solely to receive heads of legations and foreign nationals seeking business opportunities in Iran.[3] He kept in close touch with the nobility and sought their advice and counsel. He made calls at the homes of senior notables.[4] He began assiduously to court the senior and middle-ranking clergy. He made calls on them and received them regularly. More importantly, during the mourning month of Moharam he instituted prayer meetings at his own home with his family in attendance. On the tenth day of that month, the anniversary of the martyrdom of Imam Hosein and the most solemnly observed day of mourning in the Shi'ite world, he led a large contingent of mourners, including high-ranking military commanders, on a march through the bazaar performing acts of mortification and penance.[5]

An event that was to shatter the apparent tranquility in Tehran and have far-reaching consequences for Reza Khan, enabling him to strengthen his hold on the Government, was the murder of the US Vice Consul Robert W. Imbrie. The incident had its beginnings in early June 1924 when rumours began to spread of the healing powers of a public fountain in the centre of Tehran. A lame person had been ostensibly cured by drinking the water. A disbeliever, purported to have been a Baha'i, who had refused to give alms to a beggar sitting near the fountain had been blinded. Soon there were mass visits to the site by the lame, the blind and the infirm, many having come from long distances and some carried on stretchers.

On 18 July 1924 Imbrie, who had come to Tehran some four months earlier, decided to visit the site with an acquaintance, Melvin Seymour, an oil driller who probably had been seeking employment in Iran but had entered the country without the necessary papers. Seymour had been placed in the custody of the US Legation pending a decision on his continued stay or deportation. Before coming to Iran Imbrie had been provided with a camera by *National Geographic* so that he could record subjects of interest during his stay.[6] They arrived at the fountain at about 10am and took some photographs. People objected as there were women on the scene and also because it was considered blasphemous for non-Moslems to set foot on a Moslem shrine. Soon some in the crowed began to shout that the two Americans were Baha'is who had come to poison the well. The crowd became threatening and Imbrie and Seymour returned to their carriage, the driver attempting to get away as quickly as possible. A large mob had formed by now and some pursued and stopped the carriage. Imbrie and Seymour were beaten and badly injured. Some soldiers from nearby barracks had been at the fountain and on the attempted escape route but failed to intervene. Finally the police arrived and took the two Americans to a nearby police infirmary. The mob, now numbering over a thousand and led by a man in clerical garb, entered the infirmary and a youth of 16 killed Imbrie with a stone. Seymour, who had been kept in another room, somehow was spared. The victims had been exposed to the fury of the mob for almost three quarters of an hour without a shot having been fired to disperse the crowd. Worse yet, it appeared that a soldier or soldiers had taken part in the final assault on Imbrie as there was a sabre wound on his face.[7] Martial law was declared on the following day. All the foreign legations lodged strong protests and demanded the arrest and punishment of those found guilty of the assault and murder. Seymour, still in a critical condition, gave a deposition some five days after the incident wherein he stated that soldiers had hit him with gun butts and an army officer had punched him with his fists. Seymour also confirmed that the mob attack on the infirmary had been led by a cleric.[8]

There previously had been a similar setback for Reza Khan. Some two weeks earlier in Tehran unknown assailants had killed a much admired journalist and poet, Mohammad Reza Mirzadeh Eshqi, who had been an early supporter of Reza Khan's quest for a strong government and as a symbol of resurgent nationalism. However, recently Eshqi had voiced harsh disapproval of Reza Khan's autocratic behaviour in closing newspapers. Although the assailants were never identified, some placed the blame on Reza Khan and his supporters. There were now murmurs that Reza Khan had failed in his primary mission to bring security to the country. Even the capital was not free from lawlessness, not to mention soldiers having taken part in mob violence. Many in the intelligentsia held that Reza Khan had inflamed religious fervour by his courting of the clergy and ostentatious demonstrations of piety. Reza Khan had no choice but to declare martial law. If there were any other incidents or riots his opponents would have used it against him and his reputation would have eroded further.

Newspapers in Tehran began to accuse an unnamed foreign country of complicity in the outbreak of violence (under the recently-passed press law, foreign countries could not be named by newspapers if the contents could be deemed defamatory). When the British press routinely reported that soldiers were involved in Imbrie's death Tehran newspapers in retaliation all but pointed a finger at Britain, probably with the encouragement of Reza Khan. They began to hint that the unnamed though easily identified foreign country's intentions in initiating the riot was to discourage Sinclair Oil from pursuing its concession. Strong protests from the British Legation put an end to these speculations.[9]

Charles Evans Hughes, the US Secretary of State, had sent a harsh note to the Iranian Government demanding punishment of those guilty of Imbrie's death, compensation of his widow and reimbursement of the cost of sending a cruiser to the Persian Gulf to carry the body to the United States. There was an implied threat of breaking off relations if any of these demands were not met.

Commercial relations with European countries, and at this juncture the hope of US investment in Iran, were most important to Reza Khan. He had to show he was against lawlessness. The Iranian Foreign Ministry officially apologised to the United States and unequivocally agreed to pay the compensation and reimbursement of expenses demanded. It further promised to seek out the perpetrators and punish those found guilty. The monetary claims were settled quickly. Sixty thousand dollars was paid to Imbrie's widow and $110,000 to the United States Government as reimbursement of expenses for the dispatch of the cruiser. As a gesture of good will the US Department of State announced that the $110,000 would be earmarked for the education of Iranian students in the United States.[10] The fund was never so utilised as the US Congress objected to the arrangement and in any event, it was deemed too small a sum for such a purpose. Seymour meanwhile recovered and received a small compensation.

The question of punishment of the mob leaders was more difficult. How could the leaders be identified from among such a mob? Three people were finally revealed as the more serious offenders: a cleric who had led the attack on the infirmary; a soldier who had inflicted the head wound; and the youth of 16 who had attacked Imbrie on the operating table and had inflicted the fatal blow. The soldier was executed in early September. But the question of punishment of the cleric and the youth posed grave problems for Reza Khan. It was argued by some clerics that under Islamic law three people could not be executed for a single death.[11] Reza Khan was apprehensive that the trial of the two once again could alienate the masses and the clergy at the very time when he had mended fences and silenced them. It was not until November that the remaining two offenders were executed.[12] The executions passed without incident as the army stood solidly behind Reza Khan.

The killing of Imbrie and mob violence created the worst impression in the New York financial community as it was said that 'Persia is a country that God forgot as there is no such thing as stability and order'.[13] Furthermore, when the transport of oil through the Soviet Union was blocked by Moscow, US banks refused financing. Sinclair gave up the concession in 1925. Standard Oil also withdrew its bid in 1927. Some Iranian writers have made much of foreign involvement in the riots and have pointed an accusatory finger at APOC as the instigator. There is not a scintilla of evidence and such charges can be safely dismissed. The root causes lay in religious fanaticism exacerbated by the passage of the mourning month's holiest days immediately preceding the discovery of the 'magic' fountain.

Reza Khan had been weakened by the Eshqi killing. Now after the killing of Imbrie he was attacked not only for lawlessness in Tehran but additionally for the imposition of martial law. At the same time there were renewed revolts in the provinces, especially the Turkamans in Gorgan and north-western Khorasan, and Kurdish tribes in western Azarbaijan. Ahmad Shah now entered the picture as well. He felt the situation ripe to stir the pot. He had telegraphed two senior members of the ulama that he would return as soon as his health permitted and had voiced dissatisfaction over the imposition of martial law. Moddares and his supporters in parliament also sensed that the time was opportune to make another attempt to dislodge Reza Khan. Moddares put awkward questions to the Government in parliament hoping it would lead to a new vote of confidence. Foremost he attacked the imposition of martial law as contrary to the constitution. He further accused the Government of having appropriated the assets of subdued rebellious tribal chieftains without a proper accounting. He asked for written confirmation that all such items had been credited to the national treasury.[14] Another event that encouraged the opponents of Reza Khan was the threatened resignation of Millspaugh. There had been criticism by the Tehran press that Millspaugh had failed to improve the financial condition of the country and to attract foreign capital. Millspaugh complained that he was not consulted on important decisions by the Government which constituted a limitation of his powers, contrary to the terms of his contract.[15] He threatened to resign immediately unless his conditions were met but the threat was ultimately withdrawn.

As the day set for a vote of confidence approached, Moddares realised that despite Reza Khan's setbacks there were not sufficient votes to topple him, and tried to delay the process. Reza Khan nevertheless decided to seek a vote and went to parliament on 19 August, the day fixed for the vote by the minority. The morning session had been stormy, with vituperative language on both sides. On leaving parliament, Moddares and two of his colleagues were assaulted in the street. Moddares and his supporters chose not to attend the afternoon session. Only one member of the opposition (Bahar) was present, and he argued that the vote be deferred until his colleagues could attend with assurances of personal safety. Reza Khan's supporters maintained that since a valid quorum was present to transact business, the mere absence of a few members should not delay the vote. Failing a request by the opposition for a secret ballot, a voice vote was taken and it was unanimous for the retention of Reza Khan.[16]

Prior to the vote Reza Khan had committed himself to cabinet changes, and he presented his new Cabinet to parliament on the first day of September. The Socialist members were replaced. Soleiman Mirza and Amanollah Ardalan would soon take their seats in the new parliament. Reza Khan felt secure with the Socialists. He could count on their support whether or not they were included in the Cabinet. Foroughi was moved from the Ministry of Foreign

Affairs to Finance and Hassan Moshar (Moshar al Molk) replaced Foroughi as Foreign Minister. Ja'far Qoli Khan As'ad (Sardar As'ad)* became the Minister of Post and Telegraph. Abdol Hosein Teimurtash (Sardar Mo'azam) was appointed Minister of Public Works; Hosein Samii, Minister of Justice; Maj. Gen. Mahmoud Ansari (Amir Eqtedar), Minister of Interior; and Nezam al Din Hekmat (Moshar al Dowleh)† acting Minister of Education.

The most important feature of the new Cabinet was its decidedly pro-British bent. Reza Khan had probably decided to confront Sheikh Khaz'al's autonomy with force. He knew this presented the risk of a serious clash with Britain and he did not want Britain to have any added cause for antipathy. Foroughi enjoyed the confidence of the British Legation. Moshar at the Foreign Ministry was even closer to the Legation as succeeding chapters will reveal. Sardar As'ad was one of the most prominent leaders of the Bakhtiari tribe with a history of protecting British interests in Iran. Furthermore, his inclusion in the Cabinet would reduce the possibility of the

---

* Ja'far Qoli Khan Sardar Bahador, later Sardar As'ad III, 1879–1934, was the eldest son of Sardar As'ad II and grandson of Hosein Qoli Khan Ilkhani Bakhtiari, the two most renowned Bakhtiari leaders of the late nineteenth and early twentieth centuries. Ja'far Qoli Khan was one of the better educated tribal chieftains and established a reputation as an energetic and successful military leader. He was one of the liberators of Tehran (with his father) in 1909, leading to the dethronement and expulsion of Mohammad Ali Shah. In 1911 he helped defeat the main army of the former Mohammad Ali Shah, who had invaded Iran seeking to reclaim his throne. In 1917 he was appointed Governor of Arak (Sultanabad), in 1918 Minister of Post and Telegraph, between 1919 and 1920 Governor of Kerman and between 1923 and 1924 Governor of Khorasan. He was Minister of Post and Telegraph from 1924–1926 and Minister of War 1927–1934, when he was arrested for allegedly re-routing a large shipment of rifles to fellow Bakhtiaris. He was murdered while in detention. Most Iranian observers, including the impartial Mehdi Qoli Hedayat believe the charges were false.[17]

† Nezam al Din Hekmat (Moshar al Dowleh), 1883–1937, was born in Shiraz. His father's title was bestowed on him after the former's death. He studied briefly in Paris in 1913. As deputy in the Third Parliament he threw his lot with the Iranian emigrés of World War I and lived in Turkey for the duration of the war, returning in 1919. He was Under Secretary of War in 1920, Governor of Persian Gulf Ports in 1922, Acting Minister of Education in 1924, Governor of Esfahan in 1927, Governor of Lurestan in 1931 and later Governor of Kurdestan. In 1934 he was appointed Minister of Post, Telegraph and Telephone. He died in 1937, survived by a brother and cousin who played prominent roles during the Reza Shah reign and after.[18]

Bakhtiari tribe supporting Khaz'al. Teimurtash's past quarrels with Norman were forgotten and he was now perceived as a friend. Moshar al Dowleh Hekmat received the highest accolade in being described by the Legation as 'a true Anglophile'.[19]

As mentioned earlier, when Reza Khan became Minister of War only Tehran and a few other cities were under the control or effective sovereignty of the Central Government. The province of Gilan was ruled by Kouchek Khan; inner Mazandaran was under the virtual control of Amir Moayed Savad Kouhi; eastern Mazandaran and parts of northern Khorasan were ruled in effect by two Turkaman tribes; north-west Khorasan was dominated by Sardar Mo'azez Bojnurdi and his Shadlou tribe; and in eastern and southern Khorasan some ten different tribes held sway. Northern Azarbaijan and the area on the Russian border were under the rule of Eqbal al Saltaneh Makou'i; Esma'il Aqa Semitqu controlled all the areas west of Urumieh to the borders of Turkey; and the Shahsavan tribe controlled eastern Azarbaijan. Various Kurdish tribes controlled areas near Hamadan. Areas around Kermanshah were under the power of Sanjabi and Kalhor tribes. Lurestan was ruled by Lur tribesmen and central and parts of western Iran by the Bakhtiaris. Fars and the Persian Gulf areas were ruled by the Qashqa'i, Khamse, Tangestani, Kohgilouye, Mamasani and Boyr Ahmadi tribes. The province of Baluchestan and areas east of Bandar Abbas were the domain of Baluchi tribes. Their authority was so dominant that the Baluchi chief Doost Mohammad Khan had minted a coin with his name prominently displayed on it.[20] Then there was the virtually independent province of Khuzestan, renamed Arabestan and ruled by Sir Sheikh Khaz'al Ibn Jabir Sardar Aqdas.

It is worth noting that since the decline of the Safavids early in the eighteenth century, the very vastness of the country, the absence of a sizeable standing army and the increasing inroads made by foreign powers had produced in Iran a political culture that was opposed to ther concentration of power in any one individual, group or institution including the monarch, the Russian or the British Legation, or any single tribal leader. Iran's élite including the great landlords, the ulama, tribal leaders and merchants all sought access to any source of power that would optimise their own roles and positions. It is against this setting that Reza Khan was intent on imposing his will by creating a strong central government and eradicating diverse pockets of established power, of which the tribes were the most blatant example.

Reza Khan's entire effort from the time he became Minister of War had been to put an end to tribal independence. Probably as early as 1911, and later in his campaign as a junior officer against tribal insurgency, he had realised that Iran would never be regarded as independent, nor in fact be so, until all the tribes were subdued and there was only one government which ruled the entire country. It was not merely that the tribes controlled over three-quarters of the geographical area of Iran and paid no heed to any central government, but some wittingly and some unwittingly had become pawns of European powers serving their interests and objectives. From the end of the nineteenth century tribes had been used by foreign powers to weaken the Central Government or undermine one another's influence in the country as during World War I.

For Reza Khan the taming and even the elimination of tribal leaders posed no moral problems. In addition to their serving foreign powers he had other deep reservations about tribes and their leaders.

> [Reza Khan] felt that most of the tribesmen were of an alien culture... [He] did not think that tribes belonged to 20th century [Iran]... Besides he was hypersensitive to any criticism in the foreign press and was haunted by the fear that Persia might be regarded as a backward country... To him, tribes constituted a shameful anachronism and the very sight of camels, tents and tribal attire [so picturesque to Western eyes] was repugnant'.[21]

He also felt they contributed nothing to the country. Almost all tribesmen were illiterate. Their manpower could not be utilised for the development of the country as long as they led a nomadic existence. They were not to be counted in the work force and they contributed in no way to attempts to modernise and industrialise Iran. The tribal culture ran counter to the creation of a modern nation state.

It is against this background that Sheikh Khaz'al's autonomous rule so preoccupied Reza Khan and every nationalist politician in Tehran. Until the Sheikh could be subdued all of Reza Khan's prior efforts to bring security to Iran would prove in vain. Tribes in other parts of the country that had been subdued would rise again. Iran would never be a cohesive entity or truly independent. Sheikh Khaz'al would remain an anachronism and a relic of the pre-nationalist era, and his mere presence would negate everything Reza Khan and his supporters had striven for.[22]

Khuzestan is located in the south-western corner of Iran bordering Iraq to the west and the Persian gulf to the south. The majority of its population in the 1920s were Arabic-speaking nomadic tribesmen. The Karun River which begins in the mountains of the Bakhtiari region, runs the entire length of Khuzestan and empties into the Euphrates. In the nineteenth century the river afforded one of the most favourable routes of communication between the Persian Gulf

and the plateau to the north. In 1888 Britain obtained a concession
for navigation on the Karun from Naser al Din Shah and soon established a close relationship with Sheikh Maz'al, the chieftain of the
dominant local tribe the Muhaysin. Thereafter Maz'al 'held himself
and his tribe at the orders of the British Government'.[23]

In 1897 Maz'al was assassinated by members of his tribe, insti-
gated and led by his brother Sheikh Khaz'al, who inherited his
brother's considerable wealth and assumed the leadership of the
tribe.[24] Khaz'al further cemented the relationship with Britain and
soon the Government in Tehran came to be totally ignored. The
Tehran-appointed Governor of the province warned Atabak, the
then Prime Minister, that unless Khaz'al's powers were curbed
'Arabistan will in a few years pass into the hands of Britain'.[25]
Successive Iranian prime ministers, fearing Britain, refused to act
and even enhanced Khaz'al's stature and powers by granting him
the sole right to collect customs dues at the port of Mohammareh
(Khoramshahr) without even asking Khaz'al to give an accounting of
the receipts.[26]

From early 1901 Khaz'al sought assurances 'that he was recognised by the British Government as a servant of the British Legation
so that he could oppose the Central Government's action [which was]
against his interests'.[27] In June 1903 Britain gave written assurances
similar to those given to the Sheikh of Kuwait that Britain would
protect Khaz'al against any Russian attacks and would prevent any
attempt by the Iranian Government to curtail the Sheikh's authority
in the region. Soon afterwards one of Khaz'al's many daughters married a senior Bakhtiari leader. There were to be more intermarriages
among Khaz'al's immediate family and Bakhtiari Khans. These marriages allowed Khaz'al to extend his influence in the region and even
over the other smaller Arabic-speaking tribes in Khuzestan.[28]

Under the 1907 Anglo-Russian convention which divided Iran,
Khuzestan (called Arabestan) was not even mentioned as part of the
country. The British, with Russian acquiescence, acted as if it were
a protectorate under British rule.[29] The Government in Tehran raised
no protest and in effect permitted the continuation of the status
quo. When in May 1908 oil was discovered at Masjed Soleiman in
Khuzestan, Britain's relations with Khaz'al assumed even greater
significance. Earlier Britain had entered into several financial agreements with the Bakhtiaris to guard drilling operations. Britain was
now eager to enter into similar arrangements with Khaz'al. Later
that year Khaz'al asked Britain to undertake:

... [to the] utmost of its powers to prevent his absorption by any power
and to guarantee him and his heirs of continuing rule... immunity

against inroads by Majliss against his powers... and if Persia is divided he would retain power in the province.[30]

Sir Percy Cox, British chief Resident in the Persian Gulf, recommended that Britain extend the assurances Khaz'al sought, and in 1909 the British Government agreed; Khaz'al even received some shares in APOC gratis.[31] Also at Cox's recommendation, in 1914 Khaz'al received further assurances and guarantees of his rule.

In 1917 Sheikh Khaz'al, in a public ceremony, received the GCIE decoration and thereafter was addressed as Sir Sheikh Khaz'al. At about the same time Cox recommended that Arabistan should be absorbed officially by Britain making it part of Iraq.[32] At the end of World War I Khaz'al for a brief period was considered as a possible king of Iraq. The idea was soon discarded when the plan for the 1919 Agreement came to the foreground. Both the idea of incorporating Khuzestan as part of Iraq and any consideration of Khaz'al as the ruler of the new country were deemed unnecessary by British policymakers. Besides, there were the former rulers of Arabia who had to be awarded new kingdoms. Britain felt that the 1919 Agreement would protect all of her strategic and financial interests in Iran without any change of boundaries. To compensate Khaz'al and soothe his disappointment Britain made a gift of over 2,000 of the latest rifles, ammunition, four mountain guns, a river steamer and even ceremonial saluting guns. Ahmad Shah was prevailed upon to bestow on Khaz'al the glorified warrior title of Sardar Aqdas.[33] By early 1919 Khuzestan had become a virtual British protectorate with a ruler free from the control of Tehran.

By the time of the coup of February 1921 Sheikh Khaz'al had reached the zenith of his power. He was regarded as the ruler of an independent country. But the Government in Tehran had slowly prepared a strong and valid case against the Sheikh, who had paid no taxes since 1913 nor accounted for any customs receipts that he had collected. In 1922 the Central Government being pressed for funds made a formal attempt to collect at least part of the back taxes. Khaz'al was urged by the British Consul in Ahwaz to reach some kind of settlement with Tehran. Too proud and confident, he ignored both the Consul and the Tehran Government. For the first time the Central Government was given legal cause to proceed against Khaz'al. There was even talk of sending troops to the region to forcefully collect the back taxes. Percy Loraine could see the hazard and in a telegram to Curzon warned of impending dangers as long as Khaz'al remained 'obstinate and uncompromising'.[34]

Reza Khan had his own timetable. He knew all along Khaz'al's continued autonomy posed the single greatest obstacle to the unification of Iran. Unless Khaz'al were subdued the pacification of other tribes would not mean much and sooner or later they would rise again and there would not be a moment of peace. However, the army at this early juncture was not ready and, more important, Britain's response was unpredictable. Reza Khan had not consolidated his power sufficiently to be able to impress upon Britain that it would not be worth her while to use force to defend the Sheikh. Being cautious as always his first move had been the probing operation ostensibly against Lurs and Bakhtiaris in the summer of 1922. In reality he had planned for troops to advance to northern Khuzestan to ascertain the responses of Khaz'al and Britain.

Khaz'al had not been idle. He knew Reza Khan sooner or later would mount a military operation against him. His response to the rise of Reza Khan had been to persuade the Bakhtiaris, Lurs and some of the lesser southern tribes that they had a common interest in preventing Reza Khan from becoming too powerful. The ambush at Shalil in the summer of 1922 by Lur tribes in an area adjacent to northern Khuzestan had been organised by Khaz'al and Amir Mojahed, a Bakhtiari chieftain, some months earlier.[35] Reza Khan had guessed at Khaz'al and Bakhtiari complicity from the outset but there was not much he could do. He had to wait until the army had been built up further and his own position in Tehran made secure in order to mount the Khuzestan operation.

Loraine went on an extended leave in early March 1924. He had known all along that sooner or later Reza Khan would make his move to disarm Khaz'al. While on leave in London Loraine attended a meeting of the Committee of Imperial Defence on July 28. He analysed the political situation in Iran and reported that there could be a clash of forces in the oil region before the end of the year. The Defence Committee, as a precautionary move, decided that the Government of India should be alerted and be prepared to dispatch a military force to Khuzestan if it were found necessary.[36]

By mid April Reza Khan had weathered the republican storm and consolidated his position in Tehran. He began preparations to send troops south when the extremely hot weather of Khuzestan abated. His first step was to ensure that other southern tribes would not join forces with Khaz'al and would remain neutral. In the past he often had used one tribe to neutralise another, with varying degrees of success. In early 1923 he had used a small Bakhtiari contingent to keep Turkamans in Khorasan quiet. Qashqa'is had been used to crush Boyr Ahmadi in south-western Fars.[37] Reza Khan had established reasonably good relations with the Qashqa'i leader Sowlat al Dowleh, who had become an admirer of Reza Khan's nationalism. In early September 1924 Sowlat al Dowleh came to Tehran to take his seat in the Fifth Parliament.[38] As we shall see the Qashqa'i tribe stood aside in the operation against Khaz'al even though Government troops crossed Qashqa'i territory on the last leg of their march.

Reza Khan, like the Qajars, exploited the friction among Bakhtiari tribal leaders. The younger khans had always been in revolt against their elders residing in Tehran. They felt disenfranchised and left out of any decision making. In 1921 the younger Khans had formed a Bakhtiari Soviet and published a 'manifesto of sorts aimed at more equal and egalitarian relations within the tribe'.[39] While Reza Khan was planning the Khuzestan expedition most of the senior Bakhtiari chieftains were in Tehran and Sardar As'ad was in his Cabinet as Minister of Post and Telegraph. Equally important had been the gradual disarming of the Bakhtiari and Qashqa'i tribesmen begun in the spring of 1924.[40] By the end of that summer the army was equipped with rapid-fire weapons of recent vintage as well as a few armoured cars. Reza Khan had more than a dozen observation planes, some two or three with bombing racks. He had also built enough dirt roads for the troops to travel.[41]

Sheikh Khaz'al had realised by now that the ambush at Shalil had not dissuaded Reza Khan from going forward with his plans for a major thrust to the heart of Khuzestan. His response to the threat was both military and political. He had mobilised his tribal forces and had been promised the support of the Lurs and Bakhtiaris. In mid June he informed the British Consul in Ahwaz and the Legation in Tehran that his troops were in a state of full alert and ready to confront and repel any forces Reza Khan may send his way.[42] On the political track he telegraphed the Shah in Paris on 14 September and 'invited him to Mohammareh asking him to return via Arabistan'. On 16 September he sent a letter to the President of parliament, heads of all foreign legations in Tehran and some senior members of the clergy accusing Reza Khan of violating the Constitution of Iran and having wrongfully usurped the powers of the Shah. The Sheikh promised the recipients of his letters that he and his supporters would do 'their utmost to ensure the definite establishment of constitutional principles and the indispensible return of the Shah'.[43] In his letter to the clergy Khaz'al denounced Reza Khan as an enemy of Islam, the Shah and the constitution and 'he was determined to overthrow Reza Khan or perish in the attempt'.[44]

Khaz'al was unaware that his support among British officialdom in Iran was dwindling. His main backers numbered only the British Consuls serving in various posts in southern Iran who mostly had been recruited from the Government of India. E.G. Peel, the Consul in Ahwaz, was a strong champion of Khaz'al and had been advocating for several months the removal of the 'Anti-British Reza Khan from office'. During September he wrote a number of reports to the Foreign Office espousing Khaz'al's position. He wrote:

> Centralising policy of Reza Khan appears definitely to have failed. Bakhtiaris are on the side of Sheikh Khaz'al who can on his own mobilise 25,000 Arabs. This force can defeat Reza Khan if Britain adhered to its policy of neutrality... [The Sheikh] was confident [he could] compel the resignation of Reza Khan and protect British lives and property.[45]

Another strong supporter of Khaz'al was the Consul in Bushehr, Prideaux, who wrote to the Foreign Office arguing that all Britain had to do was to indicate that it was more sympathetic to Sheikh Khaz'al than to anyone else. Reza Khan would then fall, the Shah would return and the Sheikh 'would protect all our interests'.[46]

The single most important supporter of Khaz'al had been Sir Percy Cox, who was now retiring as the High Commissioner of Iraq. He could do little with Curzon out of office and the changing post-war world. As one of the key architects of the 1919 Agreement it must have been galling to him to witness the rise of Reza Khan and his attempts to cut down the Sheikh, thus dismantling one of Cox's major achievements in the protection of British interests in Iran.

Against these supporters of Khaz'al there was Esmond Ovey, Loraine's stand-in for the duration of the latter's leave, who like Loraine had become a vigorous supporter of the strong central government thesis and hence an advocate of Reza Khan's policy. Ovey was disturbed by reports of the British Consuls and wrote to MacDonald:

> I am appalled at the liberty with which the Consul General in Bushehr openly suggests that His Majesty's Government should lend themselves to the plot to overthrow the Prime Minister and recall the Shah.[47]

Ovey also criticised Peel, who had reported that in a clash of forces Sheikh Khaz'al would be the winner. Ovey had earlier asked MacDonald to order the consuls either to co-operate with the Legation in Tehran or to remove them from their posts.[48] The Foreign Office concurred with Ovey. Oliphant wrote to Peel on behalf of MacDonald that it was not for the Consul 'to anticipate the political situation in the Capital, 700 miles away... of which Mr Ovey can be the sole Judge'.[49] Victor Mallet, who had replaced G.P. Churchill at the Persian desk was a forceful supporter of a strong central government and argued that there was not much Britain could do as Reza Khan 'was too big a personality to be easily shifted from the

17. *Ahmad Qavam (Qavam al Saltaneh)*. Twice prime minister between 1921 and 1922, this younger brother of Vosouq was a wily and corrupt politician who broadened Iran's contacts with the US.

18. Hosein Pirnia (Mo'tamen al Molk). The Speaker of the Majlis between 1922 and 1925 was a highly respected and principled guardian of the sanctity of parliamentary supremacy.

19. Seyyed Hassan Moddares. An excellent parliamentarian, his vanity drove him to see himself as an indispensable advisor to kings, princes and prime ministers. But he was outflanked by Reza Shah and was eventually put to death.

saddle as previous [Persian] Prime Ministers'.[50] Finally MacDonald himself instructed Peel in Ahwaz and Prideaux in Bushehr 'to speak [with] one voice with the Legation' and to discourage the Sheikh's bellicose inclination.[51]

The attitude of APOC also played a crucial part in the final resolution of the conflict. Few in APOC sympathised with Reza Khan. Most dismissed the argument that a strong central government would safeguard British oil interests in the region. Nevertheless APOC was much concerned and apprehensive that Khaz'al's disobedience and belligerent rhetoric could start a civil war in the very heart of the oil fields. Another compelling argument against the Sheikh was that even if Reza Khan were to fall there would be no guarantee that succeeding Iranian governments would not move against the Sheikh. The APOC representative in Tehran wrote:

> There is a liklihood even if Reza Khan is eliminated, the administration of the army will continue present policy regarding the Sheikh of Mohammareh which is backed by public opinion.[52]

The issue of public opinion bore significant weight with the British Legation and the upper ranks of APOC. Khaz'al was extremely unpopular. Even Moddares, to whom Khaz'al had written, thought it unwise to speak up for him. The enemies of Reza Khan felt that to support Khaz'al was to be tainted with a pro-British brush and appear as anti-nationalist and opposed to Iran's attempt at national unity.

In late summer MacDonald wrote to Ovey:

> [APOC] is very disturbed. [The Sheikh] is telling Bakhtiaris and Qashqai and others that he will protect his region. It [APOC] is equally confused about Sheikh Khaz'al's invitation [to Ahmad Shah] to come to Mohammareh as his guest to elaborate plans for an independent south Persia.

MacDonald instructed Ovey to send the following message to Sheikh Khaz'al:

> While he may rest assured that His Majesty's Government is doing its best for the Persian Government to accord just consideration to his rights and interests, I feel obliged to remind him that our assurances [to Khaz'al] are dependant upon his loyalty to Central authority and urge him in a friendly way to abstain from any violent action which would be highly prejudicial to his own interests and to ours. Resident in Bushehr to deliver message personally.[53]

With all the conflicting advice, APOC in London never could make up its mind definitively although its foremost authority on Iranian tribes, Dr M.V. Young was on the side of a strong Central Government.[54] The mere fact that APOC's directors remained undecided opened the field for ad hoc decisions by the Foreign Secretary and the diplomats in London and Tehran.

Another element that began to concern British policy makers was the entry of the Soviets in the propaganda war waged by the Sheikh. Newspapers in Iraq had begun openly to support Sheikh Khaz'al. Their common theme was that 'Arabs will unite to defend the Sheikh' and Arabistan.[55] In response the Soviet news bureau, Rosta, began a campaign against the Sheikh and his backers, whom they viewed as perpetrators of a nefarious British plot. The Sheikh was accused of sending money to Reza Khan's opponents in Tehran and of sending emissaries to the Shah in Paris with the object of reaching an arrangement for establishing a separate kingdom in Khuzestan.[56] The involvement of the Soviets in the war of words had a pronounced effect on British thinking. Once again the growing Soviet menace became part of the equation. It reinforced the thesis that it is better to have a strong man in Tehran to keep the Bolsheviks at bay. The supporters of Reza Khan argued that if any-one were to be forced to give in it should be Sheikh Khaz'al whose sole ambition was to increase his own power and wealth.[57]

Reza Khan, having totally recovered from his reverses and sensing overwhelming support in the country for the impending expedition, began to speak in confident tones to the British Legation. He let the British Military Attaché know that he could raise a force of 40,000, sufficient to defeat the Sheikh even with Bakhtiari intervention. He was prepared for war whatever the consequences. Any damage to the oil installations, would be solely the responsibility of Sheikh Khaz'al. Ovey, who had supported Reza Khan from the time he arrived in Tehran, now argued that Sheikh Khaz'al, by rebelling against the Central Government and refusing to pay taxes, had forfeited his right to invoke British pledges to protect his local autonomy as these pledges had been conditioned upon his loyalty to the Central Government.[58]

In 1923 Reza Khan had authorised the US financial advisers to prepare and make public a detailed account of taxes owed by Khaz'al going back almost ten years. Khaz'al could have defused the situation by making some partial payment but badly miscalculated the political situation in Tehran and his eroding base of support at the British Legation. With his background of fratricide, his cruel and arbitrary rule in Khuzestan and long servitude to his British masters there were few people willing to defend him publicly. At the end of the summer of 1924 Ovey attempted to arrange for the Sheikh to come to Tehran to settle his tax arrears and make peace. Khaz'al refused. With Khaz'al's rejection of any compromise, MacDonald was forced to write to him:

> ... but I must warn Your Excellency that the patience of the Persian Government will soon become exhausted and that in the regrettable event of hostility you must expect no sympathy whatsoever from me.[59]

Khaz'al also was beginning to lose support among senior Bakhtiari leaders. Although most of the Khans sympathised with the Sheikh they had no alternative but to remain silent. There had been a gradual disarming of the tribes and in mid October some 1800 troops were sent from Tehran to support pro-Central Government tribal governors. Peel, although instructed to follow the policy adopted by the Legation in Tehran, remained unchastened and wrote to the Foreign Office:

> [Reza Khan] 'insists Sheikh Khaz'al must submit otherwise troops would cross Bakhtiari territory to the border of Arabistan. Reza Khan is a bluffer. I do not believe he will attack. Turkamans have risen. Baluchistan is still independent country. Luristan is still unsubdued. The Sanjabi, Kalhor and Wali Pusht-e-Kuh would seize the opportunity of harrasing government if hostilities broke in the south. Reza Khan should be thankful to us. Tehran is quiet only because of martial law. Reza Khan needs us... Basically he should be thankful to us for keeping the tribes quiet.[60]

Peel had not ceased his advocacy of the Sheikh. He was indirectly saying that if Britain stirred the tribes, Reza Khan would have to think twice before sending troops to Khuzestan. Peel was to be reassigned and he left Iran by the beginning of 1925.

Reza Khan had completed preparation for the movement of troops. He informed Ovey that he had made up his mind and Government troops numbering 15,000 would shortly start their march to Khuzestan. Reza Khan himself left for Esfahan on 5 November. Foroughi, the Minister of Finance, was to act for him during his absence.[61] There was little Britain could do now. The Foreign Office turned to Loraine to mediate and defuse the crisis. Loraine, while on leave, had married and was on his honeymoon. He cut short the honeymoon and with his bride left London. He stayed in Paris 24 hours, saw Ahmad Shah briefly and set out by boat to Egypt. Loraine's plan was to arrange a meeting between Sheikh Khaz'al and Reza Khan with himself as mediator and hope for some face-saving compromise.[62]

With the movement of Government troops, Peel was instructed to compel Khaz'al to write a letter to Reza Khan apologising for his slanderous remarks. The Sheikh was prevailed upon and wrote a letter on 14 November asking forgiveness for his past deeds. Reza

Khan telegraphed the British Legation in Tehran that he accepted the apology but the movement of troops could not be stopped as winter was approaching and troops had to reach warmer territory. Loraine, who by now had reached Baghdad, was upset over Reza Khan's response. He telegraphed Peel to warn of the impending offensive of Reza Khan and to release Khaz'al from his promise of non-belligerency but 'also to remind him of his responsibility for British lives and property'.[63]

There was not much Khaz'al or his coalition of tribes could do. Britain had restrained the tribes and now they were paralysed. The tribal leaders had no idea of where Britain stood and what she expected them to do. The only viable option was the intervention of British troops, which had been entertained as a measure of last resort. Loraine had written some eight months earlier that 'Reza Khan does not understand any barrier to his activity unless they are made perfectly clear to him nor what the consequences would be'.[64] Loraine had also maintained that Reza Khan was an excellent bluffer in certain situations. To test his appraisal of Reza Khan's immediate plans, Loraine requested a battalion of troops from India as well as the dispatch of three gunboats to be sent to Basra.[65]

On 7 November 1924 MacDonald and the Labour Government had lost the general election and Stanley Baldwin, the leader of the Conservative Party, became the new Prime Minister, with Austin Chamberlain as Foreign Secretary. Chamberlain was faced with several problems soon after he took office. In Egypt Sir Lee Stack, Governor of Sudan and Acting Commander of the Egyptian army, had been assassinated. Chamberlain had written to Loraine even before the latter had requested troops, 'We must avoid if we can too many crises at one time'.[66] Now in response to Loraine's request he wrote:

> I cannot emphasise too strongly the reluctance with which His Majesty's Government would embark on any military intervention in Arabistan [in view of the situation in Egypt]. We must go to the utmost length and even take some risks in order to avoid complications in south Persia at the present moment.[67]

The request for troops was hence rejected but three gunboats were sent to Basra with one taking position in Abadan.

Britain began to fear that Khaz'al would leave Iran and settle on his estate in Basra. The possible flight to a neighbouring Arab land would not reflect well on Britain. It would appear that Britain had let down an ally to whom she had given guarantees and with whom she had contractual obligations.[68] The situation remained fluid. A few days later the Foreign Office changed its mind and began to reconsider sending troops when Loraine warned it would be difficult to persuade Reza Khan to compromise and grant Sheikh Khaz'al terms favourable enough for the Sheikh to consider it worth his while to remain in Iran. The dispatch of British troops to Khuzestan may have been the only way Reza Khan could have been impelled to allow the Sheikh to keep his position and at least some of his former powers.[69] A note of caution crept into the thinking of the Foreign Office when the legation in Tehran reported that the Soviets had offered to send troops 'to protect the Persians'.[70] The situation once more was reassessed and the risk of military intervention by Britain was reconsidered.

The options for Britain were dwindling. Reza Khan had overwhelming troop superiority and there was little chance for the Sheikh of help from neighbouring tribes. The fear of Soviet intervention introduced a dangerous dimension. Equally important to Loraine was the fact that if Reza Khan were unsuccessful in his attempt to bring down the Sheikh his enemies in Tehran would have a great chance to remove him from office. After lengthy deliberation Loraine requested that the gunboat harboured in Abadan be withdrawn. The only way now for Britain to preserve its prestige was to arrange a meeting between Khaz'al and Reza Khan and hope some face-saving device would emerge.

In late October, before Reza Khan had left Tehran, Ovey, at the urging of Loraine, had attempted to arrange a meeting of Reza Khan, Loraine and the Sheikh somewhere between Tehran and Moham-mareh. Reza Khan had refused and stated that he would meet Khaz'al only in Tehran. He rightly believed that a meeting with Khaz'al anywhere in southern Iran before Khaz'al had surrendered would be ruinous to his prestige 'since it would be tantamount to accepting British influence in the affairs of Persia'. Reza Khan had further insisted on a letter of apology from Khaz'al and disbanding of his troops.[71] As already mentioned the Sheikh did send a letter of abject apology when it had become obvious that his forces had disintegrated.

When Reza Khan reached Shiraz another attempt was made for him to meet Loraine and Khaz'al, this time in Bushehr. Reza Khan again refused and announced that he intended to continue to Khuzestan.[72] He had probably initially agreed to meet Loraine and Khaz'al in Bushehr, but when news of the impending meeting had been leaked by Reuters, he changed his mind. In Reza Khan's own version of events he stated that the Soviet Legation in Tehran had sent him a message that it was disturbed over the news. Reza Khan in a double-edged reply intended for both the Soviets and British telegraphed the Soviet Legation in Tehran:

I have never accepted the interference of a foreign power. Otherwise I could not protect the independence of my country... Sheikh Khaz'al is an Iranian subject and only those in power in Iran can forgive or punish him.[73]

Reza Khan next went to Bushehr, where he met G. Havard, the Oriental Secretary who had travelled to Bushehr at Loraine's instruction. Reza Khan told Havard he would be willing to see the Sheikh only in Mohammareh or Ahwaz provided the Sheikh travelled a considerable distance outside town to greet him. He would also be willing to meet Loraine provided their meeting was not publicly announced. Loraine seized the opportunity and asked Peel to compel the Sheikh to accept. This was the best face-saving situation Loraine could have obtained for the Sheikh, and Loraine left Baghdad for Basra. Reza Khan arrived at the borders of Khuzestan on 27 November, having received further telegrams from Khaz'al which were tantamount to outright surrender.[74] The leading column of the army had preceded him and encountered no opposition. The main body was to arrive in two weeks.

Reza Khan met Khaz'al in Ahwaz on 6 December. He next met Loraine with Havard as translator. He assured Loraine that 'he did not want a fight with Britain' and that the Sheikh could have his position and privileges but he had to take certain measures to acknowledge the authority of the Central Government. Troops would have to occupy Khuzestan at least until the spring, but if the situation remained calm they would then be withdrawn. Loraine dealt in generalities and tacitly endorsed Reza Khan's plan.[75] In just two weeks after the meeting with Loraine, the main body of Government troops occupied the entire territory. Brig. Gen. Fazlollah Zahedi, who commanded the leading force, was appointed Governor General of the province which reverted to its ancient name.[76] Khuzestan once again had become an integral part of Iran and would be governed as any other province.

Ironically Loraine's reputation as a master diplomat soared. The mere fact that a bloody clash had been avoided with no loss of life and no damage to APOC installations was highly gratifying to the Foreign Office, which was greatly impressed by Loraine for diffusing the situation. Chamberlain was elated and wrote to Loraine, '[Your] dispatch is as admirable in its kind as [your] action throughout these difficult and perilous negotiations'.[77] The Sheikh was now regarded as an anomaly whose fate must be made 'subsidiary to the main consideration', a unified and stable Iran as a bulwark against the Soviet threat to the Persian Gulf and India.[78]

Following the meeting with Loraine, Reza Khan paid his first visit to the oil fields. After a short visit to Mohammareh he made a pilgrimage to the Shi'a shrines at Najaf and Karbala before returning to Mohammareh where he saw Sheikh Khaz'al again.[79] On 20 December 1924 Reza Khan signed documents pardoning the Sheikh and agreeing to respect the Sheikh's ownership of his lands and possessions and promising that he and his dependents would not be harassed or molested.[80] The Sheikh in return promised he would settle his tax indebtedness. It was obvious to all including the British Legation that the repossession of Khuzestan was permanent, irreversible and that neither the Sheikh nor any other tribal chieftain would ever exercise the powers and independence previously practiced.

When some three months later news reached Tehran that the Sheikh might leave Iran and settle on his estate in Basra, Reza Khan became apprehensive that Khaz'al would continue to be a source of concern if he were unwatched and out of reach. He could incite his own and neighbouring tribes to cause mischief and the army garrison in Khuzestan would be tied down trying to pacify them. In April 1925 Reza Khan raised the matter with Loraine and stressed that the question of Khaz'al's unpaid taxes had remained unresolved and it would be helpful if the Sheikh could be induced to come to Tehran to settle his affairs. Loraine wrote to the Foreign Office and the new British Consul in Ahwaz, Moneypenny (who had replaced Peel), to urge the Sheikh to come to Tehran to settle his back taxes, thereby removing all encumbrances on his property.[81] Khaz'al became agitated and delayed giving an answer. In late April, at Reza Khan's instructions and without the knowledge of any British official, Iranian soldiers boarded Khaz'al's boat, removed him and one of his sons and sent them by car to Tehran. They were housed at one of the numerous residences Khaz'al had maintained in Tehran.[82]

Loraine was continuing his interrupted holiday and was in Persepolis when he received a telegram from Chamberlain informing him of the forced transfer of Khaz'al to Tehran. Loraine placed the blame on the Sheikh for not having accepted previous advice to come voluntarily to Tehran. He informed Chamberlain that there was not much he could do as the Sheikh did not 'behave sensibly'.[83] Reza Khan's only explanation sent through intermediaries was that he had to bring Khaz'al to Tehran. If he had stayed in Khuzestan there would have been constant trouble with the tribes.

Khaz'al and his son reached Tehran on 10 May. Loraine sent him a welcoming letter but the messenger was refused admittance by the guards around the Sheikh's house. Havard paid a call but he too was denied entry. Loraine instructed Havard to see Reza Khan and receive permission for unhampered access by British Legation officials. Reza Khan turned on Havard furiously, and with expletives

and foul language told him that Sheikh Khaz'al was an Iranian subject and that neither Havard, Loraine nor others could visit Khaz'al
without his express permission. He had to think of the security of
the country and could not be bothered with social calls by British
officials on someone who until recently had been a rebel. Havard
had no choice but to lodge a protest and leave.[84]

A few days later Davoud Meftah (Meftah al Saltaneh), the Deputy
Foreign Minister, called on Loraine to discuss an unrelated matter.
At the end of the meeting Meftah explained that Havard's call on
Reza Khan had been at an inopportune time. Reza Khan had been
deeply upset over a recent Turkaman uprising in northwest
Khorasan, otherwise he would not have used abusive language.
Meftah further suggested that in view of Reza Khan's tempestuous
temperament he hoped Loraine would forget the matter.[85] Loraine
had no choice but to forego the official protest. A few days later Reza
Khan himself attended a large dinner at the British Legation and
told Loraine that Khaz'al would continue to be guarded but he could
receive visitors.[86]

Sheikh Khaz'al was not allowed to leave Tehran, although he was
subsequently received regularly by Reza Shah and treated deferentially. When some two years later he asked to go to Europe for
medical reasons as he was gradually losing his eyesight, Reza Shah
ordered his Minister of Court, Teimurtash, to have one of the best
ophthalmologists from Europe come to Tehran.[87] Khaz'al never settled
the issue of his back taxes and he was not able to exercise full control and dominion over his vast properties. He died in 1936 and only
when Reza Khan abdicated was Britain able to force the Iranian
Government to return his properties to his heirs.[88]

The subjugation of Sheikh Khaz'al was the last step in the unification of Iran. If Khaz'al had remained in his former position he
would have been an ever-present danger to the Iranian state. With
the enormous power and prestige of Britain and its domination of the
League of Nations, Khuzestan could have been made independent
with no recourse by Iran, or remained a vassal state always in danger
of absorbtion by Britain if the policies of the Iranian Government
were deemed inimical to the interests of Britain or APOC. Chamberlain had later reviewed the 1914 guarantees and assurances to
Sheikh Khaz'al and wrote:

> We are living in a different world to that in which assurances were given
> and must walk warily. I do not say in every respect it is a better world
> but certainly it is not an easier world in which to carry out our former
> policy... but we must take care that we are not arraigned on any ground
> on which we cannot defend ourselves.[89]

Britain finally appeared to have adjusted its policy toward Iran and to have accepted new realities.

Reza Khan had made a triumphant entry into Tehran on 1 January 1925. He entered the city 'like a Roman Emperor returning from a great and distant campaign', except that the enemy had abjectly surrendered with no blood having been shed. 'Yet it must be remembered that the mere exercise of energy and determination constituted heroism in a country that had not seen these qualities in many years'.[90]

NOTES ON CHAPTER 12
Further details of publications and documents in Bibliography

1   FO 371/10146, Ovey to MacDonald, 31 July 1924.
2   Richard W. Cottam, *Iran and the United States*, pp 42–43.
3   Soleiman Behboodi, *Khaterat Soleiman Behboodi* (*The Memoirs of Soleiman Behboodi*), pp 145–148.
4   *Ibid.*, p 149.
5   *Ibid.*, p 155; Amin Banani, *The Modernization of Iran*, p 42.
6   Donald N. Wilber, *Riza Shah Pahlavi*, p 87; Hosein Makki, *Tarikh Bist Saleh Iran* (*A Twenty Year History of Iran*), vol. 3, pp 92–106.
7   FO 416/79, Ovey to MacDonald, 19 July 1924.
8   FO 416/75, Ovey to MacDonald, 24 July 1924.
9   FO 416/75, Ovey to MacDonald, 24 July 1924.
10   DoS 891.636/392, Soaper, Washington DC to W. Murray, Chargé at US Legation in Tehran, 28 August 1924; FO 371/10156, Ovey to MacDonald, 10 October 1924.
11   FO 416/75, Ovey to MacDonald, 10 October 1924.
12   FO 416/75, Ovey to Austin Chamberlain, 17 November 1924.
13   DoS, Soaper to W. Murray, 28 August 1924.
14   FO 371/10146, Ovey to MacDonald, 31 July 1924.
15   FO 416/75, Ovey to MacDonald, 19 August 1924.
16   FO 416/75, Ovey to MacDonald, 20 August 1924.
17   Mehdi Bamdad, *Tarikh Rejal Iran Quroun 12, 13, 14* (*Dictionary of National Biography of Iran: Twelfth, Thirteenth, Fourteenth Centuries*), vol. 1, pp 245–247; Sardar As'ad Bakhtiari, *Khaterat Sardar As'ad Bakhtiari* (*The Memoirs of Sardar As'ad Bakhtiari*) ed. Iraj Afshar; Mehdi Qoli Hedayat (Mokhber al Saltaneh), *Khaterat va Khatarat* (*Memoirs and Hazards*), p 514.
18   Mehdi Bamdad, *Tarikh Rejal Iran Quroun 12, 13, 14* (*Dictionary of National Biography of Iran: Twelfth, Thirteenth, Fourteenth Centuries*), vol. 5, p 318.
19   FO 371/10146, Ovey to MacDonald, 10 September 1924.
20   *Tarikh Artesh, Novin Iran*, Part 1, 1300–1320 (*History of the Modern Iranian Armed Forces*), Part 1, 1921–1924.
21   Pierre Oberling, *The Qashqa'i Nomads of Fars*, pp 149–150.
22   Ervand Abrahamian, *Iran Between Two Revolutions*, p 120.
23   William Theodore Strunk, 'The Reign of Sheikh Khaz'al Ibn Jabir and the Suppression of the Principality of Khuzistan', unpublished PhD thesis, p 6.
24   *Ibid.*, p 8; Lord Hardinge, *Old Diplomacy*, p 65; Hosein Makki, *Tarikh Bist Saleh Iran* (*A Twenty Year History of Iran*), vol. 3, pp 240 and 294.
25   William Theodore Strunk, 'The Reign of Sheikh Khaz'al Ibn Jabir and the Suppression of the Principality of Khuzistan', unpublished PhD thesis, p 11.
26   *Ibid.*, p 23.
27   *Ibid.*, p 28.
28   *Ibid.*, pp 99 and 102. Despite these marriages Bakhtiari-Khaz'al relations were always tenuous as each looked to Britain for increased favours.
29   *Ibid.*, p 139.
30   *Ibid.*, p 240.
31   *Ibid.*, p 243.

32 *Ibid.*, p 314.
33 *Ibid.*, p 316.
34 FO 371/7804, Loraine to Curzon, 25 April 1922.
35 FO 371/7807, Minutes by Peel, 4 August 1922.
36 Gordon Waterfield, *Professional Diplomat: Sir Percy Loraine*, p. 82.
37 Pierre Oberling, *The Qashqa'i Nomads of Fars*, pp 150–151.
38 FO 416/75, Ovey to MacDonald, 10 October 1924.
39 David Brooks, 'The Enemy Within', Chapter 12 in Richard Tapper (ed.), *The Conflict of Tribe and State in Iran and Afghanistan*, pp 358–359.
40 Lois Beck, *The Qashqa'i of Iran*, p 131. Sardar As'ad accompanied Reza Khan during the entire journey to Khuzestan.
41 Pierre Oberling, *The Qashqa'i Nomads of Fars*, pp 150–151.
42 FO 371/10134, Ovey to MacDonald, 28 June 1924.
43 FO 371/10136, Ovey to MacDonald, 9 September 1924.
44 FO 371/10135, Ovey to MacDonald, 11 and 17 September 1924: quoted by Houshang Sabahi, *British Policy in Persia 1918–1925*, p 179.
45 FO 371/10135, E.G.P. Peel to Foreign Office, 23, 25 and 27 September 1924.
46 FO 371/10135, Prideaux to Foreign Office, 15 September 1924.
47 FO 371/10135, Ovey to MacDonald, 16 September 1924.
48 FO 371/10146, Ovey to MacDonald, 20 August 1924.
49 FO 371/10135, Minutes by Oliphant, 18 and 24 September 1924.
50 FO 371/10146, Minutes by Mallet, 3 September 1924; Houshang Sabahi, *British Policy in Persia 1918–1925*, p 180.
51 FO 371/10135, MacDonald to Peel, 10 October 1924.
52 FO 371/10135, W.C. Fairly, Tehran, to APOC, London, 3 October 1924.
53 FO 416/75, MacDonald to Ovey, 23 August 1924.
54 FO 1011/128, Dr M.V. Young to Loraine, 3 September 1924; R.W. Ferrier, *The History of British Petroleum Company*, vol. 1, pp 390–394. Houshang Sabahi, *British Policy in Persia 1918–1925*, p 181.
55 William Theodore Strunk, 'The Reign of Sheikh Khaz'al Ibn Jabir and the Suppression of the Principality of Khuzistan', unpublished PhD thesis, p 392.
56 FO 371/10135, Ovey to MacDonald, 3 August 1924.
57 Houshang Sabahi, *British Policy in Persia 1918–1925*, p 181, quoting Minutes by Mallet, 18 and 24 September 1924.
58 FO 371/10146, FO 371/10135, FO 371/10134 and FO 371/10136, Ovey to MacDonald, 14 and 20 August, 15, 17, 24 and 29 September, and 9, 10 and 23 October 1924.
59 FO 371/10136, MacDonald to Tehran Legation for transmittal to Khaz'al, 11 October 1924.
60 FO 371/10146, Peel to Foreign Office via Ovey, 1 November 1924.
61 FO 416/75, Ovey to Austen Chamberlain, 17 November 1924.
62 FO371/10136, Minutes by Oliphant, 11 October 1924; FO 1011/128, Ovey to Loraine, 8 November 1924. Houshang Sabahi, *British Policy in Persia 1918–1925*, p 184.
63 FO 371/10137, Loraine to Peel, 25 November 1924.
64 FO 371/10137, Loraine to MacDonald, 11 February 1924.
65 FO 371/10137, Foreign Office to Loraine, 25 November 1924.
66 FO 371/10137, Minutes by Chamberlain, 20 November 1924.
67 FO 371/10137, Chamberlain to Loraine in Baghdad, 25 and 28 November 1924; Houshang Sabahi, *British Policy in Persia 1918–1925*, p 187.

68 FO 371/10780, Memorandum by Mallet, 3 and 6 December 1924.
69 FO 371/10138, Loraine to Chamberlain, 3 December 1924.
70 FO 371/10138, Monson to Chamberlain, 3 December 1924.
71 FO 371/10136, Peel to Ovey, 24 October 1924; Houshang Sabahi, *British Policy in Persia 1918–1925*, p 184.
72 FO 371/10137, Monson to Foreign Office, 24 November 1924.
73 Reza Shah, *Safar Nameh Khuzestan dar Sal 1303 (Khuzestan Travel Journal of the Year 1924)*, pp 47–53. It is generally accepted that the book was written by Farajollah Bahrami (Dabir A'zam), a close associate of Reza Shah in his early years who served as confidential secretary. It is a fairly reliable though self-laudatory and highly selective account of the campaign in Khuzestan. The passage quoted has been condensed and translated into English.
74 FO 416/76, Monson to Chamberlain, 15 December 1924.
75 FO 371/10843, Loraine to Chamberlain, 22 December 1924. Houshang Sabahi, *British Policy in Persia 1918–1925*, p 191.
76 FO 416/76, Loraine to Chamberlain, 31 December 1924.
77 FO 371/10138, Chamberlain to Loraine, 10 December 1924.
78 FO 1011/131, Loraine to Osborne, 7 February 1925. Houshang Sabahi, *British Policy in Persia 1918–1925*, p 192.
79 Gordon Waterfield, *Professional Diplomat: Sir Percy Loraine*, p 92.
80 FO 371/10843, Loraine to the Foreign Office, 12 March 1925.
81 FO 371/10843, Loraine to the Foreign Office, 7 April 1925.
82 FO 371/10843, Moneypenny to Loraine, 23 April 1925.
83 FO 371/10843, Loraine to Chamberlain, 4 May 1925.
84 FO 371/10843, Loraine to Chamberlain, 12 and 25 May 1925.
85 FO 416/76, Loraine to Chamberlain, 19 May 1925.
86 *Ibid.*
87 Soleiman Behboodi, *Khaterat Soleiman Behboodi (The Memoirs of Soleiman Behboodi)*, pp 314–315.
88 Gordon Waterfield, *Professional Diplomat: Sir Percy Loraine*, p 132.
89 FO 371/10843, Minutes by Chamberlain, 11 May 1925.
90 Vincent Sheean, *The New Persia*, p 52.

13

The Abolition of the Qajar Dynasty

Reza Khan had been away for over two months. Five planes escorted him into the city and one of Sheikh Khaz'al's sons, having been appointed as an aide-de-camp, accompanied him. Although his supporters had made extensive arrangements for Reza Khan to enter the capital in glory there was also a genuine and most impressive display of popular feeling for his bloodless victory in the south. The illuminations and fireworks in Tehran and the provincial centres were to last three days. The official welcoming committee comprising leading officials including most members of the Cabinet, members of parliament and high-ranking military officers met Reza Khan some 40 kilometres outside of the city. Many notables had gone as far as Hamadan to greet him. On reaching Tehran, Reza Khan ordered a curtailment of the celebrations and retired to his house in the north of the city. From 5 January he held separate receptions for representatives of foreign legations as well as Iranian dignitaries.[1]

There was one remaining serious insurrection which demanded Reza Khan's attention. Turkaman lawlessness still prevailed in eastern Mazandaran and northern Khorasan. In October 1924 they had escalated their attacks on neighbouring villages and blocked the Tehran-Mashad road. They had also attacked Astarabad (Gorgan) and laid seige to Bojnurd. The local garrisons had been too weak to

withstand the attacks and Reza Kahn, whose pirority lay in subduing Khaz'al, had done little to relieve the situation except to
dispatch a nominal force to check further advances and to open the
main road between Tehran and Mashhad. Reza Khan now focused his
attention on this situation and by late May Bojnurd was relieved and
the Turkamans fled across the border of Soviet Turkamanistan. They
were to cause little trouble thereafter and were gradually disarmed.

An important element in quelling the Turkaman uprising and
generally facilitating the control of nomadic tribes was the slowly
emerging air wing of the armed forces. As early as 1922 Reza Khan
had been convinced that an air force would cost a fraction of what
it would cost to raise the army to the strength he felt was essential
for the internal security of the country. Aeroplanes also would be far
more effective in putting down revolts by tribes and, more important, could provide timely information of tribal movements outside
their zones.[2] Planes would also have commercial value as they could
facilitate communication. With the war over in Europe and a vast
surplus of planes available, the cost became affordable (about £300
– £400 a plane). The first purchases of planes were from France in
autumn 1923, but they proved unsuitable in that they were aged
and not well-adapted to Iranian conditions. Reza Khan stopped purchases from France and subsequently bought eight planes from
Germany and two from the Soviets. These planes were more suitable
and pilots from these countries were employed. Reza Khan was
especially eager to purchase British planes stationed in Iraq as they
would be best adapted to the climatic conditions of the area and the
supply of spare parts would be easier. Britain delayed the sale and
it was not until 1933 that Britain became Iran's major supplier of
planes. The Soviets became the next largest source and pilots were
trained by manufacturers either in Britain or the Soviet Union.[3]

In the campaign against Sheikh Khaz'al only a few planes occasionally flew over Ahwaz, principally for psychological purposes. In
the campaign against the Turkamans the use of a few planes also
had a great psychological effect on the rebels although the material
damage was insignificant. The first military use of the planes was in
Lurestan in the summer of 1924 when the Lurs laid siege to
Khoramabad and all communications with the outside were cut. In
the absence of other means, aeroplane reconnaisance missions provided valuable information. Later some bombs were dropped, which
dispirited the Lurs and the siege was lifted.[4]

With all parts of the country now quiet, Reza Khan's prestige was
at its height in the early months of 1925. Not a word of criticism was
uttered publicly against him. There were no longer large organised

hostile factions in the Fifth Parliament. The groupings now could be categorised generally as those who supported Reza Khan and his entire Cabinet; those who supported Reza Khan as Prime Minister but wanted changes in the Cabinet; and a small minority opposed to the entire Government and Reza Khan personally. In their rare public utterances the most this last group were prepared to say was to acknowledge Reza Khan's past and continued services but express veiled dismay over the Shah's continued absence and further express the hope that the Shah would return as soon as possible.[5] What these few deputies really wanted was for the Shah to come back and either remove Reza Khan from office or at least act as a counterbalance against Reza Khan's growing power. The composition of these groupings were not permanent. There were constant realignments in parliament which occured for personal reasons or reasons of expediency rather than on grounds of political beliefs or deeply held convictions. Insofar as economic and social policy were concerned there continued to be what could be called the conservatives and progressives. The progressives were still represented by Soleiman Mirza. The conservatives were against any social or economic change and also strongly against any Soviet influence in Iran. The most effective spokesman of the right, Moddares, wanted the Shah to return as soon as possible and in the meantime to have as many of his protegés as possible included in the Cabinet.

The most important political development in parliament at the beginning of 1925 was the loss of considerable prestige by Moddares, Reza Khan's chief adversary whose prestige had been at an all-time high when he had led the anti-republican movement and had been chiefly responsible for its collapse. He had squandered a great deal of goodwill in siding with Sheikh Khaz'al and even acting as an advocate and go-between for the Sheikh. Although a man of sincere beliefs Moddares:

> ...was not too particular about the means he employed for the attainment of his objectives.... he used tactics which could easily be taken as evidence of hypocricy and inconsistancy... For example he surprised many by his defence of Firouz's credentials [for admittance to the Fourth Parliament] barely six months after the latter's [prominent role] in the implementation of the 1919 Agreement and when he made the tactical mistake of contacting Khaz'al... who stood accused of being a separatist, a tyrant and agent of imperialism.[6]

Centre stage amidst all these manoeuverings was the overwhelming presence of Reza Khan who almost everyone knew had not yet played his last card. After the republic fiasco, one thing was certain and Reza Khan knew that if he were to become the king or absolute ruler it had to be with the overwhelming approval of parliament. He had also learned that he could not browbeat the deputies. He could promise the deputies everything they asked and hoped for. He could call in past favours. But there must be no use of force or overt coercion. There could be no semblance of violence and he had to have public approval at all levels of society.

It was at this juncture of Moddares's decline in prestige that Reza Khan made a blatant attempt to court and engage him in serious dialogue. He began to see Moddares on a regular basis. The meetings were mostly at one of Reza Khan's two residences in Tehran and always before sunrise when a trusted factotum would be sent to fetch Moddares. Reza Khan also began to extend other courtesies. When Moddares needed to travel to the environs of Tehran, Reza Khan would instruct the head of the Tehran municipality to arrange for private transportation.[7] These meetings began in early January 1925 and continued even after Reza Khan's coronation in 1926 when they abruptly ceased as Reza Khan no longer needed Moddares's support.

On these occasions Reza Khan put forth his case. He had brought security to the country; he had created and moulded a military force that would ensure continued security; he had tamed troublesome tribes and unified the country; he now had a legislative agenda that could bring prosperity, free Iran from foreign influence and gain respect from its neighbours. All this could be undone by the Shah who was constantly plotting to remove him as commander of the army. Reza Khan further argued that he could no longer work with either the Shah or the Vali'ahd, in whom he had lost all confidence. The country was still far from safe as various tribes could rise again as the Turkamans had done in the north. If he were to leave Tehran the Shah could take the opportunity to plot his removal. Reza Khan wanted assurances that his position was secure, expecting to have the same personal security as that which he had provided for the country.

Shortly after the coup in 1921 Reza Khan had started to sign letters emanating from the army as Commander-in-Chief of All the Forces. This was in direct contravention of the constitution, which invested that office and title in the person of the reigning monarch. Ahmad Shah had never conferred the title on Reza Khan and had refused to do so. The matter had lain dormant although Reza Khan had continued to sign documents with that title. Most observers, including Loraine, believed this was one of the principal reasons for the Shah's suspicions that Reza Khan had ambitions of higher office and was partially the cause of the Shah's prolonged absence.[8]

Moddares, whose vanity was his principal weakness, could not avoid the temptation of power offered by his association with Reza Khan. He had always wanted to be counsellor to kings, princes and prime ministers. He became the main sponsor of an act of parliament which would confirm Reza Khan's position as Commander of All Armed Forces, thus assuring that he could not be dismissed by Ahmad Shah acting solely on royal prerogative. On the other hand, Reza Khan had to acknowledge and confirm the authority of parliament over himself, an authority parliament constitutionally possessed but which it had been too timid openly to assert, much less to exercise and enforce. Moddares may have genuinely believed that he had extracted a key concession from Reza Khan. Although the powers of the Shah had been curtailed, parliament had reasserted its authority over Reza Khan and could withdraw at its pleasure what it had granted. On 12 February 1925 parliament passed the following law:

> Majles [Parliament] hereby acknowledges that the supreme command of all defensive and security forces of the country should rest exclusively with Reza Khan who with full powers shall fulfill his functions within the bounds of the Constitution and all prevailing laws of the land. This function shall not be rescinded without the approval of the Majles.[9]

In return for his efforts in sponsoring the Commander of Armed Forces Act, Moddares extracted what appeared to him further concessions from Reza Khan. Since his return from the south, Reza Khan had not called on the Vali'ahd. The argument of his supporters had been that the Vali'ahd had not sent the state carriage to meet Reza Khan on arrival at the outskirts of Tehran. Reza Khan considered this slight as justification for not paying a courtesy call on him, but now agreed to call. On 17 February he visited parliament in open session and thanked the deputies for their confidence in him and passage of the recent law. Two days later he called on the Vali'ahd and ostensibly established cordial relations with him.[10]

Moddares had also pressed for the return of all prominent Iranians now either exiled or living abroad of their own volition. In addition to the Shah, Moddares wanted Naser al Molk (Qaragozlou), the former regent, and Vosouq, Qavam and Seyyed Zia, all former prime ministers, to come back. The Shah publicly pleaded that he was in Europe for health reasons, but the public knew his itinerary by now: Paris, Deauville, Biarritz, Nice and Geneva. Moddares had earlier sponsored a motion for parliament to officially ask Ahmad Shah to return to Iran. The motion had been overwhelmingly defeated.[11] Reza Khan's argument was that the Shah

could come back any time he wanted to and his absence had nothing to do with him. As far as the others were concerned, they too
would be welcome to return any time they chose. Moddares wanted
these former prime ministers, especially Vosouq and Qavam, to
return as a balance against the increasing power of Reza Khan and
regarded them as potential prime ministers in case Reza Khan fal-
tered.[12] As it happened, Vosouq, Naser al Molk and Qavam all came
back in stages after the coronation of Reza Shah. Seyyed Zia's
return took place after Reza Shah's abdication.

The only firm *quid pro quo* Moddares obtained was Reza Khan's
promise to bring into his cabinet two of Moddares's nominees. In
August 1925 Reza Khan reshuffled his cabinet and Firouz Firouz
(Nosrat al Dowleh) and Shokrollah Sadri (Qavam al Dowleh)* were
respectively appointed as Ministers of Justice and Interior. These
appointments were not well received and led to harsh criticism by
Soleiman Mirza. Were it not for the direct intervention of Reza Khan,
who was in parliament that day, Soleiman Mirza would have tabled
a motion of no confidence against the Government.

Firouz was destined to play an important role in the first three
years of Reza Shah's reign. After his release from imprisonment he
had taken his seat in the Fourth Parliament with great difficulty. His
leading an anti-British faction had proved futile and had aroused
the bitter enmity of Norman and Loraine. Sensing no bright future
ahead in parliament, he had resigned his seat and had been
appointed Governor of Fars, where he served capably. He had been
elected to the Fifth Parliament but was undecided as to whether he
should resign his governorship and take his seat in parliament.
Feeling his career at an *impasse* and believing that the United States
was emerging as a leading nation, Firouz sought to be appointed as
Minister to Washington DC. He also felt that an absence from domestic politics for a time would make his association with the 1919
Agreement fade from memory so that he would become less contro-
versial. Neither his sought-after appointment to Washington nor a
later attempt to head the Iranian Legation in London materialised.[13]

---

* Shokrollah Sadri (Qavam al Dowleh), 1875–1926, was born in Esfahan
the son of a chamberlain at the court of Mozaffar al Din Shah, a position
he himself later filled, although he fell into disfavour and was exiled to
Mazandaran. He went to Europe, returning in 1909 and becoming active
in the rebellion against Mohammad Ali Shah. He was made Governor of
Tehran in 1909; Minister of Commerce in 1910; Minister of Post in 1920.
He was Governor of Esfahan and later Lurestan and a deputy in the Fourth
and Fifth Parliaments. He became official representative of Sheikh
Khaz'al in Tehran and was a favourite of successive British Legations.[14]

Despite encouragement from Moddares, Firouz did not return to Tehran. It was at the urging of Davar that Firouz finally relinquished his governorship and returned. Davar assured him that Reza Khan needed capable supporters in and out of parliament and would be pleased to have Firouz as an ally. Davar also urged Firouz to sever his association with Moddares and join the new parliamentary majority.[15] Firouz soon disassociated himself from Moddares and became a staunch supporter of the pro-Reza Khan faction. Davar also played a key role in convincing Reza Khan of Firouz's fidelity. Although Firouz served loyally and introduced innovative measures at the Ministry of Finance, Reza Khan never fully trusted him, always aware that Firouz had at one time entertained higher ambitions. Distrust of Firouz probably had its origins in Reza Khan's attitude towards the grandees of the Qajar era.[16] Reza Khan also appears to have been reminded that he had served as a junior officer under Firouz's father, Abdol Hosein Mirza Farmanfarma. Despite Farmanfarma's repeated offers of material help and protestations of loyalty, Reza Khan had preferred to maintain his distance.[17]

Firouz also tried to mend relations with the British Legation. Loraine wrote to Chamberlain:

> Firouz has faithfully observed the understanding with me in August 1923 to cease his opposition to British interests and as Governor of Fars he acted most courteously towards British Consul.[18]

Chamberlain, however, was not all-forgiving. He wrote to Loraine:

> You can tell him [Firouz] I am willing to regard the period of his recent activities as a closed chapter. But his relations with us can not be those he enjoyed before the year 1921...[19]

Firouz's relations with Britain remained stable until he was appointed Minister of Finance in February 1927. As an early advocate of the establishment of a national bank of Iran and recinding the British-owned Imperial Bank's concession to issue currency in Iran, he again aroused the bitter enmity of the British Legation.

In the reshuffle of August 1925 Reza Khan made one further change in the Cabinet. Mehdi Fatemi (Emad al Saltaneh)† was appointed Minister of Education. The changes in the cabinet were not really a concession to Moddares. Firouz had broken with

---

† Seyyed Mehdi Fatemi (Emad al Saltaneh), 1888-1962, was born in Esfahan the son of the factotum to Zell al Soltan, and married his daughter. He was Deputy Governor of Fars and was elected to the fifth and sixth sessions of parliament. He was made Minister of Education in August 1925; Minister of Justice in December 1925; Minister of Interior

CONTINUED OVER PAGE

Moddares by then and Reza Khan personally wanted him in the Cabinet at the recommendations of Teimurtash and Davar. What Reza Khan gained from Moddares's support for the Commander of Armed Forces Act far outweighed any concessions he had made. The Shah had been rendered powerless and Reza Khan's overwhelming support in parliament made it highly unlikely that it would rescind the powers granted to him by the law.

The change of Cabinet was basically aimed at gaining influence with the conservative opposition elements in parliament. Reza Khan knew there would be no opposition from the socialists. In any drastic steps contemplated against the Qajars it was the Moddares group he had to mollify.[21] As in the prelude to the move against Sheikh Khaz'al, the Cabinet assumed an even more pro-British look. He did not want a hostile British Legation when he made his next move.

With the compact with Moddares secure, Reza Khan was to press for the approval of the backlog of his proposed legislation. In quick succession, beginning on 1 April 1925 parliament passed the 'Law of Rectification of the Official Calendar' which changed the names of the months of the year from Arabic and Turkish to their pre-Islamic names. The first six months of the year were to have 31 days, the following five months to have 30 days and the last month to be 29 days and in leap years 30 days. It was a solar calendar and the year commenced on the vernal equinox, about 21 March, and the traditional Iranian New Year's day. On 21 April the law for the establishment of the first Iranian bank was approved. The capital of the new bank was to be raised from the pension fund of military officers. The bank was initially named Bank Artesh (Army Bank), later briefly Bank Pahlavi and finally Bank Sepah.

On 5 May parliament approved a far-reaching and important piece of legislation. All civilian and pseudo-military titles were abolished and in accordance with the 'Law of Identity and Personal Status' all Iranians were required to adopt a family name and register their names, date of birth and marital status at Registrar Offices soon to be established. The award of titles had reached preposterous proportions and had become the subject of much ridicule and derision by European travellers and by Iranians themselves. In the latter part of the Qajar era, especially during the last years of Naser al Din Shah, upon

---

Seyyed Mehdi Fatemi CONTINUED FROM PREVIOUS PAGE
between February and May 1927. He fell out with Teimurtash, therefore was not elected to the Seventh Parliament, but was elected to the Eighth Parliament. He was Governor of Gilan between 1933 and 1937 and head of the municipality of Tehran in 1943. Elected to the Fourteenth Parliament, he became a Senator in 1950.[20]

the donation of a few gold coins, and sometimes without a gift but merely as someone had pleased the monarch or his senior courtiers, people in and out of government service received ludicrous titles.[22]

Reza Khan himself abandoned the title of Sardar Sepah and adopted the family name Pahlavi. The name was that of an ancient language of Iran and embodied connotations of history, tradition and dynasty, probably chosen in anticipation of soon becoming ruler of Iran. Some seven months later, when he became king, Pahlavi became the name of the new dynasty. Reza Khan based his dynasty's legitimacy not on tribal power as did the Qajars nor as the alleged descendants of Shi'ite aristocracy as in the case of the Safavid dynasty but solely as the patriotic son of a soldier from Savad Kouh, representing the emerging new nationalism of Iran.[23]

On 22 May a law creating the state sugar monopoly was passed. The proceeds from the monopoly were to partially finance the construction of a trans-Iranian railway. (The enabling law for the construction and financing of the railway would be approved in the next session of parliament.) The last important law enacted by the Fifth Parliament was the 'Compulsory Military Service Conscription Law' of 8 June 1925. Under the law all Iranian males residing in Iran and abroad reaching the age of twenty-one were required to undergo two years of military service. The law was passed despite opposition by the large landowners and clergy. The landlords were against the measure initially because such conscription would erode their patriarchal authority and draw essential manpower from their farmlands. As far as the ulama were concerned two years of indoctrination in a secular institution administered by anti-clerical officials, i.e. the officer class, would undermine and corrupt the religious beliefs of the recruits. A number of middle-ranking clerics declared in separate fatwas that military service endangered the principles of Shi'ism and the fundamentals of Islam.[24] The opposition of the landlords was neutralised by pressure from the officer class and the intervention of Reza Khan. As for the opposition of the clergy, Reza Khan had the prior consent of two senior clerics, Ayatollah Na'ini and Ayatollah Esfahani. The agreement of Moddares not to stand in opposition in parliament ensured the passage of the law. In the initial draft of the bill the only blanket exemption was for men on whom an entire family was dependent.[25] As a concession to the clergy an exemption was granted to theology students. The law was amended in 1926 and again in 1931 limiting this exemption. Students at seminaries had to provide documentation and pass an examination ensuring that they were in fact full-time students making progress toward a clerical vocation and did not intend to become professional life-long students.

In 1926 a Department of Compulsory Service was established and the country was divided into recruiting areas.[26] The goal of Reza Khan was to have a standing army of 50,000.

The minorities, Christians, Jews and Zoroastrians, strongly supported the measure, and their deputies in parliament insisted:

> ... they too should share the burden as well as the privileges of citizenship... Although little remarked at the time the opening of the army to non-Moslem minorities represented a complete break with the past and symbolised the triumph of nationalism over religious and communal identities.[27]

In July 1924, while Loraine was in London during his home leave with his new wife, two of the Shah's uncles, Nosrat al Saltaneh and Azd al Soltan, had travelled to London with the message that Ahmad Shah wanted to see Loraine in Paris. Loraine had answered that he must have prior permission from the Foreign Secretary. Lancelot Oliphant, the senior official for Iranian affairs at the Foreign Office, recommended to MacDonald that such a visit could serve no purpose and the Shah would use it solely to irritate Reza Khan. Oliphant had further recommended that Britain should adopt a hands-off policy regarding any move towards a republic or even a change of Shah were these issues to arise.[28]

At a prior meeting between Nosrat al Saltaneh and Davoud Meftah (Meftah al Saltaneh), the Chargé d'Affaires at the Iranian Legation in London at the time, Meftah had been asked whether the Foreign Office still thought highly of Vosouq and 'would it view with pleasure the return of Vosouq to power'. The question went unanswered by the Foreign Office. Seyyed Zia was also in London at the time, probably lobbying for the Vali'ahd or Vosouq. However, there is no record of his having had a conversation with anyone at the Foreign Office.[29]

That was how matters stood until Loraine, on his way back to Iran during the Khaz'al crisis, stopped overnight in Paris and saw the Shah. Loraine advised the Shah he should return to Tehran hinting that prolonged absence would put his throne in jeopardy.[30] It appears that Loraine's meeting with Ahmad Shah was unauthorised. Loraine had called on the Shah purely as an act of courtesy. The next day the Shah saw Armitage Smith, formerly the financial adviser to the Iranian Government under the 1919 Agreement and now Britain's representative at the Paris Reparations Commission. The Shah told Armitage Smith that he had seriously considered the advice of Loraine and had decided to return by the end of November. The Shah's decision was probably more motivated by Sheikh Khaz'al's invitation to return to Iran via Khuzestan than the advice offered by Loraine. The Shah asked Armitage Smith to inform

Loraine, who was on his way to Cairo, that he had heeded his advice and was making preparations to leave.[31] MacDonald immediately telegraphed the British Ambassador in Paris to return the Shah's message to Armitage Smith. The Shah 'could send any message he wishes to anyone but not through the Foreign Office'. MacDonald added that Britain should not be involved in the matter of the Shah's return. This was the first and only rebuke Loraine was to receive from his superiors. Although mildly worded Loraine was being criticised for having seen the Shah in the first place.[32]

In order to exonerate himself for having acted as an unauthorised go-between for Ahmad Shah, Armitage Smith sent the following report to the Foreign Office:

> I now realise that [Ahmad Shah] lied to me. He had made up his mind to return to Tehran even before he had talked to [Loraine]... There are now in Paris one sovereign, two Imperial Highnesses [Azd al Soltan and Nosrat al Saltaneh], three ex prime ministers [Vosouq, Qavam and Seyyed Zia] and one ex regent [Naser al Molk]. They all turn up and expect to be fed, a touching but somewhat expensive tribute to their confidence in their ex financial adviser... Also when they get into a mess they expect me to get them out... I will ignore the Shah... for his contemptible cowardice, avarice and treachery... but this time I believe he would go back...[33]

Ahmad Shah's latest manoeuvre had not worked. Whether he intended to go back or not, it was obvious that he wanted it to appear that it was the British Minister in Tehran who had urged his return.

The year 1924 passed without the Shah returning. The efforts of Moddares in early 1925 to have parliament pass a resolution officially asking the Shah to return had failed by a large margin. Equally unsuccessful was the Moddares campaign for the return of the Shah as part of an assemblage which would include the three former prime ministers and the former regent. Reza Khan had neutralised this argument by saying that he had nothing to do with their absences and, that in any event all would be welcomed back if they chose to return. Next, Moddares and his allies began to sound out British officials in Tehran on their reaction to a return by the Shah.[34] They also sought assurances that Britain would guarantee the Shah's safety if he returned. The answers they received were the standard reply to such queries that 'Britain does not interfere in Persia's domestic affairs'. All questions probing Reza Khan's ultimate intention also went unanswered or ignored.[35]

Soon after Reza Khan's return from Khuzestan his supporters began to float the idea that the best solution for resolving the issue

of the absentee Shah would be to place an elderly Qajar prince or a
minor on the throne. These supporters were careful not to specify
what role Reza Khan would play in such an arrangement. Loraine
also reported that Ahmad Shah had two adult brothers in addition
to the Vali'ahd who had seniority over the Shah's infant son, for
whom a regent would have had to be found if the infant were to be
appointed the next Shah. No-one was certain what plans Reza Khan
had to assert total control over the state. Would it be the outright
deposition of the Qajars, the removal of Ahmad Shah and the Vali'ahd
and placing a minor Qajar prince on the throne with himself as
regent, or keeping the existing monarchy intact and assuming dictatorial powers delegated to him by parliament? All these alternatives
were difficult to resolve constitutionally and by the beginning of
spring were discarded. There soon began amongst Reza Khan's supporters a slow but perceptible agitation for a change of dynasty as
the only viable solution.[36]

Loraine knew that many people, probably including Reza Khan,
thought Britain was behind the campaign for the Shah's return.
Loraine himself was ambivalent as to whether it was in Britain's best
interests for Reza Khan to supplant the Qajars. Despite the respect
and even admiration he had acquired for Reza Khan's abilities, he
was still wary that if Reza Khan were to attain absolute power, relations with Britain might deteriorate. More probably, having witnessed
the turmoil over the republican issue and how close Reza Khan had
come to being toppled, Loraine felt it was better to keep the monarchy
intact with Ahmad Shah serving as a ceremonial figurehead.

Sensing that something drastic was afoot Loraine felt he should
seek specific instructions from the Foreign Office. He wrote to
Chamberlain:

> Poor as is my opinion of the Shah I do now consider his return desirable
> on several grounds. Would you object to my expressing privately to the
> Valiahd the opinion that the Shah would be unwise to reject an invi-
> tation made by the government?[37]

Chamberlain immediately objected to the proposal and reasoned
that the Shah's return would cause strife, threaten the stability of
the Government, resulting in strained relations between Britain and
Iran.[38] Victor Mallet of the Persian Desk added '... the Shah has done
nothing to earn him the gratitude or support of His Majesty's Government'.[39] The message was clear. Loraine was not to interfere. Britain
was to stay clear of the controversy for another eight months.

Ahmad Shah remained silent in Paris for some three months. In
early June he instructed his relatives in Tehran to inform members

of the Government as well as the British Legation in Tehran that before he made a final decision on his return:

> ... two emissaries worthy of the Imperial confidence should be sent to Paris to discuss with him certain matters which he is unable to refer to in telegrams and letters.[40]

As we shall see these confidential matters were principally that he would agree to abdicate provided that the Iranian Government would pay him a guaranteed pension such as his father had received, a lump sum and an annual pension guaranteed by the Czarist Government, for his abdication in 1909.[41]

By the beginning of the summer the prevailing mood in Iran was that it wanted the presence of the monarch and continuation of the monarchy. It was becoming more difficult, however, to deal with an absentee Shah who appeared indifferent to the fate of his country. If Ahmad Shah had returned after the demise of the republican movement his throne may have been safe. Now the longer he waited the more questionable became his hold on the throne. The Shah had lost a great deal of prestige by his contacts and involvement with Sheikh Khaz'al's machinations at the end of 1924. Reza Khan, who had stood alone in subduing a despised foreign lackey, was now basking in triumph. It appeared more and more that Ahmad Shah would not come back as long as Reza Khan retained the reigns of power. He mistakenly believed that time was on his side. He was fighting a war of attrition against Reza Khan and hoped that he somehow could be removed. Even a sympathetic Loraine was beginning to despair. In a report to Chamberlain he wrote, '[The Shah's] refusal to come back is one of the meanest and most contemptible that could be conceived'.[42]

Reza Khan, being very aware of the failure of his attempt to dislodge the Shah and change the existing order to a republic, was most hesitant to make any drastic moves. He had decided to play a waiting game in the hope that the Shah's reluctance to come back would alienate even more people. Many senior Qajar Princes were in fact losing confidence in the Shah and made their sentiments public. The Vali'ahd by contrast was gaining some support. He had shown character in refusing to yield to Reza Khan during the height of the republican campaign by neither resigning his office nor leaving the country. He had remained loyal to his brother but had not failed to express his dismay over the Shah's absence.[43] With the Vali'ahd being talked about as the logical successor to the Shah, Reza Khan had to act cautiously, and the summer passed without Reza Khan making any overt move.

In mid September, news reached Tehran that the Shah and his mother accompanied by a large entourage had booked passage for Iran.[44] Shortly after, probably at the direct orders of Reza Khan, the Government Grain Department began to release less wheat to Tehran bakers. There had been a failure of the harvest in that year with resulting shortages and poor quality bread. Soon there were mass demonstrations in the city. On 22 September a crowd of thousands gathered at one of Tehran's largest mosques. Several people began addressing the crowd, laying the blame on the Shah and asking for his dethronement. The Shah had already acquired an odious reputation when during the last year of the First World War he had been accused of hoarding grain and profiteering. Pro-republican sentiments were also chanted. However, the crowd failed to respond and instead marched and broke into parliament asking for bread. The next day the bazaar closed. Several hundred people then sought refuge at the Soviet Legation because a rumour had spread that the Russians had offered to sell wheat to the Iranian Government at a reasonable price but the Iranian Government had refused the offer because of British disapproval. It soon became apparent that the Government, at the orders of Reza Khan, had started the whole episode, and as soon as the demonstrations appeared to turn against the Government, they were stopped. On 24 September the Government issued larger quantities of wheat and gradually calm prevailed.[45]

Ahmad Shah, heartened by the news of dissatisfaction amongst the populace, sent a telegram to Reza Khan in late September which read: 'I will be leaving Paris via Bombay on 2 October. I am pleased to return to my beloved country and look forward to meeting your excellency'. Reza Khan in reply sent the following message:

> Your Imperial Majesty's telegram was received. It is indeed a pleasure. I beg to ask His Majesty to inform us at which Iranian port he will disembark, signed Reza Commander in Chief of Armed Forces.[46]

It appears, however, that Ahmad Shah had no intention of coming back. In making the announcement of his departure at a date certain he was merely testing the reaction of Reza Khan. Whatever the Shah's true intentions, the measured response of Reza Khan and the failure of any of his supporters to speak up made him change his mind. Nevertheless the news of the Shah's impending departure brought matters to a head and spurred Reza Khan into action. Some ten days after the Shah's announcement partisans of Reza Khan staged large demonstrations against the Shah and the Qajar dynasty in Tabriz which soon spread to Rasht, Esfahan and Mashhad.[47]

These demonstrations were a prelude to prepare parliament for action on the future of the Shah. Leaders of the demonstrations made clear that there was no longer thought of a republic but a change of sovereign.

Publicly the Soviets stood clear of the issue, but their emissaries in Tehran had made it known for some time that they were unequivocal supporters of Reza Khan. Newspapers in Turkey, with obvious official sanction, began to publish articles in support of Reza Khan and a change of dynasty, and their embassy in Tehran made its sentiments public.[48] Britain was still sitting on the fence but it was obvious they had to make a move soon. Hassan Moshar, the Foreign Minister and a tested confidante of the British Legation would now play the key role in alerting the Legation to the urgency of the matter. Moshar's past association with Vosouq had established him as one of Britain's stalwart allies in Iran. He had had a rift with Norman, who held him partly responsible for the fall of Seyyed Zia. Later he had been forced into exile as a result of allegations that he had led a plot to topple and murder Qavam, then Prime Minister. He had returned from Europe with Reza Khan's blessing and had been restored to his former prominence. Reza Khan had counted on his closeness to the British Legation, and prior to the expedition against Sheikh Khaz'al, Moshar had been appointed as Minister of Foreign Affairs, a position he was to hold for over 18 months. Moshar had been an asset during Reza Khan's difficult campaign against Khaz'al. Now with the issue of change of dynasty, Moshar was to be equally helpful to Reza Khan's plans. As early as the beginning of the summer of 1925 Moshar had intended to resign as Foreign Minister and retire from Government service. A rivalry had developed between Foroughi and Moshar for the attention of Reza Khan, who had more often sided with Foroughi. During Reza Khan's absences from Tehran Foroughi had been appointed Acting Prime Minister. Moshar had been talked out of resigning by Loraine and remained as Foreign Minister.[49]

At two meetings with Loraine on 21 and 22 October Moshar made Reza Khan's thinking clear. Loraine had not seen Reza Khan for over two months and had no idea of his true intentions and how far he was prepared to go in his campaign against the Qajars. Moshar told Loraine that Reza Khan was determined to be rid of the Qajars but was apprehensive of the disapproval of the British Government. Reza Khan believed the announcement by the Shah to return must have been with Britain's blessing and considered 'Britain's silence as inconsistent with her friendly protestations' towards himself. Moshar further explained that Reza Khan believed that 'In all Persian crisis British influence had been felt and prevailed and it is no different in this instance'. As an example Reza Khan had given the deposing of Mohammad Ali Shah which could not have taken place without Britain's approval. Loraine told Moshar that someone had to 'clear the mist from Reza Khan's mind who was fighting shadows', and explain that Britain had nothing to do with the Shah's announcement. Loraine said that if Reza Khan wanted to see him he would go immediately but added, 'I can not go to see him merely to protest our sincerity'.[50]

At the meeting of 22 October Moshar informed Loraine that sources close to Ahmad Shah had confirmed that he had no intention of returning and would abdicate if he received a handsome allowance payable by the Iranian Government and guaranteed by a third party. Loraine was left with no doubt that the Shah wanted the guarantor to be Great Britain. Moshar emphasised that an absentee Shah was harmful to the country. Furthermore, Reza Khan was obsessed with the problem and believed that unless he cleared up the question of the Qajar dynasty nothing could be done for the country. Moshar concluded that all serious work, whether internal or external, was in suspension and would remain so until the question of the Shah and the dynasty had been resolved.[51]

Despite Moshar's arguments Loraine still was not convinced that a change of dynasty was the best and only solution. He believed the deposition of the Qajars was fraught with danger and uncertainty. In his detailed report to Chamberlain he set out possible alternatives: the abdication of Ahmad Shah in favour of the Vali'ahd 'who is not that unpopular'; or the abdication of the Shah and Vali'ahd and the elevation of one of the younger sons of Mohammad Ali Shah (who were ages twenty and twenty-one) with Reza Khan as regent. Loraine admitted that perhaps neither of his proposals would be workable as Reza Khan wanted to be rid of all Qajars. He still believed that the deposition of the Qajar dynasty could bring about instability. Loraine again complained that he could not call on Reza Khan. 'I cannot discuss the dethronement of the Shah to whom I am accredited'. Loraine's final advice was that Britain should stand aloof and merely make a statement:

> [Britain] 'does not wish to intervene or be involved in this internal question... this will give courage to several factions... and also show that we are not totally disinterested... Reza Khan [then] may seek my advice... and I could point out the dangers ahead.[52]

Although Chamberlain also had not wanted Britain to be involved in the question of a dynastic change, he now realised the urgency of the situation and agreed that a statement by the British Government would be in order. He decided on a personal message to the Iranian Foreign Minister which read:

> Reports have recently reached me that it is believed His Majesty's Government lately instigated the Shah to return to Persia. There is not a vestige of foundation for this allegation. His Majesty's Government have no wish to interfere in the internal affairs of another and friendly country. His Majesty's Government have no desire to take sides in any constitutional struggle. These issues are capable of action only by the Persian people.

Chamberlain added that the entire text of the message could be published by either the Persian Government or the British Legation.[53] Moshar immediately informed Reza Khan of the contents of the communique and convinced him of British intentions to remain neutral. Moshar also informed Loraine that Reza Khan now wanted to see him.[54] Loraine personally delivered the message to Reza Khan and they had a brief conversation.[55]

Whatever lingering doubts Reza Khan had were dispelled by Chamberlain's message. For Reza Khan, who had continued to believe that Britain had been opposed to and was behind the opposition to the creation of a republic, the message from Chamberlain was essential before he would take any decisive steps. He had already taken preliminary measures. The key to his plans was to be certain that parliament would act quickly to prevent any opposition from forming. The election of a large number of the deputies to the Fifth Parliament had been heavily influenced by the military and the Ministry of Interior and the overwhelming majority were sympathetic to Reza Khan's plans. The senior clerics had remained quiet during the campaign to discredit the Shah. Moddares too had kept out of the debate. Reza Khan's parliamentary majority was secure this time and there was no chance of splintering or factionalising. The presiding officers of parliament were now Reza Khan's allies and no trouble was expected.

Parliamentary by-laws provided that at the beginning of every six months during the two-year term of each parliament there should be an election of a president, two vice presidents and the lesser administrative officers. Hosein Pirnia had been the President of the last two parliaments, the fourth and fifth. Pirnia's knowledge of parliamentary procedures and his influence over the deputies were acknowledged by his colleagues. In the mid-term of the Fifth Parliament, Mohammad Taddayon, a key ally of Reza Khan, made a bid for the presidency to replace Pirnia. Since it was anticipated that the question of change of dynasty could be discussed many

prominent deputies felt it was better to maintain the experienced
Pirnia, and Taddayon withdrew. In his speech anouncing his withdrawal Taddayon made some uncalled-for comments, comparing his
own background with that of Pirnia. Pirnia took offence and refused
to stand as a candidate. Attempts were made to change his mind but
he adamantly refused. Taddayon's remarks gave Pirnia the perfect
excuse to stand down. He knew the issue of change of dynasty
would be difficult to handle and could strain Iranian constitutional
law. Deputies turned to Mostofi, who also refused. As there were no
others with the prestige of Pirnia and Mostofi, on the next balloting
Taddayon, a sitting Vice President, was elected President.[56]

With the election of the presiding officers of parliament out of the
way Reza Khan pressed for the passage of a resolution to abolish the
Qajar dynasty. As Reza Khan had the support of an overwhelming
majority, the outcome of the vote was a foregone conclusion. His
supporters, however, were not willing to leave anything to chance.
On 30 October a large number of deputies were invited to Reza
Khan's house and all, even those whose vote was not in doubt, were
asked to sign the resolution that would be presented to parliament
effecting the removal of the Qajar dynasty.[57] On 31 October, the day
set for the vote, great care was taken to ensure that deputies would
not leave parliament, depriving it of a quorum. However, several key
members of parliament had obtained prior leave of absence.
Moddares used the excuse that since the refusal of the post of president by Mostofi had not been in writing there should be another vote
for the presiding officers of parliament. His request was denied and
he left the meeting. Mostofi, whose forefathers had served Qajar
kings in high positions, was in an uncomfortable position. It was
expected he would abstain. Reza Khan had acquired great respect
for Mostofi and planned to appoint him prime minister when parliament and the Constituent Assembly had completed their work.
Knowing that Mostofi intended to either abstain or absent himself
when the voting began, and also being aware that Mostofi's abstention
could influence some wavering deputies, Reza Khan sent a message
to Mostofi that he urgently needed to see him. Mostofi left parliament and by the time he returned voting had been completed and
the proposed resolution had been passed.[58]

The stage was now set for the final act of the drama. The resolution deposing the Qajars was introduced:

In the name of the welfare of the people of Iran, Parliament hereby
declares the abolition of the Qajar Dynasty and within the bounds of the
Constitution and other prevailing laws of Iran, entrusts the provisional
government to the person of Reza Khan Pahlavi. The determination of the

form of the permanent government shall rest with the Constituent Assembly which shall be held for the purpose of amending articles 36, 37, 38 and 40 of the Constitution.

Only four deputies chose to make their opposition public and speak against the resolution. Each of the four praised Reza Khan in one form or another and none said a word in praise of the Qajars nor in defence of Ahmad Shah. The first speaker in opposition was Seyyed Hassan Taqizadeh.* He began by praising Reza Khan for his past services and declared support for his Government. There was also a strong hint in his address that he would even support Reza Khan's accession to the throne if a valid constitutional route could be found, but that he had strong reservations about the proposed resolution which had been hastily drafted. He recommended the appointment of a commission comprised of people knowledgable in constitutional law to study the matter. Parliament could vote then on the commission's recommendations.[59] Taqizadeh believed deeply in constitutional government and institutions, but his decision to speak first was a mistake. His speech was badly organised and poorly read. Furthermore Taqizadeh was never at his best when he was under pressure. He would exhibit this weakness again and again in

---

* Seyyed Hassan Taqizadeh, 1878–1969, was the son of a preacher born in Tabriz and was self-educated. As an ardent nationalist, he was elected to the first parliament and became a prominent member. When Mohammad Ali Shah closed parliament Taqizadeh sought refuge at the British Legation. The Shah demanded that he be handed over, but was refused. He travelled to Europe under an amnesty, returning in 1908, and was elected to the Second Parliament in 1909 after Mohammad Ali Shah's fall. He went to Europe again in 1910, and did not return to take up the seat to which he was elected in the Third and Fourth Parliaments. He lived mostly in Berlin between 1914 and 1923. He edited an influential journal, *Kaveh*, which advocated modernism and the adoption of Western values, over which he was excommunicated by middle-ranking clergy. After his return to Iran in 1924 he was elected to the Fifth and Sixth Parliaments and travelled to the United States as a delegate to the Philadelphia Trade Exhibition. He was made Governor of Khorasan in January 1929, recalled the same year and appointed Minister to London between May 1929 and April 1930. He was Minister of Roads and Minister of Finance before being sent to Paris as Minister at the end of 1933. He was recalled the following year, but was granted extended leave of absence and did not return until after World War II. He became Minister to London in 1941; was elevated to Ambassador; elected to the Fifteenth Parliament; appointed to the Senate in 1950, later becoming its President. A man of considerable erudition, he was a mediocre administrator with a close-knit circle of admirers, his reputation being enhanced by his seniority in the Masonic hierarchy.[60]

his political life. The next opposition speaker was Hosein Ala, whose speech was the briefest of the four. Ala, who was neither a parlimentarian nor public speaker, argued that parliament had no authority to vote on the proposed resolution, it being against the constitution.

The third speaker was Mohammad Mosaddeq, who put forth the best reasoned, although intricate, argument, running as follows: Reza Khan as Prime Minister and chief executive of the country had rendered valuable service, and his retention in the post would continue to have a salutary effect and yield further benefits. Were he to become Shah, he could no longer assume or exercise executive authority under the present constitution and thus the country would lose an effective Prime Minister. If after ascending the throne Reza Khan continued to exercise executive authority he would be acting in direct contravention of the constitution. A constitutional monarch is not responsible to parliament. If there were to be a constitutional monarch with executive powers, it would constitute a system of government without parallel in the world.[61] Mosaddeq meant what he said. There was no sarcasm in his remarks. He genuinely believed Reza Khan had accomplished a great deal and a productive parliament had performed its proper role in approving the required legislation. He was arguing for continuance of that partnership. In reverential tones he was pleading with his colleagues not to make Reza Khan a king, as he was by nature an autocrat, soon wanting a monopoly of power. Mosaddeq was bound to clash with Reza Shah. He was exiled and did not return to the political scene until after Reza Shah's abdication in 1941.

Ali Akbar Davar, in reply to Mosaddeq, basically argued that although a monarch under a constitutional system had limited powers, the personality and competency of the monarch was crucial for the direction a country would take. A competent and well-intentioned king would play an important part in the revival, development and independence of the nation. Davar avoided the central argument of Mosaddeq and concluded that at this juncture parliament was merely faced with the simple task of removing from the throne an incompetent king.[62]

---

*   Haji Mirza Yahya Dowlatabadi, 1862–1939, was born in Esfahan. He studied at theological seminaries, was accused of apostasy and forced to leave Esfahan. He was an early pioneer in modern education in Iran, and between 1897 and c.1905 established several secular primary schools in Tehran. He was elected to the second and fifth sessions of parliament from Kerman. He left Iran in 1927 and did not return until shortly before his death in 1939. He was the author of an engaging autobiography in four volumes.[65]

20. *Abdol Hosein Teimurtash (Sardar Mo'azam).* As Reza Shah's principal policy maker Teimurtash was the king's alter ego for nearly seven years before his fall from grace, after which he was murdered on the orders of the Shah.

21. Sir Percy Lorraine. As a favourite of Curzon he arrived as British minister in Tehran in 1921, but over the course of his five year posting he came to question London's longstanding policy of undermining strong central government in Iran.

The last speaker was Yahya Dowlatabadi,* who criticised the undue haste in the preparation of the resolution. He also complained about having been pressured the previous evening by the followers of Reza Khan to sign the resolution now before parliament. He then argued that the resolution touched on separate and unrelated matters: the abolishing of the Qajar dynasty; Reza Khan as a future king; and amendment of the constitution. These three matters should be the subject of three separate resolutions. He was opposed to the Qajars and would vote for abolishing the dynasty. He had the highest regard for Reza Khan as Prime Minister and Commander of the Armed Forces and wished him continued success. He was, however, opposed to hereditary monarchies and hence to the draft resolution.[63]

All four opposition speakers left the chamber following their remarks and abstained from voting. The main argument of the four deputies who spoke in opposition as well as the other deputies who abstained from voting by having left the chamber came down to the following: deputies had sworn allegiance to the sovereign; the Constitution vested sovereignty in the Qajar dynasty; in order to depose the Qajars there must be an amendment of the Constitution; only a national referendum could authorise constitutional change. Supporters of the proposed resolution contended that the public had spoken. The mass of telegrams from the electorate to the deputies demanding the abolition of the Qajar dynasty constituted the expression of national will and was tantamount to a referendum. The deposition of Mohammad Ali Shah in 1909 by a committee of parliament was cited as precedent.

There were 80 deputies present, a valid quorum, and all voted for the resolution. Nineteen deputies were absent for cause and with prior authorisation from the President of parliament, including the two eldest sons of Farmanfarma. Thirteen deputies were listed as absent without prior notice. There were twelve deputies listed as late arrivals who took no part in the voting. A study of the absentees and late arrivals reveals that at least 25 would have voted against the resolution. Their list includes such prominent names as Mohammad Taqi Bahar, Hashem Ashtiani, Moddares, Hassan and Hosein Pirnia and Mostofi. Equally significant was that only one deputy elected from Tehran, Soleiman Mirza, voted for the resolution. The others were listed as absent.[64]

If at the outset of his campaign to depose the Qajars Reza Khan had bypassed parliament and called for the election of delegates to a constituent assembly with the pre-set agenda of abolishing the Qajar dynasty, the decision of the representatives to the assembly would have been deemed a referendum on the dethronement. Reza

Khan would have been on firmer constitutional ground and may
have been supported by a larger majority, including many of the
established names. In his haste to be rid of the Qajars he and his
advisers had decided against such a route as it would have delayed
matters for several months.[66]

The Qajar dynasty fell with a whimper. In many ways there had
been no real contest. Reza Khan's opponent had been a timid and
selfish young man who did not care about his country and had
refused to return to it. Long before Reza Khan had come upon the
scene the Qajars had been discredited and Ahmad Shah had
acquired a reputation for greed, profiteering, self indulgence and
indifference to the fate of his country.

> There was little in the last years of the Qajar Dynasty of which any
> Iranian could be proud. The regime that Reza Shah took over from
> Ahmad Shah Qajar was a mixture of political impotence, lawlessness,
> oppression, dishonesty and debauchery.[67]

Ahmad Shah was no match for a shrewd and determined rival of
exceptional ability. Reza Khan had won because he had become an
indispensible figure, both feared and respected. He had emerged
at the right time and given the people what they had desperately
wanted for 20 years, a strong central government, security and unification of the country free from foreign interference. He could not
have toppled a 130 year dynasty, however, had it not been that his
principal adversary was an irresolute, pleasure-seeking young man
who came to the throne through an accident of birth. It has been
said that of all forms of government, hereditary monarchies are the
most uncertain, dependent on the vaguaries of biology. Dynasties
have often failed to produce heirs who were old enough or capable
enough to govern effectively.

NOTES ON CHAPTER 13
Further details of publications and documents in Bibliography

1   FO 371/10140, Loraine to Chamberlain, 9 January 1925.
2   Alexander Powell, *By Camel and Car to the Peacock Thone*, pp 298–299;
    FO 416/76, Intelligence Summary, 5 June 1925.
3   Wilfred Knapp, 'The Period of Reza Shah' in Hossein Amir Sadeghi and
    R.W. Ferrier (eds), *Twentieth Century Iran*, p 33.
4   Stephanie Cronin, *The Army and the Creation of the Pahlavi State in Iran*,
    1910–1926, pp 135 and 136.
5   FO 416/76, E. Monson to Chamberlain, 19 December 1924.
6   Homa Katouzian, *The Political Economy of Modern Iran*, p 87.
7   Soleiman Behboodi, *Khaterat Soleiman Behboodi* (*The Memoirs of
    Soleiman Behboodi*), pp 199, 202, 218, 219, 222.
8   FO 371/10140, Loraine to Chamberlain, 21 February 1925.
9   Baqer Aqeli, *Ruz Shomar Tarikh Iran* (*Daily Calendar of the History of
    Iran*), translated by Cyrus Ghani, vol. 1, p 192.
10 FO 416/77, Loraine to Chamberlain, 28 February 1925.
11 Baqer Aqeli, *Ruz Shomar Tarikh Iran* (*Daily Calendar of the History of
    Iran*), translated by Cyrus Ghani, vol. 1, p 192.
12 FO 371/10140, Loraine to Chamberlain, 16 June 1925.
13 FO 371/10146, Memorandum by Oliphant, 2 July 1924.
14 Mehdi Bamdad, *Tarikh Rejal Iran Quroun 12, 13, 14* (*Dictionary of
    National Biography of Iran: Twelfth, Thirteenth, Fourteenth Centuries*),
    vol. 2, pp 151–152; FO 371/12320, R.H. Clive to Chamberlain, 13 July
    1927.
15 Firouz Mirza Firouz (Nosrat al Dowleh), *Majmoueh Mokatebat, Asnad
    Khaterat va Asar* (*Collected Documents, Correspondence and Memoirs*),
    vol. 1, pp 123, 124, 126, 128, 130, 131, 132, 137 and 170.
16 *Ibid.*, p 137.
17 Reza Khan resented Farmanfarma's attempts to make a gift of certain
    water rights. Equally unwelcome were Farmanfarma's attempts to
    donate furniture to one of the houses being built by Reza Khan:
    Soleiman Behboodi, *Khaterat Soleiman Behboodi* (*The Memoirs of
    Soleiman Behboodi*), p 132. Behboodi also records Reza Khan's deroga-
    tory comments on several occasions that Farmanfarma 'is too wealthy'
    and that his sons Firouz Firouz and Mohammad Hosein Mirza Firouz
    are better than their father: pp 131, 132 and 137.
18 FO 416/76, Loraine to Chamberlain, 25 January 1925.
19 FO 416/76, Chamberlain to Loraine, 25 February 1925.
20 FO 371/52755, J.H. Le Rougetel to E. Bevin, 27 May 1946.
21 FO 371/10140, Loraine to Chamberlain, 10 August 1925.
22 It was not difficult to create a title. As an example, by merely taking the
    Arabic root word of Nasr (meaning aid or assistance) and its derivatives
    such as Nosrat, Naser, Mansour, Entesar, Montaser and Mostanser, and
    adding a noun such as al Saltaneh (sovereignty), al Dowleh (govern-
    ment), al Molk (realm), al Soltan (sovereign), al Tojar (merchants), al Ataba
    (physicians), al Sho'ara (poets) and al Islam, one could create several
    hundred titles.
    Mozaffar al Din Shah needing money to finance his trips abroad and
    support his large court retinue began to sell titles on an even larger

scale. Tradesmen, preachers, physicians, pamphleteers and even the wives of the well-to-do and ordinary women in the Shah's harem were awarded titles. Soon there were titles such as Fakhr al Moluk (Pride of Sovereigns), Fakhr al Dowleh (Pride of Government), Fakhr al Saltaneh (Pride of Sovereignty), Hosn al Saltaneh (Beauty of Sovereignty), Efat al Dowleh (Chastity of Government), Qamar Jahan (Moon of the World).

23 Shahrokh Meskoob, *Dastan Adabiat va Sargozasht Ejtema* (*Story of the Literature and the Fate of Society*), p 11.

24 Ervand Abrahamian, *Iran Between Two Revolutions*, p 131.

25 Stephanie Cronin, *The Army and the Creation of the Pahlavi State in Iran 1910–1926*, p 128.

26 *Ibid.*

27 *Ibid.*, p 127. There had been an Armenian contingent in the army which had fought bravely in the overthrow of Mohammad Ali Shah in 1909 and also in repelling his abortive attempt to reclaim his throne in 1911.

28 FO 371/10146, Memorandum by Oliphant, 24 July 1924.

29 FO 371/10146, Memorandum by Oliphant, 2 July 1924.

30 FO 371/10146, Knatchbull Huggeson to Sir T. Spring Rice at the Foreign Office, 31 October 1924.

31 FO 371/10146, Lord Crew (Ambassador to Paris) to MacDonald, 31 October 1924.

32 FO 371/10146, MacDonald to Lord Crew in Paris, 1 November 1924.

33 FO 371/10146, Armitage Smith to Knatchbull Huggeson, 8 November 1924.

34 FO 371/10140, Loraine to Chamberlain, 22 January and 10 February 1925.

35 FO 371/10140, Col. Howard, Consul General Mashhad, report of conversation with Motavali of Shrine of Imam Reza, 27 March 1927.

36 FO 371/10140, Loraine to Chamberlain, 10 February 1925. There is no official record of Ahmad Shah having had an infant son at the time. Loraine's reference to the infant is not substantiated elsewhere.

37 FO 371/10840, Loraine to Chamberlain, 2 March 1925.

38 FO 371/10842, Minutes by Chamberlain, 3 March 1925.

39 FO 371/10892, Minutes by Mallet, 23 January and 3 March 1925.

40 FO 416/77, Loraine to Chamberlain, 16 June 1925.

41 Yahya Dowlatabadi, *Hayat Yahya* (*The Life of Yahya*), vol. 4, p 362.

42 FO 371/10140, Loraine to Chamberlain, 16 June 1925.

43 *Ibid.*

44 FO 416/77, Chamberlain to Loraine, 16 September 1925.

45 FO 416/77, Loraine to Chamberlain, 24, 28 and 29 September 1925.

46 Baqer Aqeli, *Ruz Shomar Tarikh Iran* (*Daily Calendar of the History of Iran*), translated by Cyrus Ghani, vol. 1, p 196.

47 FO 416/77, Loraine to Chamberlain, 22 October 1925.

48 FO 416/77, Loraine to Chamberlain, 18 October 1925.

49 FO 371/10140, Loraine to Chamberlain, 10 August 1925.

50 FO 371/10140, Loraine to Chamberlain, 21 October 1925.

51 FO 371/10140, Loraine to Chamberlain, 22 October 1925.

52 *Ibid.*

53 FO. 416/77, Chamberlain to Iranian Minister of Foreign Affairs, 23 October 1925.

54 FO 416/77, Loraine to Chamberlain, 26 October 1925.

55 FO 416/77, Loraine to Chamberlain, 29 October 1925.

56 FO 416/77, Loraine to Chamberlain, 29 October 1925.

57 Soleiman Behboodi, *Khaterat Soleiman Behboodi* (*The Memoirs of Soleiman Behboodi*), p 246.

58 Yahya Dowlatabadi, *Hayat Yahya* (*The Life of Yahya*), vol. 4, pp 381–385. It is not known whether Reza Khan actually saw Mostofi that day.

59 Hosein Makki, *Tarikh Bist Saleh Iran* (*A Twenty Year History of Iran*), vol. 3, pp 432 and 450, translated from the Persian and edited by Cyrus Ghani.

60 FO 371/52755, J.H. Le Rougetel to Bevin, 27 May 1946.

61 Hosein Makki, *Tarikh Bist Saleh Iran* (*A Twenty Year History of Iran*), vol. 3, pp 442–450, translated from the Persian and edited by Cyrus Ghani.

62 *Ibid.*, pp 450, 452–455.

63 Dowlatabadi was highly agitated during his speech as he was interrupted by supporters of Reza Khan. This summary is an interpretive account of his remarks.

64 Hosein Makki, *Tarikh Bist Saleh Iran* (*A Twenty Year History of Iran*), vol. 3, pp 465–466.

65 Mehdi Bamdad, *Tarikh Rejal Iran Quroun 12, 13, 14* (*Dictionary of National Biography of Iran: Twelfth, Thirteenth, Fourteenth Centuries*), vol. 4, pp 437–438.

66 At least two writers have mentioned that Reza Khan sent a personal envoy to England to ask Ironside, as a matter of honour, to release him from his promise not to depose Ahmad Shah. Neither the time of the visit nor the name of the messenger are mentioned: Maj. Gen. Sir Edmund Ironside, *High Road to Command*, p 118 and Denis Wright, *The English Amongst the Persians*, p 184.

67 Jahangir Amuzegar, *The Dynamics of the Iranian Revolution – The Pahlavi Triumph and Tragedy*, p 71.

14

The Beginning of the Pahlavi Era

As soon as the vote in parliament had been completed, a number of measures which had been planned carefully in advance were put into motion. Reza Khan resigned as Prime Minister and Foroughi became Acting Prime Minister. That afternoon Maj. Gen. Amir Tahmasebi,* the Military Governor of Tehran, together with Brig. Gen. Yazdanpanah, commander of the Central Division, Col. Dargahi, Chief of Police, and Col. Bouzarjomehri,† acting head of the Tehran municipality, took over the royal palaces. Mohammad Hassan Mirza, the fomer Crown Prince, escorted by guards, was sent by car to the border of Iraq, from whence he travelled to Paris to join his brother. He had pleaded that he was short of funds and had been given 5,000 tomans.[2]

---

* Abdollah Amir Tahmasebi, c.1878–1928, was the son of a Cossack officer and joined the Cossacks in 1898. He received promotion largely through Ahmad Shah's patronage and in 1919 became commander of the Shah's bodyguards. Initially he was ignored by Reza Khan, but he soon made him a Brig. Gen. in the new army. In 1924 he was promoted to Maj. Gen. and Commander of the North-western Division, where he probably disposed of the powerful local grandee Eqbal al Saltaneh Makou'i. He was popular in Azarbaijan; later Military Governor of Tehran; Minister of War in Foroughi's Cabinet on Reza Khan's accession to the throne; Minister of Public Works in 1927. He was killed in an ambush by Lur tribesmen. One of the better and more respected officers of his day, he spoke Russian and French and was author of *A History of the Reza Shah Period 1925–1926.*[1]

The Minister of Interior informed provincial Governors of the act of parliament and the make-up of the Provisional Government. The Minister of Foreign Affairs informed all foreign legations of the changes. On 2 November Reza Khan, with the new title of His Imperial Highness, issued a declaration as head of the Provisional Government which read in part as follows:

> All my efforts have been for the general security, the contentment of the people and the greatness of the country. I have always had in mind two important objectives which have taken precedence over all my other thoughts and I am happy that now I will be able to put them into effect, as is my duty. These long cherished dreams are the practical application of the true religious tenets of Islam and the attainment of peace of mind and tranquility of the people.[3]

The proclamation was directed primarily towards the clergy. The ulama of the holy centres of Najaf, Karbala and Qom remained silent on the changes. It appeared as if they did not mind Reza Khan as a king as long as there was no more talk of a republic. The other principal clergymen also made their obeisance to Reza Khan and remained passive.

The next day Reza Khan attended a reception in his honour at parliament to celebrate its recent decision. A three day official holiday was declared, with the streets illuminated and fireworks at night. Despite the celebrations there was no great enthusiasm among the masses and no spontaneous rejoicing. Although the Qajars were neither loved nor respected, Reza Khan was not a person who had either elicited or acquired any degree of affection. His stern appearance, rarely a smile on his face, and his outbursts of anger even in public had not endeared him to the populace. People were also bewildered by the change, and although they had come to respect Reza Khan did not know what it meant for them. As Loraine was to write:

> More than half of the intelligentsia is slightly in favour of change but only a considerably smaller proportion will commit themselves definitely to supporting it. This accounts for lack of enthusiasm and lack of opposition.[5]

---

† Karim Bouzarjomehri, c.1878–c.1947, joined the Cossack Brigade and rose from the ranks; close to fellow-officer Reza Khan, who appointed him in 1923 Head of Tehran municipality, a post he held until 1934. Between September 1929 and March 1930 he was Minister of Public Works while retaining his municipality position and between 1937 and 1939 commanded a division of the Tehran garrison, promoted to Major General. He was the chief instrument of Reza Shah's attempts to modernise Tehran: he widened streets, tore down dilapidated buildings and planted trees.[4]

Ahmad Shah sent a telegram from Paris that he did not accept the decision of parliament and would continue to consider himself monarch of the country. He further intended to take his case to the League of Nations and have himself reinstated. On the very day of Ahmad Shah's announcement, his uncles and other Qajar princes called on Reza Khan to extend their congratulations.[6]

Reza Khan's first priority was to convene the Constituent Assembly as quickly as possible. He feared that if the interval between the recent act of parliament and the assembly's vote on his accession to the throne were too long the opposition would have time to coalesce. Elections for the Constituent Assembly were controlled by the Ministries of War and Interior and no chances were taken. It was made certain that only candidates who were certain to vote to give Reza Khan the crown were elected. In some districts in the provinces elections were not even held. The nominees were notified by the Ministry of Interior that they were to be delegates to the assembly. Almost all members of parliament who had voted for the abolition of the Qajar dynasty were elected to the Constituent Assembly.[7]

Loraine was anxious that Britain recognise Reza Khan's new position as quickly as possible and called on Reza Khan on 3 November promising provisional recognition by Britain as soon as was feasible. Reza Khan, in turn, assured Loraine that all treaties between Iran and other countries would remain in full force and duly observed.[8] All heads of diplomatic missions to Tehran met and agreed to send the Foreign Minister, Moshar, a letter as an act of courtesy, with brief individual acknowledgments of Moshar's letter of 31 October informing them of the decision of parliament.[9] The United States, however, was the only country that decided it was better to wait for the decision of the Constituent Assembly before extending recognition. In the meantime the United States Chargé, Coply Amory, was authorised to express sentiments of friendship and transact official business as before.[10] Moshar, on instructions from Reza Khan, told Amory that Great Britain, Turkey, Germany and the Soviet Union were sending notes of provisional recognition the next day and Reza Khan expected the same from the United States. Frank Kellogg, Secretary of State, relented and the United States also extended provisional recognition.[11] On November 8 Italy, Belgium, Poland and Egypt joined the rest.

At this sensitive juncture, when Reza Khan was demanding acceptance and respect from the diplomatic community, a minor and unexpected controversy threatened to disrupt the smooth relationship established between Reza Khan and Loraine. The Soviet Minister to Tehran, Yureniev, had called on Reza Khan on 4

November to express the sentiments of the Soviet Union on the imminent accession of Reza Khan to the throne. He had showered Reza Khan with compliments and effusive protestations of friendship, and in the course of these amenities had enquired whether Reza Khan would agree to the elevation of Soviet diplomatic representation to ambassadorial level. Reza Khan, without giving the matter any thought and not realising that with the exception of Turkey there was no exchange of ambassadors between Iran and any other country, had answered affirmatively. A week later the Soviet Foreign Commissar informed Moshar that they would appoint an ambassador, and on 27 December Yureniev was elevated to the rank of ambassador. Loraine was the senior foreign diplomat in Tehran and the dean of the diplomatic corps. Now he would be outranked and would have to walk behind Yureniev, and it would be the latter who would deliver all formal addresses on occasions when the Shah received the entire diplomatc corps. Moreover, ambassadors not only outrank all other emissaries but have the right to demand an audience with the head of state to which they are accredited. It appears Loraine took the matter quite seriously. He may have thought this elevation of representation was a signal for a closer relationship between Iran and the Soviet Union at the expense of Britain. Loraine informed Moshar that Britain as a matter of internal policy would not elevate the existing diplomatic representation to ambassadorial level. As the diplomatic discrepancy in status would be viewed by the Foreign Office as an affront, the only alternative left for him was to be recalled to London and replaced by a new minister. When Loraine realised that the arrangement with the Soviets had gone too far to be reversed he convinced the Foreign Office to accept the situation.[12]

The first opportunity for Loraine to see Reza Khan for an extended period took place when Harold Nicolson,* the new Counsellor of the British Legation, was to be introduced. Loraine first complimented Reza Khan and said that he had come across a report he had written on 31 January 1922 wherein he had informed the Foreign Secretary that Reza Khan 'had been the first Persian of prominence whom I had

---

* Harold Nicolson, 1886–1968, was the son of Sir Arthur Carnock (later Lord Carnock) who had served as Counsellor at the British Legation in Tehran in 1885–1887 and later as Ambassador to St. Petersburg when the 1907 Convention was negotiated. Harold Nicolson joined the diplomatic service during World War I; served at the Paris Peace Conference; Tehran 1925–1927; Berlin 1927; resigned 1929; member of parliament 1935–1945; married Vita (Victoria) Sackville West; prolific writer of biographies, diaries and letters.[13]

met who had not endeavoured to enlist my sympathies in favour of his own person or other groups of partisans but had spoken to me only of the interests of his own country'. Reza Khan was pleased and stated that he hoped all outstanding matters could be cleared up soon. He acknowledged freely the assistance which Britain and her representatives in Iran had given to the country and himself. As to the status of future relationships Reza Khan went on to say:

> ... he quite realised that in the past Great Britain have been compelled to interfere in Persian affairs to an extent which would have been undesirable in a better organised country. [His goal had been] to bring about a state of affairs in which this is no longer necessary... A strong Persia might be able to take on her shoulders a part of the heavy load of responsibility which Britain bore in the East.[14]

Loraine, who had dealt with Reza Khan for four years took these remarks as a protestation of friendship but also as a warning which Reza Khan had given countless times before that the two countries should deal with each other as equals. For Nicolson such blunt talk from a former soldier who had been assisted in his career by Britain was unacceptable. As we shall see Nicolson took a dislike to Reza Khan from that very first meeting. In less than a year, when he became Chargé d'Affaires of the Legation (Loraine left in July 1926), Nicolson began to question almost everything Loraine had attempted to build upon and played a key part in the gradual cooling of relations between the two countries.

The Constituent Assembly held its first meeting on 6 December and Reza Khan gave the opening address in which he emphasised that the representatives must come to a decision in a short time, that any delay would be detrimental to the interests of the country. On 12 December the Assembly completed its work and amended the relevant provisions of the constitution. Reza Khan became the new sovereign and succession went to his male descendants in direct line, if born of an Iranian mother.[15] In the event the Shah had no son, the heir to the throne would be designated by the sovereign subject to the approval of parliament, however, no member of the Qajar family could be so chosen. The age of majority of the heir was set at twenty years and the Qajars also were barred from becoming regents. Of the 260 representatives 257 voted for the amendments to the Constitution, with three abstentions. Soleiman Mirza and two of his Socialist colleagues abstained. He argued that although he and his party had enthusiastically supported Reza Khan and his reforms, his socialist and republican principles prevented him from endorsing the establishment of monarchies.[16]

There were a few representatives at the assembly who wanted to grant the throne more powers than specified in the existing constitution, and there was some controversy as to whether the crown should descend in hereditory succession or be vested in Reza Khan only for his own lifetime. Neither issue was acted upon. On 15 December Reza Khan took the required oath of fealty, swore to uphold the constitution and was pronounced Reza Shah Pahlavi.

On 16 December the Acting Prime Minister, Foroughi, and the entire Cabinet resigned. The choice of the first Prime Minister under the new Shah had narrowed down to Hassan Moshar, the incumbent Minister of Foreign Affairs, and Mohammad Ali Foroughi. Reza Shah was probably pleased with Moshar for his role as an effective intermediary with foreign legations, especially the British, and the speedy recognition by the foreign powers. Moshar had also acted as intermediary with the British Legation during the campaign against Sheikh Khaz'al and had later deflected much of the criticism for the isolation of the Sheikh in Tehran. Moshar had harboured prime ministerial ambitions for some time and it was common knowledge that he was Loraine's choice and that he had strong support in parliament, far exceeding that of Foroughi.

Foroughi's greatest asset was Reza Khan's complete trust. On the three occasions when Reza Khan had left Tehran for a considerable length of time, Foroughi had been appointed Acting Prime Minister. Furthermore, Moshar was objectionable to the Soviets while they were neutral towards Foroughi. There were no immediate problems with Britain while Reza Shah still had weighty unresolved trade and commercial matters pending with the Soviets and he needed someone as prime minister to whom the Soviets would not be overtly hostile. The main difficulty of the introverted and aloof Foroughi[17] was his lack of support in parliament.

When Foroughi became Reza Shah's nominee, Taddayon, the President of parliament, informed Reza Shah that Foroughi had only a few supporters and could not be confirmed. Reza Shah called some 20 members of parliament to his house and asked them to give their support to Foroughi. That settled the matter and parliament voted for him by a large margin. Probably one of the key elements in Reza Shah's selection of Foroughi was to stress the appearance of stability and continuity, that nothing had changed since he had become Shah. Foroughi had been Prime Minister before and he would remain in that post for the time being. On 19 December he presented his Cabinet to parliament. Moshar was retained as Minister of Foreign Affairs; Maj. Gen. Abdollah Amir Tahmasebi was Minister of War; Hosein Dadgar, Minister of Interior; Morteza Qoli

Bayat, Minister of Finance; Ja'far Qoli As'ad, Minister of Post and Telegraph; Ali Akbar Davar, Minister of Public Works and Commerce; and Yousef Moshar, Acting Minister of Education.[18]

The most noteworthy addition to the Cabinet was the appointment of Ali Akbar Davar as the Minister for Public Works and Commerce, his first cabinet post. He soon demonstrated exceptional organisational abilities and the same feverish energy he was to bring to his future posts. Within a few weeks of his appointment he prepared a bill, approved by parliament, for the employment of a US firm to undertake a survey determining the primary route for a proposed railway system. Through his efforts the first paved road from Tehran to Mazandaran was completed. Davar's other accomplishments in this post were the establishment of a school of commerce to teach the principles of economics, management and accounting, and the award of a contract to a Danish firm to provide the first public bus service in Tehran.[19] Davar was a superb executive and a unique administrator for his time. He was the first person to employ younger educated Iranians. He trusted his subordinates and delegated the powers required by them. Davar emerged as the principal conceptual thinker of the early Pahlavi era. Most of the innovative measures adopted during that period in law, finance and administration originated with him. Later as Minister of Justice he would reorganise the Ministry and supervise the drafting of the civil code which was the first step in the secular administration of justice.

The most unexpected appointment was the selection of Abdol Hosein Teimurtash as Minister of Court. There were at least four people closer to Reza Shah who had expected the prized appointment for their loyalty and length of service. Cheraq Ali Khan (Amir Akram), a second cousin to Reza Shah, had served him for the last eight years in various capacities, principally as a trusted family member. Cheraq Ali Khan, who adopted the family name Pahlavi Nejad,[20] was the only known member of Reza Shah's family who had received a reasonable formal education, carried himself well and had achieved a social status independent of Reza Shah. Nevertheless he was passed over as Minister of Court but appointed as head of the recently established Office of the Crown Prince, Mohammad Reza, with the rank of Deputy Minister of Court under Teimurtash. Hosein Dadgar had also entertained thoughts of being appointed as Minister of Court. He had served Reza Khan since 1923, most recently as Vice President of the Constituent Assembly. Dadgar, however, had served too many masters, including Seyyed Zia, and was never regarded by Reza Shah as anything more than a mere instrument. Another intimate of Reza Shah who had coveted the post of

Minister of Court was Brig. Gen. Khodayar,[21] who had briefly served as Minister of Post and Telegraph but had remained as administrator of Reza Shah's ever-growing private estate. Another member of Reza Shah's inner circle was Farajollah Bahrami (Dabir A'zam),* who had acted as private secretary to Reza Khan from his days as Minister of War. Bahrami had also expected to be made Minister of Court. What he received was the position of Private Secretary to Reza Shah, a post which presumably gave him direct access to the Shah and control of appointments. With the selection of Teimurtash, however, the duties of all other positions at the Ministry of Court were to become academic and merely ceremonial. Bahrami maintained his position for only two years. He expected too much from Reza Shah and interfered in matters which did not concern him. He was slow to realise that their relationship had changed, and Reza Shah lost patience with him. He was appointed to other positions but was kept away from the court. Succeeding private secretaries wisely kept their distance.

The selection of Teimurtash as Minister of Court was an inspired choice and Reza Shah's success in the initial years of his rule owed a great deal to this appointment. Teimurtash had worked hard for Reza Shah from the beginning of 1925. His tireless and energetic campaign on behalf of Reza Khan to depose the Qajars had been impressive. However, many others had worked just as arduously to bring Reza Khan to the throne and furthermore Teimurtash was a newcomer to Reza Shah's camp. He had not accompanied him on any military expedition or inspection of the provinces and was not on close social terms with him. There is no record of Teimurtash having been invited to Reza Khan's home in the evenings or having a fixed day for meetings.[22] Teimurtash had his own circle of intimates with whom he would spend most evenings. When Reza Khan

---

* Farajollah Bahrami (Dabir A'zam), c.1890–c.1950, came from a large and prominent family, was born and educated in Tehran, became private secretary to Reza Khan in 1922, but lost Reza Shah's confidence, in 1927 being sent to Europe as supervisor of Iranian students. He returned in 1929, was made Governor of Esfahan in 1930; Fars in 1931; Minister of Post and Telegraph in 1933; Governor of Khorasan between 1933 and 1934. He was recalled for reporting that adequate facilities did not exist in Mashhad for the accomodation of orientalists attending Ferdowsi's millenary. He was not employed until after Reza Shah's abdication; was then Minister of Interior in 1943; and Governor of Esfahan 1943–1944. Bahrami was one of the better educated people around Reza Shah and had a flair for Persian literature. He wrote an account of Reza Khan's journey to Khuzestan and the expedition against Sheikh Khaz'al in 1924.[23]

had become Prime Minister in the autumn of 1923, Teimurtash was Governor of Kerman and did not return to Tehran until some five months later.[24] He had played a minor part in the republican movement and it was not until August 1924 that Teimurtash served in Reza Khan's Cabinet as Minister of Public Works. It was therefore all the more surprising that a relative newcomer with an association of no longer than two years was appointed Minister of Court, a position that would bring him in daily contact with the new monarch.

Reza Shah was most anxious to bring dignity to his court and receive acceptance in European capitals. Having measured the people around him it was not difficult to realise that Teimurtash would be the only person who could organise the court along the lines of European monarchies. Teimurtash was a person of immense charm who could also be forceful and bring the required discipline to administration of the Court. Having attended a prestigious military academy in St Petersburg also must have impressed Reza Shah. His knowledge of French and Russian was a great asset. Teimurtash was an excellent public speaker and an engaging conversationalist. He was to act as translator for Reza Shah at crucial meetings with foreign dignitaries and would refine in translation any rough edges in his master's remarks.

Teimurtash did establish a most respectable court for Reza Shah. He was especially sensitive to protocol and wanted Reza Shah to be surrounded with dignity. He appointed Hassanali Ghaffari,* a career diplomat who had been the chief of protocol at the Ministry of Foreign Affairs, as Grand Master of Ceremonies at the Ministry of Court.[25] Ghaffari had been educated in Europe, spoke excellent French and had travelled extensively. He was well acquainted with matters of protocol in European capitals.

---

* Hassanali Ghaffari (Moaven al Dowleh), 1888–1980, came from the most prominent family of Kashan. The family had produced the two most distinguished painters of nineteenth and early twentieth century Iran, Sani' al Molk and Kamal al Molk. His forefathers included a most seasoned Iranian diplomat of the nineteenth century, Farrokh Khan Amin al Dowleh, and a score of nineteenth century high-ranked government officials. Ghaffari was the son of the first Moaven al Dowleh (Mohammad Ebrahim) who had been Minister of Foreign Affairs. Ghaffari joined the Ministry of Foreign Affairs where he became Director of the Protocol Department; Grand Master of Ceremonies at Ministry of Court 1926–1929; Political Under Secretary of Ministry of Foreign Affairs; and briefly Acting Foreign Minister in late 1929. He was Minister to Brussels 1933–1936 and remained in Europe until 1943; in 1949 he was posted to Switzerland; and in 1951 became Ambassador to Brazil, Argentina and Chile.[26]

Teimurtash would in future become the only route of access to
the Shah. He would attend Cabinet meetings and speak for the Shah.
He was to become Reza Shah's alter ego. Prime Ministers became
subservient to him and were told by the Shah that 'Teimurtash's
word is my word'.[27] In almost every sphere Reza Shah delegated full
powers to his Minister of Court. Teimurtash became the only avenue
of contact by foreign legations. The British considered him an obstacle to their closer access to Reza Shah. He had a history of a stormy
relationship with the British Legation. Initially he had enjoyed a
fairly close rapport with Norman but had become disenchanted with
Britain when he was imprisoned by Seyyed Zia, which he considered
to have taken place with at least Norman's assent. Shortly after his
release he and Firouz had led the campaign against British influence
in Iran.[28] Subsequently he saw little of Loraine but his relationship
with the British Legation had stabilised. With the Soviet representatives in Tehran he had maintained a more even one.[29]

Teimurtash soon demonstrated his administrative capabilities by
arranging all details of the coronation, on which work had begun
immediately after the deposition of the Qajars. He ordered the
design of a new crown and preparation of various medals and decorations. Teimurtash contacted the British, Belgian, Spanish and
Swedish Legations in Tehran to submit details of their coronation
ceremonies. He devised the Iranian ceremony from their procedures
insofar as they corresponded with past Iranian practice.[30] The task
proved more difficult than anticipated as there was no tradition as
to the manner in which Iranian monarchs had been crowned in the
preceding 200 years.[31] The most common practice in the Qajar era
had been for the eldest member of the family to place the crown on
the head of the new monarch. Due to Reza Shah's humble origins
there were no members of his family who would have been suitable
and the idea had to be discarded.

The coronation was held on 25 April in the main hall of the
Golestan Palace, the ceremonial seat of Qajar kings since the days
of Naser al Din Shah. Representatives of the government, the diplomatic corps and senior members of the clergy were present. The
ceremony was simple and conducted with dignity. A senior clergyman of Tehran gave the opening speech. The newly designed Pahlavi
crown was carried by Teimurtash, who together with the senior cleric
of Azarbaijan gave the crown to Reza Shah, who himself placed it on
his head. After a fairly long oration by Foroughi in which there were
extensive recitations of the poet Ferdowsi, Reza Khan, now Reza
Shah, addressed the assemblage. One of the main points of his
address was that special attention be paid to the safeguarding of

religion as it constituted an important bond for national unity. He then stressed fundamental reforms in education, economy, transportation, agriculture and the strengthening of the military. The most urgent reform was the reorganisation of the judicial system. He expected government officials to exert energy and set examples of honesty, moral courage and perseverance.

The ceremony was an important indication of the esteem in which the participants were held by Reza Shah. Teimurtash and Foroughi rode in the same carriage. Prior to the coronation both had received the highest decoration from Reza Shah.[32] Each of the high-ranking military officers and ministers carried a bejeweled object from the collection of the crown jewels such as swords, seals and sceptres, as a symbol of sovereignty. Foroughi carried the Kiani Crown which had been designed in the Qajar era. Teimurtash carried the Pahlavi Crown with which Reza Shah crowned himself.[33] The ceremony was well received by foreign observers and the diplomatic community in Tehran. Vincent Sheean described it as 'a skillful mixture of magnificence and simplicity'.[34] Loraine considered the event 'economical, not unimpressive and short'.[35]

Clearly the charismatic Teimurtash had emerged as the dominant figure in the early Pahlavi era, but he was to be disgraced and murdered within seven years. Even the cautious and prudent Foroughi would be forced into retirement only to come back after the invasion of Iran by the Allies in August 1941.

Loraine was determined to narrow outstanding problems between Great Britain and Iran and ensure cordial relations between the two countries after his departure. One of the legitimate charges against Britain had been her close relations to the southern tribes in Iran and their use as an instrument of policy to coerce the Iranian Government. In late December Loraine arranged a luncheon at the Legation with Esma'il Qashqa'i (Sowlat al Dowleh), the Qashqa'i chieftain, Sheikh Khaz'al and Ebrahim Qavam (Qavam al Molk), the nominal head of the five Arab tribes of Fars. Britain had a history of stormy relations with Sowlat al Dowleh, who had led his tribe in numerous campaigns against the SPR and occupied Shiraz in the last days of World War I. Reza Shah had disarmed the tribe gradually and Sowlat al Dowleh was now practically a hostage in Tehran as a member of the Fifth Parliament. Loraine had re-established relations with Sowlat al Dowleh, and the invitation to him was intended to bury the hatchet and set aside the enmity of the war period. Khaz'al and Qavam al Molk had been invited principally to demonstrate Britain's support of Reza Shah. After the luncheon, at the urging of Loraine, each of the chieftains swore loyalty to Reza

Shah and 'undying friendship to the British Government whose magnanimity and wisdom each exhorted'.[36]

Beginning in 1926, and until his departure in July of that year, Loraine had a monthly audience with Reza Shah to discuss outstanding issues between the two countries such as the settlement of the amount of back taxes owed by Sheikh Khaz'al, which Reza Shah contended was in the hands of the US financial team, and the question of Iran's indebtedness for expenditures made by Britain in Iran between the years 1918 and 1921. Reza Shah had promised that the Iranian Government would soon write a letter to the British Government and officially acknowledge that Iran did owe 'some money' to Britain. On the question of a differential tariff, Loraine urged that the Iranian Government continue to apply the 1920 tariff. Reza Khan was unyielding, and repeatedly told Loraine that it was solely a decision for the Iranian Government which intended to set its own tariffs. On the question of recognition of Iraq, Reza Shah's answer had been that he must have the consent of the senior ulama, who were slowly coming around.

At a later meeting Loraine introduced two recent points of contention.[37] He expressed apprehension over the award of the fisheries concession in the Caspian Sea to the Soviet Government, as they would now have the dominant position along the whole Caspian littoral. Reza Khan ignored the objection and merely stated that he knew the Russians as well as anyone and they would not cause any mischief. Loraine was also worried about the proposed plan to build a railway from Khoramshahr to Tehran. He argued that since he assumed the railway later would be extended to the border of the Soviet Union, Russian access to the Persian Gulf would be facilitated. Reza Shah also dismissed this apprehension and added that the Russians were equally disturbed believing it to be a British scheme to keep naval vessels, including submarines, in the Caspian.[38]

At Loraine's farewell meeting on 27 June he raised two issues which he had hitherto avoided. Loraine said that he wanted to bring to the Shah's attention the prevalence of 'oppression and corruption throughout the whole Persian administrative machine... and especially in the army'. Taken aback, Reza Shah asked for specific examples. Loraine stated that it occured in the requisitioning of animals, food stuffs and means of transport by army personnel. Loraine added that the reason he had mentioned the matter was that whatever the army did reflected on Reza Shah directly and personally. The subject greatly disturbed Reza Shah, who equated the army with the security of the country and had allowed military commanders more latitude than his civilian administrators. Instead of amplifying the legitimate point he had raised, Loraine made the mistake of bringing up another issue which was spurious and self-serving. He complained that Iranian 'foreign policy was not clear'. Reza Shah then lost his composure and stated that Iran's foreign policy was perfectly clear. What Loraine was asking was that Iran move even closer to Britain and sever relations with all countries that Britain found objectionable. Reza Shah's final comment was that if he were to move Iran any closer to Britain 'it would appear to my countrymen as if we were subservient to Britain and [I] would not allow that'.[39]

Loraine had long believed that a strong and stable Iran would better serve Britain's strategic and economic interests in the East. He had accepted the fact that Reza Shah would pursue an independent national and foreign policy. The annoyance of Reza Shah over the question of foreign policy at their last meeting was natural and understandable to him. What Loraine did not know was that less than three months after his departure Harold Nicolson, the Chargé d'Affaires at the Legation, would begin to question the entire centralisation policy of Reza Shah and its endorsement by the Foreign Office. Nicolson became an implacable foe of Reza Shah, personally as well as politically, and began to erode the good will nurtured by Loraine. For reasons not entirely clear, Nicolson took an intense dislike to Reza Shah from the first visit.[40] In a report prepared on 30 September, only two months after Loraine had left, Nicolson wrote to the Foreign Secretary:

> Parliament is hostile to Reza Shah and a Constitutional crisis is looming... The personality of the Shah is alarming. It is perhaps too early to pronounce that Reza Shah has proved a failure. It is becoming doubtful however whether he possesses the intellectual or moral calibre necessary for his high functions. He is secretive, suspicious and ignorant; he appears wholly unable to grasp the realities of the situation or to realise the force of the hositlity which he has aroused... The tribes are restless and waiting for the lead. The people are impoverished and oppressed. The administration of justice is a greater scandal than before. The civil service is underpaid, corrupt and incompetent... our old tribal friends have been sacrificed to the policy of centralisation; the elder statesmen have each in turn been discredited...[41]

Nicolson by temperament and background was ill-suited to understand a changing Iran. He was still enamoured of Curzon's policy of tribal supremacy and a weak Central Government under the protection of Britain. He was later to write that 'Persia has lost much by the change... her charm, her gentleness, her culture and her dignity...' He further questioned the value of national independence for Iran.[42]

Nicolson's two years in Tehran were instrumental in a revival of Reza Shah's phobia about British intentions in Iran.

Nicolson's longing for the romantic Iran of the days before Reza Shah, with a row of camels in every town and village, is echoed by many English visitors of the same background. Writers such as Robert Byron, Christopher Sykes, David Talbot Rice and Owen Tweedy were to complain of attempts by Reza Shah to instill self-respect in his countrymen. Their recurrent complaints were: 'the arrogance of Persians; the disappearance of picturesque traditional attire'; the 'puritanism' imposed by Reza Shah as opposed to the 'gaiety' of the earlier period; the reluctance of Persians to attend social functions at the British Legation and impart useful secrets as in the Qajar era. 'Persians were always conceited. Now they have added insolence because Reza Shah has made them think Persia is important.' He even instituted border controls requiring identification for entry into the country. 'In one day he ends extraterritorial rights and privileges for foreigners... What insolence'.[43]

Loraine was more of a realist. From his first days in Tehran in December 1921 he had been a keen and fascinated observer of Reza Khan's ascent to power. He had played an important role in convincing the Foreign Office of the changing circumstances in Iran and the need for a reversal of policy. On the last day of 1925 he wrote a detailed report to the Foreign Secretary setting out some key remarks made by Reza Shah during the course of the past four years which Loraine considered 'a significant revelation of the attitude and mould of mind in the man with whom I was dealing'. Loraine gave a chronological account of these remarks.

In late 1922 when Mustafa Kamal Pasha had been trying to weld together a modern Turkey, Reza Khan had told Loraine:

At the time of the Coup in 1921 had he wished to act as Mustafa had done and seize all the reigns of authority with his own hands he had the force and authority to do so and there was no one to stop him least of all Seyyed Zia. He confessed he had been tempted to do what Mustafa had done but reflection had made him bide his time and stay his hand. He had argued [with himself] that creaky and corrupt as was the machinery of state, it had survived many centuries. During the War and post War period it had suffered the severest shock of all and was perhaps showing signs not merely of decay but of disintegration. This however was attributable more to the men who worked the machine than the machine itself. He [therefore] had reached the conclusion that the machinery would succumb altogether under the fresh shock of radical reconstruction in which case there would be nothing left to reconstruct and he had therefore decided to see what could be done by patient patching and overhauling, and by the creation of at least one sound organism in the shape of a national army, which might by its example and vigour breathe fresh vitality into the whole structure.

Loraine recounted other conversations in which Reza Khan had told him that 'he was a frank monarchist as far as his own country was concerned. He deplored the weakness, the selfishness and ineffectiveness of Ahmad Shah' but as he was the sovereign Reza Khan was bound to do his best in the circumstances. Some time after the deposition of the Qajars, Reza Khan had brought up the question of a republic. He admitted that he had pressed the republican idea, but:

... it did not take him long to perceive that contrary to his earlier expectations, the people emphatically did not want a republic and they were still fundamentally monarchists'. He could have waited for a year and then pressed again for a republic 'but he knew it was repugnant to the masses of people.

Loraine then outlined the picture that emerged:

These statements when threaded together give the real clue to the mainsprings of [Reza Khan's] actions; they show a line of consistency and indicate a development of thought accompanying a development of circumstances rather than the execution of a settled plan or the fulfillment of a long cherished ambition. They also reveal what I have noticed as a characteristic of [Reza Khan] in dealing with other... issues: a patient study of the problem at hand, the careful preparation of his measures to resolve it and a reluctance to take any decisive step until positive of its desirability and of its success. The trait is a curious one in a man possessing the present Shah's natural impetuosity of temperament... but it has manifested itself in every important measure he has taken... Simko rebellion; Sheikh Khazal's recalcitration; his own assumption of the office of Prime Minister; his campaign against the rebellious Lurs and the Turkamans; the disarmament of the Shahsavan, Bakhtiari and Qashqai. A very similar contrast can be observed in his personal demeanour. In any matter and on any occasion of real importance, his simplicity, his dignity and complete self command are striking. While in his ordinary every day relations he often terrifies those around him by the vigour of his invective.

Loraine ended his review with the conclusion he wished to draw:

We now have as king of Persia, a man who, notwithstanding his humble origin, his total lack of Western education, his inexperience of conditions in any country but his own, has some elements of real greatness; a man with an independence of judgement, altogether singular in his surroundings; a man who keeps his counsel far more closely than is generally supposed, who is not afraid of responsibility in big matters..., who believes that he has a definite mission to fulfill to his country and is determined to fulfill it... I am not blind to his shortcomings, nor dazzled by his personal success, but I do feel convinced that he is the one man able to put the affairs of his country in order and set its feet in the path of real progress. He must for this reason alone, command our sympathy and I think he is entitled to a large measure of our respect for what he has already achieved. He will as he himself realises be obliged to carry still most of the burden on his own shoulders, on account of the dearth in Persia of human material in statesmen.[44]

NOTES ON CHAPTER 14
Further details of publications and documents in Bibliography

1   FO 371/12300, Clive to Chamberlain, 13 July 1927; Mehdi Bamdad,
    Tarikh Rejal Iran Quroun 12, 13, 14 (*Dictionary of National Biography of
    Iran: Twelfth, Thirteenth, Fourteenth Centuries*), vol. 2, pp 281–282.
2   Hosein Makki, *Tarikh Bist Saleh Iran* (*A Twenty Year History of Iran*), vol.
    3, pp 470–471.
3   *Ibid.*, vol. 3, p 476.
4   FO 416/98, Bullard to Halifax, 7 February 1940.
5   FO 371/10140, Loraine to Chamberlain, 6 November 1925.
6   FO 371/10140, Loraine to Chamberlain, 19 November 1925.
7   FO 416/74, Loraine to Chamberlain, 21 November 1925.
8   FO 416/74, Loraine to Chamberlain, 3 November 1925.
9   DoS 891.01/25, Amory to Secretary of State, 2 November 1925.
10 DoS 891.01/26, Secretary of State to Amory, 4 November 1925.
11 DoS 891.01/27, Kellogg to Amory, 7 November 1925.
12 FO 416/78, Loraine to Chamberlain, 17 December 1925. Britain elevated
    its diplomatic mission to Iran only after Reza Shah's abdication.
13 Denis Wright, *The English Amongst the Persians*, pp 166, 184.
14 FO 416/78, Loraine to Chamberlain, 9 December 1925.
15 The question of 'male descendants born of an Iranian mother' was given
    a very liberal interpretation in 1939 when the Egyptian Princess
    Fowzieh, the wife of Mohammad Reza the Crown Prince, was deemed
    Iranian by an act of parliament.
16 Ervand Abrahamian, *Iran Between Two Revolutions*, p 135.
17 Nasrollah Entezam, *Khaterat Nasrollah Entezam* (*Memoirs of Nasrollah
    Entezam*), pp 193–194.
18 FO 371/11841, Loraine to Chamberlain, 30 December 1925.
19 Baqer Aqeli, *Ruz Shomar Tarikh Iran* (*Daily Calendar of the History of
    Iran*), translated by Cyrus Ghani, vol. 1, p 216; Baqer Aqeli, *Davar va
    Adlieh* (*Davar and the Ministry of Justice*), pp 91–92.
20 Cheraq Ali Khan was the only family member of Reza Shah who was
    allowed to adopt a family name which included the word Pahlavi. The des-
    cendants of Cheraq Ali Khan adopted the names Pahldad and Pahlavan.
21 For a discussion of the prospective candidates for Minister of Court,
    refer to Ali Dashti, *Panjah va Panj Sal* (*Fifty-five Years*), pp 135–136.
22 Soleiman Behboodi, *Khaterat Soleiman Behboodi* (*The Memoirs of
    Soleiman Behboodi*). Behboodi, who kept a diary of Reza Khan's appoint-
    ments, makes no mention of Teimurtash having been invited to Reza
    Khan's house for the weekly gatherings at which a Russian card game
    was played.
23 FO 416/98, Bullard to Halifax, 7 February 1940.
24 FO 371/13783, Clive to Foreign Office, 23 January 1923.
25 Ghaffari's primary task concerned diplomats and foreign dignitaries
    seeking an audience with Reza Shah. Protocol for internal functions was
    delegated to Gholam Ali Dowlatshahi (Mojalal al Dowleh), 1878–1932,
    the great grandson of Fath Ali Shah. Dowlatshahi had worked at the
    Ministry of Interior and held several governorships. His daughter,
    Esmat, had married Reza Khan in 1923 bearing him four sons and a
    daughter.

26 FO 371/52755 Le Rougetel to Bevin, 27 May 1946.
27 Mehdi Qoli Hedayat (Mokhber al Saltaneh), *Khaterat va Khatarat* (*Memoirs and Hazards*), p 512.
28 FO 416/69, Norman to Curzon, 16 July 1921.
29 As the chief executor of Reza Shah's foreign policy Teimurtash was to have an uneven relationship with both of the major foreign legations in Tehran. The Soviet Legation did not trust him but transacted business with him in a normal way. With the British Legation Teimurtash had a stormy relationship from the beginning of his political career. In November 1920, when there was a paralysing fear that Kouchek Khan and his Soviet allies would attack Tehran any day, Teimurtash together with Seyyed Zia had approached Norman and requested the British Government to finance the formation of a special army to fight the insurgents in the north. Later Teimurtash on his own had offered a modified plan whereby he would personally head the troops in the campaign. The Foreign Office had ignored both plans. DBFP doc. no. 576, Norman to Curzon, 5 November 1920 and DBFP doc. no. 586, Curzon to Norman, 25 November 1920.
      After the coup of 1921 Teimurtash had become disenchanted with the British and hostile to Seyyed Zia, by whom he was imprisoned. Upon his release, Teimurtash, together with Firouz, became active in plans to have Norman recalled and British financial advisers dismissed. Norman had written to Curzon in July 1921 that Teimurtash who was considered a 'friend of the British Legation had now turned against us because he believes I was responsible for his imprisonment'. Norman continued, 'Sardar Moazam another of our former friends exiled by Seyyed Zia for injudicious utterances... blames us and thinks I persuaded Seyyed Zia to punish him because he had said I was involved in the Coup. He made the remark in my presence but I forgot about it... I think it is his resentment against Seyyed Zia with whom he was on cordial terms and was even offered a cabinet post... which he declined... Sardar Moazam is a young man of some courage and intelligence with a considerable gift for eloquence but he is a spendthrift, a drunkard, a debauchee and a gambler who does not pay his losses and is totally irresponsible and untrustworthy. He was educated in Russia and his outlook on life resembles that of the less reputable young officers whose society he frequented there. He has now abandoned himself to Rothstein with whom he is said to work in the closest accord... He and Prince Firouz have the dubious honour of authorship of the recently published document most inaccurately headed 'A Statement of Truth'... which is very offensive to us': FO 416/69, Norman to Curzon, 16 July 1921.
      Relations with the British Legation remained cool and distant even after Loraine arrived in Tehran. Loraine also belittles him and marks him as an ally of Firouz hostile to British interests: FO 371/7803, Loraine to Curzon, 28 January 1922; FO 371/7806, Loraine to Curzon, 7 May 1922.
      After his death Teimurtash was accused by two former Soviet agents of the Soviet Secrect Service, OGPU, of having been a spy for the Soviets. Georgy Agabekov, the head of OGPU in Iran who defected to Western Europe in 1930, made the allegation in his book *The Cheka at Work – The Russian Secret Terror*. Recently Boris Bazhanov, another OGPU agent,

merely related the same story as told to him by Agabekov in *Bazhanov and the Damnation of Stalin*. The allegations have been dismissed as flimsy and without substance.

30 Baqer Aqeli, *Teimurtash Dar Sahne Siassat Iran* (*Teimurtash on the Iranian Political Scene*), pp 215–217.

31 There are no written accounts of the crowning ceremony of Nader Shah in 1736 nor of his nephew in 1747. Karim Khan Zand was never crowned and there is no account of the coronation of Aqa Mohammad Khan Qajar in 1796.

32 The British Government seriously considered the award of a decoration to Reza Shah on the occasion of his accession to the throne. For a variety of reasons the idea was discarded, the most important having been that Reza Shah probably would not have accepted: FO 371/10840, Minutes by Oliphant, 31 December 1925.

33 For detailed accounts of the coronation refer to Abdollah Amir Tahmasebi, *Tarikh Shahanshahi A'lahazrat Reza Shah Pahlavi* (*The Royal History of His Majesty Reza Shah Pahlavi*); Vita Sackville-West, *Passenger to Tehran*.

34 Vincent Sheean, *The New Persia*, p 66.

35 FO 416/78, Loraine to Chamberlain, 1 May 1926.

36 FO 371/11483, Loraine to Chamberlaine, 31 December 1925.

37 FO 371/11481, Loraine to Chamberlain, 2 February 1926.

38 FO 371/11483, Loraine to Chamberlain, 9 March 1926.

39 FO 371/11483, Loraine to Chamberlain, 27 June 1926.

40 Both Nicolson and his wife dwelt somewhat excessively on Reza Shah's physical unattractiveness. Nicolson described him as a 'bullet-headed man with the voice of an asthmatic child': Harold Nicolson, *Curzon – The Last Phase*, p 148. Vita Sackville-West described him thus: 'In appearance Reza was an alarming man, six foot three in height, with a sullen manner, a huge nose, grizzled hair and brutal jowl': Vita Sackville-West, *Passenger to Tehran*, p142.

41 FO 371/11483, Nicolson to Chamberlain, 30 September 1926.

42 Harold Nicolson, *Curzon – The Last Phase*, p 148.

43 Robert Byron, *The Road to Oxiana*, p 49; Christopher Sykes, *Four Studies in Loyalty*, pp 63–66; D. Talbot Rice, 'Introduction' in Robert Byron, *The Road to Oxiana*, p xi; Owen Tweedy, *Cairo to Persia and Back*, pp 176–181.

44 FO 371/11483, Loraine to Chamberlain, 31 December 1925.

Epilogue

In retrospect it appears that the end of the Qajar Dynasty and the crowning of Reza Shah was entirely predictable. Yet in February 1921 after the coup even the most astute observer could not have foreseen that Reza Khan was destined for the throne. It would have been a safer wager that Reza Khan would remain a dynamic and powerful minister of war for several years. After having fulfilled his primary tasks to unify the army, assert the authority of the Central Government and break the power of some of the unruly tribes, he would retire as a titled and much-decorated army officer to tend his newly acquired estates. Without detracting from Reza Khan's energy, determination and intelligence, it was taken for granted that soldiers of the Cossack Division could not become prime ministers, let alone overthrow a dynasty and supplant a Shah who was held as the 'Shadow of God' and 'Pivot of the Universe'.

There were, however, irresistible forces and trends at work which had rendered precedent irrelevant: over a century of humiliation by foreign powers; the failure of the constitutional promise; the carving up of the country into zones of influence; the attempt to impose the 1919 Agreement on a prostrate nation ravaged by foreign troop occupation during World War I; secessionist movements in four of the largest and richest provinces; the fear of a Bolshevik take-over of the northern provinces; a weak, dissolute and greedy monarch; the inability of old-line politicians to take effective action and their gradual discrediting; and the disappearance of any semblance of order and security. These all set the stage for the emergence of a strong autocratic leader.

The concentration of these factors had exhausted the population. Reza Khan's talent was in understanding that there was great yearning for a strong centralised state that would put an end to lawlessness, eliminate tribal fiefdoms and their bonds to foreign powers, and end civil wars and secessionist movements. Reza Khan, within a year of becoming Minister of War, had put down three serious revolts in the north and made inroads against tribes in central Iran. He had kept the country from splintering. Of equal importance was his awareness of 'the second goal of the Constitutional Revolution, modernising the state... Reza Khan was no less the child of the Iranian Constituional Revolution than Napoleon was of the French Revolution'.[1]

In the year leading to the overthrow of the Qajars, Reza Khan's most common refrain had been that he could not undertake any long-term planning for modernization until the question of the Qajar dynasty was resolved. As the unquestioned master of the situation Reza Shah was duty-bound to act on his long term promises. He had created a strong centralized state. Now he had to introduce and implement measures to make it viable. He faced a formidable challenge.

At the beginning of the nineteenth century the level of Iran's economy was roughly comparable to that of Turkey, India and Egypt but, unlike those economies, Iran's remained static. There were several reasons for this lag, including Iran's unfavourable location off the main sea routes that carried the flow of merchandise, men and ideas from Europe to the East.[2] But by far the main reason for the country's economic backwardness was the absence of a strong central government to provide order and undertake a systematic policy of economic development. The treaties of Golestan and Turkamanchai in 1813 and 1828 sealed the fate of Iran. Russia effectively controlled the northern half of the country and Britain gradually the southern half. Concessions and extra-territorial rights were granted to the two powers with the Shah and his chief ministers as the only beneficiaries. The increasing presence of Russia and Britain led to a gradual degradation of Iranian society. 'Loyalty went to one or the other or both powers but none to Iran... and worse, a consensus between the two powers that a weak and underdeveloped Iran would best serve their interests'.[3]

By 1921 Iran was bankrupt, her economic institutions were primitive and she was still an overwhelmingly agricultural society. 'Of its population of about ten million, ninety percent lived by farming and herding and more than half were peasants. One in four belonged to a nomadic tribe, and only one in five lived in a town. There was no such thing as an Iranian economy... Even agricultural production was mainly grain for local consumption... Modern industry was non-existent... Iran was still at the pre-industrial stage and if one had to single out one factor to exemplify the situation, it would be the absence of railways'.[4] There were a few hundred kilometers of paved road and only one port (Anzali) that had undergone any improvement. Turkey and Egypt had over 4,500 kilometers of railroads.[5]

Reza Shah's foremost objective was the creation of a modern state. This would entail the importation of the science and technology of the West as well as European principles of administration, education and economics. There was a consensus amongst Reza Shah's close advisors that the most pressing priority was the restructuring of the entire legal system and the codification and administration of laws along a secular path. The first priorities thus became reforming of the legal system and pressing ahead with the railway.

In early 1927 Davar was appointed Minister of Justice in Mostofi's third and last Cabinet.[6] He obtained parliamentary approval to close the Ministry of Justice for four months to revamp its administrative structure, reorganise the court system and dismiss incompetent and dishonest employees and judges. In the interim Reconciliation Chambers were set up to handle pressing cases.[7] In a remarkable and unprecedented exhibition of energy the work of restructuring was completed within four months and Reza Shah personally reopened the new Ministry of Justice. Most of the new judges were non-clerical younger men who had had a secular education.

Davar also established several committees to draft a new civil code. The committee that prepared the first book of the Civil Code was headed by Davar himself and included some of the most learned and respected names in Islamic law, several having a knowledge of European law.[8] In May 1928 the first part of the Code, comprising 955 articles, was submitted to parliament for approval.[9] These articles embraced laws relating to property, contracts, decedent estates, wills and inheritance and were modeled on the Napoleonic Code while observing the fundamentals of Shi'a jurisprudence. The Iranian Civil Code is a masterpiece of draftsmanship, blending Western principles of law and Islamic legal precepts. Lucidity and generality are its main characteristics. Its universality was such that the Government which followed the Iranian Revolution in 1979, despite declarations of its intention to repeal the Code, merely settled upon limited amendments.

The judicial reform initiated by Reza Shah had another immediate target. In addition to the severence of the clergy from the administration of law, it sought to end the extra-territorial rights enjoyed by foreign nationals in Iran. As soon as the drafting of the Civil Code had been completed, Reza Shah announced on 11 May 1928 that capitulation rights of all foreign powers in Iran were abrogated. Beginning in the nineteenth century Iran had relinquished to foreign governments jurisdiction over the trial of foreign nationals charged with commission of crimes or misdemeanors in Iran. It was now effectively argued that Iran had a judicial system as well as a body of law on a par with any European country and that foreign nationals would be treated equitably by Iranian courts. The abrogation of these extra-territorial rights had been one of the most cherished dreams of the early constitutionalists and a principal aspiration of the intelligentsia, who considered it an unbearable continuation of Iran's subordinate status to foreign powers. Every reformist government since the beginning of the constitutional period had declared upon taking office that it intended to end the system.[10]

As early as the First Parliament in 1907 there had been talk of building a railway system. The absence of a railway had been held out as a primary cause of Iran's backwardness, however there were no funds available and the enthusiastic deputies had no idea how to finance the project. The two powers had been willing to back only a system that ran along a route of their choosing serving their commercial and strategic interests and were adamently opposed to any other route. Britain was apprehensive that a system that extended southward would jeopardise her oil interests and pose a threat to India. Russia, in turn, had been opposed to construction of a system that would run east-west between India and Iraq.[11]

After several surveys by American consulting engineers it was decided to construct the first stage of the railway in a generally northeast-southwest direction from the Caspian Sea to the Persian Gulf. Political and military considerations were uppermost in Reza Shah's mind. Any north-south and east-west routes were to be avoided. The railway would also avoid the frontiers of India, Iraq and Turkey and would be constructed as far as practicable some distance from both the Soviet railways in Soviet Azarbaijan and the republics of Central Asia, and the British railway systems in Iraq and India. It was also decided to bypass every large city except the capital but traverse the areas inhabited by the principal nomadic tribes, the control of which was most important to the Central Government.[12]

There was ongoing debate as to how to finance the railway. Some argued that it was impossible to undertake any substantial infrastructural project without foreign capital. There was a group that admitted the advantages of foreign capital but suggested that the past history of borrowing by Qajar Shahs solely for personal use and pledging the revenues of the country as security would inevitably attach an odium to any foreign borrowing. It would be disastrous for the beginning of a new dynasty from which a great deal was expected.

The question of raising the money internally was not easy either. The institution of an income tax was thought to be premature and in any event would be difficult to assess and collect. Thus the only recourse was an indirect tax on mass-consumption goods. Parliament had already voted on a government monopoly for the import and export of tea and sugar in May 1925. A value-added tax on all such imports would provide the required funds. Sugar was not produced yet in Iran and the consumption of tea far exceeded local production.[13] At a cost of approximately $125 million the railway project was completed by early 1939.[14]

Any attempt at modernization in such a short time was bound to be costly and create hardship. Reza Shah certainly was relentless and demanded a great deal from his subjects, but the Qajars had left the entire population to suffer without anything to show for it after 130 years. Europe underwent the same and probably harsher hardship to achieve industrialisation, create railway systems and national armies. The Iranian railway, however, was more than a transportation and communication project that needed justification on purely economic grounds. It was an assertion of independence and a means of restoring the lost confidence of the nation. The Trans-Iranian Railway is the most enduring monument of Reza Shah's industrial policy. It constituted in its day 'one of the most spectacular examples of railway building in the world'.[15]

Another important contribution of Reza Shah was reform and innovation in education. Mandatory elementary education for six to thirteen-year-olds and six years of secondary education was instituted, based on the modern French curriculum. The number of elementary schools quadrupled between 1925 and 1939 and secondary schools increased sixfold.[16] Education, which had been the virtual monopoly of the clergy, became secular. Enrollment of girls at elementary and secondary schools increased almost tenfold.[17] Women were to enjoy the same educational and social rights as men.[18] There was an intense effort to train teachers. A teacher's college was established in 1933 and several more by 1940; various technical and vocational schools were established between 1923 and 1941; veterinary schools, military schools and later a Military Academy were created. The University of Tehran was inaugurated in 1935, initially with five faculties: literature, science, medicine, law and engineering. Existing colleges of theology, fine arts and agriculture were incorporated as additional faculties.[19] From 1928 a programme was established to send at least one hundred students abroad annually for higher education.[20] By 1941, 2,395 students had been sent abroad and 452 had completed their studies and returned.[21]

Reza Shah 'was neither an agnostic nor unbeholden to the Shi'ite ulama for his accession to the throne'. He simply saw no conflict between modernisation and the precepts of Islam, and the Shi'ite faith remained the official religion of the country.[22] In early 1937, on the occasion of a feast celebrating a Shi'ite holy event, he delivered a speech in which he said:

> A number of people make the mistake of thinking that the meaning of reform and progress in the world today is that they no longer need to observe the principles of religion and religious laws, or in other words, they see a contradiction between reform and progress on the one hand and religion on the other. The fact is that the great Law Giver of Islam, were he living today and confronted by the progress of the world, would himself demonstrate the conformity of the basic features of his laws with the conditions and forms of present day civilization. Unfortunately during the course of centuries men have abused his fundamental and clear ideas, and as a result, they have pulled the country backwards so that for thirteen centuries, when each century should have seen a great stride forward toward progress and perfection, it has remained backward and stagnant. We must now, frankly facing these old defects, make amends for the indolence of the past'.[23]

There were also great strides made in the field of public health. By 1929 there was compulsory vaccination against smallpox and a campaign was started to eradicate malaria, intestinal infections and trachoma'.[24] A Department of Public Sanitation was established in 1926 which became the Department and later Ministry of Health.[25] By 1932 all practitioners who held themselves out as trained physicians had to take an examination to become licensed physicians or pharmacists.[26] Hospitals were constructed in almost all provincial centres and most principal towns, a 500-bed hospital in Mashhad and a 1,000 bed hospital in Tehran being the largest. 'Charitable organizations such as the Red Lion and Sun, orphanages and the Organization for the Care of Mothers and Children are all the legacy of the Reza Shah era'.[27]

Preservation of the cultural heritage of Iran and promotion of the arts also received attention. A college of music was established to collect and transcribe folk music and traditional Iranian songs. For the first time public musical performance was given official patronage.[28] An Academy of Culture was founded to attempt to remove from the Persian language Arabic and Turkish words which had crept into it, provided a suitable substitute could be found. In 1934 the millenary celebration of the poet Ferdowsi was held in Mashhad, close to his place of birth, attended by leading Western scholars.[29] In 1930 a law was passed relating to the discovery and preservation of movable and immovable objects of antiquity, and regulations were enacted for the award of survey and excavation rights to foreign and Iranian entities. Soon thereafter an Archeological Museum was established.[30] Great efforts were made towards urban development, and imposing structures were built in Tehran.[31]

By the end of 1924 the Government had been able to exercise control over expenditures and financial solvency was restored. The fiscal system was modernised and centralised. Tariff control lost to foreign powers was regained in 1928 despite strong protests from Britain and the Soviet Union.[32] Through the levy of new and higher import duties and the establishment of some thirty state monopolies in the manufacture of consumer goods additional revenues were raised. The first National Bank of Iran was established in 1927 and in March 1932 became the sole issuer of currency.[33] The Government's success in 'urban construction, road building, transport facilities... post [including air mail], telegraph and telephone communications, radio broadcasting and overall economic development changed the country's structure'.[34] It should be borne in mind that the development of Iranian industry occurred during the world-wide depression of the 1930s when Iran's oil revenues were insignificant.

Reza Shah's foreign policy towards the great powers as well as Iran's neighbours was principally aimed at establishing the political and economic independence of Iran. He had given Iran its long-desired independence and wanted the international community's acknowledgement that Iran was no longer a pawn in the great powers' game and should be treated with respect.[35] He continued to be cautious in his dealings with Britain except during the 1931–1933 oil dispute when he ignored his ministers' warnings that in the midst of a world-wide depression it would be most unlikely that APOC would accede to Iran's demands to increase her oil revenues. He was equally cautious with the Soviets, whom he never fully trusted and always feared.

Among his immediate neighbours he secured and maintained the best relations with Turkey and a stable relationship with Afghanistan. Only Iraq gave him some difficulty in the early years of his reign. He made a lengthy state visit to Turkey in June 1934 where he cemented relations with Ataturk. With Afghanistan the only contentious issue was water rights to the Helmand river which flows from the Afghan mountains into Iran. A 1938 treaty which specified the quantity of water that could be diverted by Afghanistan was never fully observed. The matter remains unresolved to this day.[36] There were several major issues with Iraq which were fully resolved by the early thirties and in 1937 Iran, Turkey, Iraq and Afghanistan concluded a non-aggression pact and a treaty of friendship known as the Sa'adabad Pact.[37]

Reza Shah by training, experience and temperament was an autocrat. In his years in the Cossack Division he had known little

but to give or accept orders. In the four-and-a-half years he had
served as Minister of War and Prime Minister he had developed a
distrust of the parliamentary system. His experience with the republican movement and the opposition led by clerical leaders had
convinced him of the futility of a *modus vivendi* with the deputies.
He had found negotiations and compromise frustrating. Beginning
with elections to the Fifth Parliament he had begun to interfere in
favour of candidates who would follow him without a murmur. By
the seventh session, parliament had become a rubber stamp and
there were to be no disagreements with his vision and plans to modernise Iran and create a secular state. Reza Shah was not known for
his warmth or humour and was not disturbed by his reputation as
a stern autocrat. He cared little for the affection of his people and
was more feared than loved. It was important to him to have total
obedience and the respect of his people. He spoke in soft and barely
audible tones unless he lost his temper, when he would lash out and
express himself with invectives.

Reza Shah was straight-laced, taciturn and a moralist.[38] He lived
a relatively simple life. There was no court life and no entertainment.
Family life was important to him. Almost all his meals were taken
with his children.[39] Reza Shah's ambitions had not ceased when he
ascended the throne. He was desperate for the continuation of the
dynasty he had founded and for his eldest son to inherit the throne.
This concern became almost an obsession. Reza Shah ascended the
throne when he was physically past his peak. The years of soldiering
under difficult conditions and campaigns in malaria infested regions
had taken their toll. By the early 1930's he appeared much older
than a person in his early fifties. Fear of approaching or sudden
death made him distrust those around him in positions of power.
Soon he too fell victim to the ceaseless struggle of nineteenth century Iranian monarchs to discredit and eliminate persons in power
whom they considered rivals.

For obvious reasons Teimurtash became the person Reza Shah
came to fear the most. The very success of Teimurtash in running an
efficient administration soon became a liability. His vibrant personality, irreverent life-style and circle of mostly disreputable intimates,
which had been tolerated and no cause of concern, now began to
irritate Reza Shah.[40] What further fueled the Shah's suspicions were
reports he was receiving from his chief of police, a bitter rival of
Teimurtash, that Teimurtash was regarded by the Cabinet and the
bureaucracy as at least an equal of the Shah himself. Reza Shah had
delegated so much authority to Teimurtash that governments had
become subservient to him. It was therefore not surprising that the

foreign press in its occasional writings on Iran would highlight Teimurtash's role. These articles which had been ignored now came to be scrutinised by Reza Shah. Most of them were highly laudatory, praising the achievements of Iran in modernisation and emphasising the indispensibility of Teimurtash as the primary force and impetus behind the progress. There would be comments that Reza Shah was an aging monarch and his heir was still a minor who would need several years of training before he could become a seasoned ruler. These commentaries would state that fortunately for Reza Shah he had as his most trusted and competent lieutenant a person with the dynamism of Teimurtash, younger and still vigorous. If circumstances required, Teimurtash could become regent for the young heir and continue Reza Shah's plans.[41] Although the autocratic strain had been present all along, Reza Shah had allowed diverse and contrary opinions in the first few years of his reign. From about 1932 to his abdication in September 1941 he became more arbitrary and his autocratic bent became more pronounced.[42] He became a dictator in all but name.

Reza Shah's obsession with his son reaching the throne and continuing the dynasty began to assume paranoic proportions fed by succesive chiefs of police. When Teimurtash was removed as Minister of Court in December 1932, Reza Shah dismantled the ministry, not to be re-established until October 1939. Officially Teimurtash was accused and convicted of corruption, bribery and misuse of foreign currency regulations. Unofficially Reza Shah accused him of a host of crimes including plans to overthrow him and deny the Crown Prince the throne.[43] Reza Shah also appears to have believed that some of his other ministers were co-conspirators.[44] Teimurtash was murdered while in prison in September 1933. Firouz had been convicted on similar spurious charges in May 1930 and was murdered in prison in January 1938.[45] With the suicide of Davar in February 1937, the last of the the small group which had been greatly responsible for the success of the early years of Reza Shah's reign, Iran was deprived of her most dynamic figures. Their loss negates the proposition that individuals are not crucial to the shaping of events and that larger forces, whether the gods or the dialectics of history, are of sole significance.

With the loss of Teimurtash and Davar, and Foroughi's forced retirement, the burden of government fell heavily on Reza Shah himself. Economic development, which had been an uphill climb from the very beginning now became even more difficult. Reza Shah's distrust of his ministers grew and his demands on them became unrealistic and beyond their capabilities. They became only instruments of his will and no-one dared raise a voice or offer an opinion.

It should be noted that the dictatorship of Reza Khan was not an anomaly in the immediate post World War I period. There was not a single democracy in Asia and east of the Rhine only Czeckoslovakia resembled one. Even west of the Rhine there were Fascist Italy, and the dictatorships in Spain and Portugal, not to forget the fate of Germany some 13 years later. Some writers have maintained that Reza Shah's rule cut short the move toward democracy inaugurated by the constitutional revolution. There is a serious flaw in the argument as democracy never had taken root despite the introduction of a constitution and later a parliament.[46] As another writer has observed, Reza Shah 'like many nationalists was more intent on the independence of his country than the freedom of his people'.[47]

Reza Shah's single most glaring character defect was his insatiable desire to acquire land. By the time he had become Prime Minister he owned two houses in Tehran.[48] He later purchased lands in Tehran's north-western suburb (Darband) which ultimately became the summer palace,[49] and in the north-eastern limits of the city, which as Tehran grew became the north central area.[50] By 1926 he began purchases of farmland close to Tehran, land in western Iran in the Kermanshah-Hamadan region and north on the Caspian coast and plains of Mazandaran. It is reasonably certain that the administrators of his estates used the influence of their positions and in some cases used coersion and duress in compelling reluctant sellers to part with their land at prices well below market value. Large tracts of land were sequestered on the dubious claim that they were part of the crown domain.[51] It has been argued that Reza Shah's avarice was grounded in the fact that ownership of land always had been the traditional source of wealth, influence and status in Iranian society.[52] Qajar Shahs had committed worse offenses and the 'Pahlavi regime did not invent, introduce or magnify the unsavoury practice of the traditional order'.[53]

Whatever justification or reasoning is advanced it is difficult to escape the fact that Reza Shah had an almost pathological urge to acquire land. He certainly did not need it. He rarely visited his estates and seldom spent much time outside the capital. It is a matter that has tarnished his reputation and casts a shadow over his character. There is no vindicating argument other than to find the roots of this urge in his humble background.

Reza Shah's efforts towards a strong, modern, independent Iran were curtailed by the Second World War and the invasion and occupation of Iran by Soviet and British forces. On 3 September 1939, two days after the German attack on Poland, Iran declared her neutrality as she had done at the outbreak of the First World War 25 years earlier. As at the beginning of the previous war, both the Russians and the British were disliked while the Germans were generally regarded in a better light. Trade with Germany had increased from the late 1920s at the expense of the Soviets and Britain. At first it appeared Iran's neutrality would be observed.

> ...but the facts of geography and geology still held good. Iran still had a more or less undefended 2000km frontier with the USSR in the north. Britian was still the paramount power in the Persian Gulf and controlled the oil resources of southwest Iran.[54]

Relations with the USSR had already deteriorated. From September 1939 the Soviet Union had become the only route by which goods purchased in Europe could reach Iran as Britain controlled the Suez Canal and refused transport of German goods. The Soviets continued to delay and even deny transit rights and Iran's plans for a steel mill as well as stage two of the Trans-Iranian Railway came to a standstill. At the end of 1939, Reza Shah turned to Britain for an alliance but wanted it kept secret lest it provoke the Russians. Britain delayed responding as it too was fearful of the Russians. The Molotov-Ribbentrop Pact placed the USSR nominally on the side of Germany and with the slightest justification the Soviets could attack Iran for control of the oil fields in Khuzestan. Later, Reza Shah's attempt to purchase planes from Britain also went unanswered.[55] This is where matters stood until Germany invaded the Soviet Union on 22 June 1941.

By the end of the first week in July the British Cabinet asked the military to draw up plans for an attack on Iran and approached the Soviets for joint military action. The Soviets, hard pressed on other fronts, were reluctant and stated they would be satisfied if Iran allowed war materiel sent by the United States to be passed through her territory to the Soviet Union. As late as 19 July the Soviets were still against military action and believed joint British and Soviet economic pressure on Iran would suffice to make her amenable to their demands.[56] The Soviets finally acceded on 22 July[57] and by 7 August detailed plans for the attack were agreed upon by both parties.[58]

The official pretext for the two powers' unprovoked invasion of Iran was the number of German nationals working in Iran. Britain maintained a large number of these Germans were secret agents and planned to sabotage Allied interests in Iran.[59] Iran's initial answer was that the number was probably less than 1,000 and they were essential for the maintenance and operation of Iranian industries. In any event they were all under police surveillance.[60] By 28 July some German technicians were forced to leave and the Iranian Foreign Ministry informed the German Legation that the work permits of the remaining German nationals, upon expiry would not be renewed.[61] The day before the invasion, Reza Shah sent the Acting Minister of Foreign Affairs to assure Sir Reader Bullard, the British Minister in Tehran, that German nationals would be expelled at an accelerated pace and gave further assurances that 'Iran would do whatever the Allies wanted'.[62]

British and Soviet forces attacked in the early hours of the morning of 25 August. The plan was for British forces from southwest and western Iran to link up at Qazvin with the Soviet troops invading the northern provinces. Some 35,000 British, Indian and Gurkha troops took part in the invasion supported by naval bombardment of ports on the western coast of the Persian Gulf and the landing of paratroops near the oil fields.[63] Seven squadrons of RAF planes assisted in the invasion.[64]

Soviet forces crossed the Azarbaijan border and met little resistance. Other columns of Soviet troops captured all the provincial centres in Mazandaran, Gilan and Khorasan. Soviet aircraft bombed Tabriz and some 16 civilians were killed.[65] They also bombed other cities in Azarbaijan, Mazandaran and Gilan, causing three civilian deaths.[66] The exact number of Soviet troops that took part in the invasion is difficult to ascertain. From a review of their troop formations and the ranks of the commanding officers, the number 120,000, of which some 80–100,000 took an active part, is a safe estimate.[67]

In the face of overwhelming superiority the Iranian army collapsed within 48 hours and on 28 August Iran sued for an end to hostilities. Foroughi came out of retirement to head a new Government and Reza Shah was made to abdicate in favour of his son on 16 September.[68] Reza Shah was forced into exile, first to Mauritius and then Johannesburg, where he died on 26 July 1944.

From the start of the occupation, Iranians reverted to their old habits. The two foreign powers once again became the masters of Iranian political and economic life. Prime ministers, ministers, governors and members of parliament were hand-picked by the two legations. The British courted the tribes and the clergy as a post-war force against Communism. The Soviets in turn set up Communist Parties in most provinces and even in the British-controlled south. Three days after the abdication of Reza Shah and before he had left the country, the Soviets were starting separatist movements in Azarbaijan.[69] The British in turn formed the Azadi (Freedom) Party, headed by the senior Iranian at APOC and the then Minister of

Finance.[70] Furthermore, British troops began to re-arm southern tribes to safeguard their interests in southern Iran.[71]

As each of the powers strengthened their historical political and geographical constituencies they also began to dismantle the strong secular government established by Reza Shah. The existence of a strong centralised government with a powerful sovereign at the helm interfered with the Allies' need to have complete freedom of action. Britain had decided prior to the invasion that Reza Shah had to go and the Russians, who had their own post-war aims in Iran, had agreed. Reza Shah could not have accepted the presence of Soviet and British troops once more on its soil. 'The system therefore had to be broken down and the authority of the state shattered.'[72]

Although Reza Shah had no systematic blueprint for modernisation, he had implemented many of the reforms that he thought necessary to modernise Iran. On the eve of the Russo-British invasion there was a strong Central Government that Iran had not seen for 140 years, free of manipulation by foreign powers, nomadic uprisings and undue clerical influence. There was a viable financial structure and the beginning of industrialisation. In 15 years he had eradicated regressive practices that had seemed to be the very tissue of Iranian life and had created institutions that had been talked about for over 50 years but toward which not a single step had been taken.

Pre-Pahlavi Iran had been characterised by the existence of many centres of power. Reza Shah destroyed traditional leaders and groups, established new institutions and laid the basis for the state to play active economic, social and cultural roles. He brought new ideologies, particularly a new form of nationalism, and in effect established the modern Iranian nation-state.

Reza Shah was far from a philosopher king, and undeniably a flawed individual. But he was unquestionably the father of modern Iran and the architect of the country's twentieth-century history.

NOTES ON EPILOGUE
Further details of publications and documents in Bibliography

1   Said Amir Arjomand, *The Turban for the Crown: The Islamic Revolution
     in Iran*, pp. 62-63.
2   Charles Issawi, 'The Iranian Economy 1925–1975' in George Lencowski,
     Iran Under the Pahlavis, p 129.
3   *Ibid.*, p 130.
4   Malcolm E. Yapp, '1900–1921: The Last Years of the Qajar Dynasty' in
     Hossein Amirsadeghi and R.W. Ferrier (eds), *Twentieth Century Iran*, p 1.
5   Charles Issawi, 'The Iranian Economy 1925–1975' in George Lenczowski,
     Iran Under the Pahlavis, p 130.
6   Baqer Aqeli, *Ruz Shomar Tarikh Iran (A Daily Calendar of the History of
     Iran)*, vol. 1, p 218.
7   *Ibid.*
8   The most prominent members of the committee were Seyyed Nasrollah
     Taqavi, Seyyed Mohsen Sadr, Seyyed Mohammad Fatemi Qomi, Seyyed
     Kazem Assar and Mostafa Adl.
9   The second and third books of the Civil Code were completed later. Book
     II dealt with personal status, including nationality, marriage, divorce and
     offsprings. Book III dealt primarily with rules of evidence and procedure.
10   Rouhollah Ramazani, *The Foreign Policy of Iran 1500–1941*, p 243.
     Russia was the first country to obtain capitulation rights for their sub-
     jects in Iran in the Treaty of Turkamanchai in 1828. Then came Spain
     in 1842, France in 1855, the United States in 1856, Britain, Belgium
     and Holland in 1857. By 1900 more than 15 countries had obtained
     extra-territorial rights. Turkey agreed to forego them in accordance with
     the Iran-Turkey Treaty of 22 April 1926.
11   William S. Haas, *Iran*, p 212. The Russians at least had built some
     paved roads in the north between Anzali and Rasht, and Tabriz and
     Julfa: *Ibid.*, p 210. Britain had been traditionally opposed to any devel-
     opment project in any part of southern Iran, fearing local industries
     would compete with products manufactured in India: M. Reza Ghods,
     Iran in the Twentieth Century, p 19.
12   Elgin Groseclose, *Introduction to Iran*, p 147. 'Reza Shah planned his
     railway on an axis designed to thwart as far as possible any advantages
     the foreign powers might have hoped to derive from it. It was standard
     gauge as opposed to the broad gauge of the USSR or narrow gauge of
     the Iraq railway system (built by the British)'. Peter Avery, *Modern Iran*,
     p 301. Stage 2 was to link Tabriz to Tehran and Tehran to Mashhad.
     Work was to have begun in 1941 but was delayed by World War II.
13   Gholam Reza Moghadam, 'Iran's Foreign Trade Policy and Economic
     Development in the Inter War Period', unpublished PhD thesis, pp
     105–116. Tea and Sugar accounted for 28.6% of total imports, exceeded
     only by textiles.
14   William S. Haas, *Iran*, p 214.
15   In the course of 870 miles (1400km) from the Persian Gulf to the
     Caspian Sea it passes from sea level to an altitude of 3000m, crosses
     4,102 bridges and passes through 224 tunnels, some of which
     corkscrew in the mountains. Along one stretch between Andimeshk
     and Darrud, 60 miles (100kms) are inside tunnels: Elgin Groseclose,

Introduction to Iran, p 147–148. It has been argued that 'without the rail-road, the British and the Soviets would have had much less incentive to invade Iran in 1941...' Patrick Clawson quoting the President of the Cultural Studies and Research Institute in Tehran. *Iranian Studies* vol. 26, Nos 3–4, summer and fall 1993, p 250. It should be noted that an ambitious programme of road building had begun in 1929, and by 1940 Iran had over 15,000 miles (26,000km) of 'motorable roads many of them through mountain areas. Few were asphalted and by European standards primitive, but for a country that had not known anything resembling rapid transport they were a great advance'. L.P. Elwell-Sutton, 'Reza Shah the Great' in George Lenczowski, *Iran Under the Pahlavis*, pp 30–31.

16 Reza Arasteh, *Education and Social Awakening in Iran*, pp 57–68.

17 *Ibid.*, pp 57 and 67.

18 In a speech on the day discarding the veil became mandatory (8 January 1936) Reza Shah said, 'We must never forget that one half of the population of our country has not been taken into account, that is to say, one half of the country's workforce has been idle': L.P. Elwell-Sutton, 'Reza Shah the Great' in George Lenczowski, *Iran Under the Pahlavis*, p 34.

19 Amin Banani, *The Modernization of Iran*, p 99. No doctorates other than in medicine were awarded until 1941.

20 Joseph M. Upton, *The History of Modern Iran: An Interpretation*, p 60.

21 Mohammad Reza Khalili Khou, 'Tose'h va Nowsazi dar Zaman Reza Shah' ('Development and Renovation in the Reza Shah Era') unpublished PhD thesis, p 164. Reza Shah had no formal education, but he had learned to read and write at the latest by 1910–1911. This author had seen two letters from Reza Khan, a lieutenant by that time, to a minor official of the Department of Finance in the Kermanshah region. Later samples of his correspondence in the 1923–1925 period which appeared recently in the collection of Soleiman Behboodi show a firmer and more mature handwriting: Soleiman Behboodi, *Khaterat Soleiman Behboodi* (*The Memoirs of Soleiman Behboodi*), the unnumbered last section.

22 Jahangir Amuzegar, *The Dynamics of the Iranian Revolution: The Pahlavis Triumph and Tragedy*, p 121.

23 Donald N. Wilber, *Riza Shah Pahlavi*, p 180.

24 Amin Banani, *The Modernization of Iran*, pp 64–66.

25 'In 1924 there were only 905 physicians in the entire country. Of this number only 253 possessed medical diplomas from accredited universities. The ratio was one doctor to every 11,000 people... By 1935 the ratio of doctors to the population had reached one doctor to every 4,000 people': Amin Banani, *The Modernization of Iran*, pp 64–65.

26 Byron J. Good, 'Transformation of Health Care in Modern Iranian History' in Michael Bonine and Nikki Keddie (eds), *Modern Iran: The Dialectics of Continuity and Change in Iran*, pp 64–70.

27 Amin Banani, *The Modernisation of Iran*, p 66.

28 Peter Avery, *Modern Iran*, p 287.

29 *Ibid.*, p 286.

30 L.P. Elwell-Sutton, 'Reza Shah the Great' in George Lenczowski, *Iran Under the Pahlavis*, p 37.

31 Among the most notable were the railway station, the National Bank, the Ministry of Foreign Affairs, the Ministry of Justice, the Officers'

Club, the Sports Stadium, Tehran University and the Central Post Office. 'In some of the small towns and villages he arranged shopping centres and here and there in rural neighbourhoods supplied the peasants with improved standardised housing'. Reza Khan created at Fariman in Khorassan a model town complete with factories, shops and stores': A.C. Millspaugh, *Americans in Persia*, p 32. For an account of buildings constructed during the Reza Shah era and their architectural significance, refer to Reza M. Moqtader's article 'The 100 Year Period of the Renewal of City Planning and Architecture in Iran', *Iran Nameh*, No. 2, Spring 1372 (1993), pp 259–270.

32 Czarist Russia had attained virtually free trade after the Treaty of Turkamanchai in 1828. Iran could not impose a duty greater than five to eight percent on Russian imports. Britain and other European countries demanded and obtained the same privileges. 'As of 1921 Iran was bound by the Russo-Persian Tariff Agreement of 1902 and the Anglo-Persian Tariff Convention of 1920': Amin Banani, *The Modernization of Iran*, p 116. The Soviets had unilaterally abrogated the Treaty of Turkamanchai and the Tariff Agreement in 1921 but still expected Iran to adhere to its terms and maintain a low tariff on Russian imports.

33 Baqer Aqeli, *Ruz Shomar Tarikh Iran* (*A Daily Calendar of the History of Iran*), vol. 1, p 262.

34 Jahangir Amuzegar, *The Dynamics of the Iranian Revolution – The Pahlavi Triumph and Tragedy*, pp 134–135. In 1925 there were less than 20 modern plants. By 1941 there were 346, including 37 textile mills, eight sugar refineries, 11 matchmaking plants, eight chemical enterprises, two modern glass works, five tea processing plants and a tobacco processing factory. Industrial workers rose from less than 1000 in 1925 to 50,000 in 1941. Ervand Abrahamian, *Iran Between Two Revolutions*, pp 146–147. By 1941 there had been development in the silk industry with two plants; eight leather processing plants; iron smelting; sacks and bags, bottles and cement factories; canning (fruit and jam); jute and soap factories. The paid-in share capital of all private enterprises in the country rose from 143 million rials in 1932 to 1,863 million in 1941. Mohammad Reza Khalili Khou, 'Tose'h va Nowsazi dar Zaman Reza Shah' ('Development and Renovation in the Reza Shah Era') unpublished PhD thesis, pp 179–183.

35 Reza Shah was on guard that his own actions or the condition of his country 'were not the objects of critical or derisive remarks'. His diplomatic legations abroad were required to inform the Foreign Ministry in Tehran of any item 'that seemed injurious to what he considered his and the country's honor': William S. Haas, *Iran*, p 156. His demand for respect from the international community led him on several occasions to overreact and sever relations twice with France and once with the United States over relatively insignificant incidents.

36 William S. Haas, *Iran*, p 272.

37 Rouhollah Ramazani, *The Foreign Policy of Iran 1500–1941*, p 266. There were three contentious issues: activities of rebellious tribes in the frontier region; treatment of Iranian citizens residing in Iraq; and the status of the Shatt al Arab river.

38 Gordon Waterfield, *Professional Diplomat – Sir Percy Lorraine*, p 210. Lord Kinross, *Ataturk: The Rebirth of a Nation*, pp 461–462. Hassan Arfa,

Under Five Shahs, p 249. In these accounts the characters of Ataturk and Reza Shah are contrasted, Ataturk as extroverted and volatile and Reza Shah as introverted and taciturn.

39 The food was simple and the time allotted for meals rarely exceeded one hour. Conversations with General Fereydoun Jam, Ali Izadi and Gholam Reza Pahlavi.

40 For every affirmative trait Teimurtash had more than the usual flaws of character. He was an ardent womaniser and had the attributes to which women are attracted. He was handsome, charming, intelligent, generous and, more importantly, he exuded power. He made many enemies as a result of this appetite. Teimurtash was also a heavy drinker and gambler, and as he aged became more impetuous when drunk and reckless when he gambled. With the position he occupied and the power he exercised Teimurtash had collected his share of enemies over the years who exaggerated all of these negative traits.

41 Ghasem Ghani, *Yaddasht ha-e-Dr Ghasem Ghani (Memoirs of Dr Ghasem Ghani)*, vol. 1, p 218.

42 The year 1932 has been taken as an arbitrary date. Mostofi died in September of that year and it is generally acknowledged that he was the last restraining influence on Reza Shah. Reza Shah had great respect for Mostofi who time and again intervened on behalf of some who were out of favour and for the pardon of some in prison.

43 Hassan Taqizadeh, *Khaterat Seyyed Hassan Taqizadeh (Memoirs of Seyyed Hassan Taqizadeh)*, ed. Iraj Afshar, pp 224, 235.

44 Reza Shah had exempted only Foroughi, Taqizadeh and Rajab Ali Mansour. Hassan Taqizadeh, *Khaterat Seyyed Hassan Taqizadeh (Memoirs of Seyyed Hassan Taqizadeh)*, ed. Iraj Afshar, pp 224, 235. Even paranoids have real enemies and Reza Shah had his share. There was an attempted coup against Reza Shah in 1927 led by Col. Mahmoud Pouladin, who was executed in March 1928. Baqer Aqeli, *Ruz Shomar Tarikh Iran (A Daily Calendar of the History of Iran)*, vol. 1, p 228. For a detailed account of the attempted coup refer to Stephanie Cronin, *The Army and the Creation of the Pahlavi State in Iran 1910–1926.*

45 Even with his callousness towards many who had been instrumental in his rise to power, Reza Shah was an exception to the monarchs who had preceded him. The members of the Qajar Dynasty were not obliterated as members of the Afsharid and Zand Dynasties had been wiped out by the Qajars. Qajar princes and notables served him in high civilian and military positions. In an important trial after Reza Shah's abdication several men were convicted of the murders of Moddares, Sardar As'ad, Firouz and Teimurtash. One of the accused was hanged, the rest received prison sentences of varying length. Reza Shah himself was not implicated during these trials. Dr Jalal Abdoh, *Chehel Sal dar Sahne (Forty Years on the Scene)*. There was no testimony that he had ordered any of these murders. There is no doubt, however, that in the existing order none of the accused would have moved without some indication from Reza Shah. It may not have been a direct command but at least something akin to Henry II's henchmen acting on the King's plea, 'Would someone rid me of this troublesome priest,' by killing Thomas à Becket; or Henry IV's rhetorical question, 'Have I no friend who will rid me of this living fear,' which led to the murder of Richard II.

46 Dariush Shayegan, *Cultural Schizophrenia: Islamic Society Confronting the West*, p 79.
47 Malcolm E. Yapp, '1900–1921: The Last Years of the Qajar Dynasty' in Hossein Amirsadeghi and R.W. Ferrier (eds), *Twentieth Century Iran*, p 50.
48 Soleiman Behboodi, *Khaterat Soleiman Behboodi (The Memoirs of Soleiman Behboodi)*, p 19.
49 *Ibid.*, p 231.
50 *Ibid.*, pp 354–5. These plots were purchased from Farmanfarma, Mostofi, Nezam al Saltaneh Ma'afi and Abbas Mirza Salar Lashkar. Later large houses were built on them which served as residences for Reza Shah's sons and daughters. The Marble Palace was also built on these plots between 1934 and 1937. *Ibid.*, p 368.
51 Donald N. Wilber, *Riza Shah Pahlavi*, pp 243–244; Ervand Abrahamian, *Iran Between Two Revolutions*, pp 136–137.
52 Leonard Binder, *Iran: Political Development in a Changing Society*, p 67.
53 Jahangir Amuzegar, *The Dynamics of the Iranian Revolution – The Pahlavi Triumph and Tragedy*, pp 72–73.
54 John Marlowe, *Iran: A Short Political Guide*, p 64.
55 Richard A. Stewart, *Sunrise at Abadan*, pp 16–17.
56 FO 416/99, Eden to Cripps, Britain's Ambassador to the Soviet Union, (concerning report of discussions between Eden and Maisky, Soviet Ambassador to London), 19 July 1941.
57 FO 416/99, Eden to Cripps, 12 August 1941.
58 FO 371/27205, Minutes of meeting of War Cabinet, 7 August 1941.
59 The British Minister in Tehran had reported the number at 3,000 when he had meant to report 2,000, and immediately informed the Foreign Office that there had been a typographical error. Nevertheless, the Foreign Office passed on the number 3,000 to the United States. Richard A. Stewart, *Sunrise at Abadan*, p 99.
60 FO 371/27151, Bullard to Eden, 22 July 1941.
61 FO 371/27151, Bullard to Eden, 28 July 1941.
62 DoS, 740.0011, Louis G. Dreyfus Jr to Secretary of State, 24 August 1941.
63 Christopher Buckley, *Five Ventures*, pp 146–148, Richard A. Stewart, *Sunrise at Abadan*, pp 83-84.
64 Philip Guedalla, *Middle East 1940–1942 A Study in Air Power*, p 155. British troops were led by Lt Gen. E.P. Quinan under Field Marshal Wavel with two Major Generals and four Brigadier Generals. Christopher Buckley, *Five Ventures*, pp 146–148.
65 Richard A. Stewart, *Sunrise at Abadan*, p 141.
66 Baqer Aqeli, *Ruz Shomar Tarikh Iran (A Daily Calendar of the History of Iran)*, vol. I, pp 328–329.
67 Richard A. Stewart, *Sunrise at Abadan*, pp 83–84.
68 FO 416/99, Bullard to Eden, 26 September 1941.
69 DoS doc no. 158, Dreyfus to Secretary of State, 19 September 1941.
70 Mostafa Fateh of APOC and Hassan Mosharaf Nafisi, Minister of Finance. DoS, No. 136, Dreyfus to Secretary of State, 6 October 1941.
71 DoS, 891.001, p 15/220, Wallace Murray memorandum to Secretary of State, date unknown but probably late 1941.
72 Gholam Reza Afkhami, *The Iranian Revolution: Thanatos on a National Scale*, p 19.

Bibliography

OFFICIAL DOCUMENTS
Documents cited, with abbreviations used

United Kingdom and Empire
Butler, Rohan and J.P.T. Bury (ed.), *Documents on British Foreign Policy, 1919–1930* (DBFP)
Foreign Office (FO)
India Office Library (L0)
Cabinet (CAB)
War Office (WO)

United States

US Department of State, Papers on Foreign Relations (DoS)

BOOKS IN ENGLISH AND OTHER EUROPEAN LANGUAGES

Abrahamian, Ervand, *Iran Between Two Revolutions*, Princeton, 1982
Abol Hassan Khan Shirazi, *The Journal 1809–1810*, trans. Margaret Morris Cloake, London, 1988
Adahl, Andreas (ed.), *Iran Through the Ages – A Swedish Anthology*, Stockholm, 1972
Afkhami, Gholam Reza, *The Iranian Revolution: Thanatos on a National Scale*, Washington DC, 1985
Akhavi, Sharough, *Religion and Politics in Contemporary Iran*, New York, 1980
Alexander, Yonah and Allan Nanes (eds), *The United States and Iran*, Frederick, Maryland, 1980
Amanat, Abbas, *Pivot of the Universe – Naser al-Din Shah Qajar*, Berkeley, California, 1997
Amir Arjomand, Said, *The Turban for the Crown*, New York, 1980
Amirsadeghi, Hossein and R.W. Ferrier (eds), *Twentieth Century Iran*, particularly Ch. 1, '1900–1921 – The Last Years of the Qajar Dynasty' by Malcolm E. Yapp and Ch. 2, '1921–1941: The Period of Reza Shah' by Wilfrid Knapp, New York, 1977
Amory, Copley, Jr, *Persian Days*, Boston, Massachusetts, 1929
Amuzegar, Jahangir, *The Dynamics of the Iranian Revolution – The Pahlavis Triumph and Tragedy*, New York, 1991
Arasteh, Reza, *Education and Social Awakening in Iran*, Leiden, 1962
Arfa, Hassan, *Under Five Shahs*, London, 1964
Armajani, Yahya, *Iran*, Englewood Cliffs, New Jersey, 1972
Avery, Peter, *Modern Iran*, London, 1968
Bakhash, Shaul, *Iran: Monarchy, Bureaucracy and Reform Under the Qajars (1858 – 1896)*, Oxford, 1978
Baldwin, George, *Planning and Development in Iran*, Baltimore, 1976

Balfour, James M., *Recent Happenings in Persia*, Edinburgh, 1922

Bamdad, Badr al Molouk, *From Darkness Into Light – Women's Emancipation in Iran*, Hicksville, New York, 1961

Bamberg, J.H., *The History of the British Petroleum Company*, vol. 2, *The Anglo-Iranian Years 1928–1954*, Cambridge, 1994

Banani, Amin, *The Modernization of Iran*, Palo Alto, California, 1961

Bassett, James, *The Land of Imams*, New York, 1886

Bayliss, C.M. (ed.), *Operations in Persia 1914-1919*, London, 1987

Beck, Lois, *The Qashqa'i of Iran*, New Haven, Connecticut, 1986

Berlin, Isaiah, *The Hedgehog and the Fox*, London, 1953

Bill, James, *The Eagle and The Lion*, New Haven, Connecticut, 1988

Binder, Leonard, *Iran: Political Development in a Changing Society*, Berkeley, California, 1962

Bonine, Michael and Nikki Keddie (eds), *Modern Iran: The Dialectics of Continuity and Change in Iran*, particularly Ch. 3 'Transformation of Health Care in Modern Iranian History', by Byron J. Good, New York, 1981

Bostock, Francis and Jones, Geoffrey, *Ebtehaj and Economic Development Under the Shah*, London, 1984

Buckley, Christopher, *Five Ventures*, London, 1977

Bullard, Reader, *Britain and the Middle East*, London, 1951

Idem., *The Camels Must Go*, London, 1961

Idem., *Letters From Tehran*, London, 1989

Byron, Robert, *The Road to Oxiana*, London, 1950

Churchill, G.P., *Biographical Notices of Persian Statesmen and Notables – August 1905*, Calcutta, 1906

Cleveland, William. L., *A History of the Modern Middle East*, Boulder, Colorado, 1994

Collins, Treacher E., *In the Kingdom of the Shah*, London, 1896

Cottam, Richard W., *Nationalism in Iran*, Pittsburg, 1964

Idem., *The United States and Iran*, Pittsburg, 1988

Cronin, Stephanie, *The Army and the Creation of the Pahlavi State in Iran 1910 – 1926*, London, 1997

Curzon, George N., *Persia and the Persian Question*, 2 vols, London, 1892

Curzon, Robert, *Armenia: A Year at Erzeroom and on the Frontiers of Russia, Turkey and Persia*, London, 1854

Dawes, R., *A History of the Establishment of Diplomatic Relations with Persia*, Marietta, Ohio, 1887

Donohoe, M.H., *With the Persian Expedition*, London, 1919

Dos Passos, John, *Orient Express*, London, 1928

Doyle, David W., *Bazhanov and the Damnation of Stalin*, Ohio, 1990

Dunsterville, Maj. Gen. L. C., *The Adventures of Dunsterforce*, London, 1932

Idem., *Stalky's Reminiscenses*, London, 1928

Elgood, Cyril, *A Medical History of Persia and the Middle Eastern Caliphate Until the Year 1932*, Cambridge, 1951

Elm, Mostafa, *Oil, Power and Principle – Iran's Oil Nationalization and Its Aftermath*, Syracuse, New York, 1992

Elwell-Sutton, L.P., *Modern Iran*, London, 1941

Idem., *A Guide to Iranian Study*, Ann Arbor, Michigan, 1952

Idem., *Persian Oil*, Westport, Connecticut, 1975

Entner, Marvin L., *Russo-Persian Commercial Relations 1828–1914*, Florida, 1965

Essad-Bey, Mohammad, *Reza Shah*, London, 1938

Eubank, Keith, *Summit at Tehran – The Untold Story*, New York, 1985

Fateh, Mostafa, *The Economic Position of Persia*, London, 1926

Fatemi, Nasrollah Saifpour, *Oil Diplomacy*, New York, 1954

Ferrier, R.W., *The History of the British Petroleum Company*, vol. 1, *The Developing Years 1901–1932*, Cambridge, 1982

Filmer, Henry, *The Pageant of Persia*, Indianapolis, 1936

Fitzsimmons, M.A., *Empire by Treaty*, South Bend, Indiana, 1964

Forbes, Rosita, *Conflict, Angora to Afghanistan*, London, 1931

Forbes-Leith, F.A.C., *Checkmate – Fighting Tradition in Central Asia*, London, nd (c.1928)

Ford, Alan, *The Anglo-Iranian Oil Dispute of 1951–1952*, Berkeley, 1954

Fromkin, David, *A Peace to End All Peace*, New York, 1989

Garthwaite, Gene, *Khans and the Shah*, Cambridge, 1983

Ghani, Cyrus, *Iran and the West – A Critical Bibliography*, London, 1987

Ghods, M. Reza, *Iran in the Twentieth Century*, Boulder, Colorado, 1989

Goold-Adams, Richard, *Middle East Journey*, London, 1947

Graves, Philip, *The Life of Sir Percy Cox*, London, 1941

Grayson, Benson Lee, *United States – Iranian Relations*, Washington DC, 1981

Greaves, Rose Louise, *Persia and the Defence of India 1854–1892*, London, 1959

Grey, Edward, *Speeches on Foreign Affairs 1904–1914*, Paul Knaplund (ed.), London, 1931

Idem., *Twenty Five Years 1892–1916*, 2 vols, London, 1925

Groseclose, Elgin, *Introduction to Iran*, New York, 1947

Guedalla, Philip, *Middle East 1940–1942: A Study in Air Power*, London, 1944

Haas, William S., *Iran*, New York, 1946

Hall, Melvin, *Journey to the End of an Era*, London, 1948

Hamzavi, A.H., *Persia and the Powers 1941–1946*, London, nd (c.1947)

Hardinge, Arthur, *A Diplomatist in the East*, London, 1928

Hardinge, Charles (Lord Penshurst), *Old Diplomacy*, London, 1947

Hay, Sidney, *By Order of the Shah*, London, 1937

Hirszowicz, Lukasz, *The Third Reich and the Arab East*, London, 1966

Hurewitz, J.C., *Diplomacy in the Near and Middle East*, 2 vols, Princeton, 1956

Ikbal, Sirdar Ali Shah, *Eastward to Persia*, London, 1931

Idem., *The Controlling Minds of Asia*, London, 1937

Ironside, Maj. Gen. Sir Edmund, *High Road to Command – The Diaries 1920–1922*, London, 1972

Johnson, Lt Col. John, *A Journey From India, to England, Through Persia, Georgia, Russia, Poland, Prussia*, London, 1818

Jones, Geoffrey, *Banking and Empire in Iran*, vol. 1, Cambridge, 1986

Kadjar, Hamid, *Memoirs*, Habib Ladjvardi (ed.), Cambridge, Massachusetts, 1996

Kapur, Harish, *Soviet Russia and Asia 1917-1927*, Geneva, 1966

Katouzian, Homa, *The Political Economy of Iran 1926–1979*, London, 1981

Idem., *Mosaddeq and the Struggle for Power in Iran*, London, 1990

Kazemzadeh, Firouz, *The Struggle for Transcaucasia 1917–1921*, New York, 1951

Idem., *Russia and Britain in Persia 1864-1914*, New Haven, Connecticut, 1968

Keppel, George, *Personal Narrative of a Journey From India To England*, 2 vols, London, 1827

Kinross, Lord, *Ataturk – The Making of a Modern Nation*, London, 1964

Labour Party, *Persia, Finland and Our Russian Alliance – In Defence of Neutral Countries*, London, 1915

Ladjevardi, Habib, *Labor Unions and Autocracy in Iran*, Syracuse, New York, 1985

Lambton, Ann K. S., *Landlord and Peasant in Persia*, Oxford, 1953

Laqueur, Walter Z., *The Soviet Union and the Middle East*, London, 1959

Lenczowski, George, *Russia and the West in Iran 1918–1948*, Ithaca, New York, 1949

Idem. (ed.), *Iran under the Pahlavis*, particularly Ch. 1, 'Reza Shah the Great', by L.P. Elwell-Sutton, and Ch. 4 'The Iranian Economy 1925–1975', by Charles Issawi, Palo Alto, California, 1978

Lesueur, Emile, *Des Anglaise en Perse*, Paris, 1923

Longrigg, S.H., *Oil in the Middle East*, London, 1954

Lytle, Mark Hamilton, *The Origins of the Iran-American Alliance 1941–1953*, New York, 1987

Marlowe, John, *Iran*, London, 1963

Malcolm, John, *History of Persia*, 2 vols, London, 1815

Martin, Bradford, *German-Persian Diplomatic Relations 1873–1912*, Netherlands, 1959

McLean, David, *Britain and the Buffer State – The Collapse of the Persian Empire 1890-1914*, London, 1979

McDaniel, Robert A., *The Shuster Mission and the Persian Constitutional Revolution*, Minneapolis, 1974

Medlicott, W.N., *The Congress of Berlin and After*, London, 1963

Meskoob, Shahrokh and Banuazizi, Ali, *Iranian Nationality and the Persian Language*, Washington DC, 1996

Millspaugh, A.C., *The American Task Force in Persia*, London, 1926

Idem., *Americans in Persia*, Washington DC, 1946

Miroshnikov, L.I., *Iran in World War I*, Moscow, 1964

Moberly, F.J., *Operations in Persia 1914–1919*, London, 1987

Mofid, Kamran, *Development and Planning in Iran – From Monarchy to Islamic Republic*, Cambridgeshire, 1987

Monroe, Elizabeth, *Britain's Moment in the Middle East 1914–1956*, London, 1963

Motter, T. H. Vail, *The Persian Corridor and Aid to Russia*, Washington DC, 1952

Musaddiq, Mohammad, *Memoirs*, trans. and ed. Homa Katouzian, London, 1988

Nicolson, Harold, *Sir Arthur Nicolson – A Study in Old Diplomacy*, London, 1937

Idem., *Curzon – The Last Phase 1919-1925*, London, 1937

Oberling, Pierre, *The Qashhqa'i Nomads of Fars*, The Hague, 1974

O'Conner, Frederick, *Things Mortal*, London, 1940

Olson, William J., *Anglo-Iranian Relations During World War I*, London, 1984

Pahlavi, Princess Ashraf, *Faces in the Mirror*, Englewood Cliffs, New Jersey, 1980

Pahlavi, Mohammad Reza Shah, *Mission for My Country*, New York, 1961

Idem., *Answer to History*, New York, 1980

Paiforce, *The Official Story of the Persia and Iraq Command 1914–1946*, London, 1948

Pearce, Brian and Ali Granmayeh, *The Staroselsky Problem 1918–1920*, London, 1994

Persia Geographical Handbook, London, 1945

Polacco, Angelo, *L'Iran di Reza Scia Pahlavi*, Venice, 1937

Powell, Alexander, *By Camel and Car to the Peacock Throne*, New York, 1923

Idem., *The Stuggle for Power in Moslem Asia*, London, 1925

Ramazani, Rouhollah, *The Foreign Policy of Iran 1500–1941*, Virginia, 1966

Rawlinson, A., *Adventures in the Near East 1918–1922*, London, 1923

Rezun, Miron, *The Soviet Union and Iran*, Boulder, Colorado, 1988

Ronaldshay, Lord (Lawrence J.L. Dundas), *The Life of Lord Curzon*, 3 vols, New York, 1927–1928

Rubin, Barry, *Paved with Good Intentions*, New York, 1980

Sabahi, Houshang, *British Policy in Persia 1918-1925*, London, 1990

Sackville-West, V., *Passenger to Tehran*, London, 1926

Saifpour Fatemi, Nasrollah, *Oil Diplomacy*, New York, 1954

Idem., *Diplomatic History of Persia 1917–1923*, New York, 1952

Saleh, Ali Pasha, *Cultural Ties Between Iran and the United States*, Tehran, 1976

Sayre, J., *The Persian Gulf Command*, New York, 1945

Schlesinger, Arthur Jr., *The Disuniting of America*, New York, 1992

Schulz-Holthus, Berthold, *Daybreak in Iran*, London, 1954

Shayegan, Dariush, *Cultural Schizophrenia – Islamic Societies Confronting the West*, London, 1992

Sheean, Vincent, *The New Persia*, New York, 1927

Shuster, W. Morgan, *The Strangling of Persia*, New York, 1912

Sickler, Martin, *The Bear and the Lion – Soviet Imperialism and Iran*, New York, 1988

Skrine, Claremont, *World War in Iran*, London, 1962

Slim, Field Marshall William, *Unofficial History*, London, 1959

Sparroy, Wilfrid, *Persian Children of the Royal Family*, London, 1902

Stewart, Richard A., *Sunrise at Abadan – The British and Soviet Invasion of Iran 1941*, New York, 1988

Sykes, Christopher, *Wassmuss, The German Lawrence*, London, 1936

Idem., *Four Studies in Loyalty*, London, 1946

Sykes, Percy, *A History of Persia*, 2 vols, London, 1915

Tapper, Richard (ed.), *The Conflict of Tribe and State in Iran and Afghanistan*, London, 1983

Trevelyan, George Macaulay, *Grey of Fallodon*, London, 1937

Tweedy, Owen, *Cairo to Persia and Back*, London, 1933

Ullman, Richard H., *The Anglo-Soviet Accord 1917–1921*, vol. 3, Princeton, New Jersey, 1972

Upton, Joseph M., *The History of Modern Iran – An Interpretation*, Cambridge, Massachusetts, 1960

Waterfield, Gordon, *Professional Diplomat – Sir Percy Lorraine*, London, 1973

Who Was Who Foreign Office List, vol. 5, London, 1967

Wilber, Donald N., *Contemporary Iran*, New York, 1963

Idem., *Riza Shah Pahlavi*, New York, 1975

Idem., *Iran: Past and Present*, Princeton, New Jersey, 1976

Idem., *Adventures in the Middle East*, New York, 1986

Wilberham, Richard, *Travels in the Transcaucasian Provinces of Russia*, London, 1839

Wilson, Arnold, *Persia*, London, 1932

Wright, Denis, *The English Amongst the Persians*, London, 1977

Idem., The Persians Amongst the English, London, 1985
Yergin, Daniel, *The Prize – The Epic Quest for Oil, Money and Power*, New York, 1991
Yesselson, Abraham, *United States-Persian Diplomatic Relations 1883–1921*, New Jersey, 1956
Zabih, Sepehr, *The Communist Movement in Iran*, Berkeley, California, 1966

LETTERS, ARTICLES AND THESES IN ENGLISH

Bill, James, interview with Seyyed Zia, Tehran, 15 August 1966, unpublished.
Bullard, Sir Reader, 'Persia in Two World Wars', *Royal Central Asian Journal*, vol. 1, pt 1, January 1963.
Cronin, Stephanie, 'Opposition to Reza Khan Within the Army, 1921-26', *Middle Eastern Studies*, vol. 30, no. 4, London, October 1994.
Grey, W. G., 'Persia', *Journal of Central Asian Society*, vol. 3, 1926.
Hambly, G. R. G., 'Aqa Mohammad Khan Qajar and the Establishment of the Qajar Dynasty', *Journal of the Royal Asian Society*, London, 1955.
Hirschfeld, Yair P., 'German Iranian Relations 1921–1941', PhD thesis, Tel Aviv University, November 1976, unpublished.
Iranian Studies, vol. 26, nos. 3-4, United States, Summer/Fall, 1993.
McLean, D., 'Finance and Informal Empire Before the First World War', *Economic History Review*, 1976.
Martin, Vanessa, 'Mudarris, Replubicanism and Rise to Power of Riza Khan Sardar Sepah', *British Journal of Middle Eastern Studies*, vol. 21, no. 2, 1994.
Moghadam, Gholam Reza, 'Iran's Foreign Trade Policy and Economic Development in the Inter War Period', PhD thesis, Stanford University, 1956, unpublished.
Murray, John, 'Iran Today: An Economic and Descriptive Survey', Tehran, 1950, unpublished.
Rubin, Michael A., 'The US in Persia and the Standard-Sinclair Oil Dispute', *Iranian Studies*, vol. 28, nos. 3–4, 1995.
Sheean, Vincent, 'Rival Imperialism in Persia', *Asia*, February, 1927.
Strunk, William Theodore, 'The Reign of Sheikh Khaz'al Ibn Jabir and the Suppression of the Principality of Khuzistan', PhD thesis, Indiana University, 1977, unpublished.
Taqizadeh, Hassan, 'Modern Persia', *Journal of The Royal Society of Asia*, no. 32, 27 July 1934.
Varedi, Ahmad, 'Mohammad Ali Foroughi, Zoka Al Molk, 1877–1942 – A Study in the Role of Intellectuals in Modern Iranian Politics', PhD thesis, University of Utah, 1992, unpublished.

NEWSPAPERS

The Daily Telegraph, London: 27 August 1941, pp 1, 2; 28 August 1941, p 6; 29 August 1941, p 6; 30 August 1941, pp 1, 6; 1 September 1941, pp 1, 5; 2 September 1941, p1; 5 September 1941, pp 1, 6.

BOOKS IN PERSIAN

Abdoh, Dr. Jalal, *Chehel Sal dar Sahne-Khaterat*, Tehran, 1368 (1989)

Adamayat, Fereydoun, *Amir Kabir va Iran*, Tehran, 1368 (1989)

Afshar, Dr Mahmoud, *Nameha'i Doostan*, ed. Iraj Afshar, Tehran, 1375 (1996)

Alamouti, Mostafa, *Iran dar Asr Pahlavi*, vols 1 and 2, London, 1988

Amir Ahmadi, Ahmad, *Khaterat Nakhostin Sepahbod Iran*, 2 vols, Tehran, 1373 (1994)

Amir Tahmasebi, Abdollah, *Tarikh Shahanshahi Alahazrat Reza Shah Pahlavi*, Tehran, 1305 (1926)

Aqeli, Baqer, *Zoka al Molk Faroughi va Shahrivar 1320*, Tehran, 1368 (1989)

Idem., *Davar va Adlieh*, Tehran, 1369 (1990)

Idem., *Teimurtash dar Sahne Siyasat Iran*, Tehran, 1369 (1990)

Idem., *Ruz Shomar Tarikh Iran*, 2 vols, Tehran, 1374 (1995)

Ardalan, Amanollah, *Khaterat Haji Ez al Mamalek Ardalan*, ed. Dr Baqer Aqeli, Tehran, 1372 (1993)

As'ad Bakhtiari, Ja'far Qoli, *Khaterat*, ed. Iraj Afshar, Tehran, 1372 (1993)

Azari, S. A., *Enqelab Berang ya Qiyam Colonel Mohammad Taqi Khan Pesyan*, Tehran, 1328 (1949)

Azari Shahrza'i, Reza, *Dowlat Iran va Motakhasesan Mohajer Almani 1310–1319*, Tehran, 1374 (1995)

Bahar, Mohamad Taqi, *Tarikh Mokhtasar Ahzab Siasi*, vol. 1, Tehran, 1323 (1944)

Bamdad, Mehdi, *Tarikhe Rejal Iran, Qoroun 12, 13, 14*, 6 vols, Tehran, 1347–1357 (1968–1978)

Bastani Parizi, Mohammad Ebrahim, *Talash Azadi – Mohit Siasi va Zandegani Moshir al Dowleh*, Tehran, 1354 (1975)

Bayat, Kave, *Shoresh A'shayeri Fars – Salhaye 1307–1309*, Tehran, 1365 (1986)

Idem., *Majmoueh Asnad va Madarek dar 1300*, Tehran, 1370 (1991)

Behboodi, Soleiman, *Khaterat Soleiman Behboodi*, ed. Gholam Hosein Mirza Saleh, Tehran, 1372 (1993)

Behnoud, Mas'oud, *Dowlathai Iran az Seyyed Zia ta Bakhtiar*, Tehran, 1366 (1987)

Berashk, Ahmad, *Gahnameh Tatbiqi*, Tehran, 1367 (1988)

Dashti, Ali, *Panjah va Panj Sal*, Tehran, 1354 (1975)

Deldom, Eskandar, *Zendegi Por Majeraye Reza Shah*, 3 vols, Tehran, 1370 (1991)

Dowlatabadi, Yahya, *Hayat Yahya*, 4 vols, Tehran, 1331 (1952)

Ebtehaj, Abolhassan, *Khaterat*, ed. Alireza Arrouzi, 2 vols, London, 1991

Entezam, Nasrollah, *Khaterat Nasrollah Entezam*, Tehran, 1371 (1992)

Eqbal, Abbas, *Mirza Taqi Khan Amir Kabir*, ed. Iraj Afshar, Tehran, 1340 (1961)

Esfandiari, Fathollah Nouri, *Rastakhiz Iran 1299–1323*, Tehran, 1343 (1964)

Fardoost, Hosein, *Khaterat Arteshbod Sabeq*, 2 vols, Tehran, 1369 (1990)

Farmanfarmaian, Abdolhosein, *Majmoueh Asnad Abdolhosein Mirza Farmanfarmaian – 1325–1340 HQ*, ed. Mansoureh Etehadieh and Cyrus S'advandian, Tehran, 1000 (1007)

Farrokh, Seyyed Mehdi, *Khaterat Siasi*, 2 vols, Tehran, 1347 (1968)

Firouz, Firouz, *Majmoueh Mokatebat, Asnad, Khaterat va Asar*, ed. Mansoureh Etehadieh and Cyrus S'advanian, Tehran, 1366 (1987)

Ghani, Ghasem, *Yaddasht ha-e-Dr Ghasem Ghani*, ed. Cyrus Ghani and Hale Bakhash, 12 vols, particularly vol. 11, *Yaddasht ha-e-Chand Raje be*

Marhoum Davar, by Abbasqoli Golsha'yan, and conversations with Lt Gen. Morteza Yazdanpanah, London, 1980–1984

Hedayat, Mehdi Qoli, *Khaterat va Khatarat*, Tehran, 1330 (1951)

Ironside, Edmund, *Khaterat Serri*, Tehran, 1373 (1994)

Jahanbani, Amanollah, *Reza Shah Kabir Dar Ayeneh Khaterat*, ed. Ebrahim Safa'i, Los Angeles, 1986

Kahalzadeh, Abolqasem, *Dide ha va Shenideh ha*, Tehran, 1363 (1984)

Kasravi, Ahmad, *Tarikh-e-Mashrouteh Iran*, Tehran, 1363 (1984)

Khajenouri, Ebrahim, *Bazigaran Asr Tala'i*, Tehran, 1320 (1941)

Larijani, Ali, *Tarikh Khani*, St Petersburg, 1854

Makki, Hosein, *Tarikh Bist Saleh Iran*, 7 vols, Tehran, 1361 (1982)

Idem., *Zendegi Siasi Ahmad Shah*, Tehran, 1362 (1983)

Mamontof, N.P., *Houkumat Tsari va Mohammad Ali Shah*, ed. Homayoun Shahidi, Tehran, 1363 (1984)

Matin Daftari, Dr Ahmad, *Khaterat Yek Nakhost Vazir*, ed. Dr Baqer Aqeli, Tehran, 1370 (1991)

Mehdinia, Ja'far, *Zendegi Siasi Seyyed Zia al Din Tabataba'i*, Tehran, 1370 (1991)

Meskoob, Shahrokh, *Dastan Adabiat va Sargozasht Ejtema*, Tehran, 1372 (1993)

Mokhtari, Habibollah, *Tarikh Bidari Iran*, Tehran, 1336 (1957)

Morselvand, H. (ed.), *Asnad Cabine Coup d'Etat 3 Esfand 1299*, Tehran, 1374 (1995)

Mosaddeq, Dr Mohammad, *Khaterat*, Tehran, 1365 (1986)

Mosaheb, *Da'erat al Mo'aref Farsi*, vol 2, Tehran, 1356 (1977)

Mosavar Rahmani, Colonel Gholam Reza, *Kohne Sarbaz*, Tehran, 1336 (1957)

Naraqi, Hassan, *Tarikh Ettema'i Kashan*, Tehran, 1345 (1966)

Idem., *Kashan dar Jonbesh Mashrouteh Iran*, Tehran, 1364 (1975)

Niazmand, Reza, *Reza Shah as Tavalod ta Saltanat*, Washington DC, 1996

Qashqa'i, Naser, *Khaterat Rouzaneh*, Tehran, 1366 (1987)

Reza Shah, *Safer Nameh Khuzestan dar Sal 1303*, Tehran, 1354 (1975)

Idem., *Safar Nameh Mazandaran*, Tehran, 1355 (1976)

Rouhani, Fouad, *Zendegi Siasi Mosaddeq*, London, 1366 (1987)

Sadr, Mohsen (Sadr al Ashraf), *Khaterat*, Tehran, 1364 (1985)

Sa'ed Maraghe'i, Mohammad, *Khaterat*, ed. Dr Baqer Aqeli, Tehran, 1373 (1994)

Safiri, Florida, *Police Jonoub Iran – SPR*, trans. M. Etehadieh and M. Ja'far Fesharaki, Tehran, 1364 (1985)

Sa'idi, Khosrow, *Alahyar Saleh*, Tehran, 1367 (1988)

Sepehr, Ahmadali, *Iran dar Jang Bozorg*, Tehran, 1366 (1987)

Shafaq, Rezazadeh, *Khaterat Majles*, Tehran, 1334 (1955)

Sheikh ol Eslami, Dr Mohammad Javad, *Simaye Ahmad Shah Qajar*, 2 vols, Tehran, 1368, 1372 (1989, 1993)

Siasi, Dr Ali Akbar, *Gozaresh Yek Zendegi*, vol. 1, London, 1366 (1987)

Tafreshi, Majid (ed.), *Do Sal Ravabet Mahremaneh Ahmad Shah Ba Sefarat Shoravi*, Tehran, 1372 (1993)

Taqizadeh, Hassan, *Khaterat Seyyed Hassan Taziqadeh*, ed. Iraj Afshar, Tehran, 1368 (1989)

Tarikh-e Artesh Novin, Part 1 1300 to 1320, Tehran, 1343 (1954)

Yaghma'i, Assadollah, *Hamaseh Fath Nameh Naibi*, Tehran, 1368 (1989)

Zargar, Dr Ali Asghar, *Tarikh Ravabet Siasi Iran va Englis dar Dowreh Reza Shah*, trans. Kaveh Bayat, Tehran, 1372 (1993)

LETTERS, ARTICLES AND THESES IN PERSIAN

Abbasali, Dadash Beik, 'Nameh be Alireza Khan Azd al Molk', *Tarikh Mo'aser Iran*, vol. 6, Iran, 1373 (1994)

Bayat, Kaveh, 'Andishe Siasi Davar', *Goft-e-Gou*, Tehran, 1372 (1993)

Boston, R. N., '3 Hout 1299', *Rahavard*, Los Angeles, November 1992

Fatemi, Nasrollah Saifpour, 'Reza Shah', Letter to the Editor, *Rahavard*, no. 22, Los Angeles, 1989

Khalili Khou, Mohammad Reza, 'Towse'h va Nowsazi dar Zaman Reza Shah', PhD thesis, Tehran University, 1373, unpublished

Moqtader, M. Reza, 'Dowran Sad Saleh Tajadod dar Shahrsazi va Me'mari dar Iran', *Iran Nameh*, no. 2, Washington DC, Spring, 1372

Idem.,'Reza Shah', Letter to the Editor, *Rahavard*, no. 23, Los Angeles, 1989

Samii, Hosein, 'Shab Sevom Hout 1299', *Ayandeh*, Tehran, 1364

Idem., 'Khaterat', *Rahavard*, Los Angeles, Winter, 1997

Sharif Khoda'i, Majid, 'Mas'aleh Jomhouriat dar Dowran Reza Khan', PhD thesis, Tehran Teachers' College, 1372, unpublished

Sheikholesami, Dr Mohammad Javad, 'Qazieh Tamdid Emtiyaz-e Naft-e Jonoub', *Donya*, nos 1 and 2, 14th year, Tehran, 1367 (1988)

Tarikh Mo'aser Iran, vols. 1–10, Bonyad Mostazefan Iran, Tehran, 1368–1376 (1989–1997)

Teimurtash, Abdol Hosein, Letter to Hassan Taqizadeh, *Ayandeh*, nos 9–12, Tehran, 1367 (1988)

Index of Names